skills with these two outstanding resources, available with

A COACHING METHOD

InfoTrac College Edition

INFOTRAC° COLLEGE EDITION

The best resource for online research

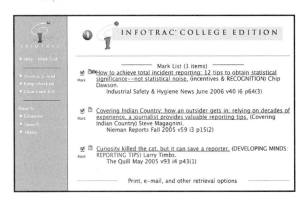

▶ More than 20 million articles from nearly 6,000 sources
▶ Articles are added daily so the most current information is available

iChapters.com

From the Wadsworth Series in Mass Communication and Journalism

General Mass Communications

Anokwa, Lin, and Salwen, *International Communication: Concepts and Cases*, First Edition

Biagi, *Media/Impact: An Introduction to Mass Media, 2009 Update*, Eighth Edition

Bucy, *Living in the Information Age: A New Media Reader*, Second Edition

Craft, Leigh, and Godfrey, *Electronic Media*, First Edition

Day, *Ethics in Media Communications: Cases and Controversies*, Fifth Edition

Dennis and Merrill, Media Debates: *Great Issues for the Digital Age*, Fourth Edition

Fellow, *American Media History*, Second Edition

Gillmor, Barron, Simon, and Terry, *Fundamental Mass Comm Law*, First Edition

Hilmes, *Connections: A Broadcast History*

Hilmes, *Only Connect: A Cultural History of Broadcasting in the United States*, Second Edition

Jamieson and Campbell, *The Interplay of Influence: News, Advertising, Politics, and the Internet*, Sixth Edition

Kamalipour, *Global Communication*, Second Edition

Lester, *Visual Communication: Images with Messages*, Fourth Edition

Overbeck, *Major Principles of Media Law*, 2009 Edition

Straubhaar, LaRose and Davenport, *Media Now*, Sixth Edition

Zelezny, *Cases in Communications Law*, Fifth Edition

Zelezny, *Communications Law: Liberties, Restraints, and the Modern Media*, Fifth Edition

Journalism

Bowles and Border, *Creative Editing*, Fifth Edition

Chance and McKeen, *Literary Journalism: A Reader*

Craig, *Online Journalism: Reporting, Writing, and Editing for New Media*, First Edition

Hilliard, *Writing for Television, Radio, and New Media*, Ninth Edition

Kessler and McDonald, *When Words Collide: A Media Writer's Guide to Grammar and Style*, Sixth Edition

Poulter and Tidwell, *News Scene: Interactive Writing Exercises*

Rich, *Writing & Reporting News: A Coaching Method*, Sixth Edition

Stephens, *Broadcast News*, Fourth Edition

Wilber and Miller, *Modern Media Writing*, First Edition

Photojournalism and Photography

Parrish, *Photojournalism: An Introduction*

Public Relations and Advertising

Diggs-Brown, *The PR Styleguide: Formats for Public Relations Practice*, Second Edition

Drewniany and Jewler, *Creative Strategy in Advertising*, Ninth Edition

Hendrix and Hayes, *Public Relations Cases*, Seventh Edition

Meeske, *Copywriting for the Electronic Media: A Practical Guide*, Fifth Edition

Newsom and Haynes, *Public Relations Writing: Form & Style*, Eighth Edition

Newsom, Turk, and Kruckeberg, *Cengage Advantage Books: This is PR: The Realities of Public Relations*, Ninth Edition

Research and Theory

Baran and Davis, *Mass Communication Theory: Foundations, Ferment, and Future*, Fifth Edition

Littlejohn, *Theories of Human Communications*, Seventh Edition

Rubin, Rubin, and Piele, *Communication Research: Strategies and Sources*, Sixth Edition

Sparks, *Media Effects Research: A Basic Overview*, Third Edition

Wimmer and Dominick, *Mass Media Research: An Introduction*, Eighth Edition

Writing and Reporting News

SIXTH EDITION

A COACHING METHOD

Carole Rich

WADSWORTH
CENGAGE Learning™

Australia • Brazil • Japan • Korea • Mexico • Singapore • Spain • United Kingdom • United States

**Writing and Reporting News:
A Coaching Method, Sixth Edition**
Carole Rich

Senior Publisher: Lyn Uhl

Publisher in Humanities:
Michael Rosenberg

Assistant Editor: Megan Garvey

Editorial Assistant: Rebekah Matthews

Technology Project Manager:
Jessica Badiner

Marketing Manager: Erin Mitchell

Marketing Coordinator: Darlene Macanan

Marketing Communications Manager:
Christine Dobberpuhl

Content Project Manager: Tiffany Kayes

Art Director: Linda Helcher

Print Buyer: Susan Carroll

Permissions Editor: Bob Kauser

Production Service/Compositor:
International Typesetting and Composition

Text Designer: Lisa Buckley

Photo Manager: Mandy Groszko

Photo Researcher: Darren Wright

Cover Designer: Rukesek Design

Cover Image:
Sergio Barrenechea/EFE/epa/Corbis

For product information and technology assistance, contact us at
Cengage Learning Customer & Sales Support, 1-800-354-9706

For permission to use material from this text or product,
submit all requests online at **www.cengage.com/permissions**
Further permissions questions can be e-mailed to
permissionrequest@cengage.com

Library of Congress Control Number: 2008928898

ISBN-13: 978-0-495-56987-9

ISBN-10: 0-495-56987-9

Wadsworth
25 Thomson Place
Boston, MA 02210-1202
USA

Cengage Learning products are represented in Canada
by Nelson Education, Ltd.

For your course and learning solutions, visit **academic.cengage.com**

Purchase any of our products at your local college store or at our
preferred online store **www.ichapters.com**

Printed in the United States of America
2 3 4 5 6 7 12 11 10 09

Brief Contents

Part One • Understanding News

1 • Changing Concepts of News 3

2 • Blogs 23

3 • The Basic News Story 35

4 • Convergent Media Writing 59

Part Two • Collecting Information

5 • Curiosity and Story Ideas 71

6 • Sources and Online Research 87

7 • Interviewing Techniques 107

Part Three • Constructing Stories

8 • Leads and Nut Graphs 131

9 • Story Organization 161

10 • Story Forms 183

11 • Storytelling and Feature Techniques 199

12 • Broadcast News Writing 223

13 • Online Journalism 251

14 • Public Relations Writing 269

Part Four • Understanding Media Issues

15 • Media Law 289

16 • Media Ethics 307

17 • Multicultural Sensitivity 321

Part Five • Applying the Techniques

18 • Profiles and Obituaries 335

19 • Beat Reporting 357

20 • Speeches, News Conferences and Meetings 377

21 • Government and Statistical Stories 393

22 • Crime and Punishment 413

23 • Disasters, Weather and Tragedies 443

24 • Media Jobs and Internships 473

Contents

Preface   xi
Acknowledgments   xv
About the Author   1

Part One • Understanding News

1 • Changing Concepts of News   3

Media Convergence   4
Changing Delivery of News   7
Economic Changes in Media   8
Changes in Online News   8
Citizen Journalism   10
    ETHICS   10
The Coaching Method   11
Qualities of News   12
    CONVERGENCE COACH   16
Hard News and Features   17
What Do You Think?   19
Exercises   20
Featured Online Activity   20

2 • Blogs   23

Blogs as News Sources   24
Citizen Journalism   26
Transparency   26
    ETHICS   27
Ethical Issues   28
Blogs in Public Relations and Marketing   29
    CONVERGENCE COACH   30
How to Write a Blog   30
Podcasts   31
What Do You Think?   31
Exercises   32
Featured Online Activity   32

3 • The Basic News Story   35

Finding the Focus   36
Nut Graphs   37
Basic Questions   37
Elements of the Basic News Story   37
    CONVERGENCE COACH   44

Examples of Basic News Stories   47
    ETHICS   49
Quotes and Attribution   50
What Do You Think?   55
Exercises   55
Featured Online Activity   57

4 • Convergent Media Writing   59

Print vs. Broadcast and Online Stories   60
    ETHICS   63
Anatomy of a News Story: P.R., Broadcast and Print   64
    CONVERGENCE COACH   66
Anatomy of a News Story on the Web   67
What Do You Think?   68
Exercises   68
Featured Online Activity   69

Part Two • Collecting Information

5 • Curiosity and Story Ideas   71

Curiosity   71
Observation   73
    ETHICS   76
Ways to Find Story Ideas   76
The Internet   81
    CONVERGENCE COACH   82
Idea Budgets   82
What Do You Think?   83
Exercises   83
Featured Online Activity   84

6 • Sources and Online Research   87

Human Sources   88
Anonymous Sources   90
    ETHICS   91
Multicultural Sources   94
Written Sources   95
Online Sources   96
    CONVERGENCE COACH   97

Public Records   100

The Freedom of Information Act   103

What Do You Think?   103

Exercises   105

Featured Online Activity   105

7 • Interviewing Techniques   107

Gathering Details   109

Sensitivity   109

Listening and Note-Taking Skills   110

The Pros and Cons of Tape Recorders   110

Listening Tips   111

Note-Taking Tips   113

Tips for Interviewers   115

E-mail Interviews   122

CONVERGENCE COACH   123

The GOAL Method of Interviewing   123

ETHICS   124

Telephone Interviewing   125

Interviewing Problems   127

What Do You Think?   127

Exercises   128

Featured Online Activity   128

Part Three • Constructing Stories

8 • Leads and Nut Graphs   131

Hard-news Leads, Soft Leads and Nut Graphs   132

Hard-news Leads   133

CONVERGENCE COACH   144

Soft Leads   145

ETHICS   146

Tips for Finding Your Lead   156

What Do You Think?   156

Exercises   157

Featured Online Activity   159

9 • Story Organization   161

The Writing Process   161

ETHICS   165

Story Structure   165

CONVERGENCE COACH   169

Making Middles Move   170

Endings   173

Body Building from Start to Finish   178

What Do You Think?   179

Exercises   180

Featured Online Activity   180

10 • Story Forms   183

Inverted Pyramid   183

The Wall Street Journal Formula   185

CONVERGENCE COACH   188

Hourglass Structure   189

List Technique   190

ETHICS   191

Question/Answer Format   192

Sections Technique   193

What Do You Think?   193

Exercises   195

Featured Online Activity   197

11 • Storytelling and Feature Techniques   199

Narrative Writing   200

Reading to Write   201

Reporting Tools   202

Writing Tools   203

Descriptive Techniques   204

CONVERGENCE COACH   212

Storytelling Structure   215

ETHICS   216

Serial Narratives   218

What Do You Think?   219

Exercises   219

Featured Online Activity   220

12 • Broadcast News Writing   223

Producing a Newscast   224

CONVERGENCE COACH   228

Writing Tips   229

Job Qualities   229

Broadcast vs. Newspaper and Web Writing   230

ETHICS   236

Teasers and Lead-ins   236

Writing for Radio   237

Broadcast Style   238

Story Structure   239

Revising Stories   245

Glossary 246
What Do You Think? 247
Exercises 247
Featured Online Activity 248

13 • Online Journalism 251

Reporting for the Web 253
ETHICS 255
Online Readers 255
Story Planning 256
Writing Techniques 258
Headlines, Blurbs and Briefs 259
CONVERGENCE COACH 260
Story Structure 263
Personal Storytelling 265
Revise 265
Take Risks 266
What Do You Think? 266
Exercises 266
Featured Online Activity 267

14 • Public Relations Writing 269

Forms of Delivery 270
Writing Skills for News Releases 271
ETHICS 272
Structure of News Releases 273
CONVERGENCE COACH 277
Video News Releases 278
Public Service Announcements 280
Media Kits 281
Corporate Publications 283
Corporate Web Sites 284
What Do You Think? 285
Exercises 285
Featured Online Activity 287

Part Four • Understanding Media Issues

15 • Media Law 289

Libel 290
The Importance of Accuracy 294
ETHICS 298
Invasion of Privacy 298

Online Legal Issues 301
CONVERGENCE COACH 303
Copyright 304
What Do You Think? 304
Exercises 304
Featured Online Activity 305

16 • Media Ethics 307

Deception 307
Plagiarism 309
Privacy Issues 310
CONVERGENCE COACH 316
Ethical Reasoning 317
ETHICS 317
Codes of Ethics 318
What Do You Think? 318
Exercises 318
Featured Online Activity 319

17 • Multicultural Sensitivity 321

The Language of Multiculturalism 321
Minorities in the News 322
ETHICS 324
Gender Differences 325
Guidelines for Writing About Special Groups 327
CONVERGENCE COACH 328
What Do You Think? 332
Exercises 333
Featured Online Activity 333

Part Five • Applying the Techniques

18 • Profiles and Obituaries 335

Turning Points 337
Profile Planning Tips 338
Basic Elements of Profiles 338
The GOAL Method 339
CONVERGENCE COACH 341
Organizing the Profile 341
Putting It All Together 342
ETHICS 345
Writing Snapshot Profiles 345

Obituaries 348
The Importance of Facts 350
Obituary Guidelines 351
What Do You Think? 353
Exercises 354
Featured Online Activity 355

19 • Beat Reporting 357
Developing Story Ideas 358
Cultivating Sources 359
ETHICS 360
Records and Research 360
Beginning a Beat 362
Covering Specialty Beats 364
CONVERGENCE COACH 366
What Do You Think? 374
Exercises 374
Featured Online Activity 375

20 • Speeches, News Conferences and Meetings 377
Media Manipulation 379
ETHICS 381
Preparation 381
Stories About Speeches 382
CONVERGENCE COACH 383
Stories About News Conferences 384
Stories About Meetings 385
What Do You Think? 389
Exercises 390
Featured Online Activity 390

21 • Government and Statistical Stories 393
CONVERGENCE COACH 395
Reporting Tips 395
Visuals 397
ETHICS 397
Writing Tips 398
Statistical Stories 402
Budget Stories 404
What Do You Think? 409
Exercises 410
Featured Online Activity 411

22 • Crime and Punishment 413
Crime Stories 414
ETHICS 426
Court Stories 427
CONVERGENCE COACH 428
What Do You Think? 436
Exercises 439
Featured Online Activity 441

23 • Disasters, Weather and Tragedies 443
ETHICS 447
Reporting Techniques 449
CONVERGENCE COACH 454
Airplane Crashes 460
Natural Disasters 461
Weather Stories 463
Personal Tragedy 466
What Do You Think? 466
Exercises 471
Featured Online Activity 471

24 • Media Jobs and Internships 473
Finding Jobs and Internships 474
Applying for a Job or Internship 475
Writing Cover Letters 477
ETHICS 482
Résumés 483
CONVERGENCE COACH 484
Interviews 486
What Do You Think? 488
Exercises 489
Featured Online Activity 489

Appendix 1—Grammar and Usage 490
Appendix 2—Style Guide 502
Credits 515
Index 523

Preface

We are living in an age of rapid changes in the media, but the basic principles of good writing, accurate reporting and ethical behavior are timeless. However, this sixth edition of *Writing and Reporting News: A Coaching Method* incorporates many of the changes taking place in the media. It emphasizes convergence throughout the book to help you prepare for careers in the media that require knowledge of print, broadcast and online journalism skills. This book includes information about blogs, podcasts, and social networking sites. As in previous editions, the coaching concepts of this book are designed to help you acquire the writing and reporting skills you will need no matter which media field you choose to enter. The book also emphasizes media ethics in every chapter so that you can gain an understanding of the problems you might encounter and learn ethical principles that will help you resolve them.

The coaching method, which is the foundation of this book, is a way of helping writers discover their problems and learn techniques to solve them. The book features tips from leading writing coaches and award-winning journalists.

New Material in This Edition

This sixth edition of *Writing and Reporting News: A Coaching Method* has been substantially revised to include an emphasis on convergence media skills in every chapter and the following new material:

- Convergence Coach boxes in every chapter
- Interactive questions—"What Do You Think?"—at the end of every chapter
- Chapter 1—Changing Concepts of News—has been completely revised and updated
- Chapter 2—Blogs—is a new chapter about blogs, podcasts and citizen journalism
- Chapter 4—Convergent Media Writing—is a new chapter that includes the anatomy of a news story for print, broadcast and the Web
- Chapter 12—Broadcast News Writing—completely revised
- Chapter 13—Completely revised chapter on online journalism including award-winning student Web sites and the Virginia Tech massacre
- Increased emphasis on public relations throughout the book
- Comparison of print and broadcast versions of stories in several chapters
- Emphasis on blogs and social networking sites in several chapters including the chapters on media law and ethics
- New examples throughout the book—including new cases in the ethics chapter such as the Duke rape case and the television show, "To Catch a Predator"

- Separate chapter on story organization, emphasizing transitions, endings, revision of stories
- Separate chapter on story forms, including models of the inverted pyramid, the *Wall Street Journal* formula, lists, question and answer and other basic structures.
- More interactive quizzes and assignments on the book Web site *academic.cengage.com/masscomm/rich/writingandreportingnews6e*
- Student workbook now incorporated into the book Web site at no extra charge
- Grammar is now in an appendix, as is an abbreviated Associated Press Style Guide

How the Book Is Organized

If you are an instructor who has used previous editions of this textbook, you will find many changes. Although this textbook is arranged sequentially to take students through the steps from conceiving ideas to constructing stories, you do not have to use the book in the order it is written. Each chapter is self-contained so that you can design the course as you prefer.

Most of the material in the fifth edition has been retained, but because new chapters have been added, the order of the chapters has changed as follows:

Part One: Understanding News

1 Changing Concepts of News (no change)
2 Blogs (new chapter)
3 The Basic News Story (was Chapter 2)
4 Convergent Media Writing (new chapter)

Part Two: Collecting Information

5 Curiosity and Story Ideas (was Chapter 3)
6 Sources and Online Research (was Chapter 4)
7 Interviewing Techniques (was Chapter 5)

Part Three: Constructing Stories

8 Leads and Nut Graphs (was Chapter 7)
9 Story Organization (was Chapter 8)
10 Story Forms (separate chapter was included in Story Organization)
11 Storytelling and Feature Techniques (was Chapter 9)
12 Broadcast News Writing (was Chapter 11 and has been completely rewritten)
13 Online Journalism (was Chapter 12 and has been completely rewritten)
14 Public Relations Writing (was chapter 10 but moved here because it incorporates print and broadcast writing skills)

Part Four: Understanding Media Issues

15 Media Law (was Chapter 13)

16 Media Ethics (was Chapter 14)

17 Multicultural Sensitivity (was Chapter 15)

(Global Journalism, former Chapter 16, eliminated)

Part Five: Applying the Techniques

18 Profiles and Obituaries (was Chapter 22; moved up to give students practice in these skills earlier in the course)

19 Beat Reporting (was Chapter 17)

20 Speeches, News Conferences and Meetings (was Chapter 18)

21 Government and Statistical Stories (was Chapter 19)

22 Crime and Punishment (was Chapter 20)

23 Disasters, Weather and Tragedies (was Chapter 21)

24 Media Jobs and Internships (was Chapter 23)

Appendix 1: Grammar and Usage (previously Chapter 6)

Appendix 2: Style Guide

Acknowledgments

I would like to thank many people at Cengage Learning who made the sixth edition of this textbook possible. They include: Lyn Uhl, publisher of English, Communication and College Success; Michael Rosenberg, publisher of the Humanities division; Megan Garvey, assistant editor of Humanities; Tiffany Kayes, content project manager for the Academic and Professional Group; Rajni Pisharody, project manager in charge of production and George Watson, copy editor.

I would also like to thank the reviewers, who contributed their time and advice for this edition. They include Barbara Adams, Ithaca College; Zita Arocha, University of Texas at El Paso; Ronald Bonn, University of San Diego; Robert Cundiff, Clearwater Christian College; George Daniels, The University of Alabama; Bonnie Davis, Virginia Commonwealth University; Kym Fox, Texas State University; Dave Garlock, University of Texas; Gary Larson, University of Nevada, Las Vegas; Carol Madere, Southeastern Louisiana University; Wanda Mouton, Stephen F. Austin State University; Sandy Nichols, Towson University; Scoobie Ryan, University of Kentucky School of Journalism and Telecommunications; Ivana Segvic Boudreaux, University of Texas at Arlington; David Smith, University of Texas at El Paso; Susan Smith, University of Wisconsin–Madison and Kate Tillery-Danzer, University of Wisconsin–Madison.

About the Author

Courtesy of Carole Rich

Carole Rich has spent 20 years teaching journalism at four universities and coaching professional writers throughout the U.S. She has taught at the University of Alaska–Anchorage and has served as chair of the journalism department at Hofstra University in Long Island, N.Y. She began her teaching career at the University of Arizona in 1985 and then taught journalism at the University of Kansas from 1987 to 1998 when she was hired as the distinguished Atwood professor in Alaska. Prior to becoming a professor, she worked for 16 years in the newspaper industry. She was a reporter for the former *Philadelphia Evening Bulletin,* city editor of the *Sun-Sentinel* in Fort Lauderdale, Fla., and deputy metropolitan editor of the *Hartford (Ct.) Courant.*

Rich has been a visiting writing coach at newspapers throughout the United States and has conducted many writing seminars at journalism organizations, including a seminar for professional journalists in Spain. She is also the author of *Creating Online Media: A Guide to Research, Writing and Design on the Internet,* published by McGraw-Hill.

1

Coaching Tips

Consider different ways to present your story for print, broadcast and online media.

Compare how similar stories are presented in print, online and broadcast media.

Ask yourself how your story affects your readers.

Consider whether your story needs a photograph, graphic, audio or video.

Plan to update your story for online delivery.

Plan interactive elements for online responses.

It [convergence] used to be defined as multiple media—a newspaper and a television station and a radio station and a Web site working together to best tell a story. . . . To me it's much more about serving the audience however the audience wants to be served, so that they can have our content whenever they want it and however they want it.

—Rob Curley, vice president of WashingtonPost.Newsweek Interactive

1 Changing Concepts of News

It's shortly after 1 a.m. and the police officer's patrol is uneventful, except for the man carrying a 5-inch-long rat on his shoulder. No crime; it was just a man who bought a rat at a pet store. At 5:42 a.m. a young mother wakes to the cries of her hungry 10-month-old daughter. At noon a homeless woman with a canister of pepper spray in her bra waits for lunch at the local soup kitchen, and as midnight approaches three fraternity members celebrate the last day of classes by climbing on the merry-go-round at a shopping mall.

These are just a few of scores of stories and photographs that chronicle one day in the life of residents in Lawrence, Kansas. The project could be done in any community. But when the *Lawrence* (Kan.) *Journal-World* tackled the subject, it created a "multimedia time capsule" by producing the story in the newspaper, on television and on its Web site with text, photos, audio and video.

That's not unusual these days. What made this project distinctive was that the newspaper and its partner TV station asked residents to participate by sending in reports about their day in any form: podcasts, broadcast, blogs, video, photos or text via e-mail.

This project was one of several innovative methods the *Lawrence Journal-World* has produced in the last several years to interact with its readers and viewers in multimedia forms. And it is an example of how the nature of news is changing.

Joel Mathis, managing editor for convergence at the *Journal-World*, says the project was created to focus on stories about how people live on a daily basis. "It was telling the stories we don't often tell because we're so busy telling stories about tax increases. Almost every news organization has done a 24-hour story but what made this different was the participation from the community."

Mathis chuckles when he talks about the entries via YouTube. "I expected something from the high schools, but we got nothing from them. The only YouTube submissions came from the senior citizens at the senior center."

In addition, reporters and photographers from the newspaper and TV station blanketed the community to document life in the city throughout the day and night.

Mathis says the project was the most complicated he has ever organized. "It involved every reporter and staff member on the newspaper and 6News (TV). We had to make sure everyone had their assignments at every hour."

Only some of the stories could be published in the newspaper for the three days of the series, but all of the stories and photos are posted on the Web where the project will remain indefinitely, Mathis says.

Not only is the delivery of information available in many forms, but the definitions of news are also evolving, and economic factors such as mergers of media companies have changed the landscape of the news industry.

Declining newspaper circulation, increased competition from cable television news stations, and access to millions of sites on the Internet are forcing news organizations to expand ways to interest readers and viewers.

Media Convergence

Good writing is still the cornerstone for all media, but the lines between print and broadcast news are blurring. The days of writing for a single medium have ended at most news, public relations and advertising organizations.

This mixture of media is called "convergence," "multimedia," "integrated media" and other terms. Although many of the skills you need to become a journalist are still grounded in basic reporting and writing principles, in today's market you'll need to gain some knowledge of how to present information for print, broadcast and online media.

Peter M. Zollman, a founder of Advanced Interactive Media Group in Florida, says news organizations must be prepared to provide information on a variety of devices: "You have to serve your audience with content and information they want in whatever form they want it. That means print, audio, video on any device they want. People will want the information they want when they want it. Your deadline is whenever the heck you get it and make it available to your audiences."

Rob Curley, who is considered one of the most innovative pioneers in online content, echoes Zollman's perspective of providing the audience news in any form they want. But he says the concept of convergence is changing. In the past a TV station would cooperate with a newspaper by telling viewers to read more about the story in tomorrow's newspaper and the newspaper would promote something on the TV station, or they would promote something on their Web sites. Curley says that was the nature of convergence, but he says it was really just "cross-promotion."

Bill Snead

Rob Curley, vice president of product development for Washingtonpost.Newsweek Interactive

At many news organizations, that concept of convergence as cross-promotion is still practiced, but more newspapers and broadcast news programs are increasing the content on their Web sites with an emphasis on interacting with readers and viewers. Although the terms "multimedia" and "convergence" can be considered interchangeable, some journalists consider multimedia as information specifically created for several media with special elements designed for the Web. The *Lawrence-Journal World* was a forerunner in this respect, due in part to Curley.

Prior to his current position as vice president of the combined interactive division of the Washington Post and Newsweek, Curley gained national attention for the innovative Web sites he created at the *Lawrence Journal-World* in Kansas. Because nearly 30,000 people are students and employees of the University of Kansas in Lawrence, Curley decided to create a separate Web site to appeal to the college audience. This site, *www.lawrence.com,* features content such as weekly drink specials, local bands, entertainment listings and the most popular feature—blogs, which are personal journals written by college students or members of the community.

"We really go all the way out with *Lawrence.com,*" Curley said in an interview shortly after he created it. "Six weeks into the site, it broke a million page views. We give a free print edition targeted to college students, but 100 percent of the content of the print edition is from the Web. We believe it is important to create separate brands. We built a really 'edgy' site. The Web site can e-mail you and remind you of items on your cell phone. The Web site will call you. It features a database of all the bands in town. The bloggers are the most visited part of *Lawrence.com.* We don't pay them. We do read all the blogs; we're looking for some stuff that could be slander or libelous. All of our bloggers have to use their real names."

Another site Curley created, geared to the KU sports-loving community, is *www2.kusports.com.* "We offer updates on game days every five minutes," Curley said. "We're trying to appeal to our audiences. We hire the smartest college kid we can find to do promotions." The site also features live chats with the coach of the KU Jayhawks basketball team and other sports-related personalities.

Curley's influence is still apparent at the *Journal-World,* which continues to publish innovative multimedia projects, such as a recent one about underage drinking. The project features an interactive map, which the reader can click on at different locations to show the number of violations for each bar and liquor store.

The innovative nature of the *Journal-World* is due largely to the vision of its owner/ publisher Dolph C. Simons Jr. In 1991, long before convergence became a popular concept, Simons declared that the newspaper was no longer the only way to operate a media business. The company publishes the newspaper and owns a cable TV station, provides an Internet service and even offers telephone service to the community.

"We believe it is important to look upon our business as an 'information business,' not merely a newspaper or a cable television operation," Simons said at an event celebrating the 100th anniversary of the *Journal-World.* "We want to stay abreast of new developments and be able to deliver news and advertising, as well as other information, however a reader or advertiser might desire."

Ten years later, Simons converted a vacant post office building into a modern convergent newsroom. A circular multimedia desk dominates the ground-floor atrium, which is surrounded by a balcony on the second floor, where the *Journal-World* and cable TV reporters work. Editors on the multimedia desk coordinate with print and broadcast reporters and editors.

Although the *Journal-World* is a morning newspaper, news is posted and updated throughout the day and night. When reporters get a story, they have to write it for the Web, where it will be posted shortly after the event occurred. Reporters may also appear on the company's cable television station, Sunflower Channel 6, where they might report their story or discuss it with the anchor on the nightly news. Then the reporters write a more complete or updated form of the story for the next morning's newspaper. The Web site also features chats with reporters and editors.

The most vivid example of convergence is the way the reporters collaborate. Reporters who share the same beats from the newspaper and TV station sit together. The *Journal-World* city government reporter's desk is next to the reporter who covers that beat for cable 6News, and the sports reporters and editors for the newspaper, the TV station, and the Web site, *KUSports.com,* also sit next to one another.

As the 21st century began, convergence took a different form. Media organizations weren't just merging different technologies in the same story; they were merging with other companies that could provide the audio and video for their online sites. Consider convergence more like a marriage or partnership, in which each type of media retains a distinct identity, but instead of competing with one another, the different media cooperate and contribute to the total product.

The Taj Mahal of media convergence is the $40 million glass and concrete News Center building, home to *The Tampa Tribune,* its partner

Bill Snead

Convergence desk at the
Lawrence (Kan.) *Journal-World*

television station, WFLA-TV, and the joint Web site, *www.tbo.com,* all owned by Media General Inc. The first floor houses a modern television station, complete with robotic cameras, and the fourth floor contains administrative offices. But the nerve centers are on the second and third floors. The heartbeat of this four-story monument is the multimedia center, a group of semicircular desks in an open atrium on the second floor. Multimedia editors can look up to the third-floor newsroom of the *Tribune,* or reporters can peer down from the balcony to the multimedia center. More often, reporters stop by the desk to pitch their stories for the Web.

Although news decisions for the TV station and the newspaper remain separate, the multimedia staff coordinates stories that both media will cover for the Web site. Kenneth Knight, multimedia coordinator of the News Center, says that despite the sophisticated computer equipment, much of the collaboration occurs by "sneakerware," running upstairs to the *Tribune* newsroom or downstairs to the TV producers' offices, which encircle the second floor. On an almost daily basis, the multimedia desk will use video from the TV station and print stories to produce multimedia packages on the Web site.

In a report on Florida's basic skills tests for students, reporters from *The Tampa Tribune* and the TV station cooperated in live chats, and the Web site featured a bulletin board for comments, a quiz, sample test questions and other content from print and video reports. A report about dangerous dogs was a TV multimedia production with video, and a report about online grocery shopping was a joint newspaper and Web product, which featured tips and an interactive poll.

As with the reporters at the *Journal-World,* the roles of print and broadcast journalists in Tampa are also converging. *The Tampa Tribune* newspaper reporters are being trained for broadcast because they may break their stories first on television, while WFLA-TV reporters may write their stories in print style for the newspaper or the Web.

Most editors in convergent newsrooms praise the partnerships, but the marriages are not without problems. Janet Coats, former executive editor of the *Sarasota Herald-Tribune* in Florida, which is a partner with cable television SNN6 (Six News Now), said staff turnover was fairly high when the newspaper began its partnership with TV. The totally digital television operation is in a converted conference room off the side of the newsroom.

"There was enthusiasm among some people and resistance among others," said Coats. "One print reporter who was initially reluctant to go on TV later relented. I don't think he felt his soul was eternally damned."

Even as the media continue to converge, it's likely that all types of media will continue to survive in their distinct forms for many years.

Changing Delivery of News

Constant changes in technology have spawned an alphabet soup of new terms related to forms of delivering news. Almost all news Web sites offer to deliver information via e-mail or to an iPod, a portable media player. Several of these forms will be discussed in more detail in the next chapter, but here are some terms that describe the changing forms of news delivery:

- **Blogs:** The term "blog" is short for "weblog" because blogs are posted on the Web, particularly in free social networking sites such as Facebook or MySpace. A blog can be a personal journal or brief commentary about any topic and can include audio or video.

- **Podcast:** This is digital media information in audio or video form distributed over the Internet for use on a portable media player such as an iPod, an instrument developed by Apple Inc., or an MP3 player. Pod is an abbreviation for "portable on demand." You don't need an iPod to hear or view a podcast; you can receive it on your computer with the use of software.

- **RSS:** These letters stand for "Really Simple Syndication," which is probably simpler to use than to define. If you want to receive certain blogs or podcasts regularly, you can subscribe to a site using a Web feed reader called an "aggregator" that will compile them and deliver them to you. You insert a link to the site into the aggregator software (see next item). Search engines such as Google or Yahoo! offer to deliver automatic updates of news via

RSS feeds. These feeds, delivered to your e-mail, contain headlines, summaries and links to the articles.

- **Aggregator:** This is software that compiles or collects certain Web sites that you want delivered to you regularly and pushes them to you via e-mail or automatically downloads them for you into a portable media player. The aggregator is also known as a feed reader because it "reads" the sites it will "feed" to you. It checks them for new material and downloads updates to your computer or portable media device.

Economic Changes in Media

The changing face of the media isn't just in the content and delivery of news; it is in the ownership of the largest media organizations. Economic forces created significant changes in major media companies at the start of the 21st century. Newspaper circulation was declining and the large media companies listed on the stock exchange were under pressure because of sagging stock profits for their shareholders. Media companies demanded cuts in staffs and resources at their news organizations, but those measures did not do enough to boost the profits so two of the largest companies were sold.

Knight-Ridder Inc. sold its 32 newspapers to the McClatchy Co. in 2006. But the new owners, concerned about unprofitable newspapers in some of the larger markets, decided to sell 12 of the Knight-Ridder papers, including *The Philadelphia Inquirer*, the *San Jose* (Calif.) *Mercury News*, and the *Star Tribune* in Minneapolis.

The Tribune Company, which owned 11 daily newspapers, 23 television stations and the Chicago Cubs, was another major media organization that was sold in 2007 to Chicago real estate magnate Sam Zell. Among the major newspapers that the Tribune Company sold were the *Chicago Tribune*, *Los Angeles Times* and the *Baltimore Sun*. The company was the second largest media company in the U.S.; Gannett Co. is the largest.

Another major acquisition was Reuters, an international news service, which was bought by the Thomson Company, a Canadian-based firm that published textbooks and educational materials, particularly business information.

Journalists who got into the business years ago with the idealistic notion that the primary concern of media companies was content became disillusioned by the emphasis on economics, and several editors at major newspapers like the *Los Angeles Times* quit in protest. The times were changing and the news business was just that— a business that was supposed to make a profit.

Changes in Online News

The Web has changed the nature of news in other ways:

Continual Deadlines: When a news story breaks, reporters at many newspaper and broadcast organizations are expected to file the story immediately for the Web and update major stories online throughout the day. Competition for readers is keen.

More news sites are competing with MSNBC and CNN, which consider themselves "24\7" sites, meaning they publish news 24 hours a day, seven days a week. They are not alone.

Interactive Content: One of the main distinctions of online news is the ability to interact with readers. Web news stories often feature polls, chats, and questions at the end of stories to prompt readers to express their views. More than ever, writers need to consider how their audience will be affected by the story, regardless of the medium.

Related Links: Online news is accompanied by links to related information, so a news story may no longer be a single entity. Traditional print and broadcast news stories also refer readers and viewers to related online information. The Web has intensified research and reporting.

Nonlinear Structure: Print and broadcast news stories are written in linear order—to be read or heard from beginning to end as if in a straight line. Because the Web features links and multimedia features, it creates a nonlinear environment, meaning readers may access content in any order they choose. Although many online news stories are still linear, original Web content is organized in more related pieces. Instead of one story containing all the information, nonlinear news might be split into separate parts for background, profiles, timelines, databases and multimedia.

Databases: Many news sites offer databases that you can search for information about health, school test scores or crime statistics in your community. For example, *The Philadelphia Inquirer* (*www.philly.com/inquirer*) offers an annual report card allowing you to search a database for public and private schools in Pennsylvania and New Jersey to find out about school test scores and related facts for schools in these areas. Many other news sites also offer searchable databases for crime statistics, school test scores and other community information.

Personalized Journalism: In addition to blogs as a form of personalized journalism, online news sites are reaching out to users by asking them to contribute their personal stories. Sunline (*www.sunline.net*), the Web site for the *Sun-Herald* (Charlotte, Fla.), led the way in personal journalism by allowing its users to post their own obituaries, war stories, pictures of pets and other personal sites.

A more sophisticated form of personal journalism is the basis of *www.musarium.com,* a site devoted to personal narratives. The site's motto is "Discovering signs of intelligent life on earth." The stories and photo essays range from a documentary about a man seeking assisted suicide to a special section called "Interviews 50 Cents." Reporters for this section of the Web site traveled around the country with a card table and a sign offering people 50 cents for their stories, which included revelations about people's fears, hopes, dreams and love stories.

Specialized Beats: Almost all news sites feature sections devoted to health, technology, money, travel and other subjects that appeal to readers' special interests. Although traditional media have always covered these subjects, sometimes limited to certain days of the week, Web news sites offer more frequent and more thorough coverage.

Citizen Journalism

The Web was not the only cause of change in the news industry. Years of declining newspaper circulation spurred a movement called "public journalism," also called "civic journalism," a form of reporting that involves readers in planning the news based on their concerns. It is an attempt to make readers care about their community and the news coverage. If unemployment is a concern to the community, the newspaper might ask readers to suggest problems they want the paper to address, such as job opportunities, retraining and resources. Editors and reporters then might plan a series based on those topics.

The Charlotte (N.C.) *Observer* was one newspaper that practiced public journalism extensively, especially in its election coverage. In one presidential election, the *Observer* conducted polls jointly with a local television station and asked voters what issues they wanted politicians to discuss. Reporters then interviewed candidates about those issues instead of letting candidates discuss their own agendas.

ETHICS   Plagiarism and Fabrication

The case: (This situation is based on the case of Jayson Blair, a former reporter for *The New York Times*.) A reporter for your campus newspaper quickly becomes a star by charming editors and professors, volunteering for stories and writing prolifically. His stories are filled with descriptive details and human-interest features that gain him a reputation as an outstanding writer. But the editor of the paper is concerned because several of his stories require corrections after they are printed, and the editor can't trace some of the sources. The editor and some staffers complain to journalism professors about this reporter's inaccuracies, but the professors dismiss the complaints as jealousy over this rising star.

The reporter lands a prestigious internship with a large daily newspaper and later is hired full time even before he graduates from journalism school. He shows much promise and gets assigned to major national stories, but during his four years at the paper his stories require 50 corrections, and one of his editors thinks he should be fired. However, top management at the newspaper excuses the reporter because he says that he has had several personal problems.

His trail of deception, plagiarism and fabrication is uncovered after the newspaper is notified that he plagiarized a story written by one of his former campus newspaper colleagues, who was working at a newspaper in San Antonio. The story, about a Texas mother whose son died in Iraq, was only one of at least 36 articles containing plagiarized or fabricated quotes and facts. The reporter resigns, and the newspaper publishes an extensive front-page Sunday story explaining the situation and apologizing to readers.

Dilemma:

■ What steps could have or should have been taken to prevent this situation from happening?

■ Should a reporter be fired as soon as the first incident of plagiarism or fabrication is discovered?

■ Should a reporter whose stories require numerous corrections be fired?

■ What would you have done if you were the campus editor or his editor at that newspaper?

■ What can be done to prevent plagiarism and fabrication in the media?

Ethical values: Accuracy, credibility.

Ethical guidelines: According to the code of ethics of the Society of Professional Journalists, "Seek truth and report it. Test the accuracy of information from all sources and exercise care to avoid inadvertent error. Deliberate distortion is never permissible."

The concept of public journalism has evolved into a movement called "citizen journalism," where members of the community contribute to the news via blogs and online interactive forums. Several television news channels such as CNN and MSNBC use citizens to report the news, particularly in times of tragedies such as floods, hurricanes, and tornadoes. It is also referred to as participatory journalism or "user-generated content," where members of the community actively contribute to the news by reporting or writing reports.

The *Lawrence Journal-World* 24-hour project was one form of participatory journalism, but it was not considered real citizen journalism. A better example is the *Journal-World*'s "Citizen Journalism Academy," which includes 25 local citizens who periodically submit news reports or work with the newspaper and its partner TV station to contribute stories for major events such as elections. The "academy" also offers the citizens five sessions of training about news writing and standards taught by *Journal-World* journalists and professors from the University of Kansas journalism program.

Citizen journalism has created controversy about whether citizens who are not employed by a news organization should even be referred to as journalists, but the movement is clearly a significant force in news media.

The Coaching Method

Whether you are writing for print, broadcast or online media, you still need to master the basic skills of reporting and writing. The coaching method is a way of helping writers discover their problems and learn techniques to solve them. An editor may concentrate on the results of your writing and fix the story, but a coach concentrates on the process of writing. A coach doesn't stress how you failed to write a good story; a coach stresses how you can succeed.

Like a basketball coach who trains players how to improve their techniques on the court, a writing coach trains writers how to perfect their techniques in the craft. This book aims to serve as a surrogate writing coach by anticipating the problems writers might have and offering solutions. It features tips from leading writing coaches and award-winning journalists.

The coaching method in this book has four phases:

1 **Conceive the idea:** At this stage you develop the idea for the story. If you are covering an event, such as a meeting or an accident, you need to start with the idea—the main point of what occurred. If you are writing a news story about a problem in your community, you still start with a central idea, which is the focus of your story. Once you begin reporting, you may discover some information that is more important than your original focus. Thus, you should be flexible and decide the focus for writing after you collect the material.

2 **Collect:** This is the reporting stage. Before you conduct your interview, you should look for background information: Check online sources and any available documents or clips from previous stories about your subject and your sources. Then interview sources, and gather as much information as you can about your topic. Don't rely on one source; seek several points of view. Ask more questions

and take more notes than you plan to use. You should also jot down your observations and gather as many details as possible.

3   **Construct:** This is the planning and writing stage. Begin with a plan for your story developed around the focus, the main idea of your story. Then go through your notes and mark only the information related to that focus. Like a carpenter building a house, you need a blueprint. A good writer does not write a story without a plan. Jot down a few key words to indicate how you will organize your story. Then write a first draft of your story. You may revise your original draft in the next step.

4   **Correct:** After you have written your story, read it and make any necessary changes. You may decide to add or delete information or to completely reorganize the story during this stage. You should also check the spelling of all names and the accuracy of facts, and you should correct grammar, style and typing errors.

These four steps constitute the basic process for all news stories. In the coming chapters you will learn many techniques for reporting and writing news. But first you need to understand what constitutes a news story.

Qualities of News

Definitions of news are changing. But these are some traditional qualities of news stories:

Timeliness: An event that happened the day of or day before publication or an event that is due to happen in the immediate future is considered timely. In broadcast and online media, timeliness is considered "immediacy" and is even more crucial. When stories are posted online immediately after they happen or broadcast several times a day, you have to consider how to update them frequently. Even print newspapers have several editions, which require updating. Some events that happened in the past may also be considered timely if they are printed on an anniversary of the event, such as one, five or 10 years after the incident. Timeliness answers this reader's question: Why are you telling me this now? The following story was timely because it was published the day after the accident:

> A bus loaded with elementary school children crashed head-on into a compact car in southwestern Jefferson County yesterday, injuring 24 students and the two drivers.
>
> —The (Louisville, Ky.) *Courier-Journal*

If that story had been written for broadcast or online media, the angle would have been updated to report the current condition of the students and drivers.

Proximity: An event may be of interest to local readers because it happened in or close to the community. This story would be of particular interest to residents in the Oregon community where the man lived:

A 71-year-old former psychologist received an eight-year prison sentence Monday for running the most sophisticated indoor marijuana growing operation ever discovered in Clackamas County.

Authorities said Arvord E. Belden of Estacada may be the oldest man ever sentenced to federal prison for a drug crime in Oregon.

—Dave Hogan, *The* (Portland) *Oregonian*

Unusual Nature: Out-of-the-ordinary events, a bizarre or rare occurrence, or people engaged in unusual activities are considered newsworthy, as in this story:

Man ticketed for walking his lizard

FORT LAUDERDALE, Fla.—Walking your dog along the beach here is illegal—and so is lounging with your lizard, Chris DeMango found out. Mortimer, DeMango's 20-pound purple-tongued monitor lizard, complete with matching pink doll sweater and leash, was out for exercise Monday. DeMango said a walk makes Mortimer more docile, but police said it makes him an illegal lizard—animals are banned on the beach. DeMango was ticketed, and his lizard law violation could cost him 60 days in jail and a $500 fine, said police spokesman Ott Cefkin. DeMango was not amused. "I would think that would be the most absurd thing, if I were to go to jail for this," he grumbled.

—*St. Petersburg* (Fla.) *Times*

Human Interest: People like stories about people who have special problems, achievements or experiences; profiles of people who have overcome difficulties or who seek to improve society inspire readers. This example about a couple who spent $6,000 looking for their lost cat combines human interest and an unusual story:

Five-year-old Marble used to hide in the box springs of a spare bed in Bill and Carol Deckers' Denver home.

Now the Deckers' cat is hiding somewhere in the woods near Carthage, Mo.

Since Marble escaped from the couple's recreational vehicle Aug. 18, the Deckers have spent more than $6,000 trying to get her back.

"We taught her to live with us and we owe it to her," said Carol Decker, 41, a part-time accountant who gave up her job to look for Marble. . . .

Since losing Marble, the Deckers have put up posters and placed newspaper ads in Colorado, Missouri and Oklahoma, and contacted a psychic to locate her, to no avail.

The Deckers have returned to the site, often sleeping outdoors in the hope that their presence would draw Marble to them.

—Tillie Fong, *Rocky Mountain* (Denver) *News*

Conflict: Stories involving conflicts that people have with government or other people are often newsworthy, especially when the conflict reflects local problems.

LANSING—Opponents of a new law that makes it easier to obtain a permit to carry a concealed weapon in most Michigan communities are preparing a petition drive to block the law's implementation.

—Dawson Bell, *Detroit Free Press*

Here is an example of a story that combines conflict with human interest and unusual qualities:

The family expected to mourn Anthony Romeo, who died of heart disease in September at his Seffner home. Instead, they found a stranger in his coffin.

The Hillsborough Medical Examiner's Office had shipped the wrong body to the funeral home.

The mix-up so upset Romeo's son Joseph that he filed suit Monday against Hillsborough County, the Brandon funeral home and the private courier that delivered the body.

—Rachel L. Swarns, *St. Petersburg* (Fla.) *Times*

Impact: Reaction stories to news events or news angles that affect readers have impact, especially when major national stories or tragedies occur in any community. Newspapers often seek local angles by writing how people in their areas are affected by the news, as in this story following a massive tsunami that killed thousands of people in 11 Southeast Asian countries:

Scientists at the West Coast and Alaska Tsunami Warning Center for years worked on a windy hilltop just outside downtown Palmer, far from the reach of potentially disastrous waves and public notice.

But with global attention on tsunami readiness galvanized by the Indian Ocean waves that killed more than 160,000 people, the center is poised for a major upgrade that could protect Alaskans as well as coastal residents around the world, a top federal administrator told staffers at the center.

—Zaz Hollander, *Anchorage Daily News*

Some additional qualities of news to consider:

Helpfulness: Consumer, health and other how-to stories help readers cope with their lives. Online news sites abound with helpful stories.

If your head spins at the torrent of medical studies that fills newspapers, magazines and TV, join the club. It seems that each day brings another round of studies contradicting last month's hot results.

One day vitamin E is found to prevent cancer. Next, it is suspected of causing it.

Margarine is good. No, it's bad.

One can almost hear a collective scream of frustration across the land.

Studies are the cornerstone of medical progress, showing doctors and patients the way to longer, healthier lives. But they can also lead us astray.

To try to help you through the hype and hustle, here's a basic outline of what studies are, how they differ, what they can tell us and where they can go wrong. Call it A User's Guide to Medical Studies. Or, How to Follow Health News Without Having a Stroke.

—Phillip E. Canuto, *Knight-Ridder/Tribune News Service*

Celebrities: People who are well-known for their accomplishments—primarily entertainers, athletes or people who have gained fame for achievements, good or bad—attract a lot of attention. But celebrity news has become so popular that some journalists are concerned it is displacing news and pandering to the public's desire for entertainment.

Ted Koppel, former anchor of the TV show "Nightline," said in a "Frontline" interview: "To the extent that we're now judging journalism by the same standards that we apply to entertainment—in other words, give the public what it wants, not necessarily what it ought to hear, what it ought to see, what it needs, but what it wants—that may prove to be one of the greatest tragedies in the history of American journalism."

Entertainment: Stories that amuse readers, make them feel good or help them enjoy their leisure time have entertainment value. In a broad sense, many of the news features in sports and lifestyle sections can be classified as entertainment. Entertainment stories often involve celebrities or have human-interest qualities. But they are also controversial. The line between news and entertainment is not clear, especially in coverage of celebrities as stated in the previous item. However, this story combines newsworthy qualities of human interest and unusual nature to entertain or amuse readers:

ODESSA, Texas—When Elbert Lewis got his draft notice, he told his wife goodbye. Then he thought of his children. And his seven grandchildren. And his great-grandchild.

The Selective Service was cracking down on potential draft dodgers, and government records showed Lewis failed to register as required by law when he turned 18.

The problem: Lewis turned 18 in 1932.

The records showed his birthdate was Nov. 11, 1976, instead of in 1914.

What's more, Lewis did register for the draft--in 1941. He served on a Navy anti-aircraft cruiser during World War II and received a Purple Heart.

When Lewis got the draft compliance notice Saturday, he broke the news to his wife, Janie.

"He came into the den and said, 'Well, I have to tell you goodbye,'" she said. "Then we called our kids. We just cut up and acted silly about it, really." "We really got a laugh out of it, and so did all four of my kids," Lewis said.

He dashed off a copy of his birth certificate and honorable discharge to the Selective Service.

The agency removed his name from its list, spokesman Lou Brodsky said.

The idea of being 18 again was appealing, to a degree.

"I wouldn't mind it, take away the war," Lewis said.

—*The Associated Press*

Issues or Problems in the Community: These stories usually include qualities such as conflict and proximity. The *St. Cloud* (Minn.) *Times* combined the trends of reader involvement with issues important to minorities in a series called "Open or Intolerant?" The newspaper sought opinions from teenagers of different races as well as from police, city leaders and residents about police treatment of young people of color.

Since moving to St. Cloud three years ago, Jacob "Cisco" Owens says he has been hassled, detained, pulled over and provoked by St. Cloud police officers more times than he can remember.

Owens, a 16-year-old Apollo High School junior, admits he's been in trouble a few times for minor things. But for every time he's done something, anything, wrong, he swears he can identify seven more times he's been confronted by police when he's done nothing at all.

"And almost all the time they ask me if I'm in a gang. It makes me angry that they just assume. It's just a given that I'm treated like that," he says. "Just because I'm young and black, I'm treated like a thug." Dozens of young people of different races in St. Cloud say it's no secret: Police here are known for targeting minority youth for bogus traffic stops, tough talk, and sometimes, rough treatment when responding to calls.

—Lee Rood, *St. Cloud* (Minn.) *Times*

Trends: Stories may indicate patterns or shifts in issues that influence readers' lives, such as increases in crime, social issues and other forces in society.

Many Milwaukee area public libraries no longer have strict "SH!" policies.

Libraries are shedding their image as quiet, somber places for bookworms and students only. Instead, today's libraries offer a wide variety of materials and programs in an effort to appeal to more people.

—Lawrence Sussman, *Milwaukee Journal Sentinel*

Convergence Coach

- Train yourself to think for multimedia. Compare online news stories with those in your local newspaper. Are they the same, or do they offer links, polls, questions and other related features? If your local TV news station has a Web site, compare that site with the newspaper's Web site.

- Learn to think interactively. Analyze interactive online features such as polls, games, message boards and databases in your local Web news sites or others, such as CNN (*www.cnn.com*).

- Plan to update stories. Analyze how major news sites such as *msnbc.com* and *cnn.com* continually update their stories.

- Consider the role of blogs. Analyze blogs for their news or entertainment value. Check journalists' blogs at *www.cyberjournalist.net*.

- Consider the importance of audience. Compare the *Lawrence Journal-World* site, *www2.ljworld.com/*, with its companion site, *www.lawrence.com*.

- Become a visual thinker. Compare the visuals for a news story covered in your newspaper, on TV and online. Consider visuals for the stories you will produce.

Hard News and Features

News falls into two basic categories: hard news and soft news. "Hard news" includes stories of a timely nature about events or conflicts that have just happened or are about to happen, such as crimes, fires, meetings, protest rallies, speeches and testimony in court cases. The hard-news approach is basically an account of what happened, why it happened and how readers will be affected. These stories have immediacy.

"Soft news" is defined as news that entertains or informs, with an emphasis on human interest and novelty and less immediacy than hard news. For example, a profile about a man who designs model airplanes or a story about the effectiveness of diets would be considered soft news.

Soft news can also be stories that focus on people, places or issues that affect readers' lives. These types of stories are called "feature stories." A story about the growing number of babies suffering from AIDS could be considered a soft-news story. It isn't less important than hard news, but it isn't news that happened overnight. However, a feature story can be based on a news event. Instead of being just a factual account of the event, it features or focuses on a particular angle, such as human-interest reactions.

If the action or event occurred the same day as or the day before publication of the newspaper, the event is called "breaking news." Here is an example of the lead of a breaking-news story from a Saturday edition:

> Tornadoes rapped Topeka and southeast Shawnee County Friday afternoon, damaging seven homes and sending residents scurrying for cover.
>
> No one was injured by the short, severe storm that struck unexpectedly.
>
> —Steve Fry, *Topeka* (Kan.) *Capital-Journal*

The preceding example of a hard-news story tells readers what happened. The newspaper also printed this feature story focusing on people affected by the storm:

> Becky Clark of Topeka was told the tornado sirens that sounded Friday afternoon were a false alarm.
>
> Then she got home from work and saw her back yard at 2411 S.E. Gemini Ave. in the Aquarian Acres neighborhood.
>
> "I couldn't believe it," she said.
>
> A tornado had lifted up the family pontoon boat, which was parked in the back yard, and tossed it into the family swimming pool, crushing part of the boat.
>
> "It just wanted to get in the water," said Joe Clark, Becky's husband.
>
> "I guess it was tired of being in dry dock. . . ."
>
> —Joe Taschler, *Topeka* (Kan.) *Capital-Journal*

The hard-news story about the storm was the main story, called a "mainbar." Because the accompanying feature story was a different angle on the same topic, it was a "sidebar" packaged with the main story.

But many other features in a newspaper do not have a breaking-news peg. They simply focus on interesting people or topics. For example, the *Boca Raton* (Fla.) *News* printed a feature story on the growing popularity of waterbeds, a topic of interest to its readers.

The Importance of Visuals

The presentation of a story with photographs or graphics is crucial. Broadcast media depend on visuals for the majority of stories. Studies by The Poynter Institute in St. Petersburg, Fla., show an increased emphasis on graphic devices and color in print media.

In one study, called "Eyes on the News," researchers measured the movements of people's eyes as they read the newspaper. The results of this study, also known as the Eye Trac study, show that readers are drawn to color photographs first, then headlines, cutlines (captions), briefs (stories abbreviated to one to three paragraphs) and a number of other graphic devices called points of entry—points where the reader enters a story. Some of those eye-catching points include subheadlines and quotations displayed in larger type within the story.

The study also concludes that most people only scan the newspaper, looking at headlines and graphics, and that they read very few stories all the way through. The average reader skims about 25 percent of the stories in the newspaper but thoroughly reads only half of those (about 12 percent), the study concludes.

Mario Garcia, who co-authored the Poynter study and is a world-renowned consultant on newspaper design, says the majority of readers today do not remember life without television, so visual elements are crucial in a newspaper. "The marriage of visual and words has to begin early—from the first time you learn reporting," he says.

A subsequent study tracking eye movements of online readers determined that graphics were less important in online news. The study by The Poynter Institute and Stanford University found that online readers focused first on text in Web news sites rather than informational graphics. Follow-up studies in 2004 and 2007 of online readers revealed that readers focused on banner graphics and photos but still focused more on text when they entered a Web site. A surprising finding in 2007 was that online readers will read a story thoroughly if they are interested in it, contrary to earlier studies that claimed online readers had short attention spans. Despite those findings about Web readers' preference for text, most online news sites make extensive use of photos. For example, *Newsday* (*www.newsday.com*) offers a regular feature called "This week in photos."

Although television news depends on video, reporters in all media need to consider audio or video that may accompany a story on the Web. In addition, reporters and public relations practitioners need to consider graphic devices that will enhance the content of a news story or news release.

That is the emphasis at the *Reno* (Nev.) *Gazette-Journal,* a Gannett newspaper that makes extensive use of graphics. Reporters are expected to visualize their stories as a total package involving photos and graphics.

The emphasis is on using verbal and visual tools that will make information clear to readers. For example, a story about rare water spouts from Lake Tahoe was accompanied by the graphic shown below, which explained how water spouts are created. The information was not repeated in the text.

In this multimedia world, planning visual elements is a crucial part of any news presentation.

Graphic explaining a natural disaster

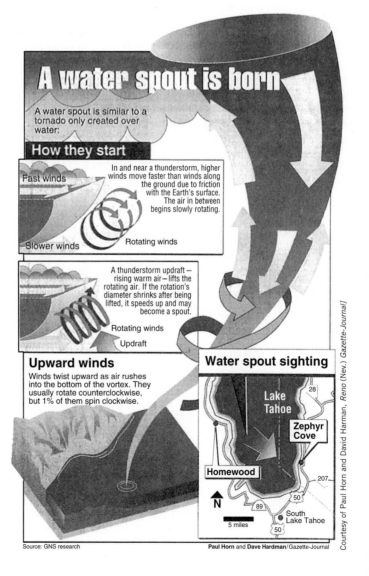

Courtesy of Paul Horn and David Harman, Reno (Nev.) Gazette-Journal

Exercises

1 **Visual awareness:** Try this experiment to test your reading habits. Bring to class a copy of a newspaper you haven't read. Read the newspaper as you would for pleasure. Place a check on the first item you look at—a picture, graphic, headline or story. Mark the stories you read, and place an X at the point in the story where you decide to stop reading. Where did your eye go first? Why are visual elements so important? Now analyze which stories you read and how much of them you read. Where did you stop on most stories? Why? Keep in mind that because you are a journalism student, you may read more than the average reader.

2 **Journal:** Keep a journal of your reading or viewing habits of news for three days. Write a paragraph each day about the kinds of stories you read and didn't read, how many you read all the way through, and how many you read just through the headline or the first few paragraphs. Do the same for stories you read online. Analyze your preferences. Record the amount of time you spent reading the newspaper for pleasure, not for an assignment. Record how much you watched news on TV. Then interview three other people—students, neighbors or strangers--and ask them what kinds of stories they do and don't read in print and online. Ask where they get the majority of their news—from print, broadcast or online media. Write a summary of your findings.

3 **Online news ideas:** Either in small groups or as a class, brainstorm topics and ideas that you would want to read in an online newspaper or magazine. Brainstorm at least three interactive features for an online college newspaper.

4 **Qualities of news:** Analyze your local or campus newspaper on the front page and/or local section. Identify the qualities of news of the main stories. Now do the same for a TV news broadcast. Jot down the stories in a 30-minute telecast and identify the qualities of news in each segment.

☞ **Featured Online Activity** Log on to the book Web site and take the interactive multiple choice quiz on qualities of news at

academic.cengage.com/masscomm/rich/
writingandreportingnews6e

Coaching Tips

Keep your blog short.

Provide links to related articles or sources.

Provide a short headline that explains the main point clearly.

Write a lead that gets to the main point quickly.

Keep sentences short.

Write in conversational tone, the way you would tell your reader a story. You may use the first-person pronoun "I" in a blog but not in a news story.

Offer a question or comment at the end that will elicit readers' responses. Most blog sites are formatted to provide posts from readers to your blog.

The popularity of bloggers is leading to a new way of thinking about news. . . . With much in common as well as many differences, bloggers and mainstream journalists should be looking to one another for ideas on how to navigate our newly revised media world.

—Steve Outing, online media pioneer

2 Blogs

Babbling Brooke runs a modeling agency in Denver and writes a blog about social events in the city. Doug Brown is a reporter who writes a blog about sex, love and life. And Slacker Bride is a Colorado resident who writes her blog about wedding plans.

These are three of more than 25 blogs posted on the *Denver Post* Web site in a section called the "bloghouse." "Think of this place as a funky old apartment building where a lot of different personalities live and hang out," *Post* editors wrote to describe the site's blog collection.

The U.S. dictionary publisher Merriam-Webster defines "blog," as "a Web site that contains an online personal journal with reflections, comments and often hyperlinks." Also known as "web logs," or "weblogs," blogs have proliferated to such an extent that they have their own world called a "blogosphere," which can be considered a social network of people who post blogs. Other blogs are more like essays commenting on news or issues with links to related articles or sources.

MySpace, the most popular social networking site for college students, claims more than 150 million subscribers who post their profiles and messages in text, photos and/or video on the free site. Founded in 2003 by an Internet company called eUniverse, it was bought in 2005 by Fox Broadcasting owner Rupert Murdoch for $580 million and is considered one of the most popular Web sites in the U.S.

YouTube is the leading free site featuring videos. A modest site started in 2005 for people to post personal videos, YouTube became so successful that a year later Google bought it for $1.65 billion. Even politicians running for office began to post videos on YouTube.

The future audiences for news or public relations information are even more likely to be part of the blogging generation. A 2007 study by the Pew Internet and American Life Project reveals that 55 percent of American youths age 12 to 17 who use the Internet have created profiles on online social networking sites, mainly on MySpace.

Some social networking sites restrict access to blogs if members specify limits to a circle of friends, but public blogs can be located through search engines. Every day millions of blogs are added to news and social networking Web sites.

How do you find them? In addition to popular search engines such as Google and Yahoo!, which feature blog searches, these sites and programs can do the work for you:

- **Technorati:** This site is a search engine that indexes millions of blogs and updates the references by tracking posts and links to them. The Technorati Web site claims there are more than 175,000 new blogs created every day. In addition, Technorati teamed up with the Associated Press to index bloggers' comments posted in the 440 newspapers that subscribe to the AP.

- **Trackbacks:** These are links at the end of a blog, like footnotes or references you might put in a term paper. Someone who posts a comment to your blog can insert a link back to his or her comment or related sites, provided that the software for both sites supports trackbacks.

- **Permalink:** Like trackbacks, permalinks are URLs (Web addresses) that link to comments or related sites. They are most often used in blogs.

- **Flickr:** This site is a photo-sharing repository where you can post photos that you may want to use in blogs or share with friends.

- **RSS:** The letters stand for "Really Simple Syndication," which is a program that automatically sends information you requested to your computer or digital media player. The RSS online tool can track information that changes, whether it is in blogs or any Web sites, through an "aggregator," which is a program that compiles the information from the sites you have selected. It basically "feeds" the information to your computer or portable media device. It can be used for news summaries, blogs or podcasts, and audio or video digital files that can be downloaded to your computer or portable media device.

Be careful what you post on a blog, especially if you are seeking a job. Employers have been known to search popular blog sites such as MySpace and Facebook when they are interviewing job candidates. In addition, posting personal information such as telephone numbers or addresses can make it easy for sexual predators or other undesirable people to contact you, despite attempts by social networking sites to protect privacy.

Blogs as News Sources

Although many blogs began as personal journals produced for friends and other people with common interests, they have become valuable sources for journalists when news breaks such as tragedies or weather disasters.

The social networking site Facebook served a crucial role in communication after a gunman massacred 32 people at Virginia Polytechnic Institute and then killed himself on April 16, 2007. Telephone communication was limited that day, so students used Facebook to let friends and families know they were safe and to seek information about other students whose fate was not yet known. "To everyone I haven't talked to yet, I'm okay," one student wrote in a Facebook group called "I'm okay at VT." Journalists searched through profiles and blogs on that site and others to find sources and quotes for their stories about the massacre.

The Virginia Tech tragedy wasn't the first time that blogs and social networking sites had become major sources for news. After Hurricane Katrina in the Gulf Coast, MSNBC recruited citizens to tell their personal stories by asking these questions: "Was your home severely damaged or destroyed after Hurricane Katrina or Hurricane Rita? If you are rebuilding, tell us your story. You may also send text, pictures and video."

A study of the future of media cites the growing "symbiotic" relationship between mainstream media such as newspapers and broadcast, and blogs or other social networks. "It has become common for mainstream media to quote blogs and bloggers, sometimes exclusively, and the conversations between bloggers often provide the ideas for media stories," according to the 2006 study by Future Exploration Network.

Another study by a Washington, D.C.-based Internet communications firm analyzed the Web sites of the 100 most circulated newspapers in the U.S. Ninety-two percent of these newspapers offer video and 95 percent offer blogs. "It is evident that newspapers value tools such as RSS and blogs as methods of gaining new Web-focused readers and also as a method of retaining former readers whose daily habits have changed to include the Internet, as opposed to print news," the study said. "Blogs are an effective way for reporters and newspaper publishers to speak directly to the newspaper's audience. . . . In addition, blogs increase interactivity and stickiness of newspaper Web sites, as features such as 'comments' encourage readers to visit the Web site on a consistent and regular basis."

Consider bloggers as a group of news tipsters. As with all news, you have to check the accuracy of a report and determine the bias of the blogger. Reporters who cover beats often check blogs on their subjects such as government and politics. Information about politics in blogs such as Power Line, Technorati and Wonkette are rich sources of news tips for reporters.

The other advantage of reading blogs for news tips is that they provide insight into what readers and viewers are concerned about, much like letters to the editor. Blogs also provide sources for human interest stories on news events.

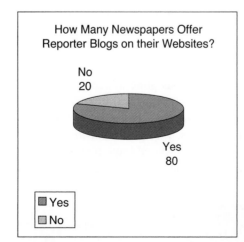
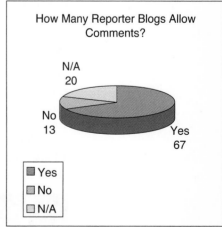

The Bivings Group, from "The Use of the Internet by America's Newspapers."

Citizen Journalism

The concept of involving readers and viewers in reporting and disseminating news is called "citizen journalism," "participatory journalism" or "user-generated-content." The movement is an attempt by media organizations to increase their interaction with their audience. The contributors are often called "citizen journalists," because they are not staff members of the news organization even though they may write blogs on a regular basis for the media Web site.

A pioneer in the user-generated-content movement is a South Korean Web site called OhmyNews. When it was created in 2000, it had 727 citizen reporters contributing content. Seven years later the number had mushroomed to more than 60,000 contributors. Oh Yeon-ho, creator of the site, said in a speech to celebrate the seventh anniversary: "Our citizen reporters work not only in Korea but also from 100 other countries. . . . We are now realizing our motto 'Every citizen is a reporter' all over the world."

In an article on OhmyNews, contributor Ashok Kumar Jha defines citizen journalism as follows: "It is about writing on issues, which the reporter feels is important. It is about telling the world a first-person account. It is about showing everyone the world through the reporter's eyes. It is about the self-confidence that your opinion does matter to thousands of readers."

The Web site has become so popular that in 2007 Oh Yeon-ho created a citizen journalism school in an abandoned elementary school in South Korea. The school will accommodate 100 students who will be trained in journalism skills. Special classes will also be conducted for media executives who want to start a new media venture.

Many U.S. news organizations are also embracing the concept of citizen journalism. *The Spokesman-Review* in Spokane, Wash., is one of them. "One only has to look at the explosion of YouTube, MySpace and the entire blog phenomenon to conclude that people are more engaged than ever in creating and disseminating information," Carla Savalli, senior editor for local news at the newspaper, wrote in a report about the newsroom of the future. "Mass-media newspapers no longer control the pipeline. It is out of this new social order that citizen-generated content springs and perhaps represents an even greater challenge for tradition-bound newsrooms than continuous news or multiplatform publishing."

Transparency

The Spokesman-Review has gone a step further than just encouraging contributions from readers. It is striving for transparency, an effort by news organizations to explain how the newspaper or television station determines the news and how it is covered. To achieve this, *The Spokesman-Review* has opened its editorial meetings to readers and viewers in several ways. It offers webcasts of the editorial meetings at 10 A.M. and 4:30 P.M. Monday through Friday so viewers can see how the decisions about the news are made.

Courtesy of OhmyNews International

The paper also posts a blog called "News is a Conversation" on its Web site with this note: "As part of our effort to increase transparency in journalism, *The Spokesman-Review* has invited readers to talk about our news coverage and content on a daily basis: what they like, what they don't like, and what they'd like to see more of. We participate, but the readers lead the conversation here." And the newspaper Web site offers another feature called "Ask the Editors" to encourage readers to ask questions about the paper's editorial decisions. The paper also invites readers to attend the daily news meetings.

Such transparency is not limited to newspaper organizations. Television news shows also offer blogs to explain their editorial decisions. The CBS News show offers a feature called "Public Eye" on its Web site to foster transparency.

"Public Eye will not just scrutinize CBS News, it will try to lift the curtain and show how the news is made—through video stories, regular news stories and even by taking our community into CBS News meetings, control rooms and edit booths," CBS editors explain on the News Web site. "Public Eye will be run by a team of independent and experienced journalists. They will take questions, criticisms and observations from our vast and articulate audience to the people of CBS News and try to come back with some answers, explanations and analyses."

NBC News also offers a blog to foster transparency. Brian Williams, anchor of the nightly news, writes The Daily Nightly blog to provide a narrative of the day's broadcast and a window into the editorial process at NBC Nightly News, the Web site says.

The movement toward transparency has been fueled in part by growth of blogs, in which citizens have more venues to publicly scrutinize and criticize media coverage, and by several scandals of plagiarism and fabrication. Bloggers have become watchdogs for the media by exposing mistakes in the news.

In one case Dan Rather, a former anchor for CBS, reported a story based on a memo that President George W. Bush received preferential treatment when he was

ETHICS

You are a reporter for a television news program or a local newspaper, and you are covering a follow-up story to a shooting at a high school in your area. You are writing a human interest sidebar and you are seeking sources. You check MySpace under high schools and find several students who have personal pages. Two of the students from the high school have posted poignant messages about the school shooting.

■ Can you quote from those messages in your story?

■ Do you have to attribute the information to the student and to the posting on MySpace?

■ Do you have to contact the students who posted the messages before you quote from them?

The solutions to this ethical dilemma are not clearly defined. Issues involving online resources are being discussed by journalism organizations, but no official codes of ethics exist. However, some general ethical principles can guide your decision. Accuracy is a main principle in journalism

so it makes sense to verify the information by contacting the student on whose Web page the message appears. Other people could have posted messages to the student's MySpace site. Attributing information you get from other sources is another ethical practice. Legally, all information published or posted on a Web site is copyrighted even if it does not bear a copyright symbol so that's another reason to attribute the information and seek permission to use it.

in the National Guard. A blogger posted a commentary on a political blog site that the memo could not be accurate because the typeface used in it didn't exist when the memo was supposedly written. That report was picked up by mainstream newspapers and television news and ultimately resulted in an investigation by CBS and an apology for the story.

Such media black eyes have prompted news organizations to publicly apologize and explain how the situations occurred and what is being done to correct them. Declining circulation of newspapers and decreasing audiences for TV news are other factors that prompt media organizations to interact more with their readers and viewers and improve trust.

Ethical Issues

Bloggers may be acting as watchdogs to improve credibility and trust in the media, but how trustworthy are the bloggers? Even though the contributors may be called citizen journalists, are they really journalists? Because most blogs are not edited and do not have to meet the standards of accuracy and fairness required by mainstream news sites, their credibility is questionable.

Another ethical issue is whether staff reporters for TV news stations and newspapers should write blogs that express their personal opinions when they are supposed to be impartial in covering the news.

Ethical issues abound in this changing world of bloggers. Although news sites may offer guidelines for blog contributors, no official code of ethics governs the blogosphere.

Jonathan Dube, creator of a comprehensive online journalism Web site that lists more than 300 media blogs, has proposed a bloggers' code of ethics on his site, *www .cyberjournalist.net*. His proposed code encourages bloggers to practice some of the same standards that journalists espouse, chiefly to "be honest and fair in gathering, reporting and interpreting information." His code is an adaptation of the Society of Professional Journalists code of ethics, which is widely followed by mainstream media organizations.

The Poynter Institute, a training facility for journalists, has also proposed guidelines for online media and user-generated content. The guidelines propose that publishers adopt clear standards for taste and judgment, anonymous posting, links and such issues as copyright infringement and moderating readers' responses to the blogs for objectionable content.

Those kinds of guidelines are what OhmyNews has posted on its site as a code of ethics site for its citizen journalists. The site requires contributors to identify themselves as citizen reporters when covering stories and to avoid writing articles based on assumptions or predictions.

Even with guidelines, citizen journalism poses several ethical issues for mainstream media publications that post contributors' blogs on their sites. Some of those concerns are:

- Is the information on blogs accurate or based on rumors?
- Should journalists use sources from social networking sites without contacting the person who posted the information?

- Should journalists use anonymous sources from blogs?
- Should blogs be edited or monitored for standards of taste?
- How should editors deal with abusive posts on Web sites that seek comments from readers and viewers? This issue has become a problem as interaction with readers and viewers increases on Web sites that seek comments, but staff to supervise the Web sites is limited at most news organizations.

Because blogs and other forms of citizen journalism are evolving, media organizations are still wrestling with solutions to these concerns.

Blogs in Public Relations and Marketing

Blogs are not limited to journalism and personal sites. Hill & Knowlton, one of the largest public relations/marketing firms in the world, supports blogs and calls them "collective communication." On its Web site, the company says, "Like many other companies, we believe that blogs have the potential to become powerful communications tools. We have created this community to give our consultants the opportunity to participate in the blogosphere, to listen to and learn from our audiences, and to contribute their own vast insight and experience on topics related to our industry. All our bloggers are employees of Hill & Knowlton somewhere."

PRWeb, a wire service Web site that distributes news releases, has also ventured into the blogosphere by using a system called TrackBacks, which enables bloggers who respond to a news release to link directly to the release in their commentary.

"Customer interaction is part of our corporate DNA. It is built into everything we do. For years, we have watched as press releases distributed through PRWeb have been the catalyst for online conversation. Adding trackbacks to our press releases completes the communications loop," according to a PRWeb news release. TrackBacks also can link one blog to another on a similar topic if both blog sites support the technology.

The Public Relations Society of America (PRSA) has joined the blog movement by operating an online media room, which includes RSS feeds to updated news releases as well as podcasts (*http://media.prsa.org*). In a survey "Wired for Change," conducted by PRSA and Dow Jones & Co., professional practitioners and students in public relations raised concerns about the credibility of information in social networking sites, but almost all of them agreed that technology had positively affected public relations practices.

"The citizen journalist with a high-tech cell phone and blog can turn the role of communications upside down—from a world of control to a world of community and conversation," according to the survey. "These tools make our work more complex, raising more questions than answers, like how to translate professional ethical standards into the world of social media."

A researcher in another study concluded that public relations and marketing firms must start using blogs if they want to survive. "Blogs will make or break your business," according to Nora Ganim Barnes, author of the study "Behind the Scenes in the Blogosphere: Advice from Established Bloggers." She says that consumers

Convergence Coach 🌐

Techniques for incorporating blogs and comments in a news Web site are similar for print and broadcast news organizations. In a television newscast, the reporter or anchor will usually refer viewers to the Web site where links, polls or surveys and comments are posted, and print media organizations also promote additional material on their Web sites. To encourage reader and viewer interaction via blogs or just comments, consider using some of these techniques.

■ Post a question at the end of a news story on the Web to seek comments.

■ Include a poll or quiz on the Web site.

■ Promote added features to the news on the Web site such as a photo gallery, full texts of speeches or documents.

■ Add multimedia features—audio and video—of news on the Web site.

■ Update your stories frequently, especially for breaking news.

want to talk about products, and if they can't talk to the vendor, they will talk to others online in blogs.

Barnes, director of the Center for Marketing Research at the University of Massachusetts–Dartmouth, concludes her study with a strong admonition: "Blogs are not a fad. They are no longer even an option. Those businesses that choose to remain outside this online conversation will be sidelined. Eventually they will become extinct."

How to Write a Blog

A blog is an online conversation you are having with the reader. Consider it like a telephone conversation; it's a two-way communication where you say something and hope for a response. You may use the first-person voice (I or me) because you are expressing your thoughts, but you should not insert yourself into a news story. Some blogs may just be one or two paragraphs with links to related stories, especially on news items, while others can be a complete journal entry. Here are some tips for writing your blog:

■ Be brief. Blogs are not meant to be term papers.

■ Be clear. Use simple sentences.

■ Be focused. Like a news story, which should have one main idea, a blog should also contain one main topic.

■ Be careful; check your spelling and grammar. Informal communication in e-mail and blogs tends to be sloppy. Errors in spelling and grammar mar credibility.

- Be interesting. Provide something new or evocative if you are writing an opinion about news. Write about a topic that would be of interest to other people in your age group or community.

- Be accurate and fair. Don't spread rumors or information that may not be truthful. The basic guidelines of accuracy and fairness that apply to news stories apply to blogs as well.

- Be conversational. Write as though you are talking to a friend.

- Target your audience. Consider the people you are trying to reach and write about topics they would want to read, especially on social network blogs. If it is a personal blog, what do your friends and family want to know? If it is a blog intended for a public audience, ask yourself why anyone would want to read your comments.

- Write a clear headline that will hook the reader.

- Add links to related sites or other blogs if relevant.

- Add a question or thought at the end that would elicit readers to post their responses to your blog.

Podcasts

If you don't want to write a blog, you can hear it or see it by producing it as a podcast. Once a combination term for broadcast and iPod, podcast is now a legitimate word. It has been added to the New Oxford American Dictionary, which defines it as "a digital recording of a radio broadcast or similar program, made available on the Internet for downloading to a personal audio player."

Although the original definition was confined to audio files, definitions and uses of podcasts have expanded to include video. A video podcast is also called a "vidcast" or "vodcast," but whatever you call it, this form of media is now a common alternative format on news sites as well as social networking sites.

You don't need an iPod, a portable digital media player by the Apple Inc., or an MP3 player, which also compresses audio files into digital form, to hear or view podcasts. You can click onto a podcast in your computer and listen to it with software for hearing audio or viewing video. You can also download a podcast to your computer and listen to it or view it with free software such as iTunes, Quicktime or Windows Media Player.

If you want to receive regularly updated information from podcasts of blogs or news, you can subscribe to a Web site that contains an RSS reader, the program that compiles sites you select and automatically delivers them to your computer or portable digital device.

Many free software programs exist for bloggers and podcasters. For step-by-step tutorials, check *www.blogger.com,* a free blogging site that uses feedburner.com, owned by Google, for posting podcasts. Technology will continue to change, and more sites and programs will provide easy ways for you to create and post your blogs and podcasts.

What Do You Think ?

Do you think citizen journalism will continue to be a major force in journalism?

- ☐ Yes
- ☐ No
- ☐ I hope not
- ☐ Not sure

Exercises

1 **Word association exercise:**

- Write five or 10 words that come to your mind associated with these words (1 minute for each word association): snow, happy, sad, dreams, goals, pain.

- Now expand your thoughts to one paragraph (3 minutes for each idea): I am afraid of . . . . I hope to be . . . . The best gift I received . . . . My worst experience . . . .

2 Write a blog on a personal topic that you think might be of interest to a campus audience. You can expand some of the thoughts you just wrote in exercise 1 into a blog or write about a new topic. Add a question at the end to solicit responses to your blog. Check *www.lawrence.com/blogs* for ideas. You can create your own blog at *www.blogger.com* or other blog sites.

3 Access *www.myspace.com* or *www.blogger.com* and study the types of blogs that are posted. Choose three blogs on either of these sites or other blog sites and write a critique of the blogs. In your critique, discuss what makes them interesting or boring and how well or how poorly are they written.

4 Access the blogs on *www.cyberjournalist.net* and critique a blog by a journalist (*www.cyberjournalist .net/cyberjournalists.php*). In your critique, discuss how the blog differs from a news story and whether the thoughts expressed by the journalist in the blog create an ethical dilemma regarding the neutrality the journalist should express in a news story.

5 **Terminology:** Access the Web site for this chapter and take the multiple choice quiz on terms used related to blogs and podcasts in this chapter.

☞ **Featured Online Activity** Log on to the book Web site and take the interactive quiz on blog and podcast terms at

academic.cengage.com/masscomm/rich/ writingandreportingnews6e

Coaching Tips

State the focus, the main idea, of your story in one sentence.

To find your lead, ask yourself: What is most important or most interesting?

Write the story in a conversational tone as though you were telling a friend.

Consider how your story will affect readers.

Consider what photographs, graphics, audio or video your story needs for print, broadcast or online delivery.

Consider interactive elements for Web versions

Too many stories fail to answer the reader's most challenging question: So what?

—Roy Peter Clark, writing coach and author

3

The Basic News Story

The basic news story is told upside down. It usually is called a hard-news story. That doesn't mean it should be hard to read. Quite the contrary. It really should be called an easy-news story because the facts are presented in a direct form that makes it easy for the reader to get the most important information quickly.

A hard-news story often presents the result of a news event first, so the key facts are in the first few paragraphs. If a news story were a mystery story, you would solve the mystery in the beginning and then devote the rest of the story to telling the reader how and why it happened.

For example, if state officials who regulate higher education—often called the Board of Regents—met yesterday to discuss an increase in tuition at universities in your state, you wouldn't write that the Board of Regents met to consider a tuition increase. You would give the results. What did the regents decide? This is a direct approach: "The Board of Regents voted yesterday to raise undergraduate tuition next fall at state universities by $100 to $4,700." Or you might stress the impact on readers by writing "Tuition will increase next fall by $100 for undergraduate students at the state's universities." Then you could explain that the decision was made yesterday by the Board of Regents and give details about the tuition increase and its impact. Here is an example:

Students at the University of Alaska will pay more for tuition next year. The Board of Regents approved a 5 percent tuition increase at its meeting Tuesday.

Students taking 15 credits a semester will pay $4,290 annually, which is $210 more than they pay this year. The cost for lower division credits will increase to $134 from the current $128.

Finding the Focus

Not all basic news stories have to start with such a direct approach. Some stories start with a storytelling approach, such as an anecdote about a person or place. Regardless of how you start your story, all news stories are developed around one main point—a focus. The rest of the story should contain quotes, facts and information to support that focus. Because readers and viewers are bombarded with so much information these days, they want to know the point of the story quickly, so you need to put the focus in the first sentence or within the first few paragraphs of the story.

In print and Web media, the focus is usually identified by a headline. In broadcast news, the anchor will lead into the story by identifying the main point. Regardless of the medium, the focus should be high in the story, but in some cases if the story is compelling enough, it could be a little lower.

Most of the techniques discussed in this chapter apply to all media. Because you will need to produce news for convergent media, the next chapter explains different techniques for print, broadcast and online delivery. Chapters later in the book will provide more detail about writing for broadcast and the Web.

The following questions will help you find a focus:

What's the Story About?   To determine the focus of a news story, ask yourself, "What's the story about?" Try to answer that question in one simple sentence. Think of focus as a headline for your story. How would you describe the main idea in a few words? What makes this story newsworthy? You could use this focus statement as your lead if you decide you want the first sentence to get directly to the point of your story.

How Are Readers or Viewers Affected?   Why should readers or viewers care about your story? This is the "so-what" factor. Is there something important or interesting or unusual that will affect your audience? If you were trying to convince someone to read or view your story, what point would you stress?

How Would You Tell the Story to a Friend?   Another way to determine your focus is to use the "tell-a-friend" technique. This is a natural conversational method, particularly important in broadcast writing.

Imagine that your friend asks what the story is about and what happened. Chances are that you might talk about the most interesting information first. Thinking in these terms will give you a clue for your lead and your organization.

In this example, the focus is in the first sentence, which is the lead. It tells what the story is about and how it affects the reader. It is also written in a conversational tone. The second paragraph and the rest of the story provide facts and information to support this main idea.

Headline	**Eye on privacy at work**
Focus in the lead	If you have a job, you have no privacy when it comes to using the office computer.
Second paragraph supporting the lead	From monitoring e-mails to capturing instant messages among friends, employers can do as they see fit with the information passing through a company network.

—*Chicago Tribune* |

Nut Graphs

The "nut graph" is a sentence or paragraph identifying the focus of the story. The term was coined more than 50 years ago by *The Wall Street Journal* in a memo to its staff. The memo said a story must have one central theme that must be expressed in a "nutshell summary" high in the story. The concept of the nut graph has since become a standard formula for all news stories.

If your lead explains the focus in the first sentence, you don't need a separate nut graph. However, if your lead does not identify the main idea of the story, you need a nut graph to explain the focus.

Lead   When freshmen begin college, they often feel like the world is their oyster.

Unfortunately, many 18- and 19-year-olds are swallowing that big oyster in one gulp—and bellying up for seconds

Nut graph   There's a name for this behavior—it's called the "freshman 15," and it has been a part of college life for about as long as young people have been heading off in pursuit of higher education. That term is used to describe the typical weight gain many freshmen experience their first year away from home.

—Jim Baker, *Lawrence* (Kan.) *Journal-World*

Basic Questions

All news stories answer some basic questions: who, what, when, where, why and how?

As newspaper readership declines and competition increases because of all-day coverage in broadcast and online media, editors increasingly want the answer to another question: So what? What is the significance to readers? How can you make readers see and care about the story?

Eugene Roberts, a former editor at *The New York Times* and *The Philadelphia Inquirer,* tells this story about how his editor influenced him to write vividly enough to make the reader see. Roberts was a reporter at the *Goldsboro News-Argus* in North Carolina. His editor, Henry Belk, was blind. Many days Belk would call in Roberts to read his stories to him, and Belk would yell, "Make me see. You aren't making me see."

Advice from Roberts: "The best reporters, whatever their backgrounds or their personalities, share that consummate drive to get to the center of a story and then put the reader on the scene."

Much has changed in the media since Roberts was a reporter many years ago. But his advice is just as relevant today. Identify the center of the story, which is the focus, gather information to make the reader see, and write a compelling story to make the reader care.

Elements of the Basic News Story

News stories in all media share some common elements. Every news story is based on one main idea—the focus. The basic news story structure includes a headline and three general parts: a beginning, called the "lead," a middle, called the "body," and an ending. After you determine the focus, write the lead and nut graph if needed. Here are the basic parts of a news story:

Headline

The headline is the line on top of the story that tells the reader what the story is about. It usually is written by a copy editor or editor, except at very small newspapers where the editor also may be the reporter/writer. The headline usually identifies the focus, especially in online stories, so the reader can decide whether to access the full story.

Online news sites and many newspapers today are using secondary headlines—called "deck heads," "summary lines" or "summary blurbs"—under the main headline. The two headlines together give the reader a quick overview of the story's content. Here is an example from a newspaper that uses summary lines on most of its major stories:

Headline	**Salmon spawn a new crisis**
Deck head, summary line or summary blurb	Dwindling numbers and fading strength threaten to add the fish to the list of endangered species. But some question if the Northwest will pay the price to save the animals.

—Los Angeles Times

Even though you may not write the headlines for your stories, you can use the concept as a writing tool. If you are having trouble identifying the main point of a story, think of a headline for it. Broadcast news scripts don't include headlines, but the concept will help you find focus.

Lead

At the beginning of the story, the hook that tells the reader what the story is about is called the "lead." A good lead entices the reader to continue reading. In a hard-news story, the lead usually is written in one sentence—the first sentence of the story—and gives the most important information about the event. But even a basic story can have a creative lead, called a "soft lead" or "feature lead."

Summary Leads: The most common type of lead on a hard-news story is called a "summary lead" because it summarizes the main points about what happened. It answers the questions of who, what, when, where, why and how. The rest of the story elaborates about what, why and how.

Hard-news leads do not have to answer all those questions in the first sentence if doing so would make the lead too long and difficult to read.

Shorter leads of fewer than 35 words are preferable, but that number is only a guideline.

The writer has to decide which elements are most important to stress in the first sentence. The summary lead in the following example stresses who, what, where and when; the rest of the story gives more details, such as the names of the professor and the suspect:

> A Northwestern University professor of hearing sciences was shot and seriously wounded in a university parking lot Thursday.

Feature Leads: A lead that starts with a story or description about a person, place or incident, is called a "feature lead" or an "anecdotal lead." Many feature leads begin with a description of a person who is a key source in the story. Because a feature lead does not explain the focus of the story immediately, you need to follow the lead with a nut graph as in this example:

Lead

When he was a little girl, Leo said he hated wearing dresses. Today the Ball State University graduate student is sitting in his office, clad in khakis and a button shirt.

At first encounter, Leo, who asked for his last name not to be used, looks like a typical thirty-something guy; sideburns, goatee, a little pudgy but nothing out of the ordinary. In a raspy tenor voice, he talks about the store he and his wife own, about their cats and about how he quit smoking three months ago and can't live without nicotine gum.

But Leo's demure appearance betrays his extraordinary past. In 1999 he began the process of physically transitioning from a woman named Lynette into a man named Leo. . . .

Nut graphs

—Adrian Sharp, *Ball State University*

Nut Graph

The "nut graph" is a sentence or paragraph that states the focus—the main point—of the story. It should tell in a nutshell what the story is about and why it is newsworthy. In a hard-news story with a direct summary lead, the lead contains the focus, so you don't need a separate nut graph. But the nut graph is crucial when a story starts with a feature lead because the reader has to wait for a few paragraphs to find out the reason for the story.

The nut graph should be placed high in the story, generally by the third to fifth paragraph. But if the lead is very compelling, the nut graph could come later. Rigid rules can ruin good writing.

Anecdotal lead

SANTA CRUZ—Until Hollywood calls, film major Wesley Adkins said he's OK with being a struggling artist. But by the time he graduates, the junior may wish he was a business major. Already his student loans total $25,000.

Nut graph

As the cost of attending UC Santa Cruz, or for that matter most any university, has skyrocketed over the past three years, mounting debt from student aid has kept pace. More and more students are leaving school, including many at this weekend's UCSC graduation ceremonies, with huge financial burdens.

—*Santa Cruz* (Calif.) *Sentinel*

Support for the Lead

The lead should be supported, or backed up, with facts, quotes and statements that substantiate information in the lead. Here is an example:

GAINESVILLE, Fla.—A University of Florida law student suffering from amnesia after mysteriously disappearing in July has recalled her abduction under hypnosis, authorities said.

Elizabeth "Libby" Morris, 32, slowly has regained memory of her life before her disappearance from the Oaks Mall parking lot but has never consciously remembered what occurred during the five days she was missing, said Lt. Spencer Mann, a spokesman with the Alachua County Sheriff's Office.

—*The Associated Press*

Quotes or Sound Bites

After the lead, the body of the story should support the focus with information from sources, quotes or facts that explain the main idea. If you have a good quote or sound bite from a source, it should be placed high in the story after the lead or nut graph. The first quote that backs up the lead is called the "lead quote" or the "augmenting quote." It is usually the strongest quote you have, and it supports the concept in the lead without repeating the same information or wording. In broadcast news a good sound bite following the lead is equivalent to the lead quote.

A lead quote isn't required in all stories, but a strong quote or sound bite within a paragraph or two after the lead helps make the story more interesting. If the lead does not contain all the information about who, what, when, where, why and how, these questions should be answered in the body of the story. In this example, the lead quote is in the third paragraph:

PENSACOLA, Fla.—Soon-to-be graduate student Michael Kearney hasn't chosen a major yet—but give him time, he's only 11.

Michael will begin tackling graduate studies at the University of West Florida in Pensacola this summer.

"We don't push him," said his mother, Cassidy Kearney. "He pushes us. We just try and keep up with him."

—*The Associated Press*

Impact

Whenever possible, the writer should explain how the news affects readers. The "impact" sentence or paragraph should answer these questions: What is the significance of this story? What in the story makes the reader care? Sometimes the impact is explained in the lead or in the nut graph; sometimes it is lower in the story, in an explanatory paragraph.

Not all stories can show direct impact on readers, but they should all have a clear paragraph explaining the reason for the story. In some stories, such as police stories, the impact is that the news happened in the community and should be of interest to local residents.

> Home users are now the top target for Internet attackers, who are launching increasingly sophisticated attacks.
>
> That's the sobering warning from Symantec's latest Internet security threat report, released today.
>
> —*The Vancouver Sun*

Online news sites provide impact in several interactive ways: Databases let readers search statistics about education, crime or property values in their communities; interactive calculators give readers a chance to figure what a tax increase might cost them; and feedback questions or polls ask readers to comment on issues.

Attribution

Where did you get the information? Who told you these facts? How can the reader be sure what you say is true? The "attribution" provides those answers. You need to attribute all quotes—exact wording of statements that people made—and much information that you did not witness. If the information is common knowledge or indisputable, you do not have to attribute it. You also need to attribute any statements that express opinions. (A more complete discussion of how to use quotes and attribution comes later in this chapter.)

The attribution should be in the lead for controversial or accusatory information, but in many other cases it can be delayed so it doesn't clutter the lead. Police stories often have attribution in the lead, especially if you get the information by telephone or if the information is accusatory:

Lead with attribution

ST. PETERSBURG, Fla.—A 15-year-old boy was stabbed twice in the chest Thursday afternoon when he apparently tried to break up a fight in a crowded parking lot at Northeast High School, authorities said.

Backup

Police and school officials said the stabbing, believed to have occurred after one student took another's hat, was the first they could recall at Pinellas County schools.

—*St. Petersburg* (Fla.) *Times*

In the next example, general attribution is in the lead, but the specific attribution is in the third paragraph. The sources for the study are too cumbersome to use in the lead.

Lead with general attribution　A smoky bar may be more harmful to your health than a city street filled with diesel truck fumes, according to a new study.

Smoky bars and casinos have up to 50 times more cancer-causing particles than air in highways and city streets clogged with diesel trucks, the study says.

Indoor air pollution virtually disappears when smoking is banned, according to the study published in the *Journal of Occupational and Environmental Medicine* and partially funded by the Robert Wood Johnson Foundation of New Jersey, a philanthropic organization devoted to health care.　*Backup with specific attribution*

Context/Background

Is there any history or background the reader needs in order to understand how a problem or action occurred? Put the story in perspective. If the story is about a fire, accident or crime, how many other incidents of this type have occurred in the community recently? Most stories need some background to explain the action, as in this example:

Lead　Lock your doors.

Nut graph　That's the advice of University of Iowa security chief Dan Hogan in light of recent reports of a prowler slipping into unlocked dormitory rooms at night.

Backup with lead quote　"I can't stress that enough," he said. "It's a very serious situation."

Background　Since Aug. 24, there have been six reports of a man entering women's rooms between 3 a.m. and 5:30 a.m. Five incidents were in Burge Hall and one was in Currier Hall.

Two times the man touched the sleeping women, Hogan said. But there was no force or violence. In each instance the man ran when the woman discovered him.

More recently, a woman in Burge Hall heard someone at her door. She opened it and saw a man running down the hall, Hogan said.

—Valoree Armstrong, *Iowa City Press-Citizen*

Elaboration

Supporting points related to the main issue constitute "elaboration." These can be statements, quotes or more detail to explain what happened, how and why the problem or action occurred, and reactions to the event.

In this part of the story, seek other points of view to make sure you have balance and fairness. A story based on one source can be too biased. The preceding story about the University of Iowa continued with more explanation:

George Droll, director of residence services, said main doors to the halls were locked from midnight to 6 a.m. But each resident has a key. Some floors have 24-hour visitation.

Often students feel more secure than they should because the buildings are large and are home to many of their friends, he said.

Fairness and Accuracy

If the story involves conflict, you should always get comments from both or all sides of an issue. Avoid one-source stories. Also, make sure you attribute your sources; including information you use from Web sites, other news organizations and quotes or statements from people you interview.

Endings

The most common type of ending includes one of these elements: future action, a statement or quote that summarizes but does not repeat the previous information, or more elaboration. If the future action is a key factor in the issue, it should be placed higher in the story. Avoid summary endings that repeat what you have already said. In a basic news story, end when you have no more new information to reveal.

The ending on the Iowa story follows the residence director's comments about why students feel secure in large buildings where they have friends:

Summary quote ending   "That's a strength, but it can also be a weakness in terms of people securing their rooms," Droll said.

A common order for a news story might look like this:

- Lead
- Nut graph (if a feature lead is used)
- Lead quote or compelling sound bite (if one is available)
- Supporting facts or impact
- More quotes and comments (or sound bites) from sources
- Additional information, facts or comments from sources
- Ending

Visuals

Visual elements such as photographs, charts and other graphic illustrations are crucial to news presentation in print and online information. They also enhance news releases or media kits in public relations. Photographs and other graphic

Convergence Coach 🌐

Focus is crucial in print, broadcast and online news. If the focus of the story is unclear to broadcast viewers, they will turn to another channel. If the focus in an online story is not clear in the headline or summary blurb under the headline, readers may not even click into your online story. Ask yourself these questions:

■ What is the most important idea that will entice viewers to listen to your story or online readers to click into your story?

■ Before you write your story for any medium, write a focus sentence in fewer than 35 words. This also can be the lead of your story for an online site or a broadcast story. Now convert the focus into a headline of no more than six words for an online site. Here's an example from an Associated Press story:

■ Headline: Campus booze arrests jump 24 percent.

■ Summary blurb under the headline: Sex, drug, weapons violations also increase.

■ Online stories often have questions or polls seeking readers' feedback. If you were seeking feedback on the main idea of your story, what question would you ask? The question may give you a clue for finding your focus.

■ Have you answered the questions of who, what, where, when, how, why and explained the impact on the reader or viewer?

■ If your story is about a conflict, have you contacted sources on both sides of the issue?

illustrations not only help make your story look good; they can also make it easier to read. Here are some other visual elements used to enhance news stories:

Summary Blurb A paragraph or sentence summarizing the story is called a "summary blurb." It is placed below the headline. When you ask yourself what the story is about, you are really envisioning a summary blurb. Even though copy editors usually write the summary blurb, you should use the concept to write your focus statement.

In online news the summary and lead of the story may be the same because the blurb may be on an index page linking to stories inside the site. The repetition can help readers know they have accessed the correct story. But in print stories when the blurb is published directly over the story, the lead does not have to repeat the summary. It can be more creative, as in this example:

Headline

Papers a lesson in criminology

Summary blurb

A USF professor follows a paper trail to a former student wanted on charges he sold term papers to criminology majors.

A. Engler Anderson's term papers weren't just bad. They were a crime, said one professor.

Anderson, 31, is wanted on charges that he sold term papers to two University of South Florida students.

Their major?

Criminology.

The charge—selling a term paper or dissertation to another person—is only a second-degree misdemeanor, but if he is caught, Anderson will be held without bail because he failed to appear for a court hearing this week.

—*St. Petersburg* (Fla.) *Times*

The story then explains how William Blount, chairman of the USF Criminology Department, received two papers that he thought were "awful" and then discovered they were written by Anderson, a former student.

Pull Quote A good quote might be broken out of the story, placed in larger type and used as a point of entry to entice the reader. Although a copy editor will decide which quotes to pull for graphic display, when you write your story, consider which quotes could be used to entice readers. Then use your best quotes high in your story. In a story explaining sexual harassment, this "pull quote" from an employment lawyer was used for emphasis:

> *"I think what the law says is that if you hit on me, and I say, 'No way, Buster,' I'm entitled to have you accept my rejection of you, and it shouldn't interfere with my work."*
>
> —Judith Vladeck, employment lawyer

Facts or Highlights Box Information from a story is sometimes set off in a "facts box," also called a "highlights box," for reading at a glance or providing key points in the story. A facts or highlights box can include the dates in a chronology or the main points of a proposal or meeting. It is especially useful for breaking statistics out of a story. Although some information from a facts box may be crucial to include in the story, the writer should guard against too much repetition.

CNN uses a highlights box at the top of major news stories on its Web site. The box contains four to five bulleted facts from the story to give readers a quick summary of the main points as in this example:

Big area of Antarctica melted in 2005

- Vast areas of snow in Antarctica melted in the summer of 2005
- Satellite data shows an area the size of California melted
- NASA: This is the most significant thawing in 30 years
- Evidence of melting in several areas, including high elevations and far inland

—CNN

Here is an example of a facts box that accompanied a story from *The Kansas City Star* about the dangers of lightning. These statistics were not repeated in the story:

Lightning deaths and injuries

Figures below were compiled from 35 years of U.S. lightning statistics.

Location of incident

- Open fields, recreation areas: 27%
- Under trees (not golf): 14%
- Water-related (boating, fishing, swimming, etc.): 8%
- Golf/golf under trees: 5%

Month of most incidents

- July 30%

Deaths by state, top five

- Florida, Michigan, Texas, New York, Tennessee

Source: National Oceanic and Atmospheric Administration

Infographic A chart, map, graph or other illustration meant to provide information is an "infographic." Examples of infographics are diagrams of plane crashes or major accidents and illustrations explaining how something works. The most common type of infographic, called a "location map," pinpoints the location of an accident, a crime or any other major news event.

It is the reporter's responsibility to supply the information for those maps. So when you report a story that may need a map, make sure you gather information about the exact location of the event by noting the streets, the number of feet or yards from a spot where an explosion or major crime occurred, or any other crucial information that would help readers visualize the location.

The University Daily Kansan, the campus newspaper of the University of Kansas, used the location map and graphic shown here to accompany a story about a traffic accident in which a student was killed.

Many of the visual elements—such as headlines, boxes of information and summary sentences—are written by copy editors, and decisions about display are made by these editors or by page designers. However, reporters are expected to plan photos for their stories and to provide information for some of the graphics. When a chart, a graphic or a facts box will accompany your story, you need to consider

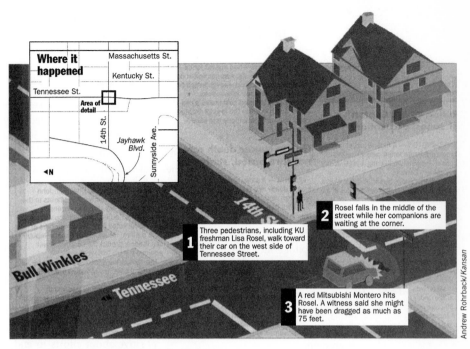

Infographic from The University Daily Kansan
Reprinted with permission

whether the story needlessly duplicates information that could be presented visually. So in the writing process, don't just think about information to put into your story; think also about information to pull out for visual devices.

Audio and Video for Online Delivery   Audio and video are crucial for television news stories, but if you are writing the story for a print publication, you still should think about sound and sight. Most news organizations have Web sites these days, so you should plan to record the interviews for posting on the organization's Web site. Even if you don't shoot the video yourself, you should discuss with an editor whether your story will need video so that a photographer can be assigned to the story.

Examples of Basic News Stories

The following examples will show you how elements of the basic news story fit together for print or online delivery. The first example is a standard news story with a summary lead. The story is organized in "inverted pyramid" form, giving the most important information first and the rest in descending order of importance. This story contains most of the basic news elements described in this chapter:

Thousands gather on Capitol steps for animal rights

By Joan Mower
The Associated Press

Summary lead: who, what, when, where, why

WASHINGTON—Thousands of animal rights activists rallied in the nation's capital yesterday, seeking to promote the humane treatment of animals in the wild, on farms and in research laboratories.

Backup for lead, with differing opinions about crowd size

U.S. Capitol Police said an estimated 24,000 people attended a rally on the steps of the Capitol after a one-mile march down Pennsylvania Avenue under sunny skies. Organizers said more than 50,000 people from around the country showed up.

Elaboration

Marchers chanted, "Animal rights—now." Many carried banners and placards with pictures and slogans saying things such as "Fur Is Dead" and "Animals Have Rights, Too." Some brought their dogs.

Background

Organizers said "March for Animals"—the first event of its kind—was a milestone in a movement they said was once viewed as outside the mainstream.

Among the groups participating were the American Society for the Prevention of Cruelty to Animals, People for Ethical Treatment of Animals, the U.S. Humane Society and the Doris Day Animal League.

Peter Linck, coordinator of the march, said the ultimate goal of the animal rights activists was to stop the use of animals in scientific research. However, he conceded it was unlikely the public would adopt that stance.

Impact

"In the meantime," he said, "we want to improve the condition of animals and promote alternatives to reform society."

Elaboration

The event attracted a wide variety of animal supporters, Linck said. They ranged from those who want protection of species, such as elephants, to those seeking to end medical testing on animals. Many were seeking changes in the way animals are raised for slaughter, as well as a ban on fur clothes.

Reaction: balance from different points of view

Health officials are particularly sensitive about efforts to end animal testing, a move they say could be disastrous for science.

Health and Human Services Secretary Louis W. Sullivan has criticized the animal-rights advocates who use violence and intimidation to block testing of animals.

"They are on the wrong side of morality," he said last week.

Sullivan said some of the greatest advances in medicine, such as the cure for polio, never would have been achieved had animals not been used in tests.

Ending: future action

Participants in yesterday's march planned to lobby Congress today in support of bills that deal with animal issues.

The next example is a basic news story with a softer lead that stresses the impact of the story. The nut graph gives the crucial information. It states the problem, the "so what" of this story. Attribution is limited in the beginning because the backup for the lead is factual: a law that has been enacted. However, note that quotes and opinions are attributed.

Throw the book at them

Deck head

Law could lead to arrests for overdue library books

Soft lead

BOSTON—Drop the novel. Step away from the car. You're under arrest for having an overdue library book.

Nut graph: what, why, when, so what, impact and background

Starting Thursday, overdue books could land you in police custody. A new law would allow the arrest of library scofflaws if they had received notice that their books were 30 days overdue.

The law also raises the maximum fine for an overdue book from $50 to $500.

Elaboration

Although the law makes no provision for an overdue book, it allows for up to five years in prison and a fine of $25,000 for the theft of library property worth more than $250.

Reaction

Gregor Trinkaus-Randall, a collection management consultant for the Massachusetts Board of Library Commissioners, said librarians needed tough enforcement tools.

Attribution for quote

"Any library book that is not returned therefore has to be replaced by the library, and that is money out of the town's pocket that could be spent on other materials," he said.

David Linsky, a defense lawyer in Cambridge, criticized the measure.

More reaction

"I think the police are having enough trouble chasing down murderers and rapists without having to keep up with people who have overdue library books," he said.

Linsky said that the law allowed the arrest of library scofflaws without a warrant, something that could not be done with an offense such as assault and battery. He said the measure was unenforceable.

Ending: reaction quote

"If the police are told by an employee of the library that you have an overdue library book, then the police can arrest you in any public place and put the handcuffs on you," he said. "That's the real horror show of this thing."

—*The Associated Press*

ETHICS

Ethical dilemma: What do you do if a source tells you not to quote him or her at the end of an interview or after the interview but before you go to press or on the air?

Ethical values: Decency, fairness, accuracy, responsibility to readers and sources, credibility.

Ethical guidelines: The decision is more difficult when sources want to withdraw their quotes after you conduct an interview. Try to avoid this situation by making it clear at the start of your interview that you want your source to go "on the record." If you still encounter a source who wants to retract a quote, you can negotiate with the source, or you can insist that you have a right to use the information because you identified your purpose clearly. But that may not help you.

Here are some questions to consider when asked to withdraw a quote:

- Are you being fair to your source?
- Are you being fair to your readers?
- Are the quotes essential to your story?

These are tough decisions. You can read more about what constitutes "on the record" and "off the record" or "not for attribution" in Chapter 7, "Interviewing Techniques."

Quotes and Attribution

Good quotes can back up your lead and substantiate information in your story. In addition, good quotes let the reader hear the speaker. But boring quotes can bog down stories. If they repeat what you have already said, it's better to paraphrase or eliminate them. In a broadcast story, sound bites take the place of quotes.

Susan Ager, a columnist and writing coach for the *Detroit Free Press,* said reporters should consider quotes as the spice of the story, not the meat and potatoes. "Readers come to the newspaper the way they come to a party," she said. "They want to talk to interesting people. Long quotes usually are not very interesting."

When to Use Direct Quotes

Here are some guidelines for deciding when to use quotes:

- Is the quote interesting and informative?
- Can the quote back up the lead, the nut graph or a supporting point in your story?
- Ask yourself: Is the quote memorable without referring to your notes? If so, it's probably a good quote.
- Do your quotes repeat your transitions? Could the quote or the transition be eliminated? In broadcast news avoid introducing a sound bite with a transition that repeats what the source will say. That is called "parroting," a technique that should be avoided.
- Can you state the information better in your own words? If so, paraphrase.
- Does the quote or sound bite advance the story by adding emotion, interest or new information?
- Are you including the quote or sound bite for your source or for your readers or viewers? That is the most important question of all. The readers' and viewers' interests always take priority.

Here are some types of quotes or sound bites to avoid:

- Avoid direct quotes when the source is boring or the information is factual and indisputable. For example, a city official who says, "We are going to have our regular monthly meeting Tuesday night" is not worth quoting directly.
- Avoid any direct quote or sound bite that isn't clearly worded. If a government official says something in bureaucratic language that you don't fully understand, ask for clarification and then paraphrase.
- Avoid accusatory quotes from politicians or witnesses of a crime. If you intend to include any accusations, get a response from the person accused. A direct quote or sound bite does not save you from libel. If police or other criminal justice officials make accusations in an official capacity, you may use direct or indirect quotes, provided that you attribute them carefully.
- Avoid quotes that don't relate directly to the focus and supporting points in your story. Some of the best quotes a source says may have nothing to do with your focus. It's better to lose them than to use them poorly.

How to Write Quotes

On the surface, writing quotes may seem easy: You just write down what somebody else has said. The format for writing sound bites in a broadcast script differs from print style and will be explained in the next chapter and in the broadcast chapter. For print and online delivery, you must observe the following guidelines if you want to use quotes correctly and effectively:

- Always put commas and periods inside the quotation marks: "There are no exceptions to that rule," the professor said.

- A question mark and other punctuation marks go within the quotation marks if the punctuation refers to the quoted material; otherwise, they go outside the quotation marks: He asked, "When does the semester end?" Who said, "I hope it ends soon"?

- Each new speaker must be quoted in a separate paragraph:

"Never place quotes from two speakers in the same paragraph," Professor Les Polk said.

"Even if it's short?" Janet Rojas asked.

"Yes, Polk answered.

- Don't attribute a single quote more than once. If you have two quoted sentences from the same speaker in the same paragraph, you need only one attribution:

"You must study your Associated Press Stylebook," the professor said. "You will have a test Tuesday on material in the first 30 pages."

- "When the quote is two or more sentences in the same paragraph, attribute it after the first sentence," Carol English said. "Don't make the reader wait until the end of the paragraph to discover who is speaking."

- Attribution in the middle of a quote is acceptable but not preferable if it interrupts the thought:

"It isn't the best way," he said, "to use a direct quote. But it is all right if the quote is very long. However, it's better to put it at the end of a complete sentence."

- Don't tack on long explanations for the quote. If the quote isn't clear by itself, paraphrase. For example, avoid the following:

When asked how he learned about the fire at his apartment complex, he said, "I heard the news on the television."

■ Just as bad:

"I heard the news on the television," he
said when asked how he learned about
the fire at his apartment complex.

■ Instead, introduce the quote with a transition:

He was at a friend's house when the fire
broke out at his apartment.
    "I heard the news on television," he
said.

■ Limit the use of partial quotes. They are acceptable when the whole quote
would be cumbersome, but too many partial quotes make a story choppy. And
the reader wonders what was left out. If you follow a partial quote with a full
one, you must close the partial quote:

McDonald says he sees the government
as "weak and inept" and fraught with
"major-league problems."
    "There's a crisis in our leadership,"
McDonald says.

■ Limit the use of ellipses, which are sets of dots that indicate part of the quote
is missing.

Use three dots for the middle of a sentence; four (one of which is the period)
for an ellipsis at the end of the sentence. Use the ellipsis when you are condensing
whole quotes or long passages from which you delete several sentences. It's useful
for stories about speeches or excerpts from court rulings. Be careful not to leave out
material that would change the speaker's meaning.

When to Use Attribution   All quotes must be attributed to a speaker. In addition, you need to attribute information you paraphrase. In print and online writing,
the attribution may follow the quote, but in broadcast writing, the attribution must
come first. In many cases in broadcast news, the name and title of a speaker may
be superimposed over the video on the bottom screen so you don't always need to
introduce the source in a sound bite.

Plagiarism   Copying the words of other writers is plagiarism, a cardinal sin in
journalism. Even if you paraphrase information you receive from other publications,

you are plagiarizing if you don't attribute it. Plagiarism is grounds for dismissal at most news organizations. If you take information from written or online resources, make sure you attribute it. Here are some guidelines for material you need and don't need to attribute:

- You don't need to attribute facts that are on record or are general knowledge:

  > The trial will resume tomorrow.
  >
  > A suspect has been arrested in connection with the slaying of a 16-year-old girl in Hometown last week.

- You don't need to attribute information that you observed directly:

  > The protesters, carrying signs and chanting songs, gathered in the park.

- You don't need to attribute background information established in previous stories about the same subject:

  > The defendant is accused of killing the three Overland Park women whose bodies have never been found.

- You do need to attribute information you receive from sources if it is accusatory, opinionated and not substantiated and if you did not witness it—especially in crime and accident stories. However, you don't always have to attribute everything in the lead. The following statement is factual, so no attribution is needed:

  > A 2-year-old girl escaped injury when a mattress she was sitting on caught fire and engulfed the studio apartment in flames at Wheatshocker Apartments.

- Attribution is needed here, however, because the cause of fire is accusatory and the amount of damage is speculative:

  > A 2-year-old girl playing with a lighter started the fire at the Wheatshocker Apartments near Wichita State University that caused about $400,000 in damages, fire authorities said Thursday.
  >
  > "She was just kind of flicking it, and she caught the bedding on fire," said fire Capt. Ed Bricknell.
  >
  > —*The Wichita* (Kan.) *Eagle*

Wording of Attributions For most hard-news stories, the word *said* is preferable. Although there are many synonyms for *said,* they make the reader pause. *Said* does not. Don't worry about overusing the word.

- Strictly speaking, *said,* the past tense, should be used if someone said something once. If someone always says the same thing, use *says,* the present tense. However, that rule is very restrictive. You could also just use *said* for most hard-news stories and use *says* for feature stories (if *says* seems appropriate to the context). In either case, keep the tense you choose throughout the story; if you start with *says,* continue using it for the rest of the story. In broadcast writing "says" gives more immediacy.

- Avoid substitutions for *said,* such as *giggled, laughed* or *choked.* It's almost impossible to giggle, laugh or choke at the same time you are speaking. If you want to convey the emotion, write it this way: "I'm going to try out for the circus," she said, laughing.

- Use *according to* when you are referring to inanimate objects: "*according to* a study." It is acceptable to say "*according to* police" but not preferable. People talk. Use *said* or *says* when you attribute to people; *according to* is vague.

- Normal speaking order is preferable. You should place *said* after the name or pronoun. If the person has a long title, *said* can be placed before the name and title.

  Awkward: "Normal speaking order is preferred," said the professor.

  Preferable: "Normal speaking order is preferred," the professor said.

Overview Attribution This is a technique that allows you to attribute information to one speaker for several paragraphs without attributing each statement or each paragraph. It is useful when you are giving a chronology of events, as in a police story. But if you change speakers, you need to use attribution for the new speaker. Overview attribution is a brief statement followed by a colon.

Police described the incident this way:

Witnesses said this is what happened:

Police gave this account:

Second References The second time you refer to a source in your story, use the last name only. If you have several sources—or two sources with the same last name, such as a husband and wife—use the full name again or an identifying phrase:

James Jones, the director of public safety, was injured in a three-car crash yesterday. Jones was taken to Memorial Hospital, where he was treated for bruises and released.

If you have mentioned several other people and want to get back to Jones later in the story, remind the reader who Jones is by using his title:

Public Safety Director Jones said he would return to work Monday.

Titles When a person's title is used before the name, capitalize it, as in the preceding example. When it is used after the name, use lowercase letters:

Police Chief Ron Olin said the crime rate has gone down.

Olin, police chief of Lawrence, said the crime rate has gone down.

Courtesy Titles Most newspapers and TV scripts no longer use courtesy titles—Mr., Miss, Mrs. or Ms.—before people's names. There are exceptions. *The New York Times* and *The Wall Street Journal* still use courtesy titles. Other newspapers use them in obituaries. For general purposes in this book, courtesy titles will be eliminated unless they are contained in examples from newspapers that still use them.

What Do You Think ?

Would you continue reading a news story if the focus is not clear in the first few paragraphs?

☐ Yes
☐ No
☐ Not sure

Exercises

1 Basic news story: Write a story based on the following information. Write a focus sentence before you start your story. For this story, your focus sentence should be the results of the study. If you want a lead that gets directly to the point, your focus sentence could also be your lead.

Once you've written a focus sentence, add a suggestion for visual presentation—a photograph, chart, facts box or other graphic illustration. Decide what facts, if any, should be duplicated in the story and the graphic. Then organize the story by placing facts, quotes and elaboration in an order with the most important information near the top of the story to the least important material and perhaps ending with a good quote. The following material is based on a story from *The* (San Bernardino, Calif.) *Sun*.

Who/what: A study comparing the death and accident rates of left- and right-handed people.

When: Study was conducted last year and was reported in today's edition of the *New England Journal of Medicine.*

Where: Study was conducted by Diane Halpern, a psychology professor at California State University at San Bernardino, and Stanley Coren, a researcher at the University of British Columbia.

Why: To determine why fewer left-handed people are among the elderly population.

How: Researchers studied death certificates of 987 people in two Southern California counties. Relatives were queried by mail about the subjects' dominant hands.

Backup information: The following points are not necessarily in the order they should be used in your story.

The researchers found that the average age at death for right-handed people was 75, for left-handed people 66; left-handed people represent 10 percent of the U.S. population; right-handed females tend to live six years longer than left-handed females, and right-handed males live 11 years longer than left-handed males; left-handed people were four times more likely to die from injuries while driving than right-handers and six times more likely to die from accidents of all kinds.

Halpern said, "The results are striking in their magnitude." Halpern is right-handed.

She said her study should be interpreted cautiously. "It should not, of course, be used to predict the life span of any one individual. It does not take into account the fitness of any individual." Left-handed women die around age 72; right-handed women die around age 78. Left-handed men die about age 62; right-handed men die about age 73.

"Some of my best friends are left-handed," Halpern said. "It's important that mothers of left-handed children not be alarmed and not try to change which hand a child uses," she said. "There are many, many old left-handed people." "We knew for years that there weren't as many old left-handers," Halpern said. "Researchers thought that was because in the early years of the century, most people born left-handed were forced to change to their right hands. So we thought we were looking at old people who used to be left-handed, but we weren't. The truth was that there simply weren't many left-handers left alive, compared to right-handers."

"Almost all engineering is geared to the right hand and right foot," Halpern said. "There are many more car and other accidents among left-handers because of their environment."

2 **Reaction story:** Interview at least three students on campus who are left-handed. Ask them what problems they encounter because they are left-handed. Using the study in Exercise 1 as a focus for your story, write a reaction story with the students' comments. Make sure you get the full names of the students, their majors and year of study (freshman, sophomore and so on) so you can identify them properly in the story.

3 **Find the focus:** Using your local newspaper, find the focus paragraph (the nut graph) in news stories on the front page and local-news pages.

4 **Online focus exercise:** Access an online news site for your community or for a national source, such as *www.cnn.com* or *www.msnbc.com,* and discuss the following points:

- Do the headlines and/or summary blurbs clearly identify the main point of the story?
- Compare the online headlines of major news stories in two online sites.
- Which headlines entice you to click into the story? Why?
- How long are the average online headlines?

- Do summary blurbs add or detract from your interest in reading the full story? How much information should the summary blurb reveal about the story? What type of summary blurbs do you prefer: a single sentence, a paragraph or a few paragraphs?

5 **Quotes and attribution exercise:** Check the appropriate column to indicate whether attribution is or is not needed:

Not Needed	Needed		
☐	☐	**a**	Two leading figures in the growing national debate about political correctness on American college campuses will be at the University of South Florida in Tampa tonight.
☐	☐	**b**	Dieting doesn't work for the vast majority of people.
☐	☐	**c**	A 40-year-old woman went berserk in her ex-boyfriend's apartment early Monday, shooting him to death with seven shots from two guns.
☐	☐	**d**	Members of a local gay rights group protested Thursday in support of a gay University of Tampa student's efforts to take an Army ROTC class.
☐	☐	**e**	City council members voted unanimously Thursday to increase city fines for prostitution.
☐	☐	**f**	A York College sophomore died early yesterday after drinking at a dormitory party.
☐	☐	**g**	Alumni members of Skull and Bones, an all-male secret society at Yale University, have voted to admit women.

6 **Enterprise:** Attend an event on your campus, and write a basic news story about it. (Look in your campus newspaper or your university's online site for a list of activities that will take place during the week, or check bulletin boards for notices of activities.) Talk to friends about other story possibilities. Here are some other possible topics for a news story at the start of the semester: a new course, problems

that students are having enrolling in certain courses, a new club or organization on campus, a student support group.

7 Class reunion feature: This exercise will give you practice gathering and writing quotes. The scenario: Imagine you are attending a class reunion of your department 25 years from now. Interview your classmates in small groups, and rotate among the groups so you get comments from at least five different students.

Ask them their ages and occupations, and make sure you spell their names correctly. For female students who may be using a married name, include their maiden names if they were unmarried when they graduated. Even though you should never make up quotes, for this exercise students can use their imaginations about their future careers, but they must give the same information to everyone who interviews them.

Write the story as though you were a reporter for a local newspaper. Do not use first-person "I" or "we"; pretend you were an observer, not part of the reunion. Give the time and place—somewhere in your school— and the number of students attending the reunion. Try a creative lead focusing on one interesting person.

Then use a nut graph: She (or he) was one of ____ students attending a class reunion of (your school). Try to get as many complete quotes as you can.

☞ **Featured Online Activity** Log on to the book Web site and take the interactive quiz on basic news qualities, quotes and attribution at

academic.cengage.com/masscomm/rich/ writingandreportingnews6e

Coaching Tips

Stress immediacy—the latest developments in a story.

Plan to post and update your story continually for the Web.

Plan to produce your story for print, broadcast and the Web.

Determine how your story will affect readers.

Read your story out loud for broadcast.

Plan audio and video elements for broadcast and/or the Web.

Plan interactive questions for the Web.

"It's mobile, immediate, visual, interactive, participatory and trusted. Make way for a generation of storytellers who totally get it."

—From "The Future of News: Media, Technology and Society," report for the American Press Institute

4

Convergent
Media Writing

The job advertisement for the small Colorado newspaper says the paper seeks a candidate with these qualities: "A person who understands that newspapers are in more than the newspaper business, but in the information business, where the Web site needs be at the forefront of thought—not an afterthought. A person who can take a complex issue and write it so it's easy to follow and relevant for the reader."

The job ad for the PBS-affiliated television station in Ohio requires a person who can do the following: "Create journalistic content across platforms of radio, TV and the Web that is of high quality, timely and relevant, and that is valued and used by audiences. Produce reports and interviews for programs across platforms of radio, TV and the Web. Adept at research, story planning and development; demonstrated broadcast production skills in radio and/or TV or a willingness to be trained to use those tools; have a crisp, clear broadcast writing style or, if a print journalist, a willingness to be trained to in those skills."

And the public relations job offered by the U.S. Coast Guard promises $4,500 a year in tuition assistance at any accredited college in addition to the salary and benefits for a candidate who has "broad experience in media relations with national print, electronic, and internet media." Job duties include: "Writing press releases, magazine articles, brochures, fliers, and other organizational materials, as assigned; an ability to work under pressure and meet deadlines, and the ability to communicate complex material in a way that is accessible to a broad audience," the ad says.

All the job ads stress the need for good writing skills and a preference for candidates with a degree from a journalism program. You may not have to excel in all areas of the media, but the ability to write for print, broadcast and the Web is an advantage for gaining employment in media careers today.

The need for training students in all media is supported by a recent study conducted for the Radio-Television News Directors' Association.

"Communications and electronic journalism have changed dramatically in recent years and promise to change even more in years to come," the association reports. "The familiar lines that once marked the boundaries between radio, television, print, computers, telephones and other media are blurring. News in the future will be a fully digital broadband mix of audio, video, print, graphics and databases. In the coming years, new technology and changing market forces will completely transform the news industry."

The study, "The Future of News," conducted by Bob Papper, a professor at Hofstra University, says that while people expressed support for traditional media in the study, "they also made clear they want a whole range of new media type options. In particular, they want news and information on demand and many want to interact with that news. . . . People want their news to be right up-to-the-minute. More than 90 percent of those surveyed say it's very or somewhat important, and the figure is even higher for young adults."

The research also suggests that news departments that survive into the future will have to operate on many technological platforms at the same time, Papper wrote.

That concept is precisely why the Gannett Company Inc., the largest media company in the U.S., revamped its news strategy in 2006 and renamed its newsrooms "information centers." In a memo to Gannett employees, Craig Dubow, the company's chief executive officer, explained the concept: "The Information Center, frankly, is the newsroom of the future. It will fulfill today's needs for a more flexible, broader-based approach to the information gathering process. And it will be platform agnostic: News and information will be delivered to the right media—be it newspapers, online, mobile, video or ones not yet invented—at the right time. Our customers will decide which they prefer."

The information center also includes a reorganization of the traditional newsroom. Instead of divisions such as the city, national and business desks, the newsroom will be organized to foster convergence in seven major areas: local news, a digital desk (to deliver news immediately), public service, data delivery (such as calendars, school information or statistical data), custom content, multimedia and community conversation. That last division includes a term called "crowdsourcing," which is another way of expressing reader and viewer participation in contributing to the news. The main point of the reorganization is to emphasize that news of the future must include ways to connect with the audience in a variety of platforms.

Convergence vs. Multimedia The terms "convergence" and "multimedia" are often used interchangeably, but many organizations that claim they are convergent produce the same material for print, broadcast and the Web with some added features for the Web. A multimedia project may be created with features that complement each other but differ for print, broadcast and the Web. Even if the news story is the same on the Web as the print or broadcast story, many news Web sites offer additional items such as chats, blogs, podcasts, interactive features, galleries of photos and video to enhance a story in print and broadcast. Whether you call it "convergence" or "multimedia," to function in these media, you need to understand some similarities and differences among them.

Print vs. Broadcast and Online Stories

The basic elements of a news story for print, broadcast and the Web are the same. In later chapters we'll study print, broadcast and online writing style in more detail. However, to succeed in communication careers today and in the future, you should develop a convergent media mindset that you can apply to skills discussed throughout the book. Here are a few principles to help you can get a head start in writing for cross-media platforms.

Immediacy The main point to stress in broadcast and Web stories is immediacy. What is happening now? What are the latest developments? How can you update the story, giving it a "forward spin" to tell what will happen next? Even if you are reporting a breaking news story for a newspaper, plan to report it first on the Web or on a partner television station. The days of waiting until the next publication cycle for a breaking news story in a newspaper are over.

Print: What happened or who did what? Past tense. Fire destroyed a duplex in midtown yesterday morning, leaving two families homeless.

Broadcast and the Web: What is happening *now* or who is doing what *now*. Present tense is preferable. For example: Two families are homeless today after a fire destroyed their midtown duplex.

Conversational Style Writing simple sentences in a conversational manner— the way you talk—is preferable for all media but essential for broadcast. Stories on the Web resemble print style.

Print: Write to be read. The reader can absorb more information in the mind's eye although conversational style is preferable. Sentences may be longer and more detail can be included in the story.

Broadcast: Write for the ear and the eye. Write in conversational style. You are talking to the viewer. Read your story aloud. Writing for the eye means you should plan your story around the images. In most cases, broadcast stories are shorter than their print counterparts. The average TV news story is 1:30, meaning one minute and 30 seconds. Keep the sentences short and simple, structured as subject-verb-object, meaning who did what or what is happening.

Here is the print lead on a story:

Talking on a cell phone while driving is as dangerous as driving while drunk, new federally funded research shows, and it doesn't matter whether you use a hands-free model or hold the phone up to your ear during the conversation.

—*South Florida Sun-Sentinel*

Here is a conversational approach to the cell phone story for broadcast:

How many times have you been cut off or otherwise annoyed on the road, only to find the other driver is talking on a cell phone?

A new scientific study says it now proves that talking and driving is as dangerous as drinking and driving!

—*KXAN-TV* (Austin, Texas)

Active Voice The structure in active voice is subject-verb-object: who is doing the action. Passive voice explains what action being done to whom. Active voice is preferable for all media but more essential for broadcast because it conveys more immediacy. In some cases the passive voice is more appropriate. For example:

Active Police rescued the woman. (Who did what.)

Passive The woman was rescued by police. (What was done to whom.)

Passive: The defendant was sentenced to 10 years in prison. In this case the emphasis on the defendant may be preferable.

Active: The judge sentenced the defendant to 10 years in prison. The emphasis here is on the judge, who may not be as important to stress as the defendant.

Impact When possible, lead with the effect a story will have on viewers. In breaking news this isn't always appropriate, but explaining the impact on the audience is a good way to grab the viewers' attention. This technique also works well for print. The following example from broadcast news would work as well in print or online stories:

> Anchorage residents will able to breathe air that's a little cleaner this weekend. A new, tougher version of the citywide smoking ban goes into effect July 1.
>
> The new smoking ban effectively updates the 2001 ban by adding day-care centers, outdoor stadiums and bars to the list of places where smoking is against the law.
>
> —*KTUU-TV* (Anchorage, Alaska)

Attribution Put the attribution at the beginning of the sentence in broadcast writing. In print and Web writing, the attribution may come at the end of the sentence. When you put the attribution last in a broadcast story, it sounds as though the reporter is the source of the information or opinion, which can be dangerous especially if the statement is an accusation.

Print: The blaze started in the basement, fire officials say.

Broadcast: Fire officials say the blaze started in the basement.

Consider how dangerous the following sentence would sound if the attribution is not clear at the beginning of this sentence: The suspect abused the animals, police say. A better way to say it is: Police say the suspect abused the animals.

If the information is on public records, a statement without attribution is OK as in this sentence: The suspect is charged with three counts of animal abuse.

Said vs. Says When you attribute information in broadcast writing, "says" gives more immediacy than "said." However, if it is awkward to use the present tense, use "said." If a source said something a week ago, using "says" would be improper. In print, "said" is used more often except in features because generally the source said the quote in the past. Here are examples from the stories compared later in this chapter.

Print: The first firefighters arrived on the scene about three minutes later, at 7:43 a.m., the Anchorage Fire Department spokesman **said.**

Broadcast: The Anchorage Fire Department **says** the blaze broke out about 8 a.m., in a child's bedroom at 8151 Northwind Ave.

Visuals   In print publications, photos and graphics enhance a story. In television news the visual elements are crucial. In this age of convergence, many news organizations publish stories in multiple media. As a result, if you are writing for a print

ETHICS

You are running a story that comes with images that you consider too disturbing to publish in your print and broadcast editions. The images include photos of dead American soldiers, some who have been beheaded and others whose dead bodies are hanging from enemy poles. The enemy is using these images in its media, particularly TV and Web media. You want to portray the brutality of the enemy, and you think the images tell the story better than just words. Your newspaper and TV station generally do not run photos of dead bodies. Discuss the pros and cons of the following issues:

■ Can you justify using these images in print or on TV? Are there any differences between using them in either medium?

■ If you decide to use these graphic images in any media— print, broadcast or online—how will you use them and how will you explain your decision to your audience?

■ Will using these images on the organization's Web site create the same concerns? Why or why not? Are there different standards for the Web?

■ What are your alternatives?

Before the 9/11 terrorist attacks on the World Trade Center, American media organizations rarely used graphic images of dead bodies. After that event and in subsequent news stories covering the war in Iraq, more of these disturbing images appeared, and editors throughout the U.S. wrestled with decisions about publishing them. A photo that created wrenching decisions by editors portrayed a man jumping from the top of one of the World Trade Center towers during the 9/11 attack. Another case involved images of three American civilians whose charred bodies were hung from a bridge by Iraqis who had tortured and burned them. One of the most difficult decisions, however, involved photos of naked Iraqi prisoners being abused by American soldiers in an Iraqi prison in Abu Ghraib.

Would you have run these images? Kenny Irby, director of visual journalism and diversity for the Poynter Institute, offers this opinion in a column he wrote: "Newsroom leaders and decision-makers agonize over 'doing the right thing' when trying to decide whether to show visual truths— and not just write about those truths—because the visual images are more searing. . . . Such images are articles of visual information that convey messages of truth and report authentic facts in immeasurable ways. Thus, decisions about compelling and often disturbing photographs will never satisfy all of the people all of the time, and that is not the role of the messenger. . . . Yet by and large the U.S. media's principle is this: Citizens can make their own best choices when armed with honest information."

You can find more articles about disturbing photos by searching on the Poynter Institute site at *www.poynter.org.*

©Fred Pearce

Students at the University of Alaska Anchorage produce information for print, video and the Web to cover the Carrs/Safeway Great Alaska Shootout basketball tournament.

publication, you should still plan photos, audio and video to post on the organization's Web site.

Interactivity Try to get readers and viewers involved in all media but particularly in broadcast and online. In print and broadcast you might add a question or poll and refer your readers to the organization's Web site. On the Web, there are several ways to interact with the reader through questions, polls, chats, blogs or requests for readers' photos and stories. Not all stories lend themselves to reader interactivity, particularly breaking news stories. However if you are reporting a controversial issue or information about a city budget or proposal, ask your readers to respond with their comments or votes on an informal poll.

Anatomy of a News Story: P.R., Broadcast and Print

Compare the following information from a news release, a broadcast story and a print news story. The news release was issued on the Web because reporters who cover police and fire departments can't wait to receive releases for breaking news by mail. Although most print and broadcast reporters supplement news releases with their own sources, these news stories relied heavily on the releases because other sources were not available or relevant to the initial story.

Note some of these differences between the broadcast and print versions:

- The sentences in the broadcast version are much shorter than in the print version. The broadcast version is spoken over images (SOT—sound on tape).
- The Web versions for both print and broadcast were written in print style.
- The broadcast news story, which was the first to report the accident, uses present tense in the lead whereas the print version, which appeared the next day, updates the lead with newly released information.

In the next two examples, the print and broadcast stories were published on the same day. The print version was published first on the newspaper's Web site the afternoon of the fire. The broadcast version was aired on the evening news the day of the fire. Note that the print version tells what happened (past tense) and the broadcast version features an updated lead with present tense to give the current condition of the families. Also note that attribution in the

News Release

Date   Contact: (Name of police spokesman and phone number)

Man in Critical Condition after Apparent Hit and Run

At about 12:04 AM on Sunday (date included) Anchorage Police mid-shift patrol officers responded to the report of a person lying in the roadway at Debarr Road and Norene Streets in East Anchorage.

Responding officers located a male adult suffering from head and torso trauma. The victim was transported to a nearby local hospital for emergency treatment. He is listed in critical condition.

Investigating officers located evidence of an apparent vehicle/pedestrian collision. The driver of the vehicle left the scene without immediate notification as required by state and municipal laws. Officers were unable to locate the suspect vehicle or the driver.

At this time, the name of the victim is unknown. The victim appears to be a white or Native male about 35-48 years of age with brown hair and eyes. The male was wearing blue jean pants, a royal blue sweat shirt and dark blue "hoodie type" sweat shirt. The male was also wearing brown leather boots.

Police are asking for anyone who has information about this incident and or the name of the victim to call the Anchorage Police Department at (number given).

Anchorage Crime Stoppers pays callers whose tip leads to the arrest of a felony crime suspect. Callers may receive a cash reward of up to $1,000.00 and may submit their tip anonymously by phone at (number given) or on the net at *www.anchoragecrimestoppers.com*.

NOTE – The Traffic Division reports that three vehicle/pedestrian collisions have occurred in the past few weeks. Motorists are advised to be especially alert as the prelude to winter solstice means shorter periods of daylight and extended periods of darkness. Pedestrians are advised to cross at designated, well-lit crosswalks.

Oftentimes, alcohol is a contributing factor with one or both parties involved. The Anchorage Police Department urges responsible alcohol consumption by those legally entitled to do so.

# # #

The broadcast version posted on the TV station's Web site (featured video with the police spokesman). This is not written in broadcast script style, which we will study later. Note the emphasis in the lead is on the perspective given at the end of the news release.

Police search for another hit and run driver

ANCHORAGE, Alaska—For the third time in recent weeks, police are looking for yet another hit-and-run driver. This time a driver left a seriously injured man behind as they fled the scene.

The collision happened at the intersection of DeBarr Road and Norene Street around midnight last night.

A Good Samaritan saw the man—whose identity is not known—lying in the street and tried to keep other cars from striking him.

Anchorage Police Department Spokesman Lt. Paul Honeman said the victim suffered serious head and leg injuries but is alive and in the hospital.

(Honeman sound bite—Honeman name superimposed at bottom screen)

"There's no real clear indication. Anybody who had been in that location just prior to, or might have seen anything or knows anything about this incident, is asked to call the Anchorage Police Department." (End of sound bite)

Police also want help identifying the victim. They said he looks to be 35 to 48 years old with brown hair and eyes. He appears to be white or Native descent. He was wearing blue jeans, a blue sweatshirt and a second, darker blue hooded sweatshirt. He was also wearing brown leather boots.

Police said he is in critical condition.

—Jill Burke, *KTUU-TV* (Anchorage, Alaska)

Print version published the next morning with new information from the police department and updates on the victim's condition.

Pedestrian in critical condition after hit-and-run

A man critically injured in a hit-and-run traffic accident over the weekend is 48-year-old Garon James Koozaata, who is originally from St. Lawrence Island, police said today.

Just after midnight Sunday, Anchorage police discovered Koozaata near DeBarr Road and Norene Street. Police believe a vehicle hit him and the driver left without reporting the collision. Police are now looking for that driver.

"It's disturbing to realize that someone will mow a human being down and they'll just keep going," said Lt. Nancy Reeder.

Koozaata remained unconscious today at a local hospital, Reeder said. He was identified using his fingerprints.

Police are asking anyone with information about the hit-and-run to call 786-8900. Callers can leave tips anonymously by calling 561-7867.

Anchorage police used fingerprints to identify the victim of Sunday morning's hit and run.

Garon James Koozaata, age 48, was struck by an unknown vehicle in the area of Debarr Road and Norene Street in east Anchorage. A passing motorist discovered Koozaata shortly after midnight and notified police. Koozaata remains at a local hospital in critical condition suffering from head and torso trauma. Koozaata is an Anchorage resident from St. Lawrence Island.

Anyone with information as to the person responsible for this hit and run is asked to call Anchorage Police at (number given). Tipsters can report information anonymously by calling Anchorage Crime Stoppers at 561-STOP or submitting their tip on the internet at *www.anchoragecrimestoppers.com*. Crime Stoppers will pay cash rewards of up to $1,000 for information leading to a felony arrest. All calls and internet submissions are confidential.

—Kyle Hopkins, *Anchorage* (Alaska) *Daily News*

Convergence Coach 🌐

Writing for print, broadcast and the Web requires careful planning and reporting for more than one story. Here are some things to keep in mind:

- Plan to file breaking news immediately on the Web.

- While you are reporting, plan for the next cycle of the story. Always consider what will happen next.

You will need a fresh angle for the next broadcast or the next day's newspaper.

- Plan for audio and video elements that might be posted on the Web site, even if you are primarily reporting the story for print publication.

print version comes at the end of the sentence and it is in the beginning of the sentence in the broadcast version.

Print version.

Child alerts family to duplex fire

A child in an East Anchorage duplex alerted his family that the house was on fire Tuesday morning, leading to a safe evacuation and only minor injury to one person.

The family of four—one adult and children ages 6, 8 and 12—were at their rented duplex unit on Northwind Avenue, near Muldoon Road, when the child roused everyone as smoke detectors started sounding, said Tom Kempton, Anchorage Fire Department spokesman.

The first firefighters arrived on the scene about three minutes later, at 7:43 A.M., Kempton said. Crews found smoke streaming from an upstairs window and the family waiting outside. The adult had a minor burn to the hand but didn't have to go to a hospital, Kempton said.

Firefighters had to wake residents in the attached duplex unit and get them out, Kempton said. But that half of the building wasn't damaged.

The fire apparently started in an upstairs bedroom. Crews kept the blaze to that area, though the rest of the unit had smoke damage, Kempton said. Firefighters declared the scene under control just before 8 a.m. Damage is estimated to be $40,000 to $50,000, and the cause of the fire is under investigation.

The occupants reportedly do not have renter's insurance. The Alaska chapter of the American Red Cross is providing the family with food, clothes, shoes and lodging.

—Katie Pesznecker, *Anchorage Daily News*

Broadcast version posted on the station's Web site.

Family left homeless after fire

Anchorage, Alaska—Two Anchorage families are safe, but one is homeless after a duplex fire this morning in the Muldoon area.

The Anchorage Fire Department says the blaze broke out about 8 A.M., in a child's bedroom at 8151 Northwind Ave. The child alerted the rest of the family while fire crews went to the adjoining unit to make sure neighbors escaped safely. Firefighters were able to safely evacuate all people and pets from the home.

The cause of the fire is not yet known.

The American Red Cross of Alaska is assisting the family who was displaced. They did not have renters insurance.

—Maria Downey, *KTUU*

Anatomy of a News Story on the Web

The Gannett Company Inc. offers a training site for delivering online information. In one section, Kate Marymont, executive editor of *The News-Press* in Fort Myers, Fla., says when news breaks, it is posted online. "We don't hold back anything. As soon as we know and it is verified, it goes online. It doesn't have to be the complete print story."

Marymont describes how this worked when news broke that a 2-year-old child had discovered the bodies of his parents, both 25, who had been murdered in their home in the Gateway section of Fort Myers. Marymont described the process as follows:

- Announce the news as soon as possible. In this case *The News-Press* posted the breaking news at 4:47 P.M. and mentioned an upcoming news conference.

- Update in increments. Tell when there is more to come. The next information was posted on the Web at 5:30 P.M., alerting viewers that *The News-Press* would soon be posting tapes of the police interviews shortly.

What Do You Think ?

Do you think the Gannett Co. plan to reorganize newsrooms from traditional departments to seven new divisions fostering convergence is a good idea?

☐ Yes

☐ No

☐ Not sure

- Promote within the site. In this case the promotion said the tapes mentioned before are live online now.
- Post multimedia—in this case exclusive audio and video.

As you study the other chapters in this book, continue to develop a convergence mindset so that you present information to your audience when they want it and how they want it.

Exercises

1 **Deconstruct a news story:** Using a news story from your local or campus newspaper or from an online site, analyze the story as follows:

- Lead: Is it a summary or feature lead?
- Nut graph: Identify the focus. If the story uses a feature lead, is there a clear nut graph and where is it placed?
- Lead quote: Is there a quote from a source high in the story?
- Supporting information: Does the story contain information that supports the main idea?
- Sources: Does the story contain information from two or more sources to elaborate upon the main idea?
- Ending: Does the story end with a quote or additional information about a future action or comment on the main idea?

2 **Update:** Take any story in today's newspaper and convert it for broadcast by updating the lead, changing the attribution to conform to broadcast writing style and condensing it.

3 **Police story—print and broadcast:** Write a brief story for print and another version for broadcast, based on the information in the following news release.

Use your city's name for the police department and attribute information to Police Spokesman John Coptalker:

At about 2:54 AM on Thursday – March 22nd (use this year) Police Mid Shift Patrol Officers responded to reports of a shooting at an apartment located at the 7000 block of Walker Road.

Responding officers located two persons who had been shot. One victim, a male adult in his mid 40s was dead of the apparent gunshot wounds. Another victim, identified as Mary Pothead—age 36—was transported to a local hospital for emergency treatment. Pothead is listed in serious condition.

Details about the incident are sketchy. Detectives believe that this incident is possibly related to illegal drug activity. Detectives are seeking a possible suspect in this case described only as an unknown male. No other information is available at this time.

Detectives are actively seeking information from any persons who may have been in the area of or have knowledge of this shooting incident. Persons with information are asked to call the (Use your city) Police at 123-4567.

Persons who wish to remain anonymous may call the city's Crime Stoppers at 123-STOP or on the web at *www.crimetips.com*. Callers whose tip leads to an arrest of a Felony suspect are eligible for a reward of up to $1,000.00.

4 Interactivity

a. Using the example about cell phones cited in this chapter, write a poll question for online readers.

b. Write a poll question or chat topic for online readers to respond to about some controversial issue on your campus or in your community for online readers.

☞ **Featured Online Activity** Log on to the book Web site and write a story for print and another version for broadcast delivery based on the news release posted on the site in Chapter 4. Access the Web site address and pull down the menu to Chapter 4 exercises.

academic.cengage.com/masscomm/rich/ writingandreportingnews6e

Coaching Tips

Record the sights, sounds, smells and other details you observe when you are reporting.

Use concrete nouns; avoid adjectives.

Use vivid action verbs to describe your observations.

Is your story idea newsworthy?

Will your story pass the "so what" test to make readers and viewers care?

Will your story include audio and video for TV or the Web?

Will your story include interactive elements on the Web?

Keep a tickler file of follow-up ideas for stories that were published or are due for an upcoming development.

Search the Internet for story ideas about your topic.

You tell your readers a story by not telling them. You show it. You write it so they feel it. Use all of your senses to put the reader there. Get in the smells and the sounds.

—Martha Miller, magazine writer and editor

5

Curiosity and Story Ideas

T he blood spots made the difference.

A woman shot her boyfriend. He fled to a nearby store to seek help, and he died two hours later in a hospital.

It was just a basic news story for Martha Miller, then a police reporter. But when she went to the scene, she saw the blood spots.

First Miller measured the spots with a dime. But they were larger than that. So she tried a nickel. That fit. Then she counted the spots. She wrote a hard-news lead stating that the woman had shot and killed her boyfriend, and in the middle of the story she wrote this:

Martha Miller

> Brown, who was shot several times, staggered out of the apartment and down two houses to the Waystation convenience store on Virginia Street—his path, easily traceable by 41 nickel-size blood splotches that dotted the sidewalk.
>
> —Martha Miller, *Reno (Nev.) Gazette-Journal*

Martha Miller, magazine writer and editor

Why bother measuring and counting the blood spots? "I was curious," says Miller, now a magazine writer and editor for *Better Homes & Gardens*. "I saw them and I wanted to follow where they led. I wanted to show how he fled and that he was dripping blood. I wanted the reader to picture that."

The technique is one you learned in kindergarten: Show and tell.

Curiosity

A good reporter also possesses a trait you had in kindergarten—curiosity.

You probably badgered your parents with questions: What's that? Why?

Those are still good questions for gathering news. Just add a few more: Who, when, where, how and so what?

Most writing teachers tell you, "Show, don't tell." But you need to do both. To show, you need to observe. To show and tell, you need to be curious. You need to ask questions the reader will want answered in the story.

In these days of convergence when your story may be published in several media, you need to observe and report sights and sounds for audio and video.

How do you know what questions to ask, what to observe and report?

Start with the basics:

Who: Get the full names of people involved, complete with middle initials, and always check the spelling. A person named "John" might spell it Jon or other ways. If your source is known by a nickname, write the full name on the first reference and put the nickname in quotes after the first name. For television, the source's name may be superimposed over the image on the screen so accurate spelling is essential as well. Ask your source how he or she prefers to be addressed. For print and the Web, use the last name on second reference except for children.

What: Get an account of what happened. In some stories, especially police stories, you may want to recount the sequence of events. You don't have to write the story chronologically, but you need to understand the sequence.

When: Note the day and time of the event. If you are writing a story for the Web, consider writing a time line as a sidebar, which might be linked to the story or placed in a box on the same page.

Where: Get the location. Describe the scene. You may have to provide details to a graphic artist for a location map, so gather specific details about the location.

Why: Understand what caused the event. What was the conflict, and what is the resolution, if any?

How: Seek more information about what happened. How did it occur? In what order did events unfold?

So What: What impact did this event have on the participants? What impact could it have on readers? What makes this story newsworthy or significant? If you were writing a poll question for television or the Web, what would you ask readers or viewers?

Now for the harder questions: What does the reader need to know to understand and care about your story? You can't explain the event unless you understand it yourself, and you can't understand it unless you dig for answers. The key is to unleash your curiosity. Here are some techniques for developing your curiosity:

Role Play: Put yourself in the role of the reader. What makes the story important and interesting? If you were affected by this story, what would you want and need to know?

Imagine that you are a reporter for your campus newspaper. The phone rings. The caller tells you there is a fire and then hangs up. You call the fire department. A dispatcher gives you the address of the fire. It's your address. What are the first questions that come to your mind? If you have roommates, chances are you would want to know if they were injured. Was anyone else in the building killed or injured? Is your cat OK? Was your apartment or room destroyed? What was the extent of the damage? What caused the fire? When did it start? How long did the building burn? Where will residents of the building live if their apartments were destroyed or heavily damaged?

Then you might be concerned about other questions: How long did it take to put the fire out? Were there eyewitnesses? Who called the fire department? How quickly did the department respond? Is this the first time this building has been struck by a fire? Did the building have sprinklers? If so, did they work?

The list could go on. That's the basic concept of role-playing, and it can generate dozens of questions for you in many stories.

Use Time Lines: Understand the sequence of events. Start with the present; then go to the past and then to the future. What is happening now? How did this action develop? In what order did the event evolve? What is the next step? Questions involving time sequence will give you information for background and chronology in your stories. Time lines are also an excellent technique to use for Web stories.

Be a Detective: Imagine that you are a detective at the scene of a crime, a protest rally or any other event that involves a mystery or conflict. What questions would you ask to solve the crime or the problem? These questions will center on what happened, the motives, the consequences and the clues to uncovering the truth.

Observation

Good writers must be good reporters first. And good reporters observe and gather details with all their senses: sight, sound, smell, and less often, taste and touch. You can use your observation powers in any story—from a fire scene to a county fair.

Mary Ann Lickteig turned an ordinary story about the Iowa state fair into a fun one by observing these details:

> Off in an exhibit room, Nancy Pelley, a home economist from Tone Brothers spice company, looked over five cakes. One of them looked back. It had teeth and a tongue hanging out between the layers. "Isn't that something," Pelley mused.
>
> "What category is that?"
>
> It was the Ugliest Cake category.
>
> A green one with gummy worms on top won first place. Eight-year-old Jonathan Eddy of Des Moines named his entry "Green Mean Wormy Machine."
>
> To satisfy the requirement to include his recipe, Jonathan penciled on an attached card: "I made a cake. I frosted my cake. I made it ugly."
>
> —Mary Ann Lickteig,
> *The Des Moines* (Iowa) *Register*

The Show-in-Action Technique

If you want the reader to visualize your source or the scene, one of the best techniques is to show the person in action. This technique is more commonly used in feature stories with descriptive writing. But it also can be used in hard-news stories or for a soft lead on a news story. Regardless of the type of story, you need good observation skills. Here is an example of the show-in-action technique:

ST. PETERSBURG, Fla.—On a palm tree at the University of South Florida's St. Petersburg campus, a squirrel munches on an acorn. A few feet below, three students quietly assemble their equipment.

One keeps an eye on the squirrel. One sets up a video camera. Another prepares the bait, a fake, Caddyshack-esque squirrel with a robotic tail.

If the tail is convincing enough, the squirrel in the tree may try to communicate with the robot on the ground. That could provide new clues about what it means when a squirrel bats its tail.

This research, conducted entirely by undergraduates, is part of a new philosophy at USF and in universities across the nation.

—The Associated Press

Hard News vs. Soft News

You need good observation for both hard-news and feature stories. Although descriptive detail based on observation is more common in feature stories, you can use the same observation techniques in gathering information for hard-news stories. Stories about weather disasters, fires and other events where the scene is crucial lend themselves to descriptive detail based on observation. At a protest, use observation to report what signs the protesters carried and what they were chanting. At a trial, use observation to help the reader see how the defendant and other people in the courtroom reacted.

If you are reporting a breaking news event for television, don't depend on video to record these observations. In any disaster, fire or similar event, the reporter needs to describe the scene and answer questions the anchor might ask. In addition, reporters may be expected to post blogs to describe breaking news events.

Such was the case when a tornado wiped out the small town of Greensburg, Kan. In addition to publishing news stories in print, photo galleries and video, the *Wichita* (Kan.) *Eagle* reporters posted their observations on blogs. Note the description based on observation in the print version of the story:

This sun-baked High Plains town no longer has a grade school, a high school, a City Hall, a hospital, a water tower, a fire station, a business district or a main street.

It has people, but all 1,400 of them live elsewhere today. The homes they kept, the rooms where they were born, where they grew old together, now lie in millions of pieces, some of them as small as matchsticks. Tatters and shards of Greensburg flew for miles across the short grass and sage and yucca outside town on Friday night. Their branches now hold the shreds of housing insulation, pieces of tin, pieces of twisted roofing, crumpled family photographs, torn documents, and bits and pieces of belongings.

—Wichita (Kan.) *Eagle*

Here are two examples of a reporter's observations in a blog posted on the *Eagle's* news site:

In a strange juxtaposition, a full set of white and blue china—including tea service—stands on display in a storefront on Haviland's main street, perfect, while Greensburg residents' dishes are strewn across their town.

People stop to hug in front of the hardware store, relieved to see one another.

Deb Gruver, *Wichita Eagle*

HAVILAND—The street in front of Haviland High School looks like an insurance industry trade show. Major insurance companies have glitzy mobile trailers parked out front with satellite capability. High-tech toys help agents and adjusters access customer records. But the gadgets are also helping customers.

"Free Internet access" signs are posted along the sidewalk for people who want to check e-mail messages.

Agents are everywhere, wearing business polos with their company logos.

—Deb Gruver, *Wichita Eagle*

Fact vs. Opinion

You need to use observation to gather facts and details about an incident, but you should not express your opinions about what you saw. In news stories, all opinions, judgments and accusations must be attributed to a source. In the past, the only places for reporters' opinions or interpretations were in columns, in stories labeled "analysis" or first-person stories, which were usually preceded by an editor's note. Now reporters may use first-person observations and opinions in blogs, but news stories should still rely on facts and opinions of other sources.

Although broadcast news can be more personal, reporters do not usually refer to themselves in news stories unless they are responding to questions from the news anchor.

In the following excerpt, the example labeled "Appropriate" is a description from a story about a plane crash. Most of this story is detail based on observation. The second paragraph contains a vivid description of the crash site. Note that an opinion is expressed in the last paragraph, although it is attributed to someone on the scene, not to the reporter. In contrast, the example labeled "Inappropriate" shows how not to write the story. Note the improper use of the first person (inserting the reporter in the story). Opinion that is not attributed to someone else is printed in italics.

Appropriate

A US Air jetliner landing at Los Angeles International Airport collided on the ground with a SkyWest commuter plane Friday night, creating a fiery tangle of wreckage. At least 12 people were killed, 24 were injured and 21 were missing, officials said.

Orange flames boiled up from the fuselage, and a huge column of smoke towered over the airport. Spotlights and the lights from police, fire and other rescue vehicles silhouetted the smoldering wreckage against the darkened sky.

"It was a sight beyond belief," said Brett Lyles, 23, of San Francisco.

—*Los Angeles Times*

Inappropriate

A US Air jetliner landing at Los Angeles International Airport collided on the ground with a SkyWest commuter plane Friday night, creating a fiery tangle of wreckage *that was horrifying to behold*.

I saw orange flames that boiled up from the fuselage, and a huge column of smoke towered over the airport. *It was eerie to see* the spotlights from police and other rescue vehicles silhouetting the smoldering wreckage against the darkened sky. *It was a frightening sight.*

ETHICS

Ethical dilemma: You belong to a campus organization that is sponsoring a charity event that you think will make a good story. Should you write the story? Is it a conflict of interest to report and write a story about an organization to which you belong?

Ethical guidelines: The Society of Professional Journalists Code of Ethics says journalists should be free of obligation to any interest other than the public's right to know. Journalists should avoid conflicts of interest, real or perceived, and should disclose unavoidable conflicts.

Observation to Find Questions

Use observation as a reporting tool, not just as a writing tool. When you observe action or details at a scene, what questions occur to you?

When Martha Miller observed the blood spots, she wondered not only how big they were but also how many there were and how long it took the man to get to the convenience store after he was shot. Details make a difference in your reporting and writing.

Observation for Visual Presentation

When you are at the scene of an accident or an event, many of the basic reporting questions are likely to come to mind. Just as important are ideas for a good photograph or graphic illustration. Does the story need a graphic to explain how something works? Would a photo, graphic or chart eliminate the need for lengthy explanation in your story? Is there information you should gather for audio and video for broadcast delivery or for posting on a Web site? What do you see that you would want the reader to see as well? Don't forget to observe locations and pinpoint them by proximity to major streets or specific distances from a site that the artist can interpret and the reader can understand. When you collect information, you need to see your story as well as hear it.

Ways to Find Story Ideas

The basic concepts for news—local interest, human interest, timeliness, unusual events, conflict, celebrity, impact of news events—can generate story ideas. A major national or local news event might be worth a local reaction story. If you are on a college campus, you are surrounded by experts in many fields. Professors can be good sources for national stories that need a local angle or interpretation.

The primary way to get story ideas, especially if you are assigned to a beat, is to contact your sources regularly and ask them what is going on in their workplace. Another way of getting story ideas is to examine records related to your beat, such as government documents.

Many good stories result from curiosity and observation. Have you noticed anything unusual or different on campus or in your community? Photojournalists usually excel at observing people and places for good pictures. An idea for a good photograph might also be an idea for a good story.

The visual concepts are as much a part of the story idea as the verbal concept. Does the story need a photograph, graphic illustration (such as a chart or map) or highlights box? Does the story need audio and video? Think about those elements when you devise your story idea.

Here are some other suggestions for ways to find stories:

Brainstorm: Discuss ideas for stories with other students and with people in your community. What topics on campus or in your community are of interest to people? Does anyone have an unusual course, a professor worth a profile or an interest in an organization that is newsworthy? Think of consumer stories—how to get the best buys on textbooks, tips for winter or spring break, and health tips for students, especially during exam periods.

Check Databases: Check computer databases of other stories. When you begin a beat or a major story, check for sources and angles in previous articles about the subject in your own publication and in other newspapers, magazines, databases and the Web. Be careful not to copy information or quotes—that's plagiarism—but use these stories for ideas.

Map the Topic: "Mapping" is a form of brainstorming suggested by researchers who have studied the functions of the left side of the brain (the logical reasoning part) and the right side (the creative part). It is a process of word association that helps you explore different facets of a topic of interest to your readers. Draw a circle or a trunk of a tree for the main topic, and list the related ideas as spokes or branches—or just write a list.

For example, you might want to explore whether tuition is increasing. Tuition is the topic in the center of the circle or on the trunk of the tree. The related topics might be the effects on out-of-state students, where the money goes, a comparison to other colleges and so on. Once you have generated several ideas related to the main focus, you can eliminate the ideas that don't seem worthy of a separate news story.

Another topic for possible mapping is a holiday. How many ideas can you devise for stories related to Thanksgiving, spring break or Valentine's Day?

Try this technique with the weather. If your area has had floods, hurricanes, tornados, earthquakes or an extended drought, think of all the people, businesses and other groups affected by the weather. The diagram on the next page shows how the topic of floods could be mapped.

Assume Other Points of View: This technique is similar to mapping. Take an issue and role-play to discover how other people might think about it. Does that process give you an idea for a feature or a profile about someone who is affected by the issue? If the state cuts funding to your university, how are students, programs, departments and related campus activities affected?

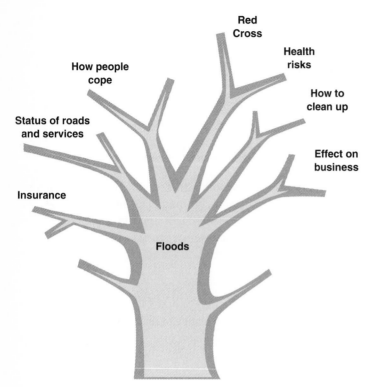

Red Cross

Health risks

How people cope

How to clean up

Status of roads and services

Effect on business

Insurance

Floods

Story ideas generated by mapping the topic of floods

Another potential source of ideas is special interest groups. What groups of people don't get much coverage in your newspaper? Do minorities on your campus have concerns that could generate news stories?

What problems do elderly residents in your city have? Do women's groups in your school or town have special problems and interests that would make good ideas for news? What are the needs of people with disabilities? Do veterans in your community have special needs that are newsworthy? Do you have an active gay rights group on campus? Contacts with members of these groups can generate dozens of story ideas.

Observe: Look at bulletin boards on campus or in local government offices. Look around your city. Are there new stores or buildings that are worth telling the reader about? Are there old buildings, landmarks or stores that are closing, such as a famous hangout? Does anything make you curious? Do you notice something new on campus or in the community? Is there a program or event that might be newsworthy?

Talk to People: Ask your friends what interests them. Eavesdrop at lunch to find out what people are talking about. When you are out in the community, ask people what they read in newspapers or view on television or the Web and what they would like to read.

Check Directories: Universities and many government agencies have directories listing departments and personnel. Do any people, places or programs seem newsworthy? Does your school directory list organizations or departments that sound unusual or worthy of a feature?

You could also check the yellow pages of your telephone book for ideas about interesting services and places. For example, are several mosques listed in your city under the category of churches? If so, does this indicate changes in the population of your community?

Read Local Newspapers and Watch Local TV News Stations: Does a news story suggest angles that could be developed into a separate story? Does it name people who could be profiled? Sometimes the best feature stories are offshoots of a breaking news story.

Is there a larger story to be developed from a news event? If an apartment building in your community or a campus building is cited for fire safety violations, is there a larger story about fire inspections or problems with apartments, especially in areas that rent to students?

When a big story breaks in your community, are there experts or other people affected by the problem who would be worth a separate story? For example, if the teachers in your town are on strike, consider all the different people who are affected. Is there an expert on campus or in your city who is worth a feature because of his or her views on the issue?

Almost all major stories affecting your community—such as disasters, strikes, crimes and court rulings—need follow-up stories to explain the next step or action resulting from the issue.

Read Classified Advertisements: Look for unusual items. An advertisement in a campus newspaper about services to provide term papers could make a good investigative story. Other ads about adoption, unusual research offers or new services could generate news stories. Also look in the lost and found column. Is there a human interest story behind a lost pet or other item?

Patricia Rojas, a former reporter for *The Des Moines* (Iowa) *Register,* was scanning the classified section of her newspaper when this ad caught her attention: LOST WARRIOR, blue tick Coonhound, male, stupid but friendly.

"When I saw 'stupid but friendly,' I had a feeling there was a good story behind this ad," Rojas said. There was. The dog had wandered two blocks from home and couldn't find his way back. It turned out that the dog had led a difficult life. One time he was stolen from his owner, Lisa Volrath of Des Moines, and he nearly starved after his captor abandoned him. This time he was luckier. Someone found him and took him to an animal shelter. Rojas ended her story with this quote from Volrath after she had recovered her dog:

"I could tell from his stupid expression that he was my dog," Volrath said.

It was just a little story, but people enjoy reading about dogs, cats and other pets. And Rojas said her editors appreciated her initiative in finding the story.

An advertisement for a lost pet cobra turned into a fun story for another reporter. This story could be broadened into a feature about unusual pets.

Localize National News: Is there a national story that you can apply to your area? What are the local angles? What are the reactions of people in your community? National elections, tragedies, terrorism, war and other national events can all be localized by focusing on people in your area who are affected. In many cases when a natural disaster occurs in another state, people from your community might volunteer to help, so check churches and local agencies to find out if there is a local angle.

Seek Profiles: Is there a person who is in the news or someone who should be in the news because of his or her accomplishments? Is an expert mentioned in a story worthy of a separate profile?

Can you find stories about people who have accomplished something special, triumphed over adversity, or experienced pain or joy in relation to a news event? Or can you find stories about people who represent a particular aspect of a news event? Such stories often make good human-interest features.

If you are writing for a campus newspaper, you can find many people to profile, including new professors, retiring professors or campus employees and staff members who provide important functions behind the scenes,

Read Letters to the Editor, Blogs and Feedback on Web Sites: You can get many story ideas from the problems and reactions that people express in letters to the editor in print or online forums.

Track Programs and Events: Check your campus Web site for upcoming events, speakers and scheduled entertainment. Is there a campus or government program that would be of interest to your readers? Is it a new program? Is an old program approaching an anniversary? Has it been effective or ineffective? Is there a program that a private citizen or group is trying to establish? Is the program related to the season or to an event in the news? For example, is there a program at your university affected by budget cuts?

Holidays, news events and anniversaries of major news events also make good features. Plan ahead and think of stories related to these topics.

Good editors and reporters in all media keep tickler files, which are organized by weeks or months to remind them about stories that should be followed. When you are reporting, especially on a beat, you should start your own tickler file so you can remind yourself about stories you should follow. You could keep a calendar in your computer to create a digital tickler file listing story ideas that need updates during each month.

Rewrite News Releases: Government agencies, organizations in your community and campus organizations issue news releases about events. These news releases often contain ideas for features. If you are assigned to cover a specific beat, ask the key sources to send you any news releases they issue.

In some cases you can subscribe to an organization's news releases, using RSS, the technology that automatically sends material to your computer or portable digital device when you subscribe to a site. Many government agencies have embraced technology by offering media information in print, audio and video. You can get a list of all the U.S. government agencies that offer RSS feeds at *www .usa.gov/Topics/Reference_Shelf/Libraries/RSS_Library.shtml.*

For example, NASA (National Aeronautics and Space Administration) offers multimedia news releases and audio and video feeds as podcasts, including one specifically geared to career opportunities for students.

Courtesy of NASA

If you are covering a major weather problem such as floods or storms in your area, the National Oceanic and Atmospheric Administration (NOAA; *www.nws .noaa.gov/pa/*) also offers RSS feeds in audio and video formats. In addition, the agency offers story ideas for reporters.

When you use a news release, regardless of the format, remember that it is not a balanced news story. It is written by an advocate for the organization. Even though you may copy information in the release without plagiarizing, you should always check the information. You should also try to contact sources listed in the release and seek other sources to confirm, deny or give other points of view.

If the news release contains quotes, you may use them, but it is better to get the comments directly from the source. If you can't, you should attribute the comments to the release—for example, "the chancellor said in a prepared statement" or "according to a news release."

If you use a video news release in a TV news show or Web site, you should attribute it to the organization that created it. News organizations that have used video news releases without divulging the sources have been accused of unethical practices. By failing to reveal that the video was promotional material that could be biased, the stations that presented the videos as their own were accused of misrepresenting the information and deceiving the viewers.

Follow Issues and Trends: Are there problems on campus or in your community that reflect national problems? Do any local news events reflect a larger problem? For example, if four women have been attacked on campus in separate incidents, is there a larger story about rape on campus or lack of security?

When you write issue stories, make sure that you have a narrow focus. A topic such as AIDS or homeless people is too broad. Focus the story on one aspect of the problem. You might do a story about how your city is or isn't caring for AIDS patients. Or you might do a story about an aspect of the homeless problem in your city, such as an increase in the number of homeless women with children.

Be Curious and Concerned: These qualities, above all, will lead you to good stories.

The Internet

The Internet has exerted a profound influence on the way reporters and editors in all media are gathering story ideas. Almost all online media sites post feedback questions or polls attached to stories or major issues. These responses can generate ideas for follow-up stories.

Weblogs: Also known as "blogs," these are personal essays or journals that have proliferated on the Web in recent years. Some blogs are written by reporters who give their "behind-the-scenes" or personal views of an event, while other blogs are posted by people who just want to express their thoughts. Blogs may generate story ideas because they express problems or thoughts about which people are concerned.

Be careful about quoting or using information from blogs in a news story. Although some blogs may contain factual information, they are unedited journals

Convergence Coach

- Use the Internet for ideas, but do not copy information from a Web site without attributing it to the source. That's plagiarism. Ideas are not copyrighted, but the information on the site is protected by copyright laws even if the site does not have a copyright symbol or notice.

- Use blogs for story ideas, but check the information and attribute it to the blog author.

- Subscribe to RSS feeds from news and government agencies related to a beat or topics you want to cover regularly.

- If you post audio or video from a news release on your Web site, attribute the source.

- If you refer to an online source, The Associated Press Stylebook recommends that you cite the URL (the Internet address) as the last line in a story. However, Web URLs are often included in the text of online stories these days because Internet users have become more sophisticated about using links and returning to the text if they are interested in the story.

or essays that do not have to adhere to principles of journalistic credibility. Because they are not checked for accuracy even if they are written by journalists, blogs have spawned a controversy in the media over whether they can be considered journalism. Regardless, they are a popular form of expression on the Web. Jonathan Dube, a journalist who authors a comprehensive site called *Cyberjournalist.net,* lists more than 150 blogs by journalists and dozens more by news freelance writers. You can also use blog search engines such as Technorati (*http://technorati.com/*) or Blog Search Engine (*www.blogsearchengine.com*) where you will find blogs grouped by topics such as politics, health and travel.

Search Engines: The ability to search the Internet by topic provides an incomparable way of gaining story ideas. If you type a key word into Google, one of the most popular search engines, you may get millions of responses. Narrow the search term if you want more specific information. The Internet also provides access to thousands of online news sites. By surfing through such news sites, you can gain story ideas about issues that you can tailor to your community.

Idea Budgets

Some story ideas are assigned by editors, but most editors expect reporters to provide their own story ideas, especially if the reporter covers a beat. The daily "story budget" contains a brief description of each story planned for the next day's newspaper, TV news show or online news site. Each budget item, or "budget line," begins with a "slug" (a one-word title) and is followed by a few sentences describing the story. Many news organizations also use a planning story budget, describing story ideas for the week and long-range stories.

The budget line is also a tool to help you focus your ideas. As you write your budget lines, you should be keeping the "so what" factor in mind. Your budget line is your way of selling the story idea to your editor, so you need to make it sound like an essential news story or a compelling idea.

To write a budget line, give your story a slug, and describe the idea in a paragraph or two. Include potential sources and possibilities for photos or graphics. Here's an example of a budget line by Buddy Nevins, a reporter who covered the transportation beat for *The Sun-Sentinel* in Fort Lauderdale, Fla.

Pedestrians: Broward has one of the highest rates of pedestrian deaths in the nation. One problem is that the roads haven't been designed for pedestrians, and many don't have sidewalks or crosswalks because of a lack of money. What is being done to solve the problem?

Graphics: Charts, maps of worst roads

A good budget line should summarize the main point of your story. It will also give you a head start in writing your lead or nut graph.

What Do You Think

How observant are you? When you drive or walk to campus, do you notice anything new or unusual that might generate a news story idea?

- Often
- Never
- Occasionally
- Only if it's threatening to hurt me

Exercises

1 **The dart method:** This idea comes from Alison Plessinger, Ph.D., an assistant professor at the Defense Information School in Virginia. It's like playing a game of darts except that wherever the dart lands on a map, you write a story about that place. Here's how it works: Take a large campus or community map pasted to a corkboard, and throw a dart at the map. Using that area of town or campus, write a story about someone or something in that area. For example, Plessinger says, you could go to the room or apartment where you lived as a freshman and interview the current occupant. Or you could use the campus or local phone directory and select a name at random to write a profile about the person. The concept, she says, is that everyone has a story to tell. Plan a backup of a few names in case the first person you contact is not available or willing to talk to you.

2 **Role-playing for curiosity training:** You have lent your car to a friend. You find out that your friend has had an accident with your car. Write a list of questions that come to your mind. Now add any questions you might need to answer to make the incident a news story. Write a list of the sources you would contact.

3 **Description for observation training:** Describe in detail some statue, painting or special landmark at your school.

4 **More description for observation training:** Without looking at the person next to you, write a brief paragraph describing what he or she is wearing and everything else you can remember about the person's appearance.

5 **Show-in-action technique for observation training:** Write a descriptive paragraph about a professor, a relative or a good friend. Use the show-in-action technique to describe the person's mannerisms, characteristic expressions and other details.

6 **Observation:** Describe the office of a source you have interviewed or of a professor you confer with frequently. List at least 10 items that are memorable. Do not include such standard items as desk and bookcase.

7 Graphic exercise for observation training: Imagine that a rare painting was stolen from a museum on your campus or in your city but was discovered the next day in a recycling bin or large trash receptacle on your campus. Go to that site (choose any area containing a large bin), and collect all the information you can for a location map or graphic illustration describing exactly where the painting was found. Write a list of information that you would give to an artist for drawing a location map. Make sure that you include nearby streets, the number of feet or yards from a recognizable spot, dimensions of the garbage bin and other details you think would be helpful to the artist. Then, using your own directions, draw a location map to test whether you have gathered good information.

8 Create a mood piece or scene: Go to some favorite or interesting place on campus or in your community (a park bench, for example), and observe the surroundings and people. Use all your senses. Write a few paragraphs or a brief essay creating mood as though you were describing the scene for a feature news story or a short story. Include dialogue if you overhear people speaking or any other details that might help create the mood. If you use a demonstration or rally for your observation exercise, write a feature story about the event.

9 Field trips: Talk to people on your campus and in your community about what they read or don't read in the campus or local newspaper and what kinds of stories they would like to see in their newspaper.

10 Look in your local newspaper for ideas for profiles. People used as sources might be interesting subjects for a separate story. Pick at least three names of people who might be newsworthy to interview.

11 Read the classified advertising section of your newspaper, and look for items that could generate stories of human interest, new businesses, trends or unusual news.

12 Write a story budget with three ideas for stories you would like to cover. Identify some sources you would interview, and consider photo or graphic possibilities. Use the story budget format in this chapter, or modify it as you or your instructor wishes.

13 Take a walking tour of your campus or your community (individually, in small groups or as a class). Write as many story ideas as you can based on your observations.

14 Localize a news story based on a national issue. For example, localize a story about the problems and legal issues of gay marriages or gays in the military. How would you localize your story, and whom would you contact?

15 Enterprise: Write a news story from one of your story ideas. If you are still having trouble, consider a story about an upcoming holiday. You might get some other ideas if you check the office of institutional research at your college or university for any studies the office has done. Check some club sports that don't regularly get covered in your campus newspaper or check clubs and support groups on your campus or in your community. Who are some of the people behind the scenes who perform valuable services in your community? You could do profiles such as a day in the life of a postal carrier, the city clerk, a sanitation worker or other people in service jobs. You might also check news releases on your school's Web site to gain story ideas of interest to your community.

☞ **Featured Online Activity** Log on to the book Web site for Chapter 5 and do the exercise to generate story ideas from the trigger words listed from A to Z.

academic.cengage.com/masscomm/rich/ writingandreportingnews6e

Coaching Tips

Use the matchmaking technique: Ask one source to recommend another one who is knowledgeable about the subject you are researching.

Check previous stories about the subject in your organization's databases before you begin your reporting.

Check any records or documents related to your story.

Check the Internet for information about your sources or topic.

Check the credibility of Web sites before you use information from them. Does the site date its information, attribute sources, list authors, and provide e-mail and/or telephone contacts?

Attribute sources. Avoid anonymous sources.

Contact sources who have opposing points of view.

Anonymous sources challenge our credibility with readers.

—Peter Bhatia, executive editor, *The* (Portland) *Oregonian*

6

Sources and Online Research

Mark Potter calls his source book his "bible." He takes it with him everywhere. It is a 7-by-9-inch address book, so worn that it is held together by sturdy strips of packing tape. Potter, a reporter for NBC, says he couldn't function without his source book. It is so crucial to his job that he keeps a duplicate in his home.

Potter cross-indexes his source book three ways: by the source's name, occupation and location. If he wants to contact an FBI agent he once interviewed in Detroit but whose name he may have forgotten, Potter looks up the agent's name under *FBI* or *Detroit*. Under each listing, Potter records the source's addresses and telephone numbers for work and home.

Getting the home phone numbers is not always easy, especially for police officers, who keep their numbers unlisted. So Potter asks for the information this way: "How can I reach you in the off hours?" That way, if the source does not want to reveal a home number, he or she can give an option of another way to be contacted, Potter says. It avoids placing a negative tone on the interview.

Here is some information that you should include in your source book:

- Name of source.
- Phone numbers (include work and cell phone). If possible get a home phone number for your source.
- E-mail address.
- Physical address.
- Notations: Add any information such as important dates (a birthday, for example) to remember or personal information (family members) that you might use if you contact the source frequently and want to be thoughtful.

It's not too early in your career for you to start a source book. The people you interview in college, such as professors who are experts on foreign policy or the economy, may be good sources for stories later in your career. If you are creating your source book in your computer or personal digital assistant, be sure to back it up on a storage device. And although it may seem old-fashioned in these days of digital devices, it's a good idea to have a printed copy of your source book.

Mark Potter, NBC reporter (third from left)

A good reporter needs people to interview and written sources, such as public records. But how do you get sources, and how do you know which ones to use for a given story?

Before you begin reporting for any assignment, check previous stories about the topic in databases and do online research. Most print and broadcast newsrooms maintain databases of stories the newspaper or television station has done, making it easy to search for previous stories about the person or topic. You can also find sources on the Internet in news groups, social networking sites and blogs. If you are searching for a source by name, check to make sure that the source is the person you want; many people have the same name, and the information you retrieve may not be for the correct source.

When you are assigned to a breaking-news event, such as a fire or accident, you may not have time to check previous stories before you leave the office. But you should check them before you begin writing. The building that burned may have had problems with sprinkler systems or previous fires in the past.

The same recommendation applies to crime stories. A suspect arrested on charges may have been arrested previously for the same or other charges. If you find a story about a suspect's previous arrest, make sure that you find out if the charges were dropped or what happened in the case.

Use caution: Newsroom files and videotapes may not be up-to-date, and follow-up stories may not have been written or aired about crime suspects. Even more problematic is the Web, which can archive everything, but if the document is not dated, you may not be getting the most accurate information.

Human Sources

Newswriting needs human sources to make the story credible and readable. Information from eyewitnesses and participants lends immediacy to a story, and direct quotes and sound bites make a story interesting. You can find human sources in a number of ways.

- **News releases:** All news releases list a contact person, usually a public information officer or public relations contact. Contact that person first but don't stop with that source. Whenever possible, ask to speak to the people mentioned in the news release.

- **Up and down the ladder:** Who's in charge of the organization or department? You could start at the top by contacting the department head. On many other stories, you should also go down the ladder and try to contact the person closest to the incident. For example, if you are writing a police story, try to contact the officer who was at the scene. If you are writing about a study, contact the professor or researcher who did the study.

■ **Names in the news:** If you read or view a news story from a newspaper, telecast or from the Internet, don't just quote the news story. Contact the primary source—the person involved. That is particularly true when you read about a survey or a study.

■ Get to know administrative assistants, sometimes still called "secretaries," of officials in a corporation or a department. This is especially important if you have a beat—a specific area of coverage such as education, government, police or other specialties you are responsible for covering regularly. Without the cooperation of the administrative assistant, you may not get to the sources you need.

■ **Community and campus leaders:** Find out who are the leaders of groups in your community and campus. Don't limit your sources to these people, but they could be valuable initial resources who can lead you to other people.

■ **Sponsorship:** This technique is a method of introducing yourself to a source by using a contact the source might know. Someone you know can "sponsor" you to contact the source you want. For example, when Mark Potter was working on a story about the problems of Haitians in Miami, the Haitian refugees were reluctant to talk to him. Many of them were illegal immigrants. Potter said they thought he was an immigration official who was seeking to deport them. So he asked a community social worker who had gained the trust of several Haitians to recommend him to one of the Haitians. The social worker introduced him to a Haitian named Pierre, but Pierre didn't have the information Potter wanted. However, Pierre said his brother-in-law might help, and Pierre introduced Potter to him. After establishing trust with the brother-in-law, Potter asked him to get other Haitians to talk to him. And that's how he got the sources he needed for his story.

■ **Self-sponsorship:** If you have reported and written a previous news story about a subject of interest to the source you are trying to contact, you can sponsor yourself. When you contact the source, introduce yourself by referring to the relevant article or newscast you reported.

Nancy Tracy, a former reporter for *The Hartford* (Conn.) *Courant,* was working on a follow-up story about three people who survived when the Mianus River Bridge in Connecticut collapsed and their vehicles plunged into the river. But a key source, Eileen Weldon, wouldn't talk to her or anyone else in the media. Weldon had severe injuries and was tired of press coverage.

So Tracy tried self-sponsorship, a way of recommending herself. "I'm going to send you some clips of other stories I have done to show you that I am a very sensitive reporter," she told Weldon. "Please read them. I'll call you in a few days. If you don't think I can be fair, I won't ever bother you again." Tracy got the interview. Her clips "sponsored" her.

■ **Matchmaking:** Once you have contacted a source and want to find others, use the matchmaking technique, which is related to the sponsorship method. Ask the source who else you might contact about the situation.

■ **Fairness:** If you are writing a story involving conflict, find sources who have the opposing points of view. Do not report any accusations about a person without contacting the target of those comments.

USA Today library

■ **Primary and secondary sources:** When you are conducting an interview, if your source says something about another person, particularly if it is derogatory or controversial, make sure that you check with that other person. The first source's statements not only could be wrong; they could also be libelous. You should even check out written information about sources to make sure that it is accurate.

■ **Blogs:** Postings on the Internet from people who have written blogs about an issue can be good sources for you to contact. Don't quote from a blog without trying to contact the writer. Also, don't consider information from blogs as accurate news. Blogs are usually opinion columns and personal reflections, but they can be valuable for finding human sources.

Anonymous Sources

Many people will be willing to talk to you if you promise not to use their names. An anonymous source is one who remains unnamed. (The terms "anonymous source" and "confidential source" are used interchangeably by most people.) But should you make this promise? Most editors today would say no, unless there is no other way to get the information. And even then, many editors would refuse to grant that immunity from identification. The more you rely on unnamed sources, the less credibility your story has.

The Associated Press policy on anonymous sources is as follows: "Reporters should proceed with interviews on the assumption they are on the record. If the source wants to set conditions, these should be negotiated at the start of the interview. At the end of the interview, the reporter should try once again to move some or all of the information back on the record."

In the past, reporters who promised their sources anonymity had a good chance of honoring their promise even if they were subpoenaed to reveal their sources. Most news organizations successfully fought any court attempts to reveal sources. But in the last few years, judges in several courts penalized reporters by sentencing them to jail for refusing to reveal their sources.

One of the most publicized cases occurred in 2005 when Judith Miller, then a reporter for *The New York Times,* spent 85 days in jail for refusing to testify to a federal grand jury about the name of a confidential source who had revealed the identity of an undercover CIA agent, which is a federal crime. When the source gave Miller permission to reveal his name, she was released from jail and testified. An unusual factor in this case was that Miller never wrote a story about the agent. Miller claimed her refusal to reveal sources was a matter of principle. "I do not make confidential pledges lightly, but when I do, I keep them," Miller told U.S. District

Court Judge Thomas F. Hogan when he sentenced her to jail. Miller resigned from the *Times* a few months after she testified because of objections from some of her colleagues about her actions and because she had become the news, she said in her resignation letter.

Matt Cooper, then a reporter for *Time*, did write a story about the CIA agent, Valerie Plame, but he reluctantly revealed his sources to the grand jury after his appeals for immunity from testifying were rejected by the Supreme Court.

The case has prompted support for a federal shield law that would prohibit federal courts from forcing reporters to reveal their confidential sources. In 1972 the U.S. Supreme Court ruled that journalists have a duty to provide grand juries information relevant to criminal trials. Since then, all states except Wyoming offer some protection of journalist-source privileges either by shield laws or precedents from case law, but these state statutes do not apply to federal courts.

The issue of using anonymous sources has been controversial for many years. A recent survey by the Associated Press Managing Editors organization showed that one in four newspaper editors refuses to allow reporters to use anonymous sources. But investigative reporters insist that they need to rely on them as sources.

"The anonymous source is a tool like any tool. But it tends to be overused," Peter Bhatia, executive editor of *The Oregonian*, said in a forum at the Poynter Institute, a training organization for journalists. "We don't use anonymous sources unless there is no other way to get the story in the paper and the story is of such compelling public interest that we must get it in the paper."

Despite the problems with anonymous sources, it's unlikely that news organizations will eliminate them altogether. If you must use anonymous sources because you have no other alternative, you should check the information with other sources, preferably ones who will allow use of their names, and check documents. Many sources, named or unnamed, have their own agenda and want to manipulate reporters so the sources can promote their cause. For fairness and balance, it is crucial for reporters to check with other sources to confirm, deny or provide other points of view.

ETHICS

Ethical dilemma: Should you show your story to a source before publication?

Discussion: Most journalists are opposed to prepublication review by a source because of fears that the source may recant statements or may wish to change the copy. Steve Weinberg, an author of several books and former director of the Investigative Reporters

and Editors organization, strongly favors checking the story with a source because, he says, it will ensure accuracy. Other journalists have always favored reading parts of a story, especially technical or sensitive information, back to a source. In most cases, deadline pressure prevents journalists from waiting for sources to review the whole story. But if such review is

possible, should it be allowed? What do you think?

Ethical guidelines: Fairness, credibility, accuracy. The Society of Professional Journalists Code of Ethics says journalists should "test the accuracy of information from all sources and exercise care to avoid inadvertent error."

When using unnamed sources, you may identify the person with a vague reference, such as "according to one official." Or you might give the person a pseudonym, a false name. Although most editors discourage pseudonyms, they are sometimes allowed in feature stories about sensitive subjects such as rape. But they are rarely used in hard-news stories. It is preferable to use no name or a first name only. If you use a full-name pseudonym, which is not preferred, you should check your local telephone directories to make sure that you aren't using the name of someone in your community. And in all cases, to protect the identity of the source, you must tell the reader that this is a false name.

Janet Cooke didn't do that. And she touched off a furor in the newspaper industry that persists years after the incident. Cooke, then a reporter for *The Washington Post,* won the Pulitzer Prize in 1981 for a story called "Jimmy's World," about an 8-year-old heroin addict. There was only one problem: Jimmy didn't exist. When Cooke first discussed the story with her editors, she said she had located the child's mother, who was reluctant to talk. Her editors said she could grant the mother anonymity. Cooke turned in a compelling story about the child and his mother. But when Cooke won the Pulitzer and was profiled in newspapers, some discrepancies in her résumé were discovered. That led to questions about her story. She ultimately admitted that she had made up the story about Jimmy and his mother. The *Post* returned the Pulitzer, and Cooke resigned in disgrace.

Cooke's story wasn't based on an anonymous source; it was a fabricated source. The impact was a crisis of credibility for the press. Newspapers throughout the country began developing policies against using pseudonyms, and many editors banned the use of anonymous sources altogether.

Fabrication of sources and other information in news stories surfaced as a problem again in the 1990s and later in several high-profile scandals. Most notorious was the case of Jayson Blair, a reporter for *The New York Times,* who made up quotes, fictionalized scenes and plagiarized material in dozens of the stories he wrote during his four years at the newspaper. His deception was discovered after he plagiarized material from a story written by a Texas newspaper reporter with whom Blair had worked when he was a reporter on the student newspaper at The University of Maryland. Blair never graduated from the school and was hired by the *Times* after his internship there because he showed so much promise. After the discovery of this and other stories that were fabricated or plagiarized, Blair resigned in disgrace, and the *Times* published an extensive front-page story about his deception.

Blair's trail of fabrication and plagiarism mirrored the pattern of Stephen Glass, a rising star at *The New Republic,* who was fired after his editor discovered that he had fabricated sources in many of his stories. His deception was discovered when a reporter for an online site questioned a story Glass had written about a convention of hackers. The convention didn't exist, nor did the software company cited in the story. Glass even created a phony Web site for the nonexistent software company. A complaint from an online magazine spurred the investigation, which revealed that the article was a hoax, and several others Glass had written were also fiction. A few years later, Glass published an autobiographical novel called *The Fabulist* about a reporter who fabricates stories. The Glass story also became the subject of a movie called *Shattered Glass.*

Both Blair and Glass were reporters in their 20s with limited experience but great promise that landed them these prestigious jobs. On the other hand, Jack Kelley was a veteran reporter with 21 years of experience at *USA Today* when he resigned at age 43, after evidence surfaced that he had fabricated sources. His work was questioned after he submitted a story about a woman who died fleeing from Cuba by boat. The woman whose photo Kelley submitted with the story was a Cuban hotel worker who had neither fled from Cuba nor died. Further investigation by the newspaper revealed problems with numerous stories, including one for which he had been a Pulitzer-Prize finalist.

Patricia Smith, a former columnist for *The Boston Globe*, had also been nominated for a Pulitzer Prize. She resigned after the *Globe* discovered that she had fabricated sources and quotes in her columns. In her last column she apologized and explained why she had attributed quotes to people who didn't exist.

"I could give them names, even occupations, but I couldn't give them what they needed most—a heartbeat," she wrote. "As anyone who's ever touched a newspaper knows, that's one of the cardinal sins of journalism: Thou shall not fabricate. No exceptions. No excuses."

A few months later, Mike Barnicle, a famous *Boston Globe* columnist, was also fired after editors checked some of his columns and concluded that he had fabricated sources in a column. They also accused him of plagiarizing material from entertainer George Carlin in another column. He denied the accusations and has since been hired as a columnist for another Boston newspaper.

Promises: Dan Cohen made the issue of anonymous sources even more complicated. He was a public relations executive. In 1982 he gave reporters from the (Minneapolis) *Star Tribune* and the *St. Paul* (Minn.) *Pioneer Press* damaging information about a candidate for lieutenant governor in Minnesota on the condition that they would not reveal him as the source. The reporters agreed to grant Cohen anonymity. But editors of the two newspapers overruled the reporters and insisted on printing Cohen's name in the story. The editors decided that since Cohen was working for the opposing political party, the readers had a right to know the source of the information.

Cohen sued on the grounds of breach of contract. He claimed that the newspapers had violated an oral contract of confidentiality and that, as a result, he had suffered harm by losing his job. A jury at the first trial level agreed that a reporter's promise of confidentiality is as legally binding as an oral contract. The newspaper appealed and lost. The case went all the way to the U.S. Supreme Court, which ruled in 1991 that the First Amendment does not protect journalists from being sued if they break promises of confidentiality. The high court sent the case back to the Minnesota Supreme Court for a ruling on damages, and Cohen was awarded $200,000.

Before you agree to grant anonymity to a source, you should check with your editors to determine the policies of your organization.

Even when sources agree to be identified, they often ask for anonymity for portions of the interview. They'll say, "This is off the record." Sometimes they aren't even aware of what the term means.

Here are some definitions of the terms used most often to establish ground rules in an interview:

On the Record: The source agrees that all information can be used in a news story and that he can be identified as the source of it. The easiest way to establish this understanding is to identify yourself as a reporter immediately and state your purpose for the interview. If you are interviewing people who are not accustomed to dealing with the media, you may need to remind the source during the interview that you are quoting him about the material, especially if you are writing about controversial issues. Such a reminder may jeopardize your chances of using some of the material, but it is better to take that chance during the interview than later in a courtroom after you have been sued.

Off the Record: The information from this source may not be used at all. If you can get the same information from another source, you may use it, but you may not attribute it to the source who told it to you off the record.

Not for Attribution: You may use the information as background, but you may not identify the source.

Background: This is similar to the term "not for attribution." Generally, it means that you may use the information but can't attribute it. Some reporters define background as the ability to use the information with a general attribution, such as "a city official said." If you are in doubt during the interview, ask the source how you can identify him, and give the specific wording you intend to use.

Deep Background: This term is rarely used or understood by most sources except for officials in Washington, D.C. It means you may use the material for your information only but may not attribute it at all, not even with a general term, such as "government official."

Multicultural Sources

One of every three people in the United States is a member of a minority racial or ethnic group, according to recent U.S. Census figures. Projections indicate that by 2050 minorities will make up nearly half of the country's population, which is expected to add another million people to its current 300 million. Asians are expected to be the fastest growing group, increasing by 213 percent to 33 million people, and Hispanics will be the next largest group with an increase of 188 percent from 36 million to 103 million people. Do your local media reflect this diversity? Do your stories include sources from the minority members of your campus or community?

Members of minority journalism organizations have often complained that minorities are represented in the news media in stereotypical ways especially in sports pages and crime stories but not enough in the basic news stories. As this population increases, it is incumbent upon you to include diverse points of view in articles, photographs, video and other media.

In addition to racial and ethnic diversity, there are many other minority groups such as members of the gay community and people with disabilities who are often neglected by the news media until a controversy develops or when they are subjects of a special feature story about their differences. Strive for inclusiveness in all media, including news and public relations materials. How can you develop multicultural sources?

- Identify leaders of minority groups, including religious organizations, and put them in your source book. But don't anoint them as the only spokespeople for their groups.
- Use the matchmaking technique when you are contacting these leaders and ask them to connect you with other members in their community.
- Be sensitive. Ask people of diverse backgrounds how they would like to be described. Some Hispanics prefer to be called "Chicanos," some blacks prefer the term "African-American," and people with disabilities have several preferences about how they want to be referred to in stories. The Associated Press Stylebook recommends that you avoid describing anyone as "disabled" or "handicapped" unless it is pertinent to the story. Instead describe the disability and avoid euphemisms such as "mentally challenged."
- Use racial or ethnic labels only when they are relevant to the story.
- Rely on visuals. Photographs and videos can demonstrate inclusiveness.

USA Today has a strong commitment to diversity. The newspaper urges reporters to make an effort to get views in all news stories from people of both sexes and various ethnic and racial groups.

"It comes up in every story conference or in every photo/graphic assignment," says J. Taylor Buckley Jr., a former editor at *USA Today.* "If you are doing a story on the new techniques of orthodontia, it's just as easy to find a black kid with braces as a white kid. It's not only the right thing from a standpoint of fairness and equality, it's smart. The opportunities are there, and anyone who fails to exploit them is stupid.

A related issue is the identification of people in newspaper stories by race or ethnicity. Almost all newspapers have policies against mentioning a person's race or ethnic background unless it is relevant to the story. To show that it uses multicultural sources, *USA Today* prints pictures, especially in columns containing readers' points of view.

Written Sources

You can find many additional clues for human sources and other information from a variety of written sources. Even though you may rely on Google and other Internet search engines, don't overlook some traditional printed sources.

Telephone Directories: The white and yellow pages of telephone books are primary places to locate sources. Most local telephone books also contain information about city and county government agencies, utilities and other frequently used services.

Reverse Directories: These directories, also called "city directories" or "cross-directories," list residents of a community three ways: by name, address and telephone number. Imagine that you are on deadline and have the address of a woman whose house is on fire and that you want to reach her neighbors for comments. How can you do this if you don't know the neighbors' names? You can look in the cross-directory under the address you have. The adjacent homes will be listed first by address, with names and telephone numbers of the occupants beside the address (unless they have unlisted telephone numbers). If you have a phone number but not the name, check the section for phone numbers.

The reverse directory is one of the most useful ways of locating people for comment when you can't go to the scene. These directories are published by real estate firms in most major communities and are kept in most newsrooms and libraries. Some online search engines, such as *www.reversephonedirectory.com,* will provide the same information.

Libraries: Your local public library and your college library contain a wealth of source material to help you find background about a story. Some of the most useful reference works are *The Reader's Guide to Periodical Literature,* encyclopedias, almanacs and other books of facts, population data and financial records of major corporations. Many of these resources are also online.

Most college and university libraries also have a section devoted to federal and state documents and publications. In this section you can find transcripts of congressional hearings, publications from federal and state agencies, and reports from all sorts of government offices.

Online Sources

You are writing a story about sexually transmitted diseases among college students. You check the Web for background by typing "sexually transmitted diseases" in a search engine such as Google. You will get more than 2 million listings.

Although the Web is an essential tool for finding background information, how do you know what information is credible? Stephen C. Miller, assistant to the technology editor at *The New York Times,* offers his "trust-o-meter," a technique he uses to determine credibility of Web information. Miller says his first choice is government sources because the information is official and public. For background in the story about sexually transmitted diseases, the National Institutes of Health or the Centers for Disease Control would be considered a reliable government source. Information from national health organizations might also be credible in this case.

Next, Miller likes university studies because they are peer-reviewed, but he says they should be linked to university sites or research journals. He finds personal sites the least trustworthy.

You might still check personal sites for ideas or contacts, but be wary of citing them without checking the information. Even if the information is trustworthy, you can still spend needless hours wading through it if you don't search effectively.

Effective Searching

Narrow Your Search: Try to be as specific as possible when you type a request in a search engine. For example, if you just want definitions of sexually transmitted diseases, typing those last three words will give you general sites. But if you are seeking rates of these diseases among college students, add *rates* and *college* to your search request.

Understand Domains: You can guess the address of many sites by using their domain extension. The domain is part of the address that identifies the type of site: *.gov* for government, *.edu* for education, *.com* for commercial, *.org* for organization and *.net* for network. If you were looking for the U.S. Census Bureau, you could guess *www.census.gov,* and you would be correct.

In 2000 additional domain names were added—*.biz* and *.info* for general-purpose sites; *.name* for personal sites; and *.museum, .aero, .coop* and *.pro* for community sites—but the primary endings are still the most common.

Find Site Contacts: If the site doesn't list contact information, you may find who owns or operates the Web site by using "whois" databases (*www.betterwhois.com*). These databases are not inclusive, but they will list owners and addresses of sites registered with a domain server if you type the site name and domain.

Check State Sites: State government sites are good places to seek background information for state-related news. All states with Web sites have a similar address formula: the word *state* followed by the postal abbreviation and *us* for

Convergence Coach

Here is a checklist to help you determine credibility of Web sites and search more effectively:

- **Who:** Is an author, site owner or name of sponsoring organization listed on the site? Avoid unnamed sites.

- **What:** Is the site affiliated with a government agency, an educational institution or a nationally credible organization? Check the site index for an "about us" page for further information.

- **When:** Is the site dated? This is crucial. Use the most current information you can find.

- **Where:** Does the site have any contact information—a phone number, address or names of individuals, not just "webmaster"?

- **Why:** Does the site have a bias or promotional agenda? If so, either avoid it or get other points of view, and check the accuracy.

- **How:** Narrow your search by typing specific key words instead of a broad topic.

- **Attribution:** Print the information you plan to use so you can document it; sites frequently disappear. Copy the site name and URL (address) for a link or citation. Don't copy anything from a site without attributing it.

United States or *ca* for Canada. For example, the state government address for California is *www.state.ca.us*.

If you are writing a crime story or you just want to check a source's background to make sure that the person is not a sexual offender, nearly 40 states have sex offender registries. An easy way to find these registries is to start with your state site. In one case a student doing a background check on a candidate for the campus student senate found the person on a local sex offender register.

Understand Search Engines and Directories: Search engines will locate sites with the specific words you seek, while directories such as Yahoo! group documents by categories such as news and travel. If you have no idea what kind of information exists in a topic you are researching, you might try a directory.

Use Metasearch Engines: If you want to save time and find out the responses to your request from several search engines simultaneously, use a metasearch engine. This type of multisearch engine queries several search engines and lists the relevant returns. For information on how search engines work and which ones are the most comprehensive, check *www.searchenginewatch.com*.

Use Journalism Directories: Several journalists have created Web sites with links to all sorts of valuable resources for the media. From government agencies to businesses and public records, you can find useful sources without scouring the Web yourself. For example, the Investigative Reporters and Editors organization has a Web site with links to topics for numerous beats in its resource center*: www.ire .org*. One of the most complete sites is "A Journalist's Guide to the Internet," *http:// reporter.umd.edu*, created by Christopher Callahan, former associate dean of journalism at the University of Maryland and now dean of the journalism school at Arizona State University.

Find Experts: From anger management to zoo animals, an expert on almost every topic is willing to provide information to journalists. You can find these experts easily in *www.yearbook.com*, a site created to provide journalists with expert sources. Profnet (*www.profnet.com*) is another site devoted to serving journalists with expert sources throughout the world. Designed for professional journalists by PRNewswire, this resource should be used for publications, not for term papers.

Find a Map: If you are seeking directions to a location for an assignment or for personal use, use a mapfinder such as *www.mapsonus.com, www.mapquest.com* or any other maps linked to most search engines. They will pinpoint the location and even provide you with driving directions.

Find Press Releases and Wire Services: Check *www.prnewswire.com, www. prweb.com, www.uwire.com* (for college wire stories) or *www.businesswire.com* (for business news).

Build an Online Source Book: When you find sites that you plan to use frequently, bookmark them. But computers can crash, and you may lose your bookmarks. You should also build a source book with the names and URLs of your most helpful sites just as you would create an address book for your favorite sources. When you interview people, make sure that you ask for their phone numbers and e-mail addresses, and add them to your source book.

Find Media Jobs and Internships: Job sites abound, but if you are seeking a job or internship in the media, you will find opportunities faster by checking media organizations such as PRSSA (Public Relations Student Society of America), RTNDA (Radio-Television News Directors Association), ASNE (American Society of Newspaper Editors) and minority media groups.

Find People: Almost all search engines have yellow and white pages where you can search for people's phone numbers, addresses and e-mail addresses. However, many of these are inaccurate. Although it's still worth a try if you are trying to locate a source, it's best to ask sources for their e-mail addresses and phone numbers when you interview them.

Use E-mail and Discussion Groups: Several media discussion groups that send messages to your e-mail are good ways to find sources in your field. You have to subscribe to these groups, but most are free. It's best to "lurk" for a while and read the messages before you post your own so that you can understand the nature of the discussions. Most media discussion groups involve professionals, so you should take care not to post questions about research you could have done yourself. You'll find links to media discussion groups for American and Canadian groups at *www.journalismnet.com.* Julian Sher, a Canadian investigative journalist who created the site, gives tips on how to search for sources and even how to spy on people in news groups or chat groups. He suggests going to Google's news groups, selecting a topic and clicking on the name of the person who sent the message. Other sources for media news groups are listed on Christopher Callahan's Web page under listservs *(http://reporter.umd.edu/listserv.htm).*

Usenet is a group of more than 30,000 public discussion forums to which anyone may post a message. In many cases, people don't use their real names on these groups. They are not as credible for sources, but you can find topics and people in *www.google.com* under "groups."

Social networking sites: These days social networking sites such as MySpace, Facebook and YouTube have become more popular than Usenet. While social networking sites may be useful for locating sources, you should be wary of the credibility and should check with the sources before using the material in a news story.

Databases: A database is a collection of information. The term now generally refers to massive collections of information stored in computers. Many newspapers subscribe to databases containing newspaper and magazine stories compiled by a commercial company.

For daily news stories such as meetings, local events and other breaking news, checking a database is too time-consuming. But when you are seeking background for an in-depth story or feature, databases are worth checking. For instance, if you are working on an in-depth story about date rape on college campuses, a database check would be helpful. By reading other stories, you can get ideas for an angle on your story or find expert sources to contact.

The best way to learn how to use a database is to go to the library and ask for assistance. Each database has a different set of instructions; many include charges for use. One of the most popular databases for newspaper and magazine writers is NEXIS, a collection of newspaper, business and trade sources. It is available in some libraries but often with restrictions for users. LEXIS, the other part of this service, contains the text of court decisions, legislative records and legal resources. It is available in most law libraries. It is also available online for a fee.

Many other databases contain only an abstract (a summary) of the article in a journal, newspaper or magazine. You still have to look up the paper or microfilm version to see the entire article.

Public Records

Many government records, such as data from state and local agencies, may be obtained from databases consisting of public records. Access to such records has spurred a type of reporting called "computer-assisted journalism." Using software programs that have sophisticated mathematical tools, reporters have been able to do complicated searches and analyses of huge banks of data that they would not be able to do with paper records. For example, if you want to find out who earns the highest salaries in each department at your university or college, you could spend days sifting through a printed version of the budget and trying to compare salaries. But if the budget is available on a database, you can use a computer program to analyze this information for you in minutes. However, a large database can still be time-consuming to interpret, which is a deterrent to computer-assisted reporting at some publications.

Other Public Records

An official at your university tells you that there are no serious fire safety violations on campus. But you want to be sure, so you decide to check the state fire marshal's report on the last fire safety inspection of campus buildings. The report may list many violations that the official might not have deemed serious. Records on paper or in computer form are valuable information sources.

Not only do such records as fire and police reports provide detail about investigations; they also give names of people to contact. When police officers investigate an accident or a crime, they fill out reports with details of the scene and crucial information about the people involved, including names, addresses, birth dates, physical descriptions and other material. Most of the records are public.

The following list mentions just a few of the public records that should be available to you locally. In addition, government offices in your state capital contain records from all state agencies, including your college if it is state-owned. Federal offices in a state capital contain many records of federal agencies and of federally funded programs in your locale. The location of these records varies from city to city, and access may also vary.

Political Contributions: To check campaign contributions to candidates for state offices, you can access a searchable database for each state at *www. followthemoney.org.*

Real Estate Records: Mortgages, deeds (which record the property owners, purchase date and sale price in some states), the legal property description, indexes listing previous property owners, and commercial property inventories (lists of everything the commercial property owner has, such as trucks, supplies and equipment) are available in the Register of Deeds office. This office also has maps showing all the property in the county and individual maps called "plats," which show the zoning of each piece of property. Records for tax rates and the assessed value of the property are located in the county assessor's office. If you don't have a property description or know what property your subject owns, the county clerk's office has a listing of who owns what. Some states post property records online.

Voter Registration Records: These records, located in the county clerk's office, list people's political party if they are registered voters, as well as their addresses and dates of birth. They also list telephone numbers. In some cases, people who have unlisted telephone numbers may have listed their numbers on these records.

Fish and Game Licenses: These are also recorded in the county clerk's office.

Salaries of County Employees: The salaries are listed by position only (usually not by employees' names) in the county clerk's office. In some counties or cities, names may be included.

County Government Expenses: These can also be found in the county clerk's office.

Corporate Records: Articles of incorporation, which list the officers of the corporation and the date the company registered with the state, are very useful if you are trying to find out who the company officers are. Articles of incorporation are located in the Register of Deeds office or in the state office that regulates corporations.

Court Records: Filings in all civil and criminal court cases, except juvenile cases, are open to the public. They are located in your county courthouse.

Military Records: You can find out the details of individuals' military service in the Register of Deeds office in some municipalities, but only for people who registered for military service in that county. Otherwise, you have to file a request under the Freedom of Information Act to the individual branch of the service.

Personal Property Loans: If a person has taken out a loan of more than $1,000 or has used credit to buy something worth more than $1,000, such as a stereo, the information could be on file under the Uniform Commercial Code listings kept in your county courthouse. Some states also have these listings online.

Tax Payments or Delinquent Tax Records: These records are kept in the county treasurer's office.

Motor Vehicle Registrations: These records and the personal property tax are on file in the county treasurer's office.

Building Inspection Records and Housing Permits: These are available in the city's building inspection and housing department. Also available are all the complaints that have been filed against a property owner, which are useful for stories on substandard housing. This office also has records on all permits issued for construction or building improvements.

City Commission Meeting Records, Local Ordinances and Resolutions: The city clerk's office keeps these records.

City Expenses: Information about purchase orders, accounts payable, the inventory of city agencies, budgets, expenditures and the like are available in the city's finance department. Records of purchase orders and accounts payable are extremely useful if you are investigating the expenditures of any city department or the actions involving any contract the city has with a vendor or builder.

Public Works Records: Plans for public works projects—such as sewers, traffic signals and traffic counts—should be available in the public works department of your municipality.

Fire Department Records: These include records of all fire alarms, calls (including response times), fire inspections, and firearms owners and registration (which may be in a different location in some cities). Also on file, but not available to the public, are personnel records, including pension records and other items of a personal nature. However, salaries are public record. These are in the fire department or in your city or county clerk's office.

Police Records: Criminal offense reports, statistics of crime, accident reports and driving records are in the local police department and the sheriff's department. Records of ongoing investigations are generally not available to the public.

Utility Records: Water records—such as bacterial counts, water production, chemical usage and other items pertaining to the city's water and sewage operations—are available in the city utilities department.

School District Records: Almost all information pertaining to the expenditure of public school funds—including purchase orders, payroll records, audits, bids and contracts—is available from the school district. Personnel records of employees are also available in limited form. Names, addresses, home phone numbers, locations of employment, birth dates, dates hired and work records are available, but information about employee work performance and other personal information is not public. Information about students, other than confirmation that they are enrolled, is not public.

The Freedom of Information Act

The Freedom of Information Act was established by Congress in 1966 to make federal records available to the public. It applies only to federal documents. In addition, the act allows for several exemptions that prohibit the release of documents. Records classified by the government because their release would endanger national defense or foreign policy are exempted. So are certain internal policies and personnel matters in federal agencies, as well as a number of records involving law enforcement investigations. If an agency refuses to release documents you have requested through the FOIA, you may appeal the decision.

In many cases, the document you request comes with information blacked out or cut out. Some documents look like paper doll cutouts by the time they are released. Another drawback to using the FOIA is that it is time-consuming. Although an agency is required by law to respond to your request within 10 working days, delays are common.

However, many reporters have found the FOIA invaluable. The documents they have received have led to major investigative stories.

For questions or more advice, you can call the libel and FOI hotline, 24 hours a day, seven days a week: 800-F-FOI-AID. You can also access a complete online guide to the FOIA through the Internet:

- **Freedom of Information Center:** *http://web.missouri.edu/~foiwww*
- **FOI Resource Center:** *www.spj.org/foi.asp*

Before you file an FOIA request, try the direct approach: Ask the agency for the records. You might get them. If you must file a formal FOIA request, it is a good idea to check first and make sure that you are contacting the appropriate agency for your request.

When you file your request, be sure to write "Freedom of Information Request" on the envelope and on the letter. You do not have to explain your reason for the request. The agency may charge copying and processing fees, but if you are not using the material for commercial purposes and the material is likely to contribute to an understanding of government operations, you may be entitled to a fee waiver.

You can access an interactive sample FOIA letter generated by the Reporters Committee for Freedom of the Press at *www.rcfp.org/foi_letter/generate.php*. Here is a print version:

You can use a form letter for your request. The sample shown here is recommended by the Society of Professional Journalists. If you prefer to be contacted by mail, omit your telephone number.

What Do You Think

Would you be willing to go to jail to protect an anonymous source if you were forced to reveal the name in court?

- Yes
- No
- Maybe
- Not sure
- It depends on how long I'd have to stay in jail

Sample Freedom of Information Act request

[Date]

[Agency head or Freedom of Information Officer]
[Agency]
[City, State, Zip Code]

Freedom of Information Act Request

Dear [FOI Officer]:
    This is a request under the federal Freedom of Information Act.
    I request that a copy of the following documents [or documents containing the following information] be provided to me. [Identify the documents or information as specifically as possible.]
    In order to help determine my status to assess fees, you should know that I am [suitable description of the requester and the purpose of the request, such as

■ A representative of the news media affiliated with the newspaper (magazine, television station, etc.), and this request is made as part of news gathering and not for a commercial use

■ Affiliated with an educational or noncommercial scientific institution, and this request is made for a scholarly or scientific purpose and not for a commercial use

■ An individual seeking information for personal use and not for a commercial use

■ Affiliated with a private corporation and seeking information for use in the company's business]

[Optional] I am willing to pay fees for this request up to a maximum of [dollar amount].
    If you estimate that the fees will exceed this limit, please inform me first.
    [Recommended] I request a waiver of all fees for this request. Disclosure of the requested information is in the public interest because it is likely to contribute significantly to public understanding of the operations or activities of government and is not primarily in my commercial interest. [Include a specific explanation.]
    Thank you for your consideration of this request.

Sincerely,

[Signature]
[Your name]
[Address]
[Telephone number]
[Fax number]
[E-mail address]

Exercises

1 Reverse directory: Imagine that the mayor of your town, another city official or a university official has disappeared. You want to talk to members of his or her family and to the neighbors. Find the missing person's telephone number in the cross-directory or an online search engine such as *www.reversephone-directory.com.* Now find three neighbors you could interview by using the street address searches.

2 Databases: Select a topic for a feature story about an issue on your campus, such as date rape, racial tensions on college campuses, alcohol bans, political activism or a health issue such as sexually transmitted diseases among college students. Now check the Internet or go to your library and use a database to find stories about your topic. Make note of any national experts on the subject and any statistical material or reports you would find helpful in your story.

3 Primary Sources: Get copies of a police report, a university study, or any other report that has been released at your school or in your community. Make note of the primary sources (officers, investigators or researchers) you would contact.

4 Record search: Conduct a record search of a person, preferably a politician or other person in your community who owns property. Your task is to construct a paper-trail profile. Try to find out all you can about the person without ever talking to him or her. However, you may drive by the person's home to observe the property and include that information in your report. Write the profile based only on records and observation. You may be surprised how much you can write.

Here are some suggestions for records that should be available to you:

- Land records, which should include a complete description of the person's house
- Court records of criminal and civil suits, possible marriage or divorce, or even birth records
- Delinquent tax records
- Corporation records for ownership of personal property or corporation papers (if applicable)
- Records of voter registration, auto registration and tax liens
- Educational background, including curriculum vitae for university employees
- Financial disclosure (for politicians)
- Check the Internet by conducting a search for your source.

5 FOIA request: Write a Freedom of Information Act request for some information from a federal agency that funds a program in your school or community.

6 Enterprise: Write a story about the people for whom buildings or landmarks on your campus are named. Using your campus library, check the archives to find the background of these people. Then conduct interviews with students who use these buildings, or who live in them if they are residence halls, and find out how much or how little the students know about these people. In the clips, try to find interesting anecdotes about the namesakes and reasons for naming the buildings for them.

☞ **Featured Online Activity** Log on to the book Web site for Chapter 6 and take the scavenger hunt to test how well you can find sources on the Internet.

academic.cengage.com/masscomm/rich/ writingandreportingnews6e

Coaching Tips

Write your observations in your notes; include specific details.

Mark the information in your notes, such as quotes and facts, that you plan to use when you write the story.

When interviewing athletes or people who have been interviewed frequently, try to find a new angle or a question they haven't been asked.

Always check the spelling of the source's name and the wording of job titles.

Ask the follow-up questions "why" and "how," and ask sources to give you an example.

Gather details for graphics. Get information an artist would need to draw for a map or other illustration. Details will make your writing more vivid as well.

Plan audio and video for Web publication.

In interviewing, if you are sincere and the sources know that you have compassion, they're going to talk. A lot of the skill is just being open to what they have to say."

—Barbara Walsh, Pulitzer-Prize winning reporter

7 Interviewing Techniques

Barbara Walsh says one of the "stupidest" things she ever did almost ruined the interview that led to a Pulitzer Prize. Walsh had tried for months to get an interview with convicted murderer William R. Horton Jr. Finally, his lawyer gave her permission. She walked into the jail, met Horton and learned a painful lesson.

Horton was serving two life sentences plus 85 years in a Massachusetts prison for the murder of a gas station attendant and a subsequent crime he committed while out of prison on a furlough (a brief stay in the community). He broke into the home of a Maryland man, slashed him repeatedly and raped his fiancée twice.

Walsh, then a reporter for the *Lawrence* (Mass.) *Eagle-Tribune,* faced Horton through the window that separated them. "The first question I asked was 'How the heck did you get out on furlough?' It was the stupidest thing I've ever done," she says.

Horton wanted to terminate the interview. Walsh salvaged the interview with Horton by switching to something he wanted to discuss.

"I asked him, 'What do you want to tell me?' And he said, 'I'm not a monster. You people (the press) have made me out to be a monster,'" Walsh says.

The interview then went on for two hours, and eventually Walsh returned to the tough questions she wanted to ask Horton.

The story was one of a series about the Massachusetts furlough program that earned Walsh the Pulitzer Prize. Walsh, who later worked at newspapers in Florida and Maine and now is a freelance writer, says she was lucky that Horton talked to her, but she learned a valuable lesson about interviewing techniques: "Save your tough questions for last."

She still asks tough questions—but at the end of the interview. "I've learned to be real slow and real patient," she says. "I'm more inclined to let people talk longer. You may not use all the information, but you can offend them if you rush." Walsh says the key to good interviewing is good listening. "In interviewing, if you are sincere and the sources know that you have compassion, they're going to talk. A lot of the skill is just being open to what they have to say."

But when sources are reluctant to answer her questions, she rephrases the questions and asks them again—sometimes three or four times—as in the following story about women in a Florida prison. "I asked one of the female inmates on Death Row,

'What's it like to sit there and know the state wants to electrocute you?' She skirted the question the first time. I asked it three times during the interview." Eventually Walsh got the answer. "If you ask—not in a cold way, but sincerely ask what was it like for you—they'll answer." The result was this revealing portrait (also notice how Walsh weaves in her own observations):

Barbara Walsh, reporter

Kaysie Dudley spent two years on Death Row meditating and learning more about how the state was going to kill her.

"I did a lot of research on what they were going to do to me," Dudley says. "It was very morbid, but I wanted to know." Dudley, 28, was sent to Death Row at Broward Correctional Institution in 1987 after she was convicted with her boyfriend of strangling and slicing the throat of an elderly Clearwater woman.

"My boyfriend killed her," Dudley says. "I held the woman in my arms as she took her last breath. It was a terrible experience." As she talks, Dudley sits in the cafeteria of the women's prison, nervously rubbing her fingers together, her nails raw and bitten to the quick. From her neck hangs a small silver cross.

It is cool, and Dudley wears a black sweater over her state-issued aqua dress.

"I wasn't afraid of dying," Dudley says. "But I didn't like to think about electricity running through my body...." After spending two years on Death Row, Dudley says, she feels she has suffered more than enough.

"I was 22 when they locked me up in there," she says. "I feel like in a way they've already killed me. It took me almost a year to get my facial expressions back, my emotions, my ability to laugh.

"I was a zombie when I came out of there," she says, absently twisting her hair with her constantly moving fingers.

—Barbara Walsh, *South Florida Sun-Sentinel*

Although Walsh usually takes notes, she says a notebook can be threatening. She waits until she has established rapport with her source before she opens her notebook. And she rarely uses a tape recorder—too unreliable and threatening, she says.

Her advice to student reporters? Don't overlook anyone as a source. "When I go to the courthouse, I consider anybody who talks as a source—from the janitor to the people who sell coffee. These are real people who may not be high-priced attorneys, but they know what is going on. Reporters narrow their sources too much."

Walsh certainly didn't narrow her sources for a five-part series she wrote for the *Portland Press Herald/Maine Sunday Telegram*. She interviewed more than 700 families, doctors, police officers and social workers, and reviewed more than 4,000 pages of state and federal documents and databases for the series about the effects of poverty on children in Maine's rural towns. Despite those thousands of statistics, Walsh humanized the plight of the children by her intensive reporting and use of details as in this story about a 16-year-old girl who was abandoned by her mother:

It was the dolls that she wanted. The porcelain dolls her mother kept in the china closet. Delicate faces, their eyes painted black, lashes long and lacy, their dresses, puffy, purple and pink, tiny princesses.

It was the dolls that Jillian Higgins remembers most in the trailer where she lived. The dolls and their beauty stark against the inside of a trailer filled with trash, dog feces, floors covered with everything "you can imagine."

"My mom had these dolls she got for every birthday from the time she was like 5 'til she was 17," she says. "They were so cool and I wanted them. I always wanted them. I'm not sure why."

—Barbara Walsh, *Portland Press Herald/Maine Sunday Telegram*

Gathering Details

Like Barbara Walsh, Edna Buchanan won a Pulitzer Prize—in her case, as a police reporter for *The Miami Herald*. Buchanan recounts one of her mistakes when she didn't ask the right question. Now an author, Buchanan offers this advice in her book *The Corpse Had a Familiar Face*:

What a reporter needs is detail, detail, detail.

If a man is shot for playing the same song on the jukebox too many times, I've got to name that tune. Questions unimportant to police add the color and detail that make a story human. What movie did they see? What color was their car? What did they have in their pockets? What were they doing the precise moment the bomb exploded or the tornado touched down?

Miami Homicide Lieutenant Mike Gonzalez, who has spent some thirty years solving murders, tells me that he now asks those questions and suggests to rookies that they do the same. The answers may not be relevant to an investigation, but he tells them, "Edna Buchanan will ask you, and you'll feel stupid if you don't know."

A question I always ask is "What was everybody wearing?" It has little to do with style. It has everything to do with the time I failed to ask. A man was shot and dumped into the street by a killer in a pickup truck. The case seemed somewhat routine—if one can ever call murder routine. But later, I learned that at the time the victim was shot, he was wearing a black taffeta cocktail dress and red high heels. I tracked down the detectives and asked, "Why didn't you tell me?"

"You didn't ask," they choroused. Now I always ask.

Sensitivity

The way you deal with sources can differ, depending on whether they are public or private individuals. Because public officials are accustomed to dealing with the media, you have a right to expect them to talk to you. Private individuals do not have to deal with the media, and you need to operate with more sensitivity when interviewing them. If a public official utters an outrageous quote, it's fair game. When a private individual does, you could remind the person that it will be published and make sure that the source will stand by the comment. Although many reporters believe that once they have identified themselves as members of the media, anything in an interview is fair game, reporters who display extra sensitivity usually end up with more information.

All sources, public and private, want to be portrayed well in the media. Many sources, especially public officials, will manipulate reporters by revealing only information that furthers their cause. As a result, reporters need to be aware of the source's bias and ask probing questions that go beyond what the source wants to reveal. It is also crucial to check the information and seek alternative points of view.

Listening and Note-Taking Skills

Truman Capote knew how to be a good listener. He didn't take notes during his interviews for his book *In Cold Blood*. Nor did he use a tape recorder. He was convinced that a notebook or a tape recorder would inhibit his sources. "People would reveal themselves, he maintained, only in seemingly casual conversations," wrote his biographer, Gerald Clark.

With his childhood friend Nelle Harper Lee, Capote conducted scores of in-depth interviews for the book, a nonfiction story recounting how two men murdered a family in rural Kansas. Each night Capote and Lee would return to their hotel and write notes about the interviews they had conducted that day. "Each wrote a separate version of the day's interviews; then they compared notes over drinks and dinner. . . . When their combined memory failed, as it sometimes did, they went back and asked their questions in a slightly different way. On occasion they talked to the same person three times in one day," Clark wrote in his book *Capote: A Biography*.

That technique is impractical for a reporter on a daily newspaper. And these days, when the credibility of newspapers is under attack, trying to reconstruct interviews and direct quotes from memory is downright dangerous. When freelance writer Janet Malcolm reconstructed quotes, she got sued for libel. Even though the U.S. Supreme Court ruled that it's acceptable to reconstruct quotes as long as the meaning isn't changed, if you don't have Capote's memory, it's better to take good notes.

Capote said he trained himself to be a good listener. "I have a fantastic memory to begin with," he said in an interview with Charles Ruas, author of *Conversations With American Writers*. "I can repeat almost verbatim any conversation up to as long as eight hours. I could never have written *In Cold Blood* if I had ever produced a pencil, much less a tape recorder."

The Pros and Cons of Tape Recorders

Capote's objections to using tape recorders are well founded. A tape recorder is not a substitute for good notes. Tapes can break, and machines can fail you when you need them most. They can inhibit a source. They can also prevent you from taking good notes if you rely on them too much. And tape recorders can't pick up observations—a smile, a nervous tic, a source's appearance or mannerisms. But in these days of convergence, they are essential for taping parts of interviews that may later be used as sound bites for video or the Web versions of your story. Just make sure you also take notes.

In addition, if you want to get the exact wording of quotes, or if you are interviewing a source about a controversial subject, a tape recorder is beneficial. But you shouldn't play back the entire tape and transcribe it before you write your story. That is too time-consuming. If you use a tape recorder, scan the tape until you get to the quotes you need.

Before you begin taping your interview, follow some etiquette. Start your interview with basic introductions—who you are and why you are there—and some opening conversation. To put the source at ease, you might even ask a question or two before you ask the source if he would object to the recorder. Then, if the source agrees to allow the recorder, don't place the machine directly in his face. Put it off to the side of the desk or table, where it is not so intrusive.

If you want to record a telephone interview, be aware of the laws in your state. Twelve states prohibit tape-recorded conversations without the consent of the person being taped: California, Connecticut, Florida, Illinois, Maryland, Massachusetts, Michigan, Montana, Nevada, New Hampshire, Pennsylvania and Washington. Other states mandate that only one person must be aware of the taping, either the reporter or the person being interviewed. For a list of laws regarding taping in each state, check the Reporters Committee for Freedom of the Press at *www.rcfp.org/taping*.

You can't secretly tape any conversation between two other people when you are not a part of the discourse. For example, if you are on an extension phone and neither party knows you are taping the conversation, you are violating a federal law against wiretapping. The Federal Wiretap Statute provides for penalties of up to $10,000 in fines and up to five years in prison.

The most ethical approach is to let your source know you are taping the interview, except in a very few situations. For example, if you are conducting an undercover investigation in a state where the one-party rule applies, you could tape a conversation without the source's knowledge. However, most editors consider the use of deception or other undercover techniques a last resort.

Listening Tips

Before you write notes or record conversations, you should follow Capote's example and develop good listening skills. Here are some tips:

Focus on the "Hear" and Now: Concentrate on what the source is saying now, not on what you will ask next. One of the major obstacles to good listening is poor concentration caused by worrying about what you will say instead of focusing on what the source is saying. Your next question will be better if you have heard the answer to your last one.

Practice Conversational Listening: Base your next question on the last sentence or thought the source expressed, as though you were having a conversation with your friend. If you want to move to another topic, you can do so either with a transition—"On another subject"—or by just asking the question. But if you are really paying attention, the order of your questions will be more compatible with the source's trend of thought.

Practice Critical Listening: Evaluate what the source is saying as you hear it. Listen on one level for facts, on another for good quotes, and on a third level for elaboration and substantiation. Is the source making a point clearly and supporting it? Do you understand the point? If not, ask the source to repeat, elaborate or define the meaning. If you listen for meaning, you can direct the interview instead of letting the source control it.

Be Quiet: Whose interview is this anyway? Do not try to impress the source with what you know. You can't quote yourself. Let the source explain a point, even if you understand it, so you can get information in the source's words.

Be Responsive: Make eye contact frequently so your source knows you are listening. Let the source know you are paying attention. If you don't understand something, say so. "Why?" "How?" "I don't understand" and "Please explain" are good follow-up reporting questions based on good listening.

Listen for What Isn't Said: Is the source avoiding a topic? Who or what isn't the source talking about—a family member (in a personal profile), a close official, a crucial part of his background? Sometimes, what is omitted from a conversation is more revealing than what is included.

Listen with Your Eyes: What kind of body language is the source displaying? Is the source fidgeting or showing signs of nervousness at some point in the interview? Is the source smiling, frowning or exhibiting discomfort when you ask certain questions? Are these telltale signs that the source may be lying or withholding information? Observation can be a good listening tool.

Be Polite: If the source starts to ramble or give you irrelevant information, don't interrupt. Wait for the source to pause briefly, and then you can change the subject.

Block Out Personal Intrusions: You've had a bad day, your car broke down, you failed a test or you have some emotional concerns. Make a determined effort to block out these personal thoughts. They intrude on your concentration while you are trying to listen. Your problems will still be there when the interview is over. The source will not.

Develop Listening Curiosity: Don't go to your interview with a rigid agenda of questions. Although you may start with prepared questions, allow yourself to be surprised when the interview goes in another direction, and follow that course if it is interesting. Listen for what you want to know and what you didn't expect to know.

Note-Taking Tips

When the late Foster Davis was a writing coach at *The Charlotte* (N.C.) *Observer,* he checked reporters' notes to determine if problems in the stories originated in the reporting process. "The quality of stories has something to do with the quality of notes," Davis once said in an interview. "Writing is the least important part of it; everything that leads up to it is what matters."

Davis said he looked at notes to see if they were legible and if they included names and dates as well as reporters' observations. "When the notes said 'trees,' were they specific trees? Were the notebooks dated? Were exact titles spelled out? Detail is what makes the difference between good and bad notes," he said.

Detailed notes give you this advantage: When you begin writing your story, you may need more information than you anticipated during the reporting process. When you take notes can be as important as how you take them. Note taking can make some sources nervous. If you are dealing with people who are not accustomed to being interviewed, start your interview slowly by asking a few nonthreatening questions. After you have established some rapport with the source, take out your notebook.

Here are some tips to help you take good notes:

Be Prepared: Bring extra pens or pencils. You may run out of ink, or your pencils may break. In addition, take *both* pens and pencils. If you do an interview in the rain, you'll want to have pencils handy. Do not rely on electronic equipment for note taking.

Concentrate: When you hear a good quote or the start of one, write rapidly. Concentrate on what you are hearing and block out everything else until you have written the quote. Even if you are concentrating on a previous thought, you will still hear what is being said. So if the person says something better than the last quote, you can switch your concentration to the new information. Thinking of your next question while you are trying to write down a complete quote will interfere with your concentration.

Use Key Words: When you are not trying to get a direct quote, jot down key words to remind you of facts and statements.

Develop a Shorthand: Abbreviate as many words as possible. The word *government* might become *gov,* and *you* could be abbreviated as *u.* Some type of shorthand is especially important when you are trying to write complete quotes.

Slow the Pace: When you are taking notes for a quote, slow the pace of the interview by pausing before your next question until you write the quote. If you think you are pausing too long, ask a question that will not require a crucial answer. You could ask the source to elaborate about the last statement. If your source is speaking too fast, politely ask him to slow down.

Request Repetition: Don't be afraid to ask your source to repeat a quote or fact you missed. Although the quote may not be worded exactly as before, it will be close enough. In fact, the repeated statement may be even better. When people have had a chance to think, they often state things more clearly.

Make Eye Contact: Don't glue your eyes to your notes. Make sure that you look at your source during the questioning and while you are taking notes. Practice taking notes without looking at your notebook.

Mark Your Margins or Notebook Covers: When you hear something that prompts another question in your mind—a fact you want to check or the name of another source you want to contact—jot it in the margin as soon as you think of it. Don't depend on your memory to think of it later. Some reporters use the covers of their notebooks to write questions that come to mind during the interview so that they can find them easily without flipping through notebook pages. And don't forget to take notes on your observations, either in the margins or elsewhere.

Verify Vital Information: Make sure that you get the exact spelling of your source's name and his title during or at the end of the interview. Don't go by a name-plate on a door or desk. That could be a nickname. Ask the source for the name he prefers to use, and ask for the spelling even if you are sure of it. A simple name such as "John Smith" could be spelled *Jon Smythe.* If you get this information at the end of your interview, you also could ask for a home telephone number and an e-mail address at this time. Even if you are reporting for television, you will need the spelling of the name, which may be superimposed on the screen during a sound bite.

Double-Check: If your source says he has three main points or reasons for running for office, make sure that you get all three. Write "3 reasons" in the margin, number them as you hear them and check before you conclude the interview.

Be Open-Minded: You may have one idea for the story when you begin taking notes. But don't limit your notes to one concept. Your story angle could change at any time during the interview. You can't always envision how you will write the story. When you do, you may be sorry you didn't take better notes, especially if you decide to change the focus during the writing process.

Use a Symbol System: To save time writing your story, while you are taking notes, put a star or some symbol next to the information or quotes you think will be important. Develop your own system.

Stand and Deliver: Practice taking notes while you are standing. You will not have the luxury of sit-down reporting, especially at the scene of fires, accidents, disasters and most other breaking-news stories.

Save Your Notes: You should save your notes before and after the story is published. How long you should save them is debatable. Lawyers disagree whether notes are helpful or harmful in court cases if you are sued for libel or any other reasons. But most editors advise saving the notes at least for a few weeks after the story in case any questions about it arise. For this reason, it is helpful to date your notebooks.

Transcribe Notes Only for Major Stories: Should you transcribe your notes in your computer before you write a story? Definitely not if you are on deadline. Some reporters find it helpful to rewrite their notes before they write a major story because it refreshes their memory, especially if a story will involve many sources and be written over a period of days. If you haven't mastered the art of writing clear notes, it may also help you to transcribe your notes immediately after your interviews. For breaking-news stories, you will most likely have to post the news on the Web or deliver it on TV, so you won't have time to transcribe notes. Clear notes are crucial.

Tips for Interviewers

An important factor leading to a successful interview is that old Boy Scout motto: Be prepared. First, consider your mission. You are a reporter, not a stenographer who just receives information and transcribes it. A reporter evaluates information for its accuracy, fairness, newsworthiness and potential to make a readable story. During the reporting process, you will look for facts, good quotes, substantiation and answers to the five W's—who, what, when, where, why—and also "how" and "so what." One question should lead to another until you have the information you need.

An interview with one source is just the beginning of reporting for most stories. For credibility and fairness, you need other sources—human and written—for differing points of view and accuracy checks.

Planning the Interview

If you are sent to cover a breaking-news story, you should get to the scene quickly and find sources there or start calling sources on the telephone. The planning stages described here apply only to interviews that you need to set up in advance. Most of the other reporting techniques apply to both kinds of stories.

Identify Your Focus: What is the purpose of your interview? Determine a main idea or goal for your story. The focus may change after you do the interview, but you need to start with a specific reason for your story so you know what kind of information you need to get and what sources you need.

Research the Background: Check news clippings and available documents—court records, campaign records or other relevant written and online sources—to familiarize yourself with the topic and the source. Check with secondary sources—friends and opponents—before or after you interview the subject of a story. Ask the source's friends, secretaries or co-workers to give you anecdotes and tell you about the person's idiosyncrasies.

Identify Your Goals: What kind of information are you hoping to get from this source? Is it primarily factual, as in an interview with a police officer for a story about an accident? Or do you want reaction from the source to an issue or to something someone else said? Is the source going to be the central focus of the story, as in a profile, or just one of several people cited in the story? Get a general idea of why you need this source so you can explain briefly when you call for an interview.

Plan Your Questions: This step may seem premature, considering that you haven't even been granted an interview. However, if the person refuses to see you when you call for an interview, you might be able to ask a few questions while you have the source on the phone. If you are a good interviewer, you can prolong the conversation and wind up with a good interview.

Prepare your list of questions in two ways: Write all the questions you want to ask, preferably in an abbreviated form. Then mark the questions you must ask to get the most crucial information for your story. If your source refuses to grant you the time you need, you can switch to the crucial list during your interview.

Request the Interview: The most important point is to plan ahead. Officials, educators and many other sources are busy people. They may not be able to see you on brief notice.

When you make the call, first state your name and purpose. Or try the sponsorship technique: "I'm working on a story about date rape on campus, and Officer John Brown suggested that I call you. I understand that you have some information about a survey the university conducted on this subject." Then ask what time would be convenient. If you want an hour but the source can't spare the time, settle for a half-hour.

If you are calling an official, you probably will have to negotiate through an administrative assistant. Be courteous and persuasive. First, ask to speak to the source. If that's not possible, tell the assistant that you would like to interview his boss about a story you are writing. You don't need to elaborate unless you are asked to do so.

You can also try contacting a source by e-mail to set up an appointment. Often it is easier to reach busy people by e-mail than by telephone. State your name, affiliation and purpose. Save your questions until you find out if you can get a telephone or face-to-face interview. (Interviewing by e-mail is discussed later in the chapter.)

Don't wait several days to hear from your source. Try calling again or e-mailing the source on the same day or next day if your deadline permits.

Dress Appropriately: If you are interviewing a source on a farm, don't wear a business suit. On the other hand, show your source respect by dressing neatly. However, if you are interviewing corporate officials or people in more formal business settings, you should dress as though you worked there.

Arrive on Time: You could arrive 10 to 15 minutes early, but don't arrive too early because you could inconvenience people who are busy. And never come late.

Conducting the Interview

Interview questions can be classified as two types: closed-ended and open-ended. You need both types.

- Closed-ended questions are designed to elicit brief, specific answers that are factual. They are good for getting basic information, such as name and title; yes or no answers; and answers to some of the who, where, when questions. For example, these are closed-ended questions: How long have you worked here? Who was at the meeting? How many people were at the rally? When did the accident occur?

- Open-ended questions are designed to elicit quotes, elaboration or longer responses. Avoid being judgmental in the way you frame your questions or respond with follow-up questions. The more neutral you are, the more responsive your source is likely to be. Keep your questions brief and simple; don't ask a double question or precede a question with a long explanation.

The questions that will elicit the most quotes and anecdotes start with *what, why* and *how*:

- What (What happened? What is your reaction? What do you mean by that? Can you elaborate?)
- Why (Why did you do that . . .? Why do you believe . . . ?)
- How (How did something happen? How did you accomplish that?)
- Give me an example (a follow-up question to explain how the source felt, thought, acted in a specific situation)

Keep your questions brief. Ask questions in simple sentences—one question at a time. Don't combine two questions into one sentence. A long lead-in to a question can confuse the source. Slow the pace between questions so you can take notes. Ask unimportant questions or ask for elaboration while you are writing down quotes. Remember to be responsive by making eye contact frequently during the interview.

The Dumb Factor: Beginning reporters often worry that they will appear dumb to sources. Don't worry about what you don't know. You are there to listen and learn, not to be the expert. The whole point is to get information from the source. In fact, acting dumb can give you an advantage. Even if you know the answer to a question, you should ask it anyway so that you can get the information in the source's words. If you think a question is too simple, you might apologize for not knowing more about the subject. You might say, "I'm sorry I don't understand this. Could you explain so I can write it clearly for my readers?" Most sources enjoy taking the teaching role or showing off what they know.

Acting dumb does not mean forgetting about preliminary background work. It is dumb if you can't tell your readers something because you were afraid to ask. It's better to feel dumb during the interview than afterward, when you turn your story in to an editor or when you read it in the newspaper or hear it on a broadcast.

Here are some ways to conduct the interview and some types of questions to ask. Not all of these techniques and questions apply to every story.

Start Out by Using Icebreakers: Introduce yourself and briefly state your purpose. Be friendly. Establish rapport with some general conversation. Don't pull out your notebook immediately. Try to sit at an angle to your source so you are not staring directly at him in a confrontational manner. A desk might serve as a barrier and provide enough distance so you don't appear threatening.

Observe the surroundings. Do you notice something you can mention as an icebreaker, a way to establish rapport? Don't be artificial. If an official has a picture on his desk of his family, don't get overly familiar. Use good judgment. Then explain a little more about what you are seeking in your story.

Plan Your First Question: Try to find a question or approach that would interest the source, especially if the person is a celebrity, an athlete or an official who has been interviewed often. These people often give standard answers to questions they consider boring because they have been asked the same questions so many times. If you research well, you will find some tidbit or angle to a story that might lead to an unusual question—and an interesting answer.

Put Your Questions in Nonthreatening Order: In most cases you will want to follow Barbara Walsh's advice and start with nonthreatening questions. However, if you have only five minutes with a source, you may have to ask your toughest question first or whichever one will yield you the most crucial information for your story.

Ask the Basic Questions: Who, what, when, where, why and how are the most basic. Then add the "so what" factor: Ask the significance. Who will be affected and how? This question will give you information for your impact paragraph.

Ask Follow-Up Questions: These are the questions that will give you quotes and anecdotes. Use a conversational technique. Let the interview flow naturally. When a source answers one question, follow the trend of thought by asking why and how, and asking the source to explain or give examples. Frame your next question on the information you have just heard by focusing on key words in the last answer. When you want to change the subject, ask an unrelated question or use a transition: "On another topic . . ." or "I'd like to go back to something you said earlier. Could you explain why you were at the scene where the murder occurred?" Use follow-up questions to go from the general to the specific. If the source makes a vague statement, ask for specific examples.

You may have a long list of questions, but don't let your source see them. A long list can make the source watch the clock. One student reporter took out a press release during the interview. When the source saw it, he told the student to use the comments in the release and terminated the interview. It would be better to write your questions on the front or back of your notebook so you can refer to them easily without turning pages frequently.

Here are some general follow-up questions to provide context and interesting material:

- What was your reaction?
- What do you mean by that?
- How did that happen?
- How did you do that?
- What is the significance?
- Who will be affected?

Keep Quiet: Do not talk too much or try to impress your source with your knowledge. Don't insert your opinions or comments. Let the source talk. You need to quote the source, not yourself.

Be Nonjudgmental: Don't insert your comments or opinions into your questions. Nor should you judge your source's actions or answers. You should remain neutral and strive for fairness. You can get an opposing side of a dispute or other points of view from other sources. If you have to ask a controversial question, use the "blame-others" technique: Your opponent says that . . . . How do you respond?

Control the Interview: If your source rambles or prolongs an answer and you want to move the interview in another direction, don't interrupt. Wait for a natural pause and ask your next question, using follow-up question techniques.

Repeat Questions: You've asked an important or sensitive question, and the source has given you an evasive or incomplete answer. What should you do? The best tactic is to drop the question and continue the interview. After you have discussed a few other points, repeat the question you want answered, but state it in a slightly different way. Sometimes a source will recall more the second time the question is raised.

Ask Background Questions: Get the history of the issue, if applicable. How and when did the problem or program start? Why?

Ask About Developments: Go from the present to the past and to the future. What are the current concerns and developments? How did the issue evolve? What is likely to happen in the future? The answer to the question about the future may provide you with a good ending for your story. In some cases, it may give you a lead and a new focus for your story. The next step in an action is often the most newsworthy angle. Many newspapers, broadcasters and online producers prefer this approach, which is called "advancing the story." Because you may have to post your story immediately for the Web, you will need to update the news anyway for your next broadcast or newspaper edition.

Construct a Chronology: This tip is somewhat related to the previous point. When appropriate, ask questions to establish a sequence of events. You don't need to write the story in chronological order, but you need to understand the order in which events occurred.

Role-Play: If you were in the reader's place, how would you use the information? For example, if you needed to apply for a loan, what steps would you have to take, and where would you go? What does the reader need and want to know?

Ask About Pros and Cons: Ask your source to discuss both sides of an issue, when relevant. Who agrees and disagrees with his point of view? What are his responses to the opposition?

Ask for Definitions: Your job is to translate jargon for readers. So always get your source to define any bureaucratic or technical terms in language that you and your readers will understand. Don't accept or write any information that you can't explain. To clarify, you might restate the information in your own words and ask the source if you have the correct interpretation. For example, you might ask, "Do you mean that . . . ?" or "Are you saying that . . .?"

Verify: Ask questions even if you know the answers. You need to quote or attribute information to your source, not yourself. Always check the spelling of your source's name—first and last names and middle initial. Check the person's title and the dates of crucial events. Check the accuracy of information on a résumé or news release. You don't have to repeat everything, but you should ask the source if the information released is correct. Then ask some questions that expand on the basic information. For example, if you are interviewing the president of MADD (Mothers Against Drunk Driving), you might ask, "Have you ever been involved in an accident involving a drunken driver, or were you ever arrested for drunken driving?" Such a question may not be as insensitive as it seems because many people get involved with causes after they have had a personal experience with the problem.

Also, remember that if the source tells you something about another person, you must check it out with that person.

Use the Silent Treatment: Pause for a few seconds between questions to let the source elaborate. If the pause seems uncomfortable, the source may break the silence first. One reporter was writing a profile of a nun. He asked her if she missed having a sex life and how she coped without one. She gave a brief, expected answer that she had made a conscious choice of abstinence when she took vows of celibacy. The reporter was disappointed with the answer. He said nothing. She said nothing. For several seconds they just sat in silence. Both were slightly uncomfortable. Then she broke the silence and began elaborating about how difficult celibacy was for her at times. Sometimes the best follow-up question is no question.

Use the "Blame Others" Technique: When you have to ask tough questions, blame someone else: "Your opponent says you cheated on your income taxes. How would you respond to that?" Reporters and editors have mixed feelings about warning the source that a tough question is coming. Don't do it, they say, in confrontational interviews when you are trying to get a source to reveal information that could be damaging. It puts the source on notice and gives him a few seconds to become defensive and evasive. But do warn the source or apologize if it's going to be a tough, emotional question, especially if you are interviewing grieving people, says Jacqui Banaszynski, who won a Pulitzer Prize for a series about a man with AIDS. She tells sources that she will ask tough questions, but they don't have to answer them. "But I'll try to convince them to do so," she says.

Handle Emotional Questions with Tact: Emotional questions can be difficult. Ask your source to recall how he was thinking or feeling at the time of an incident. "Were you frightened when the train lost power? What were you thinking at the time?" Avoid insensitive questions. There's a saying in journalism that there are no stupid questions, only stupid answers. That's not exactly true. "How do you feel about the death of your three children?" is not only a stupid question; it's insensitive as well. Instead of asking such an emotionally loaded question, ask the person to recall specific memories about his children, or ask how the person is coping with the tragedy.

Ask Summary Questions: Restate information, or ask the source to clarify the key points he is making—for example: "Of all the goals you have expressed, which would you say are the most important to you? What do you think are the three major issues you face?"

Use the "Matchmaker" Technique: Ask if anyone else is involved in the issue or if there are other people the source would suggest you contact. Remember that you will want more than one source for your story so that you can strive for fairness and balance.

Ask Free-Choice Questions: Ask the source if there is anything he would like to add. Jennifer Zilko, a reporter for a television news station in Alaska, says this is the most important question to ask.

End on a Positive Note: When you have finished the interview, thank your source. Ask if you can call back if you have any further questions. At this point, you also could ask for a home telephone number or another way to reach the source, such as an e-mail address or cell phone number.

Reporting for Visuals

Whenever you go on an assignment—especially a breaking-news story involving an accident, a disaster such as a flood or explosion, or a crime—gather information for the graphic artist. Even if you don't use all these details for a graphic, you can use many of them to make your writing more vivid. Get maps, brochures or any other written materials that might be available to help the graphics department pinpoint the location of the crime or disaster scene. Even if you are reporting for TV and you have cameras, you still need to gather information for graphics that might be posted on the Web or used in a broadcast.

If you have video, don't describe the scene that viewers can see for themselves. But if you don't have video, gather details so you can describe the scene to viewers or the anchor or use in a print story.

Locations: Get the names of streets and major intersections nearest to the site of the incident. Ask details about specific measurements: yards, feet, number of city blocks or whatever else would help pinpoint locations. How many feet or yards away from the landfill is the nearest house? What buildings are in the area? When the gas pipe exploded, how many feet from the gas line was the nearest building?

Chronology of Events: Get specific times or dates and other information to recount the sequence of events. For example, suppose a terrorist takes a hostage. When did the incident occur? At what time did each development occur before the hostage was released or killed?

Statistics: Think of charts for print, broadcast or public relations materials. If your city council has raised taxes, what have taxes been during the past five years? How much has tuition increased during the past several years? How does this year's enrollment compare with enrollments in previous years? Statistics like these can be boring to read. But they are easy to understand in chart form that can be posted in print or on the Web. Charts are also effective to include in public relations news releases.

Highlights: Gather information for a facts box, such as important dates or highlights of someone's career. Suppose you are doing a profile. Instead of listing key dates and incidents in your story, could you place them more effectively in a box? Ask about interesting hobbies, favorite books, favorite movies, marital status or other personal information that might help the graphic artist—and the reader. In the past, when a reporter turned in a story that was reported and written well, editors used to say, "Your story looks good." It's up to you to make sure that it does—both verbally and visually.

E-mail Interviews

Although e-mail is an effective tool for contacting sources, it is not an effective method for interviewing people. But in some cases, it may be the only way you can get comments from a source. Use it as a last resort if you can't interview a source in person or by telephone.

Advantages: E-mail gives the source some time to think about responses to your questions. It also saves you from taking notes, and you can get accurate quotes when the source responds in writing.

Disadvantages: E-mail interviews prohibit spontaneity and good follow-up questions. You also can't observe the source's reactions and body language, nor can you gather descriptive detail.

Convergence Coach 🌐

The basic techniques of interviewing are similar for print, broadcast or online reporting. You still need to decide the focus or main reason for the interview, research the background and prepare good questions. But much of broadcast and online reporting may be for spot news. In a convergent media world, you need video and audio for online delivery even if you are a print reporter. Setting up cameras for TV may make your source nervous, so use that time for icebreakers or for getting background information from the source. For broadcast and online audio and video, you are seeking good quotes, so open-ended questions are preferable. Here are some tips especially geared to broadcast interviews:

- Ask open-ended questions to elicit quotes such as how, why, what was your reaction, what were you doing at the time of the incident. Avoid questions that can be answered "yes" or "no."

- Keep questions brief in simple sentences. Don't ask two questions at one time.
- Don't ask questions that express your opinion; that works for any medium. Avoid leading questions such as "Don't you think that . . ." and similar ones that include preconceived suggestions.
- Ask questions that your audience would want answered.
- Gather information that an anchor might ask you for elaboration.
- Listen carefully.
- Ask free-choice questions: At the end of the interview, ask the source if there is anything he would like to add.

Tips for E-mail Interviews

- **Limit the number of questions:** Sources will respond better to one or two questions than to a long list. Strive for a maximum of five questions.
- **Clarify your purpose:** Make it clear that you intend to use the e-mail message in a news story. Personal e-mail messages are not intended for publication.
- **Verify the source's full name and title:** E-mail addresses do not always include the source's proper name.
- **Limit your follow-up e-mail messages:** You may have to reply to the source's e-mail with another question or a request for more information. But don't badger the source with several e-mail messages.
- **Attribute to e-mail:** Although not required, it is preferable to explain in your news story that the source made the comments in an e-mail interview.

The GOAL Method of Interviewing

The GOAL method is a concept to help you frame questions for a variety of stories, especially profiles, features and stories about programs and issues. It is a variation of a technique devised by LaRue W. Gilleland, a former journalism educator. It does not work with all stories, nor should you limit your questions to these concepts. But it is a starting framework. Here's what the letters stand for:

G = goals

O = obstacles

A = achievements

L = logistics

Many interviews can be designed around the GOAL concept, especially for profiles and features about new programs. If you structure your questions around these ideas, you will get answers to the questions of why, how and what. Here are some ideas for specific questions using this method:

Goals: "What are or were some of your goals in this program (or in your career)? What are you trying to accomplish? Why do you want to do this?" Try to discern the person's motivation for his actions.

Obstacles: "What were some of the obstacles you faced (or are facing)?" Get specific examples or anecdotes. "What is one example of a difficult problem you experienced?" Try not to qualify your question by asking for the most difficult problem or the funniest or happiest moment. People have difficulty deciding what is best, worst, hardest, easiest, happiest or saddest. They need clues, such as a specific period during their life.

Achievements: "How did you overcome these obstacles? How did you achieve your goal (or how do you plan to achieve it)?" Again, get specifics.

Logistics: "How did you or the program get to this point?" This is the background: past, present and future. "How did your background affect your goals, obstacles and achievements? What factors in your background relate to the focus of the story? Is there a chronology of events that will help the reader understand the story?" Weave in the background where it will be interesting and relevant.

ETHICS

Ethical dilemma: Should you accept gifts from sources? Does the value of the gift make a difference?

The case: You are working on a feature story about a new music store in your community. After you finish the interview, the store owner offers you some gifts, such as a CD case, a baseball cap and a T-shirt with the store logo, and a few CDs featuring your favorite musical artists. You do not plan to write reviews of the CDs. The total worth of the gifts is about $35. Should you accept some, all or none of these gifts? If you plan to review the CDs, should you keep them after you review them?

Ethical values: Credibility, conflict of interest

Ethical guidelines: The Society of Professional Journalists Code of Ethics says journalists "should refuse gifts, favors, fees, free travel and special treatment and shun secondary employment, political involvement, public office and service in community organizations if they compromise journalistic integrity." Several newspapers, such as the *Detroit Free Press* and *The Philadelphia Inquirer,* prohibit reporters from accepting any gifts, books, records or other items of value from news sources who will be included in a news story.

Telephone Interviewing

Edna Buchanan was persistent. The former *Miami Herald* police reporter spent much of her life making difficult phone calls to people who were grieving. If a source hung up on her, Buchanan waited a minute or two. Then she called back. The second time she identified herself again and said, "We were cut off." Sometimes her sources changed their minds, or someone else who was willing to talk answered the phone. But if they hung up again, she didn't call a third time.

More often than not, people are willing to talk to reporters, especially on the telephone. For many sources, talking about a loved one who died is cathartic.

Not all telephone interviews involve difficult situations. Reporters on a daily newspaper get many of their stories by telephone—from daily checks with police about crime stories to interviews with politicians, government officials and community leaders for reaction stories, issue stories and a wide range of features.

Nancy Tracy, a former *Hartford* (Conn.) *Courant* reporter, had a way of almost seeing through the telephone. She would ask her sources for details. She asked what they were wearing, what they were doing, what they were thinking, how they were coping and reacting. She was always empathetic. Sometimes she would apologize for asking difficult questions; sometimes she would sympathize. Then she would ask more questions. And rarely did anyone refuse to answer her.

Here is an excerpt from a story Tracy did about a Georgia couple who survived when their truck plunged into the Mianus River in Connecticut when the bridge collapsed. In her telephone interview with David Pace, Tracy asked such questions as "Where are you sitting now? What is your daily routine? What do you think about and dream about?" and even "What is the weather today?"

Some days when the pain isn't too bad, he stands by the front door, watching trucks roll by on Highway 41 on their way to Macon. Then the memories come flooding back, the crash, the pain.

Inside the small mobile home, his wife also remembers the day their world fell apart, when a metal and concrete span that was the Mianus Bridge split, sending them and four others tumbling 70 feet to the Mianus River in Greenwich.

It is a year today since the bridge collapsed, but for David and Helen Pace of Perry, Ga., it's as if it happened yesterday. It still figures in their nightmares, still limits their days.

A living hell, 27-year-old David Pace calls the past year.

It is raining. Helen Pace has taken to her bed. On damp or rainy days, her back hurts more than usual. On the days she is up, she wears dark stockings to cover the scars on her legs. She used to be proud of those legs, her husband says.

They had been married six months, and he'd gotten into the habit of bringing her with him on the long-distance runs. The night the bridge fell down, they were on their way to New Hampshire with 26,000 pounds of empty beer bottles in their semi-trailer.

He loved trucking—the good money it brought, the chance to see the country. Now, David Pace says, his and his wife's injuries are so severe that his parents are afraid to leave them alone.

"I've had to turn to my mother-in-law, my father-in-law, my mom and dad," he says. "It kind of takes a part of my manhood away from me. It hurts. It hurts bad."

—Nancy Tracy, *The Hartford* (Conn.) *Courant*

Tracy got all that information by telephone.

Although interviewing people in person is preferable, it is often not practical, especially if you are on deadline. You won't be able to observe facial reactions, gestures and surroundings when you conduct telephone interviews, but you still can gather information accurately and thoroughly.

The techniques of telephone interviewing are very similar to the methods of interviewing in person. The major difference is that you need to work harder at keeping the source's attention and focusing your questions. Researchers suggest that the average telephone interview should be limited to 20 minutes. After that, the attention span of the person responding wanes. If you call a source at home, he or she may be further distracted by children or other family concerns.

Here are some guidelines for telephone interviewing:

Identification: Immediately state your name and affiliation and the purpose for the call.

Icebreakers: These may not be necessary. Get to the point quickly. If you use any icebreaker to establish rapport, keep it very brief.

Length of Questions: Keep questions very short. Phrase each question clearly and simply. Limit questions to no more than two sentences; one is better.

Clarification: Make sure that you understand the information you receive. It may be harder to understand information in a telephone interview, so clarify anything that is confusing. Repeat any confusing terms or information in your own words, and ask your source to verify your interpretation.

Specifics: Ask for details and examples. If you want to describe the scene, ask your source to give you the descriptive details.

Chronology: A chronology is especially important in police and fire stories you receive by telephone. If you do not understand how an event occurred, try restating the chronology: "Let me understand—is this how it happened?" Or after a source tells you the high points of what happened, you could ask him to explain the order in which events unfolded.

Limits: Because your time may be limited by many events beyond your control, limit the number of questions in a telephone interview. Plan two lists: all the questions you want to ask and crucial questions. If you have time for only a few questions, switch to the crucial list. You may also want to ask your questions in a different order. Don't wait too long to ask the crucial ones. You never can tell when the source will be interrupted and will terminate the interview.

Control: Changing the subject to get to the questions you need to have answered is even more crucial in a telephone interview than in person. You can't spare too much time for establishing rapport or engaging in nonproductive conversation. Be mindful of the information you must get for your story.

Verification: Double-check the spelling of the name, title and other basic information. If you haven't heard it clearly, spell it back to the source. This basic information is crucial when dealing with police officers. They usually do not identify themselves by their full names when they answer the phone on duty, so make sure that you get first and last names and the proper rank, such as lieutenant, sergeant or captain.

At the end of the interview, thank the source and ask if you may call back if you have more questions. Use judgment here. Don't ask this of police or reluctant sources; just call back if you must have more information.

Interviewing Problems

- **What do you do if the source says something is "off the record" during an interview?** Ask the source why the information should be off the record (meaning you can't use it) and try to convince the source that the information is not harmful. Ask the question another way during the course of the information to see if you can get the information on the record.

- **What do you do if the source tells you not to use his name after the interview?** Try to prevent this by making sure you identify yourself and your purpose clearly at the start of the interview. If you suspect that this might happen, set ground rules at the beginning of the interview by explaining that you cannot use anonymous sources. If this happens at the end of the interview, negotiate. Try to convince the source to be identified. If the source still refuses, ask if you can identify the source by a vague title or position such as a source in the administration.

- **What do you do if the source gets emotional and starts to cry during the interview?** Pause. Give the source a chance to regain composure. Offer to get the source a drink of water or something else that might be helpful. Be understanding and sympathetic but don't start to cry as well.

- **What do you do if the source terminates the interview abruptly before you have the information you need?** Ask if you could contact the source again for further questions.

- **What do you do if the source gives you information that is inaccurate or false?** Check your facts and if you discover inaccuracies or falsehoods, contact the source again and confront him with the problems. Ask for an explanation.

Exercises

1 Interview a reporter from your local newspaper, radio station or television station about his reporting techniques. Or choose a reporter whose stories you like, and interview him about techniques.

2 **Icebreakers:** Make a list of questions you would use as icebreakers to interview a professor or a source whose office you have visited.

3 **Reporting scenarios:** Develop questions for the following situations:

- You learn that there is a fire in a residence hall on your campus. List at least 10 questions you would ask. List five sources you would contact. What kind of background information do you need?

- A professor on campus has received a $1 million grant to study plagiarism among college students. List at least five questions you would ask if you were interviewing the professor. What other sources will you use to make this a good story?

- A study at another university says college students are sleep-deprived. Women students get less than six and a half hours of sleep, and men get seven to eight hours of sleep. You are writing this story for your campus newspaper. How will you localize this story? What sources (other than students) do you need to make this a credible story for your university audience? Where will you find them?

4 **Note taking:** The object of this exercise is to see how accurately you can quote sources. Tape an interview from any television news show. Use a VCR or a voice recorder. As you are watching the show, write down some direct quotes. If you use videotape, watch the screen periodically as though you were making eye contact with a source. Then play the tape and test your accuracy. If you do this in a classroom, you can compare your notes with classmates' notes. Analyze what caused you to be inaccurate—if you were—and how you can improve your note taking.

5 **Notes:** Submit your notes for the last story you wrote. Share your notes with another student, and critique each other's notes on the points Foster Davis recommends in the preceding "Note-Taking Tips." Are your notes legible? Do they have names, dates, titles and details? Compare your rating of your notes with another student's evaluation of them. Discuss improvements in your note taking that might have helped your story.

6 **Technical clarity:** This exercise was suggested by Jacqui Banaszynski, Knight Chair in Journalism at the University of Missouri. Interview a source about some technical information you don't understand. The source could be anyone from an auto mechanic to a scientist. Work on clarifying jargon and other information you don't understand. Then write the results of your interview in a brief story or several paragraphs explaining the technical information clearly.

7 **Graphics:** Check your local newspaper or another newspaper that uses graphic illustrations. Study a graphic, and write a list of questions you would have asked to gather the information that the artist used to design it.

8 **Enterprise:** Conduct an interview in order to write a news story about an issue on your campus or in your community. Here are some suggestions:

- Write a reaction story based on interviews with students or local residents about any controversial topic in the news.

- Attend a demonstration, rally, meeting or other public event on your campus or in your community.

- Check your campus and local newspapers for clubs and support groups in your community.

- Write a story about the economic or psychological impact that any unusual weather in your area may have had on businesses, agriculture or people.

☞ **Featured Online Activity** Log on to the book Web site and take the interactive quiz for Chapter 7 to test your listening skills.

academic.cengage.com/masscomm/rich/
writingandreportingnews6e

Coaching Tips

Keep leads short—preferably fewer than 35 words.

"What struck you as most important or interesting?" Ask yourself that question to find your lead.

Write a headline for your story; that could be a clue for your lead.

Write a focus sentence at the top of your story.

Points of emphasis: Place the key words at the beginning or the end of the sentence for emphasis.

Avoid suffering: If you can't devise your lead, start with your nut graph and write your lead later, or write several leads and choose one later.

Don't invent your lead. Base it on the backup in your notes.

The best day is the one when I can write a lead that will cause the reader at his breakfast the next morning to spit up his coffee, clutch at his heart and shout, "My God! Martha, did you read this?"

Edna Buchanan, former police reporter,
The Miami Herald

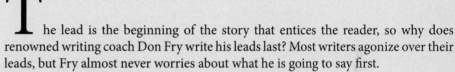

8

Leads and Nut Graphs

The lead is the beginning of the story that entices the reader, so why does renowned writing coach Don Fry write his leads last? Most writers agonize over their leads, but Fry almost never worries about what he is going to say first.

Fry says he begins the writing process long before he sits down at his computer. "I'm imagining the story while I'm reporting it," he says. Fry concentrates on what he calls the "point statement," also known as a focus graph or nut graph. He asks himself what the story is about and what the point of the story is. Any information that doesn't relate to the point statement doesn't get included in the story.

And then he starts writing. Not at the beginning, but at the paragraph containing the point statement. He continues writing until he gets to his ending, which he calls the "kicker." Then he writes his lead. After that he revises.

Don Fry, writing coach

The point statement, which we've discussed throughout the book as a focus statement, may end up being the lead, or it will give you the idea for the lead. You may still prefer to write your stories by starting with the lead, as most writers do. But thinking about your story before you write it will give you a better chance of writing a good lead.

Mervin Block, a leading writing coach for broadcast journalism, has similar advice. "Think. Don't write yet. Just think," he says in his book, *Writing Broadcast News*. "Think about what you want to say and how best to say it: clearly, concisely, conversationally. . . . Start strong. Well begun is half done."

The lead is crucial in any medium, especially these days, when readers and viewers are bombarded with so much information from print, broadcast and online sources. If you access any online news site, you may get a choice of 20 or more stories with headlines and leads on the main page. Studies show that most newspaper and online readers are scanners, who just read headlines. How can your leads entice the readers, listeners or viewers to continue? Take a clue from television teasers: Does the anchor tease you about a story that makes you stay tuned after the break? Leads should entice the reader to stay tuned into the rest of the story.

Hard-news Leads, Soft Leads and Nut Graphs

The lead (originally spelled *lede* to differentiate it from "lead" type) tells the reader what the story is about. Think of the lead as a teaser or foreshadowing of what will come in the story. No matter what type of lead you write, you must back it up with information that substantiates it. If you haven't got material to support your lead, you have the wrong lead.

If you have been writing focus statements above your stories, you have a head start on writing leads. To write a focus statement, you asked yourself: What is the story about? What is the most important information? What is the point of this story? Those are the same questions you need to ask yourself to write a lead or a nut graph.

Sometimes nut graphs and leads are the same; sometimes they aren't. Here's how to tell the difference:

Hard-news Leads: Also called a "summary lead," a hard-news lead summarizes in the first sentence what the story is about. A hard-news lead is usually only one sentence or two at most. It gets directly to the point. Summary leads can be used in any medium. Public relations practitioners use summary leads in news releases, which need to be brief and newsworthy. In these examples, note that the broadcast version uses present tense and a more current angle:

- **Print version:** A 20-year-old Franklin and Marshall College student was shot a block from campus early this morning during an attempted robbery, police said.
- **Broadcast or Web version:** A 20-year-old Franklin and Marshall College student is in critical condition today after he was shot early this morning during an attempted robbery a block from campus.

Nut Graphs: Also called the "focus graph," the nut graph is a paragraph that explains the point of the story—what the story is about. A summary lead often tells that information and takes the place of a nut graph. In this example, the lead is purposely vague, and the nut graph is in the third paragraph:

The Alpha Gamma Rho fraternity president says it was a practical joke that got blown out of proportion.

Police say it was a hazing incident that involved new AGR members preparing to have sex with a goat.

Nut graph   And Western officials are still trying to determine if AGR members violated university policy by having a goat in their house that may have been used to intimidate new members.

— Corey Paul, *College Heights Herald*, Western Kentucky University

Soft Leads: Also called a "feature lead" or a "delayed lead," a soft lead can be several paragraphs long and can take a little longer to get to the main point of the story. It delays telling the reader what the story is about by teasing the reader with a description or a storytelling approach as in the previous example. With a soft lead, you must tell the reader the point of the story in the nut graph. In these days of impatient readers, the nut graph should be early in the story—usually by the third to fifth paragraph. Here is an example of a soft lead and a nut graph:

Soft lead: who, what	SAN JOSE, Calif.—A nervous flight attendant was having trouble taking a urine drug test. So she drank a glass of water—and another—and another.	The unidentified San Mateo County resident is the first drug-test taker known to suffer from "water intoxication," doctors reported yesterday in the *Journal of the American Medical Association.* There have been only seven other reported cases of healthy people with the dangerous condition, which causes waterlogged brain cells and a dilution of body minerals. One died.	*Nut graph The focus tells "so what." The story is about the dangers of water intoxication in connection with drug testing.*
More what	After guzzling three liters in three hours, she still couldn't urinate.		
Where	But hours later, the 40-year-old woman staggered into a Burlingame, Calif., hospital, her speech slurred, her thinking fuzzy.	*—Knight-Ridder/Tribune News Service*	
	The diagnosis: She was drunk—on water.		

How do you decide whether to use a hard or soft lead? The choice depends on several factors: the significance of the news, the timing, proximity (interest to your local readers or viewers), subject matter, and in many cases, your editor's preference. If the subject is serious—death, disaster, a major change in the law—consider a hard-news approach. Breaking news that happened yesterday or today also lends itself to a hard-news lead.

Hard-news Leads

Summary Leads

A summary lead should answer several, but not all, of the basic questions: who, what, when, where and why, plus how and so what. If you cram all of them into the lead, it could be cumbersome.

Choose the most important factors for the lead. Save the others for the second or third paragraph. This example stresses who and what, the most common type of summary lead:

Who, what, when, why	TALLAHASSEE, Fla.—A Florida law student was held Tuesday on a charge she hired a hit man to kill a secretary who found out the student had stolen an exam, police said.

This example stresses who, what and why:

> WASHINGTON (AP)—The Federal Aviation Administration said Tuesday it would hire 12,500 new air traffic controllers over the next decade to off-set a wave of looming retirements.

Subject–Verb–Object Order: Summary leads are most effective when they follow subject–verb–object order (who did what or what happened). This order is also favored for broadcast writing. The following lead, which works for print, broadcast and the Web, starts with who, what, why and when:

> A 22-year-old Mesa resident is accused of offering an undercover police officer $1,000 to kill a woman who appeared on her boyfriend's MySpace.com Web page.
>
> —*East Valley Tribune,* Mesa, Ariz.

Avoid writing long summary leads that begin with clauses, as in this example:

> Declaring that property owners must be protected from an arrogant government, House Republicans are nearing approval of legislation that would weaken federal efforts to protect wetlands and endangered species.
>
> —*The Associated Press*

This lead would have been clearer if it had begun by explaining who is doing what: "House Republicans are nearing approval . . . ."

Order of Information: When you write a summary lead, how do you decide which basics to include and in what order? The points of emphasis should be the first or last words in the lead. Decide which elements are the most important—who, what, where, when, why, how or so what. Usually it is safe to use a subject-verb-object format: who did the action, what happened, to whom. But sometimes the how or why is most important.

Here are some facts presented in a story:

Who: Three boaters

What happened: Two killed, the third injured when the boat capsized

When: Sunday

Where: Lake Harney near the Volusia-Seminole county line in Florida

Why: High winds and waves

How: Explained later in the story

The lead that appeared in the newspaper stresses who first, followed by what:

> Two boaters were killed and a third was injured Sunday when their small boat capsized in high winds and waves on Lake Harney near the Volusia-Seminole county line.
>
> —*The Orlando* (Fla.) *Sentinel*

Now look at the way the lead would read with different elements placed first:

What
A small boat that capsized in high winds and waves on Lake Harney near the Volusia-Seminole county line caused the death of two boaters and injuries to a third Sunday.

When
On Sunday two boaters were killed and a third was injured when their small boat capsized in high winds and waves on Lake Harney near the Volusia-Seminole county line.

Where
On Lake Harney near the Volusia-Seminole county line, a small boat capsized Sunday in high winds and waves, causing the death of two boaters and injuries to a third.

Why
High winds and waves on Lake Harney near the Volusia-Seminole county line caused a small boat to capsize Sunday, killing two boaters and injuring a third.

The actual lead from the newspaper seems the most logical because the point of emphasis—the important news (boaters died)—is first. The last lead, focusing on why, is the next best option; the point of emphasis (boaters died) is at the end.

If you were writing that story for broadcast news, you would update the information and use present tense:

> Two boaters are dead and a third is suffering from injuries caused when their small boat capsized today on Lake Harney near the Volusia-Seminole county line.

Most of the time when you write a hard-news lead, you will put the most important information first. Or you might want the point of emphasis at the end of the sentence, as in this example:

> A consumer group said Thursday that some sunscreens and cosmetics contain an ingredient that can promote cancerous skin tumors, and it called on the government to halt their sale.
>
> —*The Associated Press*

Active vs. Passive Voice: Active voice is generally preferable to passive in print and always preferred in broadcast writing. Active voice stresses who is doing the action; passive voice stresses those to whom the action is done. But you may need to use passive voice when the emphasis is on what happened instead of who caused it to happen, especially in police or court stories.

Active voice is stronger for the following example, because it emphasizes the iguana as the subject; for broadcast put the attribution first:

Active	A pet iguana started a fire in a split-level house in Hillsmere Shores by knocking over a heat lamp with its tail, fire officials said.	A fire in a split-level house in Hillsmere Shores was started by a pet iguana that knocked over a heat lamp with its tail, fire officials said. *Passive*
Broadcast version with attribution first—still active voice	Fire officials say a pet iguana started a fire in a split-level house in Hillsmere Shores by knocking over a heat lamp with its tail,	

In the next example, however, passive voice is preferable because it gets to the point faster:

Passive   A former employee of the University of Pennsylvania's Van Pelt Library was sentenced to seven years of psychiatric probation yesterday for the theft of $1,798,310 worth of rare books and documents.

—The Philadelphia Inquirer

The sentence was imposed by Philadelphia Common Pleas Court Judge Russell M. Nigro, as the story later explains. The emphasis in the lead is on the employee who was sentenced. Here is how the lead would sound in active voice:

Active   Philadelphia Common Pleas Court Judge Russell M. Nigro yesterday sentenced a former employee of the University of Pennsylvania's Van Pelt Library to seven years of psychiatric probation for the theft of $1,798,310 worth of rare books and documents.

In the active version, it takes longer to get to the point of the story, and the emphasis is on the judge, not the employee.

Where to Say When: The time element can be confusing in a lead. In breaking news, when something happened yesterday, the time element usually does not come first in the sentence. But you need to place it where it is accurate, even if it sounds awkward.

Here is an example of a confusing time element:

> University officials agreed to raise
> tuition by $100 Monday.

As written, the lead indicates the tuition will increase on Monday. Wrong. Tuition won't go up until next fall. Here's what really happened:

> University officials agreed Monday to
> raise tuition by $100.

Delayed Identification: When the *who* in your lead is not a well-known person in your community or in the nation, you can identify the person by age, location, occupation or another modifier in the first paragraph. Then identify the person by name in the second paragraph. When you use delayed identification, even if your story involves several people, the first name you use should be the one you referred to in your lead.

All states have laws restricting the release of juvenile offenders' names, and several states prohibit the release of names of rape victims. In addition, many newspapers and television news organizations have policies to withhold names of criminal suspects until they are formally charged with crimes. Therefore, you need to use alternative forms of identification in these situations as well.

The following examples show how to say who in the lead and delay identification:

Age

An 18-year-old Tampa man was shot and killed Wednesday after he and two friends confronted a gunman who had beaten a friend of theirs, Tampa police said.

Warren Smith III, of 3524 E. 26th Ave., was shot behind his right ear at 6:40 P.M. and was pronounced dead shortly after arriving at Tampa General Hospital, police said.

—*St. Petersburg* (Fla.) *Times*

Occupation

Two Minneapolis meter monitors have been charged with stealing an estimated $35,000 worth of nickels, dimes and quarters from parking meters.

Dale Timinskis, 42, and Leroy Siner, 40, both of Minneapolis, were arrested Tuesday after police watched their activities.

—*Minneapolis Star Tribune*

Location

An Anchorage woman who embezzled more than $450,000 pleaded guilty Friday in U.S. District Court in Spokane, Wash., to charges of identity theft and filing a false tax return.

Jana J. Josey, 44, who now lives in Wenatchee, Wash., used various schemes to embezzle money while working as an accounts payable clerk for Quality Asphalt Paving, an Alaska construction company.

—*The Associated Press*

Other identifier   A former Duke University student who posed as a wealthy French baron was a con artist with lavish desires, said a judge who sentenced the imposter to three years in prison for fraud.

Maurice Jeffrey Locke Rothschild, 38, who changed his name from Mauro Cortex Jr., was sentenced in Greensboro, N.C. for bilking two banks by posing as a nobleman from France's wealthy Rothschild family. The charges involved $12,000 Rothschild received after submitting false information on credit card applications.

—Newsday

If you are writing a story about a person who has been in the news frequently, such as a suspect in a trial, you may use the name, but add a phrase or clause to identify the person, as in this example about a woman on trial for the murder of her former fiancé.

Prosecutors in the trial of former stripper Michele Linehan want the jury to watch a movie called "The Last Seduction," about a woman who tried to manipulate her lover into killing her husband for $1 million.

Updated Leads

The summary lead usually stresses basic facts about the news in the immediate past, and it is usually written in past tense. This type of breaking-news lead is often referred to as a "first-day lead," as if readers were hearing the news for the first time.

Because television and online news sites require immediacy, leads are often updated by advancing the story to the next step, a process called "forward spin" or "advancing the lead." Newspapers also refer to updated leads as "second-day leads." *USA Today* uses this approach regularly.

The first example is a standard summary lead that appeared in a morning paper. It stresses what happened yesterday in the search for a missing University of Arizona professor.

Rescue workers combed a rugged area in the Tucson Mountains yesterday evening in search of a UA music professor who has been missing since Tuesday night.

—The (Tucson) *Arizona Daily Star*

The second example appeared in a competing afternoon newspaper. It gives the story a forward spin, stressing what will happen today even though there is no new information; this would work better for broadcast:

Deputies plan to resume a search this morning in rocky terrain in the Gates Pass area for missing University of Arizona music Professor Roy Andres Johnson, 58, who they fear was killed.

—Tucson (Ariz.) *Citizen*

A few days later the professor's body was found; he had been murdered.

Here is an example of how you might update a lead, especially for broadcast:

Original version Princeton University officials have placed a cap on the number of A's that professors can award in an effort to crack down on grade inflation.

Updated version Students at Princeton University won't be receiving as many A's this year. School officials are cracking down on grade inflation by placing a cap on the number of A's professors can award.

Impact Leads

The "impact lead" explains how the readers and viewers will be affected by an issue. This type of lead is also good for broadcast stories. It is an excellent tool to make a story seem fresh and relevant. The impact lead is especially helpful on bureaucratic stories. It answers the questions "So what? What does this news mean to a reader?"

Impact leads can be written in a hard-news summary form or in a more creative form, such as a soft lead. The information you give must be factual, not your interpretation. And if you use an indirect lead, you must write a clear nut graph early in the story.

The previous updated lead is also an example of an impact lead because it starts with how students at Princeton University will be affected by the new grade restrictions.

This impact lead uses a direct summary approach:

Summary lead with impact Southwest Missouri State University must release its campus crime reports to the public, a federal judge ruled Wednesday in a case that could affect colleges across the nation.

U.S. District Judge Russell G. Clark called the withholding of those reports unconstitutional and ordered university officials to provide the public and media access to them.

Backup with more impact The ruling, thought to be the first of its kind in the nation, has prompted the U.S. Department of Education to begin re-evaluating its stand on the release of campus reports.

—*The Kansas City* (Mo.) *Star*

Here is an impact lead that directly addresses readers and viewers; this lead that would work equally well in print, broadcast or on the Web:

> Are you avoiding the bathroom scale? Is it a struggle to pull on last year's clothes? If the answer is "yes," you probably need to take off some extra pounds. But what you might not know is that a little extra sleep could be the answer.
>
>   Studies show that people who sleep too little are actually more likely to raid the refrigerator.
>
> *—Fairbanks* (Alaska)
> *Daily News Miner Webcast*

Attribution in Leads

Attribution tells the reader where you got your information. Too much attribution can clutter a lead. Too little can get you in trouble. For print and Web stories, you may put the attribution at the beginning or the end of the sentence; for broadcast, attribution must come first. Here are some guidelines about whether you need to use attribution:

- If you know the information is factual and you witnessed it or have firsthand knowledge that it is true, you may eliminate the attribution. If you received the information by telephone, as in police or fire stories, attribute it to your source.
- Whenever you are saying anything accusatory, as in police or political stories, you must attribute the information.
- You also must attribute the quotes or partial quotes you use in a lead.

To keep attribution clutter to a minimum, you may give a general reference to some sources—such as "police said" or "experts say"—if their titles are long. Then, as in delayed identification, give the specific name and title in the second reference.

In broadcast news, if the source is shown on videotape, the name and title may be superimposed under the video so you may not need to attribute by name and title. If you do use attribution, put the source's title before the name:

Right: Police Chief John Law says the suspect is in custody.

Wrong: John Law, police chief, says the suspect is in custody.

Fact vs. Opinion Here are some examples that demonstrate when to use attribution:

Fact: No attribution is needed.	An 88-year-old man died Monday afternoon when fire spread through his second-floor apartment at the Wellington Arms Apartments in north St. Louis County.
Opinion: Speculation about the cause needs to be attributed.	An 88-year-old man died in north St. Louis County Monday afternoon, apparently after he started a fire while smoking in bed, authorities said.
Attributed fact: Attribution for fact is needed because the reporter got the information secondhand (by telephone).	The body of a man who had been fatally stabbed was discovered Monday morning in a city trash bin in the Lewis Place neighborhood, police said.

—*St. Louis* (Mo.) *Post-Dispatch*

Accusations A person is innocent until proved guilty in court. In crime stories, attribute any accusatory statements to police or other authorities, especially when you are using a suspect's name. If the person has been charged with a crime, you may state that fact without attribution. The word *allegedly* can be used when the charges have not been proved, but direct attribution to the police is preferable. Here are some examples:

No attribution is needed.	A University of North Florida chemistry major has been charged with building a 35-pound "megabomb" powerful enough to destroy everything within a radius of 150 yards.

—*The Associated Press*

Attribution is needed for an accusatory statement.	David Roger Flint killed 16-month-old Brittany K. Boyer on Monday by dangling her by the arms, swinging her side to side and beating her head against the floor and wooden furniture, police say. The 23-year-old Flint was arrested about 10:30 P.M. Tuesday and accused of murder.

—Jane Meinhardt, *St. Petersburg* (Fla.) *Times*

The word **allegedly** *is used because it has not yet been proved that the kidnap and rape occurred.*	A 38-year-old paroled murderer has been arrested in St. Croix County, Wis., for allegedly kidnapping and raping two 16-year-old girls in Minneapolis last month. . . .

Later, the lead is backed up this way.

He was charged with two counts of first-degree criminal sexual conduct and two counts of kidnapping.

—*St. Paul* (Minn.) *Pioneer Press*

This lead would be a safer alternative.

A 38-year-old paroled murderer has been charged with kidnapping and raping two 16-year-old girls in Minneapolis last month.

Quotes Whenever you quote someone directly, indirectly or partially, you need to attribute the statement.

Full quotes are difficult in leads and can be awkward. Reading a story that starts with a full quote is like coming into the middle of a conversation; it's hard to tell the context and meaning of the quote. Full quotes are also ineffective for broadcast writing.

A more effective technique is the use of partial quotes, especially when the speaker says something controversial or dramatic. Leads may also contain reference quotes, a few words referring to something controversial. Both partial and reference quotes should be backed up later in the story with the full quote or with the context in which the statement was made.

A full quote is used in this lead because it is dramatic, but it is still confusing.

"I've done everything out there," 31-year-old Gilbert Franco told his wife Thursday. "All that's left to do is learn the Bible and to die."

The next day, San Jose police say, Franco entered the C&S Market at East Julian and 26th streets and shot to death Katherine Young Suk Choe, 40, whose family owns the store.

Seconds later, 50 yards away, Franco fatally shot himself in the head.

—*San Jose* (Calif.) *Mercury News*

In this example a partial quote is used and backed up later with the full quote, a technique used more often in stories about speeches, politics and court stories:

A reference quote is used in the lead.

The University of Pennsylvania announced yesterday that it was penalizing a senior scientist for "lapses of judgment" in an experiment last April in which more than 120 people may have been exposed to a virus that can cause a fatal form of leukemia. . . .

The backup puts the partial quote in context.

The committee concluded that the professor was not guilty of research misconduct as defined in a school policy. However, the committee concluded that there were "lapses of judgment and failures of communication" in the experiment.

—*The Philadelphia Inquirer*

Attribution First or Last The rule of thumb in the lead is to put the most important information first. If the attribution is cumbersome and will slow the lead, put it at the end. If it is brief, you can put it first. In broadcast writing, however, you need to put the attribution first. If the attribution is cumbersome, refer to the source broadly as in "a new study" or "a state official," and state the full attribution in the next paragraph.

Attribution last

Casual drug use has dropped sharply during the last five years, but the number of addicts using cocaine daily has not changed significantly, the federal government reported yesterday.

—*The Philadelphia Inquirer*

Attribution first (acceptable, and preferable for broadcast writing)

The federal government reports that casual drug use has dropped sharply during the last five years, but the number of addicts using cocaine daily has not changed significantly.

Attribution last (because name is cumbersome and not as important as conclusions)

In a typical week, about 85 percent of the adult U.S. population uses a newspaper, according to a landmark study of daily newspaper readership released today.

The Impact Study of Newspaper Readership is part of a project to help the country's nearly 1,500 daily newspapers gain readers. The study was conducted by the Readership Institute of the Media Management Center at Northwestern University, Evanston, Ill.

Cluttered Attribution In the example that follows, note how a long attribution at the start of the sentence clutters the lead:

Cluttered

Karen Davisson, child protection worker with the Kansas Department of Social Rehabilitation Services district office in Emporia, said Tuesday that only rarely are neglected or abused children removed from their parents' care and placed in foster homes or put up for adoption.

Uncluttered

Neglected or abused children are rarely removed from their parents' care and placed in foster homes or put up for adoption, a state social worker said Tuesday.

Karen Davisson is a child protection worker with the Kansas Department of Social Rehabilitation Services district office in Emporia.

One of the most common causes of clutter in leads is too much information about where and when something was said. Put some of this material in the second paragraph. Put the location of the meeting much farther down in the story, or eliminate it altogether unless it is important to the reader.

Cluttered   Fort Riley is being considered as a possible host for the proposed joint landfill for Geary and Riley counties, Riley County Director of Public Works Dan Harden said during an informational meeting Tuesday night at the Geary County 4-H Senior Citizens Center.

Fort Riley is being considered as a possible site for a landfill, a Riley County official said Tuesday. Dan Harden, director of public works said. . . .   *Uncluttered*

Convergence Coach

The basic techniques of writing leads apply to all media, but broadcast leads should stress the most current information. If you are posting the information first on the Web, you will need to update the lead for the next print edition as well as the next broadcast.

Online writing is similar to print, but summary leads are often preferred because readers are impatient to discover the main point of the story. Summary leads are also preferred for public relations writing in news releases.

If the headline and blurb are in summary form, the lead might be descriptive or anecdotal. But make sure that the nut graph is high in the story if you use a soft lead. With millions of Web sites competing for readers' attention, readers will click to another story or site if the lead or nut graph is not clear. Because the content on most online news sites mirrors print versions, you need to consider how your lead and nut graph will work both in print and online. Descriptive and anecdotal leads work well for feature stories, trends and profiles in broadcast writing and on the Web.

Here are some guidelines for broadcast and online writing:

■ Use active voice, with an emphasis on short, uncomplicated sentences. State who is doing the action rather than to whom the action was done.

■ Use simple sentences, preferably structured in subject–verb–object order (who did what). Avoid long sentences that begin with clauses.

■ Put the most important information first in the sentence.

■ Use a conversational tone. Addressing the reader as "you" works well in broadcast and on the Web.

■ For broadcast, place attribution first, not at the end of the sentence; either order works for the Web. If the attribution is cumbersome, put it in another paragraph, as in this example:

New research indicates that eating lots of red meat may create about as much of a certain cancer-promoting chemical in the colon as smoking does.

The findings, presented Saturday in Lyon at the European Conference on Nutrition and Cancer, were part of a study that also appears to revive the theory that fiber wards off colon cancer, the second most deadly cancer worldwide.

—*The Associated Press*

■ Most important, get to the main point quickly. This story begins with a soft lead sentence, but the main point is still in the lead:

Never mind what the label says. The new brands of energy drinks are aimed more at marathon partiers than serious athletes. And that has health officials worried.

The drinks come in flashy cans and bottles with names like Red Bull, Adrenaline Rush and Jones Whoop-Ass Energy Drink. They don't taste great by almost universal consensus, but they're the fastest-growing segment of the beverage market because they deliver a quick punch of energy.

—*The Associated Press*

Soft Leads

Coaching Tips

- Try writing many different leads instead of struggling to find the perfect one. Don't wait for a creative muse.
- Make sure that your lead is related to your focus and can be backed up in your story.
- Do not strain to "create" a lead from your head. Pull from the story, not from your head, for inspiration.

Soft leads can be fun to write and fun to read. They can also be painful. If you don't get to the point quickly, they can also be tedious. They can be as effective in broadcast writing as in print.

Although soft leads are also called "delayed leads," the lead is still first. Only the nut graph is delayed. Remember that all leads, especially soft leads, must be backed up in the story and must lead to a nut graph. It is preferable to place the nut graph high in the story, by the third to fifth paragraph.

Most breaking-news stories contain summary leads, but in 2005 the Associated Press announced that it would begin offering two types of leads—hard and soft—on many of its stories, especially spot-news stories that happen early in the day. "One will be the traditional 'straight lead' that leads with the main facts of what took place. The other will be the 'optional lead,' an alternative approach that attempts to draw in the reader through imagery, narrative devices, perspective or other creative means," according to an article in *Editor & Publisher*.

That's a major change for the news wire service, which primarily offers the summary lead. It's a recognition that readers need different approaches to stories.

There are many types of soft leads. They can be used on both news and feature stories. Most of them follow a simple concept: specific to general. Use a specific example at the beginning to illustrate the main point of the story.

People like to read about other people. As a result, many soft leads start with something about a person who is one of many people sharing the same problem. The idea behind these soft leads—called "anecdotal leads"—is that readers can relate better to one person's problem than to a general statement of a problem.

Other common types of soft leads are descriptive and narrative. "Descriptive leads" describe a person or a scene. "Narrative leads" are storytelling leads that recount the event in a dramatic way to put the reader on the scene as the action occurs.

And then there are leads that are just clever or catchy.

It's not what you call soft leads that matters; it's how you write them. The important point is to tell a good story. When writers struggle with soft leads, it is often because they think they must create something clever. All too often, the result is a cliché. It is best to look at your notes and build a lead based on something interesting in the story, instead of waiting for the creative muse.

The sections that follow show a variety of ways to structure a soft lead. The basic techniques are descriptive, anecdotal and narrative.

ETHICS

Ethical dilemma: You want to write an anecdotal lead focusing on a person for your story, but you don't have a real source. Should you use a hypothetical person without telling the reader?

Should you use a hypothetical situation at all?

Ethical values: Credibility, accuracy, truthfulness.

Ethical guidelines: The Society of Professional Journalists Code of Ethics says, "Seek the truth and report it. Avoid misleading re-enactments or staged news events."

Descriptive Leads

This type of lead describes a person, place or event. It is like the descriptive focus-on-a-person lead, but it doesn't have to focus on a person who is one of many. It can be used for news or feature stories.

In this example, the story focuses on the man who is causing the problem:

Skippack farmer John W. Hasson stood ankle-deep in mud, pumping milk into a wooden trough as his pigs, squealing and grunting, snouts quivering, climbed over each other to get to their feed.

Hasson inhaled deeply.

"Does that smell sour to you?

That's what they call noxious fumes," he said with a sniff toward his new neighbors, Ironbridge Estates, a subdivision of two-story colonial houses costing $200,000 plus.

Ironbridge's developers say Hasson's farm smells.

And his 250 pigs squeal too much.

So they have filed suit in Montgomery County to force him to clean up his act. The case is scheduled to be heard May 8.

Nut graph

—Erin Kennedy, *The Philadelphia Inquirer*

Anecdotal Leads

This type of lead starts with a story about a person or an event. In a sense, all soft leads are anecdotal because they are all storytelling approaches. Many combine descriptive and anecdotal techniques.

This lead is an anecdote—the story behind a woman's court case:

Late one spring night, after drinks at a bar and a bit of protest, Elaine Hollis agreed to her boyfriend's desire to capture their passion on videotape.

Inside Edward Bayliss' apartment, the video camera rolled at the foot of his bed.

He promised to erase the tape.

Seven years later, Hollis, who has a son with Bayliss, was in Delaware County Court accusing him of contriving to bring her into disrepute by exhibiting the tape. Bayliss, president of Philadelphia Suburban Electrical Service in Upper Darby, admitted showing the tape to one of his friends.

Nut graphs

Hollis contended he showed and distributed the tape in Delaware County and surrounding areas, as well as gave copies of it to two bar owners in Darby, who played it for customers.

Last week, after three years of litigation, a county judge upheld an Oct . 15

Common Pleas Court order that mandated Bayliss pay Hollis $125,000 to settle her lawsuit.

—Patrick Scott, *The Philadelphia Inquirer*

The next example contains another anecdotal lead that tells a story but incorporates the news in the first sentence. It is a good example of how to update the news about a minor earthquake that occurred the previous day by using a storytelling approach. (If the earthquake had been greater and had caused death or injuries, a summary lead would have been more appropriate.)

When the shock wave from a magnitude 4.7 earthquake rolled through Anchorage Wednesday morning, dentist Kendall Skinner had just inserted a 3-inch needle into the mouth of a patient and begun an injection.

"It was jarring," Skinner said. "It's such a sharp object in the back of somebody's mouth."

With a somewhat unsteady hand, Skinner finished the injection as fast and safely as he could, then pulled out. His patient, a 20-something woman who needed a filling, told him she was

fine. The numbing started before the shaking, so she didn't feel a thing.

People all over Anchorage and the Matanuska-Susitna Valley were shaken but not stirred from their regular workday routine Wednesday when a quake struck beneath the Point MacKenzie area a few miles north of downtown—then triggered an afternoon of minor aftershocks.

Nut graph

—Doug O'Harra, Megan Holland and Zaz Hollander, *Anchorage* (Alaska) *Daily News*

This lead uses both anecdotal and descriptive techniques:

Dawn Clark's cat walked carefully across the lawn, then stopped suddenly, looking bewildered.

The cat sniffed tentatively, then bolted off the grass and spent the next few minutes licking its paws—trying to clean the paint flecks from them.

The lawn had recently been mowed and was green as a billiard table, because it had just been painted with a vegetable dye.

Nut graph

Santa Barbara residents have devised innovative ways to keep their yards

green since the city, faced with an expected water shortfall of nearly 50 percent for the year, declared a "drought emergency" in late February and banned lawn watering.

Clark's cat had just experienced one: Several landscape companies now offer painting and local nurseries are stocking their shelves with green paint and pump sprayers.

Extension of nut graph

—Miles Corwin, *Los Angeles Times*

Narrative Leads

Like an anecdotal lead, a narrative lead tells a story with enough dramatic action so readers can feel as if they are witnessing the event. Narrative writing uses all the techniques of fiction, including dialogue, scene setting and foreshadowing—giving the reader clues to what will happen. It takes longer to set up the nut graph for this kind of lead, but if the story is dramatic enough, the narrative approach may work.

Police Officer Juan Cabrera felt the barrel of the gun press against his head.

"I'm gonna kill you," a voice from behind said.

"I didn't see who it was. I didn't know what was happening," Cabrera said. "I just thought someone was going to kill me." Cabrera instinctively knocked the gun away, wrestled the suspect to the ground and handcuffed him.

The suspect was a 12-year-old boy. The gun was a toy.

"It looked like a .38-caliber short-barrel revolver," said Cabrera, a five-year veteran of the force. "It was a cap gun."

The incident was no joke for the boy. He was arrested on a charge of battery on a law enforcement officer.

—Kevin Davis, *The South Florida Sun-Sentinel*

Other Soft Leads

Soft leads can be written in many other ways. The following techniques are variations on the three main types of soft leads, combining features of descriptive, anecdotal and narrative leads.

Focus-on-a-Person Leads You can focus on a person in two ways: Use an anecdotal approach, telling a little story about the person, or use a descriptive approach that describes the person or shows the person in action. This type of lead can be used in profile stories about the person or in news stories about issues, where the person is one of many affected by the point of your story. This approach, used by many newspapers and broadcast stations, is also called *The Wall Street Journal* format because that newspaper uses this format daily on its front-page features and originated the term "nut graph."

This example uses the descriptive approach:

Nita walked slowly down the narrow hall, deftly guiding her tottering 11-month-old son around the abandoned baby walkers, strollers and toys.

Inside her tiny bedroom, the 17-year-old mother pointed to photographs of her son's father and some of her friends. Cards congratulating her on her recent high school graduation were nearby. The baby's crib was crammed into an area near the door.

Nita, one of 85 residents at Florence Crittenton Services in Fullerton, is one of a growing number of teenagers having babies in Orange County—a figure that has increased 36 percent in five years.

—Janine Anderson,
The Orange County (Calif.) *Register*

Nut graph: points out that person is one of many

The focus-on-a-person lead is an effective technique for broadcast news as well, especially when the person or people used in the lead exemplify a problem shared by many other people in your community.

Nut graph: points out that these people are like many others in the community

> Judy and Jose Westbrook spent the morning cleaning up the furniture in their front yard. The Blue River had overflowed its banks and forced its way into their Independence home.
>
> More than 25 families share their predicament. Late this afternoon all of those families were awaiting word about their flood insurance claims.

Here is another example of this popular *Wall Street Journal* lead format because it starts by focusing on a person who is used to illustrate a problem that affects many others like her:

> SEATTLE—Natasha Khachatourians has so much student debt that she's working two jobs. Eight hours a day, she staffs the front window at Seattle University's financial-aid office. Three nights a week she's at her second job, working at Lovers Package until 10:30. Saturdays she pulls another eight-hour shift at the adult-entertainment store.
>
> She's barely staying afloat. Khachatourians, 23, graduated from Seattle University last year, and her debt tally is $60,000 in education loans, plus $4,500 on four credit cards. After consolidating her federal loans, her education payments are $300 a month.
>
> "I eat a lot of bread," she said. "It's cheap."
>
> *Nut graph* Her predicament reflects that of many college graduates: Students are leaving college owing more and more, and that swelling debt is out-pacing the rise in other higher-education costs.
>
> —Sharon Pian Chan, *The Seattle Times*

Contrast Leads   This type of lead can be used to set up stories about conflicts or unusual circumstances. The two most common ways to write contrast leads emphasize circumstances and time:

But-Guess-What Contrast: Contrast leads that revolve around circumstances can be used to explain something unusual:

> William Pearce, known to his patients as Dr. William J. Rick, was charming and slick, say his former associates and police detectives.
>
> He came to town with medical degrees, numerous national board certificates and myriad other qualifications.
>
> *Nut graph* But the real Dr. Rick died in 1986, police say. And now William John Pearce, 57, is in jail on charges of impersonating a doctor.
>
> —Sharon McBreen, *The Orlando* (Fla.) *Sentinel*

Here is a descriptive lead setting up contrast without the "but":

DENVER—Above a pond labeled "Industrial Waste," two bald eagles perch on a tree limb. Down the road from workers in white protective suits, scores of prairie dogs scurry across a field. Around the corner from hundreds of barrels containing remnants of mustard gas, a dozen mule deer stand in a thicket.

It's a paradox that some view as almost poetic: The Army's Rocky Mountain Arsenal—a shut-down war factory, a boarded-up lesson in how not to treat the environment, one of the most poisoned pieces of land in the United States—has become a haven for wildlife.

Nut graph

—John Woestendiek, *The Philadelphia Inquirer*

Then-and-Now Contrast: Time contrasts—then and now—are useful ways to show change. This type of lead also can be used when the background is interesting or important and is relevant to the focus.

It was March 1964 when Lewis "Hackie" Wilson, the 7-year-old son of a St. Petersburg firefighter, disappeared after stopping to pick up flowers on his way home from school.

His case received national attention a month later when a sheriff's posse on horseback, flushing out rattlesnakes ahead of a line of 80 searchers, found the child's bones in a field south of Venice.

Now the case may be revived.

Prosecutors in Sarasota County have realized that Joseph Francis Bryan, a convicted child kidnapper indicted for Hackie's murder in 1965, has never been brought to trial.

Nut graph

—Karen Datko, *St. Petersburg (Fla.) Times*

Teaser Leads These leads use the element of surprise to tease the reader into the story. The nut graph may also be a contrast, but the first sentence sets it up as a tease into something unusual. Broadcast news uses the concept of teasers before commercials to convince the audience to stay tuned after the break, but teasers are also effective in leads on broadcast stories.

BURLINGTON, Vt.—This is no ordinary public library.

For one thing, there are only four books on the shelves. For another, you won't find any of these works, or the many that are expected to join them soon, at other libraries or bookstores.

You probably never will.

That's because the Brautigan Library, which opened here last weekend, has a unique policy—it only accepts books that have never been published.

Nut graph

—Steve Stecklow, *The Philadelphia Inquirer*

Mystery Leads Like teasers, these leads promise the reader a surprise or a treat for reading on. They set up the story like a mystery novel. They're fun to write and fun to read, but they won't work unless the subject matter lends itself to this approach. They are effective for print and broadcast writing.

One technique for writing mystery leads is to start with a vague pronoun, *it* or *they,* and to delay naming the noun to which the pronoun refers: "It began at midnight." Later you specify what "it" was. Here is an example of a mystery lead:

They know who you are, what you eat, how you procreate—and where to find you.

Do you like ice cream? The U.S. government has used that information to track down draft-dodging 18-year-olds who signed up for ice cream parlor "birthday clubs." . . .

Been turned down for a Master-Card or Visa? List Brokerage and Management, a New York list marketer, may have your name. It rents a list of 1.6 million people rejected for bank cards—obtained, the company says, from the very banks that turned you down. . . .

Computer companies are hooking up with credit bureaus and massive data banks to allow people with only a desktop computer to single you out by income, age, neighborhood, car model or waist size.

Nut graph

—Stephen Koff, *St. Petersburg* (Fla.) *Times*

This next lead uses not only the mystery approach but also the format of the novel as part of the lead:

The case has all the elements of a 1950s film noir mystery.

The characters: the scheming husband, the trusting wife, the other woman.

The story: The husband, Ray Valois, buys a lottery ticket, scratches it and finds three "Spin, Spin, Spin" symbols. That makes him eligible to win up to $2 million in the California "Big Spin" lottery, but he does not want to tell his wife, Monica, according to his statement in San Luis Obispo County Superior Court records. So he gives the ticket to another woman, waitress Stephanie Martin. She agrees to cash in the ticket, according to court records, and secretly give him half.

The inevitable plot twist: Valois and Martin turn on each other. He claims that he owns the ticket. She claims that she owns the ticket.

The conclusion: Martin spins and wins $100,000. But the wife finds out and sues both of them for fraud.

Now neither Martin nor Valois has the $100,000. His wife's attorney, Gary Dunlap, obtained a temporary restraining order, restricting lottery officials from awarding the winnings until a court hearing today.

Nut graph

—Miles Corwin, *Los Angeles Times*

Build-on-a-Quote Leads If you have a great quote, build your lead around the quote that will back up your first sentence. But be careful not to repeat too much of the quote in your lead; that's boring and repetitious. Building on a quote is an easy and effective way to find a lead, provided that the quote is related to the focus of the story. This technique works equally well for hard-news leads. For broadcast news, however, you would not read a quote. Instead, you might start with a video of a person speaking, called a "sound on tape" (SOT).

ANDOVER, Kan.—Melinda Easterbrook knows exactly how long it took for a tornado to blast apart her comfortable home while she and her husband huddled in the basement.

"It lasted five Hail Marys and two Our Fathers, but you have to say them quickly," she said yesterday.

While she was praying, the concrete basement rumbled and shook. When she and her husband, Bryan, came upstairs, they were hardly prepared for the scope of the destruction that had swept through this small town about five miles east of Wichita.

Nut graph

—Larry Fish, *The Philadelphia Inquirer*

The next example is the kind of build-on-a-quote lead to avoid. The backup quote says the same thing as the lead, and it's right after the lead, so it's boring. In broadcast writing this is called "parroting," with the reporter introducing a sound bite that repeats what the source says on tape. It should be avoided as well.

A commitment to high-tech learning and small classes taught by professors has made Fort Hays State University the fastest-growing university in the state Board of Regents system, FHSU's president said today.

FHSU had the largest spring semester enrollment increase among the six regents' universities—2.4 percent compared with the previous spring.

"We've been the fastest growing of the regents' institutions over the last five years," FHSU President Edward Hammond said.

List Leads   If you have a few brief examples to lead into your focus, you may list them in parallel sentences—making sure that your sentences have the same construction, such as subject–verb–object order. Three seems to be a magic number; more than three can be awkward and tedious.

Boston College has an assistant dean for alcohol and drug education. Rutgers University sets aside dorm rooms for recovering student alcoholics. The University of Nevada bars students from leaving school sports events to make alcohol runs.

Increasingly, colleges are confronting problem drinking by providing education and rehabilitation programs, alternatives to the campus bar scene and stricter regulation of on-campus parties.

Nut graph

—*The Associated Press*

Question Leads   These can be effective if the reader is interested in finding the answer to the question you pose. If not, you could lose the reader. One way to test question leads is to determine if the answer would be yes or no. Those are the dangerous ones. A question that raises a more thoughtful, and more interesting, answer is preferable.

What are the odds of finding your true love by placing an ad with a telephone dating service?

About one in 40, according to Terry Ehlbert.

On April 13, Ehlbert is planning to marry Scott Anderson, who was the last of 40 guys she agreed to meet after placing a voice-mail ad with the 1-976-DATE service she saw advertised on TV. . . .

The phone services work in much the same way published personal ads do.   *Nut graph*

—Rick Shefchik, *St. Paul* (Minn.) *Pioneer Press*

The next example is a little dangerous. What if you don't want to buy cigarettes at all? Will you read on?

Nut graph   Want to buy cigarettes while at the gas station? Or while sipping a cocktail at your favorite bar?

Not in Lower Merion, if township officials have their way.

Officials there, concerned about the availability of cigarettes to minors, have proposed a municipal law prohibiting cigarette vending machines in the township. The law would be the first of its kind in Pennsylvania.

—*The Philadelphia Inquirer*

Cliché Leads   In general, avoid clichés. But occasionally, a play on words will work as a clever lead. Consider this:

Nut graph   Nick Agid's workshop is just a stone's throw from the Torrance post office. Good thing, too. When Agid drops a post card into the mail, it lands with a five-pound thud.

Agid is a sculptor who carves messages on leftover chunks of marble and granite. They become postcards when he adds scratched-on addresses and slaps stamps on the slabs.

—Bob Pool, *Los Angeles Times*

Leads to Avoid

The leads described in this section are strained, obtuse, rambling or just plain awful. They don't work for a variety of reasons.

Cluttered Leads: Keep Your Leads Simple, Especially for Broadcast.
Don't try to cram all the major facts of the story in one sentence. Some long leads may work but most should be fewer than 35 words, especially if you are reading

them for radio or television. This lead is too complex and contains the cliché, "killed two birds with one stone."

> Rolling up their sleeves, 20 students from Voznesenka School, near the head of Kachemak Bay, killed two birds with one stone Saturday: they washed away the grit and grime and put a shine on more than 25 local vehicles, and they raised more than $300 to help pay for next spring's graduation expenses.

Good News/Bad News Leads: The bad news is this type of lead. They're clichés, and they're used so often that they're boring. They're also judgmental.

> Some good news for city workers: The county administration has been giving signals that it might not have to give out any pink slips, at least for now.
>
> Some bad news for city taxpayers: The county administration has shown no signs of scaling back its proposal to raise taxes for the next several years.
>
> —*Newsday*

Crystal Ball Leads: These are dream-sequence leads that foretell the future. If you were writing about psychics, perhaps you could write this kind of lead. But most people can't predict the future. "John Jones never imagined when he boarded the plane that it was going to crash." Would he have been stupid enough to board it if he had known? Leads that emphasize "if only they had known" are far-fetched. Consider the following. It's unlikely that a child who is choking is thinking about the future—much less about what he can do for someone else.

> When 10-year-old Jason Finser of Clermont was saved from choking to death at a family dinner two years ago, he never dreamed he would be able to return the favor.
>
> *Nut graph*   But luckily for his classmate, 9-year-old Abby Muick, Jason knew exactly what to do when she choked on a chocolate-and-Rice Krispies treat in the lunchroom at Minneola Elementary School.
>
> —*The Orlando* (Fla.) *Sentinel*

Nightmare Leads: These are also dream leads, usually relating to a past experience. The nightmare analogy is overused: "The past three days were like a nightmare for John Jones." For the reader, too. Every bad experience someone has does not have to be compared to a nightmare.

> The nightmare became reality for local police yesterday when a Niagara Falls drug dealer was arrested at the Greater Buffalo International Airport.
>
> Hidden in his baggage were $50,000 worth of heroin, some PCP, and a sampling of a new drug he referred to as "smokable cocaine."
>
> *—Niagara* (N.Y.) *Gazette*

Plop-a-Person Leads: This type of lead is a misuse of the focus-on-a-person lead. When the writer just tops the story with a sketch of a person and does not back it up in the text, that's plopping. It's also misleading. The reader starts the story thinking that the person has something to say or do in the story. But after the lead, the person disappears.

> Tuesday was a good day for psychology professor Carnot Nelson.
>
> He spent most of it helping an honors student work on her thesis. He read another student's doctoral dissertation and two master's thesis proposals. Then he went to a meeting, which he left after an hour and a half so he could do some reading of his own.
>
> Nelson, a senior professor at the University of South Florida, who also teaches large undergraduate classes and small graduate seminars, is a good example of the range of activity involved in teaching Florida university students.
>
> "Education is a one-at-a-time, hand-made business," said state university spokesman Pat Riordan. "You can't mechanize it, you can't computerize it and you can't put it on an assembly line."
>
> But college professors in Florida are under increasing pressure to do exactly that. Recurring state budget cuts have made some classes larger and eliminated many others. And a political climate that says there can be no new taxes until a state government becomes "more productive" has fueled a drive to force professors to spend more time in the classroom.
>
> *—St. Petersburg* (Fla.) *Times*

This is the last time we hear about Nelson, despite his being a good example.

Nut graphs

Weather-Report Leads: These leads set the scene by describing the weather: "It was a dark and stormy night." Avoid using the weather as a lead when it isn't related to the story.

> It was hot and humid the day the city council decided to ban smoking from all public buildings.
>
> The ordinance, passed unanimously, will go into effect immediately.

Stereotype Leads: These are most common in features about older people, women and groups with special interests. The writer tries hard to be complimentary but instead only reinforces stereotypes. This is the lead for a story about Senior Olympics, games for people over age 60:

> At the age when most of their contemporaries are in rocking chairs, these athletes will be competing in swimming, archery, badminton, bicycle racing—just about every imaginable sport, through the long jump and shot put.
>
> —*The Baltimore Sun*

If you look around your college campus, you're likely to see many professors in their 60s, and most of them don't spend much time in rocking chairs.

Soft leads can be enticing and creative, but they must be accurate.

Tips for Finding Your Lead

To find a lead that will work for you in your story, first find your nut graph. Ask yourself what the main point of the story is. Then ask some of these questions to find your lead:

Reader Interest: What did you or would the reader find most interesting about this subject?

Memorable Item: What was the most memorable impression or fact?

Focus on a Person: Is there someone who exemplifies the problem or issue? If you tell a story about this person or show the person in action, will it lead to the point in the nut graph?

Descriptive Approach: Will a description of the scene relate to the focus?

Mystery Approach: Can you tease the reader with a surprise that leads to the nut graph?

Build on a Quote: Is there a great quote to back up the lead? If so, write the lead so it refers to the quote without repeating it.

Contrast: Would a then-and-now approach work?

Problem/Solution: Can you set up a problem so the reader wants to discover the solution?

Narrative Storytelling: If you were just telling a good story, how would you start? Can you reconstruct the events to put the reader on the scene?

Exercises

1 Hard-news leads: Write summary leads from the following information. For the time element, use the day of the week instead of *yesterday* or *today.*

  a Write this lead for a print publication: A study was released yesterday by the University of Colorado. The study was funded by the Alfred P. Sloan Foundation. The study said that 60 percent of college students who begin studying science, mathematics or engineering switch to another major. The study cited poor teaching and an aloof faculty as the cause.

  b There was a fire yesterday at a pizza restaurant. It is located at 2035 Main St. Two firefighters were injured when the roof fell in. They were treated at St. Luke's Medical Center for minor injuries. The fire started in the basement of the building. The cause is under investigation. The roof collapsed, and the inside of the restaurant was destroyed. Damages are estimated at $100,000. The information comes from fire officials in your community.

  c The Centers for Disease Control today released the results of a survey of nutritional supplements. Nutritional supplements include vitamins, protein supplements and products promising muscle growth. Only supplements in powder, capsule or tablet form were surveyed. "It turned out that at least half of the ingredients have no documented medical effect," said Rossane Philen, a medical epidemiologist at the National Center for Environmental Health and Injury Control. She was part of the surveying team. The survey said many nutritional supplements have no medical support for their advertised claims.

2 Broadcast versions: Convert the leads you wrote in Exercise 1 to broadcast leads.

3 Active/passive voice: Change this lead to active voice:

A 29-year-old Phoenix man was killed Tuesday when his motorcycle was struck by a car on East Ina Road.

Write a lead in passive voice from this information: Jones County Circuit Court Judge Billy Landrum yesterday sentenced a 17-year-old high school sophomore to two consecutive life terms for the murder of two men in a convenience store.

4 Delayed identification: From the following information, write a lead using delayed identification.

Background provided by the police: Michael Stephens, who lives in the 3700 block of North Camino Street in Tucson, was driving a flatbed truck in central Tucson early yesterday morning. He lost control of his truck, and it overturned on East 15th Street near South Kino Parkway. He died of head injuries at the scene of the accident at 2:30 A.M. He was 44 years old.

5 Updated lead: From this information, give the lead a forward spin for the next day's paper or the next edition of TV news.

Background: Vandals broke into the Midtown Magnet Middle School at 300 Fifth Ave. just before 7 P.M. on Sunday. They broke windows and damaged 11 classrooms and an office area. They damaged computers and other equipment. The cost of the damages has not yet been estimated. Classes are scheduled to resume today. School was closed Monday while school district employees spent the day cleaning up damage to the school.

6 Impact leads: Write impact leads from this information:

  a The Board of Regents (or the governing body of universities in your state) has approved an increase in rates for campus housing at your university. The biggest increase will be in residence halls, where rates will increase 14.8 percent for double-room occupancy. The current rate is $2,684, and it will increase to $3,080 next fall.

  b The Rockville City Council will meet at 7 P.M. Tuesday. The council will consider adopting an ordinance that would impose penalties for false alarms that are sent to the police department from faulty or improperly operated electronic security systems. Under the proposed ordinance, an alarm system owner would be allowed six free false alarms. The owner would have to pay a $30 penalty for each additional false alarm.

7 Attribution: Write a summary lead from the following information. Decide whether you need to include attribution.

Capt. J. Randall Ogden, a spokesman for the Tucson Fire Department (or use your local fire department spokesperson): A fire destroyed a home on East 17th Street. It was started by a cigarette that was discarded in a sofa. The fire left the husband, his wife and their four children homeless. The fire started at 1 A.M. and caused $30,000 in damages.

8 Anecdotal, focus-on-a-person lead: Write an anecdotal lead with a person focus from the following information; include a nut graph. Your focus is about the frustrations that students experience trying to park on campus because the parking department has sold too many permits.

Background: Nancy Pauw is a graduate student. One morning, she circled the parking lot east of the computer center three times before she found a parking space. Last year, there were 7,565 student parking permits sold for 3,930 spaces. "I have to get here an hour early so I can get to class on time," Pauw says. She is one of many students (on your campus) who experience the daily frustration of not finding a parking space even though they have purchased $30 and $50 permits.

9 Specific to general with nut graph: Write a soft lead, including a nut graph, that uses the specific-to-general technique to convey the following information:

Background: The General Accounting Office, the investigative arm for Congress, issued a report yesterday that said record keeping at the National Park Service is defective. The report said information in the Park Service's financial statements is inaccurate and filled with accounting errors. Property owned by the Park Service is overstated by more than $90 million, the report stated. Examples of inaccurate data in the Park Service records include a vacuum cleaner that is really worth $150 but is listed in records as worth $800,000, a dishwasher worth $350 but valued at over $700,000, and a fire truck worth $133,000 but undervalued at 1 cent.

10 Descriptive: Write a descriptive lead for a story about apartments that violate city codes and are considered hazardous but that are often rented to students anyway.

Background: You interviewed a student who lives in an attic apartment. His story is similar to the stories of many other students in this neighborhood, known as the Oread neighborhood. As you climbed the steps to his apartment, you noticed that duct tape keeps the banister in place on the stairs. You saw that the kitchen is infested with mice and roaches. The student, Ted Flis, took you to the bathroom and said it has no electricity. "It's a dump," said Flis, a senior majoring in architecture. "But it was the cheapest thing I could find." This apartment is located at 1032 Main St.

11 Narrative: Change this lead into a narrative lead:

A man threatening suicide kept police at bay for more than nine hours Sunday before he was pulled back from the ledge of a parking garage rooftop.

The man, a 36-year-old Topeka State Hospital patient and Wichita resident whose name wasn't released, threatened to jump from the south ledge of St. Francis Hospital and Medical Center's three-story parking garage at S.W. 6th St. and Mulvane.

Louis Cortez, St. Francis public safety officer, spotted the patient walking toward the ledge on the roof of the garage about 8:40 A.M. Sunday. Cortez stopped his vehicle and told the man to move away from the ledge.

The patient shook his head, "No." "I stepped out and asked him, 'Can I help you, sir?' and he said, 'I'm going to jump,'" Cortez said.

Shortly before 6 P.M., several teenagers in front of St. Francis House, 701 S.W. Mulvane, began shouting, "Don't jump!" and "It's not worth it." The patient shouted back, "You want to see me jump?"

But the teens distracted the patient just long enough for Cortez to grab him around his waist and pull him from the ledge.

12 Leads analysis: Use two or three different newspapers or online news sites so you can see if they have different writing styles for news stories. Find leads as directed, and attach copies of the leads to your report.

  a Find an example of a descriptive lead, an anecdotal lead and a narrative lead. Label each type. Analyze whether your examples are effective, and explain why or why not.

  b Find three feature news leads you like. Explain what techniques the writers used and why you like them.

  c Find three feature leads you do not like, and explain why.

13 Print to broadcast: Using your local or campus newspaper, change the leads on three newspaper stories to broadcast form.

☞ **Featured Online Activity** Log on to the book Web site for Chapter 8 and use the leads exercise to improve your skills in writing several types of leads. Access the Web site at

academic.cengage.com/masscomm/rich/ writingandreportingnews6e

Coaching Tips

Write a first draft; mark it "fix later" if you get stuck. Don't perfect every line during the drafting process.

Read your story aloud when you finish. You will hear the pacing and also catch errors.

Use lists to move the reader quickly through parts of the story.

Don't struggle to get the perfect lead. Write a few leads and continue writing the story; choose a preferred lead later.

Test your endings to see if you have overwritten or strained your last paragraph. Put your hand over your last paragraph and see if the previous paragraph is a better ending.

Try free-writing. If you are stuck organizing your story, put away your notes and just write what you remember. Then plug in the facts and quotes from your notes.

I know most newspaper readers don't read all the way to the endings. But I tell myself if I do it well enough, they'll read mine.

Ken Fuson, reporter, *The Des Moines* (Iowa) *Register*

9

Story Organization

Ken Fuson

When Ken Fuson was in high school, he played the drums. He still hears the beat of the drums when he writes his stories for *The Des Moines* (Iowa) *Register:* "I think a lot about rhythm," he says.

"I work at getting the tap, tap, tap. I want to make sure every paragraph doesn't sound the same." To achieve that musical quality, Fuson reads all his stories out loud.

Rhythm, also called pacing, helps readers move through the middle of a story. And Fuson wants to make sure that they read to the end. "I probably spend as much time on the ending as I do on the beginning," he says. He thinks a good ending makes a story memorable. "If readers remember a story I wrote, that's better than money." One time, after he won a prestigious award from the Gannett Co., which owns the *Register,* he told company executives that editors who cut the ending of a story should be executed.

Getting from the beginning to the end of a story isn't a haphazard process for Fuson. He carefully plans the parts of his stories. First, he thinks: "I look for ways to show conflict and to describe the mood. I think a lot about what is the right tone and the personality of the story."

Then he starts organizing his material. "I type up all my notes. I select what I want to use. Then I put that information in an order. I need to know where I'm going and what the ending will be. Once you know what you're going to say and the way you're going to say it, then you can worry about what goes first."

And worry he does. "The first paragraph has to be perfect," he says. "And the second paragraph has to be perfect. I wish I had learned a better way of writing instead of worrying about what I'm going to say first." It may not be the best writing process, but it works well for Fuson, who consistently wins awards.

The Writing Process

If you are going to take a road trip, chances are you would check a map before you go. When you are writing a news story, you also need a plan. Here are four steps in the writing process:

- Conceive
- Collect

- Construct
- Correct

Before you turn on your computer, you need to turn on your mind. The writing process begins long before you write your story. Writers often struggle when they begin to construct their stories because they just starting writing without a plan.

Conceive the Idea

The focus is the main idea of the story. If you don't have a clear focus for your story, you won't have a well-written story. The idea for a story may start with an assignment from an editor, coverage of a breaking news event or a topic you proposed for a story. Although you may have an initial idea for your story before you do the reporting, that focus can change after you gather the information. When you are covering a breaking news event, you won't know the focus until you get the facts and other information. These questions will help you determine a focus before, during and after the reporting and writing process.

- What struck you as most interesting or important?
- What is most newsworthy?
- What is the main point of the story that readers or viewers need to know or would want to know?

Collect the Information

When you are gathering information, consider the same points for your focus. In many cases the main idea of the story will develop as you gather the information.

- Make sure that you get the basics: who, what, when, where, why and how.
- Take good notes by jotting down details of your observations as well as the quotes, facts and comments from your sources, especially on breaking news stories.
- Tape interviews for sound bites to include on the Web, but don't rely on tape or video recorders to take the place of notes. Mark your notes to indicate the sound bites. This will help you organize your story later when you edit the audio or video.
- Make notations about information you will need to get after your interviews and additional background you may need.
- Highlight or underline your notes for important points, good quotes or interesting information that you might want to include in your story.
- Gather anecdotes—brief stories from sources about their experiences.
- Consider the focus as you do the reporting. What stands out in your mind as the most important idea or main newsworthy idea?
- Think ahead. If you will file the story on deadline for the Web or a television broadcast, gather information for the next step in the action or an updated version for the next broadcast or the next day's newspaper.

- Collect documents or complete information for the Web.
- Verify names and spelling.

Construct the Story

Find the Focus   Once again, consider your focus and decide if you need to change it. Write a focus sentence on top of your story before you begin. How can you find your focus now that you have gathered the information?

Jacqui Banaszynski, a Pulitzer-Prize winning journalist, uses a method she calls the "stoplight technique" to find focus. Imagine that you are at a stoplight and you have 30 seconds to tell your story before the light changes. Chances are that in 30 seconds you will express the focus.

Here are some additional tips:

- Write a headline for your story. Express the focus in fewer than five words.
- What is the most important or current information (especially if you are writing for broadcast)?
- What is most newsworthy?
- If you were posting a comment box or asking readers to write a blog or take a quiz on the Web, what is the main point that would elicit responses?

Plan an Order   Go through your notes and highlight or mark important quotes and facts. Then jot down a preliminary order in your notes or at the top of your story document. You can change the order when you start writing if you don't like your initial plan. Some writers need a very complete outline; others need only a few words to plan their stories. Here are some ways to organize your story:

Topics: List all the main points you want to cover. Decide which are the most important and which point naturally follows another. Arrange information from the most important to the least important. Then organize all the information—quotes or sound bites and supporting facts—related to the topics you listed.

Highlights: If you were writing a highlights box, what would your main points be? Use the highlights as a guide for organization by topics. Some Web news sites include a highlights box to summarize the main points of the story, so this technique can be useful for online stories as well.

Time Sequence: Does the story have distinct time elements? Can it be arranged in a chronology? For example, start with the present (what is happening now), go to the past (background or how the situation developed), return to the present and end with the future.

Sources: If you have several sources, you might organize the story by using all the comments from one source in one part of the story and then placing the next source's comments in another block and so on instead of going back and forth among sources.

Question/Answer: What question does one topic or paragraph raise that needs to be answered in the next paragraph?

Images and Sound Bites: For broadcast writing, arrange your story around your images and sound bites. Let the video images tell the story.

Ending: Decide how you want to end the story. Do you have a strong quote to put in the end or information about a future action? What lasting impression do you want to leave?

Free-Writing: If you are stuck and can't figure out an order, put away your notes and just write what you remember. Then review what you have written, and arrange it in an order that seems logical. Plug in quotes and facts later.

Correct the Story

Self-editing is a crucial step. Before you turn in your story, revise and correct your story. Even if you are writing on deadline, don't skip this step. These tips apply to all types of media.

- **Read your story aloud:** If you are writing for broadcast, reading the copy aloud is essential. This technique is also one of the best self-editing steps you can take for print publication. Your ears will catch cumbersome words or phrases that your eyes don't notice.
- **Basics:** Have you covered the basics—who, what, when, where, why or how—and in what order? Which of these elements is the most important (usually who or what and when)?
- **Context:** Have you included background or context to help the readers and viewers understand the significance of the story?
- **Check accuracy:** Double-check the spelling and titles of names and accuracy of facts.
- **Avoid adjectives:** Show, don't tell. Let your video tell the story if you are writing for broadcast. Let details and sources describe actions and feelings.
- **Use vigorous verbs:** Have you used strong, active verbs? Can you rearrange sentences that start with "There is" or "There are" and substitute active verbs?
- **Purge any parroting:** If your transitions repeat a quote or sound bite, rewrite or cut them. Let the quotes and sound bites move the story naturally.
- **Cut useless or excess words:** If you had to cut your story, what words, sentences or paragraphs could you eliminate?
- **Edit the pace:** Do you have a good mix of short and long sentences—most of them short? Does your story flow?
- **Check grammar:** Do your subjects, verbs and pronouns agree? Is your grammar correct?
- **Cut jargon:** Eliminate bureaucratic language and jargon (such as "hot topic") or other clichés. Does the story sound the way you would tell it to a friend?
- **Read aloud again.** Walk away from your story for an hour or at least a few minutes (unless you are on deadline) and reread it with a fresh approach.

ETHICS

Dilemma: You are writing a story about immigration, and you have interviewed a source who has entered the country illegally. The source provides some poignant quotes for your story, but he or she does not speak English well. Should you clean up the source's quotes so they are in proper English or should you use the quotes exactly as they were spoken with grammatical errors? If you are interviewing a politician who speaks ungrammatically, should you quote that source by using his or her exact words or should you clean up the quotes? Should you treat these sources differently?

Discussion: Legally it is OK to clean up quotes as long as you don't alter the meaning of the source's comments. In a 1991 case, *Masson v. New Yorker magazine*, U.S. Supreme Court Justice Anthony Kennedy wrote: "If an author alters a speaker's words but effects no material change in meaning, including any meaning conveyed by the manner or fact

of expression, the speaker suffers no injury to reputation that is compensable as a defamation." The decision came when a psychoanalyst, Jeffery Masson, sued *New Yorker* writer Janet Malcolm for libel and claimed she had made up quotes that defamed him in her article.

Editors are divided on this issue of altering quotes. Many journalists insist that a quote must be the exact words of the source, while others insist that minor changes are not only acceptable; they are often necessary.

The ethical issues in cleaning up quotes involve sensitivity, especially in stories involving a multicultural society. Would exact quotes embarrass your subject? What is your purpose in using the exact quotes? Would paraphrasing the material accomplish your purpose as well?

When in doubt, consider these guidelines from the Society of Professional Journalists Code of Ethics:

- Journalists should be honest, fair and courageous in gathering, reporting and interpreting information.
- Test the accuracy of information from all sources and exercise care to avoid inadvertent error. Deliberate distortion is never permissible.

The Radio-Television News Directors' Association offers similar advice in its code of ethics:

- Professional electronic journalists should pursue truth aggressively and present the news accurately, in context, and as completely as possible.
- Professional electronic journalists should present the news with integrity and decency, avoiding real or perceived conflicts of interest, and respect the dignity and intelligence of the audience as well as the subjects of news.

Story Structure

The two most common problems of professional writers are writing the lead and organizing the story. If you have followed the previous step in planning your story, you have a head start in organizing it. Here are some techniques to help you write well from start to finish:

Leads

Many writers insist that they can't write the rest of the story until they find their lead. That is a luxury that doesn't exist in these days of convergence when you need to file the story quickly for online delivery. If you can't figure out how to write your lead, don't suffer. Start with a focus sentence or a nut graph or write a few leads and choose the best one later. To find your lead, ask yourself these questions:

- What will hook the reader's or viewer's attention?
- What does the reader or viewer need to know first or most to understand the story?
- What is the story about?
- Check your notes and write a sentence that will lead into your strongest quote.

Once you start writing your story, you may develop an idea for a better lead. Check the chapter on leads for suggestions on ways to write direct leads or anecdotal ones.

Transition Techniques

To keep the middle of your story moving, you may need good transitions so that one paragraph flows smoothly to another. The best transition is no transition—a story so well organized that one thought flows naturally into another. But sometimes you need to pave the way for one paragraph to get to the next one.

- Use cause and effect: If one paragraph raises a question, answer it in the next paragraph or elaborate with an example or quote. Try to anticipate questions the reader might have.
- To introduce a new source after a previous source, use a statement about or from the new person. For example:

A controversial proposal that would require all Temple University undergraduates to take a course related to racism drew strong support yesterday from a racially mixed group of students and faculty members who testified at a campus hearing.

Statement introducing speaker

Anika Trahan, a junior, said the proposed requirement would encourage more dialogue among students who come to the university from largely segregated neighborhoods.

"They (white students) come from communities where they are never able to interact with black people," she said.

But opinion was sharply divided on whether the course should focus on black-white relations in America or include racism against Asian Americans and other groups.

Molefi K. Asante, chairman of Temple's African American studies department, contended that the requirement should focus on the white racism toward African Americans because that has been "the fundamental pattern of racism" in the United States.

Transition to new speaker

A white student, sophomore Amy Dixon, agreed. "Our predominant problem on campus is black-white relations," she said.

Transition to new speaker

—Huntly Collins, *The Philadelphia Inquirer*

Repetition of Key Words This is a technique that provides smooth transitions during the writing process or serves as a thought bridge to get you from one concept to the next. The technique is also known as "stitching" because it helps stitch one paragraph to the other. A word or phrase from one paragraph can be repeated in the next. In broadcast news, anchors often use repetition of key words to segue from one story to another.

As you write, look at the last sentence in each paragraph and find a key word that will lead you to the next paragraph. That key word can trigger a question you can answer in the next paragraph, or it can serve as a bridge for the next thought. You may either repeat the word in the next sentence as a transitional device or just use the concept of the word as a bridge to the idea in your next paragraph. Don't overuse the exact repetition of key words for transitions because your writing may become boring.

In the following example, the underlined key words serve as transitions to the next thought. In some cases the writer repeats the key word, and in others he uses it as a thought bridge.

Key word **drugs** *serves as a bridge to the next thought*

What we need are some mandatory classes that you would attend before you attempted to move your household. These would be much more useful than those classes you go to before you have a <u>baby.</u>

When you have a <u>baby,</u> you are surrounded by skilled professionals, who, if things get really bad, give you <u>drugs,</u> whereas nobody performs any such service when you move. This is wrong.

The first thing the burly men should do when they get off the moving van is seize you and forcibly inject you with a <u>two-week supply of sedatives,</u> because moving, to judge from its effect on my wife, is far more stressful than childbirth.

Even in the worst throes of <u>labor,</u> even when she had become totally irrational and was making voices like the ones Linda Blair made in "The Exorcist," only without the aid of special effects, my wife never once suggested that we should put wet, filthy scum-encrusted rags, which I had been cleaning toilets with, into a box and have paid professionals to transport them 1,200 miles so we could have them in our new home.

—Dave Barry, *syndicated columnist*

Key word **childbirth** *serves as a bridge to elaborate the idea*

Here is another example of this technique:

With a relentless sun beating on him as he cut through fields, swamps and shaggy forests, Earl Davis always looked ahead to the next <u>leg</u> of the project.

The <u>legs</u> were long and stretched interminably. The crews made slow progress. Mosquitoes whined about their heads, and snakes thrashed away when the right-of-way crews stumbled across them. . . .

Davis, who had lived in Pinellas County for almost 50 years, sympathized and <u>suffered</u> with them (the road builders).

The <u>suffering</u> wouldn't be over for a long time.

—Mark Davis, *The Tampa* (Fla.) *Tribune*

Transitions for Background To insert background, you can use words and phrases, such as *Previously* or *In the past,* or specific time elements, such as *Two months ago.* If you are going to recount part of the story chronologically, you can set it up with a phrase like *The incident began this way.*

To get from one point to another, especially in stories about meetings where several issues are discussed, you can use transitional phrases: *In another matter, On a related issue, Other items discussed included.*

Blocking Sources   Do you get annoyed when a person's last name is mentioned in a story on a second reference but you have forgotten who the person is? After a person is identified by full name once, newspapers use only the last name if the person is mentioned again in the story. If only one or two people are mentioned in a story, this device isn't confusing. But the reader will have trouble remembering sources by their last names if the story refers to several of them.

The blocking technique helps eliminate such confusion. It is a way of organizing information by using sources in blocks instead of placing them sporadically throughout a story. The problem of last names on second reference is even more confusing for online readers when a story spans several screens or Web pages.

Here is how the blocking technique works to avoid this problem: When you have three or more sources in a story, use each source once or in consecutive paragraphs, blocking all his or her comments in one place. Do not weave back and forth with sources unless you have fewer than three. If you must use a source again in another part of the story, reintroduce the person by title or some reference to remind the reader of the person's identity. The exception is a well-known source, such as the mayor, the governor, the president, a celebrity or the central character in a story. The name of such a source may be placed anywhere in the story without confusing the reader.

The blocking concept may also be used for a story that has several different supporting concepts. After you have determined your main focus, plan an order for each supporting point. Block all the backup material related to that point. If you have several people discussing several ideas, as in a meeting, you will have to be selective about which comments to include. Even in a story arranged by topics, you still should try to block information from each source—if you have more than three—in one place so that you don't confuse the reader by weaving too many people throughout the story.

In this example, notice how the sources are organized in blocks:

Beginning next spring, smokers at Lansing Community College will have to take their habit outside.

Focus   The LCC Board of Trustees has approved a smoke-free campus at the end of the next spring term. It is expected to make LCC the first campus with totally smoke-free facilities in the state.

1 (first speaker)   "It gives a year for the thing to settle in and for people to accept it and adjust to it," said Erik Furseth, chairman of the board.

Key word buildings leads to next thought   Under its current policy, smoking is permitted only in designated areas, such as portions of cafeterias. When the new policy takes effect, smoking will be banned in all parts of all buildings.

2 (second speaker)   "We do have a smoking area. It's outside the building," said Trustee Judith Hollister.

3 (third speaker)   Karen Krzanowski, assistant executive director of the American Lung Association of Michigan, said she believes that LCC is the first community college in the state to adopt a smoke-free policy.

"We're delighted," she said. "I think they are taking the lead and others will follow." A growing number of employers statewide are banning smoking,

Krzanowski said. Those include Michigan Bell, Comerica and the state Public Health Department.

LCC trustees adopted the policy after holding hearings and developing a comprehensive report on smoking. The one-year delay in implementation is designed to give employees and students a chance to prepare.

4 (fourth speaker)

The college will offer assistance to people trying to quit, perhaps by offering smoking cessation sessions, said Jacqueline Taylor, vice president for college and community relations.

LCC also will develop an education program to explain the policy and encourage people not to smoke.

"I think it's great," said Elizabeth Saettler, a non-smoker from Owosso.

5 (fifth speaker)

Sherry Brettin of East Lansing said she could accept the new policy. "I certainly think it benefits the majority of people," she said. "I smoke, but I'll go outside. It doesn't bother me," she said.

6 (sixth speaker)

—Chris Andrews,
Lansing (Mich.) *State-Journal*

The blocking technique is only a guideline and should not be adhered to strictly when the story order would be more logical if sources were repeated in different places throughout the story.

Convergence Coach

In a convergent media environment, where immediacy is required for posting news online or on TV before print, you may not think you have time for the correction step in the writing process. But you can actually save time writing because you can write your copy quickly if you know that you can revise it. The writing process tips in this chapter apply to all media, but here are some suggestions targeted to broadcast copy in the correction step:

■ Read your copy aloud.

■ Check your copy to see if the text corresponds to your video. Does the text lead smoothly to sound bites? Does the video enhance your story?

■ Now read your text aloud without viewing the video. Is the text clear?

■ Remove adjectives that express your opinion, such as descriptive terms—tragic, frightening, beautiful, etc.

■ Do your transitions flow smoothly from the videotape to the text?

■ Remove and revise any transitions that repeat sound bites.

■ Rewrite any bureaucratic terms such as police lingo (perpetrator) or government jargon (infrastructure) and others.

■ Check spelling and grammar and make sure names are spelled and pronounced correctly.

■ Check your facts for accuracy.

And take this writing process tip from Wayne Freedman, a TV reporter who wrote the book *It Takes More than Good Looks To Succeed at Television News Reporting:* "Here's a trade secret—with a proper beginning and ending, the middle of a story will usually take care of itself. You'll always find it easier to write a piece if, before leaving a location, you already know how it will start and finish. Think of this as planning your entrance and exit routes."

Making Middles Move

If you have planned a good entrance and exit, how do you maintain interest in the middle of the story? Transitions are one method, but these other writing techniques will help keep the middles moving:

Vary the Pace Follow long sentences with short ones. Pacing is even more important in broadcast writing when you are writing for the ear. If you use complex sentences, follow them with short, punchy ones:

Pamela Lewiston thought she was leading a normal life as the daughter of Dr. Normal Lewiston, a respected Stanford University physician, and his wife, Diana.

She thought wrong.

Her father had been married to—and lived with—two women besides her mother, all at the same time. His carefully managed deception ended in a cascading series of revelations after his death from a heart attack in August.

—S. L. Wykes, *San Jose* (Calif.) *Mercury News*

Parallelism Parallel sentences help the reader move quickly through the story. Parallel construction means the sentences are worded in the same grammatical order. Some of the words can be repeated for effect, especially those at the beginning of sentences. In this example, the writer uses parallelism at the beginning of the story, but you can use it anywhere:

Rudolph Almaraz kept his battle with AIDS his personal business, even though his professional business was surgery.

He didn't tell his patients. He didn't tell officials at Baltimore Johns Hopkins Hospital, where he was a cancer surgeon.

He didn't tell the doctor who bought his medical practice earlier this year.

But now the case of Dr. Almaraz, who died of AIDS on Nov. 16 at the age of 41, has frightened his patients.

—Matthew Purdy, *The Philadelphia Inquirer*

Pacing Vary the length of sentences. Follow long ones with short, punchy ones.

On New Year's Eve Lisa Botzum visited the emergency room of the Hospital of the University of Pennsylvania, complaining of nausea and vomiting. She was given a pregnancy test. She was elated by the result.

Few others were.

—Loretta Tofani, *The Philadelphia Inquirer*

Dialogue When possible and appropriate, use dialogue in your story. It works well in feature stories, news stories about council meetings and especially in stories about court cases. For broadcast stories, sound bites and video constitute dialogue. In this print feature story, "13: Life at the Edge of Everything," *St. Petersburg* (Fla.) *Times* reporters spent several months reporting about the lives of middle school students. Then they wrote a series in dramatic storytelling form, making extensive use of dialogue to put the reader on the scene. In this section, Joanne, the mother of a teenage girl, Danielle, is worried about her daughter, who is starting to date:

> A few months ago, when Danielle started to show more interest in boys, Joanne cornered her.
>
> "You're not doing anything, are you?"
>
> Danielle looked at her. "What do you mean?"
>
> "You're not doing anything with that boy that calls up?"
>
> Meaning Nelson.
>
> "No," said Danielle. "We're just friends."
>
> —Thomas French, Monique Fields, Dong-Phuong Nguyen, *St. Petersburg Times*

BBI: Boring but Important Stuff   Many stories, especially government stories, need explanation or background that could be boring. Don't put all the boring information in a long block. Break it into small paragraphs and place it where it will fit, but not in one long, continuous section. Also consider graphics as a way to present statistics and other information that could clog a story.

Simple Sentences for Complex Information   The more difficult the information is, the simpler your sentences should be. Use short sentences with simple construction, especially for bureaucratic information that would be hard for the reader to comprehend. This excerpt is from a story explaining how the judiciary committee of the Connecticut legislature works:

> The judiciary is one of the legislature's busiest. By the end of the five-month session in June, the committee will have drafted, amended, approved, or killed about 500 bills—about 14 percent of the 3,649 bills filed with the Senate and House clerks.
>
> Judiciary's 14 percent will touch nearly everyone. The committee considers matters of life and death, marriage and divorce, freedom and imprisonment.
>
> This year's issues include surrogate parenting, birth certificates, and adoption. The death penalty and letting the terminally ill die. Longer prison sentences and home release. Committing the mentally ill to hospitals.
>
> —Mark Pazniokas, *The Hartford* (Conn.) *Courant*

Lists   Itemizing information is an excellent way to keep the flow going through the middle of your story. Lists work well in results of studies, reporting statistical information or summarizing the main points in government actions. They also work well on the Web where readers tend to scan stories. You may use lists in a couple of ways:

- To itemize a group of statistics or any other cumbersome information
- To highlight key points within a story

Lists are usually preceded by a dot called a "bullet" or by some other graphic device as in this example.

A 10-year analysis of enrollment patterns at Kansas University and five other state universities revealed two dating tips for college students:

■ Men hoping to improve dating prospects might consider attending Emporia State University, where 60 percent of students are women.

■ Women interested in more dating opportunities should look to Kansas State University, the only state university in the area with more men than women.

—Tim Carpenter,
Lawrence (Kan.) *Journal-World*

Use Active Voice Whenever Possible Here's an example of active voice:

She will always remember her first story.

Here is the same sentence in passive voice:

Her first story will always be remembered by her.

The active voice has more impact.

Write Short Sentences On average, your sentences should have fewer than 25 words.

Write Simple Sentences Keep the subject and verb close together. This example shows what happens when you don't. It is from a story about school board approval of remodeling and construction projects at the city's two schools.

Those two projects—calling for construction of classrooms, office area and media center at Wakefield and construction of a new district-wide kitchen and computer lab plus remodeling projects at the high school—will be paid for by using approximately $800,000 of the district's special capital outlay fund.

Whew! That's a long sentence. The subject is *projects,* and the verb is *will be paid.* They are separated by too many words. Split it into three sentences:

One project will involve construction of classrooms, an office area and a media center at Wakefield. The other includes building a new district-wide kitchen, a computer lab and remodeling projects at the high school. The $800,000 approximate cost of the projects will be paid from the district's special capital outlay fund.

Avoid Jargon Translate bureaucratic terms into simple ones; define technical terms. Here's advice from writer George Orwell:

> Never use a metaphor, simile or other figure of speech which you are used to seeing in print. Never use a long word when a short one will do. If it is possible to cut a word out, always cut it out. Never use the passive when you can use the active. Never use a foreign phrase, a scientific word or a jargon word if you can think of an everyday English equivalent. Break any of these rules sooner than say anything outright barbarous.

Here's an example of garbled writing from the U.S. federal budget:

> Funds obligated for military assistance as of September 30 may, if deobligated, be reobligated.

Write the Way You Speak Unless you speak like the bureaucrat who wrote that budget item.

Endings

Call them lasting impressions. To many writers, the ending is as important as the beginning of the story. Unfortunately, many readers don't get that far. But if they do, you should reward them with a memorable ending.

The ending also is called the "kicker." Think of it as a clincher. It should give a summary feeling to your story without repeating any information you have stated previously.

For columnists, the ending is more important than the beginning. The twist or main point the writer is trying to make is at the end of the column. In many cases the lead could be an ending. And returning to your lead as a way to find your ending is an excellent technique.

Don't use the ending to summarize information as you might in a term paper. Instead of repeating information, cut the story to the last important point or last good quote.

The following sections describe some ways to form your endings.

Quote Kickers

The most common type of ending is the quote kicker. Look for a quote that sums up the mood or main idea of the story. When you end with a quote, put the attribution before the quote or, in a two-quote ending, after the first sentence. Do not let the last words the reader remembers be "he said."

Hotmail, the free e-mail service from Microsoft, is divulging subscribers' e-mail addresses, cities and states to a public Internet directory site that combines the information with telephone numbers and home addresses.

Hotmail customers are automatically added to Infospace's Internet White Pages directory unless they remove the check from a box in their registration form and "opt out," company officials said. . . .

John Mozena, spokesman for Coalition Against Unsolicited Commercial E-mail, said the public lists are a problem.

Last three paragraphs and quote kicker

"Spammers never do anything one-by-one," he said.

Hotmail user Chris Livermore of Redmond, Wash., said he keeps one Hotmail address private, given out only to friends. But now he gets almost 20 unwanted e-mails a week. His address is on the White Pages lists.

"Within a couple months, the account will be unusable," Livermore said. "To try to wade through about 20 spam messages to get to your own messages, it's horrible."

—*The Associated Press*

Circle Kickers

Circle kicker, which ties together the lead and the ending]

When you return to your lead for an idea to end your story in a full circle, you are using a circle kicker. Ken Fuson frequently uses this technique to devise his endings. In this example from a story about how families cope with Alzheimer's disease, Fuson repeats phrases from the lead—but ends with a twist:

"Mother, mother, mother, other, other, other. . . ."

The sound comes in short, grating bursts, like a children's record played at too high a speed.

Every day, relentlessly, another small slice of the person that once was Betty Jennings disappears. The brand of hell called Alzheimer's disease has reduced the 58-year-old woman to a stoop-shouldered, hand-wringing blabber of meaningless words and phrases.

She must be fed, bathed and diapered. Some mornings, after a particularly brutal night, Gordon Hanchett will look in the living room and see that his sister has attacked her plastic diaper, ripping it apart with her fingers and leaving small pieces littering the floor.

"It looks like a miniature snowstorm," he says.

The limits of devotion are stretched thinnest in the homes of Alzheimer's victims. Often operating on little or no sleep and frequently ruining their own physical health, family members witness the disintegration of a loved one's mind with the understanding that no matter what they do today, tomorrow will be worse.

The story continues with more about the family in particular and the disease in general. Here's how it ends:

"Mother, this mother, this other . . . Daddy, daddy, daddy."

The chatter is loud, constant and haunting. His sister's voice fills the house.

"Oh that," says Hanchett, waving his hand. "I don't even hear that anymore."

—Ken Fuson, *The Des Moines* (Iowa) *Register*

Future-Action Kickers

Many stories end with the next step in the development of an issue. But this technique only works if the story lends itself to a future element. If the next step is crucial to the story, it should be higher in the body. But if it works as a natural conclusion, then it can be the ending. It can be in the form of a statement or a quote.

> HERRING BAY, Alaska—World attention focused Friday on the attempt to rescue birds and animals from the oil spilled in Prince William Sound. Cameras in Valdez focused on the few animals saved—fewer than 20 birds and four sea otters by evening Friday. The birds on the evening news were expensive symbols for Exxon, costing more than $1,000 apiece to rescue.
>
> But on the water, the rescue efforts getting all the attention stumbled along with the air of a Sunday outing. In this bay at the north end of Knight Island, a diverse and committed group of people tried to learn to perform a futile task.

The story continues with detail about the rescue operation. Here is the ending:

> By Friday afternoon, about two miles of the shore of Herring Bay had been thoroughly searched.
>
> Only a few thousand left to go.
>
> —Charles Wohlforth,
> *Anchorage* (Alaska) *Daily News*

Climaxes

This type of ending works on stories written like fiction, where the reader is kept in suspense until the end. It is more suited to features in narrative style or short news stories that tease the reader in the beginning and compel the reader to find out what happens.

> Scott T. Grabowski sat Tuesday in the courtroom where a federal judge would determine his future, hoping that when the words were pronounced he would hear probation and not prison.
>
> But Grabowski, 27, of Greenfield, is an admitted drug dealer. Early last summer, he pleaded guilty to a charge of possessing 3 ounces of cocaine that he intended to sell on behalf of an international drug network.

The story continues with the arguments from Grabowski's defense lawyer and the prosecutor. But what sentence did he receive? The reader doesn't find out until the end.

> Finally, after a 2 ½ hour hearing, Curran (the judge) sentenced Grabowski to 30 months in prison, to be followed by three years of parole.
>
> And with a nod to the parents, Curran told Grabowski: "I'm sure their hearts are aching as they sit here today."
>
> —Jill Zuckman, *The Milwaukee Journal*

Cliffhanger, or suspense ending

Cliffhangers

Every day millions of people watch soap operas. The concept is a simple one: Give the readers or viewers a mystery, and make them want to find out what happens next. In writing, this kind of suspense ending is called a "cliffhanger." It is usually reserved for the endings of stories arranged in sections or series that will continue on another day. But it also can be used in the middle of stories to compel the reader to continue.

Cliffhangers are excellent devices for stories on the Web. At the end of a cliffhanger in the middle of a story, you could place a hyperlink to entice readers to click to the next section.

Not all stories lend themselves to cliffhangers. But many could be structured that way by putting the key points of the story on the front page and stopping with a question or suspenseful point in the last sentence before the story continues or "jumps" to another page.

This method is much more conducive to narrative storytelling, especially in a long feature, but it can be applied to hard news if the story stops at a crucial point.

This is only the beginning of a story that uses cliffhangers. Would you want to turn the page to continue reading?

In Fort Myers: Money, mercy and murder

Patricia Rosier's death was supposed to be peaceful and dignified.

She had made all the arrangements. Ordered food for the wake. Said a final goodbye to friends and family. Put the children to sleep.

On the nightstand rested a bottle of Seconals, powerful sedatives prescribed by her husband, Dr. Peter Rosier. Suicide would finally free Pat, 43, from the pain of invading cancer.

When the time came, she downed Seconals like "jellybeans," one witness recalled.

Cliffhanger

But something went wrong in the Rosier's stylish Fort Myers home that January night in 1985.

Pat wouldn't die.

Peter frantically began injecting doses of morphine to finish the job.

Pat's breathing slowed to a rasp.

But after 12 hours of the grim ritual, Pat would not die.

Finally, Pat's stepfather, Vincent Delman, decided something had to be done. Pat, he would later tell prosecutors, was suffering too much.

He took Pat's two half brothers into the bedroom and closed the door.

Twenty minutes later, the door opened. The Delmans walked out, their faces sullen. Peter was waiting in the living room, calming his ravaged nerves with a beer.

"Patty is dead," Vincent said.

After the funeral, the Delmans left Fort Myers. They carried with them the dark secret of what happened behind the bedroom door.

Another cliffhanger

On Monday, Peter Rosier, 47, is scheduled to go on trial for the first-degree murder of his wife of 22 years.

The Rosier story has it all—sex, love, wealth, murder and a major mystery: Who really killed Pat Rosier?

And another cliffhanger

—Mark Stephens and William Sabo, *Fort Myers* (Fla.) *News-Press*

On the jump page you would find out why Peter is on trial and what kind of evidence exists to try him. You also would find out why this is an unusual case: There's no body and no autopsy report. Pat's body was cremated. There are no morphine syringes; they were thrown away when she died. And there is one other unusual twist: Peter wasn't even in the room when Pat was killed.

Court stories lend themselves to this kind of dramatic structure. But so do many others.

Factual Kickers

These are strong factual statements that could sometimes substitute as leads. They are statements that summarize the mood, tone or general character of the story. They are harder to write than quote kickers, but if done well, they give the reader a powerful punch. They are truly kickers.

Strive for a very short, simple sentence that states a fact. But choose a meaningful fact that will leave a lasting impression.

Julie Sullivan is a master of the factual kicker. In the following example, she is writing about a man who lives in a run-down hotel in Spokane. This ending is a simple statement that is circular in its reference to the lead.

Here is the lead:

> Joe Peak's smile has no teeth.
>
> His dentures were stolen at the Norman Hotel, the last place he lived in downtown Spokane before moving to the Merlin two years ago.
>
> Gumming food and fighting diabetes have shrunk the 54-year-old man's frame by 80 pounds. He is thin and weak and his mouth is sore.
>
> But that doesn't stop him from frying hamburgers and onions for a friend at midnight or keeping an extra bed made up permanently in his two-room place.
>
> "I try to make a little nest here for myself," he says.

The story continues with detail about the difficulties that Peak encounters living in the Merlin. It ends with factual statements. Here are the last few paragraphs:

> When conditions at the Merlin began worsening three months ago, junkies and gray mice the size of baby rats moved in next door. He hated to see it, but he isn't worried about being homeless.
>
> He's worried about his diabetes.
>
> He's frightened by blood in his stool and sores on his gums. He wonders whether the white-staffed hospitals on the hill above him will treat a poor black man with no teeth.
>
> —Julie Sullivan, *The* (Spokane, Wash.)
> *Spokesman-Review*

Out-of-Gas Endings

You can always just end when you have no more to say. This method is appropriate for hard-news stories, particularly those structured with a summary lead and arranged with supporting points in descending order of importance. You can end on a quote, future action or another fact in the story.

Here is a story with a factual out-of-gas ending:

> TAMPA, Fla.—For the first time, a shrimper has been imprisoned for failing to use a federally mandated turtle protection device on his boat, the National Marine Fisheries Service said.

The story continues with the basic who, what, why, when and where and ends with this fact:

> The government estimates more than 11,000 sea turtles drown in shrimp nets in U.S. waters each year.
>
> —*The Associated Press*

Body Building from Start to Finish

Here is a short story that could have been written as a routine police story. The writer makes it interesting by using many of the techniques described in this chapter. Note how the writer uses good pacing, parallelism and a circle kicker:

Mystery call has police barking up wrong tree

Mystery lead

The following nail-biting police drama probably won't find its way onto the "Rescue: 911" TV show, but it's had some folks around Eldridge talking about it since it happened at the end of last week:

Short sentences

A call comes to the Eldridge police dispatcher over the 911 emergency line. The dispatcher answers and asks what the problem is.

Fragments for emphasis and drama

No response. Silence. The dispatcher can hear very heavy breathing. That's all. Pretty obvious somebody's in trouble.

Pacing: long sentence followed by short ones

Police Chief Martin Stolmeier, on patrol in the area, takes 20 seconds to get to the Frank and Paula Griggs residence, where the dispatcher's computer says the call is originating.

Key word: **still** *for parallelism*

The caller is still on the line.

Still breathing heavily. Still needing help.

Short, choppy sentences to build drama

Stolmeier arrives. Announces loudly that the police are there, begins a room-by-room search. Stolmeier knows somebody needs help. He enters the situation assuming someone may have broken into the house. Maybe some sort of struggle.

Foreshadowing

Stolmeier nears a downstairs bedroom. The dispatcher hears him over the phone getting closer. On the other side of the door is the situation—the burglar, killer or heart attack victim.

Cliffhanger

Right about now, if this were a movie, the camera would zoom in very close on Stolmeier's perspiring face and the music would be building to a crescendo of tension and you would be going crazy as Stolmeier at last comes face to face with . . . with . . .

Paragraph could also work as a climax kicker

Blaze. A 6-month-old black Labrador who seemed very energetic and very happy to see Stolmeier. In a fit of rambunctious puppyness, Blaze had knocked the phone off the wall and somehow dialed 911.

Circle kicker (returns to concept in lead)

No word on whether Blaze's phone privileges have been restricted since the incident. But they'd better not tell him about 900 numbers or the Home Shopping Network.

—Patrick Beach,
The Des Moines (Iowa) *Register*

Tips for Tightening Stories

Although you may need additional information, more often you will need to cut the story. *USA Today,* which is known for brevity, offers these guidelines to its writers for focusing, tightening and revising stories:

Squeeze a fact on every line: Allow one idea per sentence.

Focus Tightly: Think about what the real story is, and choose a slice of it. Emphasize what's new, what's coming and what it means to readers. Tell them the impact, how they can act on or use this information.

Use Impact Leads: Don't ignore the news just to be different, but avoid rehashing what readers already know. Think forward spin. Instead of writing "A jet crashed Tuesday, killing 534 people," write "Airline takeoff procedures might be overhauled after Tuesday's crash that killed 534 people." This is especially useful in broadcast news.

Make the Story Move: Make your point early. Use only the information that helps make the point.

Keep it Tight: Propel the story with punctuation. Colons, semicolons and bullets can replace some words and help the reader move faster.

Use Specific Details Instead of Adjectives: Instead of writing "the ancient windmill," refer to "the 100-year-old windmill."

Don't Over-Attribute: You don't need a "he said" after every sentence, although it should be clear where the information came from.

Use Strong, Lively Verbs: Instead of writing "There were hundreds of people in the streets to see the pope," write "Hundreds of people lined the streets to see the pope" (or *jammed, crowded* or *thronged* the streets). Sentences that start with *there* force you to use a weak *to be* verb.

Avoid Weak Transitions: A well-organized story needs only a few transitions.

Choose Quotes that Advance the Story: Avoid quotes that merely illustrate the last point made. And don't paraphrase if you have a good quote. Be selective. Don't repeat.

What Do You Think ?

Where do you struggle most when writing your stories?

- Leads
- Organization
- Transitions
- Endings
- I don't struggle at all.

Exercises

1 **Pacing exercise:** Listen to classical music or other music of your choice. With your eyes closed, draw lines on a piece of paper to express the rhythm or movements of the music. Then find a story that you think has good pacing and analyze it for the mixture of short and long sentences and paragraphs.

2 **Read aloud:** Read aloud any story you have written and note any errors you have made. Analyze how the story sounds for pacing.

3 **Endings:** Take any story you have written and try different endings, using a circle kicker, quote kicker or factual kicker.

4 **Analyze endings:** Using any local news story from your campus or community newspaper, analyze which stories have quote endings, circle kickers or factual endings. Watch your local TV news station and note how the reporters end their stories before questions from the anchor or a sign-off ending.

5 **Correction process:** Take any story you have written and check it for accuracy, grammar, spelling and other factors in the correction process.

☞ **Featured Online Activity** Log on to the book Web site for Chapter 9 to test your skills in revising stories.

academic.cengage.com/masscomm/rich/ writingandreportingnews6e

Envision your story order as a blueprint for designing a building. What shape will it take?

Consider a structure for your story when you are reporting. Does the information lend itself to a hard-news or anecdotal approach? Gather information for both types of story structures.

Gather information during the reporting process for several versions of a story: for broadcast, print and the Web.

We haven't had many names for story structures. A lot of writers get halfway through a story and don't realize that they are writing in a particular structure.

Jack Hart, writing coach and managing editor of
The (Portland) *Oregonian*

10 Story Forms

Jack Hart, writing coach

When Jack Hart coaches writers at *The* (Portland) *Oregonian,* he sounds like an architect. He talks about writing as a process and stories as structures with distinct shapes.

"Beautiful writing is built one step at a time, just like a house," he writes in his book, *A Writer's Coach: The Complete Guide to Strategies that Work.*

As managing editor and writing coach for *The Oregonian,* Hart has helped writers win Pulitzer Prizes with his methods. He tells writers to think logically when they organize their stories. He calls the process "sequencing." He says writers should organize the information in a sequence that helps readers understand how one item leads to another.

Hart also says writers should visualize a shape for their story, and he assigns names to the story shapes so writers will remember them.

"I think we are lexicon impoverished," Hart says. "We haven't had many names for story structures. I am a firm believer that if you walk through the woods and you know the names of all the plants, you'll see a lot more. A lot of writers get halfway through a story and don't realize that they are writing in a particular structure."

Hart is particularly fond of using the narrative writing structure, which is nonfiction storytelling, described later in this chapter.

Models of story structures can help you plan the organization. Your choice of structure depends on the type of material you have. Although there are many structures, the following are the most common:

Summary lead

Backup (quotes or facts)

Supporting points

Ending

Inverted pyramid structure

Inverted Pyramid

The inverted pyramid is one of the most basic story forms for print, broadcast and online news as well as news releases. It is used most often for hard-news stories. The story is structured with the most important information at the top of the story followed by supporting points in descending order of importance. It usually starts with a summary lead that gives some of the basics: who, what, when, where, why.

If you were watching a mystery TV show or movie, you would have to wait until the end to find out who was guilty. But with a story using the inverted pyramid, you tell the outcome in the lead.

The advantage of this form is that the reader gets the crucial information quickly. The disadvantage is that the reader may not read past the crucial information.

How do you decide what information should be arranged from most to least importance? Use your judgment. Some questions to ask: What will affect the reader most? What questions does the lead raise that need to be answered immediately? What supporting quotes are strongest?

This form is the primary structure for breaking news, and it is an important form for online journalism, where readers have unlimited choices. It is a useful way to let readers determine immediately whether they are interested in the story.

Regardless of the medium, stories still must be well-written to entice readers. Adding an impact paragraph—explaining how the story affects readers—is one way to strengthen the inverted pyramid. Here is an example of a basic inverted pyramid story:

Headline

Teen sentenced to read book about Holocaust

Summary headline

He must write report on "Diary of Anne Frank" for his role in cross burning on black family's lawn

Summary lead: who (delayed identification), what, why

SEATTLE—Instead of being sent to jail, a teenager was sent to the library to read the grim Holocaust tale, *The Diary of Anne Frank,* for his part in a cross burning on a black family's lawn.

Backup: who, when

Matthew Ryan Tole, 18, was sentenced Friday to read the famous story by a young Jewish girl of her family's failed attempt to escape Nazi persecution during World War II.

Supporting facts: why

King County Superior Court Judge Anthony Wartnik said Tole received a light sentence because he was not one of the leaders in the April 16 cross burning in Bothell, a suburb north of Seattle.

Supporting quote

"The Anne Frank book is great for someone to get a picture of the most extreme thing that can happen if people aren't willing to step forward and say this is wrong," Wartnik said. "I'm hoping it will make him more sensitive."

More explanation

Wartnik told him to write a book report on *The Diary of Anne Frank* within three months.

Background

Tole pleaded guilty to rendering criminal assistance in the cross burning, which involved at least a dozen Bothell High School students. The cross was built during a party at Tole's home.

Factual ending

Tole did not help build or light the cross, but some of the materials belonged to him.

—*The Associated Press*

Here is an example of an inverted pyramid story for TV news:

Lead

The Anchorage Fire Department is investigating an early morning fire in the Fairview neighborhood.

Supporting facts

Officials say the blaze started outside of the house in a pile of tires that were nowhere near an electrical or power source. Fire officials have also ruled out a carelessly discarded cigarette as the cause.

Background/ elaboration

Firefighters were called to the scene around 1:30 Wednesday morning, after two men walking by reported it to neighbors.

Sound Bite (Blayne Larsson identifier on screen)

"We were standing on the corner just talking and the first thing I saw were some flames come through the house right there and we both started running and I said we need to make sure nobody's in the house, call 911."

Factual ending

Firefighters say no one was injured in the fire.

—Yvonne Ramsay, *KTUU* (Anchorage, Alaska)
Channel 2 News

The Wall Street Journal Formula

The Wall Street Journal format starts with a soft lead, focusing on a person, scene or event. The idea is to go from the specific to the general, starting with a person, place or event that illustrates the main point of the story. The concept, whether stated or implied, is that this person or scene is one of many affected by the issue in the nut graph. The lead can be anecdotal, descriptive or narrative. It is followed by a focus graph—nut graph—that gives the main point of the story. This paragraph should explain what the story is about and why it is important (the "so what" factor).

The story then presents backup for the lead and supporting points. The body of the story is arranged topically, with one point leading to another. The ending usually comes full circle by using a quote or anecdote from the person in the lead or a future development of something mentioned in the beginning of the story.

This structure is useful for stories about trends, major issues, features, news sidebars and news events that lend themselves to a feature approach. Although it is used in newspapers throughout the country for many news and feature stories, it is named after *The Wall Street Journal* because that newspaper originated the term "nut graph" and recommended this form to its reporters many years ago as a way to humanize business stories and make them readable for all types of readers. This technique is also effective for broadcast news because viewers relate to people, so starting the story by focusing on a person affected by a problem is a good way to hook viewers.

The technique dates back to the 1950s when *The Wall Street Journal* issued this memo to its writers about how features for the newspaper should be written:

The stories generally have one theme or point. This is usually put into a one- or two-paragraph nutshell summary high up in the story. Then the rest of the piece is made to hang together by harking back to this central theme. The story should be *clearly organized* or compartmentalized along the central thread of this theme—it should not meander around without a perceptible organization.

We want to tell the story in terms of the *specific,* not in generalized or vague terms. One way we do this is to pack the story with lots of *detail.*

Another way we reduce the general situation to the specific is to give lots of colorful examples, anecdotes or small case histories to *illustrate* the overall situation we are describing.

We also lean heavily on illustrative *quotes*—attributable if possible though not necessarily so. The quotes need not be from government officials only; they could be from businessmen, shopkeepers, men-in-the-street, anyone who can shed some *color* on the situation or who can illustrate the general in specific, *individual terms.*

Be sure to include all *background* the reader might need. We can assume no prior knowledge by our readers of the subject or of financial lingo. We try to spell out all situations *with super-simplicity and clarity*—from how France's inflation has been brought about over the years to the recent economic history of Australia and what led up to its present economic situation. Please explain everything in clear-cut fashion.

We try to achieve very tight writing—short, punchy sentences and all essential information on the subject conveyed *concisely.*

At the same time, these leaders aim at being pretty *thorough* studies of the particular subject or trend. This means the inclusion of all detail and background and interpretation mentioned above. It also means we take pains to make sure the story contains the answers to every question that the story and its statements are likely to raise in the reader's mind. We can't use a story that raises questions it does not answer, so please re-check copy for this possible pitfall—and again, be sure all points are fully and *clearly explained,* and solidly *nailed down with fact.*

This is a very versatile formula that can be applied to many news and feature stories. It is useful for brightening bureaucratic stories. While you are reporting, seek out a person who is one of many exemplifying your point, or try to find an anecdote that illustrates the main point of your story.

The following story uses the *Wall Street Journal* formula. It is a trend story about casino gambling among college students. Note that the story starts with an anecdotal lead, that the sources are blocked, and that the ending is circular, returning to the person in the lead.

Soft lead

Nut graph

Backup for lead and nut graph

Supporting points: quotes, facts, anecdotes

Developments: cause/effect, explanations, points of view

Circle kicker: anecdote, description, future action related to lead

The Wall Street Journal *formula*

Casinos sinking college dreams

College students who live close to casinos may be more prone to gambling addiction. Numbers have been increasing in recent years.

By Kia Shanté Breaux

Associated Press Writer

Soft lead: focus on a person who illustrates the main point of the story

KANSAS CITY, Mo.—Michael Hudspeth started gambling when he was in junior high, shooting craps for lunch money on the cafeteria floor. When he went off to college, he played dice aboard Missouri's riverboat casinos.

His losses grew from the $2 a day his mother gave him for lunch to $2,000 he once borrowed as a student loan—and he lost that in one night.

Backup quote

"I would go to the boat every day," said Hudspeth, 24, who often skipped his classes at Missouri Western College in St. Joseph to gamble five minutes away at the St. Jo Frontier Casino. "I don't know; it's just something about all the people and excitement that keeps me going back."

Nut graph

The spread of casinos around the country may be contributing to problem gambling among college students.

Supporting information

Students who live close to casinos are more prone to gambling addiction,

said Michael Frank, a professor of psychology at Richard Stockton College in New Jersey, which has a dozen casinos in Atlantic City. "It seems to be increasing in recent years."

According to a study by Harvard Medical School's Division on Addictions, about half of the college students surveyed in the United States and Canada said they had gambled at a casino during the previous year.

At Louisiana State University in Baton Rouge, with two riverboats less than two miles from campus, a student was accused recently of bilking the school out of about $3,000 in a payroll scheme to support his gambling.

In New Jersey, "gambling is festering in every high school and college in New Jersey," said Edward Looney, director of the New Jersey Council on Compulsive Gambling. "It's absolutely epidemic. Just about any college in the country has students who gamble at racetracks and casinos."

At Kansas University, which is within an hour's drive of six casinos, students formed a Gamblers Anonymous chapter last year.

"Given that statistics show there's a tendency for younger people to develop gambling problems, it is of particular concern having casinos so

More supporting information

close to college campuses," said Steve Taylor, spokesman for the Missouri-based Casino Watch, an anti-gambling organization.

The legal age to gamble is 21 in most states, and casino operators can face big fines if a minor is caught gambling. But underage students have found ways to get in, just as they've managed to buy alcohol or get into bars.

Many use fake or borrowed ID or get through the door without being asked for proof of age. Many college students have easy access to cash either from a parent or from a student loan. Students are also flooded with credit card offers, and a parent usually is not required to co-sign.

All 11 of Missouri's riverboat casinos have adopted a program called Project 21 to remind minors that it is illegal for them to gamble and to teach staff members how to spot underage gamblers.

Jeff Hook, director of marketing at Harrah's North Kansas City Casino & Hotel, said Harrah's staff checks identification before a patron gets on the boat and again afterward if there are questions about the person's age.

Circular ending

Hudspeth was raised in Kansas City, Mo., and gambling had been around him all his life. He would borrow a driver's license from his best friend to get into the casinos, and also bet on sports, sometimes with money his mother sent him for rent. He maxed out his credit cards and took out student loans to support his addiction. He did not finish college, and instead went to work full time to pay off his debts.

A version of the Wall Street Journal formula also works well for some broadcast stories, especially when you want the lead to focus on a person to explain a larger issue, a program, a trend or a study. The structure would look like this:

- Anchor lead-in setting up the problem
- Lead focusing on a person who exemplifies a problem
- Nut graph explaining the problem
- Supporting information in sound bites, facts and other sources
- Circular ending returning to the person in the lead or main point

The following story, produced by students in a convergent media class at the University of Kansas, is a version of the *Wall Street Journal* structure.

Anchor lead-in

A fast-growing trend in tobacco products may be causing more harm than first believed. KUJH-TV's Dylan Schoonover reports that college students who use hookah tobacco may be causing greater damage to their lungs than those who smoke cigarettes.

Reporter—Lead focusing on a person

Smoking hookah is generally described as a social event that draws in experimental and young crowds for a so-called healthier and more arousing way of smoking tobacco. Many college students across the nation have caught on to this Middle Eastern tradition, including KU junior Pat Sullivan, who owns a hookah and uses it regularly.

I've read some stuff on it (hookah) and it's not a healthy alternative to smoking cigarettes, but I don't know, I think it's a lot cooler than smoking cigarettes and it's more relaxing.

Sound bite— Sullivan identifier superimposed on screen

Smoking hookah can actually be more dangerous to the lungs than cigarettes. A recent report issued by the World Health Organization claims that one 45-minute smoking session of smoking hookah

Reporter—nut graph

Supporting information introducing next source

exposes the user to as much as 200 times the volume of smoke inhaled in one cigarette.

Hazem Chahine, owner of the Hookah House, said customers smoking hookah generally do it for the company and relaxation of a session.

Sound bite with identifier of Chahine superimposed on screen

People don't smoke it all time. It's not like a cigarette and you just pick it up and smoke it, you know? Customers come in one time a week; three times a week is the maximum people you've got coming in here. I see them regularly.

Reporter—More supporting information

According to the American Cancer Society, nearly one third of all cancerous deaths results from tobacco use. Despite the risk hookah smoking is becoming

more and more popular. Eighty six percent of colleges and universities have at least one hookah lounge within close proximity of the school.

Saudis, Egyptians, Americans, Japanese, Italians, Germans, French people; all of them have a great time. We offer them drums. Basically we give them a drum so they can loosen up a little and hit it hard.

Sound bite with Chahine

Despite the health risks, Chahine is confident that students like Sullivan will continue to frequent his Hookah House.

Reporter— Circular ending

—Dylan Schoonover, *KUJH-TV News, University of Kansas*

Convergence Coach 🌐

Basic Story Structures for Broadcast

When you are writing a story for print, broadcast and online publication, you will probably rely on the two most common formats: the inverted pyramid and a version of the *Wall Street Journal* formula. Basic news stories for the Web resemble print formats, but broadcast news stories must be developed around sound and images. The broadcast story structure may be interpreted as sequences, developed around a chronology:

- Lead-in tells who or what happened
- Current situation
- Background
- Ending with current or future developments.

Another version of the inverted pyramid format for broadcast is chronological storytelling. After the hard-news lead, the story may be told from beginning to end. If the story starts with a soft lead, such as a focus on a person, the structure resembles the *Wall Street Journal* formula. As with a print story, the story is organized from the specific to the general information. It still follows a sequence developed around a basic chronology:

- Lead-in focuses on a person who exemplifies the problem
- General idea: statement of the problem or situation (equivalent to the nut graph in print writing)
- Background or past issues that led to the current situation
- Return to current or future developments

This storytelling model may be preferable for broadcast, according to Annie Lang and Deborah Potter in their article "The Seven Habits of Highly Effective Storytellers," written for Newslab, a training center for broadcasters. As they explain, "To engage your viewers, tell stories on television the way you tell them in person. Use strong, chronological narratives whenever possible. Studies have found that narrative stories are remembered substantially better than stories told in the old 'inverted pyramid' style. Whatever structure you choose, don't make viewers search their memories in order to understand your story. Give them the information they need when they need it, so they can follow each part of the story. Use words which connect the pieces of the story to each other, and which make the chronology of events clear."

Hourglass Structure

The hourglass form can start like the inverted pyramid, giving the most important hard-news information in the top of the story. Then it contains chronological storytelling for a part or for the rest of the story. This approach also works for broadcast news.

Use the hourglass structure when the story has dramatic action that lends itself to chronological order for part of the story. The technique is useful in crime or disaster stories to recount the event.

To set up the chronological narrative, you can use an overview attribution such as "Police gave the following account" or "Witnesses described the accident this way," followed by a colon. However, this type of attribution should be used only for a few paragraphs so the reader does not forget who is speaking. All quotes still need attribution. If the speaker changes, you must attribute the new source.

Advantage: Narrative storytelling in the chronological portion adds drama to the story.

Disadvantage: The chronological portion of the story may repeat some of the key information in the top of the story, making it longer than a basic inverted pyramid.

Hourglass structure

Boy, 3, shoots 16-month-old

Summary lead

TAMPA, Fla.—A 3-year-old boy shot and seriously wounded his 16-month-old half brother Thursday after he found a .32-caliber pistol under a chair cushion in the family's apartment, Hillsborough sheriff's deputies said.

Attribution

Backup for lead

Melvin Hamilton, shot once in the chest about 9:30 a.m., was flown by helicopter to Tampa General Hospital, where he was in serious but stable condition late Thursday after surgery, hospital officials said.

Attribution

Otis Neal, who pulled the trigger, did it accidentally, authorities said.

Basic inverted pyramid structure with attribution for each point

Sheriff's officials said they did not know who owned the handgun but were still investigating. Under state law, the gun's owner could be criminally liable for leaving the gun in a place where a child could get it. . . .

Observation: no attribution needed

Hours after the accident, Otis sat bewildered on a curb outside his family's apartment as television camera crews and reporters jockeyed around him. "He is saying very little. I don't think he really knows what is going on," sheriff's spokeswoman Debbie Carter said.

Facts

Otis and Melvin live with their mother, Dina Varnes, in the Terrace Oaks Apartment complex at 6611 50th St.

Overview attribution: chronological narrative begins and continues to the end

Relatives and sheriff's officials gave this account: The two youngsters were downstairs in the living room playing Thursday morning, while a 15-year-old friend of the family slept on the couch. Ms. Varnes was upstairs.

Melvin was walking around the living room when Otis found the gun under the seat cushion. He pulled the gun out and fired one shot.

Arabell Ricks, Ms. Varnes' aunt and neighbor, said she was walking to the store when her niece ran out of the apartment screaming.

"She said, 'Melvin is shot.' She said the oldest shot Melvin," Ms. Ricks said. "I went in and looked at him, and then I just ran out of the house and started praying." She said she flagged down a sheriff's deputy who was patrolling the area.

"I said, 'Lord, please don't let him die,'" Ms. Ricks said.

—Heddy Murphy, *St. Petersburg* (Fla.) *Times*

Ending reaction quote

Summary lead and backup☐
☐
Key points

• • •

List technique

List Technique

Lists can be useful in stories when you have several important points to stress. Think of a list as a highlights box within the story or at the end of the story. This technique works well for stories about studies, government stories such as meetings, and even features about people or programs if there are several key points to list. This structure is useful for online stories because readers often scan the text. It is also an effective technique for news releases, which should be brief.

When using a list for the body and ending of a story, you can start with a summary lead or a soft lead followed by a nut graph. Give some backup for the lead with quotes, facts or both. Then itemize the main points until the ending. Investigative reporters often use the list high in the story to itemize the findings of their investigation.

Limit lists in the beginnings and middles of stories to five items or fewer; lists at the end can be longer. Parallel sentence structure is most effective, but not essential, for lists. Each item should be in a separate paragraph. Lists are often used in stories about meetings to itemize actions not related to the lead. The list is preceded by "In other business" or a similar transition or sentence ending with a colon as in this example:

Finally, some facts to justify cursing at people with car phones.

A recent study of car phoning showed that drivers involved in car-phone conversations were 30 percent more likely to overlook potential hazards, such as your rear bumper.

"They were so engrossed in the phone call that they were oblivious to what was going on," said James McKnight, whose experiments with 51 drivers were the basis for the findings.

What McKnight found through controlled tests on driving simulators was this:

■ Even casual chitchat or just dialing a car phone distracted drivers enough so that they failed to respond to hazards nearly 7 percent more often.

■ When talk turned to solving simple math problems—designed to simulate business conversations—drivers failed to respond to hazards nearly 30 percent more often.

■ When engaged in casual or businesslike conversations, drivers 50 or older failed to respond to hazards 38 percent more often than younger drivers.

■ Drivers who had experience with car phones were as easily distracted as drivers who were using the phones for the first time.

—Mark Vosburgh, *The Orlando* (Fla.) *Sentinel*

Here is an example of how the list technique works in a news release:

News Release

U.S. Census Bureau News
U.S. Department of Commerce, Washington, DC. 20233
FOR IMMEDIATE RELEASE

Date   Contact information: (includes name of spokesman, phone and fax numbers and e-mail
                                                             address)

Earnings Gap Highlighted by Census Bureau Data on Educational Attainment

Adults with advanced degrees earn four times more than those with less than a high school diploma, according to tabulations released today by the U.S. Census Bureau.

The series of tables, "Educational Attainment in the United States: 2006," showed adults 18 and older with a master's, professional or doctoral degree earned an average of $79,946, while those with less than a high school diploma earned about $19,915.

The tables also showed adults with a bachelor's degree earned an average of $54,689 in 2005, while those with a high school diploma earned $29,448.

Other highlights from the tables:

- In 2006, 86 percent of all adults 25 and older reported they had completed at least high school. More than one-quarter (28 percent) of adults 25 and older had attained at least a bachelor's degree.

- High school graduation rates for women 25 and older continued to exceed those of men, 86 percent and 85 percent, respectively. However, a larger proportion of men held a bachelor's degree or higher (29 percent compared with 27 percent of women).

- Non-Hispanic whites had the highest proportion of adults with a high school diploma or higher (91 percent), followed by Asians (87 percent), blacks (81 percent) and Hispanics (59 percent).

- Minnesota and Alaska had the highest proportions of people 25 and older with a high school diploma or higher (around 93 percent).

- The District of Columbia had the highest proportion of people 25 and older with a bachelor's degree or higher (49 percent).

The package contains 14 tables of data on educational trends and attainment levels. Data are shown by characteristics such as age, sex, race, Hispanic origin, marital status, occupation, industry, nativity and period of entry, as well as metropolitan and nonmetropolitan residence. The tabulations also include data on earnings. Although the statistics provided are primarily at the national level, some data are shown for regions and states.

The data are from the 2006 Current Population Survey's Annual Social and Economic supplement, which is conducted in February, March and April at about 100,000 addresses nationwide.

Statistics from sample surveys are subject to sampling and nonsampling error. For more information on the source of the data and accuracy of the estimates, standard errors and confidence intervals, go to Appendix G of www.census.gov/apsd/techdoc/cps/cpsmar06.pdf.

ETHICS

You are covering a deadly automobile accident in your community. When you arrive on the scene, the bodies of two victims are still on the ground. A third person covered in blood is weeping beside one of the victims. Police tell you that the accident was caused by a drunken driver, who has been taken into custody. You want to convey the deadly consequences of drunken driving in your story. Should you use the graphic images of the bodies and the blood-soaked survivor?

How do you know when to use disturbing images?

The Radio/Television News Directors' Association suggests that before you air graphic content, consider the following questions:

- What is the journalistic purpose behind broadcasting the graphic content? Does the display of such material clarify and help the audience understand the story better? Is there an issue of great public importance

involved such as public policy, community benefit or social significance?

- Is the use of graphic material the only way to tell the story? What are your alternatives?

- If asked to defend the decision to your audience or the stakeholders in the story, such as a family member, how will you justify your decision? Are you prepared to broadcast your rationale to your audience? If not, why?

Question/Answer Format

Organizing a story by questions and answers is an effective technique for print and Web stories, and it can also be effective in some news releases. The Q and A, as it is commonly called, is often used for profiles, and it can be a helpful way to explain issues such as a budget increase or any controversial proposal. Even though the answer part of the story is verbatim quotes, the writer still has to be selective about which questions and answers to include from a lengthy interview. Some stories in this format just use Q for the question and A for the answer while others use names or initials for the questions and answers as in the following example. Here is an interview from the University of Alaska Anchorage college newspaper, the *Northern Light,* which used the question/answer technique in a profile of a professor:

Mariano Gonzales, Associate Professor of Art

Northern Light: How long have you been teaching?

Mariano Gonzales: Full time since '88, part time since '80.

NL: How have you changed your style since you started teaching?

MG: I have much more experience now, and I have a better idea of what works in sharing knowledge and ideas with students. (Or, I'm an older guy who hates to waste time.)

NL: What have you taught at UAA and what are you currently teaching?

MG: I have taught a wide range of art subjects: drawing, painting, printmaking, metalsmithing, photography, digital art and graphic design. I am currently focusing on color and design (an arts foundation course), computer art and design, illustration and color photography.

NL: What rewards do you personally get from teaching?

MG: Teaching is like showing visitors what's cool about where you live. You get a charge out of hearing the sounds of appreciation, even if the sounds are barely audible.

NL: Where did you go to school? What was your major?

MG: I earned a bachelor's from UAA, majoring in painting (anthropology minor), and a Master of Fine Arts from the Rhode Island School of Design in metalsmithing in '79.

NL: What drew you to this field?

MG: The discipline of art, in its purest form, is an analogue or the core of all that is worthwhile in humanity. Also, I thought I could make a living at it.

NL: What was your worst or most interesting job as a student?

MG: I created Alaska "artifacts" for the tourist trade. It was good practice, not enough money, and occasionally now I find these items at thrift stores. Fortunately no one has proof that I did them.

NL: Born and raised?

MG: I was born in El Paso, Texas, in '51, moved to Anchorage in '59 and have been a resident ever since.

NL: Favorite movie(s)?

MG: Anything by John Waters, Tim Burton, the Coen Bros, Jean-Pierre Jeunet and Michael Moore.

NL: Favorite book, poem or screenplay?

MG: Frankly, I can't read anything that doesn't have the word "spank" in the title.

NL: Favorite music or artist?

MG: Among my favorite artists are Miles Davis, Jimi Hendrix, Stravinsky, George Tooker, George and Robert Crumb, Robert Williams . . . the list goes on.

NL: What are your favorite pastimes and hobbies?

MG: These days my favorite pastime is stewing about the medieval darkness that has descended on my country and creating art that hopefully illuminates.

NL: What are you most passionate about in life?

MG: Finding the time to do what I need to.

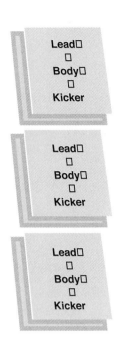

Sections technique

Sections Technique

This is a technique of dividing a story into sections, like book chapters, and separating them by a graphic device such as a large dot or a large capital letter. It works best for in-depth stories such as investigations or long features. The most effective section stories have good leads and good endings for each section. This form lends itself to cliffhanger endings for each section or for each day's installment if the story is presented as a series. Think of the sections as separate chapters, complete in themselves but tied together by the overall focus and story plot. This technique is used often in nonfiction storytelling called "narrative writing."

One common way to organize section stories is by points of view. For example, in a story about a controversial government issue, such as a new landfill, you could arrange the story in sections for each group affected by the proposal.

The other way frequently used to organize section stories is by time frames—starting with the present, then moving to the past for background and back to present developments, and ending with the future. Although the order can be flexible, the opening section must contain a nut graph explaining why you are telling the reader this story now. This technique is very effective for stories written in narrative style.

To determine whether your story is suitable for sections, envision subheads for it. Then decide if you have enough information in each subhead group to warrant a separate section.

The following story uses a combination of points of view and time sequences to organize the sections. This is written in dramatic narrative form, using storytelling that reconstructs the event. Notice how the sections are structured as separate chapters with kicker endings.

What Do You Think

When you read a news story online, which form do you prefer:

- Inverted pyramid
- Lists
- Hourglass
- Sections
- Question/answer
- I don't read news stories online

They got out alive, but no one was spared

BOULDER, Colo.—For weeks after the crash, David Hooker found the love notes his fiancee had hidden around the house.

In the medicine cabinet: "David, I love you this much."

In the sock drawer: "Poo—Here's a hug for you! Susan."

In the silverware tray: "I'll miss you! Take care."

Five months have passed since Susan Fyler boarded United Airlines Flight 282. Hooker carefully stacks the yellow slips of paper into a neat pile on the corner of his dresser, next to the framed photographs of Fyler and the mahogany box that holds her ashes.

***

This paragraph tells why you are reading this story now

Less than a half-hour away in Denver, Garry Priest can't sleep.

He watched a movie—he doesn't even remember what it was about—and one scene stuck. A woman is thrown from a car and the pavement scrapes her skin raw.

Suddenly it was July 19 again and Priest was back in Sioux City, Ia., escaping from the plane, racing along the runway, seeing the debris, the charred metal, the boy's body.

Then he thinks of Christmas.

And his eyes will not close.

***

This section gives the crucial information that ties the story together

Five months ago, they were strangers, bound only by an airplane flight.

Susan Fyler was headed to Ohio to surprise her parents with news of her engagement. Garry Priest was going to Chicago on business.

Both boarded Flight 232 in Denver. She sat in seat 31K, he in seat 15G. Fyler was one of 112 people killed in the crash. She was 32. Priest was one of 184 survivors. He is 23.

For those most directly affected—the family and friends of the victims, the survivors and their families—the holidays are proving that time has not healed all wounds. . . .

Five months later, they are strangers, but David Hooker and Garry Priest share a common grief.

***

This section is about David Hooker and how he is dealing with the loss of his fiancee

Every night, David Hooker walks into his bedroom, lights a candle and shares his day with Susan Fyler. Shortly after the crash, a friend admonished Hooker to stop feeling sorry for himself and to ask Fyler for guidance.

"I asked Susan to come live with me inside my body and to stay alive inside my body," he says, "and right after I did that, I felt a very dramatic change going on in me. I just felt all this energy coming over me."

After he lights the candle, Hooker may read the Lord's Prayer or flip through the love notes Fyler left him or look at the five photographs on his dresser.

***

It didn't make sense.

Why, Garry Priest wondered, were people acting this way? He had survived one of the worst airplane disasters in U.S. history. He had seen horrible things, scenes that made his legs shake, pictures he will remember the rest of his life.

So why was everyone calling him lucky?

"People want to pinch you," he says. "They say, 'Let's play bingo,' or 'Let's buy a lottery ticket.' They pat your head.

"I don't feel lucky at all. If I was lucky, I wouldn't have been on that plane. Nobody would have been on the plane."

This section gives the story from Garry Priest's point of view

***

They are strangers, but Garry Priest would like David Hooker to know that he, too, mourns Susan Fyler.

"Could you do me a favor?" Priest asks. "Could you tell all the people who lost loved ones and all the people who survived that I wish them a merry Christmas and that my thoughts and prayers and love are with them?"

—Ken Fuson, *The Des Moines* (Iowa) *Register*

Two more sections follow before this ending section

Exercises

1 **Inverted pyramid exercise:** Organize the information for this story in the inverted pyramid order for print or broadcast. Here are your notes, based on a story from The Associated Press:

Who: Connecticut State Police

What: Ordered ban of hand-held radar guns

When: Yesterday

Where: Meriden, Conn.

Why: Because of concerns that troopers could develop cancer from long-term exposure to the radiation waves emitted by the devices. The ban was ordered as a precaution while researchers study the possible links between cancer and use of the devices.

How: The ban affects 70 radar guns, which will be withdrawn from service. State troopers will continue to use radar units with transmitters mounted on the outside of their cruisers.

Source: Adam Berluti, a state police spokesman

Backup information: "The feeling here is to err on the side of caution until more is known about the issue," Berluti said. "The whole situation is under review." The move is considered to be the first of its kind by a state police agency. It comes two months after three municipal police officers in Connecticut filed workers' compensation claims, saying they developed cancer from using handheld radar guns.

2 *Wall Street Journal* **formula exercise:** Here are some excerpts from a story that was originally written according to *The Wall Street Journal* formula by Matt Gowen of the *Lawrence* (Kan.) *Journal-World.* Rearrange the paragraphs to conform to *Wall Street Journal* style. Use an anecdotal lead followed by a nut graph and a circular ending.

College students are most susceptible to online obsession, experts say

Jonathan Kandell, assistant director of the counseling center at the University of Maryland, has found that college students—especially those in the 18 to 22 age range—are quite susceptible to an Internet obsession. Kandell, an assistant professor of psychology at Maryland, recently published his theories in the journal "CyberPsychology and Behavior."

A few years ago, Stacie Kawaguchi started tinkering with the Internet. She clicked her mouse, surfed around and delved into an international pen-pal site. At the time a Kansas University graduate student in botany, Kawaguchi "met" folks from Canada, France, Japan and Brazil. Through the Internet, she even met her eventual fiancé, a Ph.D. candidate in engineering at Virginia Tech University.

"When you first start, you get really into it," said Kawaguchi, 26. "You get stuck on it for long periods of time."

The search for identity, the need for intimate relationships and the need for control often play a significant role in this potentially unhealthy behavior, Kandell said. Logging on, whether in chat rooms or through Web sites, can help students ranging academically from the inept to the astute cope with life's hardships. "If it's fulfilling a need, it's hard to give it up," Kandell said.

Simply put, Kawaguchi was online and overwhelmed. "You stay up late instead of going to sleep," she said. "It sucked up a lot of time." In a few months, the novelty began to wear off. "After a while, it was like, geez, this is enough," she said, adding that many of her chatmates were there night after night, even when she was gone for weeks at a time. "Basically, their whole world revolved around being there."

Studies on college campuses have shown between 6 percent and 12 percent of students may be spending too much time online, thanks in part to the ease of campus Internet access.

Kawaguchi saw the obsessive side of the Internet and managed to escape it. Others aren't as lucky.

Kandell was quick to note, however, that "addiction" was probably not the most accurate term in these cases. He compared overuse of the Internet to compulsive behaviors such as pathological gambling.

"I do see it as a psychological dependency," Kandell said. Kandell's evidence is mostly anecdotal, culled from student clients and classrooms filled with students who say they're downloading to the point of distraction.

In one class he visited, between 70 percent and 80 percent of the students raised their hands when asked whether the Internet was their chief obstacle to concentrating on projects and papers. "People are staying up all night, not going to class, not doing their homework—ultimately flunking out of school," Kandell said. "It's more pervasive than people think. There's something inherently tempting about the Internet."

For example, administrators at New York's Alfred University have found a correlation between high Internet use and a dropout rate that more than doubled. And the University of Washington has limited the amount of Internet time available to students to cut down on overuse. Several other colleges have set up support groups for Internet addiction.

Kawaguchi sees both good and bad in the Internet. The native of Oahu, Hawaii, considers it an effective communication tool but not a surrogate for human relationships. She calls it "luck" that she met her Iowa-born husband-to-be online. They traded photos and talked on the phone for a long time before taking the big step of meeting in person. The couple plan to wed in June in Lawrence. "Personally, I wouldn't recommend someone going out to look for someone on the Internet," she said. "I completely lucked out."

In addition to academic problems, jobs and relationships can be affected as social isolation grows. The Internet can provide an arena for people to simulate personal contact without actually having to meet face to face.

The underlying problem may be that the Internet's many facets are still new and somewhat unfamiliar. "I think we're just kind of scratching the surface," Kandell said. "I think it'll be a good five or 10 years before people have a good understanding of everything that's going on right now."

3 **Hourglass structure exercise:** Arrange these facts in hourglass order, placing attribution where it is needed. (This story is taken from the *St. Louis Post-Dispatch* of Missouri.) Attribute information to Capt. Ed Kemp of the Jefferson County Sheriff's Department unless otherwise noted.

Who: Two bank couriers

What: Helped police capture three suspects in a robbery

When: Last night

Where: At the Boatman's Bank of Pevely, Mo.

How: One courier, Dennis Boushie, who lives near Festus, chased a suspect on foot. The other courier, Willie Moore of St. Louis, drove a bank van, chasing a getaway car.

Police have booked three people on suspicion of drug possession. The three, who were found in the getaway car, are being held in the jail at Pevely.

Backup information: "This is beyond the call of duty. They acted more like police officers than private citizens or bank couriers," said Capt. Ed Kemp.

Boushie said he had asked the teller who was robbed if the robber had a weapon, and she said he did not. He said his pursuit of the robber had been "just common sense."

A man entered the bank shortly after it opened Tuesday morning and shouted, "Give me the money or else!" The teller gave the man an envelope containing the money, and the man ran out the front door.

Boushie chased the man on foot, and when the suspect jumped into a car, Boushie pointed the car out to Moore, who pursued it in a bank van. A few minutes later, Boushie got in a police patrol car and helped police track the getaway car.

Police broadcast a description of the getaway car, which had continued north on I-55 carrying two men and a woman. Police spotted the car, stopped it and arrested three suspects.

Police said they had found several thousand dollars in the car. The female suspect had stuffed money down her pants, police said.

Police were seeking federal warrants for bank robbery.

4 **List technique exercise:** Write a news story based on this information from the National Science Foundation.

Who: Jeffrey Cole, director of the Center for Communication Policy at the University of California. The center organized the World Internet Project, and the National Science Foundation is the sponsor.

What and why: A report, "Surveying the Digital Future," part of the World Internet Project, based at UCLA. The report is part of a multiyear study of how the Internet is affecting Americans' behavior and attitudes.

When: The first results of the report were released today.

How: The study evaluates what users do online, how they use—and whether they trust—the media, how consumers behave, how the Internet affects communication patterns, and what social and psychological effects ensue. The 2,096 respondents in the study, both Internet users and nonusers, will be contacted each year to explore how Internet technology evolves for continuing users, those who remain nonusers, and those who move from being nonusers to users.

Elaboration: The findings of the report show that Americans use the Internet exclusively without sacrificing their personal and social lives. It also revealed that users and nonusers have strong concerns about privacy.

"Our findings refute many preconceived notions that persist about how the Internet affects our lives," said Cole, founder of the World Internet Project. "Yet deeply rooted problems still exist that have long-range implications for this powerful technology."

The study found that more than two-thirds of Americans have some type of access to the Internet. More than half use e-mail (54.6 percent), and 51.7 percent of Internet users make purchases online. Nearly two-thirds of users (66 percent) and nearly half of nonusers (49.3 percent) believe that new communication technologies, including the Internet, have made the world a better place.

"Historically, Americans have been quite concerned about their privacy," Cole said, "but those concerns focused on government intrusion in their lives. Today, the concerns about privacy are quite different and focus directly on perceptions of private companies collecting information and tracking our movements on the Internet."

☛ **Featured Online Activity** Log on to the book Web site and take the interactive quiz for Chapter 10 to get more practice in writing stories in the structures described in this chapter.

academic.cengage.com/masscomm/rich/ writingandreportingnews6e

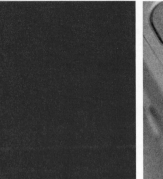

Coaching Tips

Gather details and take notes of your observations.

Use show-in-action techniques. Describe what people are doing.

Use vivid action verbs.

For narrative writing, try to envision yourself at the scene.

Get a chronology to reconstruct events as they occurred.

Think of your story as a plot with a beginning, middle and climax. Envision your sources as characters in a book; make your reader see, hear and care about them.

To write well, read well. Read as much fiction and nonfiction as you can, and study the writing styles.

We're supposed to be tellers of tales as well as purveyors of facts. When we don't live up to that responsibility, we don't get read.

Bill Blundell, *The Art and Craft of Feature Writing*

11

Storytelling and Feature Techniques

Tom French was fascinated by Karen Gregory's case. He wrote a 10-part series about her murder and the man on trial for it. It was called "A Cry in the Night."

Something very unusual happened when the series began. Readers ran out to greet the newspaper delivery trucks each day to get the next chapter in the series. Why were they so eager to read these stories? You decide.

> The victim wasn't rich. She wasn't the daughter of anyone powerful. She was simply a 36-year-old woman trying to make a life for herself. Her name was Karen Gregory. The night she died, Karen became part of a numbing statistic. . . . It was what people sometimes casually refer to as "a little murder."
>
> —Tom French, *St. Petersburg* (Fla.) *Times*

This passage was the introduction to the series. The first story began with a description of the trial of George Lewis, a firefighter who lived across the street from Karen Gregory and the person who was charged with her murder:

His lawyer called out his name. He stood up, put his hand on a Bible and swore to tell the truth and nothing but. He sat down in the witness box and looked toward the jurors so they could see his face and study it and decide for themselves what kind of man he was.

"Did you rape Karen Gregory?" asked his lawyer.

"No sir, I did not." "Did you murder Karen Gregory?"

"No sir."

He heard a scream that night, he said. He heard it, and he went out to the street to look around. He saw a man he did not know, standing over in Karen's yard. The man said to go away, to not tell anyone what he'd seen. He waited for the man to leave—watched him walk away into the darkness—and then he went up to Karen's house. There was broken glass on the front walk. He knocked on the front door. There was no answer. He found an open window. He called out to ask whether anyone needed help. There was still no answer. He looked through the window and saw someone lying on the floor. He decided he had to go in. He climbed inside, and there was Karen. Blood was everywhere.

He was afraid. He ran to the bathroom and threw up. He knew no one would believe how he had ended up standing inside that house with her body. He had to get out of there. He was running toward the window to climb out when he saw something moving in the dark. He thought someone was jumping toward him. Then he realized he was looking at a mirror, and the only person moving was him. It was his own reflection that had startled him. It was George.

—Tom French, *St. Petersburg* (Fla.) *Times*

The entire series was written like a mystery novel. But it was all true, based on interviews with more than 50 people and 6,000 pages of court documents. The writing style, called narrative writing, is a form of dramatic storytelling that reconstructs the events as though the reader were witnessing them as they happened. French later turned the series into a book called *Unanswered Cries*.

French says he never believed his series would be so popular. "The way the readers responded was so gratifying," he says.

French relied heavily on dialogue throughout the series, even from the dead woman. Although most of the dialogue and description are based on interviews and his own observations, Karen's dialogue was second-hand information, based on recollections about her.

"After I wrote it, I spent three weeks checking everything with all the participants," French says. "I read it to them word for word to make sure it was accurate."

In 1998 French won the Pulitzer Prize for another narrative series about murder. This time he researched 4,000 pages of police reports and court documents and conducted scores of interviews to reconstruct the chilling story of an Ohio woman and her two daughters. They were on vacation in Florida when they were raped, killed and dumped into Tampa Bay. Once again, French wrote a gripping account of their murders, the three-year search for their killer and his trial. The killer was convicted and sentenced to death.

Tom French

Narrative Writing

"Narrative writing" is a dramatic account of a fiction or nonfiction story. Newswriting in this style requires thorough reporting and descriptive detail. Dialogue also enhances the storytelling. Narrative writing is more like a novel or a play than a hard-news story, and the sources are like characters who relive the events in their lives. The story still must include the basic factual elements of news, but the presentation differs.

Jeff Klinkenberg, a *St. Petersburg* (Fla.) *Times* writer, views the five W's this way: *Who* is character, *what* is plot, *when* is chronology, *why* is motive and *where* is place.

French uses all these elements in his stories by weaving facts with description and dramatic tension. In this section from his Pulitzer Prize-winning series, "Angels and Demons," French uses descriptive detail to reveal how the bodies of the women were found.

It was a female, floating face down, with her hands tied behind her back and her feet bound and a thin yellow rope around her neck. She was naked from the waist down.

A man from the *Amber Waves* (sailboat) radioed the Coast Guard, and a rescue boat was dispatched from the station at Bayboro Harbor in St. Petersburg. The Coast Guard crew quickly found the body, but recovering it from the water was difficult. The rope around the neck was attached to something heavy below the surface that could not be lifted. Noting the coordinates where the body had been found, the Coast Guard crew cut the line, placed the female in a body bag, pulled the bag onto the boat and headed back toward the station. The crew members had not yet reached the shore when they received another radio message: A second female body had just been sighted by two people on a sailboat.

This one was floating to the north of where the first body had been sighted. It was 2 miles off The Pier in St. Petersburg. Like the first, this body was face down, bound, with a rope around the neck and naked below the waist. The same Coast Guard crew was sent to recover it, and while the crew was doing so, a call came in of yet a third female, seen floating only a couple of hundred yards to the east.

—Tom French, *St. Petersburg* (Fla.) *Times*

In the following section, French uses dialogue to reconstruct the scene when Hal Rogers, the husband and father of the dead women, tells the boyfriend of his daughter Michelle that his wife and daughters won't be coming home:

That day, Jeff Feasby phoned the Rogers house again, hoping Michelle would be back.

Hal picked up. His voice was strange. He sounded furious.

"Who is this?" he demanded.

Jeff told him who it was and asked if he'd heard anything. With that, Hal broke down.

"They're not coming home," he said, his voice trembling.

Jeff paused for a second. He didn't understand.

So Hal told him. They were gone, he said. All of them.

—Tom French, *St. Petersburg* (Fla.) *Times*

Reading to Write

French did not become a compelling storyteller without effort. Good writers are good readers, and French said he was inspired to do narrative writing after he read a book by the great Latin American writer Gabriel García Márquez. *The Story of a Shipwrecked Sailor* is a riveting story about a man who survived 10 days at sea without food and water.

French was also influenced by the literary journalists, a group of writers who, in the 1960s and 1970s, used the storytelling techniques of fiction for nonfiction newspaper and magazine stories. These journalists—Joan Didion, John McPhee, Tracy Kidder and Tom Wolfe—were influenced by Truman Capote's nonfiction book *In Cold Blood.* The literary journalists immersed themselves in a subject and wrote their stories with characters, scene, dialogue and plot. These were factual stories written like fiction.

Journalists often think storytelling techniques are limited to feature stories, but as you will see, you can apply this kind of writing to news about crime and courts and many other daily news stories.

Reporting Tools

Mary Ann Lickteig has a storyteller's instincts. A former feature writer for *The Des Moines* (Iowa) *Register,* she knows how to find extraordinary angles in ordinary events.

It is summer, and Lickteig is covering the annual Iowa State Fair. She is strolling from one booth to another in search of a good feature story. A pitchman is hawking a Robo-Cut slicing machine. Space-age plastic, he bellows. Lickteig laughs. Great angle for a story, she thinks.

Backstage at the pageant to choose the state fair queen, 77 girls are primping and practicing to compete for the crown. Lickteig decides that will be a good angle for another story. Now it is midnight. The fairgoers have gone home. Lickteig has not. In the center of the midway, a Catholic priest is baptizing four children. Lickteig listens. She can hear pool balls cracking in the background, where carnival workers may be playing.

The next day *Des Moines Register* readers will hear them, too, when Lickteig writes about the baptism and describes the empty paths in the midway—quiet "except for the hum of a giant generator and the occasional crack of pool balls." Or when she describes the sights and smells of the fair in this excerpt:

> The day before the fair opened to the public, hot dogs spit as they turned on roasters; tattooed midway workers smeared with grease hauled pieces of steel out of the back of trucks and turned them into carnival rides; brand new pig feeders stood waiting to be admired under a sign that pronounced them non-rusting, non-caking and non-corrosive.
>
> Odors emanating from the horse barn indicated the exhibits had arrived.
>
> —Mary Ann Lickteig, *The Des Moines Register*

Lickteig, now a freelance writer in Vermont, always looks for a good angle or theme for her stories. The focus is the reason for the story, which should be stated in a nut graph, but the theme is a literary device of an angle or unifying approach.

"You hope the theme will present itself," Lickteig says. "Usually, if you see something that fascinates you, it probably will fascinate the readers."

That's one way to find either the theme or just an idea for a story, she says. "I don't think about covering the whole Iowa State Fair. You need to break it down—show

Mary Ann Lickteig, feature writer

the fair through one family, one idea, one theme." The key to good feature writing is gathering good details and then selecting the ones that will work in your story.

"You want people to be able to see your story," Lickteig says. "Choose the details that stick out in your mind, the ones you remember when you run back to the office and tell somebody what you've found."

Like the last 83 steps of a man's life. Lickteig was writing a story about a man who had murdered three women and had spent 17 years on death row. He was scheduled to be executed. Lickteig wanted to convey what steps were involved in execution—figuratively and literally. So she walked from the inmate's cell to the electric chair, in 83 steps.

These kinds of observation techniques are crucial tools for a storyteller.

William Ruehlmann, author of *Stalking the Feature Story,* says writers must concentrate when they observe and then analyze what they observe. He gives this example: "Flies take off backward. So in order to swat one, you must strike slightly behind him. An interesting detail, and certainly one a writer would be able to pick up on. Other people see flies; a writer sees how they move."

During the reporting process, you don't always know what details you will need when you write your story. So gather all the details you can—from how many steps to the electric chair to what the inmate had for his last meal. Ask what were people thinking, saying, hearing, smelling, wearing and feeling. Be precise.

To help you gather specific details, envision a ladder with rungs leading from general to specific. Start with the broadest noun, and take it to the most specific level, as in the adjacent diagram. Then use those details to write. For example:

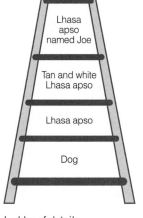

Ladder of details

> A tan and white Lhasa Apso named Joe ran onto the baseball field and interrupted the game when he stole the ball. It was only natural. After all, his namesake was Joe DiMaggio.

Writing Tools

Once you've gathered all those details, what do you do with them? The better you are as a reporter, the more you will struggle as a writer deciding what information to use. The three basic tools of storytelling are theme, descriptive writing techniques and narrative writing techniques.

Theme

Before you begin writing a feature story, develop a theme—a concept that gives the story meaning.

David Maraniss, a *Washington Post* writer who won a Pulitzer Prize, describes it this way:

> The theme is why readers want to read the story, not the nut graph required by many editors. To write something universal . . . death, life, fear, joy . . . that every person can connect to in some way is what I look for in every story.

Descriptive Techniques

Too much description will clutter a story. Too little will leave the reader blank. How much is enough? First decide if the story lends itself to description of the scene or person. Then take the advice of Bruce DeSilva, a writing coach for The Associated Press:

> Description, like every element in either fiction or nonfiction, should advance the meaning of your story. It would be a good idea to describe the brown house in more detail only if those details are important. Description never should be there for decoration. It never should be there because you are showing off. And when you do describe, you should never use more words than you need to trigger that mental image readers already have in their minds.

Techniques for good descriptive writing include the following:

Avoid Adjectives Write specific detail with vivid nouns and verbs, but avoid modifiers. When you use adjectives, you run the risk of inserting your opinions into the story. Author Norman Mailer put it this way:

> The adjective is the author's opinion of what is going on, no more. If I write, "A strong man came into the room," that only means he is strong in relation to me. Unless I've established myself for the reader, I might be the only fellow in the bar who is impressed by the guy who just came in. It is better to say: "A man entered. He was holding a walking stick, and for some reason, he now broke it in two like a twig." Of course, this takes more time to narrate. So adjectives bring on quick tell-you-how-to-live writing. Advertising thrives on it. "A super-efficient, silent, sensuous, five-speed shift." Put 20 adjectives before a noun and no one will know you are describing a turd.

Use Analogies A good analogy compares a vague concept to something familiar to readers. For example, what is a "fat" man? David Finkel leaves no doubt in his story about a circus performer. How do you visualize the "World's Biggest Man" at 891 pounds? Finkel uses familiar items to help the reader see.

> Now: 891 and climbing. That's more than twice as much as Sears' best refrigerator-freezer—a 26-cubic-footer with automatic ice and water dispensers on side-by-side doors. That's almost as much as a Steinway grand piano.
>
> —David Finkel, *St. Petersburg* (Fla.) *Times*

Limit Physical Descriptions Use physical descriptions only when they are relevant to the content. They work well in profiles; in stories about crime, courts, and disasters; and whenever they fit with the context. They don't work when they are tacked onto impersonal quotes.

Avoid stage directions—descriptions of people's gestures, facial expressions and physical characteristics inserted artificially as though you were directing a play. You don't need to describe what city commissioners are wearing at a meeting or how they gesture unless their clothing and movements enhance what they are saying and doing.

Effective

The 50-year-old airline pilot—who prosecutors say killed his wife by unknown means, cut up her body with a chain saw, and disposed of it with a wood chipper—testified with a voice and manner that was so calm it bordered at times on nonchalance.

—Lynne Tuohy, *The Hartford* (Conn.) *Courant*

The study shows college students are becoming more conservative, the researcher said, blinking her blue eyes and clasping her carefully manicured hands.

Ineffective

The color of the researcher's eyes and her hand motions have nothing to do with her comments about the study.

Avoid Sexist/Racist Descriptions When you decide to include descriptions of people, beware of sexism, racism or other biased writing. Writers often describe men with action verbs showing what they are doing and women with adjectives showing what they are wearing and how they look. One way to avoid bias is to ask yourself if you would use a similar description for both men and women or equal treatment for all racial and ethnic groups.

Consider this example:

Ineffective

Even Chandra Smith, busy being adorable in her perky non-runner's running outfit, actually looked at the track. A minute later, she was jumping around and yelling, along with most of the other 41,600 people on the old wooden benches at Franklin Field.

—*The Philadelphia Inquirer*

The story about the Penn Relay Carnival, a track meet in Philadelphia, also mentions a few men among those 41,600 people, including some volunteers who wear gray trousers and red caps. But they aren't adorable or perky.

Show People in Action One of the most effective ways to describe people or places is to show action. For example, Tom French doesn't write only about murder. In a series about life in a Florida high school, he used the show-in-action technique extensively, as in this passage about a history teacher's first day on the job. The teacher, Mr. Samsel, has given his homeroom students some forms to fill out:

The future leaders of America sit silently, some of them slumped forward, staring into space through half-closed eyes. Over to the side sits a boy. He is wearing a crucifix, blue jeans and a T-shirt. On the front of the shirt is a big smiley face. In the center of the face's forehead is a bullet hole, dripping blood. . . .

Around the room, students begin writing.

"Isn't this great?" says Samsel. "Just like real life—forms and everything."

Smiley Face looks at one of the sheets in front of him. He reads aloud as he fills it out.

"Please list medical problems."

He stops.

"Brain dead," he says.

—Tom French, *St. Petersburg* (Fla.) *Times*

Use Lively Verbs News is action, says Jack Hart, *The* (Portland) *Oregonian*'s writing coach and managing editor. But writers often "squeeze the life out of an action-filled world," he says. "We write that thousands of bullet holes were in the hotel, instead of noting that the holes pocked the hotel. We report that a jumper died Monday when his parachute failed, instead of turning to action verbs such as *plummeted* or *plunged* or *streamed*."

Mitch Albom, a sportswriter and author of three best-selling books, knows the value of action verbs. Notice the ones he uses in this story about the day Detroit Tigers baseball player Cecil Fielder hit his 50th home run. Also notice the analogies and the show-in-action description.

He swung the bat and he heard that smack! and the ball screamed into the dark blue sky, higher, higher, until it threatened to bring a few stars down with it. His teammates knew; they leaped off the bench. The fans knew; they roared like animals. And finally, the man who all year refused to watch his home runs, the man who said this 50 thing was "no big deal"—finally even he couldn't help himself. He stopped halfway to first base and watched the ball bang into the facing of the upper deck in Yankee Stadium, waking up the ghosts of Maris and Ruth and Gehrig.

And then, for the first time in this miraculous season, Cecil Fielder jumped. He jumped like a man sprung from prison, he jumped like a kid on the last day of school, he jumped, all 250 pounds of Detroit Bambino, his arms over his head, his huge smile a beacon of celebration and relief.

The Big Five-O.

—Mitch Albom, *Detroit Free Press*

Set the Scene You need to set the scene by establishing where and when. Although it is common to establish the time and weather, often in a lead, beware of using that technique unless time and weather factors are relevant to your story. "It was 2 a.m. and the wind was blowing" is akin to the cliché "It was a dark and stormy night." In this story from a California State University student newspaper, the time and weather conditions are relevant to the story:

TIJUANA, Mexico—Shivering in the mud under a 2-foot high chaparral, Jose carefully lifts his head into the cold night mist to monitor the movements of the U.S. Border Patrol.

On a ridge above a small ravine, patrol trucks scurry back and forth while a helicopter above provides the only light, turning spots of the night-time terrain into day. In the distance, guard dogs growl, bark and yelp.

At one point a patrol truck speeds toward Jose and his group of six Mexican farm laborers. Squatting in the brush, they quickly slide flat into the mud like reptiles seeking shelter.

Within seconds the helicopter hovers above them as its searchlight passes nearby, then at once directly over them. All their faces are turned downward to avoid detection by the brightness of the light that illuminates every detail of the soil, roots and insects that lie inches under them.

Soon, the truck and helicopter make a slow retreat. Jose and his group, safe for the moment, will remain motionless in that same muddy spot for the next three hours as the mist turns to rain and the rain turns back to mist.

Nut graphs

To those who have never passed this way before, the sights and sounds are of another world. But to the expert scouts called "coyotes," this alien land between Mexico and the United States is home.

Every weekday evening, approximately 2,000 people attempt to illegally cross the border from Mexico to the United States. On weekends the numbers can climb to between 5,000 and 10,000, said Victor Clark, director of the Binational Center for Human Rights in Tijuana, Mexico.

—Brett C. Sporich, (Long Beach, Calif.)
Daily Forty Niner

In the next example, the story is about a reading program. Although the lead about the weather is backed up by a quote, the weather has nothing to do with the focus or the rest of the story.

It was a beautiful spring-like Sunday, and the heat on the first floor of the Kansas City Public Library Downtown was on full-blast. But that didn't stop about 400 people from crowding inside to read and hear their favorite selections from African-American authors.

The crowd, people of all ages and races, was there to take part in the national Read-In sponsored by the Black Caucus of the National Teachers of English.

"That is true commitment," said Mamie Isler, program director for Genesis School, which helped coordinate the event in Kansas City.

The second annual Kansas City Read-In opened with a performance by 30 students from the Genesis School choir.

—*The Kansas City* (Mo.) *Star*

Narrative Techniques Narrative writing combines show-in-action description, dialogue, plot and reconstruction of an event as it occurred. This type of writing requires a bond of faith with the reader because attribution is limited. You need to make it clear where you got the information, but you don't need to attribute repeatedly. You can also use an overview attribution for portions of the story and then attribute periodically, especially when you are quoting sources.

Before you can do narrative writing, you need to do thorough reporting. It takes a different kind of questioning to gather the information you will need to reconstruct a scene with dialogue and detail. Narrative writing is not fiction. You must stick to the facts even though the story may read like a novel. You need to ask questions like these: What were you thinking at the time? What were you feeling? What did you say? What were you wearing? What were you doing? You need to get details about colors, sounds, sights, smells, sizes, shapes, times, places.

If you were witnessing the event, you would see, hear, smell and feel—perhaps even taste—the experiences of your subject. Because you are reconstructing the event, you need to ask the questions that will evoke all those images.

Those are the kinds of questions Jane Schorer asked when she wrote this Pulitzer Prize–winning story about a woman who had been raped. The woman had agreed to use her name. In this opening part of her series, Schorer sets the scene (with relevant weather and time references) and reconstructs the woman's experience so the reader is a witness to the event:

She would have to allow extra driving time because of the fog.

A heavy gray veil had enveloped Grinnell overnight, and Nancy Ziegenmeyer—always methodical, always in control—decided to leave home early for her 7:30 a.m. appointment at Grand View College in Des Moines.

It was Nov. 19, a day Ziegenmeyer had awaited eagerly, because she knew that whatever happened during those morning hours in Des Moines would determine her future. If she passed the state real-estate licensing exam that Saturday morning, she would begin a new career. If she failed the test, she would continue the child-care service she provided in her home.

At 6 a.m. Ziegenmeyer unlocked the door of her Pontiac Grand Am and tossed her long denim jacket in the back seat. The weather was mild for mid-November, and her Gloria Vanderbilt denim jumper, red turtleneck sweater and red wool tights would keep her warm enough without a coat.

The fog lifted as Ziegenmeyer drove west on Interstate Highway 80 and she made good time after all. The digital clock on the dashboard read 7:05 as she pulled into a parking lot near Grand View's Science Building. She had 25 minutes to sit in the car and review her notes before test time.

Suddenly the driver's door opened. She turned to see a man, probably in his late 20s, wearing a navy pin-striped suit. He smelled of alcohol.

"Move over," the man ordered, grabbing her neck. She instinctively reached up to scratch him, but he was stronger than she was. He pushed a white dish towel into her face and shoved her into the front passenger seat, reclining it to a nearly horizontal position. Then he took her denim jacket from the back seat and covered her head.

He wasn't going to hurt her, the man said; he wanted money. She reached toward the console for the only cash she had with her—$3 or $4—and gave it to him. He slid the driver's seat back to make room for his long legs, started the car and drove out of the parking lot.

"Is this guy going to kill me?" Ziegenmeyer wondered. "Is he going to rape me? Does he just want my money? Does he want my car?" She thought about her three children—ages 4, 5, and 7—and realized she might never see them again.

—Jane Schorer, *The Des Moines* (Iowa) *Register*

Use Foreshadowing When you give a clue about something that will happen later in the story, you are using foreshadowing. It is a way of providing mystery and teasing the reader to continue. In this example, the writer teases the reader by indicating that more ghostly experiences are coming:

SULLIVAN HARBOR, Maine—Gail Stamp was doing the dishes when she heard a noise in the hall stairway. Her husband was away, and she thought she was alone in the living quarters over the store here.

Stamp doesn't scare easily, so she went to investigate. She entered the hallway, and there, at the top of the stairs, she saw the gray form of a man.

"I stopped dead in my tracks," she said. "We both kind of froze for a second." Then the form turned and went down the stairs.

"It shook me up a little bit," she said. "But I knew right away who he was." It was the ghost of Cling Clang, she said, a man whose life, marred by tragedy, ended about 130 years ago, next to the building the Stamps now own.

That was the first encounter she had with a ghost.

But it wouldn't be the last.   *Foreshadowing*

Now she and Jim, her husband, are convinced they are not alone. They believe the ghost of Cling Clang inhabits their home with them.

And therein begins this story of spirits of the dead.

—Tom Shields, *Bangor* (Maine) *Daily News*

Create Tone Hard-news stories often have an objective, factual tone, mostly an absence of mood. But in storytelling, you should create a "tone," or "mood," such as happiness, sadness, mystery, excitement or some other emotion.

You don't need to tell the reader that the mood of the place was festive or mournful. You can show it by the images you select for your story.

Another way of creating tone is by your writing style. Mary Ann Lickteig creates a lighthearted tone by writing this profile of a hypnotist as though the reader were undergoing hypnosis:

You will read this story.

You will hang on its every word, and you will not get sleepy.

As you proceed, you will learn about hypnosis and a Clive hypnotherapist whose work has led her to the International Hypnosis Hall of Fame.

You are ready to begin. Shari Patton is sitting on the couch in her home telling you that she first went for hypnosis "like a doubting Thomas." She was a student at the University of Minnesota when a friend was going to be hypnotized and wanted Patton to come along.

Listen, now, to what she has to say:

"My friend had said, 'Go with me.' And I had said no, and after several requests begging me, I said 'All right. I'll go.' And I went to stop smoking, not believing that it would work, but very much wanting to stop smoking, and I was so amazed and delighted that it worked for me that I went back and started using hypnosis for weight control and lost 90 pounds." That's how she got started.

—Mary Ann Lickteig,
The Des Moines (Iowa) *Register*

In contrast, Saul Pett wanted to create a somber tone to reflect the mood of the nation when President Kennedy was killed. Pett chose vivid details that showed what people were feeling, and he did something else that was quite unusual. He established the reverent tone of his story by emulating biblical style.

Another way Pett created the mournful tone of his story was through the length of his sentences. Short, choppy sentences can reflect fear, excitement, anxiety or stabbing pain. Long sentences can project suffering, thoughtfulness or a quiet mood.

Pett broke many traditional journalistic rules in his article describing the four days after Kennedy was shot: His sentences were long, he used the first-person *we* and he made no attempt to write objectively. Yet his story is one of the great feature articles of the 20th century. Here is an excerpt:

And the word went out from that time and place and cut the heart of a nation. In streets and offices and homes and stores, in lunchrooms and showrooms and schoolrooms and board rooms, on highways and prairies and beaches and mountaintops, in endless places crowded and sparse, near and far, white and black, Republican and Democrat, management and labor, the word went out and cut the heart of a nation.

And husbands called wives and wives called friends and teachers told students and motorists stopped to listen on car radios and stranger told stranger. Oh, no! we cried from hearts stopped by shock, from minds fighting the word, but the word came roaring back, true, true, true, and disbelief dissolved in tears.

Incredibly, in a time of great numbers, in a time of repeated reminders that millions would die in a nuclear war, in a time when experts feared we were being numbed by numbers and immunized against tragedy, the death of a single man crowded into our souls and flooded our hearts and filled all the paths of our lives.

A great shadow fell on the land and the farmer summoned to the house did not find the will to return to the field, nor the secretary to the typewriter, nor the machinist to the lathe.

There was a great slowing down and a great stopping and the big bronze gong sounded as a man shouted the market is closed and the New York Stock Exchange stopped, just stopped. The Boston Symphony Orchestra stopped a Handel concerto and started a Beethoven funeral march and the Canadian House of Commons stopped and a dramatic play in Berlin stopped and the United Nations in New York stopped and Congress and courts and schools and race tracks stopped, just stopped. And football games were canceled and theaters were closed and in Dallas a nightclub called the Carousel was closed by a mourner named Jack Ruby.

In Washington, along Pennsylvania Avenue, they had waited all that Friday night outside the iron picket fence, their eyes scarcely leaving the lovely old house. Early in the morning the guards had kept them moving and so they walked slowly down the street, eyes right, and at the corner they turned and came back on the street side of the sidewalk, eyes left. They looked like a strange silent group of mournful pickets demonstrating love, not protest.

In the chill darkness before dawn they were still there, now motionless, standing, staring across the broad lawn and through the bare elms at the house, at the softly lighted windows in the family quarters, at the black crepe lately hung over the door under the north portico.

They saw the blinking red lights of the police cars up Pennsylvania Avenue and they knew this was the moment. The president was coming home. No sirens, no police whistles, no barking of orders that usually accompanied his return. At 4:22 a.m., Saturday, Nov. 23, 1963, there seemed to be no sound on the street or in the land.

The gray Navy ambulance and the six black cars behind it paused at the northwest gate and turned in. And along the fence, men removed their hats and teenagers removed their hands from the pockets of their jeans and women tightened their fingers around the pickets of the fence. Tears stained their faces, their young and their old faces, their white and their black faces.

At the gate the procession was met by a squad of Marines and led in along the gracefully curving drive between the elms. In days to come there would be larger and more majestic processions, but none so slow, none so geared to the rhythm of tears, as the cadence of the Marines this Saturday morning. In two straight lines, glistening bayoneted rifles held across their chests at port arms, they marched oh so slowly up the drive and all that could be heard was the sound of their shoes sliding on the macadam.

Under the portico, under the handsome hanging lantern, they stopped and divided and lined up with the soldiers and sailors and airmen on the sides of the steps, at the stiffest, straightest attention of their lives.

Jacqueline Kennedy emerged first from the ambulance, still wearing the same pink suit stained through eternity the afternoon before.

With her husband's brother, the attorney general of the United States, with his other brother, the youngest member of the United States Senate, with his sisters and his friends and aides whom he had led to this house, this far and now no farther, Jacqueline Kennedy waited in motionless silence while the flag-covered casket was removed from the ambulance. Then she and they turned in behind it and walked up the steps and through the glass doors and into the lobby and down the long corridor lined with stiff, silent men in uniform and finally came to a stop in the East Room.

There the casket was laid gently onto the black catafalque that held Mr. Lincoln on another dark incredible night almost 100 years ago. There, the kneeling priests began praying as they and others would through the long day and night by the flickering light of the candles, which silhouetted the honor guard riveted to the floor.

It was now 10 o'clock in the morning of a Saturday and Jacqueline Kennedy, still sleepless, returned to the silent East Room. She kissed her husband for the last time and the casket was sealed. A few moments later, she returned with her children and spoke to them quietly, trying to tell them something of the fact and the meaning of death. A fact and a meaning for which millions groped that day.

—Saul Pett, *The Associated Press*

Human-Interest Feature The next example is the type of human interest story that Charles Kuralt would have enjoyed reporting. It is also the type of story you might do if you work in a small community for a newspaper or TV station.

Convergence Coach

Charles Kuralt was a consummate storyteller who wrote human-interest features for "On the Road," a series for CBS-TV's "Sunday Morning" show. Long before convergence became a buzzword for a type of journalism merging print, broadcast and the Web, Kuralt epitomized a multimedia journalist. He began his career as a print reporter for the *Charlotte News* in North Carolina, where he won the Ernie Pyle Memorial Award in 1956 for his offbeat human-interest columns. When he joined CBS in 1957, he continued producing human-interest features and later wrote several books about his adventures on the road and the people he met. He loved storytelling about people in newspapers, television and books, but he was a bit baffled by the Web.

"For most of my career I didn't do stories about things that go wrong," he once said. "I did stories about unexpected encounters, back roads, small towns and ordinary folk, sometimes doing something a little extraordinary. I would not argue that it was important to society at large; it was just fun," according to the Web site Annenberg/CPB learner.org (*www.learner.org/catalog/extras/interviews/ckuralt/ck02.html*).

Kuralt always found something extraordinary in the people and places he visited. "I don't know what makes a good feature story," he said. "I've always assumed that if it was a story that interested or amused me, that it would have the same impact on other people."

Kuralt learned early in his career at CBS that a good feature story for television was dependent on

visuals. He said a CBS writer told him that "you must never write a sentence that fights the picture."

"If you're conveying some information that is not in tune with the picture that's on the screen, the viewer's going to be watching the picture and miss entirely what you're saying," Kuralt said. "It's always possible to fashion a sentence, it seems to me, so that it complements rather than struggles with the picture."

Whether you are writing feature stories for print, broadcast or the Web, take Kuralt's advice and find a story that interests you. Seek universal qualities of human interest such as people's hopes, fears, dreams, love, hate, the ability to triumph over adversity or the ability to achieve something special—like a story Kuralt did about the fellow in Indiana who could hold more eggs in his hand than anybody else.

Then, if you want to become a good feature writer for print or broadcast, take some tips from Kuralt, as he related in an interview with the Web site of Academy of Achievement: "I think good writing comes from good reading. And I think that writers, when they sit down to write, hear in their heads the rhythms of good writers they have read. Sometimes I could even tell you which writer's rhythms I am imitating. It's not exactly plagiarism, but it's just experience. It's falling in love with good language and trying to imitate it."

(To read the entire interview with Kuralt, access the Academy of Achievement Web site at *www.achievement.org/autodoc/page/kur0int-1.*)

Chances are you will seek stories about people who are doing interesting or unusual things in your community. Compare the print and broadcast versions of this story:

Print version
Cooper Landing man revels in clover collection

KENAI—Some people believe the Kenai Peninsula is the luckiest place on Earth. Cooper Landing resident Ed Martin Sr. said he believes it is time somebody proved it.

Martin has been finding four-leaf clovers since his childhood and started to save them only two years ago. Since then he has rounded up more than 76,000 clovers.

Some people likely would ask why a person would be so concentrated on how many mutated clovers they found, especially a collection well into five figures. The answer is it has to do with a little competition, and a little bit of pride.

Martin has surpassed the previously largest known four-leaf clover collection held by George J. Kaminski, who collected 72,927 clovers within prison grounds in Pennsylvania (Guinness World Records). Kaminski has held the record since April of 1995.

Although Martin's world record-breaking application still is being completed, he is confident it will stand officially. The city of Soldotna, where many of the clovers were found, is handling the paperwork.

Kathy Dawson, assistant to Mayor David Carey, is making sure the project stays within the Guinness office record guidelines. This includes clear documentation in multiple forms.

"This is just amazing. I've got file cabinets full of clovers," Dawson said. "The mayor had kids from the schools counting all these clovers, and there are still more to be counted."

Actually finding 76,000 clovers, let alone a handful, is a difficult task, so Martin shared his secret:

"I look for mutated clovers, ones with four clovers and above. Now, you're not going to believe this, but once I found 880 in one day. I found 90 percent in the Soldotna-Kenai Borough area."

It's a knack, Martin said. "People just don't see what I see," he said.

Martin expects to break a world record, but he says the accomplishment goes beyond that.

"I'm interested in the good that will come out of this," he said. "We have a wonderful country, a wonderful state and community. We are all lucky to be living here. It's just a fact of life. I really think this is the luckiest place in the world, and this will prove it. Maybe this is why the fishing is so good here."

Martin, a former member of the Matanuska-Susitna Borough Assembly, said he hasn't been as involved as he used to be—although competing for a world record in the name of your homeland seems to be a good contribution.

"When you're meeting a challenge, when you do your best in anything, there is a feeling of pride that goes with it," Martin said. "I'm going to keep looking for clovers."

—Layton Ehmke, *The Associated Press*

Broadcast version:

Note that the reporter's comments in the broadcast version are written around the images and sound bites. The text is written in capital letters and sound bites and the technical crew instructions are in lowercase. A TV script is normally printed in two columns with the directions on the left and text on the right. However, computer programs in broadcast newsrooms automatically format the script into two columns so the reporter just writes the text and directions above it in one column. The reporter's text is double-spaced in capital letters and the sound bites are in upper- and lowercase in this example:

Anchor introduction:

THE CHANCES OF FINDING A FOUR-LEAF CLOVER ON A PATCH OF GROUND ARE SLIM.

BUT ONE ALASKAN HAS BEATEN THOSE ODDS. . . . MORE THAN 100-THOUSAND TIMES.

IN TONIGHT'S ASSIGNMENT ALASKA, CHANNEL TWO'S SEAN DOOGAN TAKES US TO COOPER LANDING TO MEET THE LUCKIEST MAN ON EARTH.

The package opens with a scene setter; shot of ground and the image of Ed Martin bending over looking for clover on the side of the road.

Reporter Sean Doogan:

WHEN YOU FIRST MEET COOPER LANDING'S ED MARTIN, SENIOR . . . CHANCES ARE YOU WON'T BE SEEING HIS BEST SIDE.

Ed Martin, Sr. (laughs and says): That crazy guy with his rear-end in the air. . . . There's a nice one. . . . I got another one.

More natural sound and image of scene
Reporter Doogan:

SURROUNDED BY A NATURAL CATHEDRAL. . . . ED PREFERS THE VIEW UNDER HIS FEET. . . . HUNTING FOR WHAT MOST PEOPLE WOULD CALL ELUSIVE QUARRY. BUT NOT SO ELUSIVE FOR ED.

Ed Martin sound bite and image of him picking clover: That's a four-leaf. . . . I got another one.

Image of Martin's home and Martin holding Guiness World Record:

Martin sound bite: I have the largest collection of four-leaf clovers in the world. It's real. . . . I didn't print it.

Reporter: MARTIN'S RECORD COLLECTION OF 111-THOUSAND AND 60 CLOVERS WOULD BE MUCH BIGGER. . . . IF HE WASN'T SO DETERMINED TO SHARE HIS LUCK.

Martin sound bite: Why count them, I am going to give them away.

Reporter: MARTIN SAYS HE HAS GOTTEN MUCH MORE FROM HIS CLOVER COLLECTION . . . THAN A WORLD RECORD.

Martin sound bite: It seems when I give a four-leaf clover to anyone, I always get a smile. What's wrong with getting a smile from somebody.

Scene of town store with clover on the wall:

Reporter: CLOVER DECORATES THE TOWN STORE.

Sound bite: Glenda Mitchell, co-owner of Cooper Landing General store:

We have some on the wall here; I also have some in my wallet. I would say he's kind of like the good luck guy because when he sees you, he'll always give you one of the four leaf clovers and wish you the best of luck.

Reporter: AS LONG AS MARTIN IS AROUND, IT SEEMS . . . YOU CAN'T TRAVEL THROUGH COOPER LANDING . . . WITHOUT ENDING UP WITH SOME FRESH CLOVER.

Scene: Martin gives girl a four-leaf clover:

Martin sound bite: See . . how many guys get to see pretty girls all the time . . . see I'm lucky . . . how lucky can a guy get?

Reporter: MARTIN CLAIMS THE CLOVER ITSELF ISN'T WHAT BRINGS GOOD FORTUNE.

Martin sound bite: I've got as many as 1000 in one day. . . . It's an attitude change. . . . When you have a four-leaf clover, you believe in luck, you believe in things happening. That's what luck is all about.

Reporter: EVEN WITH THE RECORD FIRMLY IN HAND . . . MARTIN SAYS HIS SEARCH FOR LUCK ISN'T OVER.

(Video of Martin picking clovers)

Martin sound bite: I will go 'til the good Lord pulls the chain and says, I want you up there.

Reporter:

MARTIN SAYS HE CURRENTLY HAS 165-THOUSAND FOUR-LEAF CLOVERS.

AND WITH THE ODDS OF FINDING A LUCKY PLANT AT 10-THOUSAND TO ONE. . . .

ALL THE CLOVER MARTIN HAS LOOKED THROUGH OVER THE YEARS . . . IF LAID END-TO-END . . . WOULD STRETCH MORE THAN 13-THOUSAND MILES: MORE THAN ENOUGH TO GO FROM THE NORTH POLE TO THE SOUTH POLE.

SEAN DOOGAN, CHANNEL TWO NEWS.

—Channel 2 News, KTUU-TV, Anchorage, Alaska

Storytelling Structure

Up to this point in the book, even though you have had many story structures from which to choose, you probably have been organizing your stories by focus and supporting topics or in chronological order. Even with a storytelling approach, you still need to get the focus first. A narrative story can then be arranged topically or chronologically, or it can follow a literary plot form—with a beginning, a middle and an ending called a "climax."

"Most news stories are endings without beginnings attached," says Jon Franklin, a Pulitzer Prize–winning writer and author of *Writing for Story.* Reporters miss the dramatic point of view when they concentrate only on the result instead of on the actions leading up to the event. Franklin says stories should be built around a complication and a resolution. In the middle is the development, how the central character gets from the problem to the solution.

If you have a story that lends itself to this kind of plot, your focus would be the complication that the main character has to overcome. The organization could be chronological, starting with the inception of the problem. The middle would be how the character wrestles with the problem, and the climax would be the resolution of the problem.

Bruce DeSilva, writing coach for The Associated Press, says the writer must determine a resolution to do narrative writing. "That's one of the most important things for people to understand about narrative storytelling: picking the problem," DeSilva said at a Neiman Conference on narrative writing. "When you get to the resolution, the story's over."

DeSilva says that in narrative writing you should write the ending first. "So many people write the lead first. They slave away at the lead and spend lots of time on it before they write the rest of the story. Don't do that. It's almost always a bad idea. . . . When I write narratives, I always write the ending first. Try it. Try it. When you write the ending first, then when you go back to the top of the story and start to write it, you know what your destination is. You know where you're going."

The technique of developing the story in sections, perhaps arranged by points of view, can also work in a narrative story. You can start the story in the middle of the action, as long as you explain to the reader why you are telling this story now (the "so what" factor). This approach is somewhat like using the time frame organization—starting with the present, going to the past, back to the present and on to the future. Regardless of the technique you choose, you should plan your order before you write.

William Blundell, who spent years writing features and profiles for *The Wall Street Journal,* suggests in his book *The Art and Craft of Feature Writing* that features should be organized around "The Laws of Progressive Reader Involvement":

Stage one: Tease me, you devil. (Give the reader a reason to continue reading.)

Stage two: Tell me what you're up to. What is the story really about?

Stage three: Oh yeah? Prove what you said. (Include the evidence to support your theme.)

Stage four: Help me remember it. (Make it clear and forceful, and give it a memorable ending.)

Blundell says features should include the following elements, but not necessarily in this order:

Focus: What is the central theme?

Lead and nut graph: What is the point of the story? (Often, it is introduced anecdotally or descriptively.)

History: How did the problem develop?

Scope: How widespread is the development?

Reasons: Why is this problem or conflict happening now?

Impacts: Who is affected and how?

Moves and countermoves: Who is acting to promote or oppose the development, and what are they doing?

Future: What could happen as a result of the situation and developments?

Blundell also suggests blocking material from any one source in one place in the story, especially if the story has many sources. The organization is not as rigid as the list implies. If the material lends itself to narrative storytelling, it can be told in chronological order or natural story order: beginning, middle, climax, and ending.

Here are some reminders of good storytelling techniques:

- Use concrete details rather than vague adjectives.
- Use dialogue when possible and appropriate.
- Set a scene.
- Use action verbs.
- Observe or ask questions involving all your senses.
- Use show-in-action description.
- Tell a story like a plot, with a beginning, middle and climax. Get a chronology or sequence of events. You may want to use the chronology in all or part of your story. Even if you don't use chronological order, you need to understand the sequence of events.
- Follow Mark Twain's advice: "Don't say the old lady screamed—bring her on and let her scream."

ETHICS

Ethical dilemma: Is it OK to make up quotes? Is it OK to reconstruct scenes in feature stories?

Tom French reconstructed scenes, quotes and dialogue in his story about the murdered woman in one story and the other women in "Angels and Demons" based on court documents and interviews with sources who knew the women. How does that differ from cases of Jayson Blair, a former reporter for *The New York Times,* and Stephen Glass, a former reporter for *The New Republic,* who were both fired in disgrace for fabricating information in their stories?

Ethical values: Credibility, truth, accuracy, fairness

Narrative Storytelling

Martha Miller interviewed Vietnam veteran Dan Vickroy several times before she wrote this story about his injuries in the war. Each time he remembered more. She asked him to recall what he was thinking, feeling, saying and experiencing when he was injured, 25 years earlier.

Miller also reconstructed dialogue, based on Vickroy's recollections as he related them to her. The technique is acceptable if you are basing your information on documents and sources, but it is not preferable. If you can't confirm the dialogue with the original source, you can attribute it to the source who related it. If it is not controversial and you are sure it is accurate, you can reconstruct it as Miller has done.

After she finished all her interviews and filled several notebooks, Miller sat down to write the story. She was overwhelmed. She planned the story and organized it by different periods of Vickroy's life. Then she tried free-writing, just writing what she remembered to get it out of her head. After that she began refining the story, and before she revised her final draft, she read the story aloud.

The part of the story included here, the second section, contains almost no direct attribution. It is all based on Vickroy's recollections. Do you as the reader need attribution? Is the story believable without it?

A soldier's story

By Martha Miller

Iowa City Press-Citizen

Descriptive beginning for section: sets scene

Two hands lifted the sheet that covered what was left of Dan Vickroy's body.

"You're one tough son of a bitch," the surgeon said from behind a green mask.

Reconstructed dialogue

"I'm a Vickroy," Dan said. "Take me in and sew me up." They did.

Narrative chronological storytelling through Vickroy

Vickroy regained consciousness. He figured he was in the base hospital at Cam Ranh Bay. He could see nothing through the bandages over his eyes, but he could hear the squeaks of rubber soles in the hallway and hushed conversations between doctors as they hurried from bed to bed. It sounded like a busy place.

He was scared, scared to death he was blind.

His ears wanted to believe what he heard, but his eyes would believe what they saw.

The nurses told him they were bandages and that he was strapped down. They told him he had been in bed for almost two weeks. And they told him he had a 104-degree temperature. He knew that. He couldn't stop shivering.

As he lay there, his memory returned. He knew the mine had exploded and that he was badly hurt. He remembered waking up twice in surgery. The last time, he felt a surge of pain. He saw a surgeon cutting off his leg with a bone saw.

Clues of attribution without direct attribution (he remembered)

The days and nights came and went. All the same. Dark.

This time, it was night. Someone shut off all the lights in his hospital room. The doctors were back. Slowly, they unraveled the gauze around his eyes.

Scene

Vickroy held his breath. He opened his eyes and saw a faint light. It burned, but this time it was a good sign. Doctors had worked through the night cleaning his eyes. What he saw made him want to put the bandages back on.

There were wire stitches in his stomach and his right hip. There were tubes in his nose and left arm. Instead of legs, he saw blood-soaked gauze wrapped around two stumps.

The doctors told him what happened: His right leg was blown away by the explosion and his left leg was amputated in surgery; his right arm was amputated below the elbow; and he had lost part of his stomach. Being so close to the mine saved his life; the blast threw him up and out of the way.

His face was intact, saved by that last glance back to camp. Vickroy took the news better than most.

Direct quote with no attribution: speaker understood

"Psychologically, I was pretty positive." He had no legs, but he did have a wife and new baby. He had married Sharon Kay in 1968 in Tulsa. She was 8½ months pregnant when he left for Vietnam. Danny Ray was born March 28, 1969.

Baby pictures were taped, one under the other, on the side of his bed so Vickroy could look at Danny Ray while lying on his back.

Those pictures and thoughts of heading back to the United States kept Vickroy's hopes up. But back home, his family wasn't so positive.

Dan's mother, Louise, was waiting tables in a Cedar Rapids restaurant when an Army officer handed her a telegram. She cried.

Louise had never wanted her youngest to join the service. She wouldn't sign his enlistment papers and couldn't see him off.

Vickroy had started to believe he could live without legs until the day a nurse read him a letter. It had arrived at Cam Ranh Bay several days earlier, but nobody wanted to read it to him.

It was from his wife. She wanted a divorce.

"She told me she didn't want half a man."

Short sentences and pacing

Punch ending to this section: short sentences

Reporting Techniques: Establishing chronology, gathering detail, asking questions to get source to reconstruct specific events using all senses.

Writing Techniques: Organized by sections technique in time sequences; although most of the story takes place in the past, each section deals with a different part of the character's life. Primarily follows chronological order, with cliffhanger endings for each section. Other techniques: short sentences, pacing, dialogue, definitions, description, narration.

Serial Narratives

Stories written like novels in chapter form are called "serial narratives." The form is related to the sections technique, but each part is a separate story in a continuing saga. Tom French has been writing his stories in this form for many years.

This style of storytelling has become very popular for long stories presented in a series, with each part published on a separate day. If the story is compelling enough, readers will come back for the next part. The format is well-suited for the Web, where each chapter can be presented on separate Web pages.

A serial narrative needs a compelling plot with these elements:

- A character coping with a problem
- Development of the situation
- Resolution

Narrative writing puts the reader on the scene by recreating the events. The story often includes dialogue, suspense and chronological order of the plot rising to a climax just as in a fiction story. But all the information must be true, based on interviews and documents. Cliffhangers at the end of each chapter entice the reader to seek the next part of the serial.

Roy Peter Clark, a senior scholar at The Poynter Institute, experimented with a short form of the serial narrative called "Three Little Words." Each chapter of this story about a woman coping with her husband's death from AIDS was limited to about 1,000 words, approximately three screens on the Web. He likened it to a "breakfast serial," where readers could read each part while having their morning coffee.

To write a story in this form, you need to start with a good plot. Organize the story by dividing it into parts with logical breaks, just as in the sections technique. One organization technique is time frames:

- Past and present—what led to the situation and the current status to explain why you are telling the reader this story now
- Past—development of the situation
- Present—return to present
- Future—what lies ahead

Web Storytelling

The Web is an ideal medium for storytelling in many forms. Short segments are preferable to long stories that span several screens. But the Web is a perfect place to experiment with new forms of storytelling, especially nonlinear treatment with links to elements of the story. We'll discuss more about writing for the Web in Chapter 13.

No single form is right for all stories on the Web or in any other medium. Consumer journalism with helpful tips is another storytelling form that works well on the Web.

But innovative story forms abound on the Web. Storytelling on the Web can be in multimedia format, photo essays, short chunks or serial narratives. Most of all, storytelling can be interactive on the Web. Stories can involve readers by asking them to participate in polls, answer questions, write their own endings or opinions, or submit their own experiences. For an example of innovative storytelling, access Musarium (*www.musarium.com*), a site that offers stories in several creative forms.

What Do You Think ?

Do you think it is OK to reconstruct dialogue as shown by Tom French and Martha Miller in this chapter?

☐ Yes

☐ No

☐ Maybe—explain

☐ Not sure—explain

Exercises

1 **Scene:** Go to a busy place on campus or to the cafeteria and listen to people talking. Gather information about the scene. Then write a few paragraphs setting the scene and weaving in dialogue.

2 **Analogies:** Study some objects on your campus. Write similes and metaphors to describe the objects.

3 **Narrative writing exercise:** Interview a classmate about any experience he has had, preferably a traumatic or

emotional one. If your subject can't think of one, ask him to describe the morning routine from today or yesterday. Imagine that the nut graph is "And then (your subject) disappeared and hasn't been seen since." You will need to ask specific questions, such as what was the person wearing, what color and kind of car was he driving (if a car is involved), what time of day did the events occur, what was he thinking, feeling, doing, saying. Get the person to reconstruct the event exactly as it happened by asking questions about the sequence of events and details. Then write the information in narrative style in a few paragraphs or a brief story.

4 **Timed free-writing:** This exercise, borrowed from Lucille deView, a former writing coach for *The Orange County* (Calif.) *Register,* requires you to write very quickly—in 10 to 15 minutes. Write a story about a personal experience and let your mind ramble, or

write your thoughts about a topic. Remember that you are just getting your thoughts on paper. You can take any words that trigger thoughts—*soup, pizza, cars*—or a topic the instructor gives the class. Some topic suggestions from deView:

The happiest day of my childhood

My favorite assignment

My worst assignment

The most interesting person I interviewed (or know)

A turning point in my life

5 **Read well to write well:** Copy the leads or some excerpts from three news stories you read this week or copy excerpts from other fiction or nonfiction stories that you consider examples of great writing. Try to find examples of the kind of writing you wish you could write.

☞ **Featured Online Activity** Log on to the book Web site for Chapter 11 and access the exercises to practice storytelling forms of writing at

academic.cengage.com/masscomm/rich/ writingandreportingnews6e

Coaching Tips

Update leads: Tell what is happening now.

Use conversational style of writing.

Read your copy out loud before recording it or going on the air.

Use active voice.

Use short sentences—one idea per sentence.

Use present tense when possible and appropriate.

Use subject–verb–object order: Who did what.

Give attribution first; tell who said what before telling what was said.

> Good writing counts for more than anything else. . . . I don't care how pretty you are; I don't care how good looking you are or how well you can chat on the air. The fundamental value around here is breaking news and reporting it well. Everything goes back to writing well.
>
> Ed Bennett, assignment editor, KTUU-TV, Channel 2, Anchorage, Alaska

12 Broadcast News Writing

John Tracy, news director, KTUU
(courtesy Channel 2, KTUU-TV)

KTUU reporter Jennifer Zilko takes notes
while photographer Mike Nederbrock
videotapes eagles being washed.

It's 9:15 on a Monday morning and News Director John Tracy is conducting the daily planning meeting at KTUU-TV. Its' going to be a busy day. A press conference is scheduled for 10 a.m. about a major donation for the library; a national story about MySpace needs to be localized and more than a dozen American bald eagles covered with slime are being cleaned at the bird rescue center in Anchorage. That's going to be a very visual story. Too many good story ideas; too few reporters and photographers to cover them; something has to be scrapped.

"I don't want just 20 seconds of eagles," Tracy says. "I don't think you need the ice fishing story."

Reporter Jennifer Zilko is assigned to the eagle story. She heads to the bird rescue center with a photographer. Workers at the Bird Treatment and Learning Center are in a turmoil. They have 18 birds that were flown in by airplane from Kodiak Island, 252 miles south of Anchorage, and they are expecting 13 more in the afternoon. The eagles usually nest outside a fish processing plant in Kodiak, but when a dump truck left the plant with fish guts, about 50 eagles dove into the uncovered rear of the truck in search of an easy meal. Twenty of the eagles were crushed or drowned in the mucky guts. The others were covered with the sticky fish slime, which glued their feathers and prevented them from retaining body heat. Volunteers at the bird rescue center were trying to save the big raptors from certain death by washing them off with Dawn detergent.

Photographer Mike Nederbrock enters the small washing area to videotape the volunteers as they wash an eagle, and Zilko stands by taking notes. Zilko asks one of the volunteers if she can interview her a little later so she can get a human angle to the story. A press conference follows and Zilko asks several questions. At the end, Zilko asks the director if there is anything else she would like to add.

"If I could give any advice to students, that would be the question to ask: 'Is there anything else you want to share?' And ask them (the sources) to spell their first and last name," Zilko says.

Six months ago Zilko was a student herself at the University of Alaska Anchorage. Although she has only been reporting for KTUU-TV since her graduation, she has been working at the station for two years, converting broadcast scripts into print-style stories for the station's Web site. One of her professors mentioned that the station needed a Web writer, so Zilko applied, took an Associated Press style test and got the job. "The AP Stylebook was my bible for two years." She says students really need to know AP style even if they are going into broadcast and especially if they are planning to work in public relations.

Before she could become an on-air reporter, however, she received training by shadowing a KTUU reporter on assignment. "Then I came back and wrote my own version of the story," she says. "Almost everything I know, I learned on the job."

Producing a Newscast

Zilko's story is only one of 14 news stories to be squeezed into a 30-minute broadcast that also includes weather, sports and commercial breaks. The process of producing a newscast is complex. It involves several editors and producers who must plan every second of the broadcast and adapt to constant changes throughout the day as news breaks.

Logging the Tape

When Zilko returns from the eagle assignment, Nederbrock hands her his videotape, and she inserts it into a machine so she can watch the video and choose the sound bites she wants to use. This process is called "logging" the tape. She types the complete sound bite with the time listed on the tape. Some TV stations require scripts that just use the first few words and last few words of a sound bite, but at KTUU reporters type the entire sound bite so it can be read on the screen as closed captions for hearing-impaired viewers. This also helps the Web editor so he doesn't have to listen to the tape when he converts her script into an online story, Zilko says.

She types quickly as she listens to the tape. "Grammar is not my best part when I'm logging, so I fix it later," she says. "The goal is not to go over 15 seconds on your bites. If they can say it in a shorter bite, that's better." Sometimes Zilko will ask the photographer to recommend his best shot to open the story, but today he has been called away to another assignment.

Planning a Rundown

The photographer shot 32 minutes of tape, but Zilko will have only one minute and 30 seconds (1:30) for her story for the 30-minute newscast at 5 p.m. and 2 minutes (2:00) for the hour-long 6 p.m. newscast. "It may not seem like it's very

Courtesy of Carole Rich

Jennifer Zilko listens to the videotape to log in sound bites for her script.

Producers Aniela Whah (front) and Tracy Holenport.

much time, but I write short so it's fine," she says. The introduction to her story, which she writes for the anchor, will run 15 seconds before the story and 20 seconds for a question-and-answer with the anchor at the end of the story. "I sometimes come in under the time they (the producers) give me, which they like because they're always over."

The producers determine how much time each story can run. Everything is timed to the second in a television newscast. KTUU has two producers: one for the 5 p.m. newscast and one for the 6 p.m. show, but they work together throughout the day.

As soon as the morning planning meeting ends, Aniela Whah starts drafting a schedule called a "rundown" for the 5 p.m. newscast in which she allocates minutes and seconds for every story. Then she begins writing promotional briefs called "teasers," news briefs of about 20 to 25 seconds that will air a few times a day to encourage viewers to tune into the evening newscast. That's not always easy. A story might fall through or breaking news may force a story to be canceled. Writing teasers is an art.

"You have to keep it really short and not give too much away," says Tracy Holenport, the producer for the 6 p.m. newscast.

Scheduling the stories isn't easy either. Every story has to be timed to the second. "I would say that's the hardest part," Holenport says. If a story runs over the allotted time, she has to subtract time from another report such as weather or sports. The time allocated to news is especially limited. The 30-minute newscast at 5 p.m. has only 14 minutes and 9 seconds for news, and the hour-long newscast at 6 p.m. has 22 minutes for news. Weather runs eight minutes and sports runs six minutes. The rest of the time is allotted to teasers before the breaks and advertisements.

In addition to scheduling the rundowns and writing teasers, the producers write most of the anchor's material and some of the smaller stories, including rewrites of national stories. "I probably end up writing about 10 stories per newscast; it depends on the day," Holenport says. "If we are short of reporters, those days are tough on producers."

Before a show, the producers check all the graphics and names flashed on the screen to make sure they are accurate. The producers work closely with assignment editor Ed Bennett, whose desk is a few feet away from theirs.

Assigning the Stories

Bennett starts his day by checking his e-mail, wire stories, Web sites and other news media. Then he reviews the 30-day file of story ideas that he keeps in his desk. He prefers keeping paper records of news releases and other items in his "sacred file," a manila folder he keeps on his desk with a warning that it must not be removed. "That way I have an ability to cover the day's news even if the computer crashes," he says.

Courtesy of KTUU-News Channel 2, Anchorage, Alaska

Page	Story Slug	Segment	Story Writer	Source Tape	Source	Key	Graphic
A16		A	JM		INTV		
A17	ANADARKO GAS DRILLING	BTS	JM		INTV		
A18		QA	JM		INTV		
A19		INTRO	JZ		ROOF	TREATING THE EAGLES	
A20		A	JZ		ROOF		
A21	EAGLE CLEAN UP	B+	JZ		ROOF		
A22		C	JZ		ROOF		
A23		QA	JZ		ROOF		
A24	5P TEASE 2	FOSTER TRIAL SETTLEMENT	AW			in court today	
A25		MYSPACE RULES	AW			myspace	
B0	COM BREAK 1						
B1	REOPEN	((BLUE))					
B2	MYSPACE RULES	A	LT			SAFETY RULES	
B3		B	LT				
B4		A	AB			CASE SETTLED	
B5	FOSTER TRIAL SETTLEMENT	BTS	AB				
B6		GFX	AB				
B7	JUNEAU SESSION ADVANCE	INTRO	WM		FIBR	LEGISLATIVE SESSION	

This is page 2 of the rundown sheet for the 5 p.m. newscast. The story slug is Eagle Cleanup; the intro to the story is on p. A19 of the script; the writer is JZ for Jennifer Zilko, and the source is where she will report the story—on the roof of the KTUU building so that the background is outside when she is talking. A teaser to the MySpace story will come just before the commercial break.

He creates an assignment sheet as a starting point for discussion at the morning planning meeting. Then he adds or changes the story list depending on the discussion and story suggestions from the reporters, who are expected to come to the meeting with some story ideas based on their beats.

"I try to have one or two stories every day set up and ready to shoot or in certain cases ready in the can for the air," Bennett says. He can count on some stories every

Assignment Editor Ed Bennett discusses a story with a reporter.

week because the station airs regular features each day: a business story called "The Bottom Line" on Monday, health news on Tuesday, consumer news on Wednesday, movie reviews on Thursday and an unusual feature about Alaska on Fridays. And Bennett keeps his ears on the police scanner for breaking news.

"Some days it's completely slow; other days are just running and gunning from dawn to dusk so it varies a lot," he says.

He also assigns the photographers to pair with the reporters. "This is TV; the pictures often come first. The availability of a photographer determines when we go on a story or if we go on a story," Bennett says.

He says the Web doesn't affect his job too much, but if a big story breaks, he makes sure the Web editor is aware of it. "The way you cover TV news is to go quickly, go now. It's a very nice marriage with the Web because the Web is also aimed at getting information out there as soon as it comes."

But immediacy can pose problems. The Web editor might hear about a story on the police radio and want to post it, Bennett says. "Sometimes you have to wait for official confirmation. Standard journalism rules do apply to the Web and must be enforced," he says.

In addition to planning the news, Bennett edits scripts along with other newsroom managers. He looks for spelling, accuracy and completeness. He speaks emphatically when he talks about writing:

"This is the thing that people don't understand: Good writing counts for more than anything else, at least in this television newsroom—period. I don't care how pretty you are; I don't care how good looking you are or how well you can chat on the air. The fundamental value around here is breaking news and reporting it well. Everything goes back to writing it well."

Here are his recommendations for writing well:

- Clarity and brevity.
- Use of plain English.
- Avoiding repetition especially repetition between the reporter's writing and the sound bite.
- Picking sound bites that have emotion. "A reporter can give you the facts," Bennett says. "I don't need people telling you what the facts are. A reporter can do that better and faster."

It's Showtime

It's time for the 5 p.m. show. News director John Tracy heads for the studio where he anchors the 5 p.m. show. Tracy reads from the teleprompter, a machine that contains the scripts, which scroll as he reads.

Jennifer Zilko is told to go up to the station's roof to introduce her story. She's not happy about that. It's 10 degrees below zero today, but Tracy likes reporters to appear against a natural background. Zilko's story comes near the middle of the newscast.

Convergence Coach

Eric Adams, Web editor for KTUU-TV, spends much of his day checking for breaking news to post on the station's Web site. If a major story breaks, Adams sends e-mail to the 8,000 people who signed up to receive the station's news alerts. "I want to make sure it's something that 8,000 people want in their e-mail," he says. After the reporters write their scripts for the evening newscasts, he checks them to prepare them for the Web. A style editor will rewrite them later in print format with AP style for the Web.

Adams is convinced that the future of journalism is on the Web. "I would say the biggest obstacles that broadcasters need to overcome and be aware of when they are writing stories and reporting for air is that they also need to be cognizant of online elements," Adams says. "They need to think of how they can present their story in an interactive way on a Web site, which is where people might see it first or might follow up for information as opposed to just writing for broadcast."

Here are some tips to help you prepare for the Web:

■ Gather more information than you need for your TV story so that you can offer additional material for the Web. Consider the viewer. What information related to your story would the reader or viewer find helpful?

Courtesy of Carole Rich

Eric Adams, Web editor for KTUU-TV

■ When you log in your tape, consider the sound bites and video that will look good on the Web.

■ Gather full text of speeches, budgets or other material that would not be in your broadcast story but could go on the Web.

■ Consider an interactive question or poll that might work with your story on the Web.

Courtesy of KTUU-News Channel 2, Anchorage, Alaska

John Tracy

Tracy introduces the stories before the reporters deliver them, and at the end of the story, Tracy asks the reporters some questions to provide additional information. That's called a "tag." Usually the reporters write the questions, but today Tracy asks Zilko a background question about her eagle story that she didn't include. Fortunately she knew the answer regarding how many eagles had died. The show ends promptly at 5:30 to be followed by "NBC Nightly News."

KTUU is an NBC affiliate and one of three network-affiliated television news stations in Anchorage, but it has the largest audience in Alaska. Nationally it is ranked 155 out of 210 markets for television stations. Tracy has been at the station since 1985 and has won more than 100 awards for writing and reporting. He says anybody can deliver a report, but he expects reporters to tell stories, which include details and information that make viewers care.

Writing Tips

Here are excerpts from a booklet of writing and reporting guidelines that Tracy wrote for his reporters:

- **Why should I care?** In every story you write, think about the viewer. Why should they care about your story?

- **What's it all about?** You should be able to state your commitment (called the focus sentence throughout this book) with a simple sentence containing a subject, verb and object. Who is doing what to whom?

- **So what?** Does your story meet the "so what" test? Does it address a larger issue? Did I learn anything new by watching the story?

- **Attribution:** Who said what? If you are going to state anything but the most obvious fact, back it up with attribution. We don't use unnamed sources without the permission of the news director.

- **A good lead:**
  - Captures the viewer's attention
  - Is conversational
  - Uses active voice
  - Moves the story forward

- **Guillotine the Gimmes:** In the body of your story, get rid of the information that people already know. Focus on what they don't know. What's new?

- **Write to the corners:** It still amazes me when reporters *describe* the video to me. "The suspect was visibly upset." No kidding. I can see the picture. Your words should complement the video, not describe it.

- **Bounce the babble:** Don't write like a police report. People are caught, not apprehended.

- **Sound:** Use it whenever you can. It takes the viewers out of the studio and puts them at the story.

- **Sound bites:** Write to them. They shouldn't come out of nowhere, and they should not repeat what you said leading up to the bite.

- **The end:** All good stories build to a strong finish. You can only finish strong if you know how you are going to finish in the field. Your story should leave the viewer feeling something. A successful story evokes an emotional response. Does your story close the circle? Sometimes you can end your story by returning to the start of the story, having answered the question you posed.

Job Qualities

When John Tracy wants to hire a reporter or producer for KTUU, he seeks candidates who have enthusiasm, good writing ability and at least two years of experience at another station. "We all commit the same mistakes; I would like to hire someone who has already committed them so they're not making them on my air," he says.

But even more important is the candidate's writing ability. "Writing is paramount," Tracy says. "They must be good writers. I look for their ability to tell the difference between delivering a report and telling a story."

What is the difference? A report is just an account of what happened. To Tracy, a story involves and affects people. A story includes context—background that puts the story in perspective. "They (reporters) must have the ability to empathize with the subject of their story because we really write about people," Tracy says. "Find the person impacted by that policy or that story. Every story is found in the details. Apart from the skill is enthusiasm. Most of the other stuff you can teach, so I take people with very little experience. I don't believe they have to have a journalism degree—although they need a college degree—as long as they have the passion for writing."

Broadcast vs. Newspaper and Web Writing

Good writing is crucial in every area of the media, including public relations, which involves writing for print, broadcast and the Web. Here are a few major differences between print and broadcast writing:

Attribution:

Always first in broadcast: The bird rescue center's director says one of the eagles died.

First or last for print and the Web: One of the eagles died last night, said the director of the bird rescue center.

Active Voice: Who is doing what, not what was done to whom. Active voice is preferable for print but even more necessary for broadcast.

Active: Volunteers at the center washed the eagles with Dawn detergent.

Passive: The eagles were washed with Dawn detergent by the volunteers at the center.

Present Tense: Use when possible for broadcast; past tense is more common in print and the Web.

Present: One eagle remains in critical condition.

Past: One eagle remained in critical condition.

Update Leads: Use the latest information. This technique is recommended for all media, but especially for broadcast and the Web.

Old news: Eighteen eagles were flown to the bird rescue center Saturday.

Updated: Eighteen eagles are recovering at the bird rescue center, where they were flown Saturday.

Broadcast Script Format

Broadcast scripts are written in two columns, with directions for the technical crew on the left and the story text on the right. Most newsrooms use a computer program that automatically formats the scripts. The reporter's text is usually in capital letters, while the sound bites are in uppercase and lowercase letters. Sources for sound bites are identified by a machine called a "character generator," which produces titles that are superimposed under the video to identify the speaker.

TV stations have different methods of writing directions. Some stations identify sound bites as SOT, meaning sound on tape. At KTUU each sound bite is on a different tape so the bites are identified as A roll on one tape, B roll on another tape and so on. Many of the terms previously used in scripts are changing. The script should contain a slug (a one- or two-word title), which is usually assigned by the producers. The reporter's copy is usually written in capital letters, and the sound bites are typed in uppercase and lowercase letters. While you no longer have to be concerned about typing directions in columns, you should not split or hyphenate words at the end of a sentence. Remember that the script will be read on a teleprompter, and the anchor or reporter needs to see the whole word.

Here is Jennifer Zilko's script about the eagle story; compare it with the print story that follows from the *Anchorage Daily News*.

EAGLE CLEANUP-PKG

SHOW EAGLES IN SOAP
TREATING THE EAGLES
Reporter—Jennifer Zilko
Anchor—John

{***JOHN***}

Readrate 13:75

THE BIRD TREATMENT AND LEARNING CENTER IS TRYING TO SAVE THE LIVES OF MORE THAN A DOZEN EAGLES.

SINCE LAST NIGHT 18 BALD EAGLES HAVE BEEN BROUGHT TO THE CENTER AFTER DIVING INTO THE BACK OF A TRUCK FULL OF FISH SLIME IN KODIAK…AND MORE ARE ON THE WAY.

TAKE: TAKE SPLIT

{***TAKE SPLIT***}

AND AS CHANNEL 2'S JENNIFER ZILKO TELLS US – WASHING AMERICA'S CHERISHED BIRDS IS A LENGTHY PROCESS.

JENNIFER?

JOHN – ACCORDING TO

<shot- EAGLE CLEANUP>
Readrate 13:75

VOLUNTEERS, IT TAKES ABOUT AN HOUR TO CLEAN EACH EAGLE.

TAKE: A ROLL (Jennifer speaking)
(also called SOT—sound on tape)

{***A ROLL***}

FIRST EACH BIRD IS DUNKED INTO A WARM BATH OF SOAPY WATER.

THE SECRET WEAPON?

DAWN DISH SOAP.

AFTER BEING METICULOUSLY SCRUBBED, THEY'RE THEN RINSED.

VOLUNTEERS GO THROUGH EVERY FEATHER ON THE EAGLE TO MAKE SURE ALL THE SOAP IS WASHED OUT.

BUT EVEN AFTER THE WASH— SOME OF THE EAGLES AREN'T DONE YET.

TAKE: B ROLL (also called SOT)
AT: 12:53
TO: 13:03
DURATION: 0:10
(This is the sound bite
and the time on the tape plus the CG)
Cindy Palmatier, director of Avian care,
Bird Treatment Center
TAKE: AUDIO CUE

{***B ROLL***}

<12:53 We have to wait until they're dry and then we go through a sniff test. If they smell like a wet eagle, you're good. If they smell like Dawn, you're good. If they smell like fish, not good.03>

{***AUDIO:CUE***}

IF THE EAGLE SMELLS LIKE FISH IT IS SPOT WASHED AGAIN.

THE REASON IT'S SO CRITICAL TO GET ALL THE OIL OFF IS THAT EAGLES REGULATE THEIR TEMPERATURE WITH THEIR FEATHRS AND THE OIL INHIBITS THAT ABILITY—MAKING THEM SUSCEPTIBLE TO HYPOTHERMIA.

BUT EVEN THOUGH IT'S GOOD FOR THEM SOME OF THESE EAGLES DON'T EXACTLY LIKE HAVING A BATH.

ONE VOLUNTEER GOT NIPPED TWICE TODAY.

TAKE: C ROLL (third sound bite)
AT: 27:31
TO: 27:38
DURATION: 0:07
CG—Gina Hollomon, volunteer,
Bird TLC

{***C ROLL***}

<27:31 No hard feelings, none whatso-ever.33 If I was being manhandled, I might nip myself. 38>

TAKE: LOSE IT	{***LOSE IT***} THE CENTER SAYS EACH OF THESE EAGLES EATS ABOUT 400 GRAMS OF SALMON A DAY SO THEY'RE ASKING FOR PEOPLE TO DONATE IF YOU HAVE SOME EXTRA SALMON IN YOUR FREEZER.
Anchor: JOHN Readrate 13.75 TAKE: QUESTION TAKE: ANSWER	{***QUESTION***} JENNIFER—WHAT CONDITION ARE THE EAGLES IN AT THE CENTER? ***ANSWER***} ACCORDING TO CINDY PALMATIER, THEY'RE ALL DOING WELL EXCEPT FOR ONE OF THE BIRDS. THE CENTER DEEMED THAT EAGLE IN CRITICAL CONDITION BECAUSE IT'S HAVING A LOT OF PROBLEMS WITH TEMPERATURE REGULATION. THE CENTER WAS EXPECTING TO GET 13 MORE EAGLES IN TODAY BUT THE WEATHER IN KODIAK WAS TOO BAD TO FLY THEM TO ANCHORAGE.

Web Versions

The story posted on KTUU's Web site was offered in video, not text. This is how the Web page appeared after the eagle story aired:

The Web site for the *Anchorage Daily News* also featured the eagle story with a photo slide show:

Courtesy of Anchorage Daily News, Anchorage, Alaska

Newspaper Version

Here is how the story was reported in the local newspaper, the *Anchorage Daily News*. Note that in the print version of the story, the reporter used description that would be unnecessary with video. Also notice that the print version is more thorough than the broadcast version, and attribution is usually at the end of the sentence.

Slimed eagles get baths, TLC in Anchorage

SURVIVORS: 20 others died in a truckload of fish waste.

The hot, humid air inside the warehouse smacked of fishy funk, giving away the 18 bald eagles tucked into kennels inside. They, along with 13 others still in Kodiak, were the lucky ones.

About 50 eagles swarmed into an uncovered dump truck at a Kodiak processing plant Friday, leaving 20 dead after being either crushed or drowned in the fish-gut sludge inside, according to the U.S. Fish and Wildlife Service. Now the survivors need a bath.

"We've never seen a flood of bald eagles like this before," said Megan Pool, events coordinator at Anchorage's Bird Treatment and Learning Center.

"It's definitely more than we've dealt with at one time, ever."

The last batch of surviving eagles was scheduled to arrive Monday afternoon but could not get off the ground in Kodiak because of inclement weather, Pool said. The U.S. Coast Guard hopes to fly them up today, she said.

The influx has strained the resources of the center, which has three paid staff members and about 60 volunteers, Pool said. Despite the strain, volunteers were on track to finish hour-long baths for each of the raptors on hand by late Monday, she said.

Cleaning the eagles requires scrubbing them off with unscented Dawn dish detergent to remove the fish oil and slime that soaked their feathers, then rinsing them in a wood-framed structure covered in plastic to keep things hot and humid.

After they are rinsed, the birds are placed into individual kennels in a warming room, where propped-up hair dryers blow hot air on them, though they continue to need supervision.

"They can overheat, now that they're clean," said Barbara Callahan of the International Bird Rescue Research Center. "These birds are exhausted, and they really couldn't be more stressed."

After they dry, the birds are re-evaluated to see if they are completely rid of the oil, which keeps them wet and reduces their ability to retain their body heat. Those that still need scrubbing are spot-cleaned, particularly under their wings and on their upper legs, Pool said.

While most of the eagles looked understandably irritated at the process, one, No. 08-03, remained in critical condition, its listless body leaning against the back of the dog kennel where it was drying. Its blood work—yes, the eagles are having lab work done—didn't show any problems, but its body temperature remained low, Pool said.

Like all the rest, No. 08-03 is a male, said Mary Bethe Wright, a board member at the center. Nobody knows why female eagles escaped the stinky fish waste, but the women workers seemed to enjoy the gender bias.

"I don't think we have any idea. The females were smarter, maybe," Wright said with a laugh.

The opportunistic scavengers eat about a pound of salmon a day at the center, which cared for 44 bald eagles all of last year and is asking for help with heating costs—the building is being kept near 80 degrees—and donations of unprocessed salmon.

Recovered eagles should be released in a few days, Pool said, but getting them back down to Kodiak may be a challenge because of weather and expenses. Even if they make it to Kodiak, they won't be released in the same area, she said.

"We always try to release the birds as close to where we found them as possible, but we're not going to release 30 birds back at the processing plant," she said.

The fish and wildlife service is investigating to see if Ocean Beauty Seafoods will face charges because of the incident. In general, a first offense of this type would be a misdemeanor, said spokesman Bruce Woods, though intent factors into the decision about whether charges will be filed.

In a prepared statement, company spokesman Tom Sunderland said the plant adhered to its normal policies for transporting fish waste. The shipment was bound for a fish meal plant, and company procedures call for the load to be covered after the truck exits the garage, Sunderland said.

"In this case, the birds went to the waste trailer before the cover could be applied," he said.

—James Halpin, *Anchorage Daily News*

ETHICS

The Radio-Television News Directors Association (RTNDA) is the largest organization for electronic journalists. Although many television stations have their own codes of ethics, the RTNDA code of ethics serves as a guide for the broadcast industry. You can find the entire code online at *www.rtnda.org;* link to the code on the navigation bar. Here are a few of the main principles:

■ Professional electronic journalists should recognize that their first obligation is to the public.

■ Professional electronic journalists should pursue truth aggressively and present the news accurately, in context, and as completely as possible.

■ Professional electronic journalists should present the news fairly and impartially, placing primary value on significance and relevance.

■ Professional electronic journalists should present the news with integrity and decency, avoiding real or perceived conflicts of interest, and respect the dignity and intelligence of the audience as well as the subjects of news.

■ Professional electronic journalists should defend the independence of all journalists from those seeking influence or control over news content.

Teasers and Lead-ins

A teaser, also called a "tease," is a short blurb to entice viewers to tune in or stay tuned to a newscast. It is broadcast during the day before the newscast or during the newscast before a commercial break. Don't tease the regular segments in general terms like weather and sports; tease something interesting or unique in your program that will affect the viewers. Write a tease as though you were telling a friend, "Guess what?" or "You won't want to miss this!" Teasers can include audio and video.

Here is a mid-day tease of two items for the 5 p.m. newscast on KTUU:

GOOD AFTERNOON. HERE'S WHAT'S GOING ON AT THIS HOUR.

LAWMAKERS ARE BEGINNING TO ARRIVE IN JUNEAU . . . AHEAD OF TOMORROW'S START OF THE LEGISLATIVE SESSION. WE'LL TAKE YOU TO THE CAPITOL FOR A PREVIEW TONIGHT.

AND, MORE THAN 45 STATES SIGN ON WITH NEW RULES TO KEEP TEENS SAFE FROM SEXUAL PREDATORS ON MYSPACE.

THE STORY . . . TONIGHT ON CHANNEL TWO NEWS.

And here is a tease that anchor John Tracy read before the commercial break that came in the middle of the 5 p.m. newscast after the eagle story on KTUU.

COMING UP ON THE 5 OCLOCK REPORT . . . TWO FOSTER CARE TEENS SUED THE STATE SAYING IT DID NOT KEEP THEM SAFE. NOW BOTH SIDES AGREE TO A SETTLEMENT.

AND KEEPING KIDS SAFE ONLINE . . . MYSPACE JOINS FORCES WITH 49 STATES INCLUDING ALASKA TO CHANGE THE RULES.

Other introductions to teasers before the commercial break can be phrases such as "Just ahead," "Still to come," or "When we come back . . . ."

Sometimes fragments can get the point across better than complete sentences.

In a moment . . . sex behind bars. A scandal brewing in Georgia.

—CNN

Lead-ins: The anchor reads a lead into a package by a reporter. The lead-in should give the essence of the story and sometimes the context for how it occurred. It should not repeat the reporter's lead. It ends with a statement that the reporter, cited by name, has more information or just the reporter's name as in this example:

MANY WOMEN EXERCISE HARD TO GET IN SHAPE. BUT A NEW STUDY SAYS TOO MUCH EXERCISE CAN OFTEN LEAD TO SERIOUS HEALTH PROBLEMS FOR WOMEN. ILEANA BRAVO TELLS US HOW SOME FEMALE COLLEGE ATHLETES COULD SUFFER FROM EATING DISORDERS AS A RESULT. . . .

—NBC News Channel

Writing for Radio

Writing for radio news follows many of the same principles as writing for television news, but the copy is shorter. Stories can be more like the TV teasers in length. A radio newscast may total about 90 seconds with six or seven stories unless it is National Public Radio, which offers longer stories. A typical story might contain fewer than 100 words. And because you can't show video; you should create word pictures by describing the scene.

Peter King, CBS News Radio correspondent, covers complicated stories in a clear, concise way. In an interview with the Al Tompkins, the Poynter Institute's broadcast leader, King offers this advice for writing radio news:

"You have to be able to pick out the most important information and not get caught up in the minutiae. And you have to keep it simple. It's a big mistake to try to cram too much information into too little time, which is why you have to prioritize and do it quickly."

King says most of his sentences last only five to six seconds on the radio. "My rule of thumb is, 'If it seems awkward and long when you say it aloud, it probably sounds that way to the listener.' I try to keep each sentence focused on a single thought, and keep it simple. And keep in mind: You have to keep asking what the listener will and won't be able to digest."

Scripts for radio can be written in uppercase and lowercase letters instead of all capital letters, depending on the preference of the radio station. The following terms are used in radio:

Reader: a script that a newscaster reads without any background noise or comments from sources.

Actuality: the equivalent of a sound bite.

Natural sound: also called "ambient" sound. This is background sound, the same term that's used in television news.

Wrap: a story from a reporter that may include actualities.

Voicer: a story a reporter reads; it may contain natural sound but does not include actualities.

Here are examples of public service announcements written for radio:

30-second script   Soon, all over-the-counter medicines will have one thing in common: simplicity. That's because all over-the-counter medicines will feature new, easier-to-read labels that clearly show their ingredients, uses, warnings and directions. Because if there's one symptom we all want to relieve, it's confusion. For more information, call the Food and Drug Administration at 1-888-INFO-FDA. Again, that's 1-888-INFO-FDA. The new label—It's clearly better.

—Food and Drug Administration

15-second script   Tired of being confused when comparing over-the-counter medicines? Soon, all over-the-counter medicines will feature new, easier-to-read labels. For more information, call the Food and Drug Administration at 1-888-INFO-FDA. The new label—It's clearly better.

—Food and Drug Administration

Broadcast Style

Punctuation   Avoid quotation marks. Generally, sound bites take the place of quotations. But if you want to quote someone, write out the word *quote* in this way: "She said . . . quote . . . this situation is impossible" or "and these are her exact words. . . ." Don't end the quote by saying "unquote." The reader's emphasis should make the end of the quote clear.

Limit punctuation to the comma, period, question mark and dash.

Numbers   Round off numbers when possible. Write out the numbers one through nine; use numerals for numbers over 10. Write out hundred, thousand, million, billion and trillion.

Write numbers to be read as follows: 13-hundred, two-thousand, 14-thousand, one-million, 17-million. More complicated numbers would be written this way: 320-thousand, not 320,000; 15-million-230-thousand, not 15,230,000.

Spell out fractions: one-half, three quarters.

For decimals, write out the word *point:* "It comes to 17-point-two-million dollars." Write out the word *dollars* also, instead of using the symbol.

There are some exceptions. Addresses, telephone numbers and time of day are written in numerals, even if the figures are lower than 10: "She lives at 5 Westbrooke Avenue"; "The accident occurred at 10:30 this morning" (avoid *a.m.* and *p.m.*); "The telephone number to call for information is 5-5-5-1-2-3-4" (separate the numerals with dashes so they are easier to read).

Limit the Use of Numbers: They can be numbing, especially to the ear. Use percentages to give comparisons when possible. If you must use numbers, round them off and reinforce them with a graphic. Say "320-million dollars," not "320-million-122-thousand-three-hundred-44 dollars." Whenever possible, use an analogy to help viewers visualize numbers. The world's largest oil tanker is 15-hundred feet, equivalent to five football fields.

Names and Titles Spell difficult pronunciations of names and locations phonetically. Some anchors prefer only the phonetic spelling instead of the real name followed by the phonetic pronunciation. John Blum would be written as it is pronounced—John Bloom. Identify a person's title before the name: "State Attorney General John Lawmaker is pleased with the results of a crackdown on fraudulent coal dust testing," not "John Lawmaker, state attorney general, is pleased with the results. . . ."

Use Contractions with Caution Write them out. Let the anchors contract them if they want to. Avoid *can't*. It may sound too much like *can*.

Omit Needless Words Words like *that* and *which* aren't always needed.

Timing of Copy Broadcast scripts use 1:30 for one minute and 30 seconds; 2:00 for two minutes and so on.

Story Structure

Like a newspaper story, a broadcast story needs a clear focus, a lead, a body and an ending. Unlike newspaper writing, however, broadcast writing should be geared to audio and video.

Bob Dotson, an NBC correspondent awarded more than 70 times for his good writing, calls the focus sentence a "commitment" statement. It is still a one-sentence summary of the story, but it is centered more on visual impact—what you want the audience to take away from the report. Provide the commitment visually.

In speeches he makes to journalism groups, Dotson offers these tips:

Beginning: Write to your pictures first. Build your lead around a visual that foreshadows the story to come.

Middle:

Usually no more than three to five points, which you prove visually.

Use strong natural sound to let the viewer experience what happened.

Use people engaged in compelling action that is visual.

Use surprises to keep viewers involved and lure uninterested viewers.

Use short sound bites.

Ending: Build to a strong ending throughout the story, and make it visual. Make your viewers care about the story and the people.

Here are some ways to structure each part of a package, a story that contains video and sound bites:

Leads

An anchor will introduce your story, but every story in a package needs its own lead. Max Utsler, a broadcast journalism professor at the University of Kansas, said the No. 1 consideration for a lead is that it must fit the pictures the viewer sees. "Good television writing is not the craftsmanship of words; it is the presentation of the words and pictures fitting together," he said.

Once you have decided which images to use at the beginning of your package, you can decide whether the story needs a hard or soft lead. Feature stories may take softer leads; a breaking-news story calls for a direct approach. In all cases, you must get to the focus—the nut graph—very quickly, generally by the second or third sentence.

Put a human face on the story whenever possible: Try to find someone personally affected by the issue. You can start with the specific, using a person first, and then going to the nut graph:

IRIS DUNCAN WOKE UP ONE MORNING AND SAID SHE THOUGHT SOMEONE HAD PUT WAXED PAPER OVER HER EYES.

SOUND BITE: IT WAS ALL FUZZY AND CLOUDY AND I COULDN'T SEE. I HAD NO IDEA WHAT WAS WRONG.

SHE WENT TO HER DOCTOR THAT AFTERNOON. SHE LEARNED SHE HAD GLAUCOMA. THE DISEASE STRIKES ONE OF EVERY 200-THOUSAND PEOPLE.

Starting with a general statement and going to a specific person is less effective:

GLAUCOMA STRIKES ONE OF EVERY 200-THOUSAND PEOPLE.

IRIS DUNCAN IS ONE OF THEM. SHE WOKE UP ONE MORNING AND SAID SHE THOUGHT SOMEONE HAD PUT WAXED PAPER OVER HER EYES.

The You Voice: Not all stories directly affect viewers' lives. But when possible, try to stress the impact within the first few sentences. Use an element that will make viewers care or understand why this story is important, unusual or of human interest.

Don't be afraid to use the pronoun "you," especially in consumer stories, to heighten impact. Instead of writing a story about a drought in California that will cause lettuce prices to increase, try this approach:

> YOU'RE ABOUT TO PAY MORE FOR YOUR SALAD. A DROUGHT IN CALIFORNIA IS RAISING THE PRICE OF LETTUCE.

Impact Leads: Lead with the effect on viewers as in the previous lead. An impact lead often uses the you voice.

> IF YOU TOOK YOUR CAR TO SEARS FOR REPAIRS IN THE PAST TWO YEARS, YOU MAY GET A REFUND.
> THE COMPANY AGREED TO SETTLE CHARGES THAT IT CHEATED CUSTOMERS BY DOING SHODDY OR UNNECESSARY CAR REPAIR WORK.

> AN ESTIMATED 12-THOUSAND-500 MISSOURIANS WILL BE ELIGIBLE TO RECEIVE 50-DOLLAR CREDIT COUPONS FOR ANY SEARS MERCHANDISE.

Advance the Lead: When you can, advance the lead by stressing the next step to gain immediacy:

Immediacy: TWO PEOPLE REMAIN IN SERIOUS CONDITION FOLLOWING A CAR ACCIDENT THIS AFTERNOON.

No immediacy: TWO PEOPLE WERE INJURED IN A CAR ACCIDENT TODAY.

Focus on a Person: The focus-on-a-person lead works as well in broadcast as in print, especially for a feature or a news story that the anchor introduces with a hard-news lead-in. Like *The Wall Street Journal* formula, this type of lead goes from the specific to the general. The person is one of many affected by the problem.

> JUDY AND JOE WESTBROOK SPENT THE MORNING CLEANING UP THE FURNITURE IN THEIR FRONT YARD. THE BLUE RIVER HAD OVERFLOWED ITS BANKS AND FORCED ITS WAY INTO THEIR INDEPENDENCE HOME.
> MORE THAN 25 FAMILIES SHARE THEIR PREDICAMENT. LATE THIS AFTERNOON ALL OF THOSE FAMILIES WERE AWAITING WORD ABOUT THEIR FLOOD INSURANCE CLAIMS.

Mystery-Teaser Lead: The mystery-teaser lead is another effective soft-lead technique, as long as you don't keep the viewer wondering what the story is about for too long. You must get to the point within the first few sentences.

IN SOME WAYS IT LOOKS LIKE AN ORDINARY CAMP. IT HAS HIKING TRAILS, A SWIMMING POOL AND TENNIS COURTS.

BUT YOU DON'T HAVE TO WORRY ABOUT WHAT CLOTHES TO WEAR. IN FACT, THIS IS ONE OF THE FEW PLACES WHERE YOU'LL FEEL OUT OF PLACE WEARING CLOTHES.

AT THIS CAMP NEAR DENVER MEN AND WOMEN OF ALL AGES FROLIC IN THE NUDE.

SOUND BITE: NUDISM IS ABOUT THE ONLY RECREATION THAT ANYBODY CAN DO WHETHER THEY'RE RICH OR POOR. WE ALL SHARE IN THE SAME SATISFACTION, SO IT'S A VERY GREAT EQUALIZER.

—*Adapted from NBC News Channel*

Body of the Story

As with all story structures, you must identify your focus first. Then jot down the order of your supporting points—facts or quotes from sources in sound bites.

Limit transitions. One point should follow another one naturally. You have little time for wasted words or redundant transitions that parrot what the source will say in a sound bite. If you need transitions from the present to the past in your story, you can start the sentence with the time element—"yesterday" or "earlier today," for example.

One common transition device in broadcast news is the key word technique, picking up on a word in the last sentence and repeating it in the next. It's also a useful technique for bridging thought from one story to the next in the newscast. In this example, the reporter uses the word "shoes" as a transition device for the next paragraph:

THE NIKE COMMERCIAL TOUTS MICHAEL JORDAN'S BASKETBALL PROWESS. SPIKE LEE SAYS IT'S GOTTA BE THE SHOES.

BUT MIKE AND HIS BUDDIES WOULDN'T EVEN HAVE TO WEAR SHOES TO WALTZ TO THE OLYMPIC GOLD.

Most of the basic news elements—who, what, when, where, how and so what—must be included in the story but not all in the same paragraph. In broadcast writing, placement of points of emphasis for these elements differs from print.

Where: Because most radio and television stations reach such a broad audience, the location of a story is even more important in broadcast than in print. Broadcast reports can superimpose the name of the location on the screen, but you also need to say it in the story. If the story follows a series of other stories from different regions, you might start this way:

> IN PAWTUCKET, RHODE ISLAND, POLICE ARE LOOKING INTO THE SUSPICIOUS DEATH OF A 15-MONTH-OLD BABY.

When: Almost all broadcast stories have a "today" element. Avoid using a.m. or p.m. If the specific time element is important, say something like "An earthquake struck Southern California at 7:15 this morning"; or "earlier today" is sufficient. Place your time element after the verb, which is a more natural, conversational order.

> *Awkward:* AT LEAST FIVE PEOPLE TODAY WERE ARRESTED IN AN ANTI-ABORTION PROTEST OUTSIDE A MILWAUKEE CLINIC.
> *Preferred:* AT LEAST FIVE PEOPLE WERE ARRESTED TODAY IN AN ANTI-ABORTION PROTEST OUTSIDE A MILWAUKEE CLINIC.

Who: Avoid using unfamiliar names in a lead and too many names in a story. When you have video sound bites, you may not even need the name in the story. The person can be identified by a superimposed title under his image in the taped segment. For delayed identification, follow the same guidelines as for print journalism. Identify the person by an age, a location, an occupation or some other generic identifier. Then follow with the person's name. If you do have to identify a speaker, use his title before the name:

> *Say:* BROWARD COUNTY SHERIFF JOHN LAW SAID TODAY HE WOULD NOT SEEK RE-ELECTION WHEN HIS TERM ENDS NEXT YEAR.
> *Do not say:* JOHN LAW, SHERIFF OF BROWARD COUNTY, SAID TODAY . . .

Here are some ways of organizing broadcast stories:

Problem/Solution: The most common structure starts with a statement of the problem, provides support in sound bites and facts, offers background, and discusses the solutions if any exist. It often ends with the next step in the action.

Time Sequence: A story may lend itself to order by time. Because broadcast stories need immediacy, the time sequence is usually a reverse chronology that starts with the present action, goes to the past (background) and ends with a future element. Here is an example of reverse chronology:

Present

ANIMAL-RIGHTS ACTIVISTS ARE PROTESTING THIS MORNING OUTSIDE THE PITTSBURGH HOSPITAL WHERE DOCTORS TRANSPLANTED A LIVER FROM A BABOON TO SAVE A MAN'S LIFE.

Past (background)

ABOUT 15 PROTESTERS CARRIED SIGNS AND CHANTED AT THE ENTRANCE TO THE UNIVERSITY OF PITTSBURGH MEDICAL CENTER. ONE MEMBER OF THE PITTSBURGH ANIMAL ACTIVISTS SAYS THEY DON'T BELIEVE ONE SPECIES SHOULD BE SACRIFICED FOR ANOTHER.

DOCTORS SAY IF THEIR PATIENT CONTINUES TO RECOVER FOR THE NEXT MONTH OR MORE, THEY'LL DO THREE MORE OF THE SAME TRANSPLANTS.

Future

—*The Associated Press*

Hourglass: This structure is a type of time sequence. However, you start with a hard-news summary lead and then rebuild the story chronologically.

Summary lead

A TOXIC CHEMICAL SPILL NEAR SUPERIOR, WISCONSIN, FORCED HUNDREDS OF RESIDENTS FROM TWO CITIES TO FLEE THEIR HOMES. AT LEAST TWO CHILDREN RECEIVED HOSPITAL TREATMENT. A HOSPITAL OFFICIAL SAYS MORE PEOPLE WILL NEED TREATMENT.

Beginning of chronology

THE PROBLEMS BEGAN THIS MORNING WHEN 13 FREIGHT CARS DERAILED JUST OUTSIDE SUPERIOR. ONE BURLINGTON NORTHERN CAR FELL INTO THE NEMADJI (NEH-MA'-JEE) RIVER, SPILLING SOME OF ITS CARGO OF BENZENE. BENZENE IS A FLAMMABLE SOLVENT, AND ITS FUMES CAN CAUSE HALLUCINATIONS, DIZZINESS AND COUGHING.

IN SUPERIOR AND NEIGHBORING DULUTH, MINNESOTA, OFFICIALS ORDERED THE EVACUATION OF HUNDREDS OF HOMES WITHIN A MILE OF THE RIVER. AND THE COAST GUARD SAYS IT'S PLACED A BOOM ACROSS SUPERIOR BAY TO PREVENT THE BENZENE FROM SPREADING.

—*The Associated Press*

Circle: Envision your story as a circle. The main point is the lead. All supporting points should relate to the focus in the lead. Unlike an inverted pyramid, where points are placed in descending order of importance, in a circular construction, each part of the story is equally important. Your ending can refer back to a point in the lead, as in this example about a water problem in a Kansas community:

Lead

IF YOU LIVE NEAR BALDWIN CITY, YOU MAY WANT TO AVOID DRINKING THE WATER TONIGHT.

Supporting points

THE KANSAS DEPARTMENT OF HEALTH AND ENVIRONMENT IS WARNING FOLKS IN WATER DISTRICT NO. 2 IN DOUGLAS COUNTY ABOUT THE WATER. OFFICIALS FOUND BACTERIA IN THE WATER THAT MAY BE HARMFUL.

SOUND BITE (from Greg Crawford, an official with the Kansas Department of Health and Environment):

THESE ARE INDICATOR BACTERIA, WHICH MAY INDICATE THE PRESENCE OF MORE SERIOUS BACTERIA. BACTERIA CAN CAUSE A NUMBER OF GASTROINTESTINAL PROBLEMS. AND WE WOULD LIKE PEOPLE TO PREVENT THOSE PROBLEMS BY BOILING THEIR WATER OR USING BOTTLED WATER OR PERHAPS TREATING THEIR WATER WITH CLOROX OR OTHER LIQUID BLEACH.

CRAWFORD SAYS BACTERIA COME FROM DEAD ANIMALS. UNTIL OFFICIALS CAN CLEAR UP THE PROBLEMS, PEOPLE IN THE AREA SHOULD TAKE PRECAUTIONS.

Ending referring back to lead:

—*KSNT-TV*

Ending

In broadcast writing, endings are called "tags" or "wrap-ups." Newspaper stories often end with a quote from a source, but in broadcast writing, the reporter has the last word in a package, followed by his name and the station identification. Often the only time the viewer sees the reporter is at the end of the story. However, many news directors now prefer using reporter stand-ups within the story rather than at the end.

The most common endings:

- **Summary:** A fact that reinforces the main idea without repeating previous points.
- **Future:** The next step in some action.
- **Factual:** A background statement or just another fact.
- **Consumer:** Helpful items, such as where to call or go for additional information. If this information is important to the viewer, avoid giving it only one time. Warn the viewer that you will be repeating telephone numbers or locations later in the program. Plan to have phone numbers posted on the screen. You can also refer to your station's Web site for additional information.

Revising Stories

When you write the ending for your story, you are not at the end of the writing process. Revision is an important part of writing your story.

- Read your story aloud. Rewrite any sentences that sound strained.
- Check all your sources' names and titles for spelling and accuracy.
- Eliminate any bureaucratic language and replace it with simple, clear terms.
- Delete adjectives. Let the video show the viewers the scene.
- Make sure your transitions don't repeat the sound bites.
- Look at the video without the sound; then listen to your story without the video.

Glossary

Here are some basic terms used in broadcast news:

Actuality: A radio term for recorded comments from a news source. Same as a sound bite, the term used in television.

Anchor: The person who reads the news on the set in the studio.

Backtiming: Exact time in the newscast that a segment will air. For example, a story that will air 12 minutes and 15 seconds into the newscast will be labeled 12:15. If the last segment in a 30-minute newscast is one minute, the backtiming will be 29, alerting the anchor that the segment must start at precisely that time or it will have to be cut.

Brief: Abbreviated news story, from 10 to 20 seconds long.

Character generator: Computer-type machine that produces the letters, numbers or words superimposed on the screen to label a visual image, such as a person or place. Also called a *Chyron,* the brand name of the machine that generates these titles.

IN: Indicates the first few words of the source's quote to start a sound bite and the time on the tape, used at stations that don't include the entire sound bite in the script.

News director: Oversees all news operations at the station.

One-man-band: Based on the definition of a musician who plays a number of instruments, in television a one-man-band refers to a reporter who shoots, tapes and writes the story—a person who does it all.

OUT: Indicates the last few words of the source's quote, ending the sound bite.

Package: Reporter's story that includes narration, visual images and sound bites from sources.

Producer: Plans the newscast and often writes teasers and some copy for the anchors.

PSA: Abbreviation for a public service announcement.

Reader: Story the anchor or radio announcer reads without visuals or sound bites.

Rip-and-read: Copy from the wire services that is read exactly as it was written instead of being rewritten.

Seg time: Length of time for a news segment. A brief may be :10, or 10 seconds; a reporter's package, including the lead-in by an anchor, may be 1:45—one minute and 45 seconds.

SOC (standard out cue): Reporter's sign-off comments at the end of the story. For example, "This is Jennifer Zilko for KTUU Anchorage."

SOT (sound on tape): Similar to a sound bite; indicated in copy along with the amount of time the taped comments will take. For example, SOT:15 means the comments on the tape will take 15 seconds.

Sound bite: Video segment showing the source speaking.

Stand-up: A part of the story in which the reporter talks on camera at the scene; sometimes at the end of a story.

Super: Letters, numbers or words produced by the character generator and superimposed over visual images; often used to identify the person appearing on the tape. At some stations, the letters CG—for character generator—are used to indicate the super.

Tag: The closing sentence for a TV or radio story or package.

Teaser: Introduction to a story on the next newscast, to tease viewers to tune in.

Teleprompter: Video terminal that displays the script for the anchor to read. This term was previously a trademark, but AP style now considers it generic.

VO (voice over): Anchor's voice over video images. Words and images should coincide.

VOB (voice over bite): Anchor's voice over video images with a sound bite from a source.

VO-SOT (voice over sound on tape): Anchor's voice over video and sound bite; same as VOB but more commonly used.

What Do You Think ?

Would you prefer to read stories or view the video on broadcast Web sites?

- ☐ Read
- ☐ View video
- ☐ Both
- ☐ Neither
- ☐ I prefer to receive them on my iPod or by e-mail

Exercises

1 Write a broadcast brief, about 15 seconds, based on this information from an NBC News Channel story:

Who: A consumer group, the Florida Consumer's Federation.

What: Filed a suit charging the Publix Grocery Store chain with discrimination.

Why: Group claims that the grocery chain failed to put enough women, blacks and Hispanics in management jobs and that the company doesn't have enough stores in minority neighborhoods.

When: Today.

Backup information: Publix management agrees with some of the complaints but says it is working to overcome them, according to Publix president Mark Hollis.

2 **Convert the following broadcast story into proper TV news script form.**

ANCHORAGE, Alaska—Social network giant MySpace is stepping up its online security, partnering with law enforcement to make the Web site safer for kids.

Alaska has joined an effort with the site, along with attorneys general from 48 other states and the District of Columbia, to protect children, purge predators and get rid of inappropriate content, specifically pornography.

More than 70 million users are registered on MySpace and the site is spending big to protect those members, especially those under 18. The plans were announced Monday at a press conference in New York.

"Rather than treating the off-line and online worlds differently, our goal has been and will continue to make our virtual neighborhoods as safe as our real ones," said Hemanshu Nigam, MySpace chief security officer.

The Web site already makes the profiles of its 14- and 15-year-old members as "private." That designation will soon extend to 16- and 17-year-olds.

"Setting that default to 'private' definitely is a protection mechanism but it's not going to keep your child safe," said Clark Harshbarger, an Anchorage FBI agent.

Harshbarger says MySpace is making progress in its efforts to increase security but acknowledges the changes are difficult to implement.

MySpace directors also said they are working to develop technology that would help parents prevent their children from using the website. An e-mail registry would allow parents to add their children's addresses.

The Web site would then block the user.

Cynthia Drinkwater, an assistant attorney general for Alaska, says the partnership between law enforcement and MySpace has been two years in the making.

"It made a large step and it should be commended," she said, adding that the Web site made great progress last year cracking down on users who are registered sex offenders.

In July, MySpace announced that it deleted the profiles of as many as 30,000 sexual predators.

"MySpace has agreed that online identity verification is very important and that they are going to take steps to analyze the programs, that technological answers that are out there and work on developing things that might really work to make sure that people who want to use the MySpace Web site are who they say they are," Drinkwater said.

—*Lori Tipton, KTUU-News, Anchorage, Alaska.*

3 Convert the following newspaper story into a TV story.

A 16-year-old boy, driving without a license, led Louisville police on a 13-minute chase yesterday afternoon, driving at up to 80 mph on streets in the Highlands sections where the sidewalks were crowded with pedestrians.

The pursuit ended at 5:05 p.m., when the boy—whose name police did not release because of his age—rammed his father's 1991 Honda Accord into the rear of Officer Bob Arnold's patrol car on Trevilian Way just east of Valley Vista.

No one was injured, and the police car suffered only a minor scrape on the rear bumper. The other car was damaged more.

Officer John Butts said the chase started near Cherokee Park when he tried to stop the boy for running over a stop sign, and the boy refused to pull over. Butts radioed for help and Arnold joined the chase.

"I was concerned, because he came close to hitting several pedestrians who were out walking because of the nice weather," Butts said last night.

"Anxiety sets in when a chase continues on for this amount of time," he added. "It's longer than any officer would prefer to be in a high-speed vehicle pursuit."

Butts said the boy forced several cars off the road during the chase, which came to an end when Arnold managed to get in front of the boy and slowed down. He said the boy will be charged with numerous felonies and traffic violations; among the charges are wanton endangerment and resisting arrest. The boy was taken to the Jefferson County Youth Center.

Butts said he did not know why the boy refused to stop, but added, "He has no license, and he was not supposed to be driving his father's car."

—*The* (Louisville, Ky.) *Courier-Journal*

Coaching Tips

Plan interactive elements such as polls or discussion questions.

Provide blogs or forums for readers.

Write short, simple sentences.

Write enticing headlines and blurbs.

Plan photo, audio and video elements.

Consider summary or highlights boxes.

The most critical need is the ability to file material to online quickly and regularly. We believe that most reporters will soon be mojos, producing information seamlessly across platforms.

Kate Marymont, executive editor, *Fort Myers* (Fla.) *News-Press*

13 Online Journalism

Amojo is a magic charm or spell, but in Honolulu and Fort Myers, Fla., a mojo is a new breed of journalist.

Mojos are mobile journalists equipped with notepads, cameras, recorders, cell phones and laptop computers so they can file community news stories for the Web at a moment's notice. They don't go to a newspaper office; their office is in their cars. They don't wait for deadlines; their deadlines are whenever they get their information.

The mojo concept was initiated at the *Fort Myers News-Press* and is being used at the *Honolulu Advertiser* in Hawaii and *Florida Today* in Melbourne, Fla. All three newspapers are owned by the Gannett Corp., which intends to expand the use of mojos to many of its 82 other newspapers.

As competition for readers and viewers increases because of blogs, social networking sites and millions of Web choices, news organizations are seeking ways to connect with their audiences. Gannett is trying to do that by providing "hyperlocal news," community stories that matter to residents—from traffic reports to interactive graphics explaining where people can get the cheapest gas. The company has also reorganized its newsrooms as "information centers" that provide news in many platforms—from brief news delivered to cell phones to complex, interactive multimedia Web sites.

Gannett is not alone. News organizations throughout the country are using the Web in innovative ways to lure readers and viewers to their sites. Changes in news coverage and delivery—via text, photos, audio and video for mobile phones or company Web sites—affect what, when and how you need to write for the Web. Journalists today must be prepared to post news anytime, anywhere and any way.

The basic concept for breaking news on the Web is short, fast and frequent. The Web is no longer the last place to post news; it's the first. Web skills are no longer an optional asset; they are crucial for media careers in print, broadcast and public relations.

In the past most news organizations just published the same information on their Web sites as they had in their newspapers or TV report, but now news organizations are using the Web for original material such as multimedia presentations and interactive features that include blogs, games and searchable graphics or databases.

Mobile journalism may be a wave of the future for print reporters, but television stations have been using mobile vans to cover breaking news for many years. The difference between mojos and traditional reporters is that these mobile journalists live, work, and play in the communities they cover. The news is posted on "microsites," subsidiary sites of the newspaper's main Web site. These microsites contain breaking news, community profiles, searchable databases, archives and places for readers to post comments and blogs.

Mary Vorsino, a mojo for the *Honolulu Advertiser*, described a typical day for editors of Gannett in a teleconference training session:

"A typical day varies greatly," she said. "Most days start with a check of any breaking news in my neighborhood. Many days I have interviews or events happening in my region. The difference from a conventional regional beat, however, is that throughout the day I post breaking news or update items on the *Honolulu Advertiser* Web site. This allows me to give readers up-to-date information on everything from car wrecks to an upcoming informational meeting happening in their neighborhood."

Courtesy of The News Press, Fort Myers, Florida

Mark Krzoz, mojo for Fort Myers News-Press

Mark Krzos, a mojo for the *Fort Myers News-Press*, files his stories from his car throughout the day. He says you need to "get it fast and get it online." In a podcast on the Gannett Web site, he said his stories can range from writing about a different way around traffic to telling people what concerns them.

From brief neighborhood stories to complex multimedia sites, the Web is changing how journalists need to report and write news. Some of the main qualities of journalism in a Web-centric society are:

Immediacy: News must be updated throughout the day. As soon as news breaks, it should be posted on the Web. It can be delivered to cell phones, e-mail or Web sites via automatic updates called RSS (Really Simple Syndication) feeds.

Interactivity: Journalists aren't the only providers of news anymore. Web sites feature blogs and messages posted by subscribers to the site. Interactive graphics allow readers to click on a map or illustration to find the cheapest gas prices or check crime rates in their neighborhoods.

Courtesy of The News Press, Fort Myers, Florida

Graphic from the *Fort Myers News-Press* for mobile news delivery

Multimedia: In the past, multimedia projects were limited to major projects. Now multimedia is prevalent on many print and broadcast Web sites. A multimedia story is any story that uses a variety of media such as text with photographs, video, audio and graphics. Sophisticated multimedia projects feature several of these elements and interactivity.

Students at several universities are winning awards for multimedia mastery. University of Arizona students in Tucson garnered first place in the Online Journalism Association awards for their multimedia magazine called *Border Beat*. The magazine aims at providing fresh perspectives about people and issues of the U.S.-Mexican border.

Border Beat magazine produced by students in the Department of Journalism at the University of Arizona

Innovation: Storytelling on the Web can take many forms. Be imaginative. You can still use the inverted pyramid for breaking news stories, but you can also tell stories in many other ways. Think long and short—full-length stories or miniprofiles; question/answer instead of text; photographs to tell the story, quizzes, lists and games. For inspiration, check the annual awards from the Online News Association for innovative news Web sites at *www.journalists.org/awards/*.

Reporting for the Web

Good reporting is similar in any medium, but you need some additional tools and reporting steps for the Web.

Plan for Full Coverage: Be prepared to report your story for text delivery and for audio or video elements. Plan to get the full text of a speech, a city budget, a list of contest winners or other additional information to post on the Web.

Equipment: For basic reporting, in addition to a notebook and pens or pencils, take a tape recorder to get audio sound bites and some form of digital storage media such as a jump drive for the extended information mentioned in the previous point. Other necessities include a cell phone to call in your story, digital camera, extra batteries and a notebook computer if you are going to transmit a story from your location.

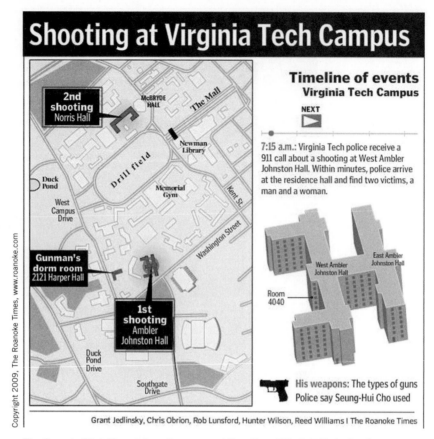

Grant Jedlinsky, Chris Obrion, Rob Lunsford, Hunter Wilson, Reed Williams I The Roanoke Times

The Roanoke (Va.) *Times* interactive map and time line of Virginia Tech shooting.

Jane Stevens, a professor of multimedia instruction at the University of California Berkeley, suggests some other practical equipment for a "backpack journalist," like a mojo. She suggests a video camera and lens cleaners to clean the video camera lenses, duct tape in case your camera breaks, plastic bags for digital video tapes and a water bottle and power bars for you.

Time Lines: When you are covering a major disaster or crime event, mark your notes with time periods for a time line that might be posted on the Web. For example, the *Roanoke* (Va.) *Times* posted a time line and an interactive map to describe events during the massacre at Virginia Tech. in 2007.

Updates and Follow-Up Stories: Plan to file your story in a brief form as soon as the news breaks. Then plan an updated version for your next print or broadcast edition. If you are covering a major breaking-news story, plan to file for the Web every time you receive new information. Think ahead. Plan to write a follow-up story for the next edition of your broadcast or print publication.

E-mail Reporting: Don't depend on it for deadline. E-mail is a good way to reach people and get limited information, but face-to-face or telephone interviewing is still preferable.

ETHICS

The Society of Professional Journalists' Code of Ethics (*www.spj.org/ethicscode.asp*), referred to throughout this book, is considered a standard for most media professionals. But no clear code of ethics exists for online journalism. However, the Poynter Institute has recommended a set of guidelines for online journalism. Some of the recommendations are as follows:

■ Journalists should avoid conflicts of interest.

■ News organizations should clearly label news and opinion.

■ Journalists who work for news organizations may keep personal blogs, but they should discuss their plans with an editor to avoid potential conflicts.

■ Professional journalists should not write an anonymous blog or comment anonymously on other blogs. "Reporters are expected to own responsibility for their work, and commenting or blogging anonymously compromises that core principle."

Jonathan Dube, director of digital programming for CBS news, has created Cyberjournalist.net, a Web site with extensive resources for online journalism. He has proposed a blogger's code of ethics that is based on the SPJ code but addresses some specific blogging issues (*www.cyberjournalist.net/news/000215.php*).

Check Accuracy and Timeliness: If you are using information from the Web, check the date of the information and the reliability of the Web site for accuracy. Is the information from a site by a government agency, a university, a respected media organization or is it from a personal site?

Online Readers

Many Web stories are versions of a print or broadcast story. But online users don't read the same way on the Web as they do in print publications.

Eye Track Studies

The Poynter Institute and Stanford University have conducted several studies to test how people read online stories. Using specially fitted glasses on the subjects, the researchers watched and recorded the readers' eye movements in these studies called "Eye Track." The original Eye Track study in 1991 tested how readers reacted to color, headlines and text in newspapers and concluded that readers looked first at headlines and photos. A study in 2000 tested on how people viewed Web sites and the conclusions were opposite from those for newspaper readers. The study showed that Web viewers looked first at text and briefs, not images. Another study in 2003 concluded that the first three words in headlines and blurbs are the most important to attract Web readers. Smaller type encourages more thorough reading; larger type encourages scanning.

The Poynter Institute/Stanford University/Eye Track Study

Headgear to track online readers' eye movements in Stanford University/Poynter Institute Eye Track study

The most recent Eye Track study in 2007 was the first to compare print and online reading habits. The most significant findings are:

- People will read a story online thoroughly if they are interested in it. This is a major change from past thinking that Web readers only scanned stories.
- Both print and online readers rarely read stories to the end, but online readers read more of a story on the Web than print readers.
- Alternative story forms such as question/answer, time lines, lists and fact boxes help readers remember facts.

Linear vs. Nonlinear

The interactive nature of the Web makes it nonlinear, meaning users may access information in any order they choose. Conversely, print and broadcast stories are written in linear order from beginning to end, as in a straight line, offering readers no choice except to stop reading. Although many Web stories are still written in linear order, Web readers have nonlinear choices of accessing related elements linked to the story or the site.

A Web package created in nonlinear order might be divided into smaller chunks spanning several pages, or it might contain links to time lines, related stories, polls and other interactive elements.

Embedded or External Links Should you include links within the text (embedded) of your story or at the end (external)? The AP Stylebook says to include the URLs (Internet addresses) within the text if they refer to a site being discussed but place them at the end if they provide additional information. In the past, most Web designers and usability experts recommended that links be placed on the side or at the end of a story because a reader who clicked on an embedded link might not return to the article. However, the current thinking is that online readers have become so sophisticated that they will return to articles they want to read even if they access a link on another page.

Story Planning

Whether readers scan or thoroughly read Web stories, the hyperlink nature of the Web changes the way writers need to plan their stories. You need to plan the story *before* the reporting process so you know what information to gather. Most news organizations use formatted programs for Web stories, so you don't have to worry about designing the Web page for your story. If you are planning to create a multimedia package or Web site, you should take a course in Web design, which is beyond the scope of this book.

Web designers plan sites by drawing a "storyboard," which is similar to an organizational chart, to show the main parts and related pieces. A storyboard can be used for news stories as well. You could also draft a simple outline to plan elements of the story.

First decide the best way to tell the story. Not all stories need to be written in linear text format. A story or some of its parts may be presented in alternative forms. Before you write your story, you should plan the organization. Writing for the Web requires envisioning a story in layers. Will your story be one page of text or will you write it in chunks? Will you use photos, audio and/or video? Will you have sidebars? These are some elements to consider:

Time Lines: Does the story lend itself to background created as a time line?

Frequently Asked Questions: Would a question/answer format or FAQ (Frequently Asked Questions) be a good way to present the story or accompany it?

Interactivity: Will the story feature a discussion question, poll, quiz, searchable databases or other information the reporter may need to gather for reader involvement?

Lists or Data for Full Coverage: Will the story be accompanied by a complete list of contest winners, school test scores or other information?

Miniprofiles: Does a story about candidates or a long feature series need short biographies of the sources?

Multimedia: Will the story include audio or video? Do you need to tape an interview for sound bites?

Related Links: Although some organizations have researchers or Web producers who find related links, when you are producing your own stories, add the relevant links.

E-mail Addresses of Reporters: Not all news sites include these addresses, but it's a good idea to add your e-mail address to your byline.

A checklist for your story might look something like this:

- Headline
- Highlights (above or on the side—optional)
- Summary blurb
- Main story—one scrolling text page or divided into chunks of several Web pages
- Breaking news brief or updates
- Links to related stories and sources (preferably on the side or at the end)
- Time lines
- Short bios of main sources
- Full text of speeches, reports, budgets or lists of winners
- Photos/graphics

- Multimedia (audio or video)
- Searchable databases
- Interactive elements: polls, games, quizzes, blogs, discussion questions or places for readers to post messages.

Courtesy of Jakob Nielsen

Jakob Nielsen

Writing Techniques

There is no single way to write for the Web. Choose the form that best fits the story or purpose. Is your purpose to inform or entertain or do both? If you are writing for a corporate or public relations site, determine the best way to convey information quickly and clearly. If you are writing news, consider the inverted pyramid for breaking or serious news. If you want to tell a good story, perhaps a narrative form might be suitable.

Jakob Nielsen, often considered the world's leading expert on Web usability, originally set the standards for online writing. He influenced a generation of Web designers and writers with his biweekly columns about Web usability (*www.useit.com/alertbox/*). Nielsen's early recommendations about how to write for the Web were based on studies he conducted in the late 1990s about how people read Web content. Many of his writing guidelines are still valid, but he admits that "because people read differently, you have to write differently."

Some of his early writing guidelines that he still espouses include:

- Write short.
- Write for readers who scan Web sites instead of reading thoroughly. "Users won't read your text thoroughly in a word-by-word manner. Exhaustive reading is rare," he says.
- Write to the point; avoid "fluffy marketese."
- Use common language, not made-up terms.
- State the most important information in the first two paragraphs.

"But the very best content strategy is one that mirrors the users' mixed diet," Nielsen said in a 2007 column. "There's no reason to limit yourself to only one content type. It's possible to have short overviews for the majority of users *and* to supplement them with in-depth coverage and white papers for those few users who need to know more."

Here are some other writing tips that apply to most Web stories:

- Write a clear focus statement or nut graph high in the story, especially if you use an anecdotal lead. Readers should know what the story is about and why they are reading it within the first few paragraphs.

- Write short, simple sentences. Reading on computer monitors is more difficult than in print. Avoid sentences with long clauses and complex sentences. Be concise.

- Use bulleted lists to help readers scan text when the story lends itself to itemized information.

- Limit each paragraph to one idea.

- Write in active voice: Who did what rather than what was done to whom. *The student won an award,* not *An award was won by the student.*

- Avoid last name only on second reference in subsequent screens or Web pages unless the source is well known or is the main person in the story. Apply the blocking technique of restricting each source's comments to one block in the story so the reader doesn't have to scroll up and down a page or refer to a previous page to remember someone's name.

- Keep paragraphs short.

- Use conversational style. Write as though you were talking to a single reader. Borrow from broadcast writing. The "you" voice works well online. Try to let readers know what the story means for them.

Headlines, Blurbs and Briefs

Headlines, summary blurbs and briefs are called "microcontent," the smaller elements of a story. But they are the biggest factor in determining whether someone will click into the story. Clarity is crucial. The headline and a summary blurb of one or two sentences should accurately summarize the story. Readers in a rush want to know exactly what they're getting when they link into a story. Unlike a newspaper, which offers only a handful of stories on each page, a Web page offers scores of headlines and links competing for attention.

Most Web experts advise against writing catchy, teaser headlines because they could be misleading. A teaser headline may work if it is accompanied by a clear summary blurb. But Web pages with many headlines may not contain summary blurbs, so the headline must tell the story by itself.

Although headlines are often written *after* the story is submitted, one of the best ways of focusing your story is to write a headline and summary blurb *before* you write the full story. Because most major news organizations also require reporters to submit briefs for the Web before publication in a newspaper or on a broadcast newscast, writing a brief first is another good way to identify the essential information for a fuller story.

Here are some guidelines for Web headlines that link to the main story:

Write Brief Headlines: Fewer than six to 10 words create better links than headlines that span two or three lines:

Study: Kids are solicited online (or)

Kids are solicited online, study says

Convergence Coach 🌐

Most of these tips apply to online writing for print, broadcast or public relations sites.

- Enlist "crowd sourcing," contributions from readers and viewers in blogs, messages or just contributions to news
- Use photos, graphics, audio and video that compliment your story; don't just add multimedia for its own sake. Just because you can create multimedia doesn't mean you should. Choose the form that best fits or enhances the content.
- Gather more information than you need for a single story. Always plan follow-up stories, full text of

documents and other materials for the reader who wants in-depth material on your Web site.

- Check the date of information from the Web.
- Add contact information to your Web site. Don't just say contact Webmaster. Provide a name, e-mail address, phone number and physical address, especially on corporate sites or public relations materials.
- Add information such as "About Us," especially for corporate information or multimedia projects. Explain who created the project and other pertinent information for viewers.

Use Strong Verbs: Some headlines may be written without verbs:

Lose 10 pounds in five weeks

(No verb) Top 10 diet tips

Put the Most Important Words First:

Cookie Monster assaulted, police say

Avoid Articles: Don't use *the, a,* or *an* at the start of a headline:

Net makes cheating easy

Not: The Net makes cheating easy

Use Question Headlines If the Subject Is Interesting Enough to Entice Readers:

Is work a pain in the neck or in the hands?

Blurbs

The majority of news sites just repeat the story lead for the blurb under the headline. That's fine if it's a summary lead. But if the lead doesn't give the main point of the story, write a clear summary or use the nut graph as the blurb.

For example, this headline from online *The Tampa Tribune* is vague standing by itself. It needs the summary blurb that accompanied it: The next headline is somewhat catchy, but it depends on the summary blurb for clarification:

Checking it out for themselves

LAKELAND—With a customer and brand base on its side, Publix is going after an online home-delivery market in a venture where others who tried it have seen their businesses marked down or shelved.

The next headline again is somewhat catchy, but it too depends on the summary blurb for clarification:

Woman seeks divorce over mynah indiscretions

A Chinese woman launches divorce proceedings after the family's pet mynah bird blabs about husband's affair. The bird began repeating words, "I love you" and "divorce" from the husband's phone calls to his lover.

Blurb Tips

Write a Clear Summary: If the lead is creative, choose the nut graph as the summary blurb. The Cookie Monster headline mentioned on the previous page may provoke curiosity, but it could use a blurb for clarification:

Headline **Cookie Monster assaulted**

Blurb Maryland dad charged with attacking Sesame Place worker. Police say the father was upset that the giant Cookie Monster would not pose for a picture with his 3-year-old daughter.

Avoid Writing Summaries that Repeat the Headline: The first sentence in this blurb is too repetitive:

Headline **Is work a pain in the neck . . . or hands?**

Blurb Has work become a real pain? If so, the problem might not be your job but your workstation. Judy Gibson, manager of the Physical Therapy department at Fairbanks Memorial Hospital, says proper ergonomics is essential to preventing problems.

Address the Reader When Appropriate: Use the "you" voice:

Headline **Get free cash for college**

Blurb You can collect thousands of dollars in scholarship money just by filling out a form.

Briefs

Blurbs are usually a few sentences. A brief can be a few paragraphs. A brief can stand alone in place of a story, while a blurb is meant to entice readers to read more. Sometimes there is not much difference between a blurb and a brief. In a majority of cases, the blurb and the brief repeat the lead or the first few paragraphs of full text. The main reason to use blurbs and briefs is to offer readers a choice of layers. Some Web readers want to read only the headline, others want a brief summary and others want the complete story.

Headline **Missing pet pig turns up as meal**

Blurb A woman who went looking for her family's missing pet pig says she found it—as the main course at a neighborhood barbecue.

Brief A woman who went looking for her family's missing pet pig says she found it—as the main course at a neighborhood barbecue.

Sadie Emerson said she and her 3-year-old son drove up and down their neighborhood streets, looking for the Vietnamese potbellied pig, Tiny Boo. They spotted a group of people having a party near a mobile home, and on the table was a mound of meat that turned out to be Tiny Boo.

—*The Associated Press*

If you wanted to find out what happened to Tiny Boo, you would link to the full story, which starts the same way. You would find out that the mobile home owner who shot Tiny Boo claimed the pig tried to attack him. He was accused of cruelty to animals.

Summary highlights

Another tool that serves as a quick summary for Web readers who are scanners is the highlights box on top of the story. For example, CNN tops its Web stories with a bulleted list of the main points in a story as in this example:

Eight killed in ski tour bus crash

Story Highlights

- Death toll rises to eight as tour bus runs off highway, rolls over

- Bus was carrying at least 50 people when it crashed in southeastern Utah

- Bus was en route from Telluride, Colorado, to Phoenix, Arizona, after weekend ski trip

Story Structure

Get to the point of the story quickly—within the first 50 words. If you picture a news Web site with a title image and possibly a banner advertisement at the top of the page plus the story headline, this doesn't leave you much room. To complicate matters, readers may be using small portable devices to get their news. In addition, text on most news sites is enclosed in tables about 4 inches wide to facilitate reading. That translates to about 100 to 150 words per screen.

Inverted Pyramid

The inverted pyramid is a favored form for Web stories because the main idea is in the lead or the first few paragraphs. The inverted pyramid form places the main point at the top of the story with the rest of the information in descending order of importance. This form is good for basic news stories, but it is too restrictive for features and other types of storytelling. As long as the nut graph expressing the main point is high in the story, writers may have as much flexibility for Web stories as for print.

The headline, blurb and lead may be repetitious, but this doesn't harm readability because it helps readers know they have accessed the correct story from the scores of others that may be linked to the site.

Here is an example of the inverted pyramid with a summary lead:

Headline	**School official cuffed, led away by couple**
Blurb	Deputies arrest pair, who were unhappy with materials given students
Lead	LUCERNE VALLEY, Calif.—Two parents barged into a school superintendent's office, handcuffed him, announced he was under citizen's arrest and drove him away in their vehicle, authorities said Friday.

Sheriff's deputies pulled them over 10 miles away, freed the school's official and arrested the couple, who said they were taking the superintendent to the district attorney's office.

—*The Associated Press*

This example also uses an inverted pyramid form with a creative lead, but the nut graph is in the third paragraph.

Headline	**Officials seize hurt animals**
Blurb	Animal control authorities haul away more than 150 injured and neglected animals—some close to death. The sign on the stable welcomes visitors to the "Heaven and Earth" animal sanctuary.

But authorities say the so-called animal shelter was a living hell. |

Lead Animal Control officials spent Friday seizing more than 150 animals from the 20-acre property where they say pets and livestock were neglected, some of them almost to the point of death.

—Jamie Malernee, *St. Petersburg* (Fla.) *Times*

List Format

Lists within stories break up the text and help readers scan Web stories quickly.

Headline **Something unspoken**

Blurb What not to say in an interview

If you're a smart job candidate, you've thought about the points you want to make to sell yourself in an interview. Maybe you've even practiced your spiel. That's good, but know too that career experts caution that saying *too* much in an interview can hurt your prospects.

You already know to avoid mentioning the office-supplies pilfering complaint filed against you in your last job—and that reprimand for arriving late on 18 days in one month. But here are some less obvious things you should avoid saying at a job interview.

- Don't address your interviewer by his or her first name, unless and until it's clearly established that the session is on a first-name basis. Here, the rule is to let the interviewer speak first.

- Don't use the wrong name. First or last.

- Don't say anything that conveys you're desperate for the job. Even if you are.

—Larry Keller, *CNN.com*

Question/Answer Format

A question/answer format is a good alternative form for Web writing. The story still needs an introduction. This CNN example includes an interactive poll, an ideal feature for online stories. It also has a question lead, which works better online than in print stories. Note the conversational "you" voice, also good for online writing.

Headline **Selling yourself again: The job interview revisited**

Lead "If you were a squirrel, which commodity would you inventory first—the nuts or the berries?" May you never encounter that question in a job interview.

But the knee-knocking trial of it all, the sleepless nights leading up to it, the 18 cups of coffee before you get there, the sudden feeling that your resume belongs to someone else and your clothes do, too, for that matter . . . it's all here again for a lot of people. Some may have thought they wouldn't be facing this particular ordeal again soon, if ever.

It's a job interview. And with the wake of layoffs widening—nearly 300,000 in the United States in the first quarter of this year, according to data from Randstad North America and Roper Starch Worldwide—a lot of people are finding themselves back in that very hot seat.

CNN: So we applied ourselves to ETICON'S Ann Humphries, asking her to tell us what's important to know from the business etiquette standpoint, what to do when it's time to grip 'n' grin.

And before we give you Ann, any squirrel knows the answer is berries, inventory them first—nuts have longer shelf life.

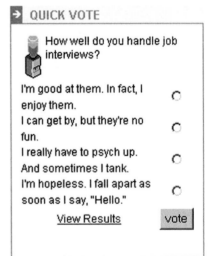

QUICK VOTE

How well do you handle job interviews?

I'm good at them. In fact, I enjoy them. ○

I can get by, but they're no fun. ○

I really have to psych up. And sometimes I tank. ○

I'm hopeless. I fall apart as soon as I say, "Hello." ○

View Results   vote

The story continues with the question/answer format from professional management consultant Ann Humphries and is accompanied by this interactive poll.

Storytelling Format

Narrative writing also can be compelling on the Web, especially if it is split into several pages with cliffhanger endings that entice readers to continue. The Web specials on the *St. Petersburg Times* site offer several examples, including this narrative story, "28 Seconds," about the mystery of USAir Flight 427. The four-part Web package was organized in chunks and featured this enticing one-screen introduction:

> 28 . . . 27 . . .
>
> It happened in little more than the time it will take you to read this paragraph.
>
> 19 . . . 18 . . .
>
> It felt like turbulence at first, but then the plane twisted left, and it was clear something was wrong.
>
> 6 . . . 5 . . .
>
> Twisting, turning.
>
> **What the hell is this?**
>
> Impact.

The rest of the story continues in dramatic storytelling.

Personal Storytelling

Human beings have been telling stories since prehistoric man drew pictures on caves and recited stories around a fire. The Web is simply a new cave blending old and new techniques. People still want to hear, read and *share* stories. And that's how the Web can exceed any other medium in history. Personal storytelling thrives on the Web, and it is increasing on news sites.

Some of the best personal storytelling sites are not traditional broadcast or newspaper sites. Musarium (*www.musarium.com*), a site devoted to photography and storytelling, is an example. "Just when you think that television has mind-numbed the brains of most people, these presentations celebrate and enforce the power of still photographs to affect people and tell great stories," the site says. The site features innovative multimedia packages with personal stories in several formats. Some of the storytelling is told in photo essays.

One of the most chilling is "Without Sanctuary," a multimedia photo essay of lynchings documented in old postcards. This story has since moved to its own site (*www.withoutsanctuary.org*).

For more innovative personal storytelling and Web design, turn to Derek Powazek, creator of Fray (*www.fray.com*), a site that features chunk-style writing with cliffhangers to entice readers to continue. Both of these sites encourage readers to share their stories.

Revise

Don't eliminate this crucial process. Be concise. Cut every word or paragraph that does not advance the story. Short sentences, short paragraphs and active verbs make Web writing more readable. The same principles that William Strunk Jr. offered for print writing in E. B. White's *The Elements of Style* apply to the Web: "Vigorous writing is concise. A sentence should contain no unnecessary words, a paragraph no unnecessary sentences. . . .This requires not that the writer make all sentences short, or that he avoid all detail and treat his subjects only in outline, but that every word tell."

Take Risks

Writing for the Web will continue to evolve as technology improves accessibility of multimedia. Basic journalistic concepts of accuracy, structure and simplicity will remain, but new forms of online writing may emerge. Start with a good story, and find an interesting way to tell it. The Web is a flexible medium.

Andrew Nachison, former director of the Media Center at the American Press Institute, is a risk taker in new media. He now heads a media think tank and futures lab called iFOCUS, to encourage innovation in Web media. Nachison said that some of the best online storytelling is distinctly different from the typical text narrative of a newspaper story.

"The challenge is to think of the Web as a different medium, not merely an extension of the newspaper. You don't have to be an MSNBC to do great stuff. Some newspaper stories may translate perfectly well as big blocks of text. But some stories can be more compelling when they're presented in completely different ways." Nachison offered these tips:

Be Flexible: Different stories call for different approaches.

Be Smart: For some stories, you may have the luxury of time and creative people to do something innovative. For other stories, you may have to shovel text online to get the story out quickly.

Be Daring: Enjoy the creative freedom the Web offers to do great journalism.

Remember the thrill of telling a great story and telling it well.

"Do great journalism whenever you can," Nachison said. "One of the great things about the Web is that you can do it all."

What Do You Think [?]

Do you prefer to scroll Web stories presented on one page or read shorter portions of stories linked to several pages?

☐ Scroll on one page.
☐ Split and spread over several pages.
☐ Both, depending on the story.

Exercises

1 **Headlines and blurbs:** Using your local or campus newspaper, write Web headlines and summary blurbs for news and feature stories.

2 **Personal essay:** Study the stories on Derek Powazek's site, *www.fray.com,* and write a personal essay in chunk style on a topic of interest to you. Try to include cliffhanger endings for each chunk to entice readers to click into the next part.

3 **Convert a story to the Web:** Using any news or feature story you have written for this course, convert it to Web style as suggested in this chapter. Add a discussion question.

4 Web story: Write a story for the Web based on this information. Include a headline and summary blurb. Use a bulleted list, add a discussion question to the end of your story and consider creating a poll. Use Web style—a space between each paragraph.

New data on marriage, divorce, and remarriage in the United States show that 43 percent of first marriages end in separation or divorce within 15 years, according to a report released today by the Centers for Disease Control and Prevention (CDC). The report, "First Marriage Dissolution, Divorce, and Remarriage: United States," also shows that one in three first marriages end within 10 years and one in five end within five years.

The findings are based on data from the National Survey of Family Growth, a study of 10,847 women 15–44 years of age.

"Separation and divorce can have adverse effects on the health and well-being of children and adults," said CDC Director Jeffrey Koplan. "Past research has shown that divorce is associated with higher rates of mortality, more health problems, and more risky behaviors such as increased alcohol use."

The study also showed that duration of marriage is linked to a woman's age at first marriage; the older a woman is at first marriage, the longer that marriage is likely to last. For example, 59 percent of marriages to brides under 18 end in separation or divorce within 15 years, compared with 36 percent of those married at age 20 or over.

About 97 percent of separated non-Hispanic white women are divorced within five years of separation, compared with 77 percent of separated Hispanic women and only 67 percent of non-Hispanic black women. Younger women who divorce are more likely to remarry: 81 percent of those divorced before age 25 remarry within 10 years, compared with 68 percent of those divorced at age 25 or over. Non-Hispanic black women are less likely than other women to remain in a first marriage, to make the transition from separation to divorce, to remarry, and to remain in a remarriage.

"These data offer an important glimpse into the social fabric of this country," said Dr. Edward Sondik, director of CDC's National Center for Health Statistics, which conducted the study. "The implications of divorce cut across a number of societal issues—socioeconomics, health, and the welfare of our children."

☞ **Featured Online Activity** Log on to the book Web site for this chapter and explore the links to innovative and multimedia sites at

academic.cengage.com/masscomm/rich/ writingandreportingnews6e

Coaching Tips

Study your audience. Find out if the editors you want to reach prefer hard-news or soft-news style, short or in-depth releases, and single releases or media kits.

Find your focus. Use the focus statement as a headline or guideline for your lead.

Consider visuals—charts, illustrations, photographs, diagrams—to make your package more appealing.

Plan video opportunities for broadcast news.

Offer delivery of releases via e-mail, Web, podcasts or other multimedia

Write a fact sheet. Even if you don't include a separate fact sheet with your release or media kit, use it as a writing tool to make sure that you have provided crucial facts about the organization in your story.

Always include contact information: name, address, telephone numbers (including cell phone and fax), e-mail address and Web site.

You have to write as professionally in public relations as if you were writing in a newspaper. Avoid hype and be realistic about what you are selling.

Evie Lazzarino, assistant vice president for public affairs,
Claremont McKenna College

14 Public Relations Writing

When Evie Lazzarino studied journalism in college, she didn't think it would lead to an all-expense-paid trip to China. But just a few years after she graduated, she wound up in front of the Great Wall of China with a bunch of dolls called Cabbage Patch Kids. She was coordinating part of a world tour featuring children from America who went to seven foreign countries as "ambassadors" for the dolls, then among the most popular toys in the United States.

"The Chinese people had never seen a Cabbage Patch doll. It was fun to see people's first reaction to them," says Lazzarino, who was then working for a Los Angeles public relations agency that handled the Cabbage Patch Kids account. "My job was like an advance job for a politician. I went to China to set up a party, places we could visit, and I met with all the Western press, such as bureaus of *The New York Times* and *Los Angeles Times*. I tried to get them to cover what we were doing. We did a photo shoot on the Great Wall, and the photo moved worldwide."

The trip to China was one of the high points in a varied public relations career. Lazzarino began her career as a reporter for her local newspaper in Kansas after graduating from the University of Kansas with a journalism degree. She is now director of public affairs and communications for Claremont McKenna College in California. But along the way she has worked as an information specialist at Hallmark Cards in Kansas City, manager of community affairs for the *Los Angeles Times* and communications director for the Richard Nixon Library and Birthplace in Yorba Linda, Calif.

Lazzarino's experience reflects the wide range of jobs in the public relations field. In addition to working with the media, she has been responsible for developing products, writing speeches for corporate officials, coordinating trade shows and promoting plans for several major accounts, including Polaroid and Mercedes-Benz of North America.

Whether you work for one client or an agency that serves many, in public relations you are serving several masters at once, Lazzarino says. If you are writing a press release, you are not only trying to please your client; you also have to please an editor at a newspaper, magazine or television station. So in a sense, you are working for several people. She says her journalism background helped her understand the kind of writing the media wanted.

Evie Lazzarino, director of public affairs and communications for Claremont McKenna College

Evie Lazzarino

Cabbage Patch doll at the Great Wall of China

"You have to write as professionally in public relations as if you were writing in a newspaper. Avoid hype and be realistic about what you are selling." Students going into public relations may think deadlines in public relations are not as strenuous as they are in newspapers. But you have many deadlines because you may have five or 10 clients you are trying to serve at one time, Lazzarino says. "People are paying a lot of money for your services. When it's someone else's money, there's a real sense of risk that you could lose clients."

One of her main suggestions is to know your audience. "You have to know different styles. Some magazines may prefer something clever, but if you are pitching something to *The Wall Street Journal*, you should have a great news story. You have to study your market. Go out and meet editors, and find out what they want."

Forms of Delivery

One of the things editors want these days is access to company information on the Web. A survey conducted for the Public Relations Society of America (PRSA) revealed that 100 percent of the respondents said it was important for companies to have a Web site for news releases. "No longer can a PR professional say that journalists don't visit online newsrooms of small companies or won't enter password-protected sections," according to the study conducted by TekGroup International in 2007. "It also can't be ignored that 98 percent of journalists preferred to receive information through e-mail alerts generated via an online newsroom."

PRSA has been following that advice since 2005, when it created its own online newsroom to offer news releases and other information via e-mail alerts, podcasts and updated information via RSS (Really Simple Syndication) readers, which are software programs that automatically deliver newly posted information to subscribers of the site.

The study also showed that journalists wanted photographs of people named in news releases, graphics, audio and video especially for online delivery. Another finding was that public relations practitioners should include their cell phone number as well as their office number in news releases.

Blogs are also gaining popularity in corporate public relations, as discussed in Chapter 2. PRWeb, a wire service for news releases, and various corporation Web sites encourage customers to respond to information on the site by posting blogs or comments.

Elizabeth Albrycht, author of the CorporatePR blog, is a strong advocate for using new technology in public relations. But she has this advice for students seeking careers in the field: "All these new tools are additives. All the old skills don't go away; you just have to learn more," she said in an interview with PR Quest, a site created by Robert French of Auburn University. The site features podcast interviews with public relations practitioners. "Blogging is writing. Writing is the single most important skill that you have to have," Albrycht said. "You need to be able to write accurately and quickly if you are going to be in public relations."

Writing Skills for News Releases

Many news releases are not read all the way through. But most editors at least skim the releases to find out if there is some newsworthy information. Community newspapers and local television stations rely heavily on news releases about events in their area.

If you want your news event to be covered, you need to consider that you are competing with many other events and stories that these media will cover. How do you get the attention of the assignment editors? Here are some tips for writing your releases:

- **Target your audience.** Make sure that your information is newsworthy for the publication. Check the name and spelling of the person who should receive the release. Don't use nicknames (unless you are very familiar with the source), and make sure that you have the correct gender. Don't send duplicate releases to several editors. You might also send a copy to a reporter assigned to the beat covered in your news release. Ask if the publication prefers a faxed release, an e-mail release or other type of delivery via the Web.

- **Find a newsworthy angle.** If you are targeting a local newspaper or TV station, localize the angle. The qualities of timeliness, local interest, new information and unusual nature are the main factors in determining newsworthiness.

- **Identify the news element in the headline and lead.** Don't make your intended reader wade through several paragraphs to determine if the event or news you are touting should be covered.

- **Consider a visual element.** If you are targeting a television station, the visual impact is crucial. You should list photo opportunities for print and video possibilities for television and the Web.

- **Relate your information to your audience.** How will readers or viewers be affected in this target area? Why is your information or event important to them?

- **Keep your information factual.** Avoid adjectives, superlatives and promotional language.

- **Provide diverse sources.** Consider how to include multicultural segments of the community in your projects, visuals and materials. The Public Relations Society of America has launched a campaign to promote diversity in the organization and to foster "ideology that promotes the coexistence of different cultures in America." For more information, access the society at *www.prsa.org.*

- **Allow lead time.** Send your releases in advance of the publication's deadlines. A magazine might have a lead time of several months. Some TV stations might prefer only a few days of lead time. Check with the publication or organization for preferred advance notice. Include the release date, preferably "For Immediate Release," unless there is some important reason for an "Embargoed Until . . ." date.

- **Use active voice.** Who did what, not what was done to whom.

- **Use present tense when possible.** In most cases you will want to promote an event or some information in a timely manner, not after the fact.

- **Check grammar and spelling.**

ETHICS

Ethical dilemma: How truthful should you be when you are faced with a conflict between protecting your client and dealing with the media?

The case: You are the public relations director for a company that manufactures portable baby cribs. The chief executive officer of your company informs you that two babies died when their cribs collapsed. However, he is reluctant to issue a recall because more than 100,000 cribs of this particular model were sold, and it would cost the company a fortune.

He says the product development team warned him a few years ago that the sides of the crib were not secure but that to replace the design would have been too costly. He wants you to reassure the media that the cribs are safe and that there is no proof the deaths of these children were a direct result of any faulty crib parts. If the media asks, he wants you to deny that the company ever had any indication the cribs might be defective.

Will you lie or withhold information to protect your employer? What steps will you propose to the CEO?

Ethical values: Truth, credibility, fairness, loyalty to your client.

Ethical guidelines: The Public Relations Society of America offers these guidelines in its code of ethics:

- A member shall adhere to truth and accuracy and to generally accepted standards of good taste.

- A member shall safeguard the confidences of present and former clients.

- A member shall not engage in any practice that tends to corrupt the integrity of channels of communication or the processes of government.

Structure of News Releases

News releases differ very little from basic news stories. Although some news releases may have feature leads, most use a summary lead that gets to the main point quickly. If you use a soft lead, put the nut graph high in the release, preferably by the second paragraph.

Mark O'Brien, a former media communications representative for Binney & Smith, makers of Crayola products, says brevity is an important factor in news releases. "You have to listen to the editors out there," O'Brien says. "They get a lot of material across their desks each day. If you have to read a page before you get to the meat of the subject, that's too much. Very few newspapers are going to print your story exactly. The release is just to pique their curiosity."

O'Brien, who now operates his own public relations agency, began work in public relations for General Foods after graduating from the University of South Florida. He says he studied what worked by comparing releases and newsletters that got published and those that didn't. He also included fact sheets in a media kit with product samples, all enclosed in a folder with a bold graphic.

Here are some basics for print releases; the format for online releases is discussed later in this chapter.

Style: Use one side of the paper. Double-space the body copy (or use 1.5-line spacing). Keep the release short, preferably one page and no more than two. Use single spacing with a space between paragraphs for releases on the Web or e-mail releases. Use Associated Press style for releases to newspapers and most magazines.

Number Pages: If the release continues to more than one page, write "more" at the bottom of the first page and number each page.

Timeliness: Send out news releases in advance of the intended publication date. Although most news releases say "FOR IMMEDIATE RELEASE," you should send them out several days or a few weeks before an event is going to occur.

Major Elements in This Order:

- **Company name** or logo at the top and company's address (street, city, state and ZIP code) or Web site if the company is only on the Web.
- **FOR IMMEDIATE RELEASE** (preferably in caps and boldface).
- **Date of release:** (This could be placed under the previous item or attached to the dateline.)
- **Contact information:** Place contact information justified on the left side of the page. Write "CONTACT:" followed by the name, title, phone numbers (telephone, cell and fax) and e-mail address of the person to contact. This information can be placed on the left or right side; it can be single-spaced.
- **Headline:** Skip two lines after your contact information. Boldface is optional but suggested. Although some firms prefer writing the headline all in capital letters, Web sites such as PRWeb recommend that headlines be written with

uppercase and lowercase letters. Limit the headline to one line, especially for Web releases.

- **Dateline:** This is the city of origin for your press release, followed by the state abbreviation if not a major city. You may put the date here, preceded by a hyphen.
- **Lead:** A direct lead is preferable, including who, what, when, and where, but a feature lead immediately followed by the key information is acceptable.
- **Body:** Briefly summarize the key points. Include a quote or comment from a company official if possible. Keep paragraphs short. Use lists if you have key points.
- **Ending:** End with a brief sentence or paragraph about the company—if relevant. Repeat a contact or other relevant source for further information. Include a Web site if available. Skip a space and type a symbol for the ending: three # # # or —30—Your format should look like this:

Organization Name on Letterhead

[Heading information can be single-spaced]

For Immediate Release   Contact: *(This information can be in single space)*
Date of release   Name, title of contact person
                                                Telephone number
                                                Cell phone number
                                                Fax number
                                                E-mail address

[Leave some space before the headline]

HEADLINE

[Double-space body copy]

DATELINE—[Location for the origin of the release (in capital letters) plus a dash, followed by the first line of the lead]

Lead: Preferably start with some hard-news lead, especially on releases for news events or announcements.

Body: Write tightly. Limit copy to one page if possible, no more than two. If you have two pages, write "more" at the end of the first page and number the pages.

Ending: As part of the ending, you could tell where more information is available, such as graphics and Web sites. A standard ending for a corporate news release includes a few lines about the company, including the company Web site.

—30— or # # #

Here is an example of a news release that Mark O'Brien sent to newspapers, including *USA Today,* which published the story on the front page.

Illustration from media kit

Press Release—Print version

Binney & Smith Inc.
1100 Church Lane
P.O. Box 431
Easton, Pennsylvania 18044-0431
[company telephone number]

For Immediate Release

Contact: Mark J. O'Brien
Media Communications
[office telephone number; cell phone number]
[e-mail address]
[date]

CRAYOLA INTRODUCES NEW CRAYONS THAT ARE LITERALLY "OFF THE WALL"

EASTON, Pa.—Parents can put away the scrub brushes and stain remover, thanks to Binney & Smith. The maker of Crayola products has introduced a totally off-the-wall product—washable crayons.

Unlike the billions of crayons produced before them, Crayola washable crayons are made from a patented formula that washes from most surfaces, including walls and fabric.

"Washable crayons address our No. 1 consumer complaint—getting crayon marks off different surfaces," says Mark O'Brien, Binney & Smith spokesperson.

"Each year we receive thousands of calls and letters regarding crayon stains, mainly from parents of preschool children. With the introduction of washable crayons, parents can breathe a little easier when it comes to crayon mishaps."

The difference between traditional and washable crayons is in their formulas. Washable crayons contain special water soluble polymers found in many health and beauty aids. This allows them to be removed from most surfaces by simply using soap and water. Tests have shown washable crayon marks can even be removed from walls and fabric one to two months after being stained. However, crayon marks are easiest to remove if washed soon after they happen.

Crayola washable crayons are non-toxic and available in two sizes. The So Big size, for younger children, comes six to a box and has a suggested retail price of $2.99. Boxes of eight, large size washable crayons will sell for approximately $2.59.

# # #

Web releases are generally shorter. These days Crayola provides news releases in several formats, including HTML for the Web or PDF (portable document format), which includes more information. A Web or e-mail news release could include contact information at the top of the screen but should repeat it or include it initially at the bottom of the release so viewers don't have to scroll back to find it.

Here is how the Crayola release might look for Web distribution:

FOR IMMEDIATE RELEASE

CRAYOLA Introduces New Crayons Washable Crayons

EASTON, Pa., Date—Crayola products is introducing a totally off-the-wall product—washable crayons. Unlike the billions of crayons produced before them, Crayola washable crayons are made from a patented formula that washes from most surfaces, including walls and fabric.

"Washable crayons address our No. 1 consumer complaint—getting crayon marks off different surfaces," says Mark O'Brien, Binney & Smith spokesperson. "Each year we receive thousands of calls and letters regarding crayon stains, mainly from parents of preschool children. With the introduction of washable crayons, parents can breathe a little easier when it comes to crayon mishaps."

The difference between traditional and washable crayons is in their formulas. Washable crayons contain special water soluble polymers found in many health and beauty aids. This allows them to be removed from most surfaces by simply using soap and water. Tests have shown washable crayon marks can even be removed from walls and fabric one to two months after being stained. However, crayon marks are easiest to remove if washed soon after they happen.

Crayola washable crayons are nontoxic and available in two sizes. The So Big size, for younger children, comes six to a box and has a suggested retail price of $2.99. Boxes of eight, large size washable crayons will sell for approximately $2.59.

Binney & Smith, maker of Crayola® crayons and markers since 1903, became Crayola LLC in 2007, reflecting the company's No. 1 brand.

For more information, contact Mark J. O'Brien, director of media communications, at (phone numbers office number, cell phone number and e-mail address). Visit the Crayola Web site at *www.crayola.com.*

Mark J. O'Brien
Phone
Cell
Fax
e-mail

# # #

Another form that would work for e-mail, Web distribution or print is a simple list of the basics: who, what, when, where, why and how. Here is an example from the American Red Cross of Alaska:

NEWS RELEASE – Date

Red Cross Smoke Alarm Drive

Contact information
Photo opportunity: Anchorage Fire Department Engine Number 5 will meet Red Cross staff and volunteers for a photo opportunity at the Benson Park at 10:30 A.M. on Jan. 15. The American Red Cross emergency response vehicle will also be at the event with coffee and hot chocolate for the community and volunteers.

   WHO: American Red Cross of Alaska and the Anchorage Fire Department

WHAT: Anchorage citizens will show their concern for the safety of their neighbors by helping the American Red Cross of Alaska distribute free smoke detectors and batteries. The group will visit at least 1,000 homes and will be attended by firefighters from the Anchorage Fire Department.

WHEN: Saturday, Jan. 15 (year), 10 A.M. – 1 P.M.

WHERE: Smoke detectors and batteries will be given away in the neighborhood bordered by Benson to the north, 36th Avenue to the West and C Street to the east.

WHY: Working smoke detectors are a crucial tool in the early detection of domestic fires, which can dramatically assist with the prevention of the loss of life and reduction of injuries. According to statistics, up to 50 percent of the smoke alarms in the U.S. don't work because there is not an operable battery in the smoke detector. We have chosen this time of year to distribute smoke detectors because most house fires occur during the months of December, January and February.

HOW: This event is made possible by a generous grant from the Allstate Foundation.

Note: For more information, please call Heather Adams at 907-000-0000. The American Red Cross is a humanitarian organization led by volunteers that provides relief to victims of disaster and helps people prevent, prepare for and respond to emergencies.

Contact information repeated here.

Convergence Coach

E-mail News Releases

- Online news releases must be shorter than print so the information can be seen on the first screen. Limit the release to one or two screens, about 500 words at most. Use single-spaced copy with a space between paragraphs. In most cases, you should put the contact information at the bottom of the release.

- Target your audience. Ask sources if they prefer to receive releases by e-mail. Don't send unsolicited e-mail. Personalize the release if possible.

- Write a brief summary of the topic in the e-mail subject line.

- Headings: Insert company name and contact information at the top, FOR IMMEDIATE RELEASE and date of release. Insert a space or two before the headline.

- Write a clear summary headline. Insert another space.

- Write a summary lead with basic information: who, what, where, when. Make sure that it is visible in the first screen.

- Use lists to itemize information when relevant.

- Avoid adjectives and superlatives. Keep the writing simple and newsworthy.

- Proofread. E-mail is notoriously filled with typos, spelling and style errors. Sloppy work is a poor reflection on you and your client.

- Don't send attachments. Your users may not be able to open your documents.

- Insert links at the bottom to relevant information. For example, if your release is about a survey the company has done, include a link to the complete survey.

- Put the contact information (office and cell phone numbers, fax, e-mail and any related Web site) at the bottom of the release.

Video News Releases

The video versions of news releases are known as VNRs, which are basically news stories produced for television. They include footage with a series of video images plus sound bites of quotes from sources in the story. In many cases the VNRs are so well done that TV stations can air them as polished news stories without even editing them. And therein lies the ethical problem.

Many small stations that have limited resources have used these VNRs produced by the U.S. government without attributing the source, thus making the video sound as though the station produced the story. Because these releases are promotional in nature and not balanced news stories, if the station does not indicate the source of the release, the audience can be misled. That isn't the fault of the public relations practitioner; it's the responsibility of the station to attribute the source.

The use of VNRs without attribution became so widespread that the Radio/Television News Directors Association (RTNDA) issued guidelines for use of them. "Television and radio stations should strive to protect the editorial integrity of the video and audio they air. This integrity, at times, might come into question when stations air video and audio provided to newsrooms by companies, organizations or governmental agencies with political or financial interests in publicizing the material," according to the RTNDA guidelines. The organization's code of ethics says that electronic journalists should "clearly disclose the origin of information and label all material provided by outsiders."

The advantages of these video releases are that they are cost-effective for the TV station, which doesn't have to expend resources to shoot the video, and they provide the station with images and sound bites that could be inserted into locally produced news stories.

The U.S. Department of Agriculture produces such an extensive amount of video and radio news releases that it has an entire broadcast media and technology center devoted to providing this type of information. The U.S. Census Bureau also provides video and multimedia news releases and features.

The format for video news releases includes the following elements:

- A disclaimer giving the news organization permission to use the material without charge.
- A list of the contents, often including the timing of each element.
- B-roll, which is video footage and natural sound that news stations can insert into stories.
- Interviews and sound bites from sources.
- Contact information.

Here is a script for a video news release by the U.S. Census Bureau about the value of a college education:

Back to School

More Education Means Greater Earnings
Date
Slug: College Costs
Synopsis: How and why students are handling the ever-increasing cost of college.
Video Source: The U.S. Census Bureau
Super Information: (times to be inserted after client approval)
:XX (the time for the sound bite)
Mahlet "Mimi" Goitom
College Student
University of Maryland
:XX
Dr. Sandy Baum
Senior Policy Analyst
College Board
:XX
Louis Kincannon
Director
Location: Washington D.C.

SUGGESTED LOCAL ANCHOR LEAD-IN: DESPITE THE RISING COST OF COLLEGE, AMERICANS ARE MORE EDUCATED THAN EVER. AND THE CENSUS BUREAU HAS JUST RELEASED INFORMATION THAT SUGGESTS INVESTING IN A COLLEGE DEGREE PAYS FOR ITSELF AND MORE. HERE IS THE STORY.

(Open with shots of Mimi working in financial aid office)
VO: MAHLET GOITOM, (mah hoh leat goy tum), OR MIMI, A THIRD-YEAR PUBLIC HEALTH MAJOR, IS ONE OF MANY STUDENTS RELYING ON BOTH FINANCIAL AID AND WORK TO PAY THE EVER-INCREASING COST OF COLLEGE.
(Cut to Mimi on camera)

SOT: "The main way that I'm dealing with the increased finances is by taking out loans and I've also become an RA to help my parents with the burden of paying for college."

(College campus shots transition to a graphic)

VO: DESPITE THE COST, AMERICANS ARE MORE EDUCATED THAN EVER. THE MOST RECENT CENSUS DATA SHOWS COLLEGE GRADUATION RATES AT AN ALL TIME HIGH. AT LAST COUNT, 27% OF ADULTS 25 AND OVER HAD A BACHELOR'S DEGREE. AND ACCORDING TO EDUCATION EXPERTS THAT NUMBER MAY CONTINUE RISING SINCE TODAY'S STUDENTS HAVE ACCESS TO A LOT MORE FINANCIAL AID.

(Cut to Sandy Baum, on camera)

SOT: "Over 100 billion dollars of student aid was distributed to college students last year. The reality is that grant aid is growing rapidly, loans are growing even more rapidly, and there is help out there for students to pay these rising college costs."
(College campus shots transition to Census Bureau graphic)
VO: MIMI, LIKE MANY OTHER COLLEGE STUDENTS, PUTS IN THE LONG HOURS BECAUSE SHE BELIEVES IT WILL PAY OFF IN THE FUTURE. AND THE EXPERTS SAY SHE'S RIGHT.
SOT: (Kincannon) "There's no doubt there is a strong relationship between education and earnings. The more education you have, the likelier it is you'll

have a higher income. For example, high school graduates earn about $30,000 yearly, where as college graduates earn nearly 75% more."

(Shots of Mimi)

VO: AND THAT WILL HELP STUDENTS LIKE MIMI CARRY THE BURDEN OF DEBT FROM STUDENT LOANS.

(Cut to Mimi, on camera, cut to shots of Mimi walking)

SOT: "I definitely think taking out a loan is worth it, I mean, an undergradu-

ate degree is essential for any career path, and I think it's definitely worth it to take out a loan."

THIS IS HANNAH HAINES.

(Local anchor tag)

SUGGESTED LOCAL ANCHOR TAG: FOR MORE CENSUS DATA ON EDUCATION, GO TO *WWW. CENSUS.GOV.*

Public Service Announcements

Public service announcements, commonly called PSAs, are messages that TV or radio stations will air without charge, provided that the messages have noncommercial and nonpolitical content. In print media they are considered public service advertisements. Because they are used without charge, they are usually very brief. In broadcast media, PSAs generally run from 15 seconds to one minute. You should check with the stations for their requirements of formats and submission dates. In general they contain information that could be considered useful or beneficial to the audience.

- At the top of your script, write a slug, the length of time for the PSA (usually in seconds), and the agency that produced it.
- Start with a hook, a strong statement that will grab the listener's or viewer's attention.
- Read your copy aloud because the message will be heard by the audience.
- Keep it brief and include only the most crucial information.
- Include the dates and times of any event you are promoting.
- Use broadcast style of all capital letters and double-spacing for a video script.
- End with some statement that either requests an action by the listener or offers more information.
- For television broadcast of video PSAs, send your video with the PSA text.

Your format should look like this:

From: Name of organization and address

Contact: Name of contact person with phone numbers (telephone, fax and cell) and e-mail address

Length: time it takes to read the PSA

Message: Type the PSA message in paragraph form

Disclaimer: At the bottom of the page, briefly describe the organization and specify that it is nonprofit.

Here is a 15-second PSA from the Federal Trade Commission:

THE FEDERAL TRADE COMMISSION SAYS ANYONE WITH A PHONE COULD BE A VICTIM OF A SCHEMING TELEMARKETER. DON'T GIVE AWAY YOUR CREDIT CARD OR BANK ACCOUNT NUMBERS ON THE PHONE. IF YOU HAVE ANY DOUBT ABOUT AN OFFER YOU HEAR ON THE PHONE, CHECK IT OUT AND GET IT IN WRITING. A MESSAGE FROM THE FEDERAL TRADE COMMISSION AND THIS STATION.

   # # #

Media Kits

Public relations practitioners often use media kits to promote corporate products. These kits are usually included in decorative folders that contain a variety of news releases, fact sheets about the company and its products, and sometimes samples of the company's products.

Planning a media kit can be a very creative experience. You should design a striking cover or package for your print media kit and include information that will be useful for different kinds of stories. A brief sheet of facts about the company is usually helpful. If you have a product sample that is suitable for enclosure, consider it part of your media kit.

These days more media kits are being produced for the Web, which is replacing kits distributed on CD-ROMs. Online media kits can include multimedia information in audio and video, PDF files containing images of the products, plus fact sheets, backgrounders and links to other information. They may also include interactive features. If you are planning a media kit for the Web, consider how many Web pages you will need for the information and create links to each page. Most major corporate sites have a Press Room link to Web pages with information about the company, news releases, products and contacts.

A good media kit should contain these items:

Attractive Cover: The kit is usually contained in a folder with the company name and logo.

Brief Letter or Note: A very brief explanation of the purpose of the kit should be provided for the editor. It could be on the inside of the cover.

News Release: The first item after the editor's note should be a news release.

Fact Sheet: Present information about the organization in simple list form. You might use headings such as *Who, What, Where, When, Why* and *How.* Fact sheets might also briefly itemize vital statistics about the organization or the issue, such as statistics on obesity if you are promoting a weight-loss product.

Backgrounder: A backgrounder is information that can provide in-depth information that supplements the news, such as statistical research or historical developments that led up to the event you are promoting. Backgrounders might also include a feature story, such as a profile of a company executive. Don't include information in the backgrounder that should be in the news release. This is additional material, not a substitute for news.

Story Ideas: The story idea sheet is optional, but if you include it, try to offer suggestions for localizing the information. This sheet should be written in list form or short paragraphs. You might also include suggestions for photos, video opportunities or graphics.

The cover letter for your media kit should briefly state what is included. On the Web, you can create a navigation bar or box with links. Here is a cover letter for a media kit from Hallmark Cards Inc.

> Dear Editor:
>
> The latest in Easter card and gift-giving trends from Hallmark Cards is tucked inside. We hope you find this information helpful as you prepare your springtime holiday stories.
>
> Hallmark offers about 250 gift and party items. The Easter gift line includes wicker baskets, stuffed animals, activity products for children (such as washable markers, stickers and coloring books), decorations, and partyware.
>
> In addition to Hallmark's regular line of Easter products, selected Hallmark Crown stores will be offering exclusive Easter items, such as Hallmark Keepsake Easter ornaments and fresh-cut flower bouquets.

The Hallmark Web site for Easter includes a story about trends for the holiday, research about Hallmark cards, product news with photos and illustrations of new Easter cards and a box of related links to Easter symbols and Passover. Web media kits are much cheaper to produce and distribute than print kits, but you still may need to send e-mail releases to media outlets that you want to reach alerting them to the new information. Another advantage of online media kits is that you can monitor how many people visited the site and what information was viewed or downloaded.

Corporate Publications

When you are writing news releases for the media whether in print or on the Web, use newspaper style. If you are writing a company magazine with news and features about people and events in the organization, newspaper style still applies. But when you are writing a memo or proposal to the company president or other corporate officials, you need to state your position in an analytical way.

That's where many business writers have difficulty, says Anne Baber, a writing coach who conducts seminars in corporations to improve communication techniques. She has also conducted seminars for the International Association of Business Communicators and has written books and many articles about career topics.

The key factor is to know the audience, she says: "There are some psychological problems people have when they write for folks up the ladder in management. One of my theories is that power warps communication. When people are writing for a boss, it's like a teenager talking to a parent. The parent says, 'Where are you going?' The teenager answers, 'Out.' The teen isn't saying everything he knows because of the power structure. In corporations, the power structure also affects communication. The writing becomes very formal, very passive. The writers don't want to put themselves forward as being initiators of action. They hide behind the third person. They write *the employee* rather than the word *you*."

Baber bases her theories on many years of experience in corporate communications. A former director of communications for United Telecom (now called Sprint), she now heads her own consulting firm, Baber & Associates, in Kansas City, Mo.

Many of the coaching techniques she uses are similar to those described earlier in this book. But the outcome is different. "Newswriting operates on the idea that if you give the public enough information, they will inform themselves," she says. "We're not doing that in an organization. We want to create attitudes or actions. It's much more like advertising." Here are Baber's tips for writing proposals and company plans:

Reporting Steps

Make a List: Ask what the audience—in this case, management—really wants to know. Then itemize all the points you can. (This is the same as brainstorming for a news story.)

Envision the Result: Ask yourself: What kind of action is the reader expected to take as a result of this information?

Make a Checklist of What and Why: Write a sentence beginning "I want to tell you that . . . " and then answer why. Then add this teaser to support the why factor: "This is necessary because. . . ." (This teaser is similar to the focus—"so what"—sentence at the top of your news stories.)

Writing Steps

Draw a "Mind Spill": Get all the research together. Draw a circle in the center of a large piece of paper. Put the main topic in the center circle. Then draw more circles, filling each one with an idea. With a colored pencil or highlighter, mark the key links between these ideas. Draw a line to connect one related idea to another so that all like information is grouped together. Then number the points, preferably in the order you will write them in the proposal. (This is the same technique as mapping for ideas or reporting.)

Organize the Order: Write a topic sentence (the same as a focus sentence) that completes this thought: "I believe that. . . ." For example, "I believe that we should market Mother's Day cards a different way." Then write the word *because* followed by point one, point two, point three—like the list technique. The most persuasive structure is three in parallel style.

Use Inverted Pyramid Style: Put the strongest point of the proposal in the lead, and then plan your proposal with supporting points.

Put Information in Perspective: Ask yourself: What does the reader know already, and what is new? If this is one of a series of proposals, you may need just a summary sentence referring to past information the reader already knows. The reader is going to read this proposal quickly and will get irritated if he has to wade through previously known material.

Write a Strong Conclusion: Summarize, but do not repeat, your lead. If you have written a proposal about marketing Mother's Day cards and you have given the supporting points that answer why you should change the method, the ending could be a strong statement such as "We should start marketing these new cards in six months." If that time frame is part of your proposal, you could just end with a statement telling why it is a good idea.

Check Your Verbs: After you have written your draft, go back and circle the verbs and see if they are strong action words. If not, revise.

Corporate Web Sites

Jakob Nielsen, the leading expert in how people use the Web, says "corporate Web sites get a 'D' in PR." A study he conducted of how journalists use these online corporate sites showed that they found the information they were seeking only 60 percent of the time. "That percentage equals a 'D' grade," Nielsen says.

According to his study, here are the top five reasons journalists visit a company Web site:

- To find a PR contact (name and telephone number)
- To check basic facts about the company, including the spelling of executives' names, location of the company and so on
- To discover the company's "spin" on events

- To check financial information
- To download images for use as illustrations in stories

If you are writing information to be posted on a corporate Web site, keep that information in mind and follow these guidelines:

- Avoid promotional language and adjectives. Keep the writing simple and straightforward.
- Include a person's contact information, the company address and phone numbers and Web site address. Do not have as the only contact an e-mail address to an anonymous webmaster.

Elizabeth Albrycht, author of the CorporatePR blog and an expert in new technologies for public relations, has this advice on her blog, "An Open Letter to PR Students:"

"Be prepared for the unexpected. The one constant in PR is change. Stories change, people change, clients change, jobs change, technologies change, fads change, trends change. . . . PR is generally NOT glamorous. There is nothing fun about stuffing press kits at 4 a.m. in a crappy conference center hotel room when you have an 8 a.m. press conference. The PR person rarely gets thanked when things go well, and is the first to be blamed when things go badly. However, one of the great things about PR is you can immediately see the results of your work. You can make a difference." (See *http://ringblog.typepad.com/corporatepr/2003/10/open_letter_to_.html.*)

What Do You Think [?]

The Public Relations Society conducted a "State of the PR Profession Opinion Survey" and asked respondents what information they seek from online pr newsrooms. Which of these elements do you think journalists wanted most in a pr Web site:

☐ Photographs
☐ Audio
☐ Video
☐ Event schedules Videos for editorial use and online use
☐ RSS feeds
☐ All of the above

(Answers at the end of this chapter)

Exercises

1 **News release (hard-news style):** Gather information from an organization for an event on your campus or in your city. Write a news release announcing the event.

2 **Media kit:** Study a company in your community. Devise a media kit to promote some product or aspect of the company. This activity may require some coordination so that many students do not bother the same firm. If a team of students or the whole class is studying a large company, divide the responsibilities so students are studying different aspects of the company.

3 **News release (feature style):** As the contact, use your name, phone number and e-mail address. The company is Excaliber Entertainment Inc., 1955 Larkspur, San Antonio, Texas 78213. This information is adapted from a press release for a former online contest site owned by Excaliber. You may use a direct or creative lead. Assume that the Web site still exists for your news release, which should be limited to one page.

Who: *www.vaultcracker.com,* a contest Web site.

What: Sponsoring a contest, "Junkiest Dorm Room in America."

When: Use now through the next two months.

Where: *www.vaultcracker.com.*

Why: To promote the new Web site.

How: The contest will award $300 to a college student whose pictures of his or her dorm room are judged the junkiest. Second prize is $100. The contest is open to all students who are enrolled full time at a college or university in the United States.

Comments: From Richard McNairy, founder and president of *www.vaultcracker.com:* "We know how busy college students are and we wanted to turn a negative into a positive. I'm sure students with messy rooms get criticism from others. Now two students with junky rooms will be able to brag about the fact that they earned cash because of their junky rooms."

More information: Visit *www.vaultcracker.com.*

4 **E-mail news release:** Write a one-page e-mail news release (about 150 words) based on the following information; use your name, phone number and e-mail for contact information:

> The U.S. Department of Commerce's census bureau released a report today about the value of various college degrees. The report is called "What's It Worth? Field of Training and Economic Status." The data are from a panel of the Survey of Income and Program Participation. College graduates who work full time and have a bachelor's degree in engineering earn the highest average monthly pay ($4,680), while those with education degrees earn the lowest ($2,802), according to the report. "Majoring in a technical field does pay off even if you don't finish a four-year degree," said Kurt Bauman, co-author with Camille Ryan of the report. "The average person with a vocational certificate earns around $200 more per month than the average high school graduate; but if the certificate is in an engineering-related field, the boost in earnings is close to $800." At the top of the earnings scale were those with professional degrees, such as doctors and lawyers ($7,224 per month), followed by full-time workers with master's degrees ($4,635), bachelor's degrees ($3,767), high school graduates ($2,279) and those without a diploma ($1,699).

> Business was the most popular field of training beyond high school; 7.5 million people had bachelor's degrees in business and earned a monthly average of $3,962. An additional 1.9 million had master's degrees in business administration or other advanced degrees in business. The average monthly earnings of people with master's degrees in business was $5,579. Of people with managerial jobs, 46 percent had bachelor's or higher degrees. Of people in professional occupations, 71 percent held a bachelor's degree or higher degrees. By comparison, no more than 8 percent of those in craft, service, farm and production occupations had completed this much education. Associate degrees generally require a two-year course of study, but people took an average of more than four years to complete them. Bachelor's and higher degrees took an average of five or more years to complete.

5 **Public service announcement:** Write a 15-second public service announcement (about 65 words) based on this information:

This message is from the Federal Emergency Management Agency. It's about tornadoes. They can be deadly. Tornadoes strike nearly every year with the most powerful winds on Earth. Remember these three tornado danger signs: One—Before a tornado hits, the wind may die down and the air may become very still. Two—Tornadoes can be nearly invisible, marked only by swirling debris at the base of the funnel. An approaching cloud of dust or debris can mark the location of a deadly tornado. Seek shelter immediately. Three—Tornadoes generally occur near the trailing edge of a thunderstorm. When a thunderstorm moves through your area, be alert for tornadoes. For more information on tornado preparedness, visit the FEMA Web site at w-w-w-dot-f-e-m-a-dot-gov, or contact the Red Cross. Plan ahead to survive the next tornado, and listen to this station for more emergency preparedness information from FEMA.

6 **Promote a product:** Working in small groups, create a new product and a company name and address. Use your name and contact information. Each person in

the group should then write a news release promoting this product.

7 Usability study: Conduct your own informal usability study by visiting the Web sites of three to five corporations that interest you. On each site, search for basic PR information described in this chapter and note your findings. Do the sites contain the basic contact information that you would need, such as phone numbers, addresses and key corporate officers? Do the sites contain a good description of the company's purpose? What other information do you think these Web sites should contain?

☞ **Featured Online Activity** Log on to the book Web site and do the assignments at

academic.cengage.com/masscomm/rich/ writingandreportingnews6e

(The answer to the question in the What Do You Think box is: All of the above with particular interest in video and RSS feeds.)

Coaching Tips

Check your story for accuracy.

Seek documents to substantiate sources' claims.

Check résumés and other materials from sources.

Seek sources with alternate points of view.

Role-play: If you were the source or the source's attorney, what would you find libelous or objectionable in the story?

If you are writing about a police or court case, check for the latest charges or disposition in the case.

Don't copy information from a Web site without attribution or permission.

Don't use online information you can't verify, especially if it includes accusations about a person.

Congress shall make no law respecting an establishment of religion, or prohibiting the free exercise thereof; or abridging the freedom of speech, or of the press; or the right of the people peaceably to assemble, and to petition the Government for a redress of grievances.

— The First Amendment to the U.S. Constitution

15 Media Law

Test your knowledge of these legal issues:

1 You are the online editor of your campus newspaper. A person using a pseudonym has posted a message on your Web site that could be libelous. If you don't remove the posting, the paper will be liable for the information in the message if a lawsuit is filed. True or False?

2 You have visited a Web site that has a graphic you want to use in your campus newspaper or your radio station's Web site. The site does not contain any copyright notice so you can use the graphic without permission. True or False?

3 Any columns labeled "opinion" or editorials published in your newspaper cannot be considered libelous regardless of the information they contain. True or False?

4 You are posting a video on YouTube. If you use just a portion of a popular song in your video, you will not be violating copyright laws. True or False?

Many legal issues arising from the increasing use of social networking sites, blogs and other online media do not have clear-cut answers. However, the questions posed here have legal precedents. Here are the answers to the first three questions, which are adapted from information on the Student Press Law Center *(www.splc.org)*, and the answer to the last question, which is explained on the YouTube Web site *(www.youtube.com)*:

Question 1: **False.** The paper is not liable for messages posted by a third party. The federal Communications Decency Act grants immunity to Web site operators and Internet providers for messages posted by a third party. But if you create part of the message by editing it, you could be considered a "content provider," and you might be liable in a lawsuit. In addition, because the Web is a global medium, you could be liable in other countries. It is probably a good idea to check the postings and delete ones that you think are offensive or potentially libelous.

Question 2: **False.** All material on the Internet is copyrighted as soon as it is created. It does not need to have a copyright notice to be protected by U.S. copyright laws. However, some images may be available without permission if they are from government sites or from Web sites that say permission is granted

The Student Press Law Center

SPLC
STUDENT PRESS LAW CENTER

1101 Wilson Blvd.
Suite 1100
Arlington, VA 22209, USA.
Telephone: 703.807.1904

Do you have questions about your legal rights and responsibilities as a student journalist or media adviser? Or are you just interested in more information about press law? The SPLC Resource Center can help you find answers.

for specific use. In many cases the site may grant permission to use images on personal pages but not for commercial use.

***Question 3:* False.** You may express opinions without impunity, but if you publish an allegation that is false and damaging to a person's reputation, you can be sued for libel no matter where it is published in a newspaper, on a Web site or in a broadcast medium. You can criticize someone as a bad performer without being libelous, but if you falsely accuse the performer of being a drug addict, that would be libelous.

***Question 4:* False.** You are violating copyright by using all or a portion of a song or video that you did not create yourself. The YouTube site specifically states: "Be sure that all components of your video are your original creation—even the audio portion. . . . If you use an audio track of a sound recording owned by a record label without that record label's permission, your video is infringing the copyrights of others, and we will take it down as soon as we become aware of it."

Libel

"Libel is essentially a false and defamatory attack in written form on a person's reputation or character. Broadcast defamation is libel because there is usually a written script. Oral or spoken defamation is slander," according to Donald Gillmor and his co-authors in *Mass Communication Law: Cases and Comment.* The "script" is not limited to a news story, the authors explain; it can take the form of headlines, photos, cartoons, film, tape, records, signs, bumper stickers and advertisements.

Several libel suits have also resulted from messages that people posted to online discussion groups. If the defamatory statements are published—whether online or in print—they can still be considered libelous.

Truth is a defense in libel suits. Anyone can sue or threaten to sue for libel, claiming injury to his reputation. The real concern is whether the person has grounds enough to win. The key factors to consider are whether you published untrue information that hurt the reputation of an identifiable person and whether you were either negligent or reckless in failing to check the information:

- Are you publishing something that you aren't sure is truthful?
- Are you carelessly publishing something that is inaccurate?
- Are you publishing something accusatory that you haven't checked out?
- Are you publishing something that clearly identifies a person and harms that person's reputation?

If your answer is yes to any of those questions, you could be in trouble for libel.

Times v. Sullivan

Those standards were the ones the U.S. Supreme Court applied in 1964 in a landmark libel case, *New York Times Co. v. Sullivan,* and the standards have been applied since then to public officials.

The *New York Times* case stemmed from an advertisement the newspaper accepted in 1960 from a group of people in the civil rights movement. The group was trying to raise money for the Committee to Defend Martin Luther King. The ad claimed that King had been arrested seven times and that his home had been bombed. It also claimed that black students who had staged a nonviolent civil rights demonstration at Alabama State University had been the target of police brutality. The advertisement accused the police department in Montgomery, Ala., of being armed with shotguns and using tear gas to subdue students.

Even though the police commissioner, L. B. Sullivan, had not been named in the advertisement, he sued for libel. He contended that the mention of "police" in the ad referred to him as the Montgomery police commissioner, and that the ad contained factual errors that damaged his reputation. He claimed that the police did not ring the college campus or padlock the college dining hall, as the ad had claimed. Furthermore, Dr. King had been arrested four times, not seven, and three of the four arrests had occurred before Sullivan was commissioner.

Sullivan won in the lower courts and the Alabama Supreme Court. But the U.S. Supreme Court reversed the decision in its landmark ruling about "actual malice." Malice, in this context, does not mean intent to harm someone; it means that you published something knowing it was false or not bothering to check its truth or falsity. As the justices wrote,

> The constitutional guarantees require, we think, a federal rule that prohibits a public official from recovering damages for defamatory falsehood relating to his official conduct unless he proves that the statement was made with "actual malice"—that is knowledge that it was false or with reckless disregard of whether it was false or not.

The court placed the burden of proving libel on the plaintiff, the person who is suing. The justices made this a constitutional issue, applying the First Amendment right of a free press to publish matters of public concern. In the ruling, Justice William Brennan wrote the following:

> Thus we consider this case against the background of a profound national commitment to the principle that debate on public issues should be uninhibited, robust, and wide-open, and that it may well include vehement, caustic, and sometimes unpleasantly sharp attacks on government and public officials.

The *Times v. Sullivan* ruling applied only to people who are public officials. The application was later broadened to include "public figures."

Public Officials

For purposes of libel law, who is a public official? Elected officials and candidates for office are definitely considered public officials. Appointed officials may or may not be. Here are the criteria: Do they have authority to set policy in the government, and are they under enough public scrutiny to have easy access to the media?

The Supreme Court defined public officials this way in *Rosenblatt v. Baer,* a case about the status of appointed officials:

> It is clear, therefore, that the "public official" designation applies at the very least to those among the hierarchy of government employees who have, or appear to the public to have, substantial responsibility for or control over the conduct of government affairs.

Is a police officer a public official? Courts in Pennsylvania are split on that decision, but most courts have ruled that law enforcement officers are public officials because they have the power to make arrests, a form of control in government. However, teachers, professors and other employees in a public education system are not usually defined as public officials because they are carrying out policies set by other officials of the school district or university. But if they achieve fame or notoriety, they may become public figures.

Public Figures

Who is a public figure, and why is the distinction between public officials and public figures important? People may be considered public figures if their achievements or notoriety places them in the public eye or if they seek attention by voluntarily thrusting themselves into a public controversy. But if they are brought into the public spotlight involuntarily, they may not be public figures. A court will usually determine whether the person qualifies as a public figure.

Like public officials, public figures also bear the burden of proving that the information in contention was libelous. The person or organization being sued does not have to disprove libel. The courts identify three types of public figures: pervasive, vortex and involuntary.

A "pervasive" public figure is a person who has gained prominence in society or great power and influence. Well-known entertainers and athletes and people who voluntarily seek public attention are in this category.

A "vortex" or "limited" public figure is a person who has voluntarily thrust himself into a public controversy to influence the outcome. The Supreme Court has stated that people in this category are not public figures for all aspects of their lives but only for the aspects that relate to their role in a particular public controversy. A key point is the "voluntary" concept. An individual does not automatically become a public figure if he is thrust into a newsworthy situation; the involvement in the controversy must be the person's choice. Access to the media is another factor in determining whether someone is a public figure. The person must have enough regular and continuing access to the media to counter criticism and expose falsehoods.

Consider the case of *Hutchinson v. Proxmire*. In 1975, when the late Sen. William Proxmire issued his annual "Golden Fleece" awards, which satirized some government-funded research projects as wasteful, he issued a press release targeting a researcher who was using monkeys to study stress. The scientist, Ronald Hutchinson, sued Proxmire for damaging his reputation and subjecting him to public ridicule by falsely claiming Hutchinson's research was wasteful. Key to the case was determining whether Hutchinson was a public figure.

Proxmire claimed the scientist was a public figure because he had received federal grants and had access to the media when they contacted him about receiving the Golden Fleece award. A federal district court agreed with Proxmire and dismissed the suit. But Hutchinson appealed.

The U.S. Supreme Court ruled that Hutchinson was not a public figure because he was not willingly involved in a public controversy until Proxmire caused it. The court said Hutchinson did not automatically become a public figure by being thrust into a newsworthy situation. Also, the court determined that Hutchinson did not have regular and continuing access to the media. He was sought out by reporters only to respond to Proxmire's criticism. Hutchinson ultimately received $10,000 from Proxmire.

The third type of public figure, "involuntary," is someone who does nothing voluntary to garner attention or to get involved in a public issue but finds himself in the middle of a public controversy anyway. Courts have found that this category rarely fits an individual in a libel suit.

Private Figures

The difference between being a public or private figure is crucial because the standards for proving libel can differ. Many states have made it easier for private persons to prove libel than for public figures. The Supreme Court has left it up to the states to determine their own standards of liability for private figures:

> We hold that, so long as they do not impose liability without fault, the States may define for themselves the appropriate standard of liability for a publisher or a broadcaster of defamatory falsehood injurious to a private individual.

The court made this ruling in a 1974 case, *Gertz v. Welch*. Elmer Gertz was a Chicago lawyer who claimed he had been libeled when a John Birch Society magazine, *American Opinion*, published an article labeling him a Communist. He sued the publisher, Robert Welch. Even though Gertz was a prominent lawyer, the Supreme Court ruled that he was a private person under the circumstances of this case. The court also declared that because private people don't have the same access to the media to defend themselves as public officials, they shouldn't be held to the same strict standards in proving libel.

In *Gertz v. Welch*, the court decided that a private individual needs to show only that the material was published with carelessness or negligence instead of proving actual malice, which means publishing with knowledge or reckless disregard of falsity. But all libel plaintiffs, public and private, have to prove the material is false and damaging to their reputation.

Even though the Supreme Court left it up to states to determine their own libel standards in cases involving private figures, the *Gertz* case paved the way for allowing private people to abide by less rigid standards than public officials and figures. Many states have followed the "simple negligence" standard in the *Gertz* case. Others require private individuals to abide by the same "actual malice" standard as public individuals. "Negligence" in this context means you failed to exercise reasonable care in doing your job as a journalist. That type of care might include talking to all sides of a controversial issue, using relevant documents, taking accurate notes and checking your information for accuracy before publishing it.

The Importance of Accuracy

Accuracy is paramount for a good journalist. Every mistake you make jeopardizes the newspaper's or broadcast station's credibility with readers and viewers. Because of that credibility factor, newspapers throughout the country print corrections every day, many for the incorrect spelling of names. That's another reason why you should always double-check the names in your stories.

Dan Rather, former anchor for CBS News, didn't kill a story that should have been checked more thoroughly before it aired and became a scandal for the CBS network. When George W. Bush was running for re-election in 2004, Rather aired a story on "60 Minutes Wednesday," that the president had received preferential treatment when he was in the Texas Air National Guard in the early 1970s during the Vietnam War. The story was based on documents the station had received from an anonymous source. Less than four hours after the broadcast, a blogger identifying himself as "Buckhead" questioned the validity of the documents and claimed they could not have been typed in 1972 because typewriters in those days did not have the font style used for the documents.

CBS originally stood by the story but ultimately apologized. The network convened an independent panel to investigate whether the documents were forged. At the end of a three-month investigation and a 224-page report, the panel members could only conclude that they didn't know. However, they said the report was rushed onto air, "driven in part by competitive pressures," without adequate checking, called "vetting," and that it violated the network's standards of accuracy and fairness.

Rather, who had been with CBS for 43 years, announced his retirement six weeks before the investigation was completed, but he didn't tie his decision to the incident. He later sued CBS for $70 million, claiming that the network made him a scapegoat for the scandal.

Following the investigation, CBS chairman Leslie Moonves issued an apology: "As far as the question of reporting is concerned, the bottom line is that much of the September 8 broadcast was wrong. We deeply regret the disservice this flawed '60 Minutes Wednesday' report did to the American public." In addition, he created a new position of vice president of standards and special projects to review the authenticity of sources, use of confidential sources and use of hidden cameras.

The incident may soon be forgotten, just a footnote in history books about the 2004 election—one of many scandals in political campaigns. But the message was clear: Accuracy is paramount, and without it, credibility will plummet.

Showing Copy to Sources

Should you show your story to sources or read it to them before you print it? Many of your sources will ask you to do that. And many editors will say you shouldn't. They claim the risks are too great that sources will recant what they have told you or ask you to delete any information that puts them in a bad light.

Steve Weinberg, former director of Investigative Reporters and Editors and a leading authority on researching records, says it's time to change that traditional way of thinking. "I am convinced that my practice of pre-publication read-backs and manuscript submission has led to more accurate, fair and thorough newspaper pieces, magazine articles, and books," he wrote in *Quill* magazine. "There is no such thing as a minor mistake, not even just one or two little errors in a lengthy manuscript."

Weinberg makes it clear that the source who is checking the story has the right only to check for accuracy, not to make any changes.

If you don't show the entire story to your source, it is considered acceptable—even wise—to ask a source about any technical information you may not fully understand. You can read what you have written and, like Weinberg, ask the source to check its accuracy.

Corrections

The most common cause of lawsuits is carelessness. Most news media don't publish material they know or suspect is false.

Although newspapers and broadcast media get sued by people targeted in major investigative projects, the majority of libel suits stem from much less important stories. Incorrect captions, defamatory headlines, an inaccuracy in a police story or a feature can result in a libel suit.

Printed corrections or oral retractions on radio or television don't prevent libel suits. They may assuage an angered source enough to forestall a lawsuit, or they may be evidence of the news organization's good faith, but corrections do not undo the harm of inaccurate published material. It's up to a jury to decide if you were negligent, careless or reckless in your disregard for the truth.

A printed correction by the *National Enquirer* didn't stop entertainer Carol Burnett from suing the tabloid in 1976 for insinuating that she was drunk. The article said that she had an argument with Henry Kissinger, then secretary of state, at a Washington restaurant and "accidentally knocked a glass of wine over on one diner—and started giggling." Burnett denied the incident occurred, and even though the *Enquirer* apologized in a retraction, Burnett pressed her lawsuit. She was awarded a total of $1.6 million by a Los Angeles jury and ultimately settled for an undisclosed amount.

Even when you use the word *alleged,* meaning that the accusation is a charge without proof, you are on dangerous ground. This word, although widely used by reporters in police cases, does not save you from libel. It is better to attribute the information to official sources or records.

If you don't name the person against whom the accusation is made, you still can be sued for libel. A person who can claim he was identified—either by enough information to describe the person physically or by position—can then sue.

Nor does attribution save you. Say that a candidate for mayor tells you his opponent is a crook. You print the statement and attribute it to the candidate. The opponent could sue you and your newspaper. Just because you named the source of the statement, you cannot avoid responsibility for it. And if it isn't true and you haven't documented it as true, you could be considered guilty of reckless disregard for the truth.

If you are going to print any accusations that could be defamatory, you should always check with the person being accused and ask for a response. Cross-checking may not save you from libel, but it at least gives you a chance to prove you were not reckless.

There are times when you can print accusatory or damaging information, especially when you are writing about crime. You have certain privileges as a member of the press, and so do some of the officials who deal with you.

Privilege

Privilege—in a legal sense—comes in two forms: absolute and qualified.

Absolute Privilege: This means that public officials, including law enforcement officials, can make statements in the course of their official duties without fear of being sued for libel. This form of privilege extends to court proceedings, legislative proceedings, public and official meetings, and contents of public records. For example, if Senator Proxmire had announced his Golden Fleece awards on the floor of the Senate instead of in a news release, he would have had absolute privilege and could not have been sued by Hutchinson, the researcher who claimed he was libeled.

Qualified Privilege: As a member of the media, you have "qualified privilege." You may print defamatory statements made by people who are absolutely privileged as long as you are being fair and accurate and the information is from a public proceeding or public record. But if your report contains errors, you could lose that qualified protection.

If during a public meeting a city council member calls another member a crook, you may print the accusation. If the same city official makes the same comment to you during a telephone interview or after the meeting, you can't print it without risking libel. The key is that the defamatory statement must be made in an official capacity during an official proceeding. Or you may use, with attribution, something stated in court records. But you must make it clear that the accusations were made by other people in records or meetings and are not proven fact.

Suppose that a police officer tells you something about a suspect. You may print this information if the officer is acting in an official capacity and if the information is documented in a public record, such as a police report or court files. However, you still should be careful about how you word accusations in crime stories. The police officer may say the man stabbed his wife, but you may not say the same thing without attribution. If the information is not stated in a public record, such as a police report or court record, it can be libelous. Generally, statements made outside of the court by police are not privileged, but some states may extend privilege to these comments.

Never call anyone a murderer unless the person has been convicted of murder in court. Suppose that a man has been murdered and you go to the neighborhood for reaction. A neighbor says the man's wife killed him. The neighbor isn't an official acting in an official capacity, and the wife hasn't been convicted. The neighbor's comments could be libelous, and you could be sued for printing them.

Don't call suspects robbers or use any other accusatory term before they are convicted. Use terms such as "the suspect," "the man accused of murder," "the woman charged with the robbery."

Person of Interest: In recent years police have been using another term, "person of interest," to describe someone who is being investigated in a crime but has not been arrested or charged with anything. Although the term appears to be a synonym for "suspect," it does not have any legal definition and can implicate people who are just being questioned. The term has become known as "the Richard Jewell rule," because it was used in reference to Richard Jewell, the man who was initially accused of being responsible for the 1996 Olympic Park bombing incident but was never charged. He was cleared of any wrongdoing, but when he died in 2007, news stories still associated him with the wrongful accusations in the bombing incident. The lesson from that is be careful how you characterize people in criminal investigations and think before you publish names of people who have not been officially charged with crimes.

Neutral Reportage

Another type of privilege, called "neutral reportage," has been recognized in about 10 states. It gives the news media First Amendment protection in writing accusations about a public official or public figure in a public controversy as long as the reporter states them accurately and neutrally. If one official or person considered responsible and newsworthy accuses another public figure of wrongdoing, you may print the information as long as you get reactions of the accused or other participants.

Under neutral reportage you aren't responsible for determining whether the accusations are true. However, many states don't extend this type of privilege to the media, so it's always safer to beware of printing unsubstantiated accusations.

ETHICS

The case: You are attending a school board meeting as a reporter. During the public comment portion of the meeting, a woman accuses a male guidance counselor in the high school of having had sex with students. This is a small town, with only one high school and two guidance counselors, both male. The school board says it will conduct an investigation. You are on deadline and must get the story in right after the meeting. You can't reach either guidance counselor for his reaction. The comment was made at a public meeting, and it is part of the public record. Even if you have the legal right to publish this information, what are your ethical concerns? Will you include this information in your story?

The best defense for a reporter is the "truth" defense, proving that what you wrote is true. What you can do and what you should do may differ. You may have the right to print statements from court records or meetings, but if you think they could be untrue or unfair, should you print them? Those are the kinds of ethical decisions journalists must make. Most editors advise this: When in doubt, leave it out.

Fair Comment and Criticism

Suppose you are writing a review of a play, concert or book, and your review is very negative. Can you be sued? Yes. You can always be sued. But you are protected under the right of fair comment.

Writers of editorials, analysis stories, reviews and other criticism may express opinions, but they may not state inaccurate facts. A factual error can be grounds for libel; an opinion is protected.

To qualify as fair comment, a comment must generally be on a matter of public interest, it must be based on facts known or believed to be true, and it may not be malicious or made with reckless disregard for the truth. In this case also, truth is considered a good defense.

Invasion of Privacy

Issues of privacy involve ethical decisions, not matters of accuracy. However, with the proliferation of invasion of privacy lawsuits, a journalist should understand the legal issues. Privacy is not a right guaranteed by the U.S. Constitution. In privacy cases, damage is usually considered the mental anguish that results from wrongfully revealing to the public some part of the plaintiff's life. Truth may not be enough of a defense in privacy cases.

Suppose that a child drowns and a mother stands on the dock as her son's body is dragged from the river. She is hysterical. A photographer takes her picture without her consent. Has the photographer invaded her privacy? Perhaps, if the photographer was on private property. The photographer could be considered an intruder. However, it is not an invasion of privacy if the photographer was on public property. Even if a scene on private property is visible from public property, the photographer would be within his rights to take pictures.

The courts have acknowledged four grounds for invasion of privacy lawsuits: intrusion, public disclosure of private and embarrassing facts, false light, and misappropriation of a person's name or image without permission.

Intrusion into a Person's Solitude

Eavesdropping, harassing someone and trespassing on private property can be considered intrusion. So can going onto private property and using a telephoto lens, listening behind doors and using any device to enhance what the unaided eye can see or the unaided ear can hear. In other words, a journalist who uses subterfuge to obtain and publish confidential material could be risking a suit for invasion of privacy. The intrusion can be either physical or mental.

In *Dietemann v. Time Inc.*, two *Life* magazine reporters were sued for going undercover as husband and wife to do a story on a plumber, A.S. Dietemann. The plumber was believed to be practicing medicine with herbs. The so-called healer told the female reporter she had cancer and prescribed an herbal cure. The female reporter taped Dietemann's comments, and her partner took pictures with a concealed camera. Even though the plumber later pleaded no contest to a charge of practicing medicine without a license, he sued the magazine company for invasion of privacy. A California court awarded him $1,000. An appeals court upheld the award and said that the undercover methods, used without Dietemann's consent, were an invasion of his privacy. "The First Amendment is not a license to trespass, to steal, or to intrude by electronic means into the precincts of another's home or office," the court opinion said.

Unlike libel suits, publication isn't required for someone to claim invasion of privacy in this type of case. Truth isn't a defense either. After ABC-TV reporters on "Prime Time Live" used undercover techniques and hidden cameras to expose unsanitary conditions at Food Lion grocery stores, the supermarket chain sued for trespass and fraud. Reporters who had falsified employment applications to obtain jobs at Food Lion reported that the supermarket chain sold spoiled meat, fish dipped in bleach and rat-gnawed cheese. Food Lion didn't challenge the television show's findings—only the methods reporters used. In 1997 a jury awarded Food Lion $5.5 million, which was reduced to just $2 after several appeals. The rationale was the same as it was 25 years earlier in the Dietemann case: Even if the news report is true, reporters don't have license to trespass.

Public Disclosure of Private Facts

Publishing facts such as information about a person's sex life or medical history that the public considers offensive could be considered invasion of privacy, even if it's true. But if the facts are taken from the public record, such as court documents, they will probably be considered fair to publish.

In 1975 the Supreme Court ruled in *Cox Broadcasting Co. v. Cohn* that a television station in Atlanta was within its First Amendment rights to publish the name of a rape victim even though state law prohibited doing so. The victim's family had sued for invasion of privacy, claiming a private fact had been disclosed. The family had won, but Cox appealed the decision to the U.S. Supreme Court. The court said the news media had the right to report matters on the public record.

Information not on the public record is more susceptible to lawsuits. The courts have ruled that the media may be invading privacy if the private facts in question would be offensive and objectionable to a reasonable person and would not be of legitimate public concern. Community standards of what is "offensive" may vary from one place to another. That's why these are difficult cases for courts to decide.

Regarding the public concern standard, the case often cited is *Sidis v. F-R Publishing Corp.*, which involved a profile in *The New Yorker* magazine of James Sidis, a genius who had graduated from Harvard at age 16. Twenty years later the magazine wrote a profile about his life as a recluse. Sidis sued for invasion of privacy, but the courts ruled that he was a public figure who had lost his right to privacy and that his life was, therefore, newsworthy or of legitimate public concern.

Publicity that Puts a Person in a False Light

If a published story or picture gives the wrong impression and is embarrassing to the person, the possibility exists that the court will consider a "false light" verdict. For example, in one case a television station doing a story about teenage pregnancy took pictures of a young woman walking down the street. The television station did not say she was pregnant, nor did the station identify her. However, she claimed the picture put her in a false light—indicating that she was a pregnant teenager—and she won her lawsuit against the station.

False light is related to defamation, but the story or picture does not have to defame a person to be considered false light. It does have to portray the person inaccurately. Truth is a defense in these cases. Generally, the plaintiff has to prove that the media showed actual malice by knowingly publishing false information.

The case often cited here is *Time Inc. v. Hill*, because it was the first false-light case to reach the Supreme Court. James Hill, his wife and five children were held hostage in their suburban Philadelphia home by three escaped convicts in 1952. After the incident, the Hills moved to Connecticut. A few years later, *Life* magazine was planning to publish a review of a play partially based on the incident. The magazine took the cast of the play to the Hills' old home and photographed the actors in some scenes from the play. James Hill sued, saying the pictures in *Life* gave readers the impression that the scenes portrayed the family's real experiences. Hill initially won his suit. But it eventually went to the Supreme Court, which ruled that Hill would have to prove actual malice on the part of *Life* magazine. The court sent the case back for retrial to a lower court, but Hill dropped the suit.

Use of a Person's Name or Photo Without Permission

This doctrine applies when the picture is used for commercial purposes, such as advertising or promotion. For example, use of an athlete's photograph to promote a product without his consent could be grounds for a lawsuit. The easiest way to avoid this kind of lawsuit is to have the person sign a consent form.

Television personality Vanna White sued Samsung Electronics when an advertisement the firm used featured a robot that resembled White as she appeared on the game show "Wheel of Fortune." White claimed her image was appropriated without her permission, and a court agreed.

Online Legal Issues

The Internet is spawning many new legal issues and laws regarding free speech vs. pornography, libel, copyright and privacy.

Communications Decency Act

The first major test of free speech on the Internet to reach the U.S. Supreme Court was the Communications Decency Act (CDA) of 1996, a federal law that restricted distribution of indecent material on the Internet to people under age 18. The American Civil Liberties Union challenged the law, which was ruled unconstitutional by a federal three-judge panel in Philadelphia, but the government appealed the ruling in *Reno v. ACLU*. In 1997 the U.S. Supreme Court struck down portions of the act that censored online material. In the ruling, Associate Justice John Paul Stevens wrote that the CDA's "use of undefined terms 'indecent and patently offensive' raises special First Amendment concerns because of its obvious chilling effect on free speech."

One area that was not struck down was a little section that has become a big issue for Internet providers, bloggers and other people who post messages on any Internet or social networking sites. Section 230 of the act says, "No provider or user of an interactive computer service shall be treated as the publisher or speaker of any information provided by another information content provider."

As mentioned at the start of this chapter, that means that if someone posts a libelous message to your Web site, you are not responsible for the content of it unless you created part of it. Courts have held that this part of the act protects you even if you edit or delete the offensive material. If you are only providing the Web site or service, you're safe, but if you contribute to the content, you could be held responsible.

Zeran v. America Online

Online providers can thank Kenneth Zeran for that protection. He was just at home in Seattle running his publishing business from his house in April 1995 when his phone began ringing every two minutes with callers issuing death threats. The calls began just six days after the bombing of the federal building in Oklahoma City where 168 people died.

An anonymous person had posted Zeran's telephone number on an America Online message board telling readers to call him because he was selling T-shirts, key chains and other memorabilia about the bombing with such offensive slogans such as "Visit Oklahoma . . . It's a BLAST!!!" Oddly enough, Zeran wasn't even a member of AOL, and the person who posted the message had a trial membership and was never identified because AOL didn't keep records of nonsubscribers.

To make matters worse, an announcer for a classic rock radio station in Oklahoma City read the message on air and encouraged listeners to call Zeran and tell him how they felt about what he was doing. Zeran sued the radio station on grounds of defamation, false light invasion of privacy, and intentional infliction of emotional distress, but the court ruled in favor of the radio station on all counts. The court ruled that the only charge applicable to broadcast was slander and there was insufficient evidence to establish injury to Zeran's reputation or that his emotional stress was "severe" enough to prevent him from conducting his daily affairs.

More significant was his suit against AOL on charges that the service was responsible for the defamatory messages and was unreasonably slow in removing them. This was the first libel case against an online service provider to reach the U.S. Supreme Court. Zeran's case was initially dismissed in 1997 by a U.S. District Court, which ruled that Section 230 of the Communications Decency Act of 1996 protected online service providers from liability for subscribers' material. In 1998 the U.S. Supreme Court upheld that decision. So AOL was not at fault, and Zeran got nothing for his troubles.

Protection for Bloggers

Although the law is specific regarding Internet service providers, it is not as clear regarding bloggers. "Bloggers can be both a provider and a user of interactive computer services," according to 'Bloggers' FAQ,' an article on the Electronic Frontier Foundation Web site *(http://w2.eff.org/bloggers/lg/).* "Bloggers are users when they create and edit blogs through a service provider, and they are providers to the extent that they allow third parties to add comments or other material to their blogs. Your readers' comments, entries written by guest bloggers, tips sent by e-mail and information provided to you through an RSS feed would all likely be considered information provided by another content provider," according to the EFF article. But the courts have not ruled on whether you would be responsible for defamatory material if you selected the information from other blogs to post on your site.

Children's Online Privacy Protection Act

Although the Communications Decency Act provisions to protect children from Internet abuses failed, three other related efforts succeeded:

- The Children's Online Privacy Protection Act (COPPA), which took effect in 2000, makes it a federal crime—with penalties of $10,000 per violation—to collect information from children under 13 and use it for commercial purposes that could be considered harmful to minors. The law requires operators of commercial Web sites or online services to obtain verifiable parental consent before collecting information from preteens and to post notices on the site of how any information would be used. The law covers such information as the child's full name, home and/or e-mail address, telephone number and any other information that would allow someone to identify or contact the child. One company fined for violations of this act was Bonzi Software, which markets the BonziBuddy, a purple cartoon gorilla. To download the joke-telling gorilla, registration was required. The Federal Trade Commission, which enforces COPPA, fined the company $75,000.

- The Child Online Protection Act (COPA) was passed in 1998 and also went into effect in 2000, but it has been blocked by the courts as unconstitutional restriction of free speech. It attempted to protect minors from harmful material on the Internet.

- The Children's Internet Protection Act (CIPA), passed in 2000, also attempts to protect children by requiring public schools and libraries that receive federal funds to install software that would block online material considered "harmful to minors," basically pornography and obscenity. The law was challenged as unconstitutional by the American Library Association, but in 2003 the Supreme Court upheld it. In addition, more than 21 states have enacted laws to require Internet filtering software in public schools or libraries to limit children's access to sexually explicit online information.

These types of legal issues are certain to continue as the government attempts to regulate the Internet.

Convergence Coach

Whose space is liable on MySpace?

Julie Doe (known as Jane Doe in the lawsuit), was a 13-year-old teenager from Texas when she created a profile on MySpace. The next year a 19-year-old man, also from Texas, saw her profile and contacted her. They began communicating and later spoke on the phone. In 2006 the two met in person, and the man sexually assaulted her, according to a lawsuit she and her mother filed against MySpace Inc. and its partner News Corporation. The charges were negligence, gross negligence, fraud and negligent misrepresentation for failing to protect underage users from sexual predators. The court ruled that MySpace was not responsible for the content on its site and dismissed the charges against the social networking service.

The case is the first to address whether that portion of the Communications Decency Act that protects Internet providers from liability for information posted by a third party can be applied to a social networking site. It probably won't be the last. Several other lawsuits for libel, pornography and other issues have been filed against MySpace, one of the most popular networking sites.

If you use social networking sites, you should comply with copyright laws and be aware of your liability for libelous content. And if you use information from online sites for writing academic papers, blogs or any other purpose, here are a few tips on how you can prevent online legal problems:

- Don't copy material from the Internet (including images) or use it in your blog, your Facebook site or other social networking sites without permission. Many images are offered free for personal use, but check the site notices to be sure.

- Don't write any defamatory messages to an online blog or other site.

- Avoid writing defamatory or derogatory comments in personal e-mail messages. E-mail is often passed to other users without the permission or knowledge of the source.

- Consider the accuracy of material you find on the Internet. Check the site owner and organization to make sure that you are using a responsible site. You should also verify the accuracy of any information from the Internet.

- Check the posting dates of online material to determine whether the information is still accurate. Much online information may be outdated.

Copyright

If you take pictures or documents from the Internet without permission, are you violating copyright laws? Absolutely. U.S. copyright laws passed in 1976 protect everything that you or others write the minute the information is offered in "a fixed form," which includes online or print information.

Although many unresolved issues remain about intellectual property rights for online materials, additional laws to protect software and online materials were enacted in the late 1990s.

- The No Electronic Theft Act, signed into law in 1997, provides penalties of up to five years in jail and fines of up to $250,000 for individuals and up to $500,000 for organizations for copying software or online materials even if you don't make a profit.

- The Digital Millennium Copyright Act of 1998 provides further penalties of up to $1 million for copying online materials for profit. More cases continue to come before the courts regarding peer-to-peer file sharing of music, such as the controversy involving Napster, which has since transformed itself into a fee-based site for downloading files. Rulings are pending on other cases involving companies that furnish the software for file sharing, and these issues are likely to continue.

However, copyright laws allow you to copy portions of materials under a doctrine known as "fair use." The law favors academic use or use of portions of works if the copied material does not deprive the creator of profits.

Whether it is material for a blog, a profile in a social networking site or other online matter, most sites that host such content specify terms about posting pornography, defamatory messages or other unacceptable material that could be libelous. The nature of communication is changing rapidly, and so are the legal decisions, but the concepts of accuracy and fairness are timeless.

What Do You Think [?]

Do you think it is a good idea to show your story to a source before you broadcast or pubish it?

- ☐ Yes
- ☐ No
- ☐ Maybe

Exercises

1 **Actual malice:** Write a paragraph explaining "actual malice" and "reckless disregard for the truth" as defined by the U.S. Supreme Court in *Times v. Sullivan*.

2 **Libel potential scenario:** You are the editor of your local newspaper. A U.S. senator has decided to seek re-election. Five women who worked for him several years ago say he sexually harassed and abused them while they were in his office. The women refuse to be named. Their allegations range from stories that he plied them with drugs and alcohol and then sexually abused them to accusations of rape. All the women are reputable, including a political lobbyist and a former secretary to the senator, but none has gone to the police. As a result, you have no record of formal complaints about their allegations. However, three years ago a formal complaint by a former employee charged him with sexual molestation, but the charges were dropped. Will you print these women's allegations and use his name? If you do, will the senator have grounds for a libel lawsuit?

3 Privacy issue 1: A candidate for city council in your community had a nervous breakdown 10 years ago. The candidate's opponent has slipped you a hospital document confirming this fact. Should you print the story? Why or why not? If you do, does the candidate have any grounds to sue you for invasion of privacy?

4 Privacy issue 2: You are a photographer who went on assignment to the county fair. You snapped a picture of a woman whose skirt blew up to her shoulders, exposing her underwear, as she emerged from the fun house. Your editor decided that this picture captured the fun mood of the fair and used it. The woman is now furious and is suing the paper for invasion of privacy—disclosure of a private fact. Discuss whether she has grounds for a lawsuit and whether you think you should have taken the picture.

☞ **Featured Online Activity** Log on to the book Web site for Chapter 15 and take the interactive quiz to test your knowledge of media law at

academic.cengage.com/masscomm/rich/ writingandreportingnews6e

Coaching Tips

Examine all your alternatives.

Consider all the parties who will be affected. Do you need other points of view?

Weigh the benefits and harms of your decision.

Justify why you are making this decision.

If someone is going to be hurt by what gets printed or broadcast about them, then journalists need to provide a reason—a good reason—for going with it. "That's my job," doesn't cut it. Nor do appeals to First Amendment freedoms.

Deni Elliott, Poynter–Jamison Chair in Media Ethics and Press Policy, University of South Florida

16 Media Ethics

Imagine that you are a reporter for your local newspaper. A drunken driver almost kills a young girl in an accident in your town. You call the hospital for information about her condition, but officials will not release it except to family members. So you ask a fellow reporter to call the hospital and identify himself as the girl's uncle. He gets the information.

Would you do that? Is it ethical?

This was one of 30 cases presented to 819 journalists in a survey conducted by Louisiana State University journalism professor Ralph S. Izard for the Society of Professional Journalists several years ago. Eighty-two percent of the journalists who responded said they would not ask their colleague to lie to gain information. Do you think their responses would be the same today? Journalism codes of ethics say deception should be a last resort, but undercover journalism and deceptive practices still abound.

Ethical dilemmas, with guidelines from various codes of ethics, have been included in chapters throughout the book. In this chapter we'll examine some major cases, causes of ethical problems and some approaches that can be used to make ethical decisions.

Deception

A case of deception that generated considerable media discussion in the 1990s was the Food Lion/ABC-TV case. ABC television network reporters lied on job applications to get hired by the Food Lion supermarket chain and used cameras hidden in their hair. The reporters for "Primetime Live" then produced a story accusing Food Lion of selling rotten meat, fish and cheese. Food Lion didn't challenge the facts but instead sued for trespass and won a $5 million judgment. But the trial judge said that was too much and cut the award to $315,000. ABC appealed, and a federal court reduced the award to just $2—a dollar for trespassing and another dollar for breaching employees' legal duty of loyalty to an employer.

Could the reporters have gained the story any other way? ABC doesn't think so, but many other journalists have questioned the use of deception in this and other situations.

A classic case of deception occurred in 1978, when investigative reporters at the *Chicago Sun Times* set up a bar called The Mirage and posed as bartenders and waiters. With hidden cameras and tape recorders, they provided evidence that building inspectors, police officers and other city officials were soliciting bribes to allow them to operate the bar. Although the series won several awards, the Pulitzer-Prize board ruled that the reporting methods were unethical and rejected it for the media's highest award. The case renewed debate about deception, and today this type of reporting is considered a last resort by many editors.

Although print and broadcast media have used hidden cameras for many years, they proliferated in television news magazine shows during the 1990s. One reason was the improved technology of cameras, which could be small enough to be hidden in tie clips. But media critics charged that a more common reason for using hidden cameras was sensationalism.

More recently an NBC-TV Dateline show, "To Catch a Predator," has garnered media criticism for its deceptive tactics in conducting a sting operation to lure alleged pedophiles to homes outfitted with hidden cameras for the show. The station hired a civilian watchdog group, Perverted Justice, whose members posed as underage boys and girls in online chat rooms to converse with adults seeking sex with minors. These decoys would then lure their chat-room acquaintances to the homes for a meeting, supposedly to have sex.

When the potential pedophiles entered the home and began conversing with the Perverted Justice decoys, Dateline's reporter Chris Hansen emerged and confronted them with their chat-room conversations and questions about their intentions. Police waited outside the homes to arrest them.

Over the course of three years, more than 200 potential predators were caught by the show. In one case a Texas assistant district attorney pursued by Dateline as a pedophile suspect committed suicide when police entered his home to arrest him. The TV station has been criticized not only for its use of hidden cameras but also for paying Perverted Justice volunteers and for its cooperation with police. Hansen defends the show by saying that it has alerted parents to the dangers of online chat rooms and it has resulted in convictions of many sexual predators featured in the series.

But deception remains controversial in ethical terms. Before using any form of deception, ask yourself if there is any other way to get the story. Louis Hodges, professor emeritus of ethics at Washington and Lee University, suggests that you apply three tests: importance, accuracy and safety. Ask yourself these questions:

- Is the information of such overriding public importance that it can help people avoid harm?
- Is there any way you could obtain the information through conventional reporting methods, such as standard interviews or public records?
- Are you placing innocent people at risk? For example, you should not pose as a nurse, law enforcement officer or employee in a job for which you might not be trained.

Deceptive reporting techniques are fraught with risks, such as lawsuits for invasion of privacy. On the other hand, deception may be the only way to reveal matters of great public concern. Even with such reasoning, using deception may still be unethical.

Plagiarism

The subjects of plagiarism and fabrication have been discussed in several other chapters in this book. Why so much attention to something you surely wouldn't do? Even though technology has made it easier to plagiarize because accessibility to thousands of news sources is so easy, stealing words from someone else without attribution is not a new phenomenon. Nor is fabrication, which is making up quotes, adding false description and basically passing fictional material off as news.

Despite considerable publicity about Jayson Blair, a *New York Times* reporter who plagiarized and fabricated stories he wrote for the newspaper, journalism students and veteran journalists are apparently not getting the message that plagiarism and fabrication are serious infractions that can lead to firing and ruined careers. Since the Jayson Blair affair in 2003, which led to his dismissal and the resignation of two top editors at the *Times,* numerous cases of plagiarism have occurred.

Size doesn't seem to matter when it comes to plagiarism. From college newspapers and small newspapers to large newspapers, journalists have been fired for plagiarism. Here are just a few examples of such ethical infractions that occurred in the last few years:

- *The University Daily Kansan* at the University of Kansas suspended a reporter who was copying material for its "Weekly Choice" calendar items from the local newspaper's Web site, *www.lawrence.com.*

- *The Cavalier Daily* at the University of Virginia fired two student reporters after discovering they had written movie and music reviews lifted from other publications.

- An entertainment editor for the *Macon* (Ga.) *Telegraph* resigned after editors discovered that he had copied material about a Ringling Bros. and Barnum and Bailey circus from the Ringling Bros. Web site. A few months earlier, another *Telegraph* reporter had been fired for plagiarizing material in several stories from other stories in newspapers or on Web sites.

- A sports editor for the *Bozeman* (Mont.) *Chronicle* was suspended without pay for plagiarizing a column taken from another columnist in North Dakota.

- A reporter from the *Sedalia* (Mo.) *Democrat* was fired after a reader called to complain about similarities between the reporter's movie review and one by syndicated movie reviewer Roger Ebert.

- *USA Today* veteran reporter Jack Kelley, a foreign correspondent who was nominated for a Pulitzer Prize, resigned after being told he would be fired for fabrication in numerous stories over a 10-year-period, and three top editors at the paper subsequently resigned for failure to catch the problems. *USA Today* hired an independent panel to research stories Kelley had written. The panel concluded that "Jack Kelley's dishonest reporting dates back at least as far as 1991. . . . Policies, rules and guidelines in place at the newspaper, and beyond that, routine editing procedures, should have raised dark shadows of doubt about Kelley's work, had his editors been vigilant and diligent. They were not."

Despite a *USA Today* policy prohibiting use of anonymous sources, Kelly routinely used them, according to the report. In one highly publicized story he used a snapshot of a Cuban hotel worker to illustrate a story he wrote about a woman who died while fleeing from Cuba in a boat. The hotel worker was alive and had never attempted to leave Cuba. "In Kelley's case, he acted duplicitously for years in the way he handled unnamed sources—and his editors let him get away with it," the panel concluded.

The list of cases involving fabrication and plagiarism could go on—at least 13 newspapers have reported incidents in which they fired or suspended reporters for these problems in the few years following the Jayson Blair case. Prior to this case (between 1991 and 2001), at least 20 reporters were fired for plagiarism or fabrication. Why is this happening at such alarming rates?

Lori Robertson, author of the article "Ethically Challenged," in *American Journalism Review,* concluded from a dozen interviews that the Internet was the main culprit. "It used to be to plagiarize from another publication, you'd have to type the information letter by letter, staring at your source," she wrote. "It took a little more effort than what you can do now: cut and paste."

Using someone else's idea for a story is usually not considered plagiarism. U.S. copyright laws don't protect ideas. In the news business, it's considered good practice to localize a national story idea or use an idea from another newspaper and do original reporting. The key is "original reporting." If you use all the same sources and the same anecdotes from another publication or broadcast, it may not constitute plagiarism, but it raises ethical questions.

Privacy Issues

Some of the most wrenching ethical dilemmas the media face involve people's privacy. You may have the legal right to publish certain information, but do you have the ethical right?

To understand the ethical concerns, it may help to define "ethics." Ethics is the study of choices about what we should or should not do, whereas morality is concerned with behavior. So ethics can be considered the process of making decisions about the way a person behaves. Some of the thorniest ethical dilemmas facing journalists concern public officials, celebrities, rape accusers and photo subjects.

Public Officials

Would you print information about the sex life of a politician? When is the private life of a public figure relevant? When does it serve the public interest to publish such details?

In the summer of 1987, reporters and editors at *The Miami Herald* decided that the private life of a politician was relevant. Former Sen. Gary Hart was seeking the Democratic nomination for the presidency. Rumors of Hart's infidelity to his wife had circulated for months, and during the campaign the rumors called into question his character and credibility. When asked about the rumors, Hart challenged reporters to "follow me around. . . . They'd be very bored." Acting on a tip that Hart had a relationship with a Florida model, *Herald* reporters staked out his townhouse. They revealed that Hart spent the night with the woman, Donna Rice. Hart never admitted that the relationship with Rice was sexual. Nevertheless, he withdrew his candidacy the day before *The Washington Post* was set to reveal evidence about his involvement in another affair.

At the time of this incident, although previous presidents and presidential candidates had engaged in extramarital affairs, their private lives had not been dissected in public. The sexual affairs of President Kennedy were not revealed until long after his assassination. But the Gary Hart case changed the nature of political reporting.

The nature of sexual revelations in political reporting changed even further during Bill Clinton's second term as president when former White House intern Monica Lewinsky testified to a grand jury that she had engaged in a sexual relationship with the president during her internship. Clinton denied the allegations when he testified in a court case brought against him by an Arkansas woman, Paula Jones, who claimed sexual harassment against Clinton when he was Arkansas governor. Then the day after his testimony, in a dramatic reversal of his previous denials, he admitted on national television that he had engaged in an "inappropriate relationship" with Monica Lewinsky.

The media followed Lewinsky day and night. Competition for any tidbit of information was keen. The media published unsubstantiated rumors, including sexual details, and relied heavily on anonymous sources and other media for news.

Thus far, media references to sex were tame compared to what was about to happen. Kenneth Starr, a special prosecutor investigating Clinton for obstruction of justice and perjury, released a grand jury report that contained graphic sexual details of the Clinton-Lewinsky relationship. The majority of newspapers in the United States either printed the entire report in a special section or posted it on their Web sites. Many newspapers offered a disclaimer that the content might be considered offensive. This report laid the groundwork for impeachment hearings on the charges that the president had committed perjury under oath when he originally denied having an affair with Lewinsky.

In November 1998, almost four years after the case began, Clinton agreed to pay Jones $850,000 to drop the case. But it didn't prevent him from being impeached.

Despite the serious turn the case took, media critics and the public still questioned whether the media had acted responsibly in relying heavily on anonymous sources and publishing rumors in the early stages of the saga. And the debate raged about whether a politician's private life should be dissected in public. The ethical dilemmas these stories posed will continue to be debated for years.

Reporters also face other ethical dilemmas about privacy when covering politicians. For example, is it in the public interest to reveal the criminal background of a candidate if he withdraws from the race before you can print the story?

Editors at the campus newspaper of the University of Kansas faced this dilemma after they found out that a candidate for student government had been convicted of indecent solicitation of a child six years earlier. When the candidate learned that the newspaper was planning to print the information, he held a press conference to resign his candidacy. He claimed it was because he had just learned he was HIV-positive. At the same time, he resigned as director of the

Brian Vandervliet

University of Kansas students dumping the campus newspaper to protest a story

organization representing gays and lesbians on campus. He never referred to his criminal record, nor would he answer reporters' questions.

Was his criminal record relevant to the public now that he was no longer a candidate for office or leader of the gay rights group? What harm would the publication of his record cause him? The student's friends pressured the editor not to run the story, saying it would cause their friend immense personal suffering when he was already suffering from the HIV-positive news. In addition, they said, he had already paid his debt to society by serving time in prison.

Stephen Martino, editor of *The University Daily Kansan* at the time, said the decision was the most difficult one he ever had to make as an editor. He said he decided to run the information because it was relevant; it was why the candidate resigned. Martino said the candidate had learned about his HIV-positive status three weeks earlier and had made no attempt to resign then. "To my way of thinking, omitting the truth is the same thing as lying. Had the *Kansan* not reported the full story as it knew it, it would have been accused of a cover-up, and its credibility would have been destroyed," Martino wrote in an editorial page column the day the story ran on the front page.

Angry students protested the next day by dumping copies of the *Kansan* on the lawn in front of the newspaper offices in the journalism school.

Naming Suspects

Consider another case that has given the media an ethical black eye. A pipe bomb had exploded in a park on the site of the Olympic games in Atlanta on July 27, 1996. One person was killed, and 111 others were injured. Initially, a security guard at the site, Richard Jewell, was declared a hero for alerting police to the bombing. Three days later, Jewell became a suspect when law enforcement officials leaked his name to the press.

Most newspapers withhold the name of a suspect until formal charges are filed. But this was a case of great national interest. Would you have published his name? The *Atlanta Journal-Constitution* did, stating that Jewell was a "target" of the investigation. That was just the beginning.

For the next 88 days, Jewell was profiled and followed by the media, and his past, present and future were the subject of news stories. Only one factor was missing: He was never charged in the crime. On Oct. 26, 1996, the FBI apologized and publicly admitted that Jewell was no longer a suspect. Eric Rudolph, accused of this bombing and several others at women's clinics where abortions were performed, was subsequently convicted charged with the crime and sentenced to life in prison.

But Jewell claimed that his life had been ruined. In an emotional press conference after he was vindicated, he said: "For 88 days, I lived a nightmare. . . . Now I must face the other part of my nightmare," he said. "While the government can tell you that I am an innocent man, the government's letter cannot give me back my good name or my reputation."

Jewell died in 2007, but news stories and obituaries still bore headlines identifying him as the Olympic Park bombing figure or suspect. The case has become a classic example in media ethics literature as a warning about the harm the media can cause in naming or pursuing suspects before they are formally charged with a crime.

Rape Cases

Whether to name rape accusers is another continuing ethical debate in the media. Because of the stigma associated with rape, most news organizations withhold the names of people who claim they have been raped. The accuser cannot legitimately be called a "victim" until the case is decided.

That issue became apparent in a scandal involving three Duke University lacrosse players accused of rape. The case involved all the elements of a TV drama—racial conflict (a poor, black single mother with a troubled background who was earning money as a stripper vs. three white students from wealthy families), a prosecutor who refused to release evidence that would have cleared the suspects, a prestigious university protecting its reputation, and a community torn by racial tension surrounding the case.

The case began when one of two strippers hired to dance at a party for the lacrosse team accused three of the players of raping her. The three players she identified were charged with rape, kidnapping and sexual offense. But DNA tests of the three players and all the other lacrosse team members did not match the rape-kit swabs taken from the woman at the hospital where she was examined after the party.

However, Durham County District Attorney Michael B. Nifong withheld this DNA evidence from the players' defense attorney and issued statements to the press calling the athletes "hooligans." Although the accuser changed her version of the story several times, the prosecutor persisted in trying the case. After a year-long investigation, the players were exonerated and the district attorney was disbarred for unethical behavior.

"This woman has destroyed everything I worked for in my life," one of the players said on CBS's "60 Minutes" after the players were exonerated. "She's destroyed two other families and she's brought shame on a great university. And worst of all, she's split apart a community and a nation on facts that just didn't happen and a lie that should have never been told."

The accused players were named in the press while the accuser was not named until the case was resolved. One of the players said after all charges were dropped that he would probably always be known as that Duke lacrosse player in the rape case. For that reason, the players' names will not be used in this textbook.

The case was reminiscent of the media treatment of Richard Jewell. Although the players were charged and Jewell was not, the intense media scrutiny of the players raises the question: Did the media act properly in the publicity it gave to this case?

Not according to Rachel Smolkin, author of "Justice Delayed," an article in *American Journalism Review*. "Unquestionably, the media too readily ran with a simplistic storyline, sacrificing a search for truth. Not only were the accused innocent of rape, the allegations of racial taunts that received so much media attention appear to have been exaggerated," she wrote.

"The lessons of the media's rush to judgment and their affair with a sensational, simplistic storyline rank among journalism's most basic tenets: Be fair, stick to the facts, question authorities; don't assume; pay attention to alternative explanations," Smolkin wrote.

The Duke case raises these other ethical issues:

- Will the case set back progress made in getting women to file charges in rape cases? Only time will determine the answer to that.
- Should accused and accusers be named before the outcome of a rape case?

The majority of news organizations still protect the accuser and name the suspects in rape cases, and the Duke case is unlikely to change those policies.

Geneva Overholser, former editor of *The Des Moines* (Iowa) *Register*, is a staunch advocate for naming both the accuser and the accused. Years ago she wrote a column saying the stigma of rape would be reduced if it were treated like any other crime and the names of rape victims were used. As a result, Nancy Ziegenmeyer agreed to let the newspaper use her name in a story relating her ordeal as a rape victim. Reporter Jane Schorer, who won a Pulitzer Prize for the story, said she received scores of calls from rape victims who expressed gratitude that the story had been told.

Overholser, who now teaches at the University of Missouri School of Journalism, still feels strongly that failing to name both parties in a rape case only prolongs the stigma of the crime for women. In a column for the Poynter Institute, she wrote: "The responsible course for responsible media today is this: Treat the woman who charges rape as we would any other adult victim of crime. Name her, and deal with her respectfully. And leave the trial to the courtroom."

Photo Subjects

Many privacy issues involve photographs. Should a photographer take a picture of a grieving mother whose son has drowned even if she doesn't want the picture taken? At what point is a photograph an invasion of privacy?

Another concern for photo editors is taste: what the reader needs to see versus what the reader wants to see. For example, should newspapers print pictures that depict gore and tragedy even if they would upset readers?

In 1987, Pennsylvania state treasurer R. Bud Dwyer convened a press conference the day before he was scheduled to be sentenced for conviction of mail fraud, perjury and racketeering. At the end of the conference, he took a gun from his briefcase, put the barrel in his mouth and pulled the trigger, killing himself instantly. Stunned photographers for television stations and newspapers shot vivid pictures of the event.

Many television stations did not air the footage of him with blood gushing from his head, and several newspapers did not publish that picture. But other newspapers published three photos, including a gory one of his head as the bullet pierced it. Readers in several locations protested loudly.

More recently, the media faced ethical decisions about publishing graphic video and photographs of Iraqi prisoners who were abused by U.S. soldiers at the Abu Ghraib prison outside Baghdad during the war in Iraq. The story, initially aired by CBS on "60 Minutes," and subsequently detailed in a *New Yorker* magazine article by Seymour M. Hersh, revealed torture inflicted on the prisoners by U.S. soldiers. Although *The New Yorker* did not print the photos, CBS showed some video, and *The Washington Post* published some photos in the newspaper and more photos and video on the *Post*'s Web site. The photos, released to newspapers around the world, showed naked prisoners being taunted and humiliated by soldiers. One of the most dramatic photos shows two U.S. soldiers smiling in front of a human pyramid of naked prisoners. Another shows a soldier holding a leash around a naked man's neck.

The *Post* posted this note on its Web site with the photos: "Some of these photos may be disturbing because of their graphic or violent nature." The *Post* and other news organizations cropped or blurred photos that showed the prisoners' genitals. Both *The New York Times* and *The New York Daily News* ran a front-page photo of a naked prisoner being menaced by dogs used by the soldiers. Television news anchors also gave a warning to viewers about the graphic nature of the images they were about to see.

The public was incensed, and editors throughout the country wrestled with what they should print or air. In many cases, news organizations offered more photos on their Web pages but limited images in print. In a *New York Times* article, writer David Carr wrote that "the news media are wrestling with how many and how much of the graphic photographs they should show." Some critics accused the media of promoting an anti-war agenda. But Leonard Downie, editor of *The Washington Post,* echoed the sentiments of many other news editors when he was quoted in the article as saying "We decided that the importance of the news was the most important consideration."

The prison photographs constituted one of many ethical dilemmas that editors faced about graphic images during the war in Iraq. When Americans civilians were burned, dismembered and hanged from a bridge by Iraqis in Fallujah, editors again agonized over printing or airing photos of their charred bodies, but many newspapers printed a photo in some form on their front pages. *The Philadelphia Inquirer* received 185 complaints about showing the charred bodies. In an article for The Poynter Institute, Anne Gordon, then managing editor of the *Inquirer*, said she told the paper's staff in an e-mail: "We do our job when we give readers all the news—no matter how painful or ugly. My heart bleeds for the families of these men. But personal feelings cannot dissuade us from our mission to provide the facts upon which an informed citizenry can make decisions."

Such ethical dilemmas arise daily at newspapers and television stations, although rarely involving photos as graphically disturbing as these. But how do editors make those decisions, and how can you decide what is ethical?

Convergence Coach

Print and broadcast journalists and public relations practitioners have codes of ethics that govern their media. Although codes don't resolve ethical dilemmas, they can serve as guides. But who tells bloggers and citizen journalists what ethical principles to follow? The blogosphere is like an unruly Wild West with no sheriffs to enforce law and order.

With the proliferation of blogs and social networking sites, journalists have raised concerns about the lack of any ethical codes to address these forms of media. But several news and blog organizations have proposed codes of ethics and some require bloggers to adhere to ethical principles stated on their sites.

The Media Bloggers Association (*www.mediabloggers.org*) encourages its members to follow these standards:

- Honesty, fairness and accuracy. Use links to supporting documents whenever possible.
- Transparency. Clearly disclose conflicts of interest.
- Accountability and trust. Use your own name and offer a means for readers to communicate with you.

OhmyNews International, the South Korean site that has one of the largest numbers of citizen journalists, requires its contributors to adhere to an agreement and a reporter's code of ethics. In addition to requirements to be accurate, some of other principles in that code are:

- The citizen reporter does not spread false information.
- The citizen reporter does not use abusive, vulgar or offensive language.
- The citizen reporter uses legitimate methods to gather information.
- The citizen reporter does not damage the reputation of others by composing articles that infringe on personal privacy.

In the United States, Jonathan Dube, creator of Cyberjournalist.net, has proposed a code of ethics for bloggers based on the code from the Society of Professional Journalists (*www.spj.org/ethicscode.asp*). His model includes these main points:

- Be honest and fair. Never plagiarize; identify and link to sources when feasible.
- Minimize harm.
- Be accountable. Admit mistakes and correct them promptly.
- Disclose conflicts of interest.

With the exception of OhmyNews, which requires adherence to its agreement, the other groups only propose these ethical guidelines. But even in journalism organizations, ethical codes can only serve as guides.

Whether it is a photo or a story, ethicist Louis Hodges suggests this guideline for privacy issues: Publish private information about public officials or public figures if it affects their public duties. But for victims of crime, publish private information only if they give their permission because these are people with special needs and vulnerability.

Ethical Reasoning

Journalists use several methods to justify their decisions. In most ethical dilemmas, editors and reporters discuss the issue and the consequences of publication before making the decision. They consider how newsworthy the story is and whether the public really needs this information. The process of ethical reasoning generally involves these three steps:

1   Define the dilemma. Consider all the problems the story or photograph will pose.
2   Examine all your alternatives. You can publish, not publish, wait for a while until you get more information before publishing, display the story or photo prominently or in a lesser position, or choose other options.
3   Justify your decision. Weigh the harms and the benefits of publication, or weigh such factors as relevance and importance of the story to the public.

The Poynter Institute Model

Robert M. Steele, The Poynter Institute's expert in ethical issues, suggests that journalists ask these questions before making decisions in ethical dilemmas:

■ Why am I concerned about this story, photo or graphic?
■ What is the news? What good would publication do?
■ Is the information complete and accurate, to the best of my knowledge?

ETHICS

The case: Your campus newspaper has received an advertisement that promotes the revisionist point of view that the Nazi Holocaust of World War II never occurred. The ad, accompanied by a $125 check, was sent by the Committee for Open Debate on the Holocaust, an organization run by Bradley R. Smith from his home in Visalia, Calif. He sent the advertisement to colleges all over the United States.

In a cover letter he urges campus editors to run the ad to promote dialogue and to support the First Amendment.

You are aware that when the University of Miami campus newspaper, *The Miami Hurricane,* ran the ad, nearly 400 students demonstrated outside the newspaper. A wealthy alumnus threatened to withdraw a $2 million gift but later recanted when the school promised to offer courses on the Holocaust. Other school newspapers have refused to print the ad. You know that this ad will offend many people on your campus and in your community, but you want to uphold the First Amendment. Will you run this ad or reject it and return the check? Justify your decision.

- Am I missing an important point of view?
- What does my reader need to know?
- How would I feel if the story or photo were about me or a member of my family?
- What are the likely consequences of publication? What good or harm could result?
- What are my alternatives?
- Will I be able to clearly and honestly explain my decision to anyone who challenges it?

Codes of Ethics

In addition to making decisions about what to report and write and how to present stories, journalists must consider whether their behavior is ethical as they perform their professional duties.

Many newspapers have devised codes of ethics that govern the behavior of employees. These include policies about accepting gifts or freelance assignments, as well as guidelines about conflicts of interest.

Staff members who violate these policies at newspapers can be fired, and many have been. In some cases, reporters have been fired for entering into business relationships with a source or for using for personal gain information they get from sources. Journalism societies, such as the Radio-Television News Directors Association and the Public Relations Society of America, also have basic codes of ethics to guide members.

Principles common to all the codes include adhering to accuracy, telling the truth, minimizing harm and avoiding conflicts of interest.

For links to codes of ethics, check the Web site for this chapter: *academic.cengage.com/masscomm/rich/writingandreportingnews6e*

What Do You Think

Do you think news organizations should require bloggers to their sites to abide by a code of ethics?

- Yes
- No
- Not sure

Exercises

1 Apply ethical reasoning, using the Poynter Institute guidelines, to the following cases (or to other cases described in this chapter):

a An anonymous source tells you that a U.S. senator for your state has voted against many gay rights issues even though he is gay. You have heard other rumors that the senator is homosexual, but the senator has denied that the rumors are true. What will you do about this story?

b You have heard rumors that your local nursing home is abusing its clients. However, no complaints have been filed with state regulatory agencies or with the police. You have contacted some of the clients' family members, who say they are concerned but have no proof. Will you go undercover as a volunteer aide at the nursing home (no special training required) to investigate?

2 Discuss the ethical dilemma, described in this chapter under "Public Officials," about revealing the criminal record of the student government candidate who resigned before the story could be published. What would you do if you were the editor of your campus publication or broadcast station? Do you agree or disagree with the decision made by the editor of *The University Daily Kansan?*

3 You are writing a story about problems of online pornography and the groups that oppose it. The story will be published on your campus Web site. Will you link to the pornography sites that the groups find objectionable?

☞ **Featured Online Activity** Log on to the book Web site for this chapter and take the interactive ethical dilemma quiz and discuss the other ethical cases at

academic.cengage.com/masscomm/rich/ writingandreportingnews6e

Coaching Tips

Seek sources from different racial and ethnic backgrounds for all kinds of stories, not just stories about minorities.

Ask your sources how they prefer to be addressed.

Ask yourself if you would write the same type of description for a man as for a woman, for a white source as for a person of color, for a disabled person or member of any other ethnic or special group.

We need to be aware of how we communicate—of our built-in biases. Language is not a neutral thing.

Tim Gallimore, consultant

17

Multicultural Sensitivity

W hat do you think of when you hear the word "alien"? Does it conjure up an image of a creature from outer space? Now add the word "illegal," and you get a term that the National Association of Hispanic Journalists (NAHJ) considers derogatory.

"The association has always denounced the use of the degrading terms 'alien' and 'illegal alien' to describe undocumented immigrants because it casts them as adverse, strange beings, inhuman outsiders who come to the U.S. with questionable motivations," according to the NAHJ in a news release. Even more objectionable to the association are headlines using the word "illegals" as a noun. Instead of terms such as "illegal aliens" or "illegal immigrants" used by many news media, the NAHJ prefers the terms "undocumented worker," or "undocumented immigrant."

As the population of the U.S. continues to change, journalists and public relations practitioners will need to exercise sensitivity about multicultural issues.

In 2005, one in every three U.S. residents was part of a nonwhite group. But by 2050 nearly half the population in the country will be a mixture of Hispanics, Asians and blacks, with Hispanics making up nearly 25 percent of the residents, according to the U.S. Census Bureau. And the term "minority" has already changed. One out of every 10 counties in the county is considered a "majority-minority" county, meaning the population of nonwhites is in the majority.

Tim Gallimore

Tim Gallimore, consultant

The Language of Multiculturalism

Even if you choose your words carefully, you can't be sure how they will be interpreted. Gender, race, and geographical and ethnic background influence interpretation, says Tim Gallimore, a former journalism professor who conducted a study about the interpretation of mass media messages. In his study, Gallimore asked students to define a number of words, including *majority, ghetto* and *inner city.* He concluded that it is hard, if not impossible, to get people to agree on one meaning for a word.

Consider, for example, the word *majority.* "It is remarkable that women view themselves as minorities although they are a majority of the population in every society," he says. "This can be explained only through the connotation of majority as possession of power—the white male-dominated majority."

Other loaded terms are *ghetto* and *inner city,* which Gallimore's students at the University of Missouri tended to define as an area with drugs, poverty, crime and gangs rather than as an urban geographical location. On television, when a news anchor says "inner-city youth," the phrase is almost always followed by descriptions and visuals of young blacks killing one another for crack or high-priced athletic shoes, Gallimore says. "Language is not a neutral thing."

Language changes, too. *African-American* is the term preferred by many blacks, but it is not accepted at all newspapers and television news organizations. *Chicano* is preferred by Mexican-Americans in some parts of the country, yet it is offensive to many older members of the group. *People of color* is a term preferred by many organizations with a majority of nonwhite members.

How can a journalist know the proper term to use? Any terms that might be acceptable today could be out of vogue tomorrow. In fact, the whole concept of political correctness has become unpopular. But sensitivity to other people—regardless of gender, race or ethnic background—will always be an important tenet of journalism.

Instead of memorizing the popular term of the day, Gallimore suggests that reporters ask people of different ethnic or special interest groups how they prefer to be addressed. "The newspaper can demonstrate sensitivity with the words the person uses to define himself or herself," he says. "That gets the newspaper off the hook. If someone objects, you could say that is the person's term."

Jose D. McMurray, former executive director of the National Association of Hispanic Journalists, also stresses dealing with people as individuals, especially before using labels. "*Hispanic* is a generic term created in Washington so bureaucrats can conglomerate an ethnic group," he says. "In California, second and third generation Hispanics prefer to be called *Latinos;* some second and third generation Mexican-Americans prefer *Chicano.* It is very much an individual decision. I'm Irish Basque. I prefer to be called Latino. But I'd rather be called Jose."

McMurray says it is also a misnomer to refer to Latinos as a minority in some areas of the country. "We are not a minority in El Paso, San Antonio or Los Angeles. *Ethnic* is a better term."

Minorities in the News

Gallimore recommends gathering a list of advocacy sources for different groups: by race, age, disability, gender and so on. If you choose a person from a group to check things out that might be insensitive or controversial, you have a better chance of being sensitive, he says. "We make most of our mistakes in the information gathering," Gallimore says. "No amount of expert wordsmanship can overcome faulty materials. Go to a variety of sources. Be more aware of different points of view. If the story involves some statement about a group, go to members of that group."

Mervin Aubespin, former president of the National Association of Black Journalists, says one way the media can become more sensitive to the needs of minorities is to hire more minorities. As the U.S. population becomes more diverse, the need for minority representation in the media workforce and in media coverage is only going to increase. But newspapers and broadcast media do not reflect the nation's diversity. Here are some figures of minority representation in newsrooms, based on surveys reported in 2006 and 2007:

- Minorities make up 13.87 percent of the 54,809 full-time journalists at newspapers, much less than the 33 percent of minorities in the U.S. population. However, 377 newspapers have no minorities on staff, according to surveys by the American Society of Newspaper Editors.

- Minorities make up 21.5 percent of the workforce in television and radio, a slight decrease from the previous year, according to a 2007 survey by Hofstra University professor Bob Papper, who conducted the survey in conjunction with the Radio/Television News Directors Association (RTNDA). In local television, minorities represent 21.5 percent of the workforce, a slight decrease, but minorities in radio news slid to the lowest point in the past 13 years: 6.2 percent. The number of African-Americans rose in broadcast media while all other minority groups decreased. "The bigger picture remains unchanged. In the last 17 years, the minority population in the U.S. has risen 8.6 percent; the minority workforce in TV news is up less than 4 percent, and the minority workforce in radio is down more than 4 percent," Papper wrote.

- The percentage of women in TV news remained steady at 40 percent at network affiliates, with 26 percent of them as news directors.

Because the Hispanic population is increasing so rapidly, newspaper companies have launched several publications written in Spanish for that market. The *Dallas Morning News* created *Al Día*, which appears six days a week. In Long Island, N.Y., where the Hispanic population is increasing, *Newsday* launched a daily newspaper in Spanish called *Hoy*. The major newspaper companies now publish 46 Hispanic publications, most of them weeklies. But these publications don't resolve the problems that still exist in the mainstream media.

Aubespin says hiring minorities is only the first step; editors have to encourage minority reporters to express their diversity. One of the problems is that white editors "really want black faces that write like whites," he says. "There is no formula, no one way to write about a minority group. The best guideline is to treat each person as an individual. We are as different as you are."

Jose McMurray is also concerned about stereotypes in coverage of Latinos. "I would like to say there is a stereotype of Latinos as hard working, family oriented, loyal people but I seldom see that," McMurray says. "Instead I get the sense there is this group of people—Lord knows where they come from—that are not trustworthy, that point guns."

Representatives of Asian groups say they are also victims of stereotypes, such as claims that Asian students are either mathematical geniuses or gang members.

Multicultural sensitivity involves not only the sources you use but also the kinds of stories you choose. Innumerable studies have been conducted to show how women and minorities are portrayed in biased or stereotypical fashion. Minorities are often featured in stories about crime but excluded as sources in general stories about lifestyles, the economy and other stories where experts are cited. Conversely, women and minorities are often portrayed as unusual if they have operated a successful business or accomplished some of the same newsworthy feats as white males.

Keith Woods, a faculty member at The Poynter Institute, says news organizations need to make different editorial decisions to overcome a history of poor and injurious coverage of minorities. "Coverage of ethnic and racial minorities still reflects too many festivals and football games and not enough family issues or finance," Woods wrote in an article for *Presstime,* a publication of the Newspaper Association of America.

The Asian American Journalists Association (AAJA) goes a step further in its "Media Watch" group; it writes letters to editors or publishers when it finds stereotypical or offensive portrayal of Asian-Americans, such as this note to *The Wall Street Journal* in reference to an article entitled "Furniture—Coping with the Asian Invasion."

> "Asian invasion" implies something ominous and dangerous; it also reinforces the bigoted belief—it continues to fester in some quarters of our society—that people of Asian descent are foreigners who are to be kept out at all cost.

The newspaper editor responded, saying no bigotry was intended but also thanking the association for calling the item to his attention.

In another letter to an editor at KTNV-TV in Las Vegas, Nev., the president of AAJA applauded the station for including people of color in its newscast about a memorial to the late President Reagan but complained about a phrase:

> We want to caution you on the use of the phrase, "yellow faces," in describing Asian Americans. It is a misnomer and an outdated one at that. Asian Americans are not yellow-skinned, after all.

Even when media organizations try to include diversity, reporters tend to go to the same sources for each minority group in the community. One source does not represent the points of view of all the members of that group, so you should try to develop many minority sources in your community.

ETHICS

Ethical dilemma: A Danish newspaper publishes some cartoons showing the prophet Muhammad in an unflattering light, including one showing a Muslim wearing a turban with a bomb. The Islamic culture forbids depiction of the prophet. The newspaper editor said he was publishing the cartoons to incite debate about censorship by Muslims. Danish Muslim organizations conducted protests, which escalated as the cartoons were published in other newspapers. Some of the protests became violent and more than 100 people were killed. The issue became a world-wide controversy, especially after the violence erupted.

If you were publishing a news story about the violent protests to the cartoons, would you publish any of the cartoons along with a news story? Why or why not? How would you explain your decision to Muslims in your community?

Gender Differences

Although inclusion of women on news pages and in TV broadcasts has improved, some stereotypes remain. The old stereotypes of the apron-clad housewife have given way to new ones of Superwoman moms.

"News media have long been fond of features that focus on the difficulties working mothers face when they try to 'have it all,'" writes Jennifer L. Pozner in an article on the Web site for Fairness and Accuracy in the Media. "Tales of strained Superwomen can serve to reinforce the underlying notion that unlike fatherhood, motherhood and work outside the home are naturally in conflict. . . . Media never question why fathers want careers, and rarely if ever imply that their presence in the workplace is bad for their children."

Just as women are victims of stereotypes, so are men. Women are supposed to be emotional; men are supposed to be strong. More often, the men featured in the news have no feelings at all. Women have an agenda of child support and social issues; men want to read about sports.

Nonsense, says Jack Kammer, a freelance writer about gender issues. In an article in *Editor & Publisher,* he says it is a mistake to conclude that women have no interest in sports or business sections and that men have no interest in lifestyle sections. In fact, he says, one study showed that 84 percent of the men surveyed said family mattered most to them. Men also want a say about child care, sexual harassment and social issues.

Shifts in treatment of women and men are apparent in advertising as well. To reach the huge female buying market, advertisers have overcompensated, particularly in several television ads, by portraying men as stupid or incompetent. The use of women as sex symbols in many beer and automobile ads had declined for a while, but it appears to be returning, especially in automobile ads.

The principles for coverage of gender are the same as they are for coverage of ethnic minorities. Make an effort to include female sources as experts in general stories, not just stories geared to women. Seek diversity of opinion, but write about people as being all equal. When you write about a woman, don't include descriptive details about her appearance unless you would also include descriptive details about a man's appearance.

For example, consider the following story about Dolly Parton. The writer acknowledged that Parton (the writer didn't call her anything but Dolly) has achieved great success—a $100 million fortune—from records, movies, TV shows and her Dollywood amusement park in Tennessee. But read the selection and decide for yourself if the story, despite its tongue-in-cheek tone, is offensive:

NEW YORK—No way they're real, not *that* big.

Women would kill to have them. Men would kill to somehow get them off Dolly Parton and onto their wives. They are just so . . . so . . . what, titanic?

Ooooo, the way they sit right *up there,* so prominently, so, so, so openly.

And up close, they look different from each other. The one on the left is almost square. The other's got a kind of pear shape to it. No wonder two security guards, with guns and walkie-talkies, are right outside the fancy hotel room.

But it just seems far too crass to mention them, to come right out and ask: "Dolly, are those *real* diamond rings?"

And so you don't.

Instead, you just sit there and stare at this tiny little woman, talking and giggling, giggling and talking. . . .

You've got to hand it to her—she's no different right there on the couch than she is on the teevee, just as bubbly, just as self-deprecating. And talk about *looks.*

No lie. She is sitting there in these spike-heeled, knee-high black leather boots, jeans that must've pinched her when she was 12. And for a top, she's got on some kind of black frilly, lacy thing. Whew. It's all topped off by a silver-gray leather jacket that's got Lawrence Taylor shoulder pads and surely cost about what Lee Iacocca has made in all his years with Chrysler.

Lord have mercy, why doesn't this woman just spontaneously combust?

Of course, it's a look that Dolly Parton has cultivated for years.

"I *l-o-v-e* all this gaud," she squeals. "It's like a kid with paints and crayons. I think it has to do with me growing up poor and wanting more. I lived in fairy tales with stories about kings and queens with their robes and diamonds. And that's what I always wanted to be."

Dolly giggles.

"I patterned myself after the trash in my home town. There was this woman, I swear." She giggles again, and leans in a bit to share a story.

"You know how every small town has a trollop or a tramp or a slut or whatever. Well, there was this woman when I was growing up. Every Saturday she'd walk the streets until somebody would pick her up. Men would be driving around, tooting the horn. She had long, blond hair that was peroxided. She wore bright red lipstick. She had long, bright-red fingernails, and tight skirts in these bright colors, and high heels.

"I thought, THAT IS HOW I WANT TO LOOK WHEN I GROW UP. I didn't know she was the town tramp. I didn't even know what that meant. So, sure enough, when I grew up, I looked like trash. But I don't feel like trash."

The giggle.

Oh, this woman is fun. Of course, she's not here just to explain her lifetime fashion philosophy. She is here because she's got a new movie out: "Straight Talk," which opened Friday.

In "ST," Dolly—sorry, but it just doesn't feel right calling her Parton—plays Shirlee Kenyon, a small-town Arkansas dance instructor, thrice divorced and stuck in a nowhere relationship.

—The Philadelphia Inquirer

Most sexism is not so blatant. But the writer of the article said he had excellent rapport with Parton and she was not offended by the article. Parton does enjoy discussing her figure and her style, and she refers to herself in terms that might well be considered sexist by the politically correct.

How can you avoid sexism and gender stereotypes? Here are some tips published in *The Gannetteer,* a magazine for employees of Gannett newspapers:

- When referring to any given person, avoid using masculine pronouns such as *he* or *his.* Instead of "Everyone should eat his own biscuit," say "Everyone should eat a biscuit." (*However, AP style says use the male pronoun "his" when it is not clear whether the antecedent is male or female.*)
- Avoid words that, by definition, refer to one sex or the other but not both. Instead of *governess,* use *tutor.*
- Avoid words starting or ending with *man.* Instead of *mailman,* use *mail carrier.* Instead of *fireman,* use *firefighter;* use *police officer* in place of *policeman.*
- Avoid stereotypes in illustrations and graphics. Not all quarterbacks are white. Not all basketball players are black. Not all single parents are women. Not all newspaper editors are men. Not all pro golfers are men.

- Avoid calling groups of people men, unless they are all male. A congressional group should be called lawmakers or members of Congress, not Congressmen.

- Avoid the stereotype of a mother. Don't say "chicken soup like your mother used to make." Maybe Father made the soup once in a while. Avoid such phrases as "old wives' tale," "tied to her apron strings" or "Dutch uncle."

- Avoid referring to women by their first names in stories. This is almost always patronizing, and not usually done to men.

- Avoid describing women with adjectives that dwell on sexual attributes. Ask yourself whether you would describe the walk of an IBM executive as "suggestive" if you were profiling a man, or would the walk just seem "confident"? Ditto for "feisty." When is the last time you saw a man described as "feisty"?

- Be careful with "first" stories: the first woman to pick up the garbage for a living, fly into space or run for the school board. *(However, if it is a first, it may be worth mentioning, but it does not have to be the focus of the story.)*

- Avoid phrases that carry an element of surprise such as "smart and dedicated woman." Is it unusual that someone who is smart and dedicated is a woman, too?

- Beware of approaching any story with the subconscious idea that it is more of a man's story or a woman's. Almost always we quote women in stories about child care. Why not men? A lack of child care is just as big a problem to them— or should be.

Guidelines for Writing About Special Groups

Every group has some special needs and concerns about language. A man who uses a wheelchair probably doesn't consider himself handicapped (a derogatory term). However, he may have a disability that requires him to use a wheelchair. A person who has AIDS is not a victim but rather an AIDS patient or a person living with AIDS. And not all people over age 65 are ready for the stereotypical rocking chair.

You cannot be expected to memorize dictionaries for each special interest group. However, if your beat is a specialty that frequently deals with aging, disabled people, AIDS or some other minority interest, you could call an umbrella organization and ask for guidelines. Most organizations have these printed.

However, your first source should be the people you interview. Ask them how they prefer to be addressed. Next, consult *The Associated Press Stylebook,* which includes guidelines under such listings as *handicapped* and *AIDS.* You'll minimize trouble by avoiding the use of adjectives to describe people.

People with Disabilities

Do not characterize someone as disabled unless that condition is crucial to the story. Avoid the word *handicapped,* unless the person uses it to describe himself. If the disability is a factor, don't say "disabled people." Instead, use "people with disabilities." Avoid such terms as *crippled* and *deformed.*

Many euphemisms—such as *physically challenged, partially sighted* and *physically inconvenienced*—have come into vogue. However, disability groups object to such euphemisms because they are considered condescending. The AP Stylebook also says to avoid euphemisms such as *mentally challenged* and descriptions that connote pity, such as *afflicted with* or *suffers from* a particular disease. Just say the person has multiple sclerosis or other applicable disease.

Heather Kirkwood, a former journalism student at the University of Kansas, is legally blind but can see with the use of various aids. She doesn't like being called *visually challenged* or *partially sighted*. She prefers the term *blind*. But she says organizations representing blind people disagree with her and insist that the distinction between partially and fully blind should be made.

"As far as political correctness, my own feelings are that it isn't the word, it is what the word means," Kirkwood says. "Saying 'visually impaired' instead of 'blind' doesn't really change the way the blind are viewed in society. What matters is what comes to mind when you say the word 'blind.' Progress is changing what it means to be blind, not changing the word for it."

Kirkwood acknowledges that many stories about people with disabilities have that same "gee whiz" factor as stories about successful women.

"As far as the 'amazing factor,' that must really confuse people," she says. "Many blind people truly believe they are amazing. That is because we are taught to think that from a very early age.

"While we can expect journalists to try to understand all of this, we know the general public probably won't," Kirkwood says. "We also expect journalists to understand that we are not all representative of an entire group of people, yet we know the general public won't be as fair.

"The biggest problem we face is not blindness, but rather the public's perception of blindness."

Convergence Coach

The Internet is a multicultural mecca for sources. More than a dozen journalism organizations devoted to racial and ethnic groups offer Web sites with sources and research. Here are some ways you can use the Web to improve your coverage of diversity:

■ Subscribe to blogs and social networking sites about diversity.

■ Do a search for blogs about diversity and racial issues. For example, check out the "Race Matters" blog at the Albany *Times Union.*

■ Read ethnic newspapers online, such as *The Amsterdam News* at *www.amsterdamnews.org* and

The Philadelphia Tribune at *www.philatribune.com* for story ideas and sources.

■ Check minority journalism organizations such as *www.nabj.org* for sources.

■ Check online diversity organizations for internships, job opportunities, scholarships and guidelines to help journalists become sensitive to diversity.

■ Check network and cable news stations, and analyze the coverage of people of color as well as the reporters and anchors.

■ Check the Web site for this chapter for direct links to many of the sources: *academic.cengage.com/ masscomm/rich/writingandreportingnews6e.*

The Research and Training Center for Independent Living at the University of Kansas, which offers guidelines for writing about people with disabilities, says euphemisms "reinforce the idea that disabilities cannot be dealt with up front." When in doubt, ask your sources how they prefer to be addressed. Here are some more tips:

- When interviewing people with disabilities, do not speak louder unless the person has a hearing impairment. A common complaint of people who have disabilities unrelated to their hearing is that everyone treats them as though they were hearing impaired. Treat people with disabilities exactly as you would any other source.

- Avoid overcompensating by writing about people with disabilities as though they were superhuman. The hidden implication is that all people with disabilities are without talent and that your source is unusual. The same principle says to avoid calling an African-American articulate or qualified, implying that other African-Americans are not.

- Avoid writing about people with disabilities as though they don't have any faults.

- Avoid using adjectives as nouns to describe a group of people with disabilities, such as *the deaf* or *the retarded*. Say "people who are deaf " or "people with mental retardation." For people who are blind, *visually impaired* is a preferred term.

- For mental illness, avoid such terms as *crazy* and *demented*. *Psychotic* and *schizophrenic* should be used in context—and only if they are the proper medical terms. Preferred terms are *people with emotional disorders* or people with psychiatric illness, mental problems or mental disabilities.

- Avoid "gee whiz" stories that stress how amazing it is that this person could accomplish anything special, given his disability.

Stories About Aging

If there were ever a group especially prone to "gee whiz" stories, it would have to be people over age 65. Most newspaper feature stories treat people in this age group as absolutely amazing just because they walk, run, dance or accomplish anything. People over 65 are usually described as spry, sometimes feisty, but always remarkable.

The population in the U.S. is aging and people over age 65 are among the fastest-growing group in the country, according to the U.S. Census. But for many years the journalists who write about them have been considerably younger, and much of the coverage reveals a lack of understanding and sensitivity even though the intent may have been well-meaning.

Consider this feature:

This place hops.

The food's tame, the dance steps slower than they used to be, the stiffest drink comes from the water fountain.

Still the Gray Crowd jams the Armory Park Senior Citizens Center.

Typically, 1,200 men and women gather daily for gossip, games, and yes— even to cast some plain old-fashioned goo-goo eyes.

—*The* (Tucson) *Arizona Daily Star*

Or the story will feature a twist—surprise, surprise, they're old!

> The teams, each with two rows of par-
> ticipants, face one another. As the blue
> balloon floats through the air, the two
> seemingly docile teams transform into
> aggressive competitors.
>   You'd think they were teenagers. They
> were . . . perhaps 50 or more years ago.
>
> —*Tulsa* (Okla.) *World*

Make age a factor, not the focus of a person's accomplishments. Readers can decide for themselves if the person's accomplishments are surprising because of the person's age. Especially avoid the astonishment factor: Isn't it amazing this person can accomplish such and such at this age?

Here are some general guidelines for dealing with people of this age:

- When writing about people over age 65, avoid such adjectives as *gray-haired* or other terms unless you would use the same type of description if the story were about a younger person with blond or brown hair.

- Avoid stereotypes. Don't introduce rocking chairs or similar stereotypical images if the people in the story aren't using them.

- Avoid *the graying population, senior citizens* and other group designations unless you are writing a trend story. And then use such a term only if it is relevant, necessary and appropriate—for example, if a group uses the term in its own name, as in Gray Power.

- Avoid saying such things as "She doesn't consider herself old," unless she says it. Even though you are meaning to extend a compliment, by writing such denials you are introducing a stereotype.

AIDS Stories

In the last 20 years, medical developments have improved the life span of people living with AIDS, but the disease still carries a stigma. It is a subject that still requires the reporter to use great sensitivity.

Jacqui Banaszynski, a distinguished professor at the University of Missouri School of Journalism, says one of the reasons AIDS stories differ from other stories is the social stigma. "The disease is one story, the social context of the disease becomes another story. If you ignore the opportunity to deal with the societal revulsion, you miss the whole crux."

Banaszynski knows first-hand how difficult it can be to interview people with AIDS. She did it long before the disease was understood and before medicines existed to prolong the life of patients with AIDS. Death was the only certainty when she wrote a series that won the 1988 Pulitzer Prize for feature writing.

The rules change for this kind of story, Banaszynski says. "You have to be empathetic. On the other hand, you have to be honest and true to the reader who may be hostile to the subject. You walk a fine line between not blaming and not whitewashing."

Banaszynski, then a reporter for the *St. Paul* (Minn.) *Pioneer Press*, spent 15 months reporting how a Minnesota farmer, Dick Hanson, and his partner Bert Henningson lived and died with AIDS. She became as close to them as a family member—actually, closer than some of their family members. When Henningson was dying, his family even asked her to help decide whether they should pull the plug (she refused).

Readers don't want to read about AIDS or deal with it, she says. So she decided that the best approach was to portray these two men as two ordinary Minnesotans who had a commonality with readers. "If Joe and Suzy Reader could not relate to two gay pig farmers, they could relate to two men who plant impatiens, feed kittens and tend a vegetable garden, because that's what all Minnesotans do." In her introduction, she stresses that this is a story about people living—as well as dying—with AIDS:

Death is no stranger to the heartland. It is as natural as the seasons, as inevitable as farm machinery breaking down and farmers' bodies giving out after too many years of too much work.

But when death comes in the guise of AIDS, it is a disturbingly unfamiliar visitor, one better known in the gay districts and drug houses of the big cities, one that shows no respect for the usual order of life in the country.

The visitor has come to rural Glenwood, Minn.

Dick Hanson, a well-known liberal political activist who homesteads his family's century-old farm south of Glenwood, was diagnosed last summer with acquired immune deficiency syndrome. His partner of five years, Bert Henningson, carries the AIDS virus.

In the year that Hanson has been living—and dying—with AIDS, he has hosted some cruel companions: blinding headaches and failing vision, relentless nausea and deep fatigue, falling blood counts and worrisome coughs and sleepless, sweat-soaked nights.

He has watched as his strong body, toughened by 37 years on the farm, shrinks and stoops like that of an old man. He has weathered the family shame and community fear, the prejudice and whispered condemnations. He has read the reality in his partner's eyes, heard the death sentence from doctors and seen the hopelessness confirmed by the statistics.

But the statistics tell only half the story—the half about dying.

Statistics fail to tell much about the people they represent. About the people like Hanson—a farmer who has nourished life in the fields, a peace activist who has marched for a safer planet, an idealist and a gay activist who has campaigned for social justice, and now an AIDS patient who refuses to abandon his own future, however long it lasts.

The statistics say nothing of the joys of a carefully tended vegetable garden and new kittens under the shed, of tender teasing and magic hugs. Of flowers that bloom brighter and birds that sing sweeter and simple pleasures grown profound against the backdrop of a terminal illness. Of the powerful bond between two people who pledged for better or worse and meant it.

"Who is to judge the value of life, whether it's one day or one week or one year," Hanson said. "I find the quality of life more important than the length of life."

Much has been written about the death that comes from AIDS, but little has been said about the living. Hanson and Henningson want to change that. They have opened their homes and their hearts to tell the whole story—beginning to end.

—Jacqui Banaszynski,
St. Paul (Minn.) *Pioneer Press*

Ground Rules for Sensitive Questions

When you write about AIDS, you have to ask about dying and you have to ask about sex. How do you approach either of these sensitive questions?

"The only thing to do is to set it in context," Banaszynski says. "When I get to it, I ask as directly as I can: How many men did you sleep with? I don't warn them that this is a hard question. I set that up in the ground rules. I say, 'We're going to talk about a lot of personal things, and a lot may be embarrassing. You don't have to answer, but I'll try to get you to answer.' If you ask honestly and directly with no judgment in your voice so there is no shame involved, they will answer. If you are embarrassed, they will pick it up. I ask the question as matter-of-factly as I would about the weather."

Banaszynski says people are really very eager to tell their stories. "I think you can ask anybody any question if you are nonjudgmental and a good listener. Nobody listens anymore."

She also used another interviewing technique in her many visits with Hanson and Henningson. "I did something I don't normally do," she says. "I reminded them of my mission. They got to like me so much. My job was to be responsible and remind them that I was there as a reporter. I broke rules and invented new ones. I said when the notebook was down they could talk freely. Nothing was fair game until the notebook was out. And then I would remind them again that it was now on the record."

When she wrote the stories, she also did something that is not general practice in journalism. "I called each person involved in the story and read them their quotes, and I told them the context. For example, in one case I said, 'I set you in the context of a fight with your family.' Then I told them, if you can convince me that I have erred or been insensitive, I'll consider changing it." Only one person complained. She didn't take out any of his comments, but she added a sentence that appeased him.

She also took the newspaper to Hanson and Henningson the night before it hit the morning newspaper stands so they could see it first. "They couldn't change anything, but that's just courtesy. If they allow me to invade their privacy, I owe them that courtesy."

Banaszynski says the ground rules are different when you are writing about people who are not accustomed to dealing with the media. "These people don't know the rules. I have more responsibility to tell them what I'm going to be writing, the general thrust, and what I'm trying to do."

Banaszynski predicts that it will get increasingly difficult to interest the public in AIDS stories. "The one thing you always have to remember about AIDS is that it has an overlay of homosexuality," she says. "It is a stigmatized disease that the public doesn't want to read about. You have to get past a big barrier of rejection.

"You have to focus on the common denominator. This could be your brother or neighbor or your doctor. AIDS serves as an extreme example of all the challenges in reporting more than other stories. You have got to find ways to have it connect to everyone's life."

Exercises

1 **Multicultural story ideas:** Interview members of various ethnic and racial groups in your community or on your campus about their concerns and the kinds of stories they think newspapers are not writing about them. Devise 10 story ideas based on your interviews.

2 **Sexism, ageism and racism:** Develop your own media watch group or be a member of one. Look for examples of language, description or other elements of stories that you think are sexist, racist or ageist.

3 **Gender coverage:** Using highlighters of two different colors, read the news sections of your newspaper for a few days. Use one color to mark the female sources quoted and the other color for the male sources. Analyze the types of stories that feature women more than men, and vice versa. Also try to determine if multicultural sources are used in the news stories.

4 **Multicultural profile:** Interview a person on campus who is a member of a minority group—whether because of the person's race, ethnic background or sexual orientation. The focus should be this person's feelings about how the media treat members of his or her minority. Get some background about the person. Then ask questions related to the focus. Some questions to include might be these:

■ How do you prefer to be addressed? How do you think the media portray people in your minority group? Are the portrayals positive or negative? (Ask for specific examples.) Have you ever experienced insensitivity or prejudice because of your race, ethnic background, disability or special interests? (Please specify.)

■ Have you ever been interviewed by the media? Was your experience good or bad? (Please specify.) What advice would you give to reporters about coverage of minorities such as yourself? (Again, ask for specifics.) Write your findings in the form of a mini-profile.

5 **Perceptions of language:** As you read the following terms, write the first descriptive words that come to your mind; then discuss whether your perceptions are stereotypes:

Texas	African-American	lesbian
ghetto	gay	truck driver
Hispanic	Asians	firefighter
Jewish	Native Americans	basketball player
Irish	Catholics	inner city
alien	immigrant	minority

6 **Television shows:** Discuss some of your favorite television shows. Are the characters white, African-American, Asian-American or Hispanic? What races are underrepresented in television entertainment?

7 **Advertising:** Watch advertisements on television for one or two days, and analyze whether they are more inclusive of racial groups than other media. Discuss which racial groups are most represented in television advertisements. Compare those ads with print ads in your newspaper or in magazines you read. Are the ads in one medium more racially diverse than in another? Discuss how men and women are portrayed in ads, especially on television. Do the ads reflect or promote stereotypes?

☞ **Featured Online Activity** Log on to the book Web site for this chapter and link to The Poynter Institute bias survey at

academic.cengage.com/masscomm/rich/ writingandreportingnews6e

Coaching Tips

For profiles:

Observe descriptive details about the person, and show the source in action.

Do background research to find unusual questions the subject will enjoy discussing.

Find a unifying theme that you can weave through your story.

Write an order for your story; think about organizing it by topics or time frames (present, past, back to present and future).

For obituaries:

Ask yourself what made this person memorable?

Check the accuracy of spellings and information in profiles and obituaries.

Everybody's got one good story to tell. If you talk to them long enough, you'll find it. Nobody has lived a totally uneventful life.

Alan Richman, writer, *GQ* (*Gentlemen's Quarterly*)

18 Profiles and Obituaries

Alan Richman enters the dark Manhattan hotel bar to await the arrival of Robert De Niro. The famous actor has agreed to meet with Richman for 15 minutes to decide whether he will grant the writer an interview for *GQ* (*Gentlemen's Quarterly*) magazine.

Richman is accustomed to writing celebrity profiles, but this time he is nervous. De Niro hates to be interviewed.

It's 6:45 p.m. The meeting is set for 7 p.m. Richman paces in the lobby. At 7:17 p.m. De Niro arrives. He startles Richman by asking him what his first five questions would be.

Richman is trying to come up with five questions the actor will like. He isn't prepared. The words don't come.

The actor says two questions will do.

Richman asks an obvious question: Why has De Niro agreed to consider an interview if he hates them so much?

De Niro says in jest that he's agreed because of the clothes he'll get by being photographed for *GQ*. Richman doesn't tell him he won't get to keep the clothes. The writer is ready to pose his second question.

He never gets the chance. De Niro says he has to go, and he leaves without agreeing to the interview.

Richman is stuck. He still has to write the profile for *GQ*. So he calls De Niro's friends and associates.

"After the interview failed, I went back and called all those people to figure how to make the story work," Richman says. "I asked them, what question could you ask that he (De Niro) would answer. Everybody told me something about De Niro you couldn't ask."

One actor who worked with De Niro said, "I don't think I'd ask him about his family or his love life. He's pretty private."

Another friend warned Richman not to talk about world politics, sports, fine wines or clothing because "he doesn't know a lot about those things."

Those and other comments about De Niro were probably more insightful than the actor would have been about himself. And that was the theme of the profile: how to interview a celebrity who doesn't like to be interviewed.

Richman had broken one of his major rules for conducting celebrity profiles. "You've got to nail them with a question they like," Richman says. "They are so bored.

Alan Richman, magazine writer

335

I always ask myself, 'What question can I ask this guy that he'll enjoy answering.' It takes thinking."

He didn't do enough thinking before he met De Niro to set up the interview. But he's had better luck with other celebrities and athletes in the 30 years that he has been a sportswriter in Philadelphia, a columnist and writing coach for *The Boston Globe,* a reporter for *The New York Times,* and a profile writer for *People* magazine.

These days, Richman has become a celebrity in his own right as the food and wine critic for *GQ,* contributing writer for several magazines, and dean of a program in food journalism at the French Culinary Institute in New York. He has been interviewed many times and has appeared on television shows. But he has also written several celebrity profiles for magazines.

Celebrities are considered worthy of profiles because they have accomplished something more special than the average citizen. However, many profiles focus on people in the community who have done something noteworthy but do not have celebrity status.

"Everybody's got one good story to tell," Richman says. "If you talk to them long enough, you'll find it. Nobody has lived a totally uneventful life."

To find that story, Richman uses what he calls the "Columbo school of interviewing," named after the deceptively naïve TV detective. "I sort of hang around looking harmless. I try to be an unthreatening as possible. Then I use a weave-and-jab style of questioning. You can't be afraid to be a little bit rude," he says. "If the point of the interview is that they were a bigamist, I'll say: 'We all want to have two wives; tell me how you got away with it.' If it's a profile of a man growing award-winning roses, I'll say: 'I can't believe someone would spend 15 years to grow a decent rose.'"

You may have a different interviewing style, but before you even get to the interviewing stage, you should research your subject's background. If possible, try to get a résumé or an academic vita if you are interviewing a professor. Check online as well. But don't rely on the information.

"I don't trust press releases or clips," Richman says. "I always ask the background stuff." Sometimes background questions can be boring. So Richman just puts his subjects on notice. He tells them: "'It's that time now; I've got to ask these questions.' Basically they think I have some secret that I'm going to ask them like 'Tell me about when you were 11 years old and you slept with a goat.' Then I tell them, 'I've got to go over your life.' They're relieved. I don't mess around and pretend it's going to be fun. It's more like, do me a favor. You never know what you are going to get."

Many reporters seek background from the profile subject's friends and family *before* they conduct the main interview. In De Niro's case, Richman had no choice. He had to contact the actor's friends *after* the interview failed, but he prefers that method anyway—with this caveat:

"One of my rules is never call up friends or acquaintances of stars and ask what they think of the person, because they will always lie," Richman says. "If you were doing a profile of Hitler, most journalists would call Goebbels and Himmler and they would say, 'What a guy!' Instead, ask them for facts or anecdotes."

Terry Gross has also interviewed scores of celebrities, politicians and other people for her National Public Radio show, "Fresh Air." She is renowned for her interviewing skill. In an article for the *American Journalism Review,* Thomas Kunkel wrote: "Gross's conversational interviews are marked by intelligence, preparation and a diplomatic but firm probing of what makes people tick." She told him, "My theory of interviewing is that whatever you have, use it. If you are confused, use that. If you have raw curiosity, use that. If you have experience, use that. If you have a lot of research, use that. But figure out what it is you have and make it work for you."

After 25 years of interviewing people for her NPR show, Gross decided to write a book about the profiles she conducted. She explains her interviewing techniques in her introduction to the book, *All I Did Was Ask: Conversations With Writers, Actors, Musicians and Artists.*

"I often ask my guests about what they consider to be their invisible weaknesses and shortcomings," she writes. "I do this because these are the characteristics that define us no less than our strengths. What we feel sets us apart from other people is often the thing that shapes us as individuals. . . . I also violate decorum by asking questions of my guests that you usually don't ask someone you've just met, for fear of seeming rude or intrusive. Within minutes of saying hello to a guest, I might inquire about his religious beliefs or sexual fantasies—but only if it's relevant to the subject he's come on the show to discuss. Or at some point during the interview, I might ask a question about a physical flaw, the sort that we gallantly pretend not to notice in everyday life. When I do this, my purpose isn't to embarrass my guest or to make him self-conscious. I'm trying to encourage introspection, hoping for a reply that might lead to a revelation about my guest's life that might lead, in turn, to a revelation about his art. . . . I try in my interviews to find the connections between my guests' lives and their work (the reason we care about them in the first place)."

Despite the candor Gross seeks from her sources, she also says she respects her guests' privacy. "I would never pressure anyone to reveal those thoughts and experiences he desires to keep private," she writes. "That's why before beginning an interview, I tell the guest to let me know if I'm getting too personal, in which case we'll move on to something else."

Those are the kinds of questions and tips that work well in profile interviews. They are what another editor calls "turning points."

Turning Points

Walter Dawson, a former editor for *The Commercial Appeal* in Tennessee, says that regardless of the profile subject, "the heart and soul of a profile is making sure the reader understands the twists and turns and intricacies of human life." Dawson says writers should consider the following universal elements:

- **Patterns:** Some lives build to a climax, as for a law school student who becomes a judge.
- **Decisive moments or turning points:** Most lives take turns along the way. Take the law school student; perhaps she wanted to be a great defense lawyer but became a prosecutor instead. Or maybe your subject was an accountant who became head of a river-rafting company.

Profile Planning Tips

Choose your subject:

- Why is this person newsworthy?
- What will be your focus of the profile?
- What has this person done that would be of interest to readers of your college newspaper, Web site or local publication?
- Does this person contribute to your college or university behind the scenes—for example, is he head of maintenance?
- Has this person received an award, written a book, started a new course or program?
- Is this person new in the job?
- Is this person retiring after a long stay at your college or university?

- If a student, is the person head of an organization, an athlete, or has he achieved an unusual accomplishment?
- Have a backup plan for another interview subject in case your first choice cancels the interview.

Background research:

- Check the Internet.
- Ask for a résumé or vita.
- Get a photo.
- Ask co-workers, students or other people about the person (before the interview) to get tips on questions to ask. (You also could interview these people after the interview). Check everything you can about the person's background *before* the interview.

- **Future:** Every profile subject has a future, and you need to ask your subject what could lie ahead. Let the person speculate, especially about career goals. Ask the impertinent question: If this career doesn't work out, what could you do? The answers about the future could also provide an ending for the profile.

In addition to revealing the turning points, strengths and weaknesses of the source during the reporting process for your story, here are some points to consider when you write the profile.

Basic Elements of Profiles

Focus   What is the main idea of the profile? What makes this person newsworthy? Why are you writing about this person now? Those questions should be answered in the nut graph.

Theme   What is the difference between a nut graph and a theme? The nut graph is the reason for the story, but the theme is an angle or recurring idea that weaves throughout the story. Some general themes for profiles might be overcoming adversity; succeeding against odds; or coping with failure, illness or serious problems.

For example, this chapter features a profile of Jacklean Davis, considered the most successful homicide detective in New Orleans. That's the nut graph—why she is the subject of this profile. The theme threaded though the story is how she overcame adversity throughout her life and career.

Background Profiles should not be written in chronological order. The subject's background should be inserted where it fits best, often in the middle of the story. But in some cases, when the background is the most interesting or crucial element, it may be the lead or in the beginning of the story, as in this example about the New Orleans detective:

Background

NEW ORLEANS—The white frame house on Barrone Street is small and gated, just as it was when Jacklean Davis was a shy, serious-eyed little girl in a world of grown-up horrors.

Here, 12 blocks from the muddy brown Mississippi River, Davis was raised by a prostitute, raped by a sailor, sexually molested by an uncle and pregnant at age 16. By then, folks in the neighborhood were whispering that Davis was headed for the same hard life as the aunt who had reared her: selling herself to strangers. In a sense they were right—but in an entirely different way.

Now 34, Jackie Davis cruises the city in a police car—not just any cop but the most successful detective in New Orleans, this humid capital of good times and jazz that also happens to be one of the deadliest cities in the South, with 346 murders last year.

Nut graph

The GOAL Method

To discover those turning points and other qualities of your profile subject, consider using the GOAL method (goals, obstacles, achievements, logistics). Questions about obstacles the person faced can provide some of the most interesting parts of your profile. Don't stick to any order, but consider some of these questions as they arise naturally in the conversation:

- **Goals:** What were your original goals? What are your next goals?
- **Obstacles:** What obstacles did you face in accomplishing your goals, and what new problems loom?
- **Achievements:** What pleasure or problems have these achievements brought?
- **Logistics:** What background (logistics of who, what, when, where) led to your current situation?

Here are some other elements to include in profiles:

Age and Physical Description: Help the reader visualize your profile subject. But use description only when it is relevant to the topic you are discussing. Make the details work for you. In this example from a profile of Willie Darden, a convicted killer who was interviewed while he was awaiting execution in a Florida prison, the writer weaves in the age and physical description by relating them to the pressure of waiting for death:

Darden maintains a normalcy, a serenity that is surreal. His forehead is not cleaved by worry lines. His hair has not gone gray. He lifts his shackled hands and displays unbitten fingernails. "Calmness is a nice thing to have in times of stress," he says.

He gives his age as 62, but prison records say he is 52. He looks 42. It's as if the man has not only cheated the executioner, but time itself.

Or maybe time just stops when there is no future.

"Prison does tend to sustain one's youth," Darden says with an ironic grin. "You're not doing anything that you would normally do on the outside—such as working hard every day. You've got no family problems. The wear and tear, so to speak, is on the inside."

—Richard Leiby, *Sunshine* (Sunday magazine, *South Florida Sun-Sentinel*, Fort Lauderdale, Fla.)

Other Points of View: Seek anecdotes and comments from friends, family, colleagues and other people affected by the person at work, such as students for a profile about a professor or employees for a profile about a manager.

Visuals

Use graphics as a way to visualize your story in both the planning and writing stages. Outlining your profile by planning a facts (highlights) box can help you determine what topics to include in your story.

If the background is boring, break it out of your story. You can put key dates and such information as birthplace, education, career moves or similar items in a box. But if that information is an interesting and crucial part of your story, leave it in the body of the profile. You also can use a box to add information that doesn't fit well into your story but might be of interest, such as hobbies, favorite books, favorite saying, major goal. The major goal should also be mentioned in your story, but it works well in a facts box.

Several newspapers, magazines and Web sites use graphic devices to substitute for written profiles; others use highlights boxes to enhance profiles. For example, *The Kansas City* (Mo.) *Star* Sunday magazine profiles celebrities with blurbs following these headings:

- Vital statistics (occupation, birthday, birthplace, current home, marital status and so on)
- My fantasy is . . .
- If I could change one thing about myself, it would be . . .
- The best times of my life . . .
- Behind my back my friends say . . .
- These words best describe me . . .

Convergence Coach

Check the Internet for background on your profile subject, but don't rely on the information. Make sure that you check the accuracy of anything you find in your interview with the subject. The following tips apply to profiles for print, broadcast and the Web:

- Start with a simple search for the person's name in *www.google.com* or other search engine.

- Check out any articles or books written by or about the profile subject. If the person has written books, read one, or at least read summaries in *www. amazon.com.*

- Check for personal and academic Web sites and online résumés the person might have—especially if you are interviewing professors.

- Check athletic records in sports sites for profiles of athletes.

- Check fan sites for celebrities or athletes. These sites may contain links to articles or other information. Use them only as a guide; don't trust information from personal sites.

- For profiles about candidates, check voting records of incumbents and campaign contributions at sites such as *www.followthemoney.org* for candidates to state offices and the Federal Election Commission (*www.fec.gov*) or candidates to federal offices.

- Check social networking sites such as Facebook, MySpace or YouTube for personal pages about your subject.

Broadcast Profiles

- Think visually in the planning stage before you do the reporting. Background research is essential so you can ask interesting questions that will elicit good responses from your source.

- Show and tell. Write to the video, and show your subject in action.

- Read your script aloud.

- Don't introduce your sound bites by parroting what the source will say.

Web Profiles

- Plan audio, video and graphic elements that may accompany your profile.

- Consider breaking out facts or other highlights into boxes.

- Plan links that might provide background or other elements of the profile.

- Consider writing the profile in sections; offer readers the choice of reading the parts linked on separate Web pages or on one page.

- Consider a question/answer format that is easy to read on the Web.

Those are also good questions to ask for your profile even if you don't use the items in a visual tool. However, if you mention topics in a graphic, you don't have to repeat them in the story.

Organizing the Profile

There is no one way to organize a profile, other than having a lead, a body and an ending. Just make sure that you have a focus. Descriptive show-in-action leads, anecdotes, contrast leads and scene-setting leads work particularly well in profiles. As with any lead, make sure that you back up the lead with information that supports it later in the story.

The body of the story can be organized in many ways:

Supporting Themes: Block each concept, use all relevant material, and go on to the next concept.

Time Frames: Start with the present, go to the past, go back to the present, and end with the future. Or use some variation of the time frames, possibly starting with the past and then proceeding to the present.

Chronology: Look for a place in the story where chronological order might be useful, but don't write the entire profile in chronological order. A chronology might be helpful for the background. It might also work if you are writing the profile in narrative style. In some cases, however, the story might lend itself to chronological order if a situation unfolds in that sequence. Just make sure that your nut graph tells readers why you are writing about this person now.

Point/Counterpoint: If the subject lends itself to pro-and-con treatment, you might consider this method. It can be helpful in profiles of politicians. You can include reaction quotes from other people after each controversial point is made.

Sections: Splitting the story into separate parts may work if the profile is very complex. For example, if you are doing an in-depth profile of a politician or crime victim or crime suspect, you might organize it in sections, either by time frames of the person's life, issues or different points of view.

Q and A: The question/answer format is becoming popular as a format for profiles. It works well in print and on the Web.

Several types of endings work well with profiles. A quote kicker can be used to summarize a source's feelings about the subject or to summarize the subject's accomplishments. Or, with a circular ending, you can return to the lead for an idea and end on a similar note. An ending with a future theme tells what lies ahead for the person.

Putting It All Together

Here is the entire profile of the New Orleans detective. This profile demonstrates a variety of techniques suggested in this chapter. It has a clear focus, which is the one indispensable element of a compelling profile, and a recurring theme of overcoming adversity. It includes anecdotes, the subject's turning points and several comments from other sources. Notice that the three sections feature the present, past and future, although they are not so clearly delineated.

She is the finest of New Orleans' finest

From a gritty past to the city's best detective

By Matthew Purdy

The Philadelphia Inquirer

Descriptive lead to create contrasts with past and present

NEW ORLEANS—The white frame house on Barrone Street is small and gated, just as it was when Jacklean Davis was a shy, serious-eyed little girl in a world of grown-up horrors.

Here, 12 blocks from the muddy brown Mississippi River, Davis was raised by a prostitute, raped by a sailor, sexually molested by an uncle and pregnant at age 16.

By then, folks in the neighborhood were whispering that Davis was headed for the same hard life as the aunt who had reared her: selling herself to strangers. In a sense they were right—but in an entirely different way.

Nut graph

Now 34, Jackie Davis cruises the city in a police car—not just any cop but the most successful detective in New Orleans, this humid capital of good times and jazz that also happens to be one of the deadliest cities in the South, with 346 murders last year.

Backup for nut graph (comment from colleague)

"She was the best I ever saw at solving a murder case," said David Morales, her boss during her five-year stint in the homicide unit. "There was nobody close to her in the history of the homicide division."

More backup for nut graph

Davis solved 88 of her 90 murder cases—a record better than any other detective and all the more impressive for the first black woman to join an elite corps of mostly white men who prodded her to fail.

Specifics: anecdotes

They destroyed her case reports, told tipsters she didn't work there, placed feces in her desk drawer, posted her mistakes on the bulletin board, and decorated her mailbox with a cartoon of a mop and bucket titled "black power."

Davis reacted by putting in longer hours. In solitary moments, exhausted, she would bow her head and sob.

"Every case that I got, I was looked at under a microscope: 'Well, what is she going to do now?'" Davis recalls matter-of-factly. "My biggest accomplishment, I consider, is not cracking under the pressure."

More backup for the "so what" factor

At a time when politicians have taken to bashing the poor for dragging on society, Davis stands out as a stunning example of someone who has succeeded precisely because of her harsh past. She is now the city's most celebrated officer—and the subject of a screenplay that has caught the eye of Whoopi Goldberg. . . .

In a life full of ironies and incongruities, Davis posed as a hooker, arresting so many men in the raucous French Quarter that 20 backup officers were assigned to her and her partner. But Davis' arrest rate so riled those in the tourist trade that her superiors had her wired to prove she wasn't entrapping men. Even so, business interest prevailed, and Davis was yanked off the street.

But not before she had nailed 300 johns.

"Having lived with a prostitute all my life, there are certain things you do, certain things you say," says Davis, chuckling over her record.

▪ ▪ ▪

New section: arranged topically to reveal personal side of source

Christina Davis, 17, is a prep school senior with a B average who hopes to study engineering next year at Xavier University. It's Wednesday night in the blond-brick ranch home where she and her mother live with Gigi and Snoopy, their two dogs. Christina Davis is alone.

Her mother, like most officers in New Orleans, earns such a modest wage—$225 a week in take-home pay—that she has to work late-night security details for extra cash, stretching her workweek to 60 hours or more.

"I'm proud of her, but she had to sacrifice time with me and a lot of things we could have done together," Christina Davis says wistfully.

Losing days—and really, years—with her daughter is Jacklean Davis' greatest regret, she says one evening as she steers her unmarked Chevy through the bombed-out Desire housing project.

Her career started here 11 years ago, when she was the only woman street cop in the rough-and-ready urban squad, which worked the projects. . . .

A short woman with a stocky look about her, crimped hair combed into a tight ponytail, Davis always made it a point to later return to murder scenes in street clothes. It helped, she says, that she doesn't look like a cop: being a woman, looking young, using slang.

As she rolls through the broken streets, Davis says she worries about the good people in the projects who get ground down by the force of crime and neglect.

She could have been one of them.

Davis lost her father in a car accident when she was 3. Her bereaved mother squandered the insurance and had to give her children to an aunt.

As it turned out, Davis' grandaunt was a prostitute who bedded down with sailors. But she was a protective, strong-willed woman with a heart of gold, Davis said.

Davis' aunt was married to a merchant marine. When he was home, little Jacklean lived in stifled terror. He was sexually molesting her. Her aunt didn't know until Jacklean was 14 and her uncle was dying of cancer.

Trauma set in again when Davis was raped at 12 by a sailor who visited her aunt. By 16, she was pregnant and people in her working-class black neighborhood were whispering that she had picked up her aunt's habits.

Davis' aunt died when she was 17, about the time she was about to give birth to Christina. But she still managed to graduate from high school, faltering when it came to college. A better life seemed always out of reach, she thought as she worked clearing tables at ritzy restaurants and driving a bus.

It all hit bottom one winter when Davis found herself homeless for a two-week stretch, huddled in her parked car with Christina, danger lurking all around.

"I knew this was it," she says. "There was no one else. I was on my own."

■ ■ ■

The idea to become a cop came to Jacklean Davis when she dated a rookie in the department. Problem was, when she took the exam, she flunked it—again and again and again.

It took Davis five tries to pass the test—and two to overcome her fear of guns and make it through the police academy. It was 1981 before she got her first job at the urban squad. . . .

"She puts her heart into everything," said Wayne Farve, an old partner. "I've seen her at shootings where she'll kneel down in the blood right next to them and ask them who did it and where she can get more information."

Back in the old neighborhood, Davis got out of her car one night, in front of her home, eight blocks from where she grew up.

"Sssssss," a man hissed, pointing a gun.

Davis froze. Here she was, holding two bags of groceries, her own gun in her handbag, in the car. She screamed, slowly stepping away, as he closed in.

Unable to reach her gun, Davis screamed louder—and the man fled.

Davis dumped her groceries, grabbed her gun and opened fire as she chased him. Then suddenly, he turned and fired back, hitting her in the leg.

As she recovered in a hospital, she took heart. No longer a frightened child, Jacklean Davis had fought back this time and won. A few months later, police caught the man. He had raped 14 women. Davis testified against him, helping to lock him away in Louisiana's dreaded Angola prison.

Return to present

All told, it may be the stuff of movies, Davis concedes. An agent is negotiating for her, and the latest news is that Goldberg is reading the screenplay of her life.

"I don't even like to think about it," she says, admitting superstition. "I don't want to put a mojo on me."

Quote kicker on future note

ETHICS

Ethical dilemmas: How much should you reveal about a person in a profile, and what is your responsibility for the consequences? Do the circumstances differ if you are writing an obituary? What should you do if you find that the deceased person was on a sex offender registry or discover that the deceased had a criminal background? Should you include items in the obituary that the family would not want?

The case: A reporter for *The News & Observer* in Raleigh, N.C., profiled a Mexican who was an undocumented immigrant. Reporter Gigi Anders says she asked if he understood that his name and picture would be in the newspaper and if he understood the consequences, according to an article in *American Journalism Review*. She recalled that he said if he got deported, that was his "destiny." However, Julio Granados, the subject of the profile, said he gave permission to use his name but not his status, according to the article. After the story ran, immigration officials apprehended Granados and five other undocumented immigrants, who faced deportation hearings. The Hispanic community was incensed. The newspaper editor wrote a column defending the story but said the paper should have thought more about the impact.

What would you have done? Would you have used the man's name and identified his workplace? If you don't include both, would you mar the credibility of the story? How much responsibility do you have for the consequences of a profile if the source gives you information that could be damaging? Are the circumstances different in obituaries? Should you comply with the wishes of the family to eliminate negative material about the deceased?

Ethical guidelines: On the one hand, the Society of Professional Journalists Code of Ethics says, "Seek the truth and report it." On the other hand, the code says, "Minimize harm." Editors disagree on this subject, especially concerning obituaries. What would you do in these cases?

Writing Snapshot Profiles

Julie Sullivan doesn't waste words. She writes snapshot profiles that let the reader see, hear and care about the character—quickly. Her skill earned her the Best Newspaper Writing Award from the American Society of Newspaper Editors for short news writing. The award was based on profiles she wrote for *The* (Spokane, Wash.) *Spokesman-Review.* They average fewer than 400 words. But she reveals a lifetime in her profiles.

Her method: short sentences, few adjectives, few quotes, many details.

Now a Pulitzer-Prize winning reporter for *The Oregonian* in Portland, Ore., she began writing at a weekly newspaper in Alaska after she graduated from the University of Montana in 1985. "I started out leaning toward brevity," she said. "My first editor in Alaska would always tell me, every time you finish a story, go back over it. Figure out what words are extraneous. What can you leave out?"

Julie Sullivan, reporter

That's good advice for broadcast and Web writing as well.

Sullivan takes voluminous notes but discards about half of them. "I write everything down. I don't trust my memory," she says. That includes her observations. A cracked concrete step. An automobile battery under the sink. Cockroaches scurrying across the kitchen table. A toothless smile.

How does she know which details to include in her stories? "I write what I remember without looking at my notes. What details stand out? Like Joe Peak's teeth were so significant and personal. The contrast struck me. His place was so neat that I couldn't figure out how somebody who paid so much attention to his surroundings wouldn't take the same care personally. Then I found out how he lost his teeth."

She is equally selective about the limited quotes she includes. "I really think readers glaze over quotes," she says. "I do few quotes because I think most people are pretty plain-spoken and simple. You don't need to use it just because it's in quotes."

Her tips for writing briefly: "Trust your instincts about what is important, what struck you during the interview. The rest is chaff. I generally bounce my lead and the most important details off my co-workers, and I can gauge from their reactions if I'm on the right track." That's the basic tell-it-to-a-friend technique.

She also stresses observation. "Pay attention to details, from the right spelling of names to finding out the date of people's birthdays."

On leads and kickers: "I tend to think readers read the beginning and the end. Never discount the lead you were throwing out. It could be a great kicker."

On structure: "You try to make a point with every paragraph."

On brevity: "Short has its place, but it won't replace more in-depth pieces; that's what a newspaper does best. I hope to continue to do both."

The profile that follows was part of a series about the problems of low-income residents in a deteriorating Spokane apartment building, the Merlin. Notice the details, and notice the strong factual kickers. As you read this profile, consider what information came from observations and what came from questions. And then decide how you could say it all in as few words.

It took twice as many words to describe Sullivan's style as she used in these stories.

Donald 'Joe' Peak

Joe Peak's smile has no teeth.

His dentures were stolen at the Norman Hotel, the last place he lived in downtown Spokane before moving to the Merlin two years ago.

Gumming food and fighting diabetes have shrunk the 54-year-old man's frame by 80 pounds. He is thin and weak and his mouth is sore.

But that doesn't stop him from frying hamburgers and onions for a friend at midnight or keeping an extra bed made up permanently in his two-room place.

"I try to make a little nest here for myself," he says.

Chock-full of furniture and cups from the 32-ounce Cokes he relishes for 53 cents apiece, Peaks' second floor apartment is almost cozy.

A good rug covers holes in the kitchen floor, clean-looking blankets cover a clean-looking bed. Dishes are stacked neatly in the kitchen sink.

But cockroaches still scurry across his kitchen table.

"I live with them," he says with a shrug. "I can't afford the insecticides, pesticides, germicides. I don't have the money."

With a $500 per month welfare check and a $175 rent payment, Peak follows a proper diet when he can afford it. He shops at nearby convenience stores where he knows prices are higher but the distance is right. He has adapted to the noisy nightlife in the hallways and sleeps when he is too exhausted to hear it.

Part Seminole Indian, Chinese and black, the Florida native moved to Spokane 20 years ago to be near relatives in Olympia. He quit school at 13 to help earn the family income and worked a string of blue-collar jobs. Along the way, someone started calling him Joe.

His voice is lyrical, his vocabulary huge, but Peak's experience with whites is long and bitter.

When conditions at the Merlin began worsening three months ago, junkies and gray mice the size of baby rats moved in next door. He hated to see it, but he isn't worried about being homeless.

He's worried about his diabetes. He's frightened by blood in his stool and sores on his gums. He wonders whether the white-staffed hospitals on the hill above him will treat a poor black man with no teeth.

—Julie Sullivan, *The* (Spokane, Wash.) *Spokesman-Review*

Brief profiles showing a slice of life or vignettes of people are excellent formats for the Web or for a package of stories as sidebars to a main in-depth story. An idea that works well is a package of stories about diversity on campus, with profiles of international students or those from varied ethnic and racial backgrounds. A major story about an upcoming election in your town might also lend itself to miniprofiles of the candidates.

Here are some examples of vignettes written by journalism students who were following Julie Sullivan's style. The assignment was to find people behind the scenes on the campus of the University of Kansas. Students were instructed to write profiles filled with revealing details in fewer than 500 words—about one to one-and-a-half double-spaced typewritten pages. They were also told to stress show-in-action techniques. The frame was the university at work.

Journalism school librarian

Yvonne Martinez has carefully picked out her wardrobe.

Dressed in a navy blue skirt patterned with white boxes and a white blouse with the same pattern in blue, she had come prepared for another day of work at the School of Journalism library.

However, her outfit would not be complete without her size 6 1/2 sneakers.

The 4-foot-11 librarian does not wear them simply because they help maintain a quiet atmosphere. That is just one of the added benefits.

She wears them because she is constantly on the move.

Whether it's searching for a student's request for the last two years' worth of *Folio* magazine or sorting through the seemingly endless stack of newspapers the library receives daily, she rarely has time to sit down.

Recent cuts in the library's budget and staff have increased Martinez's work load. The sneakers are crucial.

"I'd rather be comfortable than in pain," she said.

Her duties have grown during the two years she has been working behind the counter. But now her duties include repairing the copy machine.

It is the only copy machine the library can afford on its budget, Martinez said. Overuse causes it to break down at least once a day.

As she returns to the counter, she immediately is greeted by a professor who says the machine is out of ink. She reaches under the counter and pulls out a bottle of black ink.

As she pours, the bottle slips and ink covers her hands. More students who need to be helped arrive at the counter.

Martinez stands by the machine staring at her hands as if she were auditioning for the part of Lady Macbeth. She sighs and runs off to the restroom. She quickly returns to the counter and apologizes to the students.

After all, she is the only librarian on duty.

Ranjit Arab, *The University Daily Kansan*

Bus driver

The sounds of a screaming Mick Jagger shake the windows of the bus.

A basket of Jolly Rancher's candies sits on the dashboard. And the driver in the blue and white Rolling Stones baseball cap is smiling.

This is Hank's bus—slap him a high five on the way off, please.

Hank Jones, who is in the middle of his fifth year as a (University of Kansas) bus driver, likes doing something extra for his passengers.

"Why shouldn't I," he says. "A little extra effort can go a long way."

One passenger remembers Hank stopping his bus on Jayhawk Boulevard last Valentine's Day just to give her a candy heart. She's been a regular ever since.

Hank began driving those green and white buses when he needed some extra money and he enjoyed it so much, he stayed with it.

The students are the best part of the job, but Hank is not without his complaints.

"They're not too quick sometimes," he says. "But they're good kids, most of them."

He tries to keep it interesting—he never plays the same tape twice in one day on his portable Sony stereo.

"I'm always partial to the Stones," he says, cracking open his pack of Marlboro cigarettes. "But I'll play requests, too."

Hank plans to keep driving for KU as long as he still enjoys it—or until he finds a wife. At 34, he hasn't found the right woman yet.

But he's in no hurry.

"Who knows?" he says. "Maybe someone will get on my bus."

—Kathy Hill

Obituaries

Obituaries are also profiles, but the subjects are dead. However, you don't write about the person's death; you write about his life. Marilyn Johnson, a magazine writer and editor, is so fascinated by obituaries that she wrote an entire book about the genre called "The Dead Beat."

"The obituary pages, it turns out, are some of the best-read pages in the newspaper," she writes. "Obituaries are history as it is happening. . . .Tell me the secret of a good life."

A broadcast or Web obituary about a person who was in the news or an entertainer would include audio and video clips of the person's quotes and accomplishments as well as comments from other people.

Jim Nicholson ("Dr. Death"), former obituary writer for the *Philadelphia Daily News*

Jim Nicholson, a former obituary writer for the *Philadelphia Daily News,* became so famous for his obituaries that he was nicknamed "Dr. Death" by his co-workers. He called his obituaries "character portraits," filled with details of how the person lived, "warts and all," he says.

Obituaries tend to be flattering portraits. But Nicholson says they should be true portraits. He believes someone's bad habits and criminal background, if they exist, should be part of an obituary. Many editors would disagree. And families are not likely to be happy with unflattering material. Generally, news editors weigh whether a criminal background was a crucial part of the person's life and if the crime was highly publicized. If a person was arrested at one time for shoplifting or for another misdemeanor, most editors would recommend omitting such information. When you are faced with such decisions, it is wise to confer with an editor.

"Cleaning up someone's act after he or she has died does not serve the cause of the deceased or loved ones," Nicholson says. "A sanitized portrait is indistinguishable from any other. It is the irregularities that give us identity. The ultimate acclaim may be when a reader thinks, 'I wish I had known this man or woman.'"

Like the obituary for Lawrence Pompie "Mr. Buddy" Ellis, a retired maintenance man who was a leader in his church:

He came to be known affectionately among friends as "Dial-A-Prayer" for his unceasing availability to those who wanted him to pray with them. If he couldn't meet personally with someone, he would pray with them on the telephone, said his wife, Fannie, who shared 38 years with him. . . . At 5-foot-7 and 205 pounds, Ellis loved to eat. "He loved everything about a pig," said his wife, "and if he didn't watch out, he'd catch his grunt."

—Jim Nicholson, *Philadelphia Daily News*

The Importance of Facts

A misspelled name or a factual error is a major problem in any story; in an obituary it is disastrous. So you should check every fact, every name, every reference. And you should check with the funeral director and the family to make sure that the person you are writing about is dead.

Someone from the *Detroit Free Press* didn't do that. And the death of Dr. Rogers Fair turned out to be greatly exaggerated, as Mark Twain would say. Fair, a Detroit physician, woke up one morning to read in the newspaper that he had died of cancer. The newspaper had received the obituary information by telephone from a woman who claimed she was Fair's aunt. And the reporter didn't call back to check with family members or a funeral home.

Fair, 40, claimed the "aunt" was a 21-year-old woman who was infatuated with him. She had wooed him with flowers and love notes, but when he rejected her and began dating another woman, he began receiving harassing telephone calls, bomb threats and vandalism to his home.

"She is obviously an obsessed person," Fair told the *Free Press*. "She has stated that if she can't have me, nobody else can."

The follow-up story was an embarrassment to the paper:

The obituary for Dr. Rogers Fair in Tuesday's Free Press took a lot of people—especially Fair—by surprise.

"My beeper was just jumping off the hook," the 40-year-old physician said Tuesday. "My secretary called me. She was in tears. . . ."

The erroneous report of Fair's demise was the second phony obituary published by the Free Press in recent years. The first prompted a revision of reporting practices, requiring all obituary information phoned in by friends and relatives to be confirmed either by a funeral home or law enforcement officials.

But Fair's obituary wasn't properly double-checked, and a woman identifying herself as Fair's aunt was able to hoodwink the Free Press with details of his death.

—*Detroit Free Press*

Most newspapers have free or paid death notices—announcements from the family about the deceased. In addition, funeral directors and families call the newspaper to request an obituary. Almost all newspapers will publish an obituary about anyone prominent in the community.

Obituaries have become crucial to online news sites as well. In a creative twist, the Sunline Web site for the *Sun Herald* newspapers in Florida (*www.sunline.net*) offers readers a chance to write tributes to loved ones who have died.

Generally, reporters scan the paid death notices to look for interesting people, long-term residents or those active in community service. Then you make the phone calls—or double-check the validity of the ones you have received by calling a funeral home, checking the phone book, and calling the family back or calling other relatives and friends. And, as in any other story, you check newspaper clips or databases and the Internet.

Calling people about death isn't easy. But it isn't as difficult as you might expect, especially for obituaries. Most families are grateful because this is the last story—and more often the only story—printed about their loved ones. Usually, someone in the family is prepared to deal with the media.

The easiest way to start gathering information is with the funeral director, if one has been selected. The funeral director should have the basic information and should be able to tell you which family members to call and their phone numbers.

Obituary Guidelines

Obituary writing follows some basic forms, even when you are writing a special profile. All obituaries, no matter how long or short, must contain the same crucial information:

Background Research

Before you interview family members or write an obituary, you should do a background check on the Internet. Family members may have personal Web sites. The subject of your obituary could be listed online in alumni sites or sites for Rotary and other organizations.

Before you use anything from a Web site, make sure that you check it for accuracy. Was the site dated? Does it have an author? Is the site credible? Do not use anything you can't verify. If you do include something from a Web site, cite your source.

Name: Use full name, middle initial and nickname if it was commonly used. Enclose the nickname in quotation marks.

Identification: How do you describe a person's life in one brief phrase? That's not so easy to do, but most obituaries start with a lead that identifies the person and summarizes the main accomplishment of his life. Usually, people are identified by occupation or community service. Always try to find something special to use following the name, such as "John Doe, a retired salesman" or "Jane Doe, a homemaker who was active in her church."

Age: In some cases, a family will request that you withhold the age. You should confer with an editor about honoring this request.

Date and Place of Death: Use the day of the week if the death occurred that week, the date if it was more than a week prior to the obituary. State the name of a hospital, if applicable, or other location where the death occurred.

Cause of Death: This fact is not required at all newspapers, especially if the cause of death was suicide or AIDS-related, or when the family requests that the cause be withheld. This issue has become especially controversial because of the stigma attached to AIDS-related deaths and suicide. However, some news organizations require the cause of death, regardless of stigma or family wishes. So check your newspaper's policy before you gather the information. You may have to inform family members of the policy.

If a suicide occurs on a college campus, the news spreads quickly. Should it be mentioned in a campus newspaper story or obituary? That's an ethical dilemma that campus news editors and directors have debated. If it is very public and well known around the school, one approach is to do a general story about suicide, which is a significant issue on college campuses. In most cases, however, suicide is not mentioned in the obituary out of respect for the family.

Address: Tell where the person lived when he died and previous areas of residence for any major length of time. Broadcast obituaries rarely use the specific address.

Background: Specify major accomplishments, organizations, educational background, military background and any other highlights. When people are very active in their church, mosque or synagogue, this fact should be mentioned in the obituary.

Survivors: Use the names of immediate family members (husband or wife, with her maiden name, children, brothers and sisters). Grandchildren are usually mentioned only by number: "He is survived by five grandchildren." New complications are arising these days because of changes in family relationships. Most news publications still do not list unmarried partners as survivors, or "bonded" partners (homosexual couples united in a marital ceremony), but that rule is changing. In the future, these relationships may also be a standard part of obituaries.

Services: Specify the time, date and location.

Burial: Name the place, and provide memorial information when available. When the death occurred a week or more ago, it is customary to start with information about the service or a memorial if that has not yet been conducted.

This example about the death of a local citizen follows all the basic guidelines; it also includes information about contributions:

Lucy Davis Burnett, a Dallas native and longtime civic leader, died of cancer Saturday at her home. She was 79.

A graduate of Woodrow Wilson High School in Dallas and Mary Baldwin College in Staunton, Va., Mrs. Burnett was active in numerous cultural and civic affairs.

She was past president of the Southern Methodist University Lecture Series, vice president of the Dallas Junior League and president of the Junior League Garden Club.

She was a founding member of the Dallas Slipper Club and also held memberships in the Dallas Women's Club, the Dallas Arts Museum League, the women's division of United Way of Dallas and Highland Park United Methodist.

She is survived by her husband, F.W. Burnett of Dallas; a daughter, Lucy Chambers of Vancouver, British Columbia; a son, F.W. Burnett Jr. of Dallas; and six grandchildren.

Services for Mrs. Burnett will be at 2 p.m. Tuesday at Highland Park United Methodist Church.

Memorials may be made to Children's Medical Center of Dallas, the Dallas Chapter of the American Cancer Society or a charity of the donor's choice.

—*The Dallas Morning News*

Here are some style tips:

Names of Services: Mass is celebrated, not said. The word is capitalized. Find out the exact wording you should use for the particular mass, such as Mass of Christian Burial. Likewise, ask for the proper wording of a service for other denominations.

Courtesy Titles: Although many newspapers and TV news organizations have eliminated courtesy titles (*Mrs., Mr., Ms., Miss*) for news stories, several keep them for obituaries. Again, you must check your newspaper's or broadcast station's policy.

Titles for Religious Leaders: Check the proper title for a rabbi, minister or priest. When writing about a priest, do not use *Father* or *Pastor* for the title. Use *the Rev.* (the reverend) followed by the priest's name: "the Rev. Vince Krische." For a rabbi, use *Rabbi* before the name on first reference: "Rabbi Jacob Katz." On second reference for clergy, including priests, use only the last name. But for second reference to high-ranking clergy, use "the cardinal," "the archbishop" and so on. Check *The Associated Press Stylebook* for specific religious titles.

Here is a feature obituary for Dr. Seuss that follows the guidelines. The story begins with the writer's death, some basic information about his accomplishments and then a chronology of his life. It ends with information about survivors. No information was available about services at the time, but if it had been, it would have been included at the end.

What Do You Think

Should negative information, such as a criminal background or previous bad publicity, be included in an obituary about a person?

☐ Yes

☐ No

☐ It depends upon the prominence of the person

☐ Not sure

Theodor Seuss Geisel, alias Dr. Seuss, whose rhymed writing and fanciful drawings were loved worldwide and helped teach generations to read, died Tuesday night at his home in La Jolla.

Geisel's stepdaughter, Lea Dimond, told reporters the world-famous author died with his family around him. No other information was released regarding the cause of death, but Dimond said Geisel, 87, had been ill for several months.

In the 1950s and '60s, Geisel's books gave millions of children relief from the drab textbook adventures of Dick and Jane. His 48 children's books were translated into 18 languages and sold more than 100 million copies.

Geisel also drew most of the fanciful illustrations in his books, creating a menagerie of Whos, grinches, ziffs and zuffs, talking goldfish and loyal, sweet elephants. He was awarded a special Pulitzer Prize in 1984 for his contribution to children's literature.

Geisel's tales were filled with his own moral concerns, particularly for the environment and world peace. "The Lorax" warns against polluting the environment, while "The Butter Battle Book" tells of an arms race between creatures who disagree about whether it is better to eat bread with the butter side down or up.

When asked recently whether he had any final message, Geisel told a reporter from the San Diego Union: "Whenever things go a bit sour in a job I'm doing, I always tell myself, 'You can do better than this.' The best slogan I can think of to leave with the USA would be 'We can do this and we've got to do better than this.'"

Geisel was born in Springfield, Mass. His father was a brewer and superintendent of parks, which included the zoo, where Geisel said he started drawing animals.

He graduated from Dartmouth College in 1925, having drawn cartoons for the school humor magazine. He went to England to study literature at Oxford University, but dropped out, in part, after receiving encouragement in his artistic ambitions from another American student, Helen Palmer. She became his first wife a few years later.

Geisel spent a year in Paris, where he got to know Ernest Hemingway, James Joyce and other writers. He returned to the United States in 1927, hoping to become a novelist.

He wrote humor for the magazines "Judge" and "Life," adopting his now-famous pen name, Dr. Seuss, as a spoof of scientific developments.

Among his most famous books are "The Cat in the Hat," "Green Eggs and Ham" and "Horton Hears a Who!" which was made into a popular TV special, as was "How the Grinch Stole Christmas!"

He moved to La Jolla soon after the end of World War II. During the latter part of the war he served in the Army, helping director Frank Capra make training and documentary films. Two Geisel documentaries, "Hitler Lives?" and "Design for Death," co-written with his wife, won Academy Awards for their producers in 1946 and 1947.

After the war, Geisel's work continued to be translated to movies, with his cartoon short "Gerald McBoing Boing" winning an Oscar in 1951. He turned his attention to television in the 1950s, designing and producing cartoons, including the Peabody Award–winning "How the Grinch Stole Christmas!" and "Horton Hears a Who!". . .

Geisel did not have any children of his own. His first wife died in 1967. He later married Audrey Dimond, who has two daughters from a previous marriage. He also is survived by his niece, Peggy Owens, and her son, Theodore Owens, of Los Angeles.

—Laura Bleiberg,
The Orange County (Calif.) *Register*

Exercises

1 **Snapshot profile:** Write a short profile about someone on your campus, using Julie Sullivan's style. Plan it as a vignette, considering it part of a package or a larger subject so it has a frame of reference. For example, consider a package of multicultural profiles, new professors or alumni.

2 **Celebrity profile:** Plan a celebrity profile of someone you would like to interview. If you enjoy sports, plan a profile of an athlete on your campus. Use Alan Richman's tips, and plan an interesting question you would use to begin the interview, as well as a preliminary theme you might pursue.

3 **Profile coaching:** Coach a classmate on writing a profile. Ask your classmate some of the basic coaching questions: What's it about? What is the focus? Do you have a theme? Were there any patterns, any turning points? What anecdotes do you remember as most interesting? What is the point—why should the reader care? What order are you considering? As the writer discusses the profile, you as the coach can ask questions that occur to you.

4 **Slice-of-life snapshots:** Using the theme of "A Day in the Life" of your campus or your community, write

vignettes about people and places. Each person in the class can take a different part of the campus or community.

5 **Personal profile:** Write a blog or memo about a turning point in your life or a significant experience that might make you worthy of a profile. Pairing up with a classmate, exchange your memos and interview each

other for a profile. Then write your profiles and share the results with your partner.

6 **Obituary:** Gather information from news clips, magazines and online sources about a celebrity or otherwise prominent person in your community who is still alive. Write an obituary, including comments the person has made and comments about the person.

☞ **Featured Online Activity** Log on to the book Web site for Chapter 18 and take the interactive quiz on obituary style site at

academic.cengage.com/masscomm/rich/ writingandreportingnews6e

Ask one source to recommend others.

Keep a tickler file of story ideas and follow-up stories.

Contact sources regularly.

Check records on your beat.

Check blogs related to your beat.

Make stories relevant to readers.

Seek human elements in stories.

Translate jargon in technical stories or specialized fields.

Check the Internet for sources, background and studies.

To be a good beat reporter, you have to love what you're doing.

Sevil Omer, reporter, *Reno* (Nev.) *Gazette-Journal*

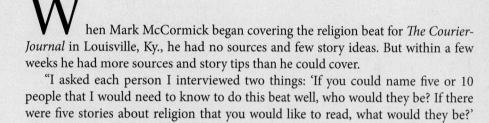

19 Beat Reporting

Mark McCormick

Mark McCormick, reporter and columnist

When Mark McCormick began covering the religion beat for *The Courier-Journal* in Louisville, Ky., he had no sources and few story ideas. But within a few weeks he had more sources and story tips than he could cover.

"I asked each person I interviewed two things: 'If you could name five or 10 people that I would need to know to do this beat well, who would they be? If there were five stories about religion that you would like to read, what would they be?' Between those two things, I amassed a large calling list," McCormick says.

McCormick kept names of all his sources in his computer. "If five people said I needed to talk to the same people, I put a star next to that person's name," he says. "I made it a point to cultivate a relationship with those people by going to lunch with them and trying to win their confidence."

He also used the matchmaker technique, asking one source to introduce him to people who might be skeptical about dealing with him or with the media in general. "I'd say, 'Would you mind telling this person I'm not a hatchet man.' That is how I made a breakthrough in the Jewish community and the Muslim community."

In the past, religion news was relegated to a page on Saturdays to announce church services and other information. But it has become a significant beat because newspaper studies have shown that religion affects people's lives as much as or more than any other news in the paper.

The religion beat was a new challenge to McCormick, who had covered police and community beats in the past. "I was a little intimidated because I am not theologically trained," he says. As he soon discovered, however, the religion beat is like any other beat. The content of the news differs, but the techniques of reporting and writing do not.

A "beat" is a specific area of coverage. It can be an entire municipality or parts of the government, such as the police department, the school board or the city officials. It can be a topical beat, such as environment, business, minorities or religion.

The skills you have studied so far can be applied to all beats in print and broadcast. Some of the following chapters will be devoted to specific beats, such as police, courts and government, but the tips from McCormick and other writers in this chapter will help you get started covering any beat.

Developing Story Ideas

Although McCormick received many tips for story ideas by asking people what they wanted to read, he also used his natural curiosity to develop ideas. One day he was covering the funeral of a 15-year-old boy who had been shot. The boy's friends showed up wearing T-shirts with the boy's picture and the words "Rest in Peace." McCormick says the shirts struck him as odd, but then he noticed similar markings on T-shirts and baseball caps after another young man died. Although it may not seem like a story for the religion beat, McCormick says this social phenomenon is, in fact, a very spiritual story.

The front of the shirts that Thomas Cooper made after the death of his friend, Tony Sullivan, read "R.I.P. T LUV" in artful script and colorful airbrushed design.

On the back was an enlarged, equally artistic design featuring "T LUV"—Sullivan's nickname.

"He's my homey; you've got to remember him," Cooper, 19, said of Sullivan, who was shot by a police officer in Lexington's Bluegrass-Aspendale housing area last month in an incident that sparked civil unrest in the city.

On Friday, Cooper was wearing a baseball cap with "T LUV" across the front. "I just got this to have something to remember him by. He was my boy."

And at Sullivan's funeral the previous week, many young people were wearing their "T LUV" T-shirts. Such shirts—with the deceased's picture or name emblazoned across them—are becoming a common sight at services for teenage victims of violence.

Some youths say wearing the shirts has nothing to do with being cool and everything to do with respecting the memory of fallen friends. Other teens and school counselors argue that many who wear the shirts don't even know the victims and are not grieving but trying to connect with a culture they see as alluring.

—Mark McCormick, *The* (Louisville, Ky.) *Courier-Journal*

One story can lead to many others, as when McCormick wrote about a hospital chapel that was closing. "I went there and talked to people about their memories," he says. "I found a woman who had spent many hours praying in the chapel 20 years ago because her husband had cancer and was supposed to die. He is still alive today." McCormick says 135 people called him or left voice-mail messages to comment about the story, and many people told him similar touching stories about how faith had affected their lives. As a result, he had many sources for another story about the power of faith.

McCormick also checks newspaper clips, journals, newsletters, press releases and national research organizations that cover religion to keep abreast of his field.

Create a tickler file. Follow-up stories are essential for beat reporters. When you cover a story that has a future element, make sure you that you follow it up and keep abreast of new developments. Develop a file organized by weeks or months and check it for upcoming or follow-up stories.

Using Blogs and Social Networking Sites

These days beat reporters also read blogs related to their beat and comments readers post to their stories online. In addition, they regularly check the Internet for documents and resources.

For example, political blog sites such as the Daily Kos (*www.dailykos.com*) and others generate hundreds of comments and provide story ideas and sources for any reporter covering national politics and government. Blogs for beat reporting have become so crucial that the Online Journalism Association created a new award category, "the best of online beat reporting." One of the first winners was a blog of Wired.com called "Danger Room" (*http://blog.wired.com/defense/*), which provides commentary on military enforcement and national security issues.

Beat reporters can keep abreast of new information added to blogs and other sites by subscribing to them via RSS, a form of technology that automatically sends them updated information as it is added to the sites.

Crowdsourcing is another way beat reporters can gather information. This is a method of involving readers or viewers in reporting and submitting information on a topic. For example, an economics reporter doing a beat story on gas prices might ask readers and viewers to submit information about gas prices in their communities. The information could also be collected via a Web site that is programmed to collect and analyze the data.

Beat reporters can also find a wealth of story ideas and information readers and viewers want by checking comments posted to stories about their beats.

Social networking sites such as MySpace and Facebook are also good places to find sources and story ideas on specific topics that beat reporters cover, whether it is environmental or entertainment issues.

But to do a good job on any beat, you also need to use the traditional reporting skills of meeting people and developing sources in person.

Cultivating Sources

Once you find sources, you need to get them to trust you. McCormick, who has since become a columnist for *The Wichita* (Kan.) *Eagle,* says when you start any beat, it's always better to write a positive story, if you can, the first time you cover a group. "I never want my first contact to be negative."

That is especially true with groups that haven't had much coverage in the past, such as the Muslims and the African-American churches on McCormick's beat. And unlike sources on police and government beats, sources in religious organizations don't expect controversy or negative coverage in the media.

But that's what they got when McCormick covered the General Association of Baptists, an organization of more than 500 black churches. The group hadn't been covered by the newspaper in the past. At the first meeting McCormick attended, the association ousted churches that had licensed women to preach. To McCormick, the association's action was a good story. The leaders of the association didn't agree. "They still won't speak to me," he says.

McCormick says he always tries to give all sources a chance to comment or to do a follow-up story that explains the issue in depth. That approach didn't work with the General Association of Baptists. However, sources will usually be cooperative if you give them a chance to explain their views and if your story is accurate and fair, he says.

Sevil Omer, who covered the police and courts beat for the *Reno* (Nev.) *Gazette-Journal,* recommends contacting sources regularly. She called her sources even when

ETHICS

Ethical dilemma: Should you become friends or get romantically involved with a source on your beat?

The case: You share a mutual attraction with a source on your beat, and you would really like to date this person. You know it would be a conflict of interest to date the source, but should you give up your rights to a personal life, or should you give up your beat? Can you maintain a relationship with a source without compromising your integrity and credibility? Does it make a difference if the relationship is just platonic or romantic?

Ethical values: Credibility, conflict of interest.

Ethical guidelines: The Society of Professional Journalists Code of Ethics says journalists should avoid conflicts of interest, real or perceived, and should remain free of associations and activities that may compromise integrity or damage credibility.

Sevil Omer, reporter

she had no specific story in mind. "I think you need to let them know you are taking an interest in them," she says.

"When you run into them, it's important to say 'Hi, how are you.' You have to make sure they know who you are and what you look like. Meet people on the scene."

Omer says regular contact is particularly important because many times police, lawyers and other sources are reluctant to give information about crimes and court cases. "A lot of times people are a bit skeptical of you; they haven't sized you up yet. In my case, some of the police who read my stories were surprised when they met me because my name confused them. They said, 'We thought you were a man.'"

Because beat reporters deal with the same sources repeatedly, it is easy to become friendly with them. But Omer says she draws the line at socializing with sources because it can cause conflicts of interest. On the other hand, if you know that a good source has a birthday or some important event in his life or has been ill, you can make a phone call or send a card. Many good beat reporters keep such notations about the source in their card file or in a computer source file.

Records and Research

Sevil Omer didn't depend exclusively on police and attorneys for information. She says all good reporters should check records, especially on the police beat: "Check the police files, public documents in courts and go to the sources. Then do what detectives do. Knock on doors and do your homework. Ask family members and victims."

In addition to covering stories as they occur, Omer watched for trends on her beat. For example, she noticed that the crime statistics revealed an increase in the number of young women arrested for violent crimes. She wondered what was causing this trend. Her investigation led to a package of stories, including a mainbar about why the trend was occurring and sidebars profiling women who were involved with gangs and with other criminal activity.

When the Bloods headed into Truckee Meadows from Southern California to organize a narcotics ring last year, they sought the toughest and brightest gang member to head the effort.

They found her in Reno.

When Harrah's officials and police reviewed a recent video of purse snatchings inside the downtown casino, they were surprised to see the suspect's young, female face.

When metal flashed at Sparks Middle School in March, security guards took two girls into custody on charges of carrying a concealed weapon on school grounds.

More and more young women are mirroring men, especially their rebelliousness, law-enforcement officials say. Increasingly, girls are committing violent crimes.

Now they call the shots and elicit fear from rivals.

"There's a large, solid group of females in gang activity," Reno Police Chief Jim Weston said about increases in the past two years.

—Sevil Omer, *Reno* (Nev.) *Gazette-Journal*

The story was accompanied by charts of statistics.

"There's a lot of mechanical work to this beat that any clerk could do. But you have to keep checking police and court files so you know the pulse and the trends," Omer says. "And despite the blood and gore, there's always a human element. You can put compassion into any story."

Online Documents

Although human sources are still the most important ones on a beat, online sources and documents have become increasingly valuable to beat reporters. One of the first steps you should take when you start a beat is to check the Internet for Web pages about your community and state. Then check more general resources and documents at online sites for organizations, government agencies, businesses and journalism organizations related to your beat.

Think in multimedia terms. Because your stories will probably be posted on the Web, you need to gather records and data in electronic form. For example:

- If you are covering a city or government beat and writing about a budget, get a copy of the complete budget in electronic form to be posted on the Web.
- If you are writing a story about restaurant inspections, get the complete list of all inspections to be posted on the Web.
- If you are covering the education beat and writing about school test scores, get an electronic copy of all the scores to be posted on the Web or created in an interactive form so readers can search for their school scores.

But remember that much of the information on the Internet is not reliable. Thousands of sites offer medical advice, but much of the information is more opinion than fact. Some sites are pure hoaxes.

Despite the accuracy and credibility problems of Web sites, the Internet is a wonderful tool for beat reporters to accumulate sources and background information.

You just have to be sure that the background, documents or Web sites come from an agency, organization, business or government institution that offers credible information.

Here are some tips:

- Check whether the site offers a contact name, postal address and phone number. Call the number and verify the contact if you are using the site as a beat resource.
- Check the date of the information posted. Not all sites offer posting dates, but you should make sure that the information you use is not outdated.
- To find out who owns or manages a site, check a Whois database. You can identify owners and contacts at nongovernmental agencies at *www.betterwhois.com,* but much of the information has not been updated in the past few years, so it may not be accurate. However, checking is still worth a try.

Beginning a Beat

The tips suggested by Mark McCormick and Sevil Omer will help you get started in any beat. If you are beginning a job or internship in an area that is unfamiliar to you or if you are assigned to cover a municipality, here are some other tips for starting your beat:

Use Shoe Leather: Get to know your community or the agency you cover. Meet its members in person. Take a walking tour of the community. Talk to people. Eat where the politicians and the city employees eat or socialize after work. Get your hair cut by the barber or beautician who has been in town a long time. Ask people what they are interested in and what they want to read in their newspaper. Get a map. Cruise the streets. See where the rich and poor, the famous and infamous live. If you have a campus beat, introduce yourself to the officials, department heads, or leaders of a department or an organization. Tell them that you are interested in what they do and are seeking story ideas on a regular basis. In many cases, the people on your beat will want the coverage.

Check Clips: The starting place for every beat and story you write is the newspaper or television database or resource room. When you find stories about major issues on your beat, consider an update story.

Let Your Fingers Do the Walking: Read the classified pages of your telephone book. How many churches are there of each denomination? Are massage parlors, astrologers or other unusual services advertised? Check the municipal services, sometimes listed in a separate section. Is there a poison control center or a government agency that sounds interesting? A quick scan of the classified section of your telephone book can give you some sense of your community and story ideas for a municipal beat. If you have a campus or city beat, check the directories of your school or city. Are there agencies or departments you don't know anything about? Find out what people in these jobs do, what they like and don't like about their jobs.

Check campus directories for clubs and student organizations that might be worth a feature.

Study the Classifieds: Check newspaper or online classified sections for your community, such as the real estate section. What is for sale? What prices are the houses? This information will give you some idea of the economic climate of the community. Maybe you can write a story about why a particular area of town has many homes for sale. Sometimes you'll find a touching story in the personal ads. Check the rewards for lost dogs, cats, birds, snakes or unusual pets. And check the legal notices. They'll tell you what the city must advertise, as in notices of meetings or for items the city wants to buy. For campus beats, check classifieds and other advertisements in the college newspaper for unusual job opportunities, new organizations and other items that could be of interest to students.

Create a Tickler File: Read the news. Are interesting people who are worth profiles mentioned in news stories? Are briefs in the newspaper worth features? Are ideas tucked into a news story that need exploring or follow-up? Start your own idea file organized by topics or dates and check it regularly.

Visit the Library: The local librarian is often a good source for information about the community.

Check Bulletin Boards: Visit the offices or agencies you cover, and read the notices on the bulletin boards. You will find notices for job openings and other interesting information that could lead to news and feature stories.

Check with Your Predecessor: If the person who previously covered your beat is still at the newspaper or TV station, ask for a briefing about the beat and for key sources.

Be a Tourist: Visit the historical society, the chamber of commerce and other community agencies. Find the places of interest, and investigate what they were like years ago. You might develop angles for features. At the very least, you will gain some understanding of your community.

Press for News Releases: Get on print and electronic mailing lists. Call the city or town clerk, and get the releases from your city and county government or from the agency you cover. Call the public relations officers of agencies and businesses in your community. Introduce yourself.

Tell them you are interested in ideas for stories. It's their job to provide them. You don't have to use their handouts, but having them will give you ideas about what is happening in your community. Call agencies such as senior citizen organizations, the Red Cross, churches and social service organizations, and make sure that you are on their mailing lists for announcements, reports and news.

Find Out Who's in Charge: Be kind to the folks who prepare the memos for officials. Get to know them, and use their names when you see them or call their offices. Talk to the janitors, the security guards and the people behind the scenes. They know what is going on, and they can be sources for tips. Meet the officials, of course, and then find out who heads the unions and professional organizations in the schools and government. The leaders of these organizations know what is going on behind the scenes. They also have stories from the workers' point of view. Use the up/down reporting principle: Go up and down the organizational ladder.

Hit Records: Know how and where to find records. Start with the city or county clerk, who will direct you to municipal offices where records are available. Visit the courthouse, and familiarize yourself with the filing system there by asking the clerks for help. These are public records, and it's the clerks' job to serve the public. If your university is part of a state system, check records on campus or at the state level for fire inspection reports, police statistics or reports on environmental hazards.

Write a Source Book: Record names, telephone numbers and e-mail addresses for everyone you interview, call or meet on your beat. Develop a filing system and a cross-listing system. Put a memo after each name. If a source tells you something personal about a child or a family member who is ill, make a note and call in a few weeks to find out how the person is doing. Or mention the ill person the next time you talk to your source. Be thoughtful. Your source will appreciate your interest and be more receptive when dealing with you. Don't forget to print out a copy or back up your electronic source book.

Join Internet Discussion Groups: You'll find journalism organizations related to your beat, and other resources, at *www.newslink.org/spec.html* and many other resources at JournalismNet (*www.journalismnet.com*), a comprehensive site created by Julian Sher, an investigative TV documentary producer and trainer of journalists around the world.

Covering Specialty Beats

You don't have to be a doctor to cover medicine or a scientist to cover the environment, but you do need to acquire knowledge of the subject in your beat. The challenge for writers of specialized subjects is to make the stories clear and to define the jargon so the average reader can understand the story in print and broadcast news. But for broadcast news beats, make sure you choose sound bites carefully to avoid bureaucratic terminology.

The Education Beat

The education beat is one of the most diverse beats. It includes stories about budgets, stories about school board meetings, crime reporting, investigative reporting, statistics of test scores and enrollment, breaking news, and most of all news and features about what is happening in the schools. Stories about school life are often the most neglected, because education reporters have so much to do to keep up with the school board and other administrative news.

The Internet is providing education reporters with an opportunity to publish expanded coverage of their beats. Several major metropolitan newspapers offer complete Web packages featuring interactive search engines that allow readers to search for test scores and other statistics for their schools.

Writing interesting stories about budgets and other technical education stories can be challenging. It requires all the skills of good writing that you have studied in other chapters, such as descriptive and expository techniques. In this award-winning story about schools in rural Alaska, called "Bush" schools and found in communities accessible only by airplane, the writers tackle a complex issue of funding and school evaluation by using a combination of descriptive and expository techniques:

Snow swirls around Bettles Field School in the Popsicle-blue light of a winter dawn.

Eight students sit at desks pushed into a circle, taking turns reading aloud from a novel. The other three classrooms are empty except for desks, chairs, cardboard boxes of books and a few computers.

All is quiet in the adjoining library, where 16-year-old Solomon Yatlin hunches in a cubicle wearing headphones and listening to the movie soundtrack "Strange Days" on a mini compact-disc player.

Solomon is the only high school student in what really should be a one-room schoolhouse.

"I'd rather go someplace bigger with a basketball team," Solomon says, looking up from his book. "It's too hard just working like this, I don't know, by yourself and all."

The Yukon-Koyukuk School District is spending $19,094 this year to teach Solomon. The same is being spent on each of his eight classmates who started the school year.

Yet hundreds of millions of dollars after a landmark court settlement 20 years ago did away with mandatory boarding schools and put students like Solomon in village high schools, most graduates are ill-prepared for college and life. A diploma from a Bush school doesn't equal one from an urban campus.

The cost of Bush education is extreme and the obstacles are many. Outsiders unfamiliar with Native ways lead the classrooms. Social problems—alcoholism, child abuse, domestic violence— keep some students from learning. When students do succeed, graduating from high school or college, they find few jobs waiting in their villages.

Critics are taking note.

As the governor and Legislature wrestle with a budget shortfall, the decline in Alaska's mainstay oil industry, and education spending that outpaces inflation, Bush high schools are under more scrutiny than ever. Lawmakers wonder: Are Bush schools making the grade?

—Wendy Hower and Kristan Kelly, *Fairbanks (Alaska) Daily News-Miner*

Here are some basic tips for covering the education beat:

■ Check educational journals for trends and national comparisons of school performance.

■ When writing about test scores or other school statistics, explain what they mean and how they affect students.

Convergence Coach

Before the Internet and electronic databases existed, newspaper stories were stored in resource rooms called "morgues." Today, with a click of a mouse, reporters can access more information on the Internet than at any time in history. The Internet should be your first stop when researching background for a story or compiling information for a beat.

▪ Join e-mail lists related to your beat. Request e-mail newsletters from public relations practitioners and other organizations related to your work in your community.

▪ Check blogs related to your beat.

▪ Always search the Internet for background on people or topics you are covering.

▪ Join journalism organizations, such as the Society of Environmental Journalists, the Education Writers of America and others related to your beat.

▪ Check government sites such as the U.S. Census and others for statistical and other information. Good starting places are *www.fedworld.gov* and *www.firstgov.gov.*

▪ Check journalism organizations and sites that compile links to resources. You'll find links to many of them in the Web sites for this book.

▪ Translate jargon.

▪ Make sure that you get into the schools to write stories about education.

▪ When you attend meetings, ask parents what they want to know about their schools. You'll find scores of links to education resources and other stories online at the Education Writers Association Web site: *www.ewa.org.*

Health and Environmental Writing

Jonathan Bor, a medical writer for *The Sun* in Baltimore, covered crime, courts, politics and education before writing medical stories. "I learned how to convert the blather of educators, bureaucrats and cops into plain English before tackling doctor-speak," he says in an article in *Coaches' Corner*, a former publication for coaching writers. "And I learned to look first for stories about real people. I believe the hallmark of good medical writing is clear, colorful prose that takes the lay reader inside a world whose inhabitants—doctors, scientists and insurers—speak a secret language."

Good medical writing, in many ways, is simply good reporting and writing, Bor says. "It is thoroughly researched. It is written cleanly, and when possible, with a human touch. Bad medical writing, among other things, is written for insiders." Here is an excerpt from a story about a heart transplant operation that Bor wrote for his previous newspaper. He witnessed the operation and wrote the story on deadline after going without sleep for 48 hours. He used the basic techniques of descriptive writing: show-in-action and details. Note how clearly he explains a complex procedure:

A healthy 17-year-old heart pumped the gift of life through 34-year-old Bruce Murray Friday, following a four-hour transplant operation that doctors said went without a hitch. . . .

The team—consisting of a surgeon, a physician's assistant and a nurse—removed the donor's heart at about 1:30 p.m. They placed it inside a plastic bag filled with an iced-saline solution, and they placed that bag inside three outer bags. The package was placed inside a blue beer cooler that bore the stamp "Transplant."

By the time their jet landed at Teterboro at 3 a.m., Murray was in the operating room where he was being prepped for surgery. Anesthesia put the patient into a deep sleep. A respirator breathed air into Murray's lungs via a tube inserted in his throat. Doctors cut a slit the length of Murray's chest. As many as a dozen doctors, nurses and technical assistants hovered over the patient, passing instruments, attending to heart monitors and swabbing the patient's bleeding chest.

Meanwhile, a state police escort ensured swift passage from Teterboro, over the George Washington Bridge and to the hospital for the vehicle carrying the transplant team and beer cooler. Within 10 minutes after landing, the transplant team was rushing the beer cooler through the hospital emergency room and up an elevator 18 floors.

By the time the heart arrived in the operating room, Murray's chest was wide open. Doctors had used a power saw to cut through his sternum, and a clamp-like retractor spread his chest apart. Murray's diseased heart, about half-again larger than normal, was fluttering inside the exposed chest cavity.

Surgeons swiftly turned the task of pumping blood over to the heart-lung machine. Their hands moving with quick deliberation, surgeons inserted tubes inside the heart's major blood vessels and severed the vessels from the heart.

The tangle of tubes carried the blood to a cylinder that supplied it with oxygen. From there, the blood traveled to a large console, which performs the job of the heart. Three spinning disks pumped the blood through the clear, plastic tubes back to the patient's body.

In one careful, spectacular moment, the surgical team made the exchange. At 4:33 a.m., doctors lifted the diseased heart—milky but purple—out of Murray's chest cavity and handed it to attendants. They, in turn, placed it in the steel bowl. On a platform at the foot of the operating table, the spent heart rested for the duration. . . .

The beer cooler was opened, and the donor heart was placed inside the patient's chest. The new heart, about as large as a relaxed fist, was attached to the blood vessels.

It jerked and fluttered and became Bruce Murray's.

—Jonathan Bor,
The (Syracuse, N.Y.) *Post-Standard*

Bor offers these tips, which apply to all beats but are particularly useful for health and environmental stories:

- Challenge the source to speak to laymen. If that fails, allow the scientist to speak his language, but constantly challenge him with your version of the facts—"Are you saying that . . . ?"
- Never forget to ask your source the cosmic questions. What does the new treatment mean for the AIDS sufferer? Will this prolong life for days, months or more? Will the patient live longer but just as miserably, or what? Does a new medical finding represent an incremental advance or a true "breakthrough" that will change the lives of many people?
- Don't forget to give your story a sense of true proportion. If health inspectors have closed down an inner-city nursing home because of rodent infestation, it

doesn't hurt to say that inspectors observed mice chewing on patients' feeding tubes and lapping the IV fluids that oozed out. If it's that bad, say it and say it vividly. Reporters need to say, however, whether the horror was an isolated finding or a condition observed throughout the nursing home.

■ Anecdotes can be wonderful or tedious. At best, they bring to life the suffering of the afflicted, the benefits of new treatments, or the breadth and social costs of an epidemic. At their worst, they turn a story into a tear-jerking soap opera worthy of a tacky TV movie. When do anecdotes work? Perhaps they work when they vividly show the human side—the joy and suffering—of an issue. They also show the practical dimensions of a problem better than some doctor or bureaucrat spouting generalities.

■ Metaphors can be nice, but they also can trivialize. I don't like stories that describe antibodies as little foot-soldiers engaged in hand-to-hand combat with disease-carrying bugs. I have seen this. Lacking something less trivial, I'd state the obvious: antibodies are substances produced by the body to fight infection.

Bor's tips apply to environmental writing as well. Stories about the environment and health have become so important that several universities are offering separate courses and programs in science writing. No single textbook chapter or portion of it can do justice to this subject. But as Bor says, these beats require the same reporting and writing techniques as any other stories.

Health writers need to be especially wary of the information offered on the Internet about diseases. Many Web sites are self-help information provided by people without medical authority, and others are offered by drug companies, which do not offer unbiased information. Check the ownership of the Web sites before you use information in a news story.

Environmental writers also have a wealth of resources available on the Internet. The Society of Environmental Journalists offers extensive links to resources and publications relating to environmental beats. You can link to it at *www.sej.org*. You can also read award-winning environmental stories linked to this site.

Business Writing

Business writing does not have to be boring. The best business writers use the same techniques of good storytelling as writers in any other field.

Fortune magazine writer John Helyar compares business writing to sports writing. "There's as much drama in the field of business as on any field of play. There are as many fascinating characters in boardrooms as locker rooms—if not more. Yet we business journalists still too often limit ourselves in how we cover the beat," he writes in a column, "Six Rules for the Business Writer's Craft." Helyar says readers can get all the financial data they want from online sites, so the business journalist should go beyond the charges and "use compelling narratives to take readers to the heart of the most important matters. . . .We need to write as if business isn't the dullest beat on the paper, but the richest—because it is."

In one of his rules, Helyar says: "You've got to put the bowl down where the dog can eat it." By that he means you should explain things clearly. "Our job is to take the jargon of CPAs and MBAs and translate it into English."

Here is an example of how Helyar translated that advice into a story about unemployment for people age 50 and over:

> When Zurich Financial let Bob Miller go in February 2003, he wasn't worried. His résumé was impeccable. He had 20 years of experience under his belt and plenty of references describing him as a high-energy, highly accomplished financial-services marketer. From his home base in Chicago, he'd racked up 100,000-plus frequent-flier miles a year, working a vast network of contacts among insurance agents and financial planners to generate millions of dollars of revenue for financial giants like CNA. Sure, it hurt to be let go. It always did. But he'd been there before—five times, in fact.
>
> "And in every situation I ended up in a better place," he says.
>
> Two years later he's still looking for that better place. Or any place, for that matter....
>
> Miller and his peers are members of a flourishing species: the involuntary retiree. When these anxious white-collar exiles aren't trying to look busy, they're going to support groups. Or worrying about the bills. Or reading advice columns about the résumé risk of fudging their age or taking a sales job at Home Depot. Or hoping that a recent Supreme Court decision on age discrimination will give them some kind of legal recourse to sue the bastards who fired them....
>
> —John Helyar, *Fortune magazine, CNN Money*

The concept of telling stories and translating business information so the average reader can understand it is at the heart of the *Wall Street Journal* formula described in Chapter 10 on story forms. The original memo the newspaper issued in the 1950s to its writers said, "Our aim is to do very complete, very thorough research-type stories—but to avoid the obvious danger in such work of becoming dull and dry. To achieve maximum readability, we try to carry the reader along with a liberal sprinkling of color, examples and other illustrative gadgets. We try to keep our stories factually complete and correct enough to interest the banker, economist or other authority on the subject—yet always bearing in mind that it must be intriguing enough and simple enough to appeal to our average reader, who might be a retailer in Des Moines, a gas station owner in Dallas, a grain merchant in Oklahoma City or someone else with no familiarity on the subject."

The technique for most stories written in this formula is to start with a specific anecdote or example and proceed to a nut graph, which explains the main point of the story. Here are some other tips for clear writing that apply to any story but particularly to business stories:

- Humanize stories by focusing on the impact of business or economic issues on people. Use a focus-on-a-person lead to help the reader or viewer relate to your story.
- Avoid using several numbers in the same sentence or same paragraph, particularly in the lead. If you must use many numbers, consider a chart or graphic instead of writing them in the text. This is especially crucial for broadcast stories.
- Simplify sentences: The more complex the concept, the simpler your sentences should be.

- Avoid jargon. Translate any bureaucratic or technical concepts into terms the average reader or viewer would understand.
- Use analogies to explain complex information. For example, *Seattle Times* business writer Peter Rinearson used several analogies like this one in his Pulitzer Prize–winning story that explained how the Boeing jetliner was created:

The complexities of the 757 passenger door are all the more remarkable because of the utter simplicity of the door's basic concept. The door is, in essence, a plug not unlike a bathtub stopper or a bottle cork.

But unlike a cork in a bottle, which is wedged in from the outside, the 757 door is wedged from the inside. The pressurized cabin air helps hold the door in place.

Sportswriting

Sportswriters have always had to rely on feature techniques of descriptive and interpretive writing, even more than other writers at a newspaper. Their readers may have seen the game, but they still want to read about it. Others who haven't seen the game want to know what happened. So sportswriters face the challenge of providing readers something more than the basic facts.

Sports reporter Mike Lopresti filing a story from a game

Unlike most news stories, where reporters rely on information from sources, sportswriters covering a game are witnessing the action first-hand. They have the responsibility for interpreting what they saw through interviews with coaches and players and their own analysis. They need to stress angles: why and how the game was won or lost or what the strategy was. How was this game different from or similar to others?

But sports stories are not limited to game coverage. The range of topics on sports pages—profiles, trend stories and general sports features—is as broad as in any other section of the paper.

Years ago, sportswriters could rely on knowing their craft and writing primarily about games and the athletes. These days sportswriters might spend their time covering athletes in courts as well as on the courts. Many stories involve athletes in legal contract disputes and court cases about drugs, violence and other criminal charges. Sportswriting also requires knowledge about games, leagues and style of sports scores. Check the Associated Press Stylebook for this information.

Some of the best writing in the newspaper—as well as some of the worst—can be found on the sports pages. Karen Brown Dunlap, president of The Poynter Institute, says all writers, especially those facing tight deadlines, could take some tips from sportswriters. She offers this advice:

- First, writers must see the same old story in different ways. . . . The characters and events in sports stories aren't necessarily more interesting than those in news stories. But in sports, more attention is paid to the people and the action. Personalities, motives and mannerisms are fleshed out to add color and meaning to stories.

- A second message from sportswriters is to keep your eyes on the story. "You can't look away when you're covering a sports story," said Merlissa Lawrence, a sportswriter for *The Pittsburgh Press*. "In that one moment something dramatic could happen."

- A third strategy is to write background information ahead of time and plan for likely eventualities. . . . It is a method commonly used by journalists covering major sports events on deadline.

- A fourth message is to give some thought to the best format for telling the story. Some games are worth only a box score. So are some meetings. Some stories require a brief; others need a long story or several textual and graphic elements.

- Finally, sportswriters write in ways that draw readers into stories. Often the readers know the score and have seen the event. The task for the writer then is to elucidate, analyze, amplify and soothe the reader with the pleasure of the words that recapture the event.

Many of the writing techniques that sportswriters use to accomplish those tasks are the same ones you have studied for other basic news, feature and specialty stories. The major difference is that sportswriters must stress interpretation, how and why, more than in basic news stories. Good sportswriters try to do that by setting a tone and developing their stories with a theme. Check your AP Stylebook for sports terminology and style.

Philip Meiring, *The University Daily Kansan*

The game itself, no longer the sole focus of sportswriters

Here are some of the basic facts to include in game stories:

- Who played, where (stadium and city), when
- Score (placed high in the story)
- Find a focus: Stress an overall theme or problem with the game
- Major plays and players
- Turning points
- Injuries
- Important statistics (conference standing, records for season)
- Weather, if it had an effect on the game
- Crowd count, if relevant (fully packed stadium or sparse attendance)

- Outcome of previous games between these two teams, if relevant
- Comments from coaches and players to explain the how and why of the game

This example incorporates most of these elements:

Not looking ahead of Big Red

With K-State coming up, KU could have played with Nebraska with a lack of motivation. The Jayhawks didn't.

A letdown would have almost been natural.

It was just two weeks ago that the Jayhawks tormented Nebraska on the road. Why take them seriously this time? A date with rival Kansas State loomed as the next game on the schedule. Shouldn't that be more important? With those circumstances, no one would have blamed the players if they lollygagged around to a 10 or 15-point victory.

But they didn't. Instead, the Jayhawks (20-0, 5-0) again showed why they are one of the best, most focused teams in the country with an 84-49 pounding against Nebraska. Take away the six-point win against Missouri, and the Jayhawks are dispatching conference opponents by more than 27 points a game.

"Everybody just does their job," senior forward Darnell Jackson said, "and we get energy from that. You don't want to lose. You don't want to go out there and disappoint the coaching staff."

Actually, Kansas was more jacked up than usual. The energy that wasn't quite there Wednesday against Iowa State reappeared Saturday in a hurry.

Russell Robinson stole the ball from Cookie Miller on the first possession. Brandon Rush picked up a steal the next time the Huskers had the ball.

By halftime, Kansas forced seven steals and had 10 points in transition. The Jayhawks only had seven steals for the entire game against the Cyclones. Their 10 fast break points were more than they had scored the past two games combined.

The small problems that had bothered Kansas were solved. The Jayhawks could run and steal again. Sherron Collins said it was about time.

"Coach said we have to start forcing turnovers on the defensive end," Collins said. "Like I said we're fine where we're at, but we have to take more steps to get more pressure. But I think we did a pretty good job today."

Of course, this wasn't against the best competition in the conference. Actually, it was against the worst. Nebraska is now 0-4 in league play, and the Huskers provided several reasons why. Shang Ping got whistled for an up, down traveling violation. Aleks Maric missed point-blank shots. Ryan Anderson bricked six threes.

They proved no match for Darrell Arthur, who scored 18, and Brandon Rush, who made five three-pointers. Russell Robinson finished with four steals, and Sherron Collins scored in double-figures for the first time since Jan. 8. The whole team seemed to be on a level above Nebraska. That's the way Huskers coach Doc Sadler saw it.

"I'm not convinced that a superior perfect game is good enough to beat these guys for us," he said.

As Sadler admitted, his team is certainly not good enough to defeat the Jayhawks, but for the first time in league play, Kansas will face a team that might be good enough. K-State is undefeated so far in conference play and has improved vastly since the beginning of the season. Wednesday night's game will surely be a challenge.

The Wildcats have gotten so much better that their star forward Michael Beasley told media his team could beat the Jayhawks anywhere—Africa, Alaska, the rec center.

"That doesn't bother me," Jayhawks Coach Bill Self said. "We'll talk to our players about that, but when a guy is averaging 24 and 13, I think he has a right to talk a little bit."

The team that gets the victory will be in position for a title run. K-State and Kansas are tied with Baylor atop the league standings, and a victory will give the winner a better path to the conference championship.

Even with that game coming up soon and Nebraska out of the way, the Jayhawks aren't ready to think only about K-State yet. They know it will be a challenge, but they're still focused on getting better for the next two days, just like they were focused for Nebraska on Saturday. Any pressure from an undefeated record and a 24-game winning streak in Manhattan hasn't entered their minds yet.

"They've kind of evolved into a group that is really looking forward to practice on Monday," Self said, "as opposed to a group that is just trying to hang on to something."

—Mark Dent, *University Daily Kansan*

Mitch Albom, an award-winning sports columnist for the *Detroit Free Press,* says good writers need to be good readers. In an interview with The Poynter Institute after he won a distinguished writing award from the American Society of Newspaper Editors, Albom said the following:

> I read voraciously, and I don't read sports things. . . . The way you get better in your own field is by making sure you surround yourself with excellence in other fields. I've never forgotten that, and I've always tried to do that with writing. Watching good movies, reading great novels, seeing great plays all help you become a better sports writer. You just have to be open to absorb it.

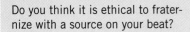

What Do You Think

Do you think it is ethical to fraternize with a source on your beat?

- ☐ Yes
- ☐ No
- ☐ Maybe - explain

Exercises

1 Choose a specialty subject of your choice—health, education, religion, sports, environment—and write a feature about a topic or program in this category.

2 Interview a beat reporter in the field that interests you. Write a story about the skills, tips, and reporting and writing techniques this reporter uses and recommends to other reporters in the field. Include specifics about problems the reporter faces on the job.

3 Choose a field of interest, and write a list of sources and government records available in this field on the Internet.

4 List the beats covered by your campus newspaper, and then list at least five beats that aren't covered but might be of interest to readers. Write a story from one of those beats.

5 Attend an athletic event at your college or university, and write a sports story.

☞ **Featured Online Activity** Log on to the book Web site for Chapter 19 and do the exercises to find story ideas for different beats at

academic.cengage.com/masscomm/rich/writingandreportingnews6e

Coaching Tips

Do your homework. Check clips and online sources for background about the speaker or issue at a conference or meeting.

Listen for what the speaker doesn't discuss. Then ask questions to find the answers that the readers or viewers will want.

Include comments from speakers at meetings and responses to questions at speeches.

Try to get as many good quotes and sound bites as possible. Favor full quotes over partial ones.

Write a highlights box—to accompany your story or to organize your story.

Get the full text of speeches and documents from meetings to post on Web sites.

Record audio for sound bites to post on the Web.

We need a press that's dedicated to the watchdog role. We don't need a pipe organ for government and politicians.

Mike Peters, cartoonist, Tribune Media Services

20 Speeches, News Conferences and Meetings

Mark Fagan calls himself a "converged reporter." Although he is primarily a print reporter for the *Lawrence Journal-World* in Kansas, when the newspaper's editors asked print reporters to appear on its cable TV station as well, Fagan took to it naturally. He says if you are a print or broadcast reporter, you are still applying the reporting and writing skills you already have. You're just learning a new way to use them. In the *Journal-World* newsroom, reporters from the partner TV station, 6 News, and the print newspaper work side by side. A multimedia desk in the center of an open atrium in the newsroom is the headquarters for coordinating stories for the newspaper, TV and Web sites.

When Fagan covers city government, he gets most of his news stories at meetings. But he gets most of his best quotes when the meetings end. Fagan, who has covered both government and business beats, says the most important part of a meeting story is what you cover before and after it.

One night the city commission was debating a zoning change. A business owner wanted to expand his electrical shop in a residential neighborhood. Commissioner Jo Andersen was angry. More business would bring traffic and crime to the neighborhood, she said.

Fagan headed straight for Andersen after the meeting. "Why were you so upset?" he asked.

"What I really wanted to say was that even if Jesus Christ himself wanted to expand his carpenter's shop in East Lawrence, we would respectfully request that he find another area that is more appropriate," she said.

"You can still say that," Fagan said. This is the beginning of the story he wrote the next day:

Not even divine intervention could help a proposal to expand an East Lawrence electric shop onto vacant lots next door.

During their meeting Tuesday night, Lawrence city commissioners denied a request from Patchen Electric & Industrial Supply Inc. to expand its 47-year-old business at 602 E. Ninth onto two lots zoned for apartments.

In the end, the request never had a prayer.

"If Jesus Christ himself wanted to expand his carpenter's shop in East

Lawrence, we would respectfully request that he find another area that is more appropriate," Commissioner Jo Andersen said after the meeting. "It has nothing to do with a person's personality. It has everything to do with zoning."

—Mark Fagan, *Lawrence* (Kan.) *Journal-World*

The story continued with explanations of how zoning had changed from commercial to residential use since the business was built and why residents objected to its expansion.

"The comments officials make during a meeting are for public posturing," Fagan says. "Some of the best quotes you get are after the meeting when you ask them to explain why they did or said something."

That advice also applies to someone from the public who speaks at a meeting. "A person may speak for 30 seconds and afterward she'll tell you, 'My kid needs a safe place to walk because he was attacked two years ago,'" Fagan says. "Don't just sit in the meeting if the person leaves; follow him or her out and get those additional comments."

What you write before the meeting is even more important, Fagan says. He writes at least one story to tell readers what officials will discuss at their next meeting. If people don't know what officials plan to do, they won't get a chance to participate in government.

Although many newspapers and TV news programs are curtailing meeting coverage because the news is sometimes dull, Fagan thinks that's a mistake. Meetings are where officials make decisions that affect the public.

Fagan goes to at least three meetings a week: the commission's public meeting; its study meetings, where officials decide what they will discuss at public meetings; and neighborhood group meetings to learn what people are really concerned about.

Courtesy of Mark Fagan

Mark Fagan (right) interviewing City Commissioner John Nalbandian

"I'll write stories sometimes and no one (from the public) will show up at a meeting, and I wonder if what I do makes a difference. Then a city commissioner will say, 'I got about 20 phone calls after your article.' So I know people are reading them."

Even if people don't read his stories or attend the meetings, Fagan thinks it's important for reporters to be there as watchdogs for the public. He says the officials know he is really there for 20,000 other people: his readers.

"I put the commissioners' comments in the paper, and everyone knows where they stand," Fagan says. "That's a great power of the press."

Whenever you are covering a meeting, it's important to look beyond what officials say publicly. Fagan says reporters should ask questions before and after the public event to find out how the story affects readers.

"An item on a meeting agenda may say they are going to award bids for highway improvements on North Second Street," he says. "I look at that and say, 'What does that mean?' Are they going to widen the street? This is the only artery that connects downtown and an old neighborhood. Are they going to close the road to traffic for eight months? This is how officials plan to spend taxpayers' money. You need to find out how it affects readers."

Fagan has also covered plenty of speeches and news conferences on his beat, especially when he is writing about elections. Many of the reporting and writing principles for those events are the same as they are for meetings. Don't just write what the officials say; find out why they are making certain comments or decisions and what the impact will be for readers.

Media Manipulation

Sources who give speeches or conduct news conferences are often using the media to further their own causes. There's nothing wrong with that. It's a way of presenting news. But a responsible reporter should ask good questions after the speech or news conference and add points of view from opposing sources when possible.

For example, Operation Rescue, an anti-abortion group, waged massive demonstrations to close an abortion clinic in Wichita, Kan. The sources from that group had a definite agenda; they were clearly trying to manipulate the press, says Steven A. Smith, former managing editor of *The Wichita* (Kan.) *Eagle*. One of the leaders of Operation Rescue conducted a news conference during which he held up a fully developed fetus, which supposedly had been aborted at about seven or eight months. Smith says the situation posed a difficult ethical dilemma for the *Eagle* staff. The leader's actions were news. But there was no evidence that the fetus had been aborted at the Wichita clinic. The result: The *Eagle* published news about the protest and the leader's actions, including the statement that there was no proof the fetus came from the Wichita clinic. But the paper did not publish a picture of the fetus. Smith says he was convinced the situation was staged to manipulate the press. Television stations also refused to show the fetus.

Protesters on both sides of the abortion issue came from around the nation to converge on Wichita, and 2,600 of them were arrested for violating city laws and defying court orders prohibiting them from blocking the abortion clinic. Both sides sought to manipulate the press.

Smith says the newspaper tried so hard to give balanced coverage that some of the editors actually measured the number of inches of type given to the pro-choice and anti-abortion sources to make sure that they had equal treatment.

The problems of manipulation were even greater for the three local television stations. Operation Rescue leaders staged their news conferences shortly before the 5 p.m. newscasts in hopes of receiving live coverage from television. News directors,

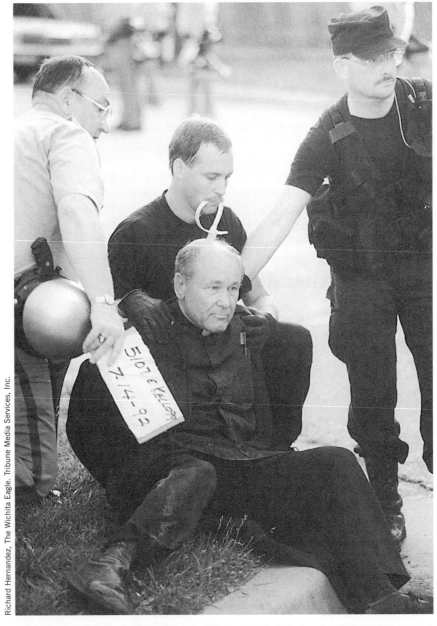

Richard Hernandez, The Wichita Eagle. Tribune Media Services, Inc.

A Roman Catholic priest, leader of the pro-life group called the Lambs of Christ, being arrested after attempting to block the entrance to the Women's Health Care Center in Wichita, Kan.

ETHICS

The case: Your beat is city government for a converged news organization, which sends you to write a story about a city council meeting for both print and broadcast. The city is going to approve an agreement with a city in Japan to become its "sister city," which will open some trade agreements and business opportunities for your city with Japan. The mayor is planning to visit the Japanese city; his trip will be funded by your city. He is planning to take his secretary, whose trip will also be covered by city funds. Rumors have circulated for some time that the mayor, who is married, is having an affair with

his secretary. He has denied that the rumors are true, but you are convinced they are.

- Will you print these rumors in your story about the mayor's trip? How will you write the story?
- Would you use the story for a print publication but not for broadcast?
- Would you post the story on the Web or in a blog?
- Does the type of media (print, broadcast, Web or blog) make a difference in your decision to publish the story?

Ethical guidelines: The Society of Professional Journalists Code of Ethics offers these guidelines:

- Seek the truth and report it. Journalists should be honest, fair and courageous in gathering, reporting and interpreting information.
- Test the accuracy of information from all sources and exercise care to avoid inadvertent error. Deliberate distortion is never permissible.
- Show good taste. Avoid pandering to lurid curiosity.

concerned about issues of accuracy and fairness, limited the live coverage. They edited the tape to be shown at the end of the 5 p.m. newscasts or only on the 10 p.m. programs so that they could have more control and present balanced viewpoints.

Preparation

Most speeches, news conferences and meetings do not pose such severe problems. Still, reporters always need to do more than listen and repeat what they hear. As Mark Fagan suggests, reporters need to ask good questions after the event as well.

To ask good questions, however, you must prepare for the event. You need to find out all you can about the speaker and the issue. Be sure to check the clips and online databases.

With a prominent speaker, you can often get the text of the speech in advance. But be careful not to rely on it. The speaker may depart from the prepared text. However, you can still use the prepared text. Just say, "The speaker said in prepared remarks" or "in a written text." Reporters sometimes have to rely on the written version, especially if their deadlines come before the speech or news conference is over.

During the speech, try to get full quotes of the important points (especially if they vary from the written text), and jot down reactions of the speaker and the audience. Note when and if the speaker shows emotion and how the audience responds. Write follow-up questions to ask the speaker after the speech or news conference.

Try to get an aisle seat. If someone asks a good question after the speech or meeting and then leaves, you should follow that person out of the room quickly so you can check the name and get more information.

Stories About Speeches

Your story should always include some basic information:

- Size of the audience
- Location of the speech
- Reason for the speech
- Highlights of the speech, including good quotes
- Reaction of the audience, especially at dramatic points during the speech

Although you need to include this basic information, don't clutter the top of your story with it—unless it is crucial to the event. Write the story just as you would any other good story.

You can lead with a hard-news approach that emphasizes a main point the speaker made or a soft-news approach that describes the person or uses an anecdote from the speech. Just don't lead with a no-news approach: Someone made a speech. Tell the reader what the speaker said.

For example, here is the kind of lead to avoid; this one appeared on a story in a campus newspaper:

> Students from Gay and Lesbian Services spoke yesterday to a psychology class about their lives and experiences.

What did they say? It's better to focus on some interesting point they made.

Speakers usually don't make their strongest points first and follow in chronological order, so your story shouldn't be written in that order. Put the most emotional or newsworthy information first. Then back it up with quotes and supporting points.

Sometimes the most interesting information isn't what happens during the speech. It can be what happens after the speech or outside the place while the person is speaking, especially if there is a protest or other major reaction to the speech.

You can also use storytelling techniques for speeches. In the next example, a journalism student used narrative and descriptive writing to convey the drama of a speech by a survivor of the Holocaust. Notice where the writer put the basic information: when, where and how many people attended the speech.

> Zev Kedem huddled in silence with his grandparents in a pigeon coop above his family's apartment while soldiers searched for them. His grandparents were prepared to swallow vials of poison as the soldiers tried the metal door they hid behind.
>
> The door held. And the soldiers went on.
>
> The year was 1942, and so begins Zev Kedem's story of survival that began over 50 years ago as Adolf Hitler orchestrated the Holocaust.
>
> A "Schindler's List" survivor, Kedem spoke for over an hour as he told the story of his childhood in a Nazi concentration camp to 750 people in the Union Ballroom last night.
>
> —Gail Johnson

Here is a basic speech story that starts with a summary lead followed by a backup quote in the third paragraph. Note that the basics of location, audience size and reaction are lower in the story.

Reporter notes lower standards in journalism

Half of the reporting duo that unearthed the Watergate scandal, which led to the downfall of President Nixon, railed Saturday against what he characterized as another downfall: the media's fascination with the "loopy and lurid."

Former *Washington Post* reporter Carl Bernstein took aim at trash television, inaccurate reporting and media monopolies, primarily that of mogul Rupert Murdoch. The media are fascinated with celebrity, gossip and manufactured controversy, and pander to viewers and readers, adding to the "triumph of trash culture," he said.

"The greatest threat to the truth today may well be in our own profession," said Bernstein, who spoke for more than an hour at Budig Hall. His speech was sponsored by Kansas University's Student Union Activities.

Although every society has an "idiot subculture bubbling beneath the surface," Bernstein said a constant diet of certain television talk shows—he twice declared Jerry Springer's show to be the worst of the worst—could cause it to boil over.

The problem needs to be addressed at the root level, with reporters refusing to limit their horizons and keep digging for the "best obtainable version of the truth," he said.

"Really great reporting almost always comes from the initiative of the reporter, not the editor," said Bernstein.

—Chris Koger, *Lawrence* (Kan.) *Journal-World*

Convergence Coach

When you cover speeches, meetings and news conferences, plan to provide additional coverage on the Web.

■ Write or broadcast a story advancing coverage of meetings and post highlights or a complete meeting agenda on the Web.

■ Tape the event to post sound bites or the entire speech or news conference on the Web.

■ Get a complete copy in digital form of budgets, proposals, speeches or other documents to post on the Web.

■ Be prepared to post a breaking news story of the event on the Web and plan a more complete follow-up story for the next print or broadcast edition of the news.

■ Focus on the significance of a news conference or meeting; find people who are affected by the news before, during or after a meeting or news conference.

■ Plan a highlights box of the key points in a speech, news conference or meeting for print, broadcast or Web publication.

Stories About News Conferences

News conferences are like speeches, except that the questions reporters ask after a news conference are often more important than the prepared comments the speaker makes. The answers to those questions are an important part of the story—and sometimes are the story. Consider news reports after the U.S. president conducts a news conference. His prepared remarks often are less interesting than his answers to the press corps.

Do your homework. Before or after the news conference, research the issue. If the conference is about a local crime, check files or background to provide perspective. How many other crimes of this nature have occurred? If the conference is about a city issue, how does the information affect your readers and viewers? Don't just recite the news; interpret it so that your audience can understand how the issues affect them.

Stories about news conferences must include the following information:

- Person or people who conducted the news conference
- Reason for the news conference and background
- Highlights of the news, including responses to questions
- Location, if relevant
- Reaction from sources with similar and opposing points of view

Stories about news conferences are like most other news stories. Although reporters' questions may prompt the most interesting information, the answers are usually

Bill Snead/The Washington Post

A White House news conference

incorporated into the story without references such as "In response to a question" or "When asked about. . . ." The main elements for coverage of a news conference are included in this story:

CINCINNATI—The mayor declared a state of emergency and announced a citywide curfew as riots over the police shooting of an unarmed black man stretched into a fourth day today.

Only people going to and from work will be allowed on the streets between 8 p.m. and 6 a.m., Mayor Charles Luken said.

"Despite the best efforts of the good citizens of our city, the violence on our streets is uncontrolled and it runs rampant," Luken said at a news conference at City Hall.

"The time has come to deal with this seriously. The message . . . is that the violence must stop."

Officials in the city of 331,000 have considered asking the state to call out the Ohio National Guard, but no decision had been made, Luken said.

The fatal shooting over the weekend of Timothy Thomas, 19, by a white officer sparked days of unrest, a federal investigation, and calls for accountability. Thomas was killed as he fled Officer Steven Roach, who was trying to arrest him for failing to appear for misdemeanor charges and traffic violations. Roach's union said he feared for his life during the encounter.

Tensions between blacks and police have heightened over the past few years. Since 1995, 15 black men died at the hands of police, including four since November. . . .

Small groups of vandals roamed several neighborhoods Wednesday night and early today, breaking windows, looting stores and assaulting at least one white motorist who was dragged from her car, police said. Others in the neighborhood came to the woman's aid. . . .

At least 66 people have been arrested on such charges as disorderly conduct, criminal rioting, obstruction, felony assault, theft and breaking and entering since the violence began Monday. . . .

A man interrupted Luken at the news conference to ask whether the mayor was ready to meet with a group calling itself the New Black Panthers. He was pulled out of the room after shouting that the mayor was a "liar." "That's the kind of incivility we've been dealing with," Luken said.

—Liz Sidoti, *The Associated Press*

Stories About Meetings

The decisions that affect readers' daily lives—such as where they take their trash, get their water and send their children to school—are made by local government officials at meetings. Yet meeting stories are often written without explaining their real impact on the reader.

Countless surveys conducted by news organizations reveal that local news is near or at the top of the list of the kinds of stories readers want. They just don't read them all the way to the end. Sometimes they don't read past the lead, especially when the lead is dull.

The stories don't have to be boring. They may not be as compelling as a story about a murder trial. But they can be written with flair and with an emphasis on the meeting's significance to readers.

All states have open-meeting laws requiring officials who have the authority to spend public funds to conduct their business in public. These boards may conduct executive sessions behind closed doors for certain discussions, such as personnel matters or collective bargaining, but all decisions must be made in a public meeting. Although open-meeting laws vary from state to state, most of them require public agencies to give advance notice—usually 48 hours—of their meetings and to conduct public hearings.

Understanding the System

When a board makes a decision at a meeting, you need to understand what kind of authority that board has. Suppose you are covering a zoning board meeting. The board is discussing a zoning application from a developer for a major shopping center. If the board approves a zoning change, is that the final decision? Probably not. Most zoning boards are advisory and must submit their recommendations to a city or county board of officials for final approval. That is essential information to include in your story.

If you are covering meetings of your university administration, find out who can make the decisions and which boards are advisory. Who can raise the tuition—school officials or a board of regents? Is the action taken at a meeting a recommendation or a ruling? You need to explain the system as well as the next step in an action.

Writing the Advance

Many times, knowing what is going to happen at a meeting is more important to readers than knowing what did happen. A story that tells readers what is being proposed can alert residents to make their concerns known before a measure is adopted by local officials. A pre-meeting story is called an "advance."

An advance is especially crucial if local officials are planning to conduct a public hearing about an issue. If the public doesn't know about it, how can the public be heard?

City and school boards usually publish an agenda in advance of their meetings. This agenda lists the items to be discussed, although new items can and usually are presented.

When you receive an agenda, look through it for items that might be of special interest to readers. Call board members and ask for comments, or ask them to pick out the items they expect to be most interesting or controversial. If the issue has previously been in the news, check clips and call other interested parties.

The point of your advance is to inform readers about items that they may want to discuss during the public comment part of a meeting or just to let readers know what their officials are proposing. If you are writing an advance for a public hearing, make sure that you give the time and location of the hearing.

Here is an example of an advance with an impact lead:

For the first time in its 107-year history, Temple University may require all undergraduates to take a course related to race and racism.

The proposal, which grew out of black students' demonstrations at Temple, is to be debated by the school's faculty senate on Friday.

Among the faculty, however, the proposal has already sparked intense discussion. The debate mirrors that of other campuses—including Stanford, Wisconsin, Michigan and Berkeley—where courses related to race are required.

—Huntly Collins, *The Philadelphia Inquirer*

The following excerpt from an advance includes the time and location of the meeting:

The stage is set for changing the city's human relations ordinance to include protections for homosexuals.

Lawrence city commissioners agreed to set ground rules for public comment on a proposal to add the words "sexual orientation" to the city's anti-discrimination ordinance.

The ground rules—such as how long people will be allowed to speak—will be determined during next week's meeting, which begins at 6:35 p.m. Tuesday at City Hall, Sixth and Massachusetts streets. A draft form of the ordinance is planned for a vote one week later on April 25.

—Mark Fagan, *Lawrence* (Kan.) *Journal-World*

Covering the Meeting

Arrive early. Find out the names of board members (usually they have nameplates), and find out who is in charge.

Ask board members, especially the head of the board, if you could talk to them after the meeting. If you know people in the audience who are leaders of a group favoring or opposing a controversial issue, greet them and tell them you would like to get comments after the meeting.

Check items on the agenda, and get any background that you need.

Check the consent agenda, a list of items on the agenda that the board will approve without discussion. They may include bids for approval or other points the board may have discussed in work sessions. A "gem" of a story may be buried in the consent agenda.

One reporter wondered why the school board had approved $30,000 in "token losses." That's a lot of money to be considered "token" losses. She discovered that it represented losses of bus tokens that the school board sold to students who had to ride public buses because there were no school buses in the city. Why $30,000 in losses? The school district had no system of monitoring the sales, and the money had been stolen at several schools. By school officials! The board didn't want to discuss this item publicly, so it was buried in the consent agenda. But the reporter wanted to discuss it. In a front-page story.

Don't remain glued to a seat at a press table. When members of the audience give public comments, get their names and more comments. Many times they will leave immediately after their testimony. Follow them out of the meeting. You can catch up with the action inside later. Or sit in the audience. Sometimes the comments of people attending the meeting are more interesting than the ones the board members make.

Stay until the end, unless your deadline prohibits staying. The most important issue could emerge at the end of a meeting when the board asks for new business or public comments. Or something dramatic could happen. The mayor could resign. Violence could erupt. You never can tell, especially if you're not there.

Writing the Story

First, how not to write it: Do not say the city council met and discussed something. Tell what they discussed or enacted. This is the kind of lead to avoid:

> The 41st Annual Environmental Engineering Conference met yesterday at the Kansas Union to discuss solutions to environmental problems.
>
> Representatives of the Kansas Department of Health and Environment, the Environmental Protection Agency and other organizations spoke to about 180 people who attended the conference.

So what did they say? This lead reveals nothing.

Some meetings are long. They can be boring. Avoid telling the reader how much you suffered listening to board members drone on and accomplish nothing in a long meeting. The reader doesn't care how much you suffer. The reader wants the news. If the length of the debate is crucial to the story, you should include it. But if the meetings are usually long and the time element is not a major factor related to the focus, don't mention it.

Here are some points to include in your story:

Type of Meeting and Location: Give this information, but if the city council or school board meets all the time in the same building, don't mention the location.

The Vote on Any Major Issue: For instance, say "in a 4-1 vote. . . ." If the issue is particularly controversial, say who voted against it—or for it, if an affirmative vote was more controversial. If the measure was approved unanimously, say so. However, don't give the vote for every minor item.

The Next Step: If a major issue or ordinance cannot be adopted until a public hearing is conducted, tell readers when a hearing is scheduled or what the next step is before the action is final.

Impact on Readers: Explain how the decision will affect them.

Quotes: Use only quotes that are dramatic, interesting or crucial to the story.

Background of the Issues: What do readers need to know to understand what has happened?

To write the story, select one key issue for the focus. If the board approved several other measures, add them at the end: "In other business." If several important actions occurred, consider breaking another key issue into a separate story, if possible. If not, try a lead mentioning both items, or put the second key point in the second paragraph and give supporting background later, after you have developed the first point—for example, "City commissioners yesterday approved plans for the city's first shopping mall but rejected plans for a new public golf course." Then proceed with the discussion about the shopping mall.

Consider advancing the story with a second-day lead, also known as an updated lead. This kind of advance tells readers what the next step is or how the story will affect them. In most newspapers, this type of lead is becoming more popular because it makes the news more timely. However, it is optional, and a first-day lead may be acceptable. For broadcast, however, an updated lead is crucial. Viewers don't want to know what happened yesterday or last night; they want to know what is happening now. If your story will appear first on the Web, you also have to consider updating the lead for a print publication that will be published the next morning.

Although many meeting stories are written with summary leads, especially if the news is significant, they do not have to follow that form. If you think a softer lead is appropriate for the type of news that occurred, you can use it. Try an impact lead that emphasizes how readers and viewers are affected by the action or lack of action that occurred at a meeting.

Here are a few matters of style for meeting coverage:

- *Board* is a collective noun and therefore takes a singular verb: The board discussed the issue at *its* meeting, not *their* meeting. If this approach seems awkward in your story, say that the board *members* said *their* next meeting would be Tuesday.

- Capitalize *city council, city commission* and *school board* when they are part of a proper name—such as the Rockville City Commission—and when the reference is to a specific commission in your town—the City Commission. If you are not referring to a specific city commission but just saying most municipalities have city commissions, use lowercase letters.

- Capitalize the titles of board members or other officials when they come before the name, as in *Mayor John Corrupt.* If the title follows the name—*John Corrupt, the mayor*—use lowercase letters.

- For votes, use *3-1*, not *3 to 1*.

Stories about meetings can take a hard, soft or advance-impact approach. Whichever one you use, make the story relevant to readers. Here's how:

What Do You Think

What are the main problems with stories about local government meetings?

- Lack of impact
- Boring leads
- Lack of interesting information
- Other—specify

Summary lead: what happened

LAGUNA BEACH, Calif.—Despite neighbors' objections, a North Laguna Beach couple were given permission Tuesday to adorn their home with a 17-foot-high outdoor sculpture of 30 water heaters and two house trailers.

Vote

The City Council, after viewing a scale model of the artwork, voted 3-1 to endorse the sculpture. It will climb around a pine tree in the back courtyard of Arnold and Marie Forde's home.

Dissenting vote   Mayor Neil Fitzpatrick dissented, saying the sculpture infringed on neighbors' views. Councilwoman Martha Collison was absent.

Reaction   "It's a victory for the freedom of expression," said Los Angeles artist Nancy Rubins, who will craft the sculpture. "It would have been a sad day if a community that sees itself as supporting the arts struck down an artwork in a private yard."

Impact: so what   The sculpture had been the focus of an intense neighborhood battle.

Residents who live near the Fordes have called the sculpture junk and complained that the artwork would block their view and spoil the neighborhood character.

More reaction   David DeLo, who lives across Cliff Drive from the Fordes, said he was considering challenging the council's action in court.

Next step   "If the council wants to place a piece of junk in a residential neighborhood, that's their prerogative, but this council has been overturned before," he said.

Backup: conditions of council action   To appease neighbors, the council approved the sculpture on the condition that the Fordes place it as low as possible in the yard and landscape the area with another tree and a hedge. The additional plants should hide the sculpture from neighbors, officials said.

Future kicker   The $5,000 sculpture will take a week to build. Rubins said she did not know when it will be finished.

—Harrison Fletcher,
The Orange County (Calif.) *Register*

Exercises

1 Speech story: If possible, cover a speech on campus or in the community. If not, you can write a story based on a speech about political correctness by Burl Osborne, former editor of *The Dallas Morning News,* posted on the Web site for this chapter, *academic.cengage.com/masscomm/rich/writingandreportingnews6e*.

2 Online speeches: You'll find many speeches online in text and audio form. If your computer has audio capacity, listen to one of the speeches and write a story. Links to these resources are available on the Web site for this chapter. If you have never read the spoof graduation speech by Kurt Vonnegut, access it online for this chapter and write a story based on it.

☛ **Featured Online Activity** Log on to the book Web site for Chapter 20 and write a speech story and a story about a news conference by linking to the suggested sites at

academic.cengage.com/masscomm/rich/writingandreportingnews6e

Coaching Tips

Write an impact, "so what" sentence on top of your story.

Try impact leads; your impact sentence could be a lead.

The more complex the information, the simpler your sentences should be.

Avoid jargon.

Write for your readers, not your sources.

Use quotes that advance the story, not the egos of the bureaucrats.

Use analogies to help readers understand numbers.

Think about graphics before you write your story. Use charts for numbers.

Gather digital copies of budgets and government proposals to post on the Web.

There are no boring government stories, but there are a lot of boring reporters and editors.

James Steele, investigative reporter

Government and Statistical Stories

Jennifer LaFleur wasn't looking for a date, but she wanted to find the best places to meet single people. Using a census database, she found the information she needed—and something she didn't want. "I threw out the data for prisons," she said. "They had a high level of single men, but not men I'd want to date." Combining the statistics with some old-fashioned reporting, she discovered that the best place to meet single men was in grocery stores.

"After I did the story, an 85-year-old woman called me and said, 'I loved your story, honey, but could you do it by age?'" LaFleur said.

LaFleur, computer-assisted reporting editor for *The Dallas Morning News*, creates fascinating stories with computer-assisted reporting. She also trains journalists throughout the country how to use databases and the Internet. She reels off stories reported from databases—for example, what color cars get the most tickets, how

Jennifer LaFleur, computer-assisted reporting editor

many dead people voted in an election, what names are most popular for the dogs in a community. And more serious stories about bus drivers with drunken-driving records, campaign finance records and foster parents with criminal records. Recently she even investigated Santa Claus by using public records.

Who's been naughty and will likely end up with a stocking full of coal?

It might just be Santa Claus or Kris Kringle.

Public records show that nationally, someone named Santa Claus has been convicted at least a dozen times during the past decade.

Mr. Claus' indiscretions include a 1996 arrest for driving while intoxicated in Jefferson County, Texas.

And Mr. Kringle has a lengthy criminal record in Oregon.

Even the Christmas crew appears to have had some troubles: Rudolph Reindeer violated a restraining order in 2004.

But don't plug the chimney and forgo the cookies and milk just yet.

Skilled backgrounders know that you can't just put someone on the naughty list based on a name. Many people have the same name, but other information would distinguish them—such as their date of birth or home address.

Unless Santa has a summer home in Beaumont, it's unlikely the Texas drunken driver with the same name is the Santa Claus. None had an address at the actual North Pole, according to public records. But several residents of North Pole, Alaska, have criminal records.

And yes, in Virginia there is a Santa Claus. In fact, there are at least four—two of whom are women. But no public records showed criminal records for those Clauses.

—Jennifer LaFleur, *The Dallas Morning News*

"I'm convinced there's not a beat that you can't use database reporting for," she said. "The biggest shortage in journalism is people with computer-assisted reporting skills."

The term *computer-assisted reporting* often refers to the use of databases, but it also refers to use of the Internet to find sources, documents and information about millions of topics. You also can download many government databases directly into your computer and analyze them in a spreadsheet program such as Excel or in a relational database program that allows you to find and compare data.

In addition to directing the newspaper's investigative reporting team and other reporters in data analysis LaFleur writes a Citizen Watchdog column in which she offers readers practical information based on public records, such as this article about the dangers of nail salons:

Searching public records might very well keep you from exposing yourself to potential health hazards the next time you pay for a little pampering.

Hundreds of people across the country get more than a pedicure or manicure when they visit a salon. They pick up nasty microbes such as *staphylococcus aureus* and *mycobacterium fortuitum* from unsanitary instruments or foot baths. The bacteria typically enter through a small cut or scratch and can cause serious or even deadly infections.

Dallas County Health and Human Resources officials received 20 reports of skin infections linked to nail salons from February 2004 to January 2006.

—Jennifer LaFleur, *The Dallas Morning News*

Convergence Coach

When you cover government agencies, think in multi-media terms. Don't just plan to write a story or script for a print or broadcast publication: Plan to provide complete versions of proposals and budgets on the Web. Get a digital version of a local government budget, school district test scores, government proposals and important statistics to accompany stories on the Web.

Here are some other tips for using the Web for government statistics and information:

- Check the date the information was posted; many reports may not be current. Contact the agency by phone or e-mail to find out if more current information is available.
- Check your city, school district and state sites for background information on government stories.
- Check if advocacy agencies and other groups in your community have Web sites. Use these sites for sources in reaction stories and human interest.

Every year, more government data are being posted to the Web. But much of the state or local information you might want is still not available on the Internet. You have to ask officials for it, and they may be reluctant to give it to you. Even if you have a legal right to the data, use the Freedom of Information Act as a last resort because responses to FOIA requests can be time-consuming.

LaFleur says reporters should try to find the person in a government agency who knows about computers and data. "It's usually a guy named Leon who works in the basement," she says. "I go to whatever agency I'm covering to find out how they do what they do. I also try to be overly cheery. I never first go in and demand a computer file."

Government databases may be available only in printout form. Ask if you can obtain the data on a disk. If not, find out the copying costs before you commit to getting the files. They could be expensive. Whether you get the data on a disk or on paper, you should check all the information carefully, especially if some of the statistics seem unusual. Data are often "dirty," meaning that they contain many mistakes.

After you get and analyze your data, don't flood your story with statistics. LaFleur bristles when people say computer-assisted stories are about numbers. They may contain only a paragraph or two of numbers, which could make the difference in the focus, but the stories still require good reporting and writing techniques.

Reporting Tips

Many stories about government often involve money and statistics. If you don't help readers and viewers understand how the information affects them, chances are that they won't read or watch the information you are trying to convey. Although much government news may come from news releases and meetings, you should also try to find stories that reveal how the government operates or fails to operate in the interests of citizens. Don't just rely on officials to give you news; find it yourself.

Here are some tips for covering local government:

Human Interest: Make government relevant to readers by finding people who are affected by the actions of government agencies.

Bulletin Boards: Check them for job offerings and other announcements that could result in stories.

Memos and Letters to and From City Officials: Check with the city clerk or administrative assistants for access to files about any issue involving public funds. Most of these—except for personnel and labor matters—are public records.

Planning Commission: Check agendas for meetings, and develop sources in planning offices. Seek information not only about future plans but also about the past. Some great stories can result from plans gone awry.

Consultants: Check who gets consulting contracts and fees, and investigate previous studies on the same subject. Sometimes, government agencies hire consultants to write studies on subjects that have already been studied frequently.

Zoning Meetings: They can be full of human interest. People care about what is going up or down in their neighborhood.

Legal Notices: Check them for bids and other notices. Government agencies must advertise for any major purchases. Check with disgruntled bidders for major contracts. Many good stories lurk behind these seemingly boring subjects.

Audits: Read them carefully. They can reveal misuse of public funds.

Union Leaders: Cultivate heads of unions in school districts and cities as sources. They know what is going on behind the scenes.

Nonofficials: Talk to the people who do the work. Get into the schools and write about what teachers and students are doing or talk to people working in government offices. Spend some time learning about what they do, how they do it and whether they do it. Many good stories can result from finding out how lower-level employees work in government.

The System: Learn how it works. Are officials in your town following the laws? If you don't know how government is supposed to operate, you won't be able to find out if it is working properly.

Records: Check expense accounts, purchasing vouchers and other records pertaining to issues or officials you are covering.

Offices: Check all the offices in your government building, and find out what kind of work the people in them do. For example, do you know the function of every office in your campus administration building? You could find features or great news stories just by checking what the people in these offices do.

The Internet: Many communities, local police departments and school districts have Web pages offering a wealth of information and documents. You can find sources, news releases and even databases on their sites. In addition, Web sites for state and federal government agencies abound.

Visuals

Before you write your story, think not about what you can put in it; think about what you can pull out of it, especially when you are writing stories with statistics. Use highlights boxes, facts boxes and charts to break out key concepts of a proposal or budget. Then you don't need to clutter the story with the same information.

Consider empowerment boxes, information that tells readers what the story means to them and what they can do. These boxes should contain information about where they can call for help, more information or other facts that would be useful. Once you have decided what can be displayed visually, you can present the remaining information verbally.

Here's an empowerment box from the *Reno* (Nev.) *Gazette-Journal* that accompanied a story about overdue parking tickets. The city adopted late fees that would add $30 to tickets not paid within a month.

To pay
- Pay at the city clerk's cashier office, using cash, check or Visa or Mastercard.

To protest
- Make an appointment. The hearing officer is setting aside time in Room 204 at City Hall. Call 334-2293.
- Hearing times are from 5-8 p.m. on Nov. 4 and Nov. 6; 1-4 p.m. on Nov. 8; 5-8 p.m. on Nov. 13 and Nov. 14.

ETHICS

The case: You are the news producer for a small television station in an agricultural community where dairy cattle are raised. You receive a video news release from the U.S. Department of Agriculture about a new program that will identify animals as they move from one location to another to track the point of origin of any animals that have diseases. The video is of excellent quality and features cattle in the background and two ranchers talking about the program. You don't have the staff or time to produce your own video on the subject, and the one you have seems perfect. After all, it's a news release, so you are entitled to use it without any copyright violation. Will you use the video news release? Will you identify the source as the USDA?

Guidelines: The Radio-Television News Directors Association says this in its code of ethics: "Clearly disclose the origin of information and label all material provided by outsiders." However, a *New York Times* investigative story revealed that many television stations are using video news releases from the government without identifying them as government sponsored. The problem has become such a concern that the Boston University Department of Journalism adopted a resolution condemning the practice. It states in part: "We find particularly objectionable the use of 'phony reporters' hired by one agency or another who deliver complete reports, including sign-offs, without ever mentioning their affiliation and, in some cases, misrepresenting it. We also condemn those stations that knowingly run news segments, written, shot and recorded by the government with no identification as to the source of the material. We regard these practices as unethical journalism that run the high risk of confusing or even deceiving the public."

Writing Tips

Presuming you have found good stories, how can you make them readable?

One way is to avoid "jargon," stilted or technical words and phrases that officials use but readers don't. Writing coaches call this artificial language "journalese," long words or phrases instead of short ones that would be clearer. Examples: *medication* for *medicine, restructuring* for *changing, funds* for *money*. When you need a loan from a friend, do you ask to borrow "funds"?

"Reading journalese is like having a series of small strokes," says Jack Cappon, writing coach for The Associated Press. "Unless you start writing the way your neighbors talk, you're not going to go anywhere."

Clichés are another common form of journalese in government stories. Journalists love to use words related to heat and cold: *heated debate, hotly contested, blasted, chilling effect, cooling-off period*. In this example, the reporter strained the lead by picking a holiday that had nothing to do with the story just so she could use these "heated" terms:

> The Fourth of July is four months away, but insults and accusations exploded like fireworks at the tumultuous Board of Supervisors meeting yesterday.
>
> The firecracker was Republican Supervisor John Hanson, who blasted his colleagues by calling them "crooks."

Here are some other tips:

Use Short, Simple Sentences: The more complex the information, the simpler and shorter the sentences should be:

Complex	*Simpler*
The City Commission last night approved a resolution to authorize the city staff to apply for funding through the systems enhancement program of the state Department of Transportation for a $3.6 million project for the expansion of U.S. Highway 77 from two to four lanes for 2.2 miles between Interstate 70 and Kansas Highway 18.	The City Commission last night agreed to apply for $3.6 million from the state Department of Transportation to expand a portion of U.S. Highway 77 from two to four lanes. The project would widen the highway for 2.2 miles between Interstate 70 and Kansas Highway 18.

Keep the Subject and Verb Close Together: Long clauses and phrases before the verb make it hard for the reader to remember what the subject is—who said or did what. Use subject–verb–object order.

Complex Rather than having government inspectors sweep through businesses, finding violations and imposing fines, in Maine, officials at the federal Occupational Safety and Health Administration, in an effort to improve work conditions and save the government money, are urging employers to identify health and safety problems and then to work with the agency to correct them.

A federal agency is urging employers in Maine to find and correct health and safety problems in their businesses instead of having government inspectors seek violations and impose fines. The move is an attempt by the federal Occupational Safety and Health Administration to improve work conditions in businesses and save the government money. *Simpler*

Use Vigorous Verbs: Whenever possible, replace *to be* verbs and other bland verbs with words that help to paint a picture of the activity you are reporting.

A 42-year-old St. Joseph man <u>escaped</u> a blazing house without serious injuries when he <u>grabbed</u> a coffee table, <u>hurled</u> it through a picture window, and then, like a movie stunt man, <u>leaped</u> through the jagged glass to escape the heat and flames.

—Terry Raffensperger,
St. Joseph (Mo.) *News-Press*

Avoid Starting Sentences with There: The word *there* forces you to use a weak *to be* verb, such as *is, are, was* or *were*.

Weak There was sadness expressed among local people gathered Thursday night to watch their team lose by two points in the NCAA finals.

Local people expressed sadness as they gathered Thursday night to watch their team lose by two points in the NCAA final. *Strong*

Interpret Information: Tell readers how they are affected.

Based on the 2008 estimate, the value of real estate in the county jumped roughly $83 million in one year—an increase of about 27 percent.

In comparison between 2006 and 2007, the value inched up 2.4 percent.

What does all that mean to the average homeowner? Most likely a lower tax rate—called a mill levy—and perhaps a lower tax bill for some, Douglas County Administrator Craig Weinaug said.

Translate Jargon: Explain terms in concepts or comparisons that the reader can understand.

A spot inventory of Jeanne Johns' freezer shows the usual stuff. Ice cream. Frozen peas. TV dinners.

Acid rain.

Acid rain? You bet.

Johns, who lives in Haslett, is one of four Michigan volunteers in the Citizen Acid Rain Monitoring Network. The network has more than 300 stations nationwide to monitor acid rain. . . .

She measures the acidity on a pH scale ranging from 0 to 14, with 0 being the most acidic. The scale increases tenfold, meaning a 4.0 reading is 10 times more acidic than 5.0.

Normal precipitation is usually about 5.6. A pH of 5.0 is equal to the acid content in cola. Frogs die if placed in water with a pH of 4.0. Battery acid is 1.5.

—Kevin O'Hanlon,
Lansing (Mich.) *State-Journal*

Vary the Pace: Avoid writing huge blocks of complicated concepts and complex sentences. Follow long sentences and long paragraphs with a short sentence as in this example:

MAT-SU—When Mat-Su school board members voted to cut three sports and millions of dollars in jobs and services earlier this spring, they said they hoped they would be able to restore some of those cuts once the borough and state budgets were finalized.

Their wish has come true.

Between the Mat-Su Borough and the state, local schools will get around $3 million more next year than district officials originally anticipated.

—*The* (Wasilla, Alaska) *Frontiersman*

Focus on a Person to Explain Impact: The way an issue affects one person makes it clear to many. That's the concept of the *Wall Street Journal* formula, and it can be used effectively in government stories. Lead with an anecdote about a person; then go from the specific to the general. It's the "one of many" technique.

Linda Green paid $42,000 in 1982 for a house on a half-acre lot in Fontana, banking on the equity that would build over the years.

But if Fontana's new general plan is approved, Green is fearful her property may be worth no more than the day she bought it.

The proposed plan would change the zoning on her half-acre so no additional homes could be built on it, making the site less attractive to buyers.

Green is not alone in her fears. She was among several landowners complaining Monday that the revised general plan—a blueprint for Fontana's growth—will put their properties in less profitable zoning areas.

"I bought my land as an investment. If they zone it down, I will lose my money, and I worked hard to put my money into it," Green told the planning commission during the first public hearing on the new 20-year plan.

More than 130 people attended the hearing.

—Tony Saavedra,
The (San Bernardino, Calif.) *Sun*

Use an Impact Lead or Explain Impact in the Story: Tell how the reader will be affected by a bureaucratic action or proposal.

> A $10,000 car would cost $25 more in taxes, a $40 power saw an extra dime and a $4 six-pack of imported beer a penny extra in Rockford if Alderman Ernst Shafer, R-3rd, gets his way.
>
> Shafer wants Rockford to join the push in Springfield for a 0.25 percent increase in the sales tax. Locally the sales tax would rise from 6.25 to 6.5 percent under the proposal.
>
> —Brian Leaf, *Rockford* (Ill.) *Register Star*

Avoid Boring Quotes: You don't have to quote an official to prove you talked to him. If you can express the official's point better in your own words, do so. You could say that park repairs included cutting trees, removing sand, adding soil for a seed bed and repairing a shelter. But one reporter quoted an official instead:

> "The total project involved tree take-downs, removal of some of the sand and replacement with some soil that would actually provide a seed bed," he said. "We also had to make some repairs on a shelter."

Use the Pull-Quote Test: Are your quotes strong enough to be broken out as pull quotes? That's one way of testing whether they are worth using in a story.

Use Conversational Style: Write the story as though you were having a conversation with a friend. Here is how one reporter used the conversational style in the lead of a government story:

> How'd you like an airport for a neighbor? Or maybe a landfill or an incinerator?
>
> Probably about as much as government officials like trying to find a site for these things.
>
> But what if you could negotiate noise insulation for your airport-area home? Or an agreement requiring the incinerator to douse its fires if it didn't burn hot enough to eliminate most pollutants?
>
> Those alternatives were offered Wednesday to a roomful of Twin Cities area public officials frustrated by their protracted and often doomed efforts to make people accept controversial facilities they don't want.
>
> In an area where officials are looking for places for new landfills, a new airport, light-rail transit routes and other public works projects, the Metropolitan Council sponsored yesterday's conference in an effort to see if there's a better way.
>
> There is, they were told by a specialist in how to make the risks of such facilities more acceptable to their neighbors.
>
> —Steve Brandt, (Minneapolis) *Star Tribune*

Use Lists: Use them in the middle or at the end of the story, especially to explain key points of an issue. Lists are particularly helpful in stories with numbers or explanations of proposals.

Avoid the City-Dump Syndrome: Be selective. Use only quotes and facts that you need. Don't dump your notebook into the story.

Use the Blocking Technique: If you have more than three speakers, block the comments from each one, and then do not use the sources again unless you reintroduce them. The reader can't remember all the officials by second reference only.

Read Aloud: If you read all or parts of your story aloud, you will catch the cumbersome phrases.

Statistical Stories

Jennifer LaFleur writes about numbers all the time, but they rarely appear in the leads to her stories. She knows how to relate to readers and make sense of statistics. Here are some of the techniques you can use in stories with statistics:

Use Analogies: Whenever you are referring to large numbers, comparisons with something familiar to readers are especially helpful. This is an analogy from a story about pollution in Alabama's rivers:

> Each minute, about 30 million gallons of Alabama river water, or the equivalent of what it would take to fill 60 Olympic-sized swimming pools, flush into Mobile Bay, washing over oyster beds in the northern part of the bay closed to harvesting.
>
> —Dan Morse,
> *The* (Montgomery) *Alabama Journal*

Round Off Numbers: In most cases it is better to round off numbers—for instance, to $3.5 million instead of $3,499,590. Make it easy for the reader to grasp large numbers. This is especially important in broadcast stories.

Avoid Bunching Numbers in One Paragraph: Spread numbers out over a few paragraphs rather than glutting one sentence or paragraph with them. Another good technique is to present numbers in lists.

This story is based on statistics, but the writer uses the list technique and breaks up numbers with quotes:

More fathers are going solo in raising kids.

It's a change that single fathers say shows greater acceptance by American families and courts that sometimes the best place for children is with Dad.

The 2000 census found:

- In 2.2 million households, fathers raise their children without a mother. That's about one household in 45.

- The number of single-father households rose 62 percent in 10 years.

- The portion of the country's total 105.5 million households that were headed by single fathers with children living there doubled in a decade, to 2 percent.

Single fathers say the numbers help tear down a long-standing conception that single fathers tend to abandon their kids, or at least not take as good care of them as single moms, said Vince Regan, an Internet consultant from Grand Rapids, Mich., who is raising five kids on his own.

"In time, it goes a long way to helping society think that single fathers do help their kids and want to be part of their lives," he said.

(The story continues with more quotes and these statistics:)

The percentage increase in single-father households far outpaced other living arrangements. The "Ozzie and Harriett" household, where both parents raise the children like on the old TV show, increased by 6 percent, and single-mother homes were up by 25 percent.

Father-headed households are still only a small percentage. Married couples with children make up 24 percent of all households—whether family or non-family. They were 39 percent of all homes in 1970. Single-mother homes made up 7 percent of all households in 2000, up from 5 percent over 30 years ago.

—Genaro C. Armas, *The Associated Press*

Interpret Numbers: Show the impact on readers in terms they can understand.

A 10-year analysis of enrollment patterns at Kansas University and five other state universities revealed two dating tips for college students:

- Men hoping to improve dating prospects might consider attending Emporia State University, where 60 percent of students are women.

- Women interested in more dating opportunities should look to Kansas State University, the only state university in the area with more men than women.

—Tim Carpenter,
Lawrence (Kan.) *Journal-World*

Use Storytelling Techniques: Even statistical stories can lend themselves to storytelling. In this example, the writer uses an anecdotal lead and limits the use of statistics, which were presented in a graphic accompanying the story:

James Frazier walked across the stage at Civic Arena on May 31 and picked up his diploma from Central High School. On Aug. 24, he'll head off to college.

Not bad for someone who dropped out of school in 1996.

He's one example of why the dropout rate in St. Joseph has fallen by half since 1989.

He's part of a trend that no other urban Missouri city can match. Not

Columbia. Not Springfield. Certainly not Kansas City or St. Louis.

With a dropout rate of 13.4 percent, according to figures released Thursday, the St. Joseph School District tops the list.

Figures for this year aren't in for the other school districts, but last year's dropout rate for Columbia was 31.5 percent. For Springfield it was 29.6 percent. The state average is the closest figure—22.8 percent.

Announcing the results, United Way cited its program, Profit in Education, started in 1989 to reduce the dropout rate. Barbara Sprong, coordinator for

Profit in Education, credited the efforts of the entire community in lowering the dropout rate. Those efforts included innovative programs at the St. Joseph School District, such as the Learning Academy.

That program, Frazier said, made the difference for him.

"The way I was going, I would have been dead or in jail," he said. He spent a rough two years in high school, missing classes and taking drugs. Academically he was on the edge.

"The Learning Academy basically turned that all around," he said.

—Dianna Borsi, *St. Joseph* (Mo.) *News-Press*

Use Graphics: Try to get the numbers out of your story and into a separate graphic. You need to mention some of the numbers, but always consider whether a chart, graph or diagram could convey the information better.

Budget Stories

Budget stories are hard to write and even harder to read if you flood them with a lot of numbers. And in broadcast stories, numbers are worse to hear. You can't avoid using numbers in all stories, but don't put several numbers in the same sentence or paragraph. Whenever you are writing about numbers, you must analyze what they mean. Most reports list numbers in comparison to a previous year or time frame. Always put numbers in perspective in two ways:

- **Explain change:** Do the numbers show an increase or decrease from a previous period?
- **State the significance:** What do the numbers mean, and why are they important? Explain what is interesting or important about these statistics in a way that will make readers care. You can even use a transition such as "Here's what this means to you."

Consider these basic questions:

Who: Who is most affected by the budget? Who are the winners and losers?

What: What are the major changes in a budget? How does it compare with previous years. Don't just say the budget or tuition has increased by 10 percent; give the figures; what is the current tuition.

When: When do the new proposals go into affect? Not all budgets have immediate ramifications.

Where: Where are the increases and decreases in the budget?

Why: Why are the cuts or in additions to the budget being proposed?

Budget planning starts several months before the budget is approved. Learn how to interpret the proposed budget by asking a financial officer of the city, school or agency to explain it to you before the budget is released. If he can't brief you on this year's proposal, use last year's budget to learn the system. In most cases, officials will be willing to cooperate because they want you to present the facts accurately.

Basically, budgets have two sections:

Revenues: The income, usually derived from taxes—primarily property taxes in municipalities. But there also are sales taxes, income taxes and fees. Look for clues about how the revenue will be raised. Will property taxes increase? If you are covering a university budget, will tuition be increased? Find out how the revenue source will affect your readers.

Expenditures: Where most of the money will be spent. Will some departments be increasing expenses more than others, such as police or fire departments? If so, why? Will salaries be increased or more people be hired? How do the expenditures for this year compare with those of the past few years?

Generally, budgets include figures from the previous year or past few years. Look for major increases and decreases in revenues and expenditures.

Before a government agency can adopt a budget, it must conduct public hearings, where the public can comment about the budget. If the budget proposal is at the hearing stage, be sure to include the dates of the hearings in your story. Taxpayers often want to attend hearings to protest cutbacks or request money for programs they support.

©Philip Meiring/The University Daily Kansan

The Kansas House of Representatives, where state budgets are hammered out

Budget and Tax Terms

If you want to explain budgets, you must know what these terms mean:

Assessments and Property Taxes: Common in municipal budgets, where taxes are based on real estate. Homeowners pay taxes based on an assessment, or estimated value, of their property. This value is determined by a city property appraiser based on a number of factors: size of the property, number of bedrooms, construction and so on. For example, suppose you decide to buy a condominium or a house selling for $160,000. That is its "market value," the price it sells for on the market. Some communities base their tax on the full market value, but most use only a percentage of the total value. The property is given an "assessed value," a value for tax purposes. If your community bases its tax on half the market value, your house would be assessed for $80,000. Your annual property taxes equal some percentage of the assessed value.

Capital Budget: Money used to pay for major improvements, such as the construction of highways or new buildings. Capital is often raised by selling bonds, and people who buy the bonds receive interest. The government then uses the money and repays the bonds, plus interest, over a period of years in what is called "debt service." The process is much like buying a house: The bank lends you money; you live in the house and repay the loan plus interest on a long-term basis, often over 30 years.

Deficit: When government spends more money than it receives. Most municipalities and states require a balanced budget: The expenses must be the same as the income. The difference between the expenditures and the income is the deficit, or debt.

Fiscal Year: Year in which budgeted funds will be spent. In government, the budget term often starts on July 1 and goes to June 30, instead of the calendar year. So if you use a fiscal year, give the dates: "in this fiscal year, which starts July 1." Or if you are writing about when the money will run out: "in this fiscal year, which ends June 30."

Mean: An average; the sum of all the figures divided by the number of items in the survey. If the salaries of 100 journalists total $3 million, they have a mean salary of $30,000. The salaries of the 100 journalists in the survey would be added and then divided by 100 to get the mean.

Median: An average; the value in the middle of a range. If 15 journalists in a survey earn from $20,000 to $65,000, you would list all the salaries in numerical order and find the one in the center of the list. The eighth number in the list would be the median.

Mill: Unit equal to $1 for every $1,000 that a house is assessed. Local school and city taxes are based on mills. Explain the impact of these taxes clearly. If the school tax rate is 25 mills, your story should say, "The tax rate is 25 mills, which equals $25 for every $1,000 of assessed property valuation." Or you could insert a definition:

"A mill equals $1 for every $1,000 of assessed value on a property." Then give an example: "Under this tax rate, a homeowner whose property is valued at $80,000 (multiplied by 0.025) would pay $2,000 in school taxes." Try to avoid using the term *mills;* just say the tax rate will be $25 for every $1,000 of assessed property value. Follow with a specific example so residents can figure out how much their tax will be.

Operating Budget: Money used to provide services (police, fire, garbage removal and so on) and to pay for the operation of government. Most of the money for this budget comes from taxes.

Other Taxes: Wage tax, income tax and sales tax. Cities and states often charge these additional taxes. Check when you write your budget stories to determine whether they will be increased or decreased. If they will stay the same, say so.

Per Capita: The rate per person. For example, if a community has 50 murders and a population of 175,000 people, the per capita murder rate would be determined by dividing 50 by 175,000, to yield 0.000286. However, such a small number is hard to comprehend, so it might be multiplied by 100,000 to give a number per 100,000. In this case the rate would be 28.6 murders for every 100,000 people.

Reappraisal: State or local decision to re-evaluate properties in the community, usually to increase their values. This action almost always generates good stories because it affects people dramatically. For example, Kansas had not reappraised properties for 20 years. When the state decided to do it, property values soared, and a tax revolt resulted. People who had been paying $200 in taxes on their homes were suddenly paying $1,000. A similar situation occurred in Atlanta:

A groundswell of protest over the mass reappraisal of Atlanta and Fulton County property is threatening to become a wholesale tax revolt.

Thousands of homeowners have turned out at meetings throughout the city and county to express displeasure with their new assessments, in some cases more than double last year's.

At the South Fulton County Annex, more than one thousand people gathered Monday to talk about fighting the assessments.

"My assessment went up 190 percent and I'll gladly sell my home to the county for what they think it's worth," said Mitch Skandalakis, a leader of the Task Force for Good Government, as the crowd roared.

—Mark Sherman, *Atlanta Constitution*

Writing Techniques

Impact is crucial in budget stories. So are graphics. A chart or list of key numbers can make a story more presentable. Also get reactions from city officials, residents at public hearings or the people most affected by budget cuts. If you are writing about university budgets, get reactions from administrators, students, professors and the officials whose departments will be affected most.

Here are some key points to include in a budget story, not necessarily in this order:

- Total amount of the budget (rounded off when possible—$44.6 million instead of $44,552,379). Most budgets are supposed to be balanced, so the figure applies to both revenues and expenditures.
- Amount of increase or decrease
- Tax or tuition levy, or how funds will be raised (impact on reader, comparison to current tax)
- Major expenditures (major increases and decreases in department funds)
- Consequences (impact on the government or agency—cuts in personnel, services, and so on)
- Historical comparisons (how budget compares with previous year and past few years)
- Reactions from officials and people affected by increases or decreases
- Definitions and explanations of technical terms

Here is an example of the kind of budget story you should avoid writing. It is flooded with statistics but doesn't clarify how the budget will affect the reader.

The recommended Rockville Centre city budget would require a 2.56-mill property tax increase.

City Manager Joan Weinman recommended to Rockville City Commission a budget of $55,672,309, which would require a local levy of 42.59 mills. Last year's budget of $50,322,409 required a levy of 42.03 mills.

A mill is $1 of tax for every $1,000 of assessed property valuation.

Weinman is recommending a 3 percent across-the-board salary increase for city employees. She is also recommending an addition of five police officers to the public safety department.

Here is the lead on another budget story, but this one explains the impact on homeowners:

HACKENSACK, N.J.—A $39.2 million budget that offers residents their first property-tax break in 20 years has been adopted by the City Council.

The budget, which includes $4 million in new state aid, was approved by a 4-1 vote following a public hearing Monday. No residents commented.

Despite a 6 percent increase in spending, the boost in state aid means that total property taxes for the owner of a home assessed at $180,000, the borough average, will drop $54 a year.

—Tom Topousis,
The (Hackensack, N.J.) *Record*

Here is another way of explaining impact in a lead that is not cluttered with statistics:

Pinellas School Superintendent Howard Hinesley has proposed a list of budget cuts for the next school year that will mean fewer textbooks, fewer teachers and fewer administrators if School Board members approve them next Wednesday.

—Patty Curtin Jones, *St. Petersburg* (Fla.) *Times*

Don't forget that budgets affect people. So when you are writing advances and reaction stories, you can use feature techniques. Here is an example of an anecdotal-narrative approach to an advance on the city budget:

It was 8:05 on a Monday in August, Rosemary Farnon remembers, when her husband, Tony, called the police to report that their rowhouse in the Juniata Park section had been ransacked.

Amid a shambles of overturned furniture, scattered papers and food taken from the fridge, the Farnons nervously and angrily waited nearly five hours before an officer appeared. He explained apologetically that the local police district had no cops to spare.

Theirs is one story, from one neighborhood, but it typifies what is happening across Philadelphia:

Taxes are up and services are down—and residents are unhappy about it.

So Rosemary Farnon and hundreds of thousands of taxpayers will be listening closely Thursday when the mayor proposes the budget for the coming fiscal year, which begins July 1.

—Dan Myers and Idris M. Diaz, *The Philadelphia Inquirer*

Here is a broadcast/Web version of a budget story; note that the end of the story refers the readers and viewers to click on a link to the complete budget and comment box:

How much does it take to run a state like Alaska? Governor Sarah Palin (R), says she needs 8.3 billion dollars.

In her Capital and Operating Budget released Monday, the governor has outlined funding priorities for the state. It contains big increases for school funding and municipal revenue sharing.

The proposed 2009 budget is up 4 percent—a smaller increase than was expected.

(VOSOT—voice over sound on tape; quotes in Web version)

"Our budget is meant to make government more responsive and responsible to Alaskans," said Governor Palin.

The governor's budget team says it's time for the state to "live within our means."

(VOSOT; quotes in Web version)

"I just think we are on track to slowing the rate of growth in government spending, and saving for the future. I think that bodes well for Alaskans' liberty," said Lieutenant Governor Sean Parnell (R), Alaska.

The proposed budget bodes well for education, adding one billion for K-12 schools and a 100 million for school maintenance and construction.

(VOSOT; quotes in Web version)

"That's a priority that we have been working on for years. And it's in the budget. Hopefully, it will be in there at the end of the day," said Representative Harry Crawford (D), Anchorage.

Also up is municipal revenue sharing. If the Legislature approves it, all Alaskan communities will split 75 million dollars of the state's oil wealth—the highest amount ever set aside for cities and villages to use how they see fit.

(VOSOT; quotes in Web version)

"This will allow our local communities to prioritize. And certainly, I would encourage local communities to use a good portion of this to reduce property tax and energy costs," said Governor Palin.

The 2009 budget is based on oil at 66 dollars a barrel. So if the price dips below that, the state gets less money. High oil prices means there's a budget surplus now; but that could change in the future. This has some lawmakers worried the governor isn't looking far enough ahead to leaner times.

(VOSOT; quotes in Web version)

"If oil prices don't stay where they are, we are going to be in a bind again. So I want to see some serious savings as well," said Representative Crawford.

(VOSOT; quotes in Web version)

"There will be some things to address with the Legislature as we get into it, and as we hear from the public about our proposals," said State Budget Director Karen Rehfeld.

Now, the real work begins to try to reach common ground on a budget to make everyone happy.

Some things that state departments thought would be fully funded will now be part of a bond vote, including 10 million dollars for the Port of Anchorage improvements and funding for a new state crime lab. Those things will now be up for a general vote.

The governor wants to know what you think about the proposed budget. To see the full budget documents, and to leave her your comments, click below: (link to full budget and comment box).

—Andrea Gusty, *KTVA, Channel 11, Anchorage, Alaska*

Exercises

1 Taxes: Figure your taxes using the following method:

a You own a home that is worth $100,000 on the market. The city appraises residential property for tax purposes at 11.5 percent of its market value. What is the assessed value of your property?

b Using your assessed value as calculated in **a**, figure your tax rate as follows:

1 Write your assessed value:

2 Divide the assessed value by 1,000 because a mill is a $1 tax on every $1,000 of assessed property value. Write that figure:

3 The tax levy in your community is 125 mills. Multiply the amount in **b–2** times the tax levy to figure your tax bill. Write the result:

c Last year your taxes were $1,250. Using the answer from **b–3** for this year's taxes, figure your tax percentage increase.

d The city had a tax rate of 125 mills last year and is raising it to 137.5 mills this year. What is the percentage increase?

2 Your dream home: Envision the home you would like to own. How much will it cost? If you want a swimming pool, sauna and other amenities, make sure that you figure them into the price along with the land value in your community or wherever you want to live. When you figure the selling price, that's the market value.

Now figure your taxes. Your community assesses property at 30 percent of its market value for tax purposes.

The tax rate for city and schools combined will be 75 mills. How much will you pay in taxes?

3 **Census data:** You want to write a story about population growth in your state. Find the statistics in the U.S. Census database for your state. Then import the data into Excel or other spreadsheet program, and analyze which counties in your state gained or lost the most population.

4 **Statistics:** Analyze the following information, and write a story about which sandwiches are healthiest (lowest in fat and sodium). These statistics are based on a study by the Center for Science in the Public Interest, a nonprofit consumer nutrition organization. The organization analyzed 12 sandwiches for fat, saturated fat and sodium. Daily limits of fat recommended by the Food and Drug Administration for adults are 65 grams of total fat, 20 grams of saturated fat and 2,400 milligrams of sodium.

Turkey with mustard: 6 grams fat, 2 grams saturated fat, 1,407 milligrams sodium

Roast beef with mustard: 12 grams fat, 4 grams saturated fat, 993 milligrams sodium

Chicken salad: 32 grams fat, 6 grams saturated fat, 1,136 milligrams sodium

Corned beef with mustard: 20 grams fat, 8 grams saturated fat, 1,924 milligrams sodium

Tuna salad: 43 grams fat, 8 grams saturated fat, 1,319 milligrams sodium

Ham with mustard: 27 grams fat, 10 grams saturated fat, 2,344 milligrams sodium

Egg salad: 31 grams fat, 10 grams saturated fat, 1,110 milligrams sodium

Turkey club: 34 grams fat, 10 grams saturated fat, 1,843 milligrams sodium

Bacon, lettuce and tomato: 37 grams fat, 12 grams saturated fat, 1,555 milligrams sodium

Vegetarian (cucumbers, sprouts, avocado and cheese): 40 grams fat, 14 grams saturated fat, 1,276 milligrams sodium

Grilled cheese: 33 grams fat, 17 grams saturated fat, 1,543 milligrams sodium

Reuben: 50 grams fat, 20 grams saturated fat, 3,268 milligrams sodium

Background: Interview with Jane Hurley, nutritionist for the center. She analyzed 170 sandwiches from Washington, New York, Los Angeles and Chicago delicatessens: "People tend to think of a sandwich as just a bite to eat, but many shops are giving you a dinner's worth of fat and calories. Tuna itself is fat free, but in sandwiches, it's drowning in one-third cup of mayonnaise. That's the equivalent of three McDonald's Quarter Pounders, fat-wise."

The center also did studies showing fat in Mexican, Italian and Chinese food. One of its most controversial studies showed that one bag of popcorn popped in coconut oil, as served in movie theaters, has as much saturated fat as six Big Macs.

5 **Crime statistics:** Access the Web site for the crime statistics on your campus. It should be on your college or university Web site, but if you can't find it there, go to the Security on Campus Web site (*www.securityoncampus.org/crimestats*) and find the statistics. They may not be as recent as they should be on your university site. You might also compare the statistics for your campus with those from a neighboring or similar-size school. Look for patterns—increases and decreases. Write a news story. If possible, call your campus police department for comments.

👉 **Featured Online Activity**   Log on to the book Web site for Chapter 21 and take the interactive quiz on government and budget terms at

academic.cengage.com/masscomm/rich/writingandreportingnews6e

Coaching Tips

Role-play: Ask yourself what you would want to know if you were affected by this crime.

Use the tell-a-friend technique.

Gather enough detail and specifics so you could draw a diagram or write a chronology of the crime as though you were designing a graphic.

Avoid the jargon of police or other legal authorities. If you don't understand a term, chances are the reader may not know it either.

Always include the background of the case, no matter how many days a police story or trial continues. Never take it for granted that the reader has read previous stories.

Be careful. Double-check your story for accuracy, and make sure that you don't convict someone of a crime before a judge or jury does.

Check the Internet and sex offender registries for background searches of suspects.

I have never understood young reporters who considered covering the cops the least desirable beat. The police beat is all about people, what makes them tick, what makes them become heroes or homicidal maniacs. It has it all: greed, sex, violence, comedy and tragedy.

Edna Buchanan, former police reporter, *The Miami Herald*

22 Crime and Punishment

The police beat, which often includes the fire department, is considered an entry-level job. Most reporters move on to other beats after a few years of covering crime stories. Edna Buchanan did not. She covered the police beat at *The Miami Herald* for more than 20 years before resigning to write books. But while she was at the *Herald,* she turned police reporting into an art form and won a Pulitzer Prize.

A soft-spoken woman, she writes with a strong punch. One Pulitzer Prize juror said, "She writes drop-dead sentences for drop-dead victims. She is never dull." Consider:

> There was music and sunlight as the paddle wheeler Dixie Bell churned north on Indian Creek Thursday. The water shimmered and the wind was brisk. And then the passengers noticed that the people in the next boat were dead.

Buchanan is most famous for the lead she wrote on a story about a man who shoved his way to the front of a line at a fried chicken restaurant. The counter clerk told the man to go to the end of the line and wait his turn. He did. But when he reached the head of the line again, the restaurant had run out of fried chicken. He battered the clerk fiercely, and he was shot fatally by a guard in the restaurant. Her lead: "Gary Robinson died hungry."

"In truth, Edna Buchanan doesn't write about cops. She writes about people," *Herald* editors wrote in the Pulitzer entry. Buchanan is the first to admit that. "You learn more about people on the police beat than any other beat," she said in a speech at a convention of investigative reporters.

She said she had reported more than 5,000 violent deaths. How did she keep from getting upset by them and burned out on the job? "The thing that keeps you going is that you realize you can make things better. You may be affected like everyone else by a terrible tragedy, but you're in a position to do something about it. That's the real joy of this job. We can be catalysts for change. We can bring about justice. Sometimes we are all the victim has got. Police stories do make a difference.

"You've got to be accurate and fair and very, very careful, particularly in crime reporting. A news story mentioning somebody's name can ruin their lives or come back to haunt them 25 years later. It is there in black and white on file. It's like a police record; you never outlive it. You can do terrible damage. So you knock on one more door, ask one more question, make one last phone call. It could be the one that counts."

When Buchanan made those phone calls and someone hung up on her, she just redialed the number and said, "We were cut off." The second time, she might have gotten a relative or someone else who was willing to talk, or the first person might have changed his mind. But she didn't try a third time; that would be harassment, she said.

Crime Stories

Buchanan gathered her information from interviews and records. And then she wove them into stories with leads that hooked the reader. She said that crime reporters need to talk to witnesses and get color, background, ages and details—what people were wearing, doing and saying when they became crime victims or suspects. In other words, crime reporters need access.

Access

If you have the police beat, you should check the daily police log, also called the "blotter," to see the listing of all crimes recorded by police for that day. The log will list the names of the victims and the nature of the crimes. This is public record and should be available to the press and anyone else. However, the supporting documents—the actual reports filed by the officer at the scene—may not be available. Laws limiting access to these reports vary from state to state. Restrictions apply especially to records for cases under investigation, but if you develop good sources in the police department, you may gain access.

Although the incident reports contain the names of the officers who filed them, many police departments with a public information officer do not allow reporters to talk to the arresting officers. It is best to abide by the department's policies. The public information officer may give you more information about the crime than the arresting officers would. Nonetheless, if access is permitted, try to talk to the arresting officers, especially in a major crime.

For details about arrests, check the jail log, which should contain the suspect's name and address, birth date, sex, race, occupation, place of arrest, and charges.

To Previous Criminal Records   If you are a good reporter, you will want to find out if a suspect has a previous criminal record for related charges. If you are lucky, you will be able to do that, but not always from the police. Again, many states restrict access to previous criminal records.

However, if someone has been convicted of a crime, that court record is usually public and should be available to you in the court jurisdiction where the person was convicted—unless the record is sealed by order of a judge. If the person was charged with a crime and found not guilty or charges were dropped, that record is also public. You need to look up the court file (and get the case file number) under that person's name.

Depending on how the records are filed in your city, you probably will need the year of the court case, too. Filing systems vary in every municipality, so ask the court clerk for help. The court file should contain all pertinent information, including names of the lawyers involved, description of the crime and all motions filed in the case. Most important, it will tell what happened—the disposition of the case—including specific terms of the sentence or probation or dismissal.

In some cases, a person convicted of a minor crime can have his record erased—"expunged"—after a number of years, with permission of the court. In other cases, a judge may permit certain records to be sealed, meaning that they will be withheld from the public and available only to law enforcement officers.

The Internet has made access to some records easier:

- Sex offender registries: 41 states have Web sites listing names and offenses of people convicted of sex crimes.

- Many court records are posted online in searchable databases.

- Public records of court cases are available online in many states and federal sites. Several other Web sites, such as *www.knowx.com* or *www.casebreakers. com,* offer background research checks on individuals for a fee.

To University Records In 1986 Jeanne Ann Clery, a 19-year-old student, was raped and murdered in her third-floor dormitory at Lehigh University. Her parents later learned that 38 violent crimes had been committed on the Lehigh campus in the previous three years, but the university was not required to divulge those statistics. Connie and Howard Clery wanted to make sure that their daughter's death was not in vain.

As a result of their efforts, a landmark federal law was enacted requiring all colleges and universities that have federal student financial aid programs to publish an annual report listing three years of crime statistics. The law, originally called the Campus Security Act, was amended in 1998 and renamed the Clery Act in memory of Jeanne Clery.

However, universities may withhold names on crime reports because of another federal law. The Buckley Amendment to the Family Educational Rights and Privacy Act prohibits government agencies from releasing any personal data about students and employees in institutions that receive federal funding. Universities have claimed that if they release such crime records, they could lose federal funding.

In 1991 a federal judge in Missouri ruled that Southwest Missouri State University must release names and records of crimes at that school after Traci Bauer, editor of the campus newspaper, sued for access. That ruling did not apply to all universities. But in 1992, a new federal law exempted campus records from the restrictions of the Buckley Amendment. Universities are still not compelled to release information on crime records, but they will no longer risk losing federal funds if they do release the names.

To Records of Juvenile Offenders All states have laws restricting the release of records that identify "juvenile offenders," people under age 18. The names are withheld by all branches of the juvenile justice system, including the social services system, but a judge can authorize their release. If a juvenile is being tried as an adult—a decision that is made by a judge—or if the juvenile's name is mentioned in open court, the name can be used. This sometimes happens when the crime is particularly heinous or the juvenile has an extensive criminal record. For example, in 1998, when juveniles were charged with shootings at schools in Jonesboro, Ark., and Springfield, Ore., with several people killed or injured, the media used the juveniles' names.

Most newspapers and broadcast stations have policies to withhold the names of juveniles, but that is more of an ethical decision than a legal one. The media may use the name if they receive it by legitimate means.

To the Crime Scene Police have the right to protect the crime scene and limit access to the press. If the crime scene is on public property, reporters and photographers can get as close as police will allow. If the crime scene is on private property, access is at the discretion of the police or the owners of the property. Generally, police will allow some access as long as the media do not interfere with the investigation of evidence at the crime scene.

Use of Names

Many newspapers and TV news stations withhold the names of suspects in crime stories until they have been formally charged with the crime. Being arrested means only that someone has been stopped for questioning in a crime. The person becomes an official suspect after charges are filed in a court, usually at a hearing called an "arraignment." (The process will be explained in the section about courts.) In recent years, police have begun releasing the name of a suspect as a "person of interest" before actual charges are filed. This term is used most often when police have good reason to believe the suspect will soon be charged with the crime, but it is controversial because it casts suspicion on someone who may not be involved in the crime.

Some newspapers also withhold the names of crime victims to protect their privacy. A growing controversy at newspapers and television stations is whether to withhold the names of complainants in rape cases. Again, the policy varies, but most of the media do not publish the names.

When names are used in crime stories, always get the full name, including the middle initial, and double-check the spelling. Do not rely on police reports; many names on reports are spelled incorrectly. Check the names in telephone directories whenever possible. If a discrepancy exists between the name in the phone book and the one the officer gave you, call the officer again or go with the information from the police.

Using full names with initials helps reduce confusion and inaccuracies; there could be a dozen John Smiths in the community. John T. Smith is more specific, especially when followed by age and address.

Wording of Accusations

Remember that all people are innocent until they are proved guilty in court or until they plead guilty. When a suspect is arrested, the person is not officially charged with anything. A person can be arrested after an officer gets a warrant or on suspicion of a crime. But the police cannot charge anyone with a crime; a member of the district attorney's office must file the charge officially with the court (more about that later). As a result, you must be careful with wording so you don't convict a person erroneously. Most media wait until the person has been charged with the crime, except in sensational cases when the arrest is important news.

If you are writing about an arrest before the official charge, do not say, "Sallie R. Smith was arrested for robbing the bank" (that implies guilt). Do say, "Sallie R. Smith was arrested in connection with the bank robbery." If you are writing about the suspect after charges have been filed, say, "Sallie R. Smith was charged with bank robbery" or "Sallie R. Smith was arrested on a charge of bank robbery."

Also be careful before you call anyone a crime victim. If a person was killed or visibly injured during a crime, it is probably clear that the person is a crime victim. In other cases, the suspect has to be proved guilty before you can say the other person is a victim. You can say "the *alleged* victim," or, if applicable, you can call the other person the accuser—for example, "The accuser in the rape trial . . . ."

Use the official charges when possible. If they are very awkward, and they often are, don't use them in the lead. Put them in the backup to the story. For example, one man who was accused of robbing a jewelry store was also accused of carrying a gun. But police didn't charge him with possession of a gun. They charged him with possession of an instrument of crime. And there are varying degrees in the charges, such as first-degree murder, which should be cited. But don't cite the other qualifications, such as Class E felony (a category for the crime), unless you are going to explain what they mean and why the reader must know. If categories are used at all, it is for explanation of the penalties: "The crime is a Class E felony, which carries a penalty of . . . ." It is still preferable to explain the penalty without the category, which is meaningless to readers.

The word *alleged* is dangerous, so avoid it whenever possible. It means to declare or assert without proof. If you allege carelessly, you can be sued. Do not say, "Smith allegedly robbed the bank." You, the writer, are then the source of the allegation—and a good candidate for a libel suit. You can say, however, "Police accused Sallie R. Smith of robbing the bank" or "Police said Smith robbed the bank." If you must use *alleged,* say, "Police alleged that Smith robbed the bank." "Police accused Smith of allegedly robbing the bank" is redundant and awkward. Besides, police rarely allege; they accuse. An accusation is OK if it comes from police (and they are citing charges on record), not if it comes from you. Other permissible uses include "The bank was allegedly robbed" or "the alleged robbery," although such uses are not preferable.

Here's an example of the proper use of *alleged:*

When basketball star Kobe Bryant was accused of rape, it would be accurate to say the "alleged rape" when referring to the incident because it was never established that the accuser was actually raped; Bryant claimed that the sex was consensual. The case was dismissed when the woman who accused Bryant of sexual assault decided not to testify. The woman also had to be considered an "alleged victim" because the charges were never proved.

Also be careful when using the word *accused.* Follow the Associated Press Stylebook guidelines: A person is accused *of,* not *with,* a crime. In addition, you should not say, "accused bank robber Sallie R. Smith" (this convicts her). Instead, say, "Sallie R. Smith, accused of the bank robbery, ..."

Attribution

In crime stories, make sure that you attribute all accusatory information and much of the information you received secondhand (not by direct observation). Factual information does not need attribution. For example, the location of a crime is usually factual. If someone has been charged with a crime, you can state that as a fact.

To reduce the use of attribution after every sentence, you can use an overview attribution for part of your story, especially when you are recounting what happened: "Police described the incident this way."

Newspaper or Television Archives

The first thing you should do before you write your story is check newspaper clips in your library, TV file tape or online archives. They may make a big difference in your story.

A reporter for *The Hartford* (Conn.) *Courant* covered the case of a man arrested on a charge of rape. Small story for a big paper. But the reporter checked clips and discovered that the man had been previously arrested on rape charges and was free on bail when he was charged with this other rape—a much bigger story. Three months later, a different reporter was making police checks. A man had been accused of rape. The reporter checked the clips. It was the same man charged with a third rape, which occurred when he was free on bail still awaiting trial in the first rape case—a very big story. And this story led to a major front-page follow-up story on the system in Connecticut that allows rape suspects to be released on bail, no matter how many times they have been arrested and charged with that type of crime. ("Bail" is the amount of money, set by a judge, that the suspect has to deposit with the court to be released from jail pending a hearing or trial. If the suspect flees, the bail money goes to the court.)

One caution: Clips and tape on file in your news organization's database may not be up to date. They may contain stories of someone's arrest but not the disposition of the case. Always check to see if charges were dropped, or if the person is still waiting trial or was convicted.

Guidelines for Reporting Crime Stories

In any story you will seek good quotes and answers to the five W's. Here are the basic questions to ask and the basic information to include in crime stories:

Victims: Get full names, ages, addresses and occupations, if available (use if relevant).

Suspects: Get full names, ages and addresses, if available; if not, get a description. Guidelines about whether to include race or ethnic background are changing. Check your organization's style. A general rule is to avoid mentioning race or ethnicity unless it is crucial to the story or to a description of a suspect.

Cause of Fatalities or Injuries: Also describe the injuries, where injured people have been taken and their current condition (check with hospitals). In stories involving property, specify the causes and extent of damage.

Location of Incident: Don't forget to gather specific information for a graphic.

Time of Incident: Be as specific as possible.

What Happened: Make sure that you understand the sequence of events; always ask about any unusual circumstances.

Arrests and Charges Filed: If people have been arrested, find out where they are being held, when they will be arraigned (a hearing for formal charges) or when the next court procedure will be. If they have already been arraigned, find out the amount of bail.

Eyewitness Accounts: Comments from neighbors may also be relevant. Be careful about using accusations against named individuals. When in doubt, leave them out.

In addition to gathering the basic information, you may want to try some of these other reporting techniques:

Role-Play: Imagine that it is your car in the accident, your home that was burglarized or burned in a fire, your friend or relative injured in a crime. What information would you want to know if you were personally affected by the story?

Play Detective: What information would you want to gather to solve the crime?

Gather Graphics: What information would you need to diagram the car accident, draw the crime scene or a locator map, write a highlights box or a chronology of events, or design a chart or graphic depicting how and where the crime occurred? Ask questions to gain the information you will have to convey to the artist who will draw the graphics for your story.

Use the Telephone: Often you will gather information for crime stories over the telephone. Usually you will get the information from a dispatcher or public information officer who was not at the scene and is just reading a report to you. Make sure that you ask police officials to repeat any information you did not hear clearly. Also ask the police officer releasing the information to give you his full name and rank. Police often identify themselves only by title and last name, such as Sgt. Jones. Ask the officer to spell the names of all people involved; you can spell them back to double-check the accuracy.

Stories About Specific Types of Crimes

For the first day of a major crime story, a hard-news approach is preferred. For follow-up stories and sidebars, consider some of the storytelling techniques.

Motor Vehicle Accidents   Vehicle accident stories usually are hard-news stories, unless there is an unusual angle. In addition to following the basic guidelines, make sure that you have this information:

- Speed, destination, and directions of vehicles and exact locations at the time of the accident
- Cause of accident, arrests, citations and damages
- Victims' use of required equipment, such as seat belts and bicycle or motorcycle helmets
- Weather-related information, if relevant
- Alcohol- or drug-related information, if relevant
- Rescue attempts or acts of heroism

It is customary to lead the story with fatalities and injuries. This example is very basic, structured in inverted pyramid form:

Summary lead: delayed identification, fatality and cause	A Santa Ana boy was killed when a van rear-ended the car he was riding in while it was stopped at a turn signal, police said. The van's driver was booked for vehicular manslaughter.
Identification	Robert Taylor, 10, died at UCI Medical Center in Orange.
When, where, other injured people	The 3:17 p.m. accident at First and Bristol streets in Santa Ana also critically injured the boy's mother, Griselda Taylor, 29, and his sister, Lynelle, 8. An 8-year-old boy in the car sustained minor injuries, police said. His name and relation to the Taylors were not released.
What happened and who was involved	Taylor was waiting on the eastbound side of First, in the left-turn lane, at a red light when a van driven by Don

Currie Edwards, 49, struck the back of her car, police said. The impact pushed her car into the intersection, and it was then struck by a westbound car driven by Phillipe Hernandez, 18.

Taylor sustained a broken neck. She was in guarded condition at Western Medical Center in Santa Ana, hospital officials said. Lynelle sustained critical head injuries, police said.   *Condition of injured people; hospital sources*

Edwards was treated for minor injuries and arrested, police said. Hernandez was not injured.

—*The Orange County* (Calif.) *Register*

Here is a broadcast accident story with similar crucial information in a brief form:

Summary lead: delayed identification, fatality

Identification and cause

Condition of victim

A man is dead after a traffic accident at Mile 66 of the Glenn Highway yesterday.

Alaska State Troopers say 50-year-old Spencer Ricketts of Anchorage was northbound on his Harley Davidson motorcycle when he crossed the double yellow line and struck a Winnebago.

Ricketts was evacuated by helicopter to Mat-Su Regional Medical Center, where he was pronounced dead on arrival.

The driver of the Winnebago, 61-year-old Robert Nastri of Arizona and his wife, who was a passenger, were not injured.

Ricketts' next of kin has been notified.

Troopers are still investigating the crash.

Who was involved

—*KTUU, Channel 2, Anchorage, Alaska*

Burglaries and Robberies A burglary involves entry into a building with intent to commit any type of crime; robbery involves stealing with violence or a threat against people. If you are away and a person enters your home and steals your compact disc player, that's a burglary. If you are asleep upstairs and the person is downstairs stealing the player, that's still a burglary. But if the person threatens you with force, that's a robbery. A burglary always involves a place and *can* involve violence against a person; a robbery *must* involve violence or threats against a person.

For both burglaries and robberies, ask the basics: who, what, when, where, why and how. Then add the following:

- What was taken and the value of the goods
- Types of weapons used (in robberies)
- How entry was made
- Similar circumstances (frequency of crime or any odd conditions)

In burglary and robbery stories, mention in the lead any injuries or deaths. Keep the tone serious when the story involves death or serious injuries. In other cases, use your judgment and lead with any unusual angles. If there are none, stress what was taken or how the burglars entered the building, if that is the most interesting factor.

Whether you write a hard or soft lead depends on how serious the crime was, whether it is the first story on the crime and whether you have enough interesting information to warrant a soft approach.

Here's a hard-news version of a burglary story:

COUNCIL BLUFFS, Iowa (AP)—A first issue of "Iron Man" was among 44 rare comic books stolen from a Council Bluffs store.

The books, some valued at $200 to $225 each, dated back to the 1950s and '60s.

Other books stolen from Kanesville Kollectibles included a 1964 first issue of "Daredevil," 17 issues of "Spider Man,"

four issues of "The Incredible Hulk," "Mystery in Space," "Tales of Suspense," "Captain Marvel" and "Thor."

Police reports said rare comic books valued at $2,950, about 300 used rock 'n' roll compact discs valued at $2,200 and $50 in cash were taken from the business.

—*The Associated Press*

In this burglary story, the tone is lighter and a soft lead is used because of the subject matter:

Someone took Burger King's "Have It Your Way" slogan too literally this week and stole a three-foot-wide Whopper hamburger display costume from a van parked in northeast Salem.

Shannon Sappingfield, a marketing representative for local Burger Kings, said the missing burger was made of sponge.

The Whopper was in a van parked at Boss Enterprise, 408-A Lancaster Drive NE. The company owns nine local Burger Kings.

When Sappingfield came to work about 6 a.m. Tuesday, she saw that the van's window had been broken. The cardboard box containing the Whopper costume was missing; two other boxes containing a milk shake costume and a french fry costume were untouched.

"I'm not convinced they realized what they had until they were away from the site and opened the box," she said.

She estimated that the costume was worth about $500. But to get another one, the company would also have to buy another milk shake and french fry costume, which cost $500 each.

—(Salem, Ore.) *Statesman-Journal*

This is a basic hard-news robbery story with a description of the suspects:

Two armed, masked men robbed a Huntington Beach restaurant late Tuesday, escaping with $2,000 in cash.

Police Lt. John Foster said the holdup occurred shortly before 11 p.m. at Jeremiah's, 8901 Warner Ave.

He said two men armed with shotguns and wearing stockings over their heads entered through the kitchen door, forced cooks into the main area of the restaurant, then made employees and patrons lie on the floor.

The robbers took the cash from a floor safe and fled, Foster said.

The men were described as Caucasian, wearing dark clothing. One was 6-foot-1 to 6-foot-3 with a thin build and dark, curly hair. The second was 5-foot-8, about 170 pounds with a medium to stocky build.

Detectives believe the same shotgun-wielding men robbed a Pizza Hut at 17342 Beach Blvd. about 9:40 p.m. Monday. The bandits took an undisclosed amount of cash and sped away in a small blue car, possibly a Toyota or Nissan.

—*The Orange County* (Calif.) *Register*

Here is how the hourglass form can be used to eliminate some of the attribution in a crime story. The story on the left does not use the hourglass structure, but the one on the right does. Attributions are highlighted with underlining (note the overview attribution in the right-hand story).

With hourglass structure

A robber took money from a clerk at Tom's Amoco, 3827 Topeka Blvd., early Sunday but had a change of heart, returned most of the cash and apologized before fleeing, police said.

The man showed no weapon but held what appeared to be a handgun

Without hourglass structure

A robber took money from a clerk at Tom's Amoco, 3827 Topeka Blvd., early Sunday but had a change of heart, returned most of the cash and apologized before fleeing, police said.

The man showed no weapon but held what appeared to be a handgun beneath his sweater, <u>said Detective Sgt. Greg Halford</u>.

<u>Halford said</u> a 19-year-old male clerk was counting money inside the business about 4 a.m. when he saw the robber walk across Topeka Boulevard toward the service station.

<u>The clerk told police</u> he tried to get the money out of sight before the man came into the service station, but was unable.

The robber gave the clerk five nickels and asked for a quarter, <u>Halford said,</u> then announced the robbery as the clerk was getting the quarter.

The clerk asked the man if he was sure he wanted to go through with the robbery. The clerk then told him that three security guards from a nearby motel often come into the service station, <u>Halford said.</u>

At that point, the nervous-looking robber went behind the counter and grabbed the money out of the clerk's hands, <u>the detective said.</u> Some of the money dropped onto the floor, so the robber picked it up, <u>Halford said.</u>

The robber started to leave, <u>Halford said,</u> then came back, apologized, returned almost all of the money, said he needed only a small amount of cash and left with a small amount.

—Topeka (Kan.) *Capital-Journal*

beneath his sweater, <u>said Detective Sgt. Greg Halford.</u>

<u>Halford described the incident as follows:</u>

A 19-year-old male clerk was counting money inside the business about 4 a.m. when he saw the robber walk across Topeka Boulevard toward the service station.

The clerk tried to get the money out of sight before the man came into the service station, but was unable.

The robber gave the clerk five nickels and asked for a quarter, then announced the robbery as the clerk was getting the quarter.

The clerk asked the man if he was sure he wanted to go through with the robbery. The clerk then told him that three security guards from a nearby motel often come into the service station.

At that point, the nervous-looking robber went behind the counter and grabbed the money out of the clerk's hands. Some of the money dropped onto the floor, so the robber picked it up.

The robber started to leave, then came back, apologized, returned almost all of the money, said he needed only a small amount of cash and left with a small amount.

Homicides *Homicide* is the legal term for killing. *Murder* is the term for premeditated homicide. *Manslaughter* is homicide without premeditation. A person can be arrested on charges of murder, but he is not a murderer until convicted of the crime. Do not call someone a murderer until then. Also, don't say someone was murdered unless authorities have established that the victim was murdered—in a premeditated act of killing—or until a court determines that. Say the person was slain or killed. Some additional information to gather:

- Weapon (specific description, such as .38-caliber revolver)
- Clues and motives (from police)
- Specific wounds
- Official cause of death (from coroner or police)

- Circumstances of suspect's arrest (result of tip or investigation, perhaps at the scene)
- Lots of details, from relatives, neighbors, friends, officials, eyewitnesses and your own observations at the crime scene

For many first-day stories about death, you may choose to use a hard-news approach. You should get the news about the death in the lead. But if there is a more compelling angle, you could put it in the second or third paragraph. Again, you must use judgment in deciding whether the story lends itself to a hard-news or a storytelling approach.

This is a hard-news approach to a homicide story:

A 32-year-old man was charged Tuesday with killing his former girlfriend when she wouldn't leave the back porch of his home.

Lester Paul Stephens of 3357 N. 2nd St. was charged with first-degree intentional homicide while armed in connection with the death of Ruby L. Hardison, 42. Hardison was shot in the head Saturday.

According to the criminal complaint, Stephens told police that he and Hardison recently had ended their relationship. But Hardison came to Stephens' home Saturday and began knocking and banging on the door and front window.

Stephens told police he got upset about the noise, and went to the back door to tell her to leave him alone. Then he went back inside and got a .32-caliber semiautomatic pistol and walked back to the porch, the complaint says.

Stephens told Hardison to get off the porch and go home, then fired one shot in the air to scare her away.

The complaint says that he then put the pistol to the right side of her head, and after they continued to argue, the gun discharged.

Stephens, who faces life plus five years in prison if convicted, was being held on $50,000 cash bail. A preliminary hearing was scheduled for April 30.

—The Milwaukee Journal

Here is an excerpt from a homicide story written in a storytelling style. This story includes reporting done according to most of the guidelines: interviews with neighbors, description based on observation, information from the police report and from officials. Remember that if you can't get to the scene, you can use your cross-directory to find neighbors to contact by telephone.

Soft lead

MELBOURNE, Fla.—June Anne Sharabati had planned every aspect of her children's lives, from their tasteful clothes to their exposure to classical music.

She missed only one detail: She forgot to plan a bullet for herself.

Backup for previous statement

The woman charged in the slaying of her two children Thursday night told deputies she would have committed suicide but she ran out of ammunition.

When deputies were called to her home at 2410 Washington Ave., they found Stephen Faulker, 14, dead on the floor of his bedroom. The Central Junior High School student had been shot in his stomach and head with a .38-caliber revolver.

Two-year-old Aisha Sharabati was in her mother's bedroom dying from similar wounds.

Basic news (five W's)

Type of weapon

Sharabati, who divorced Aisha's father in 1989, told deputies that Stephen had been a discipline problem, but she gave no explanation for her daughter's death, said Brevard County sheriff's spokeswoman Joan Heller.

Stephen's father died about nine years ago. Sharabati's former husband, Mohamad, lives in Canada and is en route to Melbourne, deputies said.

The first sign of the shootings came to light shortly before midnight Thursday with Sharabati's frantic calls to police and neighbors.

John Marrell said he was sleeping when the phone rang.

Narrative based on interview with neighbor

The call was from Sharabati, his 32-year-old neighbor. He had known her for 11 years and had helped her from time to time.

Dialogue

"She said, 'Didn't you hear the shots?' and I asked, 'What shots?'" Marrell said.

"And then she said, 'You need to get over here and get these kids. They've suffered enough.'"

Marrell said he grabbed a gun and a flashlight, thinking maybe a prowler was threatening the single parent and her children.

Instead, Sharabati met him at her screen door and told him she had "killed the kids."

Marrell said he ran home and called police, not knowing they had already been called.

Information from officials

When deputies arrived at the house, Sharabati met them unarmed on the doorstep and said, "Kill me. Kill me,"

Heller said. Sharabati was taken into custody, and deputies went in to find the bodies.

Police report

In the investigation report, Deputy Scott Nyquist said the suspect shot her son "in a fit of rage."

Reaction from neighbors

On Friday, many neighbors in the middle class neighborhood were struggling to understand how a seemingly "ideal mother" could have committed the slayings.

Occupation of neighbor (relevant to statement)

"She was the kind of mother who would attend parent-teacher conferences," said Frances Edwards, a retired high school guidance counselor who lives across the street from Sharabati. "She often said her children were her life. I sure didn't see this coming."

Observations

Sharabati's light blue, one-story home—like most in the wooded, spacious subdivision—was well maintained. In the back yard, three lawn chairs were lined up alongside Aisha's child-sized chair.

Edwards said Sharabati wanted only the best for her children.

Backup for lead

"She bought them Mozart records to listen to and dressed them beautifully," she said. . . .

Reaction from relative

"We are in deep shock—very, very deep shock," said Helen Faulker, Sharabati's mother.

Where suspect is, next step in court process

Sharabati is being held in the Brevard County jail, where she is scheduled to make her first court appearance at 9 a.m. today.

—Laurin Sellers and Lynne Bumpus-Hooper,
The Orlando (Fla.) *Sentinel*

Fires Although fire stories may not be crime stories, unless arson or other criminal behavior was involved, police reporters are often responsible for fire stories. Here are the important elements:

■ Time fire started, time fire companies responded, time fire was brought under control

■ Number of fire companies responding, number of trucks at scene

■ Evacuations, if any, and where people were taken

ETHICS

Ethical dilemma: How can you balance the desire for a great story with concern about causing harm?

The case: The situation is tense. A murder suspect is holding a hostage. The suspect had been arrested for killing his lover's 4-year-old son. He was in custody in a police car when he seized an officer's gun and shot two officers who were guarding him. After stealing a truck, he led police on a 50-mile chase and killed a state highway patrolman who was pursuing him. Then he pulled into a convenience store and held the clerk as a hostage. A local radio station called the store and broadcast a live interview with him. You are a newspaper reporter in the same area. Will you call him, too?

That was what happened in Tampa. WFLA-AM called, and then a reporter for the *St. Petersburg* (Fla.) *Times* also called and conducted an interview with the suspect. *The Tampa* (Fla.) *Tribune* reporters and editors, listening to the broadcast, decided against making a similar call. Did the reporters who called endanger the life of the hostage? What would you have done?

Ethical values: Thorough reporting, protection of the public.

Ethical guidelines: The Society of Professional Journalists Code of Ethics says to minimize harm.

- Injuries and fatalities (make sure that you ask if any firefighters were injured)
- Cause (ask if arson is suspected—intentional setting of fire), how and where fire started
- Who discovered the fire, extent of damage, insurance coverage
- Description of building
- Estimated cost of damages
- Presence and condition of smoke detectors or sprinkler system (especially in a public building or apartment building, if city requires them)
- Fire inspection record, fire code violations (usually for a follow-up story, especially in public buildings)

When fatalities or injuries occur in a fire, they should be mentioned in your lead, preferably a hard-news lead. If no one is injured or if heroic rescue attempts are involved, a soft lead may be appropriate. Follow-up stories and sidebars provide many opportunities for storytelling techniques.

This example follows most of the guidelines for reporting fires:

KODIAK, Alaska—A mother and infant escaped injury, but one of their two dogs perished in a house fire Sunday night.

Firefighters spent about a half hour battling the blaze, which started in the basement of the house, owned and occupied by Mario and JoAnn Alvarez.

"The cause of the fire is not known yet," said Kodiak fire chief Joe Hart.

When they arrived, firefighters saw smoke coming out of the upper parts of the house and found flames at the front door and coming out of the basement stairwell when they entered the building.

"There are char marks on the outside of the structure, and we had to break out some of the windows to ventilate," Hart said.

He estimated losses at $50,000, saying there was extensive damage from heat and smoke.

—*The Associated Press*

Court Stories

Writing about a crime is only the first step. The next step takes place in court. To cover courts, you need a basic understanding of the process and the terminology that is used. Court procedures vary from state to state and even in counties within states. You need to find out how the system works in the area where you are working.

A complete understanding of the courts would require a three-year course called law school. But you can learn most of what you need to know as you do your reporting. Whenever you hear a term you don't understand, seek a definition. And don't use legal terms in your stories unless you explain them. In fact, avoid them as much as possible. Go by this guideline: If you don't understand something, chances are the reader won't either. It's up to you to make the story clear.

Court cases are full of drama. They are the stuff of television series and movies. Yet newspaper stories about them are often dull. Even if you use a hard-news approach to report a conviction or testimony, you can still use storytelling techniques of dialogue, description and narrative writing for portions of the story so the reader can experience the human drama that filled the courtroom.

Here are some basic guidelines for writing court stories:

- Get reactions, facial expressions and gestures of the defendant and the accusers, attorneys, relatives and other people affected by the case, especially in trial stories and verdict stories.

- Use descriptive detail and color—lively quotes, dramatic testimony and dialogue.

- Translate all jargon, and avoid legal terminology.

- State exact charges in the story.

- Give the background of the crime, no matter how many stories have been published about this case.

- Include the name of the court where the trial or hearing is being held.

- Get comments from defendants, prosecutors, defense attorneys, plaintiffs (the people who brought suit or filed charges), relatives, and jurors in all verdict stories.

- In verdict stories, include how long the jury deliberated. Also include how many jurors were on the case; not all cases have 12-member juries, the most common number. In some cases, the amount of time the jury deliberated may be a major factor—as you will see in the following example about the O.J. Simpson case. In all cases, however, the length of deliberations is part of the story.

- Write the next step—the next court appearance or, in verdict stories, plans for an appeal if the defendant is found guilty.

The trial of former football player O.J. Simpson captured the nation's attention for nine months, but the jury deliberated fewer than four hours before reaching a verdict of acquittal. That factor was the lead on the first Associated Press stories and was still high in later editions of the stories. Even though this trial took place in 1995, references to it persist in news stories about Simpson, who has since been charged with robbery and other crimes.

> LOS ANGELES (AP)—O.J. Simpson was acquitted Tuesday of murdering his ex-wife and her friend, a suspense-filled climax to the courtroom saga that obsessed the nation. With two words, "not guilty," the jury freed the fallen sports legend to try to rebuild a life thrown into disgrace.
>
> Simpson looked toward the jury and mouthed, "Thank you," after the panel was dismissed. He turned to his family and punched a fist into the air. He then hugged his lead defense attorney, Johnnie Cochran Jr., and his friend and attorney Robert Kardashian.
>
> "He's going to start his life all over again," Cochran told reporters later.
>
> "It's over from our viewpoint," District Attorney Gil Garcetti said.
>
> After hearing nine months of testimony, the majority-black jury of 10 women and two men took fewer than four hours Monday to clear Simpson of the June 12, 1994, murders of Nicole Brown Simpson and her friend Ronald Goldman. The verdict was unsealed and read Tuesday.
>
> —*The Associated Press*

Criminal and Civil Cases

Court procedures fall into two categories: criminal and civil cases. Criminal cases are violations of any laws regulating crime. If you are arrested on suspicion of drunken driving, you could be charged in a criminal case.

Civil cases involve lawsuits between two parties. If your landlord says you have not paid the rent or you have damaged your apartment, he can bring a civil lawsuit against you. Divorces, malpractice, libel, contract disputes and other actions not involving criminal law are civil cases.

Federal Courts and State Courts

The court system functions on two levels: a federal level and a state level. Federal courts have jurisdiction over cases involving matters related to the U.S. Constitution (such as civil rights), federal tax and antitrust matters, and any other federal laws.

Convergence Coach

Use the Web to do background research and put stories in perspective.

■ Check the Web for background of criminal suspects. Start with a basic search engine and check sex offender registries—even if the person is not charged with a sex crime.

■ Check the Web for perspective on issue stories. For example, if you are writing about a local school shooting, check online for a listing of recent school shootings or similar statistics in other crimes.

■ Search blogs, and social networking sites for messages suspects may have sent.

Federal courts also hear cases between people from different states. Here is the hierarchy of the federal court system:

U.S. District Court: This is the lowest level of the federal judicial system, where most cases involving federal issues are first heard.

U.S. Court of Appeals: There are 12 of these courts for geographical areas, plus the U.S. Court of Appeals for the D.C. (District of Columbia) Circuit. It is the intermediary court, where cases from the federal district courts are appealed.

U.S. Supreme Court: This is the highest court in the nation. Cases may be appealed to this court, but the justices do not have to rule on all the cases.

Most states also have three levels of courts: a trial court, an appeals court and a state supreme court for appeals of the last resort on the state level. Cases from the state's highest court may be appealed to the U.S. Supreme Court if there is a federal angle, such as a constitutional matter—a First Amendment issue, for example—or a civil rights violation.

The names of the state courts can be confusing. In one state a superior court may be a trial-level court, whereas in others it may be an appellate court.

There also are municipal courts, where violations of local laws, such as traffic laws or city ordinances, are heard.

In addition, within the state system there are juvenile courts (for cases involving people younger than age 18) and probate courts, where disputes involving wills and estates are heard.

When you write your court story, find out the proper name of the court—whether it is called a district court, a circuit court or a common pleas court—and write that in the story.

Criminal Court Process

Crimes are classified as misdemeanors or felonies. *Misdemeanors* are considered minor offenses that carry a potential penalty of up to a year in jail and/or a fine. *Felonies* are more serious crimes punishable by more than a year in prison. Criminal procedures differ from state to state, but there are some general processes in the court system that you should understand. The following diagram outlines court procedures for both criminal and civil cases.

Arrest The person is stopped by police for suspicion of having committed a crime and is taken to the police station for questioning or further action. Police are required to read a person his rights: to remain silent (if the person does not want to discuss the issue prior to a court procedure) and to retain an attorney. These are called the Miranda warnings, based on a court case by that name.

A person can also be arrested if someone has filed a complaint with police and the police find enough probable cause to believe the complaint is true. At this point the police can notify the person of the charge that will be filed—basically, why he is being arrested—but the charge is not official yet.

Court procedures

Crimes are defined as misdemeanors or felonies. The path through the judicial process is different depending on the type of crime. However, criminal justice is just one of the types of cases that courts hear. More common, but less prominent, are civil disputes, which are usually resolved in civil court.

Misdemeanors
Misdemeanors are considered minor offenses that carry a potential penalty of up to a year in jail and/or a fine.

- ARREST
- BOOKING / BOND SET
- ARRAIGNMENT
  Case usually disposed at this time and sentence issued
- POSSIBLE TRIAL AND VERDICT

Felonies
Felonies are serious crimes punishable by more than a year in jail.

- ARREST
- BOOKING
- ARRAIGNMENT
- PRELIMINARY HEARING
- TRIAL
- SENTENCING IN GUILTY VERDICTS

Civil cases
In civil cases, a plaintiff files a suit against another party — a person or a company — seeking damages or some compensation. Divorce cases are examples of civil matters. The court procedures can be lengthy. Usually, after a suit is filed, numerous motions are filed by attorneys for both parties. Eventually the case can go to trial if it is not resolved in an out-of-court settlement.

- SUIT FILED
- VARIOUS MOTIONS
- TRIAL
- RULING BY JUDGE OR JURY
- SENTENCING IN GUILTY VERDICTS

Bill Skeet

Process of criminal and civil cases

If someone is wanted for a crime, police can also seek a warrant for that person's arrest, a legal document provided by a judge that gives police the right to make the arrest.

Booking The suspect is taken to a booking desk in the police station, where he is fingerprinted and photographed. Information about the person—age, address, physical description and so on—is then recorded in a police book, the log. At this point the person may be held in jail or released until formal charges are issued.

Charges The arresting police officer confers with a member of the district attorney's office, who decides if a charge against the suspect should be filed with the court. It is important for the reporter to find out if the person has been charged officially with the crime because many newspapers and broadcast stations don't publish or announce news of an arrest until charges have been filed.

Many states have standard bail fees for common or misdemeanor crimes, and the person may be able to post a bail bond at this time and be released without a hearing.

Arraignment Usually within 24 to 48 hours, a suspect will have a first hearing. At this point the charges are read in court. In some places, at this time the suspect can enter a plea of guilty, not guilty or no contest—not admitting guilt but not contesting the charge either. In some jurisdictions, the arraignment may be held just to formally read the charges; the plea comes at a later hearing.

If the suspect pleads guilty, the sentence can be issued at this point, and the matter can be settled—or the judge may delay sentencing for another hearing. Misdemeanor cases are often settled at this level.

If the person pleads not guilty, he has the right to a trial, and the judge can set bail at this time.

At the hearing, the judge will determine bail. If the person fails to show up for the next court appearance, the total amount of bail is forfeited to the court. When the person has no previous record, the judge may release the suspect on his own recognizance (recognition) without any bail.

Preliminary Hearing In felony cases only, a judge weighs the facts presented by a prosecutor from the district attorney's office and by the defense attorney at a special hearing. Then the judge decides whether there is enough evidence (probable cause) to hold the person for trial. If not, the person is released, and charges are dropped.

In some states, the preliminary hearing is synonymous with the "first hearing" or "first appearance," and it precedes the arraignment. In other states, "arraignment" is the term for that first court appearance.

Grand Jury In certain cases, particularly those involving political crimes or major drug cases and those in federal courts, a grand jury will be convened to investigate the circumstances of the case and determine if there is enough evidence—enough probable cause—that the crime has been committed.

Like a trial jury, the grand jury is a group of citizens, from 12 to 33 members, chosen to serve on the case. They listen to testimony from prosecutors and witnesses. Unlike the trial jury, however, the grand jury does not rule on guilt or innocence. It only recommends to a judge whether there is enough evidence to take the case to a trial.

If there is, the grand jury hands up (because the judge sits on a higher bench than the jury) an indictment, also called a "true bill." The defendant then enters a plea at another hearing. If the case goes to trial, another jury will be impaneled to serve at the trial.

Grand jury proceedings are secret; the jurors are sworn not to reveal deliberations to the media or anyone else (in most states). However, many reporters with good sources can find out the essence of what happened. After deliberations, if and when the grand jury issues a report, that is usually public record.

Pretrial Hearings and Motions Before the trial, attorneys usually file a number of motions (formal requests to the court) seeking to have the case dropped, to have the trial moved to another location (called a change of venue) or to have evidence suppressed. The judge has to rule on each motion.

Plea Bargain To avoid a trial, which is time-consuming and expensive, lawyers will often negotiate a plea bargain. This is usually a deal offering the defendant a reduced sentence in return for pleading guilty to a lesser charge. The defendant could also plead "no contest," which means the person doesn't admit guilt but won't contest the court's decision.

Trial If the case goes to trial, a jury is selected and the case is heard. In some cases, particularly civil cases, a judge may decide the case without a jury.

Unanimous verdicts are required in criminal trials in most states. If the jury can't agree on a guilty or not-guilty verdict, it is called a "hung jury," and a mistrial is declared. The defendant is then technically not guilty.

If the defendant is judged guilty, you may then call him a murderer, rapist or whatever accusatory term fits the crime involved. But do not use accusatory terms in stories before a guilty verdict.

Sentencing After the trial, if the person is found guilty, there will be another hearing. The judge will then decide on a sentence. Sometimes the judge issues the sentence immediately after the verdict.

At any time during the criminal court process, the suspect may change his not-guilty plea to a guilty one and eliminate the need for a trial.

Appeal A person convicted of a crime can appeal the decision to a higher court. It is logical to ask in all court trials with convictions whether an appeal is planned. The information should be included in the story.

Civil Court Process A civil case starts with a suit filed by a person or a company. Anyone can file a lawsuit for a fee. After filing, the lawyers for both sides file various motions with the court. If the case is not settled between the two parties at a pretrial hearing, a court hearing date is set. Civil cases may be argued in front of a judge or before a jury if one is requested. Civil suits can drag through the courts for many years. If the case goes to trial, the process is the same as for criminal trials.

Most civil cases never even get to the trial stage. At any point after motions have been filed, the judge may dismiss the case or may grant a request for a summary judgment, a ruling on the case when both parties agree to forgo a trial.

Terms Used in Court Reporting

You should become familiar with these terms so you can better understand and explain court proceedings:

Acquittal: Finding by a court or jury that a person accused of a crime is not guilty.

Adjudicate: To make a final determination or judgment by the court.

Affidavit: Sworn statement of facts.

Appeal: Plea to ask a higher court to review a judgment, verdict or order of a lower court.

Appellant: Person who files an appeal.

Arraignment: Court hearing in which a defendant in a criminal case is formally charged with the crime and given a chance to enter a plea of guilty, not guilty or no contest (nolo contendere). At this time, bail is usually set.

Bail: Amount of money set by the court that the defendant must guarantee to pay if he does not show up for a court trial. If the defendant can't raise the money through a bail bond company or personal sources, he stays in jail.

Bond: Written promise to pay bail money on the conditions stated. The bond for bail is usually 10 percent of the total amount of bail set. The term is often used interchangeably with *bail*. Very often, a person will borrow money from a bond company. Then if the person flees, the bond company loses the money.

Brief: Legal document filed with the court by a lawyer, stating the facts of the case and arguments citing how laws apply to this case.

Change of Venue: Procedure to seek a change of location of the trial, usually when defense attorneys contend that the defendant can't get a fair trial in the current location because of too much pretrial publicity.

Charge: Official allegation of criminal wrongdoing.

Civil Suit: Lawsuit to determine rights, duties, claims for damages, ownership or other settlements in noncriminal matters.

Complaint: Formal affidavit in which one person accuses another of violating the law.

Condemnation: Civil action to acquire ownership of property for public use. When a municipality wants to build a road or sidewalk, the government will condemn the property to gain right of way.

Contempt: Action that disregards the order or authority of the court. A lawyer who screams obscenities at the judge will probably be found in contempt of court.

Defendant: In a civil case, the person being sued. In a criminal case, the person charged with breaking the law.

Deposition: Written statement of testimony from a witness under oath.

Discovery: Pretrial examination of a person (including depositions), documents or other items to find evidence that may be used in the trial.

Dismissal: Order to drop the case.

Docket: List of cases pending before the court. A trial docket is a list of cases pending trial.

Extradition: Procedure to move a person accused of a crime from the state where he is residing to the state where the crime occurred and where the trial will be conducted.

Felony: Major crime punishable by a sentence of a year or more. Crimes such as robbery, homicide and kidnapping are felonies; lesser crimes such as shoplifting are misdemeanors. Legally, a felony is defined as a crime punishable by death or imprisonment in a state prison.

Grand Jury: Group of citizens selected by the court to investigate whether there is enough evidence or probable cause that a crime occurred and that the person should be charged, or indicted.

Hung Jury: Jury that cannot reach a unanimous verdict, a requirement in most criminal trials.

Indictment: Recommendation by the grand jury that there is enough probable cause to charge a person or group of people with the crime under investigation. The grand jury hands up an indictment to the judge (because the judge sits on a platform higher than the jury); the judge hands down rulings. It's preferable to use the word *issued.*

Injunction: Order by the court instructing a person, group or company to stop the action that was occurring, such as picketing. For example, an injunction can order a group to stop marching outside an abortion clinic.

Innocent: The term "not guilty" is preferable in court cases. The *Associated Press Stylebook* previously recommended using the term "innocent" in case the "not" in "not guilty" was dropped from typesetting, but that is no longer the case. AP now recommends using "not guilty."

Misdemeanor: Crime less serious than a felony; crime punishable by less than one year in jail and/or fines.

Mistrial: Trial that is set aside or declared invalid because of some mistake in proceedings or, in a criminal trial, because the jury cannot reach a unanimous verdict.

Motion: Request for the court to make a ruling or finding.

Nolo contendere: Latin for "I will not contest it" (no contest). This plea has the same effect as a guilty plea, but it is not an admission of guilt. It means the person will not fight the charge. If you agree to pay a fine for a traffic ticket but do not agree that you were speeding, you are pleading no contest. This type of plea is used as a form of bargaining to get the defendant a reduced charge in exchange for his agreement not to protest and to eliminate the need for a trial. Use the English term *no contest* in a story, and explain briefly that it is not an admission of guilt.

Plaintiff: Person who sues in a civil case. The defendant is the one being sued.

Plea: Defendant's response to a charge, stating that he is guilty, not guilty, or not willing to contest the charge.

Plea bargain: Agreement between the prosecutor and the defendant (or defense attorney) to accept a lesser charge and a lesser sentence in return for a guilty or no-contest plea. Plea bargaining is used extensively as a way to eliminate court trials. Once the defendant pleads guilty or no contest, there is no need for a trial. However, a plea bargain must be approved by the court.

Probable Cause: Determination that there is enough evidence to prosecute a criminal case. Police officials also need probable cause—enough reason to believe a crime is being committed—when they seek a search warrant or any other warrant for a person's arrest.

Probation: Condition in which the person is released from serving a jail sentence if he meets certain terms, such as serving in the community, entering drug treatment or accepting whatever restrictions the judge decides.

Recognizance: Literally, "recognition." A person may be released from jail based on his own recognizance—meaning the recognition of a previously good reputation. This ruling is essentially the judge's way of saying that, because of the person's reputation, he is not considered a high risk for skipping the next court hearing or trial.

Subpoena: Court order commanding a person to appear in court or to release documents to the court.

Summary judgment: Procedure in a civil suit asking the court to give final judgment on the grounds that there are no further questions and no need for a trial.

Summons: Document notifying a defendant that a lawsuit or complaint has been filed against him.

Suspended sentence: Court order stating that the punishment of the defendant will be suspended if certain conditions are met. A person who receives probation gets a suspended sentence.

Temporary injunction: Court order to stop an action, such as a protest, for a specific amount of time until a court hearing and ruling whether the action should be enjoined, or stopped permanently.

Tort: Civil case involving damages, pain, suffering or other allegations of wrongdoing.

True Bill: Indictment issued by a grand jury.

Verdict: Decision by a jury about guilt or innocence.

Warrant: Court order directing law enforcement officials to arrest a person. A search warrant gives officials authority to search a premises.

Court Story Examples

A court case is a continuing saga. From the time a person is arrested until the case is resolved, whether in a trial or a settlement, you will write many stories about it. But never assume that the reader is familiar with the case, no matter how sensational it may be. Always include the background.

Whether you take a soft or hard approach, make sure that your nut graph explains who is being accused of what, and place it high in the story.

If information is part of a court record, you may use it as fact—but it still may not be true. It's up to a judge or jury to decide whether the claims in court documents and trials are true. So you need to attribute your information, although not necessarily in the lead.

Unlike other stories, many court stories do not appear balanced. On any given day, one side in the case may present its arguments, so you won't always have a story that seems fair to both parties. The testimony will be biased; you should not be.

Some reminders:

- Explain charges and background.
- Describe defendants and witnesses.
- Specify the court where the proceeding takes place.
- Tell how long the jury deliberated in verdict stories.
- Tell a good story.

When the verdict is issued in a major trial that has garnered interest locally or nationally, a hard-news story is appropriate. A soft lead also may work, but make sure that you put the verdict very high in the story. The following story is an example of a basic hard-news approach. In this case, the judge sentenced the defendant immediately instead of at a separate hearing.

What Do You Think

In recent years, law enforcement officials have been releasing names of people considered "persons of interest" before charges are filed. Do you think the news media should name these people prior to any formal charges?

- Yes
- No
- Not sure

Summary lead: verdict, delayed identification

EXETER, N.H.—A high school instructor was convicted yesterday and sentenced to life in prison without parole after a sensational trial on charges that she manipulated her student-lover into murdering her husband.

Defendant's reaction, charges, name of court

Pamela Smart, 23, stood motionless as the Superior Court jury foreman pronounced her guilty of murder-conspiracy and being an accomplice to murder.

Relative's reactions

The victim's mother, Judith Smart, cried out as each verdict was read, and said afterward, "She got what she deserved."

Judith and William Smart then left the court for the cemetery where their son is buried.

"We're going to tell Gregg," William Smart said. "We're going to tell him that, by God, she did do it."

Brief background

Gregg Smart, a 24-year-old insurance agent, was murdered May 1 last year, six days before his first wedding anniversary.

More reactions

Pamela Smart's parents, John and Linda Wojas, were stone-faced as they left the courthouse.

Descriptive detail

"You know how I feel about that," Linda Wojas said when asked if she thought her daughter had gotten a fair trial. Wojas wore a yellow ribbon every day, symbolizing her belief that her daughter was a hostage of the judicial system.

Reaction quotes

"I feel terribly bad for the Wojas family," Judith Smart said. "I can imagine how I would feel and I feel very, very bad for them."

Jury information: time deliberated, length of trial and other charges

The jury, which heard three weeks of testimony, deliberated 12 hours over three days before returning its verdict. Smart also was convicted of witness-tampering for encouraging her student-intern to lie to police.

Identification of court and judge, sentencing, expected appeal

Rockingham County Superior Court Judge Douglas Gray immediately announced the mandatory life sentence for the accomplice-to-murder charge. An appeal is expected.

Background and highlights of trial

Smart was the school district media coordinator when she met William Flynn, now 17, as one of his instructors in a self-awareness program at Winnacunnet High School in Hampton.

Prosecutors said the former high school cheerleader and college honor student tantalized and seduced Flynn, then 15 and a virgin, and then threatened to end their affair unless he murdered her husband. Smart testified that she broke off the affair just before the murder.

Prosecutors said Smart feared losing everything in a divorce, including her dog and furniture.

Fate of others involved (note plea bargain)

The defense called Flynn and two confessed accomplices "thrill-killers" who shot Smart on their own, then framed his widow to avoid life prison terms. In plea bargains, they face minimum sentences ranging from 18 to 28 years.

Color details

The Boston Herald, which dubbed Smart the "Ice Princess," invited readers to call in their verdicts on a 900 number. They voted guilty, 543 to 101.

More highlights of trial

The most damaging evidence against Smart was four secretly recorded conversations she had with Cecelia Pierce, 16, her student-intern and confidante. The profanity-laden tapes, made after the murder, show that Smart urged Pierce to lie to police, that she feared being jailed herself, and that she had known her husband would be murdered.

Key testimony

Flynn, sobbing as he testified on March 12, admitted pulling the trigger on a .38-cal. pistol he held to Gregg Smart's head.

He and Patrick Randall, 17, testified that they entered the Smarts' condominium through a basement door that Pamela Smart had left unlocked for them and waited for Smart to arrive home. They also said they forced him to his knees as he begged for mercy.

Shortly before the verdict, John Wojas said people were misjudging his daughter.

Reaction quote kicker

"She's not a cold little woman like they're trying to describe her," he said. "She doesn't show a lot of outright emotion. She never has."

—*The Associated Press*

Stories about upcoming court trials lend themselves to storytelling techniques. If the story is important enough to "advance" the trial, it probably has a good story behind it. A narrative writing technique was used to advance this trial in a story that uses almost no direct attribution, except for quotes. The story is based on court records and previous admissions by the defendant. If the defendant had not admitted the crime, this story would be too accusatory.

MIAMI—He was a distraught man that day, a man who sang lullabies and wept. With one hand, he held a gun. With the other, he stroked the smooth face of his daughter, a 3-year-old existing in limbo between life and death.

An hour before, he had given her what he thought was a fatal dose of Valium. But here she was still breathing, her tiny chest rising and falling rhythmically, if ever so slightly.

She was in a crib at Miami Children's Hospital, lying on her back. She had been there for eight months, since the day she nearly suffocated. He leaned over the crib railing and looked at her eyes. They were open. They stared ahead, mirrored no emotions, saw nothing. It was the same for her other senses. The damage to her brain was total and irreversible, and because of it, she couldn't hear his weeping, and she couldn't feel his last touch goodbye before he aimed the gun at her heart.

He shot her twice. He dropped the gun. He prayed that her suffering was over. He fell into a nurse's arms, cried and said he wanted to die. He said, "Maybe I should get the electric chair to make things even. I killed my daughter. I shot her twice. But I'm glad she's gone to heaven."

On Tuesday morning in a Miami courtroom, almost five months after the death of his daughter, Joy, Charles Griffith is scheduled to go on trial for murder. The defense, says Griffith's attorney, Mark Krasnow, will be mercy. "It was an act of love," Krasnow says, "not an act of malice."

—David Finkel, *St. Petersburg* (Fla.) *Times*

The next example is a story about a lawsuit in a civil case that has not yet come to trial. When you cover a story about a suit that has been filed, always try to contact the people involved or at least their lawyers, whose names are listed in the suit. If you wade through all the legal writing, lawsuits can be very entertaining.

What has no arms or legs and wiggles in the night?

According to Gladys Diehl and her husband, John Brehm, it's their Sealy Posturpedic mattress.

In a lawsuit filed yesterday in Bucks County Court, Diehl and Brehm contend that they endured many nights of fitful slumber because an uninvited guest shared their bed—a 26-inch snake living inside the mattress.

"There was a lot of wiggling going on," said Stephen A. Shelly, the attorney representing the Quakertown couple.

Diehl and Brehm are seeking more than $20,000 from Sealy Mattress Co., the manufacturer, and Hess's department store, which sold the mattress. They say the incident traumatized them and caused sleep disorders.

According to the suit, the couple bought a mattress on May 13 from Hess's in Richland Township, Bucks County. Soon after, they began to notice an unfamiliar movement in their bed, which they "suspected could be a living creature."

In July, they exchanged the mattress at Hess's for another Sealy, hoping for a better night's sleep. They didn't get one. The replacement mattress also slithered and shimmied, according to the couple.

After four months of suspicious bumps in the night, Diehl and Brehm took the second mattress to Laboratory Testing Inc. in Dublin for examination. Inside,

workers found a dead 26-inch ribbon snake. The species is not poisonous.

The suit contends that both the manufacturer and the department store breached their warranties. . . . No date has been set for a hearing on the case.

—John P. Martin, *The Philadelphia Inquirer*

Most court stories are serious, but some have a humorous angle. Here is a light-hearted story in a conversational style that tries to involve the reader. It is an example of how a plea bargain works—or in this case, how it didn't work out very well. This story is written in storytelling form with the clincher at the end; unfortunately, the headline gives the twist away.

Man gambles on plea, loses

He admits guilt, then is acquitted

You're the defendant. You make the call:

You're Marvin E. Johnson, 40, convicted three times of drug possession.

You're facing a minimum 15 years in prison without parole if convicted of being a felon in possession of a handgun.

On Wednesday, the jury at your federal trial in Kansas City deliberates three hours without reaching a verdict. On Thursday, the jury deliberates three more hours and announces it is hopelessly deadlocked. A hung jury and a new trial loom on the horizon.

The prosecutor, Assistant U.S. Attorney Rob Larsen, offers a deal. If you plead guilty, he'll reduce the

government's sentencing request to a range of 15 to 22 months.

While you ponder that deal, the jury buzzes. It has a verdict.

Do you:

A) Sign the plea agreement and serve at least 15 months in prison? Or

B) Roll the dice with the jury's verdict? If it's guilty, you get at least 15 years; if it's not guilty, you walk away.

On Thursday afternoon, Marvin E. Johnson signed the plea agreement.

Five minutes later, the jury found him not guilty.

"I'm sure glad I struck that plea agreement," Larsen said.

"I can't win for losing," said Johnson's defense lawyer, John P. O'Connor.

—Tom Jackman, *The Kansas City* (Mo.) *Star*

1 Crime story: Although the police report shown here is labeled "Standard Offense Report," it is not. Each state has its own form; however, this one is similar to many. Most of the report is self-explanatory, with some exceptions. The case number is important for reporters; if you want to follow the case through the court system, you need this number, which stays the same for all actions in the case. Time is computed as military time, from one to 24 hours. Where the stolen property is listed, codes are used to signify the type of property. A complete code sheet is usually on the back of the police report. Write a story based on the following report:

You called the police to ask more about the theft of the bird because that was unusual. The police told you that the bird was valuable and that was probably the reason it was stolen. They told you there is no rash of bird burglars, although there had been some thefts of birds several months ago. But this bird theft does not appear to be related to those because other items were taken, the police said. Police are still investigating. Use yesterday as your time frame for the date of offense and today as the date reported.

2 **Fire story:** You are making a routine call to the fire department to find out if any fires occurred overnight. Fire Battalion Chief Stephen McInerny gives you this information:

A fire occurred in a ground-floor apartment in the 2700 block of Northeast 30th Place in your town at 1:12 a.m. today. Four fire engines and 16 firefighters responded at 1:15 a.m. Cause of fire: A stove was turned on, and some cookbooks and towels on the stove ignited. When firefighters arrived, they found a 2½-year-old cocker spaniel at the front door. Estimated damage: $9,000 smoke damage to apartment. Other units not affected. Apartment is uninhabitable. Dog's name is Tito. McInerny said the dog apparently started the fire by jumping on the stove, using one of the knobs for foothold. The setting on the burner was on medium high. The dog was apparently looking for food. The dog crawled to the front door. "The dog was clinically dead; it had no pulse and no respiration." McInerny said firefighter Bill Mock took the dog outside and gave it cardiopulmonary resuscitation and oxygen, and the dog came back to life. The dog was taken to the animal hospital and treated for smoke inhalation. McInerny said it is not unusual for dogs to be caught in house fires, but it is

---

STANDARD OFFENSE REPORT
FRONT PAGE OPEN PUBLIC RECORD

On View √ Dispatched √ Citizen	Name of Agency Your town police dept.	Agency No. 0230100	Case No. 03-123456
Incident			

Date offense started Use yesterday's date	Time 0700	Date offense ended Use today's date	Time ------	Date of report Today's date

Location of Offense 2339 Felony Lane	Time reported 22:36	Time arrived 22:40	Time cleared 22:55
Offense			

Description Burglary	Premise	Method of Entry • Force √ No Force	Type of Theft From building	Type of Force Unknown
Victim				

Name of Victim Last First Middle Smith Jon J.	**Address** Street City State ZIP 2339 Felony Lane Your town Yours Yours	Telephone no. 555-1234

Type of victim Individual	Race W	Sex M	Age 22	Ethnicity ----	Height 6-0	Weight 195	Hair Blond	Eyes Blu	License -----	Social Security No 131-300-0123

	Reporting Person		

Last First Middle Doe James Brian	Address Street City State ZIP 2337 Felony Lane Your town Yours Yours	Telephone no. 555-4321

Type of victim Individual	Race W	Sex M	Age 25	Ethnicity ----	Height 5-10	Weight 170	Hair Br	Eyes Br	License -----	Social Security No 171-009-0554

Property Description - Type of Loss
1=None 2=Burned 3=Counterfeit 4=Destroyed/damaged /vandalized 5=Recovered   6= Seized 7= Stolen 8 = Unknown

Type Loss	Property Code	Description	Est. Quantity	Value	Date Recovered
7	0618	Zenith VCR	1	300	-------------
7	0618	Sharp CD player	1	350	-------------
7	1002	Cockatoo (bird)	1	1,500	-------------

Reporting Officer John Law	Badge No. 733	Date Today	Copies to Property Total 2,150

Description of incident

At 22:56 the office was contacted by Mr. James Doe, next-door neighbor of the victim. He was watching Mr. Smith's house while Smith was away. Doe checked the door to Smith's residence at 07:00 before he went to work. When he returned home at 22:30, he again checked Smith's residence and noticed that someone had pried the deadbolt lock on the front door. I was dispatched to the residence. I searched premises but did not find any suspects. When Mr. Smith returned home, he advised that items missing were VCR, CD player and cockatoo, who answers to the name of Homer. Owner described bird as white and 10 years old. He said the bird could say his name and had limited vocabulary of "damn," "rotten" and a few curse words.

unusual for them to be revived from the dead. "That's twice in a little more than a year we've revived dogs that have been clinically dead as a result of a fire. We're getting pretty good at it."

You interview Mark Alan Leszczynski, who rented the apartment and owns the dog. He said he and a house guest went to a bar before midnight and left the dog alone. "The dog is a little mischievous. I've caught him doing this before. He has a never-ending appetite. I had just reprimanded him for going into my house guest's suitcase and stealing some candy."

3 Court terms: You may use your imagination for this exercise. The point of it is to see if you can use court terminology in the proper context and spell the words correctly. Use the following terms: *change of venue, affidavit, felony, misdemeanor, subpoena, mistrial, bond, arraignment, suspended sentence, plea bargain.*

Use the terms to write a story about this situation: A college student, 19, named Gold E. Locks, has been charged with a felony: breaking and entering into the home of Pa Pa Bear and his wife, Ma Ma Bear, who live at (you decide the address) with their child, Bay B. Bear.

4 Civil court case: Write a brief story about the following case, a petition for a name change, which was filed in the civil section of a county court (use your county court).

IN THE CIRCUIT COURT OF (YOUR COUNTY, YOUR STATE)

Joseph Weirdo, Petitioner   Case No. 99 C638

PETITION

Comes now the petitioner, Joseph Weirdo, and prays his cause of action and states as follows:

1. That he resides at 700 Louisiana St., Your City, Your State.

2. That the petitioner requests a change of name from Joseph Weirdo to Joseph Weir.

3. That the current name of the petitioner has caused him great embarrassment and suffering.

4. That petitioner is a citizen in good standing and the request for the name change is not to avoid any legal actions against said petitioner.

5. That petitioner is not seeking for redress as a means of avoiding any debts owed to any parties.

6. Wherefore, petitioner prays for favorable judgment from the court.

                Joseph Weirdo
          City, State, ZIP Code
            On behalf of himself

You call Joseph Weirdo, and he tells you he was tired of being kidded about his name. "I didn't want to go through life being a Weirdo," he says.

You check with Circuit Court Judge Jack Musselman, who approved the petition. He says he signs hundreds of these, but most of them are name-change petitions from divorced women, foster children who want to take the name of the family they have stayed with or people with "an extremely ethnic name." "I can't recall anyone looking to play games. A lot of times people are trying to avoid creditors. There's no way of checking that out."

The court clerk tells you that more than 300 people filed to have their names changed this year. It costs $200 to file the papers.

☞ Featured Online Activity Log on to the book Web site for Chapter 22 and take the interactive quiz on crime and court terms at

academic.cengage.com/masscomm/rich/ writingandreportingnews6e

Coaching Tips

Gather as much detail as possible for graphics and for your story.

Seek human-interest stories and anecdotes.

Seek citizen journalism reports and blog accounts.

Get information to reconstruct a chronology of events.

Use descriptive and narrative techniques for sidebars.

Double-check all information; initial reports and statistics will change quickly.

Use role-playing reporting techniques: If you were a relative of someone in a tragedy, what would you want and need to know?

Plan highlights boxes and empowerment boxes to provide survival tips.

Check the Internet for weather and disaster resources.

Use online sources for background perspective.

Death is always and under all circumstances a tragedy, for if it is not, then it means that life itself has become one.

Theodore Roosevelt

23 Disasters, Weather and Tragedies

David Handschuh

David Handschuh was buried alive. A photographer for the *New York Daily News,* Handschuh was driving to New York University to begin his first day as an adjunct professor of a photojournalism class. It was the morning of Sept. 11, 2001. He looked up and saw a mass of smoke. He turned on his police scanner and heard a voice screaming: "Send every piece of apparatus; the World Trade Center is on fire."

He called his newspaper and then called NYU to tell them to post a note that he would be "a little late this morning."

"All we knew is that it was an accident," Handschuh recalled. He said he turned his car around and crossed over the center divider of the highway to head toward the towers. As a photographer who had shot hundreds of fires, he knew many of the city's firefighters. He passed a fire truck with 11 firefighters who were waving to him. "All 11 firefighters in that truck died," Handschuh said. "They were on their way to their own funeral, and they didn't know it."

It was just one of many traumatic moments Handschuh would experience on that day and long after the terrorist attack of Sept. 11, 2001, in which 2,749 people died when two hijacked planes crashed into the World Trade Center towers in New York City. Terrorists had also hijacked two other commercial jetliners on that day and crashed one of them into the Pentagon; a fourth plane, headed toward Washington, D.C., plummeted into a field outside of Pittsburgh, Pa.

Although many other tragedies have occurred since then, the terrorist attack on 9/11 will endure as one of the most significant events in U.S. history.

The first attack in New York was at 8:46 a.m., and Handschuh arrived at the scene at 8:48 a.m., one of the only times he remembers that day. "At that time only one plane had hit the towers," Handschuh said. "The streets of New York were eerily quiet, as though somebody had pressed a mute button." Eighteen minutes later the second plane slammed into the south tower.

Handschuh kept shooting photos. About an hour later the south tower started to collapse. "I was standing across the street," Handschuh said. "A voice in the back of my head said, 'Run.' It was like a wave at the beach. I was running one second and flying the next. The impact of the building tossed fire trucks. I wound up partially under a fire truck. I was buried alive. I never lost consciousness, I don't think. I couldn't move my legs. A fireman came and said, 'Don't worry, Brother, we'll get you out. You're hurt but you're alive.'"

© 2001 Hectop, *http://www.maxho.com/wtc/*

The World Trade Center towers shortly after planes crashed into them

For the next nine months he went through physical therapy. "I had to learn how to walk again," he said. His right leg had been completely crushed, and his left leg had also been "messed up." His nose and mouth had been clogged with ashes. His breathing and his lungs remain only at 50 percent capacity. But even now, several years after the 9/11 tragedy, that experience scarred him in less visible but equally significant ways. He still pauses when he hears a plane overhead.

"I never want to photograph anyone dead or dying again," Handschuh says. So these days he is a food photographer.

Working with the Dart Center for Journalism & Trauma (*www.dartcenter.org*), Handschuh spends some of his time coaching journalists on how to deal with post-traumatic stress disorder, which can result from reporting and photographing tragedy. The center, based at the University of Washington, provides tips and tools to help journalists understand how to cover tragedies and how to cope with their own emotional stress that can result from this type of journalism. Until recently, little attention had ever been paid to the toll that disaster coverage can take on journalists who have to stifle their own emotions as they report and photograph the trauma of tragedy victims. But during these tragedies, journalists excel and suppress their own feelings to fulfill their mission to inform the public. Despite the personal toll, Handschuh stresses the crucial role of journalists by saying, "Our work became history."

© James Tourtellotte, Courtesy of U.S. Customs Service

Cleanup at the World Trade Center disaster area in New York

Tim McGuire, editor of the *Star Tribune* in Minneapolis, explained it this way: "When you're working at top efficiency, on the biggest story of your life, the journalist's emotions are not like the emotions of 'real people.' You become almost ashamed of how divorced you are from the suffering. And then bam! You see something on TV, or truly absorb the impact of a story you're reading, and you drown in empathy, sympathy and dread," he wrote in an article for *The American Editor,* the magazine of the American Society of Newspaper Editors.

"Our focus had to be on doing our job out of a sense of the common good," McGuire wrote. "We were charged with delivering the news and perspective on this tragedy to our readership. If we got too close to the pain, it would have impaired our ability to do what we had to do for the greater good. . . . And what we do has felt more like a calling than it has for some time. For many of us our view of our journalistic craft has been transformed."

Images from that tragedy will be seared in people's minds and in history. "We have to take those pictures," Handschuh says, "but we don't have to publish them. These were some very tough calls."

Associated Press photographer Richard Drew captured a haunting image of a man falling headfirst from one of the twin towers of the World Trade Center. His photo became the subject of ethical discussions in newsrooms around the country as editors debated whether to use it. Many did.

Bill Marimow, former editor of *The Sun* in Baltimore, was one of them. "The horror of the event determines the use of the photos," he wrote in an article for The American Press Institute. "There are so many other things that we can adjust to minimize the sensitivity aspect, but we must not minimize the horror of the event."

It was one of many ethical discussions in newsrooms throughout the country as editors struggled to document history and reporters struggled to document grief. The names and stories behind the numbers were the only way to explain the horror.

Of the 2,749 people who died in the 9/11 attacks, the remains of more than 1,000 victims were never identified, and efforts to analyze the DNA from remains have ended. The pain has not ended for families of the victims, and their stories explain the tragedy that lingers behind the numbers.

The news was disheartening for many families who say they can't find closure when they don't have a body part to place in a coffin and bury in a grave.

Joan Greene, 72, of Staten Island, said she knew in her heart that the chances of getting back remains of her daughter Lorraine Lee were not good, but had held out hope.

"This is very hard," Greene said. "I just wish I could have something of her. It's hard to put into words but I need something to go to in the cemetery to think that part of her is there. It feels very empty."

—Lindsay Farber and Carol Eisenberg,
New York Newsday

In 2004 a natural disaster usurped the death toll of 9/11. More than 180,000 people were believed to have died and another 100,000 were missing in more than 12 Southeast Asian countries bordering the Indian Ocean when an earthquake spawned a massive wall of water called a "tsunami" that swept entire towns and their inhabitants into the sea. It happened the day after Christmas in 2004, and months later, the search continued for victims of one of the world's worst natural disasters in 100 years. The final death toll may never be known.

But again the story was best told not by numbers but by the human toll on individuals—some searching for loved ones and others who witnessed the devastation and lived to describe it. Like this excerpt from a *Tampa Tribune* story:

HAMBANTOTA, Sri Lanka—When T.D. Kamaldeen's toddler son asks where his Mama is, he tells him she's working abroad, making money to buy him chocolate. Or maybe a bicycle.

Sometimes the 3-year-old boy with big brown eyes wants to call and talk to Mama. Kamaldeen doesn't know what to say. How do you tell a child his mother, grandmother, aunt, uncle and cousins—nine people in all—died in the ferocious water that he saw take his house?

Throughout the United States, news organizations sought local angles for the story by writing about disaster-relief efforts in their area and finding people personally affected by the tragedy.

Joe Hight, managing editor of *The Oklahoman* in Oklahoma City, stresses the importance of covering tragedy with sensitivity. In an article for the Dart Center for Journalism & Trauma, he reflected on the bombing of a federal building in his city.

"The bombing aftermath taught me the impact of your coverage on the victims, community and journalists," he wrote. "It taught me that a tough journalist could be a sensitive journalist. And it taught me that we live in a world in which violent acts can occur anywhere at anytime, even on a nice and sunny spring day in your community."

ETHICS

You are the news editor for a newspaper or television station in your community, and the photographer has shot images of dead bodies along with several other photos of an airplane disaster scene. The photos of the bodies strewn around the crash site are the most dramatic. Until the disasters of 9/11 and subsequent images from the war in Iraq, most U.S. media did not run photos of dead bodies. However, that changed after the 9/11 terrorist attack. Will you print or air these photos? If so, how will you justify it to the victims' families?

Guidelines: The National Press Photographers Association's code of ethics states, "Photographic and video images can reveal great truths, expose wrongdoing and neglect, inspire hope and understanding and connect people around the globe through the language of visual understanding. Photographs can also cause great harm if they are callously intrusive or are manipulated. Treat all subjects with respect and dignity. Give special consideration to vulnerable subjects and compassion to victims of crime or tragedy. Intrude on private moments of grief only when the public has an overriding and justifiable need to see."

It was in that unlikely place that journalism students at the University of Oklahoma learned how to cover a disaster that was not a class exercise.

Joy Mathis was sitting at her desk in *The Oklahoma Daily* newsroom at 9 a.m. on April 19, 1995, when someone ran in and said there had been a bomb explosion in Oklahoma City. Terrorists had bombed a nine-story federal building in Oklahoma City, 20 miles from the campus in Norman, Okla.

As managing editor of the campus newspaper, Mathis tried to find reporters to send to the scene. "No one realized what a big deal it was," she said. But within an hour after the news broke, reporters started calling Mathis and asking what they could do. Mathis didn't have a specific plan. "I was just screaming at people. I was saying, 'Get University of Oklahoma angles.' That's the kind of story I knew we could do better than anyone else."

At that time, it was the worst-known terrorist attack in the United States. Timothy McVeigh, the terrorist who bombed the building, was later convicted and executed. His accomplice, Terry Nichols, was sentenced to life in prison. The federal building was razed, and a permanent memorial and museum have been erected on the site. The memorial site includes a reflecting pool and 168 empty metal chairs, one for each of the bombing victims, each on a glass base inscribed with the name of a victim.

Like the indelible inscriptions for the victims, that tragedy remains etched in the memories of the Oklahoma students, and their coverage still serves as a lesson on how to report and write about tragedy. Within hours after the bombing occurred, Mathis had at least 20 reporters and photographers gathering news on the scene in the city and around the campus. The coverage wasn't organized at this point.

By 7 p.m., most of the reporters and photographers had returned. Mathis and Tiffany Pape, editor of the newspaper, began organizing the stories and planning the pages.

"I was feeling a little panicky because we were just getting organized, and the reporters were freaking because they didn't have much time to write," Mathis said.

Lizz Dabrowski, The Oklahoma Daily

Alfred P. Murrah building after it was bombed

Courtesy of Anita Amarfio, The Oklahoma Daily

Omar L. Gallaga (left), Joy Mathis (middle), and Michelle Fielden working on a story about the
Oklahoma City bombing

"But by 8 p.m. we had every editor reading stories." Their 16-page newspaper included six pages of explosion news and photographs, graphics, and information boxes about where to donate blood or get more information.

Omar L. Gallaga had kept his emotions in check most of the day. Now he was tired. He returned to the newsroom and then headed for Norman Regional Hospital and the Norman Red Cross. But coverage wouldn't be easy.

"At the hospital a doctor said they had their first explosion victim," Gallaga said. "The man had been walking into an elevator when the building exploded. This was exactly what I'd been waiting and hoping for. Just when I felt it was time to approach the slightly wounded man, the (public relations) woman came in. She forbade me to speak to any patients." Everyone else was too busy to speak to him.

He headed for the Red Cross. He had better luck there. People were lined up for about two hours to give blood. He went to the waiting room. "In that waiting room I saw a poster whose content would become the lead for one of my bombing stories. It read ominously, 'A disaster can happen in any place, at any time!' WOW. I scribbled it down. I talked to some students who were getting ready to donate and left the scene. I returned to the newsroom where I would spend the rest of the day and night."

Gallaga was emotionally composed until he read Rudolf Isaza's story about a grandmother who was awaiting news about her two grandchildren, ages 5 and 3, who had been in the federal building's day-care center. The woman had told Isaza about the youngest one:

"He liked to draw," she said. "Just the other day he showed me a drawing of a tall and short man. I asked him who it was. He said it was Shaquille O'Neal and me."

Seconds later, she was rushed into the hospital with the hope that there was some news of her grandchildren. After looking through pages of hospital fatalities and treated people, there came a tragic cry.

—Rudolf Isaza, *The Oklahoma Daily*

"I began to cry when I read that," Gallaga said. "As the night wore on, we all pitched in to edit stories, and the stress was starting to wear us down."

It was close to deadline. Midnight came and went. By 12:30, only a half hour after deadline, the paper was ready for the printer.

The techniques of reporting and writing these stories are the same as for any other story. But there are some differences in how you gather the information.

Reporting Techniques

Before you venture out of the newsroom to report on a disaster, you should find out a few facts and take emergency precautions and supplies. Many major metropolitan newspapers have plans for covering disasters. In Fort Lauderdale, Fla., for example, *South Florida Sun-Sentinel* has a detailed plan for coverage of disasters, particularly hurricanes. The plan spells out the responsibilities of each editor; assignments for reporters (hospitals, areas of the city, agencies); and telephone numbers of police, fire and rescue agencies, hospitals, utilities, and other places crucial to disaster coverage.

Cities also have disaster plans, and police and fire departments frequently conduct drills to test them. If you have a municipal beat, find out if the government has such a plan, and get a copy of it. If a disaster occurs, a good follow-up story is to check whether the plan was effective.

These tips are not only crucial for reporters in print and broadcast media, they also apply to public relations practitioners who might work for nonprofit organizations such as the American Red Cross or other agencies.

In the event of a disaster, you should follow these basic procedures before leaving your office or home:

- Check a map to see what routes lead to the scene. Are there alternative routes in case major arteries are blocked?
- Find out if temporary headquarters have been established for officials and media.
- Make sure that your cell phone is fully charged. But your cell phone may not work from the site of a disaster, so take plenty of change to make telephone calls to the newsroom to keep editors informed. Make sure that you have the right e-mail addresses and phone numbers stored in your computer or cell phone. If you are calling in your story on deadline, remember that information changes frequently, and you will need to keep updating your editors.
- Take proper clothing, if necessary: boots, rain gear, a change of clothes (in cases of flood coverage) and emergency rations—food and beverages if you think you'll be stuck somewhere for an extended period, flashlight, and so on. You could be reporting for a long time in an area without utilities. It's a good idea to have this emergency kit of supplies in your car at all times.
- Make sure that you have a full tank of gas for your vehicle.
- Take plenty of notebooks, pens and even pencils, which are better than pens or electronic gear in rainy weather. Don't rely on tape recorders or notebook computers at the scene of a disaster.

When you are covering the breaking news of a plane crash or earthquake or you are in the middle of a major storm, the sources of information are disorganized and unreliable. The news changes momentarily. The death toll often changes radically within the first few hours and even weeks or months later in a major disaster. Chaos reigns. You get the best information you can from eyewitnesses and officials at the scene. And then you check back repeatedly.

How do you know what to ask? You always need to ask the basics: who, what, when, where, why and how. But another way of thinking about questions is role-playing, the "what if" technique of reporting. What if I were in this person's place? What if I were waiting to find out about a relative? What would I want to know?

For example, what if it were spring or winter break and you were expecting friends or relatives to visit you? Suddenly you hear over the radio that a plane has crashed at the international airport closest to you. What do you want to know? Make a list. Chances are that the information you want to know is the kind of information any reader would want to know. What airline, what plane, how many people died, who died, who survived, what caused the crash, how did it happen, where did it crash? Those questions will produce information for your lead and the top of your story. Then you gather details.

Think statistics. You need specifics: numbers of people killed or injured or evacuated for the story and for graphics that your newspaper or TV news program might display.

Think human interest. How did people cope? How did they survive? What are their losses? What are their tragedies? Three hundred people could die in a plane crash, but the human-interest stories of a few people make that crash vivid and poignant for the reader.

Think about narrative storytelling techniques for sidebars. How would you reconstruct the incident—what was the chronology? Try to gather information about the sequence of events if the story involves such disasters as explosions, plane crashes and other events that are not acts of nature. However, even with tornadoes, earthquakes, floods and hurricanes, it helps to get the sequence of events—specific times that events occurred, the minutes involved in destruction.

Think about helpful information for empowerment boxes. Where can people get more information, donate blood, volunteer their services and so on?

Sidebars

Sidebars are not synonymous with soft news. Many sidebars are human-interest stories, but they also can be hard-news stories or informational self-help stories. A sidebar is basically a story that gives the reader some new information or more information than the main story, called a "mainbar," can provide. The main story in a disaster story is comprehensive; each sidebar should be very narrowly focused on one topic. The mainbar can allude to information that is in the sidebar, such as a quote from an eyewitness, but the sidebar should not be repetitive. A mainbar without emotional quotes from people would be boring. However, an entire sidebar about the people who have been quoted extensively in the mainbar is too repetitive.

Here are some ideas for sidebars and some questions you can ask to determine whether you need them:

Helpfulness: If I were the reader, what information would I find helpful? For example, if a disaster affects utilities, as in a flood, should you have a sidebar on how to cope without electricity or fresh water? Or if it affects roads, consider a story about alternate routes. Or a story about how to get government aid.

Human Interest: Is there a human-interest story that the reader might find compelling? Does someone have a story that is unusual?

Perspective: Would the reader find it interesting to know the history of other disasters of this type?

The Location: Is there a color piece that is compelling about the scene or a location affected by the disaster, such as a story about the hospital scene or the shelters where evacuated people were taken?

Other Angles: Is there enough information worth telling about a specific angle of the story, such as the rescue efforts, the efforts of investigators or previous problems with that type of aircraft?

Analysis: If your community has been working on a disaster plan, is there a need for an analysis piece about how rescue or government workers coordinated the disaster operations?

In most cases, especially in human-interest sidebars, you can use all the feature techniques of descriptive and narrative writing that you have studied. You should try to make the story vivid and compelling.

A sidebar still stands alone as a story, so you need to insert a reference to the main news—a brief line about the disaster or crash—especially if you have only one sidebar. If you have a huge package of several sidebars, you don't need to rehash the news statement in each one. You need to coordinate with the editor just how much of the main news needs to be in your story.

Here is an excerpt from a sidebar to the students' Oklahoma City bombing package:

Explosion prompts blood drives, donations

An ominous poster hangs in a room of the Cleveland County Red Cross. It reads, "Disaster can strike anywhere, at any time!"

As Norman residents lined up to donate blood and supplies, conversation kept going back to the explosion that ripped through downtown Oklahoma City, leaving fatalities and shock in its wake.

When the Red Cross opened its doors at 10:30 a.m., about 100 people were waiting to give blood, said Kelly Walsh, director of Red Cross donor services in Cleveland County. Kelly said her organization will continue to accept blood of all types. "We'll need blood tomorrow, the next day and next week." Particularly, the Red Cross is looking for type O blood, which can be used universally. However, Walsh said, "We need all types because all types of blood can be used for platelets."

The Red Cross will stay open until people stop coming in and as long as the staff lasts, Walsh said. Extended hours will be kept for the remainder of the week.

Those donating blood waited an average of two hours while volunteers and about 20 staff members took donations and brought in food and supplies.

Anthony Johnson, an OU microbiology sophomore, waited to donate with a group of friends. Johnson said he was angered by the bombing. "It was a big mistake. You just don't do that. Not in this country. Not in this state."

—Omar Gallaga, *The Oklahoma Daily*

Graphics

Think in multimedia terms. Almost all disaster stories in print, broadcast and on the Web, are accompanied by graphics—maps, illustrations, charts—to help the reader visualize where, when and how. The job of supplying information to the graphic designer or artist falls to the news reporter.

You need to gather details. Get information about exact locations: cross streets and measurements in yards or feet of where the accident, explosion or plane crash occurred. Try to get a map from a local gas station or convenience store. Consider whether the incident lends itself to a graphic using the time of the accident. Get a chronology in minutes or hours.

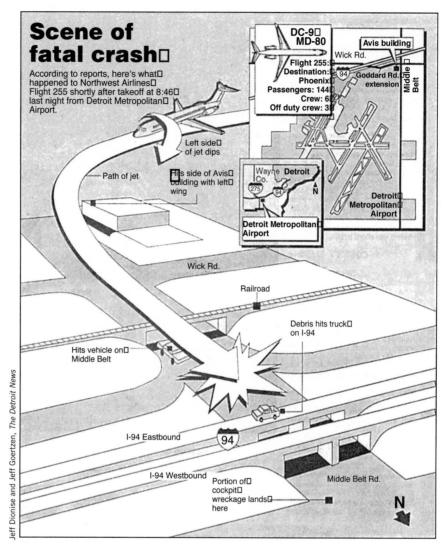

Graphic accompanying a story about a plane crash

In the process of gathering all the information you need to describe the scene to a person who will draw it, you will be gathering some details you can use in your story. And, of course, the observation skills you develop will help with all the descriptive writing you do to make the reader see and care.

Disaster Basics

Whether you are a covering a natural disaster, such as an earthquake, or another kind, such as a plane crash or explosion, you need to gather some basic facts. With the exception of the five W's, which come first, the rest of the items are not listed in order of importance.

Convergence Coach

When 33 people died at Virginia Polytechnic Institute in 2007 during the worst campus shooting in U.S. history, the conventional news media were not the only outlets for information. Social networking sites and blogs became a primary source for parents, students and other people desperately seeking information about their loved ones. The first video of the shooting was sent to CNN by a student who took the images on his cell phone. Other images of the campus after the shooting were posted on a photo-sharing site, Flickr.

The shooter, Seung-Hui Cho, a senior English major at Virginia Tech, began his rampage about 7 a.m. on April 16, and almost two hours later, he went to a classroom building and shot 32 students and professors before killing himself. The university was widely criticized for failing to alert students via text messages or other means after the first shooting. The tragedy prompted many universities to examine ways of notifying students, faculty and staff members in such crises. The event also emphasized the role that social networking sites play in conveying information during a tragedy.

Virginia Tech students posted messages on Facebook, blogs and other sites to find and provide information. And journalists turned to these sites as well to find sources for first-hand accounts of the tragedy.

This tragedy offers a lesson in how you need to think in multimedia terms when you cover a disaster.

- Plan to post information immediately to your organization's Web site.

- Check social networking sites and blogs for information, but don't trust the material as accurate. Check with the sources if possible.

- Provide links on your company's Web site to consumer information such as the Red Cross and other agencies.

- Offer ways to have citizen journalists contribute to your reports.

- Provide perspective about similar tragedies by creating time lines or lists of other disasters.

- Use the Web to provide interactive graphics if possible.

Who: How many people died or were injured, and how many survived? These numbers will change constantly, but "who" should be one of your first questions. In a plane crash, get the name of the airline, the flight number and type of aircraft, takeoff and destination sites, and the number of passengers and crew members on board.

What and Why: In many disasters, particularly airplane crashes, the cause is not immediately known. However, you should always ask and keep asking for follow-up stories. In natural disasters, get statistics about the height of rivers in floods, the intensity of earthquakes, the velocity of winds in hurricanes and similar information.

When and Where: Find out exactly what time the disaster occurred and the location. Consider graphics and a reconstruction of the event.

Weather: For a weather-related disaster, get the specifics. If it is a plane crash, always find out about the weather, which could have been a factor.

Where People Go: In case of evacuation—as in floods, hurricanes and earthquakes—find out where people are finding shelter.

Hospitals: Whenever people are injured, check hospitals.

Disaster Scene: Gather every detail of sight, sound, emotion and other sensory feelings. You will need them for description in your stories.

Estimated Cost of Damages and Property Loss: Initially, these accounts—from insurance agents, fire departments, police officials or state offices—are often inaccurate, but they add an essential element to the story.

Eyewitness Accounts: Get accounts from eyewitnesses and survivors. People make the story real and emotional. You need them for quotes in the main story and for sidebars. Ask people to reconstruct where they were and what they were doing at the time of the disaster.

Government Agencies Involved: In plane crashes, the Federal Aviation Administration and National Transportation Safety Board always get involved in investigations. In major disasters, find out whether the National Guard is helping and which federal, state and local agencies will provide relief.

Consumer Information: Find out where to go to give blood, to get help with insurance or rebuilding, to get further information. Consumer information may be included in your story or in empowerment boxes.

Red Cross and Shelters: Always check with the Red Cross and other relief agencies for their role and their needs.

Safety Precautions: Check with police and fire departments and with electric, gas and water utility companies to find out about the precautions people should take. You could refer to dangerous conditions in the main story or in a separate story.

Roads: Check highway departments to find out which roads are closed or dangerous and what alternate routes people can take.

Survivors: List those who are known to be alive.

Victims: The names of people who were killed are often not released for days, but try to obtain them from officials.

Crime: Check with police to find out about looting or other post-disaster crimes or arrests in cases of human-created disasters.

Perspective: Was this the worst, second-worst or ninth-worst disaster of its kind in a certain period of time? Check online sources or an almanac to find out how this disaster ranks against previous disasters of its kind. If it is the worst of its type, that information should appear high in the story.

Background: Check the background of the airline involved in a plane crash or a business involved in a disaster. Readers will be interested in any history that may apply to this disaster.

Medical Examiner: Check for information about progress in the identification of victims.

Here is how many of those basic elements worked in *The Oklahoma Daily*'s first-day story by Rudolf Isaza about the bombing in Oklahoma City. Many descriptive human-interest stories were in sidebars or some of the 14 other stories.

Bomb cripples Oklahoma City

Explosion leaves 31 dead, 300 missing

At least 31 people died and 300 were still missing Wednesday after a car bomb gouged a nine-story hole in a federal office building.

A 9:04 a.m. explosion ravaged the north side of the Alfred Murrah Federal Building at 200 NW Fifth St. in downtown Oklahoma City. Most of the more than 500 employees were in their offices.

As of midnight Wednesday, the confirmed death toll was 31 people, 12 of those children.

About 300 people were missing. At least 200 people were injured, 58 critically, said Fire Chief Gary Marrs. Many more were feared trapped in the rubble.

"Firefighters are having to crawl over corpses in areas to get to people that are still alive," said Jon Hansen, assistant fire chief.

Gov. Frank Keating has called a state of emergency. Nationwide bomb experts from federal agencies have been called in to decipher the cause of the bombing. The Oklahoma National Guard was called in.

Keating said he was told by the FBI that authorities were initially looking for three people in a brown pickup truck. The Oklahoma Highway Patrol put out an all-points bulletin for three individuals, described as of Middle Eastern descent. One was described as being between the ages of 25 and 30. Another may have been between 35 and 38.

Bob Ricks, head of the Oklahoma City FBI office, said the blast left a crater 20 feet long and eight feet deep directly outside the building, meaning the source of the explosion was probably outside.

An architect said the building was stable and was not in immediate danger of falling over. Ricks said the shock was felt 50 miles away. Glass was reported shattered in businesses and homes within a 30-mile radius.

The search for people trapped in the rubble started as soon as the blast occurred, starting from the top floors down. People frantically looked for loved ones, including parents whose children were in the building's day-care center. Rescuers had problems initiating the search because the elevator shaft was destroyed in the blast.

"The only way up the building is one staircase," Marrs said.

Ricks would not speculate on any suspects. "We are making no assumptions at this point," he said. "We've had hundreds, if not thousands, of leads." By midday, the government had received calls from six people saying they were from Muslim sects and asserting they were responsible for the bombing.

A police source, who requested anonymity, said FBI agents were trying to piece together a van or truck that was believed to have carried the explosives. An axle of the vehicle was found about two blocks from the scene, the source said.

General concern was that this was a direct attack on the FBI. Ricks said although the FBI did not have an office in the building, 13 brother agencies did, including the Secret Service and the Bureau of Alcohol, Tobacco and Firearms.

Also destroyed, on the second floor on the northwest side, was America's Kids, a day-care center for federal and county employees. Seventeen children had been treated as of 10 p.m. Three were treated and released, and 20 were still unaccounted for.

Oklahoma City Chief of Police Sam Gonzalez said the Oklahoma City Police Department was in charge of perimeter control and monitoring streets, and has roped off four blocks in each direction.

Oklahoma City Mayor Ron Norick requested that all people who were in the building at the time of the explosion call 297-2424 or 397-2345 to get an accurate number of people inside the building.

—Rudolf Isaza, *The Oklahoma Daily*

Death Tolls

The day after the Oklahoma City bombing, the death toll had risen to 57. Each day thereafter, the number of dead and injured increased. The final toll was 168 people, including 19 children. The opposite situation occurred in the World Trade Center tragedy, where the death toll dropped from initial reports of more than 6,000 to about 3,000 a few months later.

In disasters, dealing with numbers of victims is difficult because they change constantly. The first day you can report the facts as Isaza did, saying "At least . . . ," or use the words "an estimated" with the specific number. The following day your lead can state that the death toll has increased, or you can just write the new death toll. You don't need to correct previous information. Readers know you haven't made an error; you are just giving the facts as they become available.

Interviews with Grief-Stricken People

You have a list of people who died. Your editor wants you to call the families of victims to get biographical data and reactions. What do you do? Quit your job? Cry? Get sick? Many reporters feel like doing all three. But there are sensitive ways to cover grief. And it's difficult, if not impossible, to avoid dealing with such situations if you are going to be a newspaper or magazine reporter. So here are some concerns students have expressed and some suggestions about how you can cover such stories.

What If the Person Hangs Up on Me? You could try the Edna Buchanan technique of calling back and suggesting you were disconnected. Or you could just forget that interview and try calling someone else. Another suggestion is to call a neighbor and ask if he knows someone in the house who might talk to you. You don't have to ask for the person who is in the greatest pain. If you are on the scene and the person does not want to talk to you, you might give him card (or a note with your name and phone number) and ask if you could talk at another time.

What Questions Do I Ask? Don't ask, "How do you feel about your son's death?" Obviously, the person feels terrible. You might instead ask specific questions about what the person was like—in other words, biographical questions. What was the person planning, or where was he going when the accident happened? Then you could ask for memories about the person.

What Is the First Thing I Should Say? Introduce yourself and state your purpose. You might also express your condolences.

What If I Start to Cry? You can be empathetic and even a little teary. Try not to weep. But be sincere. Do not fake your emotions.

What If the Person I'm Interviewing Starts to Cry? Stop interviewing and ask if you can get the person a glass of water or a tissue, or just be quiet for a while. You might also ask if the person would prefer you to come back another time, depending on the severity of the situation.

What If I Say Something Insensitive Without Knowing It? Apologize.

Why Do I Have to Interview People in Times of Grief? Because these types of stories make a news event more significant and real to readers. Because people relate to other people, not to vague generalities. And remember, for some people, talking about their pain is a form of catharsis. For others, grief is a very private matter. So some people will talk to you, and others won't. Respect their needs. You won't get every story, especially if reporters from other newspapers and television stations have already talked to them. But the ones you do talk to can be wonderful.

Here is an example of how reporters interviewed friends and relatives of people who died in a plane crash. Notice from the quotes that reporters did not ask "How do you feel?" The quotes and backup information contain specific memories and details about the people who died.

Grief cuts wide swath

Relatives draw close as horror sinks in

By Jon Pepper and Rachel Reynolds

The names of the dead trickled out slowly.

Among them was a professional basketball player. A weight lifter. A high school cheerleader and a successful businessman. A nursery school teacher from St. Clair Shores.

There were boyfriends and girlfriends, granddaughters and grandsons, husbands and wives.

None of the dead were positively identified by this morning. The few names that trickled out came from friends and relatives.

Kurt Dobronski, 28, vice-president of a Scottsdale, Ariz., construction firm and a former star football player at Dearborn Edsel Ford High and Central Michigan University, had come home to Dearborn for the wedding of a friend and found his 10-day visit "the best vacation he ever had," said brother Karl Dobronski.

"Things were going great for him," Karl Dobronski said. "This is a shock." Things were also going well for Nick Vanos, a 7-foot-2 center for the Phoenix Suns basketball team. After playing only sparingly in his first two years in the National Basketball Association, Vanos was expected to start for the Suns this fall. He had come to Detroit to visit a girlfriend and boarded Flight 255 for his return to Arizona, team officials said.

"Nick Vanos was a young man who was just beginning to come into his own as a professional athlete and was about to take a giant step," said Suns general manager Jerry Coangelo. "It was very sad because he gave everything he had with his abilities. . . ."

Bill Horton of Phoenix lost his wife, Cindy, 37, who had been visiting her parents in Wisconsin. She had flown to Detroit to catch a flight to Phoenix. At midnight Sunday, he tried to calm his two stepchildren, aged 11 and 7. "They're hysterical," Horton said, sobbing. "How do you explain something like this to them?"

—*The Detroit News*

Follow-Up Stories

All major disasters require follow-up stories for many days. The second-day story should attempt to explain the cause, if that was not clear the first day. If the cause still isn't clear, you can lead with what officials are investigating. If there isn't any new information, you can describe cleanup attempts at the scene. The death toll should remain in the lead, especially if it has changed from earlier reports, or should be in the first few paragraphs. Other follow-up stories may focus on rescue efforts, human-interest elements, cost of rebuilding or any other related news.

In follow-up stories, you still need to mention what happened—when and where the plane crashed, when the earthquake occurred, and so on. In successive stories, that information can go a little bit lower. But it should still be high in the story on the second day.

Here is the second-day lead on the mainbar about the plane crash in Detroit:

Loose and broken parts caused the breakdown since mid-1985 of four jet engines like those on Northwest Flight 255, which crashed Sunday at Detroit Metropolitan Airport.

At least 154 people were killed after witnesses saw an explosion in or near the aircraft's left engine. However, the head of a National Transportation Safety Board team investigating the crash said other witnesses saw no such fire and "very preliminary" findings are that there was no failure or fire in the left engine.

Documents describing the engine failures, known to the Federal Aviation Administration (FAA) and the National Transportation Safety Board (NTSB) since April, were obtained in Washington Monday.

A U.S. Department of Transportation source claimed Monday that a serious fuel leak problem with the jet was reported by crew members less than two weeks ago. FAA officials refused to confirm such a report.

In Romulus, workers began the soul-bruising task of collecting human remains from the crash site for identification by pathologists, friends and relatives.

—Ric Bohy, Fred Girard, Mike Martindale and Joel Smith, *The Detroit News*

Airplane Crashes

You may never have to cover a major airplane crash, but small plane crashes occur in almost every community. The principles for writing and reporting the news are the same, regardless of the size of the crash.

Almost all the disaster-related information listed earlier also applies to an airplane crash. One of your first concerns should be the number of dead or injured people. Initially, you will get only estimates, and most likely they will be wrong. But some accounting of the death and injury toll should be in the lead.

Although an actual cause may not be known for months, ask anyway because you need some idea.

You should also seek the names, ages and hometowns of victims and survivors. In major plane crashes, the list of passengers and their status is usually not released for a day or more, until the relatives have been notified. The names and status of the pilots and crew members may be available sooner.

In addition to getting accounts from eyewitnesses, reactions from relatives or people at the airport, and other human-interest stories, make sure that you get the following specifics: name of the airline and flight number of the plane; the type of plane and number of engines, especially for small planes; the origination and final destination sites.

Check for comments from the air controllers. The pilot's last words are usually not available until investigators get the plane's "black box" recording, but keep it in mind for follow-up stories.

Don't forget the perspective: how many plane crashes of this type have occurred in recent years or how this crash ranks in severity.

Here is an example of a plane crash story that illustrates most of the guidelines for disaster coverage:

20 die in La Guardia crash

The Associated Press

Lead: airline, number of people aboard, where crashed, when, death toll, destination, flight number

NEW YORK—A USAir jet carrying 51 people crashed in a snowstorm Sunday while trying to take off from La Guardia Airport and skidded part way into the frigid waters of Flushing Bay. Authorities said at least 20 people were killed.

Witnesses said USAir Flight 405, bound for Cleveland, left the ground, then fell back and exploded before sliding into the water.

"It looked like the sun coming up," witness Manny Dias told WNBC-TV. "The sky lit up. It was just about to take off. It just exploded."

Sgt. John Murphy of the Port Authority said 20 people were dead, 27 were known to have survived and four others were still missing.

Eyewitness account, color quote

Backup for lead: death toll, survivors, missing

Elaboration

Divers said they found passengers, and the plane's pilot, strapped upside down in their seats in the submerged part of the wreckage.

Status of airport, diversion of flights

The airport was closed after the accident, which occurred about 9:30 p.m. Incoming flights were diverted to nearby John F. Kennedy International Airport.

Elaboration

Twenty-one people climbed out of the plane in the water and to the Delta shuttle terminal, Port Authority police said.

Suspected cause

Neither the airline nor the Federal Aviation Administration had any immediate explanation for what caused the plane to crash during takeoff or whether the bad weather was a factor. The National Transportation Safety Board sent investigators to the scene.

Detail

Port Authority police said the plane veered left at the end of the runway and hit a snow-covered barricade just before the water.

The nose, wing and engine snapped off while the rest of the plane was in the water with its top sheared off.

At Cleveland's Hopkins International Airport, friends and relatives of passengers aboard the plane were in seclusion.

USAir spokeswoman Lynn McCloud in Arlington, Va., said 51 people were on the jet, including 47 passengers, two pilots and two flight attendants. The airline said the flight originated in Jacksonville, Fla., and five passengers were booked all the way through to Cleveland.

McCloud, the USAir spokeswoman, said the temperature was 31 degrees, wind about 15 mph, and the runway was wet with patches of snow. She said visibility was three-quarters of a mile.

The aircraft was a 6-year-old Fokker-28 4000 commuter jet, McCloud said.

FAA spokesman Fred Farrar described the plane as a "relatively small two-engine jet with both engines on the rear of the fuselage."

It was the second time in three years a plane has skidded off a runway at La Guardia. Both were USAir flights.

Relatives, friends: secluded (no reaction possible yet)

Airline official's comments substantiating earlier facts

Origination point

Weather

Detail about plane

Perspective: other crashes

Natural Disasters

All disaster stories should include the same basic information: death toll, survivors, eyewitness accounts, human-interest quotes from survivors, and details of the scene and of recovery efforts. For natural disasters, add information about the natural forces at work, such as weather conditions.

Any time you are writing about a weather-related disaster, be sure to include a weather forecast. If you are covering floods, find out how high the river crested—if that was a factor—or the height of water in feet. If winds were a cause of the destruction, get the specific miles per hour of the wind velocity. In the case of an earthquake, find out the magnitude and the location of the epicenter. Explain in simple terms how the natural phenomenon occurred. A graphic may be better than words.

Tornadoes, earthquakes, hurricanes and floods all cause extensive damage and leave people homeless. Find out where people are finding shelter and what is being done to help them. Insurance is also a big factor in natural disasters. Include consumer information, such as areas that readers should avoid and the names of impassable streets, or how people can cope. Utilities are often affected, so make sure that you check about the safety of drinking water, food supplies and electricity.

Many of these consumer elements may be in sidebars. But when you write the first-day story, the format is similar to that of a plane crash or any other disaster. Give the basic facts and a death or injury toll in the lead.

> FERNDALE, Calif.—A powerful earthquake rocked California's remote North Coast on Saturday, knocking brick facades off buildings, sparking fires that destroyed several businesses and two post offices, and sending at least 35 people to hospitals with cuts, broken bones and chest pains.
>
> —*Los Angeles Times*

Here are excerpts from a weather disaster story that include all the basic information and human elements. Note the vivid verbs, descriptive writing, pacing of long and short sentences, and details of observation.

Napa, Sonoma hit by floods—again

Basic news lead

For the second time this winter, rain-swollen rivers flooded Napa and Sonoma county towns and vineyards Thursday, creating a colossal mess where weary residents were just getting their lives in order after fierce January storms.

Weather specifics

Howling out of the central Pacific, the storm slammed into the state late Wednesday with steady, torrential rain and winds blasting to 60 mph. And weather forecasters expect more of the same today.

But for a few brief respites, the relentless battering continued all day Thursday.

Power problems

Torrential rains overpowered small streams and larger rivers throughout the region, triggering floods and mudslides. High winds snapped electrical power to 540,000 customers from Big Sur to Eureka, closed highways and shut down shipping in San Francisco Bay. New snow blanketed the Sierra Nevada.

Numerous rivers and streams were at or near flood stage throughout Northern California. Among communities threatened by the rising water were Susanville, Tehama and Hamilton City along the Sacramento River.

Forecast

The National Weather Service warned residents to brace for another wave of rain spinning in from a strong low-pressure system in the northeastern Pacific before dawn today.

Forecaster Brandt Maxwell at the National Weather Service's Monterey office said some areas could get as much as two inches of rain today. "Of course, any amount is going to aggravate flooding."

The rain is forecast to taper off this afternoon, with showers tonight and Saturday.

A winter storm warning was issued for the Sierra Nevada with snow levels forecast to range from 5,000 to 6,000 feet today. As much as three feet of snow could fall above the 7,000-foot elevation, according to the National Weather Service.

History/ perspective

It's starting to look like January, when a disastrous series of storms caused widespread flooding and $300 million in damage, killed 11 people and displaced thousands throughout California.

For residents of Napa and Sonoma counties, still recovering from the floods of January, it was an all too-familiar story.

In St. Helena, a small town in the Napa Valley wine country, the Napa River flooded vineyards, homes, apartments and a mobile home park. Firefighters evacuated more than 1,000 people as the river rose to 19 feet—six feet above flood stage.

Several hundred others were rescued from the Vineyard Valley Mobile Home Park, which survived the January floods. On Thursday, two-thirds of the 300 mobile homes were under water.

Emergency workers in small boats evacuated people through waist-deep water that blocked access to apartment complexes. But even the rescuers had troubles. One rowboat, caught in the swift current, floated down the Napa River for five miles before another boat came to its rescue.

Human interest   Malia Barron Hendricks, about to give birth to her second child, and her husband, Charles, found the road to the hospital blocked by floodwaters. So they drove to a fire station where firefighters helped deliver a healthy baby girl. The woman and her newborn, Hope Bridget Hendricks, eventually were taken to St. Helena Hospital by an ambulance that had to negotiate flooded streets.

Shortly after the birth, the firefighters shared a bottle of expensive Napa Valley sparkling wine with the new mother and father.

By late afternoon, a sheet of water four feet deep covered much of the eastern Napa Valley, isolating flooded farmhouses in inundated vineyards.

Farther south in Napa, the river was expected to rise four feet above flood level, flooding Soscol Avenue, a main business artery. Helpless onlookers watched water creep into the street, growing deeper by the minute.

Mark Townsend, 41, owner of Soscol Antiques, hurriedly tried to waterproof his store, sealing the doors with tape and sandbags, putting his wares as high on shelves as he could, and hauling away the most valuable items in pickup trucks. He lost $10,000 worth of antiques in the flood two months ago.

"It's a little hard, but you have to remember we are going home tonight, and home will have booze and an espresso machine," Townsend said, "and there are a lot of people who don't get to go home tonight."

—Frank Sweeney, Janet Rae-Dupree and Michael Dorgan, *San Jose* (Calif.) *Mercury News*

Weather Stories

Not all weather stories involve disaster coverage. Weather stories can be news or features about prolonged hot, cold, wet or dry spells or just a statistical roundup of rain or snow totals for the month or year. They also can be features about interesting aspects of the weather and the ways it affects people. When a major snowstorm or thunderstorm hits an area, a weather story is expected.

Weather stories also provide drama. In 2005, *Chicago Tribune* reporter Julia Keller won the Pulitzer Prize for reconstructing the terror created by a tornado that struck one block in downtown Utica, Ill., where eight people who huddled in the basement of a bar were killed. In an article about the prize, *Tribune* editor Tim Bannon said the tornado provided all the elements of a "taut drama" that would show how a brief but devastating weather event affected people. Keller was initially reluctant to do the feature story after the event because it had been so thoroughly covered by the media as breaking news. But she persevered for seven months as she pored over weather documents and conducted hundreds of interviews to write a compelling narrative account of just 10 seconds when the "wicked wind" had ripped through the town nearly a year before. The Pulitzer judges called it a "gripping, meticulously constructed account." Here is the lead on the first of three stories:

Ten seconds. Count it: One. Two. Three. Four. Five. Six. Seven. Eight. Nine. Ten. Ten seconds was roughly how long it lasted. Nobody had a stopwatch, nothing can be proven definitively, but that's the consensus. The tornado that swooped through Utica at 6:09 p.m. April 20 took some 10 seconds to do what it did. Ten seconds is barely a flicker. It's a long, deep breath. It's no time at all. It's an eternity.

If the sky could hold a grudge, it would look the way the sky looked over northern Illinois that day. Low, gray clouds stretched to the edges in a thin veneer of menace. Rain came and went, came and went, came and went. . . .

The survivors would henceforth be haunted by the oldest, most vexing question of all: whether there is a destiny that shapes our fates or whether it is simply a matter of chance, of luck, of the way the wind blows.

Here are some other ideas for features about weather stories:

- Unusual patterns in weather for your area. Include why the weather patterns are occurring.
- Effects of weather on pets, businesses, people's moods, health. For example, many people suffer from seasonal affective disorder, a depressive state usually related to a lack of light in the winter.
- Insect infestation because of weather patterns.
- People whose occupations force them to work outside during very hot or cold spells.
- Effects of snow removal on city budgets: price of salt, sand, overtime for employees and so on.
- Excessive costs of air conditioning or heating on your school or city during hot or cold spells.
- Features about upcoming seasons.
- Consumer stories or sidebars about coping with extreme heat, cold, tornadoes, hurricanes, floods or earthquakes.

Regardless of whether you are writing a feature or a breaking-news story, include these elements in all weather stories:

Forecast: Always include the forecast for the next day or for an extended period, especially when you are writing about floods, droughts, weather-related fires, or hot or cold spells.

Unusual Angles: If the weather is unusual for your area or for the time of year, include explanations from weather forecasters.

Human Interest: Tell how people are coping. Focus on one or a few people who have interesting stories.

Warnings: Explain how extremely hot or cold weather affects people, especially very young or old people. Tell how to cope with or prevent problems. Also include warnings about keeping animals safe. Include any road or traffic information, such as road or bridge closings and alternate routes.

Records: Explain if the weather has broken any records or come near to breaking records, especially if you are doing a roundup of statistics or a story about unusual weather. Even if no records have been broken, put the weather statistics in perspective by comparing them to other months or years or using a graphic for the statistics.

Terms: Check your *Associated Press Stylebook* for definitions of weather terms. If you use such a word as *blizzard* or *hurricane,* define it by explaining how high the winds must be. In any flood story, explain the flood stages of a river and how far above or below flood stage the river is or when it is expected to crest to its highest level.

Here is a basic weather feature about an excessively hot day. It includes all the basic information, such as the forecast and human-interest elements. The writer, Cheryl Wittenauer, said she checked with the guard to make sure that she wouldn't get him fired by writing that he wasn't standing at the entrance he was supposed to guard. She also said she wanted to use the "screw it" quote "because that's the way people talk," but she cleared it first with her editor.

Weather forecast blazes on

Temperatures to soar throughout weekend

At 5 o'clock, security guard Shawn Brown was halfway through his shift watching over a parking lot under construction at the downtown post office.

The Wells Fargo employee, beads of sweat popping from his brow, is supposed to take his post at the Edmond Street entrance, where the only shelter from the sun was the bill of his cap.

Nudged by the discomfort of a 102-degree heat index Wednesday, the outdoor worker deferred to his own judgment.

"Screw it," he said. "I'm staying here in the shade. . . . This is the only post without an air conditioner. It's my second day here in a row."

The day ushered in what is forecast to be a series of blazers with above-normal temperatures and wind.

"It's blast furnace-type weather," Weather Data meteorologist Jeff House said.

Today will be sunny with a high of 96. But it will only get worse. Temperatures Friday and Saturday will soar to a searing 99, with at least 50 percent humidity.

There could be slight relief Sunday and Monday if a "cold front" produces thunderstorms. Even with the cold front, highs would hover in the middle 90s.

The above-normal temperatures are the result of a strong ridge of high pressure in the upper levels of the atmosphere.

The average high for June 24 is 87 degrees. A record high of 103 was set in 1937.

Cooper, a black poodle mix, was one of seven lucky dogs that lost a winter coat Wednesday at Jeanne's Dog Grooming, 922 Alabama St.

"They come in miserable from the heat, but they're bouncing when they leave here," groomer Colleen Whitson said. "They love it. They feel so much better."

The steamy temperatures also drew people in search of quick relief to stores and social service agencies that could supply them with fans and air conditioners.

"Sales usually hit a peak when it turns hot like this," Sears salesman Bill Patrick said. "They're replacing ones that finally gave up on them."

The Economic Opportunity Corp., 817 Monterey St., has given away more than 100 air conditioners in a four-county region since June 1. The agency has fielded many additional requests from low-income clients the last few days.

AFL-CIO Community Services, 118 S. Fifth St., is seeking donations of fans and 110-volt air conditioners that plug into a standard outlet—and are in good working condition. The agency won't accept 220-volt air conditioning units because they require electrical wiring most clients' homes lack.

—Cheryl Wittenauer,
St. Joseph (Mo.) *News-Press*

Personal Tragedy

In the beginning, hordes of reporters descended on the tiny town of Buckner, Mo., to cover the tragedy of three brothers who died in an icy pond. It was a personal tragedy of national magnitude.

Tad Bartimus, an award-winning writer for The Associated Press, was not among the initial reporters. Bartimus called the family several weeks later and said she wanted to do a story because she didn't think the real story about the boys had ever been told. To her surprise, the family consented. But Bartimus said it was a very painful story to write.

She said her reporting style for tragedy is to treat the family as though it were her own: "I can get anyone to tell me anything. And I can empathize with people. Those are my top two strengths."

But why do the media love to do stories about personal tragedies? The media are often criticized for their coverage of grieving families. A grief counselor in Bartimus' story expresses the reason well: "The human spirit is resilient beyond belief, and that is the hope here," said Ms. Howard. "At a time like this you can get swamped by the grinding pain of it. But out of that pain comes some of the most substantial character and human elegance to be found on Earth. You learn how people can rise up and care for one another."

And that is a theme of this story. Readers want to read about how people cope with tragedy.

Bartimus didn't ask the parents insensitive questions about how they felt. When parents lose their three children, the answer is obvious. Instead, she focused on how the community reacted and the parents' memories of their children.

As a reporter, you undoubtedly will have to cover a personal tragedy at some point—probably many times—in your career. Many of those stories will focus on the community and how people cope with a tragedy that happens to their neighbors or members of their

What Do You Think

If you were covering a tragedy, what would be the most difficult information for you to get?

- Interviews with survivors
- Factual information about death tolls
- Information about the cause of the tragedy
- All of the above
- Other - specify

immediate family. Bartimus' story can serve as a model for questions to ask and approaches to take.

As you read Bartimus' story, note the sources she used and the way she structured the story with a circular ending that returned to the beginning of the story for concept but focused on the future. Also note the excellent details.

Band of brothers

Tad Bartimus

Associated Press

"We few, we happy few,
we band of brothers . . ."

William Shakespeare, *Henry V*

BUCKNER, Mo.—There is so little left. A red cardboard valentine with torn paper lace, which proclaims, "I love you Mom." A carefully penned Thanksgiving essay in which the writer said he's grateful for his family "to have someone to love me." A child's "Life Story" book with extra pages left blank for future adventures.

Chad Eugene Gragg, 12, Aaron Wayne Gragg, 11, and Stephen Douglas Gragg, 8, died together at dusk on the cold afternoon of Feb. 4.

It was Aaron's 11th birthday. Despite admonishments from a teacher and a chum who rode home with him on the bus, he chose to celebrate it by sliding on the frozen surface of a farmer's pond.

The ice broke. Aaron fell into the frigid water. His big brother Chad, doing what his parents had always taught him to do, attempted to save him. He, too, fell in. Stevie, strong for his age, also tried to be his brothers' keeper. His body plunged through the thin crust.

A horrified neighbor boy ran for help. Frantic firemen pulled the brothers from the pond within 30 minutes. They weren't breathing and had no pulse. Two helicopters and an ambulance rushed them to three separate hospitals.

Thus began the agonizing pilgrimage of Charles and Mary Gragg, two ordinary people who now stagger in the footsteps of Job.

Meanwhile, word of the tragedy spread like woodsmoke over this western Missouri town of 2,800. The event would change forever Buckner's image of itself.

As doctors at St. Mary's Hospital in nearby Blue Springs told the parents their son Chad was dead, teachers and friends arrived to surround the stunned couple in a protective cocoon.

Hoping against hope, the Graggs next went to St. Luke's Hospital in Kansas City, only to be told Aaron, too, was gone.

By the time they reached Children's Mercy Hospital the Graggs were at the heart of a caravan of grief. They found Stephen on a life support system. At 10 p.m., he passed away.

In the space and time it took for the sun to set and the moon to rise, three healthy, happy, handsome little boys vanished from the lives of all who knew them.

They left behind bits of homework and smiling celluloid images, a puppy named Scooter who looks for them everywhere, empty school desks, classmates who struggle to remember their last words, teachers who wish they'd known them better.

They left behind the townspeople of Buckner, who were galvanized by the loss to dig deep within their hearts and pockets to bury the children with dignity, and continue to mourn them with honest tears.

They left behind their mother and their father, but Mary and Charles Gragg, both 41, are no longer parents. The sounds of laughter, of life, are gone from their empty house. The only noise comes from the television set. The door to the boys' bedroom is closed.

The unbearable must now be borne.

"In our age, children aren't eligible to die because our expectations have been set up that children can survive anything," said Kathryn Howard, a grief counselor with Comprehensive Mental Health Services in nearby Independence, Mo.

"All the time we read about children who fall into freezing water and survive. Why not Aaron, or Chad, or at least Stevie? They couldn't be saved because the water wasn't deep enough or cold enough. But because of modern medical miracles, we are conditioned to believe it is outrageous that they died."

Ms. Howard, whose nonprofit agency has contracts with both the local school district and fire department, had headed grief and death counseling in Buckner since the drownings. She also helped the Graggs plan their children's funeral.

"The human spirit is resilient beyond belief, and that is the hope here," said Ms. Howard. "At a time like this you can get swamped by the grinding pain of it. But out of that pain comes some of the most substantial character and human elegance to be found on Earth. You learn how people can rise up and care for one another.

"This is now a community that speaks with one voice. That phenomenon is rare—too often we are too big and fragmented a society for this to happen. But if you listen to Buckner today, what you hear is, 'We care. This matters to us. They were our children, too.'"

The Graggs had no close relatives living nearby. Acting out of instinct and compassion, Buckner Elementary School Principal Richard Thompson stepped into the abyss.

"The school in a sense became their family," said Thompson. "Working with me, Kathryn Howard, and Jerry Brown, the funeral director, Charlie and Mary decided to have the funeral in the junior high gymnasium. The parents wanted the teachers to speak, and to be pallbearers.

"This became a chance for the community to fulfill what a community is all about. Before the accident happened you could have counted on one hand the number of people who knew Charlie and Mary Gragg. Now everyone knows them and wants to help them."

The Parent-Teacher Association mobilized to take food to the Gragg home for the next two weeks. Secretly thanking God it wasn't their own kids, mothers reached into closets and brought forth suits and ties for the boys to wear to their graves.

Funds were established to accept donations to offset medical and funeral expenses. The local bank, the savings and loan and a florist donated flower sprays for the coffins.

"It is so hard to take it in," said James B. Jones, president of the First State Bank of Missouri, where nearly $20,000 was sent in the first two weeks after the accident.

Pondering the event's anguishing mathematics, Jones wondered, "If people had only one child and lost it, isn't that just as terrible as having three and losing them all? I don't know, I simply don't know, it's just so hard to make yourself think about it."

Mortician Brown tried not to think about his own boys, aged 7 and 8, as he plotted the funeral like a general planning a battle.

"We went into this with no idea there'd be any money to pay for it. I was estimating a minimum of $2,500 each. I went to my vault manufacturer and coffin supplier and explained the situation. They were willing to share the burden, no matter what happened," said Brown, whose family has served as Buckner's only morticians for three generations.

Brown decided on three identical coffins, three identical hearses. He reserved three side-by-side plots on a gently sloping hillside in the town cemetery.

From the graves you can look out over the walnut and oak trees, past the dormant farm pastures, and down toward the creek where an angry crawdad once bit Aaron's big toe, where Chad caught a two-pound lunker of a catfish, where Stevie loved to hunt for frogs.

Those are the same hills and hollows Brown scampered over as a child. He, too, remembers sliding across frozen ponds with his buddies.

Brown steeled himself not to think about any of those memories, or the event that brought him into the Graggs' circle, "because it is so overwhelming, so awesome, that it stops you in your tracks." He'd think later. First, he had a big job to do.

When he'd finished embalming and dressing the dead children in their new clothes, he tucked each boy's favorite toy into the silk-lined caskets.

As Brown ministered to the dead, Thompson and Ms. Howard, along with every clergyman in town, local teachers and reinforcements from other schools, consoled the living.

"The day after it happened we conducted emotional triage in the halls, the library, the cafeteria, and the classrooms," said Ms. Howard. "We had kids crying with counselors in corners everywhere you looked. Part of being young is learning how to deal with your pain. The kids were shown they could support one another and that they wouldn't be alone."

Teachers read "The Taste of Blackberries" to all fourth and fifth graders. The book relates the tale of a boy who loses his best friend. Younger children heard "The 10th Good Thing About Barney," a story of a little boy whose cat dies.

Thompson sent letters home with every student, detailing the day's upheaval and warning parents their children "might have tears or depression but that is expected and is normal in the grief process. . . ." Attached were four pages of guidelines for dealing with the situation.

"That day we just put a Band-Aid on it; we flew by the seat of our pants," recalled Thompson. "We decided to leave the Gragg boys' desks empty to stress the finality of death, to show some physical remains. We talked about the details. We tried to cope with the onslaught of the media but refused to let reporters talk to teachers or students. And we braced for the funeral."

Thompson is described by faculty, city fathers, and the Graggs as the glue that held everything together through that long weekend.

Besides organizing the school's response to the tragedy, Thompson set up the junior high gymnasium for the funeral, helped teachers prepare their farewell remarks, acceded to any family wishes, and comforted students who attended the open coffin visitation and closed casket funeral.

"It was tough trying to make an appropriate setting for a funeral out of a basketball court, but we did it," said Thompson.

He had a carpenter build a wooden schoolhouse which was then covered with flowers and presented by the students of Buckner. Thompson also gave the parents a brass school bell engraved with the boys' names. The gift usually is reserved for retiring teachers.

"We consider that your boys have retired to a heavenly school," Thompson told the Graggs.

More than 600 mourners heard fourth-grade teacher Jeanne Young describe the Gragg children as "three adventuresome, energetic little boys . . . each of us has a special place in our heart, locked and guarded—it's the place just for Chad and Stephen and Aaron."

Symbols of each boy's interests rested atop the blue-gray caskets: art materials for Aaron, a soccer ball for Stephen, a basketball for Chad.

Finally, the three brothers were laid to rest in the winter's hard ground.

Mortician Brown left town for a convention in Florida, allowing himself to cry most of the way.

Mental health counselor Kathryn Howard began planning a series of forums on death and dying for the Buckner community.

Principal Thompson fielded calls from People magazine and tried to get his school back to some semblance of normalcy.

"The tragedy will long be remembered in this community," said Thompson, pausing to wipe tears from his eyes and catch his breath over the big lump in his throat. "They were rambunctious country boys who were one for all and all for one.

"Two of the boys willingly gave up their lives for the other. That is the only thing that makes it comprehensible."

Mary and Charlie Gragg's relatives have gone home and neighbors visit less now. Gragg has resumed the commute to his metal treating company in Kansas City. His wife has returned to shift work for a janitorial contractor at the nearby Lake City Army Ammunition Plant.

The Graggs believe they'll stay in the neighborhood where dogs run free and kids' boundaries are defined by a stop sign on a country road.

They speak of their sons in the present tense.

Looking at a small pile of photographs, Mary Gragg remembers each of her sons as a sturdy blue-eyed, blond-haired baby.

"They were so good. They slept through the night every night.

"Aaron is my artist, my loner, he loves his dinosaurs. Chad is his daddy made over, my helper, everybody's helper, such a good student. He loves school, he never misses, and he loves riding his bicycle. Stevie's a little slow, a shy kid. Stevie loves Alf . . ."

Charlie Gragg takes up the sentence.

"You'll never see kids that alike, that close. If one goes out the front door the other two are right behind. . . . I wasn't surprised they all died trying to pull each other out of that pond.

"I always told them, 'No matter what happens, you help your brothers.' I told them that more than once. I told Chad he was responsible. He was in charge. He went to help Aaron, and Stevie followed."

Is there anything anyone can do for the Graggs? They say there is nothing. They are baffled that there might be an answer to such a question.

Soon it will be spring, time to go fishin' again, and frog huntin', and crawdad catchin'. That's when the children of Buckner Elementary School will plant three new trees in the memory of Aaron, Chad, and Stevie.

By then, the ice will be gone from the ponds.

Exercises

1 **Grief reporting:** How can you ask questions about grief? Try this classroom exercise: In groups of three or four, list all the fears and anxieties you have about interviewing people who are grieving. Then discuss some reporting techniques you can use to deal with each of these concerns. After compiling your concerns and solutions, discuss them with the class as a whole.

2 **Disaster coverage:** Brainstorm a package of stories about a disaster in your community. If you live in an area prone to weather disasters, such as earthquakes, tornadoes or floods, plan that type of coverage. Or you can brainstorm how you would cover a plane crash or an explosion in your community. List the stories you would do and places you should go for reporting on the type of disaster you have identified.

3 **Disaster plan:** Develop a plan for how you would cover a weather disaster in your area. Make a list of agencies and sources you should contact. Write a list of key questions. Develop a sidebar of consumer information with links that you would post on your campus or community newspaper or news station's Web site.

☞ **Featured Online Activity** Log on to the book Web site for Chapter 23 and write news stories based on the information provided about a plane crash at

academic.cengage.com/masscomm/rich/ writingandreportingnews6e

Coaching Tips

Call the employer to ask who should receive your application. Find out the person's title and gender and how to spell his or her first and last name.

Research the companies to which you are applying by checking the Web or library resources.

Limit your cover letter to one page.

Proofread your application carefully to eliminate spelling and typographical errors.

Make a follow-up telephone call or e-mail a few weeks after you send your application.

Be careful what information you post in blogs or social networking sites that could be found by potential employers.

Check online job sites and journalism organizations for internships and career opportunities.

I can't stress enough how important it is for the applicant to write a cover letter that is both clear and interesting. . . . If they're just saying they want a job, that doesn't excite me. I want that letter to entice me into their clips and résumé.

Paul Salsini, former staff development director
for the *Milwaukee Journal Sentinel*

24 Media Jobs and Internships

Once upon a time if you were looking for a job, you had to submit an application letter and résumé on paper. You still do for many media jobs. But these days employers don't limit their search for candidates to the printed applications they receive. They might also search Facebook, YouTube and similar sites. So beware of what you post on social networking sites. Potential employers might check out your blogs and social networking postings to find out more about who you really are. A video on YouTube showing your antics during Spring Break might be fun to share with friends but not with potential employers.

It's an asset to have multimedia skills. Video résumés may be desirable for some jobs. But don't forego the old-fashioned methods of applying for a job with a letter and printed résumé. That's especially important for media jobs, where writing well matters.

Good communication topped the list of most-desired skills sought by employers, according to recent surveys by the National Association of Colleges and Employers, a nonprofit association for college career services. But employers also cited the lack communication skills as the major problem with new graduates.

"Many employers reported that students have trouble with grammar, can't write, and lack presentation skills," according to a 2007 survey by the association. "Poor communication skills are often evident in the interview, where students are unable to articulate how what they have done relates or contributes to the position they are seeking."

As students in media classes, you probably have an advantage in gaining good communication skills. But you may not know how to market yourself well. Unless you know how to write a good cover letter and résumé, even the best grade point average may not get you the job.

"I can't stress enough how important it is for the applicant to write a cover letter that is both clear and interesting and tells me this person is a good reporter and writer," says Paul Salsini, former staff development director for the *Milwaukee Journal Sentinel*. "If they're just saying they want a job, that doesn't excite me. I want that letter to entice me into their clips and résumé. The cover letter is the only original thing they send."

If you had one sentence or one paragraph to describe yourself to a prospective employer for a job or internship, how would you persuade an employer that you are special and worth hiring? How can you tailor your application to the organization where you want to work? And how do you find jobs or internships?

These are some of the questions and answers this chapter will cover to help you find and apply for media jobs.

Finding Jobs and Internships

Q: How do you find internships and jobs?

A: The journalism and mass communications program at your school is a good starting place. It may list job and internship opportunities on bulletin boards or your department Web site. Professors in your department usually have good contacts in your field of study, so check with them as well. If you are seeking an opportunity at a specific news or public relations organization, check the Web site for that company. If you don't want to be limited to media jobs, the Associated Collegiate Press offers a more inclusive job site (*www.studentpress.org*) or general sites like jobster.com and monster.com. The next step is to check several of the Web sites offering jobs and internships in media careers, some of which are mentioned in the next few answers.

Q: How do you find internships and jobs in newspapers?

A: If you want a job or internship at a particular newspaper, first check the newspaper's Web site. Most newspapers list jobs and internship openings on their sites. Several umbrella Web sites list searchable jobs and internships by state. The American Society of Newspaper Editors (*www.asne.org*) is one of them. Another excellent searchable site for jobs and internships is journalism-jobs (*www.journalismjobs.com*). These sites and others listed on our Web site for this chapter will give you more specific information than a general search in Google or Yahoo, which will refer you to these sites anyway.

Q: How do you find internships and jobs in television or radio?

A: Some of the advice in the previous answer applies to broadcast jobs as well. First check the Web site of a specific station to see if job or internship opportunities are listed. The Radio and Television News Directors Association (*www.rtnda.org*), the main organization representing the broadcast industry, is a good place to start. It offers a searchable job base as well as information about scholarships and career resources. Some Web sites specific to the broadcast industry also provide a searchable job databases. For example, TVJobs (*www.tvjobs.com*) contains an extensive list of jobs in television and radio as well as an e-résumé database where you can post your résumé. Others include tvspy (*www.tvspy.com/jobbank.cfm*), tvandradiojobs (*www.tvandradiojobs.com*) and more linked to the Web site for this chapter.

Q: How do you find internships and jobs in public relations?

A: The public relations field is so broad that you can find opportunities in government, corporations, marketing and public relations firms. A good place to start your search is with the umbrella organizations representing public relations such as The Public Relations Society of America (*www.prsa.org*) and the International Association of Business Communicators (*www.iabc.com*). Both have searchable databases by location or position. If your school has a chapter of the Public Relations Student Society of America (*www.prssa.org*), you should consider joining because many student chapters offer networking and local job opportunities. Even if you don't have a local chapter, you can check the PRSSA site for internships and jobs. In some communities advertising and marketing firms combine with public relations positions, so you can check under advertising as well. For example, talentzoo (*www.talentzoo.com/website/content/*) contains a searchable site for advertising, publishing, marketing and broadcasting.

If you want a public relations job in government, which offers many opportunities in local and national agencies, check your state government site or the U.S. Web portal, (*www.usa.gov*), which has links to state and federal sites. Think broadly. Many organizations need publicists including hospitals, companies and nonprofit agencies, so you should consider opportunities in the location you desire.

Applying for a Job or Internship

Q: How can you find out the name of the person to whom you should send your job or internship application?

A: Start by checking the organization's Web site, a search engine or telephone book to find a phone number for the company. Even if the name of the person in charge of hiring is listed on a Web site or in a publication, call the organization and find out who should get your application anyway. Accuracy matters in media. Web sites may not be up to date and printed directories are frequently incorrect because people change jobs before publications are reprinted. Get a specific person's name and title and ask how to spell the person's name and whether the person is male or female. Don't make the mistake of addressing a letter to a female executive as Dear Mr. or worse, Dear Sir. Also make sure you spell the person's name correctly.

Q: Should you contact the editor or hiring officer first by e-mail?

A: Sure, but be careful. Check your grammar and spelling before you send any e-mail. Dan Lovely, a metro editor at a Florida newspaper, says he likes to correspond with applicants by e-mail so he can see how they communicate. He says if their e-mails are filled with typos or poor grammar, he won't hire the applicants.

Q: Should you send your application via e-mail?

A: Send an e-mail application only if the organization requests it in that form. You can send an e-mail query to find out if the organization has a job or internship, but send a written cover letter and résumé as well unless the company specifies that it prefers e-mail résumés. If so, make sure you take a print copy of your résumé with you if you get to the interview stage.

Q: Should you use your school e-mail address or a personal one?

A: Use the e-mail address you check frequently, and don't use a school address if you are graduating. Use a professional e-mail login. If you have been using an address with a login like "sexybabe," "cuteblondechick" or "studguy," change it unless you are applying for a sex-related job. Don't use smileys or other emoticons and Internet abbreviations that are often used in chats or e-mails.

Q: How many résumés should you send out?

A: Apply to as many organizations as you like, but don't send a form cover letter. Make sure you target your cover letter to the specific organization. Later in the chapter, we'll discuss how to write résumés and cover letters.

Q: Should you just send a résumé to a company on speculation without contacting an editor or hiring officer?

A: No. You can post your résumé on a job or résumé site, but don't send your résumé to a specific company without contacting someone there or receiving a request for your information.

Q: Should you include your Web sites and blog addresses in a résumé?

A: Include your Web site addresses if the sites contain professional materials. If you have a media-related blog that is relevant to the job or internship you are seeking, it might be acceptable to include a reference to it. Otherwise, keep your personal Web sites and blogs to yourself and your friends.

Q: Should you post your résumé on social networking sites such as Facebook, MySpace or YouTube?

A: It doesn't hurt to post your résumé on social networking sites, but you need to be careful about other material you have on these sites. Most reputable media companies are probably not going to be searching for candidates on these sites, but prospective employers might check out applicants who have applied to see what other information they might learn about them. If you do post a video résumé on YouTube or other site, make it professional as though you were speaking to the prospective employer.

Q: How many clips, scripts, graphics or other examples of your work should you include in a job or internship application?

A: In general, newspaper editors suggest at least six articles, preferably showing variety in styles such as features and hard news. For a broadcast job, enclose a few tapes, and for a Web job, make a copy of the sites you have created and include working links. For a public relations job, enclose a few samples you have created of news releases, brochures or other materials, especially examples of your writing ability.

Q: If you are a member of a minority ethnic or racial group, should you mention this in your cover letter or résumé?

A: A racial or ethnic minority background may be an advantage in some media jobs, particularly if the organization is in a community with a large population of minorities, such as Hispanics, Asians or African-Americans. Most news organizations are eager to increase the number of minorities on their staffs. You can refer to your racial or ethnic background judiciously in a cover letter and résumé by mentioning organizations or activities in which you have engaged that reflect this diversity or by explaining how your racial or ethnic background may help you in the job that you are seeking.

Q: What skills or qualities would be especially important to cite in your résumé?

A: Multimedia skills are valuable for most media organizations. In addition, if you are bilingual or multilingual, that could be an asset in many media jobs. However, if you make that claim, make sure you are fluent in the languages you mention; do not exaggerate. If you say you are bilingual in English and Spanish, you could be interviewed by an employer in Spanish to test your fluency.

Writing Cover Letters

Your cover letter gives employers their first impression of you. You may get all A's in your news writing and public relations classes, but do you know how to market yourself? That is the purpose of a cover letter, which is often more difficult to write than a news story because it is hard to write about yourself without appearing egotistical. However, you can use some of the same techniques that you use in a news story. Just as you need a focus in a news story, you need to get to the point of your cover letter quickly. Explain within the first three paragraphs that you are applying for a job or internship at this organization.

Cover letters can start with a straightforward approach like a hard-news lead or a more creative feature-type lead. Most important, avoid writing a form letter that you send to several employers. Each letter should be tailored to the company where you are seeking a job. To do that, you need to do research. Check out the organization's Web site. If it is a newspaper site, read the paper online for a few weeks. For a broadcast job, check out the station's site for news stories and personnel. For public relations, familiarize yourself with the material that company produces or clients the firm represents.

For many years Paul Salsini reviewed cover letters and résumés from job applicants to the *Milwaukee Journal Sentinel,* where he was the staff development director and writing coach. One of the worst mistakes applicants make is that they fail to change the text in their word processors when they are sending out multiple applications, Salsini says.

He also was appalled by the mistakes in these job applications. One applicant misspelled *Milwaukee* throughout her application. Another said, "I've always wanted to work at the *Minneapolis Star.*"

"Good for her," Salsini says. "Why should I care?" He also stresses that applicants should attach some explanation to their clips about how they wrote the story. "If they would just write a couple of sentences to explain whether this was their story idea and why the story was important, it would help to put the clip in context. It helps an editor understand the story. That doesn't take a lot of work and it is so important."

The same principles apply to broadcast jobs. When you submit a tape, you should include an explanation of how and why you did the story.

Internships and experience on campus newspapers, radio and television stations are important. Editors want evidence of how you report and write or what you can do as a copy editor, broadcast producer or reporter. They want clips of stories you have written or edited. However, clips are edited, so they aren't always indicative of the person's writing skill, Salsini says.

Technology has further complicated the job application process in the past few years. Many employers now scan applications into databases, so you need to keep your format simple and brief, preferably limited to one page each for the cover letter and the résumé. In addition, employers expect you to include an e-mail address or cell phone number, whichever way you would be most accessible.

Cover Letter Tips

Make your first impression on the editor a good one. Use proper business letter form, and keep it brief—no more than one page. Editors and other employers are busy people. Double-check and triple-check your spelling. Make sure that all the names and titles are correct. A misspelled name, typo or other mechanical error can disqualify you for consideration.

Be straightforward—not cute, not boring. Start with why you are applying to this organization or something about yourself that makes you worth noticing. But get to the point quickly: why you are applying. Specify whether you are seeking an internship or full-time job.

Here is some advice from an article that Judith Clabes, president and chief executive officer of the Scripps Howard Foundation, wrote for *Quill* magazine when she was editor of the *Kentucky Post*:

I'm editor of a medium-sized daily, and being deluged with letters to the editor comes with the territory.

Believe me, by the time I've shuffled through the "Dear Stupid" letters to the editor, the "Dear Employee" memos from corporate, and the really important "Dear Resident" mail that somehow pours into the office, I'm in no frame of mind for a job-seeker's "Dear Mr. Clabes" letter.

"Dear Mr. Judith Clabes" really ticks me off.

Now, this may seem quirky, but we editors are entitled to an eccentricity or two.

Idiosyncrasies aside, we editors do seem to agree on the issue of introductory letters from job-seekers. We prefer:

- Straightforward, one-page letters
- Simple résumés
- Well-selected clips (yes, college newspaper clips are fine)

In the end, the clips speak loudest. But the introductory letter may determine whether a busy editor will even bother to listen. . . .

The following will automatically turn off an editor:

- Grammatical errors
- Typographical errors
- Misspelling the name of the newspaper
- Misspelling the name of the editor
- Form letters
- Incorrect titles, including courtesy titles
- Cutesy letters
- Bad writing, including poor sentence structure
- Phony sales pitches
- Lengthy, self-centered letters . . .

Typos are killers. "I can't remember bothering to interview an applicant whose letter contained typos or grammatical errors," says Dee W. Bryant, former editor of *The Leaf-Chronicle* in Clarksville, Tennessee. "If a person is that careless with letters, it raises the question about carelessness as a staffer."

Bryant's pet peeve, however, is the automatic—and mindless—"Mr." greeting. "If an applicant is seriously interested, he should have taken the time to find out. It irritates me that people make the invalid assumption that editors are men." . . .

Though we editors have our own pet peeves as well as hiring strategies, we shudder over the cute stuff, the gimmicks, the overzealous attempts at creativity. . . .

What will work is a simple, professional approach. Throw away fuchsia paper and the gimmicks. Invest time in investigating the newspaper. Write a simple, well-crafted (and proofread) one-page letter that demonstrates your interest in journalism generally and in that particular newspaper specifically. Include a brief résumé and five or six well-selected clips.

Before you write your cover letter and résumé, do some research about the organization to which you are applying. If you are seeking a job at a newspaper or magazine, read the publication. You can check the Web or online databases, such as LEXIS/NEXIS, or get copies of the publication.

If you are applying to a corporation for a public relations or advertising position, check databases, such as Standard & Poor's Register of Corporations, and business publications to learn something about the organization. Don't just cite facts about the company; weave the information into the paragraph in your cover letter that explains why you want to work for the organization.

Content of Cover Letters

Try to limit the cover letter to one page. Always address it to a specific person, never "Dear Sir" or "Dear Madam." Write a good lead that tells something about you, but don't make it too flowery. Follow with a nut graph—your reason for writing. If you prefer a direct approach, lead with your reason for the letter.

In the middle of your letter, explain why you are eager to work for this particular organization. Even though you are including a résumé, mention its high points. Make special note of any unusual skills you may have, such as fluency in a second language or relevant experience. If someone at the organization has encouraged you to apply, mention this person's name. The adage "It's not what you know but who you know" has some validity.

Write a few more paragraphs briefly explaining your experience, if any, and your major assets—why anyone should want to hire you—and why you want to work for this company. Then wrap it up with a brief paragraph thanking the editor for his attention.

Consider the lead to your cover letter as carefully as you would consider the lead to a news story. It's the attention getter.

A cover letter that starts "I am graduating in May from journalism school, and I am seeking an internship (or job)" will most likely land in the trash. Thousands of other applicants are also graduating from journalism schools. That lead reveals nothing special about you.

Here are some effective types of leads:

Direct Approach: "Please consider me for a reporting internship (or job—and specify the type of position and the name of the organization) this summer." Follow with a line or two about who you are and why you are interested in this company. This approach does not reflect any creativity, but it is preferable to a strained lead.

Experience Approach: If you had a good internship or have previous journalism-related experience, consider starting with a paragraph about what your experience was and why you are interested in or qualified for this job. If you are a graduate student or nontraditional student, you might refer to your previous experience and your reasons for studying journalism.

For example, Michael Strong was a nontraditional student who was once a massage therapist. His job application began, "How many reporters do you know who have experience meeting people when they are nude? That isn't exactly traditional training for a reporter, but I'm not a traditional candidate for a reporting job."

Reference Approach: The adage of who you know, not what you know, is still somewhat true when you are applying for a job or internship. If someone in the organization referred you to the company or if you have spoken to the recruiter, you can begin your cover letter by referring to that person or conversation.

Preferably by the second paragraph, explain the purpose of your letter—similar to a nut graph in a news story. State what type of job or internship you are seeking and why you are applying to this organization.

In the body, mention some highlights of your résumé or special skills that make you qualified or valuable for the position you seek. Elaborate briefly on any experience you've had related to this position. Try to tailor your comments to this organization rather than writing a form letter with a generic tone.

At the end, mention any enclosures, such as clips or videos. You may thank the person for attention to your application or provide any contact information that you think is necessary.

Autobiographical Approach: Start with something about your background that made you want to become a journalist (or whatever type of career position you are seeking). If you use this technique, keep it short. Don't give your life story. (See the example that follows.)

Student's home mailing address
City, State, ZIP code
Student's e-mail address
Phone numbers (including cell phone)
Date

Maureen Murray, Recruiter for Account Executives
Leo Burnett Company Inc.
35 W. Wacker Drive
Chicago, IL 60601

Dear Ms. Murray:

The basket of apples in your company logo indirectly led me to seek a career in advertising and to write this letter seeking a job in your agency. When I was growing up in Chicago, my grandparents told me a story about how your company used to hand out apples to people on the streets during the Depression as a good public relations gesture. I was impressed. I thought that your company would be the kind of place where I would like to work someday. Every time I see your logo, I remember that story.

Now, as a journalism student at the University of Kansas, I am even more impressed with the Leo Burnett Company, which is ranked the No. 1 advertising agency in the Midwest. Please consider me for a position as an assistant account executive in your client services division. I will graduate in December with a bachelor's degree in journalism. I have taken several advertising, public relations and news-writing courses. I would be eager to work on any of your accounts, such as Nintendo, Reebok, Hallmark Cards or Pillsbury. Any opportunity in your agency would be challenging, but a chance to assist on the Walt Disney account is my idea of the perfect job.

Although I have gained many skills from my academic training, I believe that my internships have offered me the best education. Currently I am a public relations intern for the Nelson-Atkins Museum of Art in Kansas City. I recently promoted and publicized the autobiographical exhibit of artist Andrew Wyeth. I also gained valuable experience last winter as an advertising intern for The Pioneer Press, a suburban Chicago newspaper chain. In that position, I created target account booklets, wrote reports and assisted sales representatives. When I worked in the advertising department of my college newspaper, *The University Daily Kansan,* I won an award as the best account executive.

I work well with people, and I am a good problem solver. In addition to my sales and advertising skills, I have written news stories for the university newspaper. I understand that you are seeking applicants with a broad educational background, and I believe that the media experiences I have had make me a good candidate for your firm. Although I have much to learn, I offer boundless enthusiasm and a positive work ethic.

I will call you within the next two weeks to see if you will grant me an interview. I can be reached at (913) 000-0000. I am enclosing a résumé and some examples of my work. Thank you for your consideration.

Sincerely yours,

[Signature]

Shelly Falevits
E-mail address

Courtesy of Shelly Falevits

Sample cover letter with an autobiographical approach

Here is a more straightforward approach by another journalism student:

Student's home address
City, State, ZIP code
e-mail address
Phone numbers (including cell phone)
Date

Name and title of person to whom you are applying
Name of organization
Address of organization
City, State, ZIP

Dear Mr. or Ms. Name of person (don't use generic Dear Sir or Dear Madam):
I am seeking the position of a graphic designer for the Web pages produced by Information Network of Kansas. After corresponding with you by e-mail, I realized that my skills and training fit the needs of your state agency. My background in Web design and my experience with layout of newspapers and business communications make me a qualified candidate.

I can benefit your organization with my knowledge of several computer graphic design packages and programming languages. I have lived and worked in many different towns in Kansas and will use this knowledge to help develop services for the people who use your network. My internship with the Kansas Public Policy Institute also gave me an in-depth view of our state government and the politicians who represent the people.

The Information Network of Kansas is providing cutting-edge information, and I am interested in working for an agency that refuses to stagnate. I am also interested in working for an agency that provides an essential service to its community. I hope that my skills and your services will benefit both of us.

I appreciate your consideration. I can be reached by e-mail at ……… or by phone at …………

Sincerely yours,

Erin Rooney
Enc. Résumé

ETHICS

Case 1: You have an internship at a local newspaper or television station. A few weeks after you start working, your supervisor asks you out on a date. You like your supervisor and think you could get romantically involved. Should you go on a date? What are the ethical problems of dating your supervisor?

Case 2: You have been hired by the newspaper or television station where you have wanted to work for a long time. You have established some roots and really enjoy your job. You've been on the job for about a year. You are very attracted to your editor, and he or she feels the same attraction to you. Should you get romantically involved? If

so, what are the ethical problems and alternatives?

Case 3: You face a similar situation as in Case 2, but this time you are attracted to a source on your beat. Can you or should you get romantically involved? Do you have to give up a romantic relationship for your job? What are the ethical issues, and what alternatives are open to you?

Résumés

Limit your résumé to one page, with a possible second page for references. Arrange your topics from most recent to previous, such as current experience followed by previous jobs. White paper is preferred. Content is more important than appearance. If you have a home page and online résumé, add the Web address to your résumé.

If your experience in previous internships or jobs is more interesting than your education, put the experience category first. If you have no experience or awards, eliminate the category; don't write "none."

You can start your résumé with an objective, a sentence that explains your job goal, or a summary, a paragraph that highlights your skills and accomplishments. Summaries are gaining favor with employers these days because they offer more information in a quick format than a vague objective.

Objective: Limit your objective to one sentence. Tailor the statement to the type of job you are seeking.

- **Vague:** "Seeking to use my skills in public relations."
- **More specific:** "To use my journalism training at a small, community newspaper to gain experience in several types of reporting and writing assignments."
- **Specific:** "To use my communication skills and my background in graphic arts in a public relations and marketing firm with opportunities for creative expression and growth."

Summary: The summary should be limited to a paragraph that highlights your skills and/or experience:

- "Campus newspaper editor and journalism major with internships at two major metropolitan newspapers. I am seeking a reporting position at a small to midsize newspaper with opportunities for advancement. Versatile skills include reporting, writing, copy editing and page design."

Here are some other tips:

- Make sure that your résumé is free of typos and spelling errors.
- List two or three references, and include phone numbers and e-mail addresses where your references can be reached. Do not say "References available on request." Do everything you can to help the employer. By withholding references, you force the employer to spend more time checking on you. Make sure you ask the people you list if they agree to be references for you. Don't assume or just list their names.
- Skip the fancy paper. Scannable résumés should be as simple as possible on plain white paper with black type of at least 12 points. Your headings can be in larger type, but don't mix fonts. Also eliminate borders and underlining.
- Include five or six clips (or videotape for broadcast journalists, although scripts help in this area as well). Choose clips with good leads. Editors rarely read past a bad lead. Try to include a variety: features and hard news, short and long. Short is better, unless you have a major project. If you have some

good enterprise stories, those you developed through your own ideas, include them. The significance of the news event is not important to editors; they want to see how you wrote more than what you wrote.

- When you copy your clips, don't reduce them in size. Cut them so they fit on standard-sized paper, even if you have to use more than one page for a story.

- Templates such as those offered in Microsoft Word are acceptable provided that you adapt them by adding or eliminating categories that don't apply to you. Consider using "Education" as your first topic heading if you are just graduating, but if you have considerable experience, list that heading first. Interests are optional, but references are not. Make sure that you add a heading for references because one is not included in the templates. Then list your references' titles, phone numbers and e-mail addresses if they agree to be listed.

- Follow-up phone call: A week or two after you have sent your letter and résumé, call the organization to ask if they were received and if you may come for an interview. Find out when the editor you are calling is on deadline or in meetings, and try to avoid these times.

Convergence Coach

Online Résumés Reading a résumé online is more difficult than reading it in print, so keep your Web résumé even shorter than your print one. Try to limit it to three screens. Don't just transfer the print résumé to an online version.

Use a different format, perhaps paragraphs or lists. Don't use the column structure you might use in print; online reading is vertical, not horizontal. If you use a one-screen design, don't offer too many links to separate categories for education, experience and so on. Endless clicking can be tedious for a potential employer. Put the basic information on one page, and link to clips or your portfolio.

Here are some other tips for Web résumés:

- **Background:** Don't use a dark background with white or light type. The type may not show up if an employer wants to print your résumé. If you really prefer this type of design, offer a printable version as well, with white background and black type.

- **Privacy:** Protect your own privacy and that of your references. Consider eliminating your address and phone number in online documents, especially if you post your photograph on your site. The same is true for your references. Although providing contact information for references is preferable in print, for online sites you may have to write "References available on request."

- **Create your own online résumé:** Many Web sites include résumé forms. Unless you are applying to a company that prefers you to use its online résumé form, create your own résumé so you can demonstrate your ability to express yourself—a major qualification for media jobs.

- **Identify yourself:** If you are creating your own Web résumé, make sure that you put your name and e-mail address on every page of your site. Don't use "I" or "Nancy's résumé" as an identifier.

- **Offer a printer-friendly résumé:** If you have a fancy Web site, offer a simple printer version. Recruiters will need to print your resume and keep it on file.

Your Name
E-mail: name@ . . .
Cell phone number

Permanent Address	**Present Address**
[If home address differs from address during the semester]	
Street	Street
City, state, ZIP code	City, state, ZIP code
Phone number with area code	Phone number with area code

Objective or summary   List your career objective or a brief summary paragraph of your achievements and goals

Education:

Years   University of . . .   Location
[Give dates, from most recent to previous.]
Degree expected: B.A. in journalism, [Date]
Major: Journalism with emphasis in magazine

Other colleges attended [If any]   Location

High school attended [Optional]   Location

Experience: [List any full-time or part-time jobs, particularly any related to your field, in order starting from the most recent. Give the dates. You may add a line or two explaining your job duties.]

January–May [Year]
Reporter, *The Daily Campus* newspaper; covered university administration

July–August [Year]
Reporting internship with *City Newspaper;* covered general news for city desk and features

May–August [Year]
Server Starving Students, [City, state]

Special skills and awards: [Omit this category if you have no special skills.]
Skilled in graphics programs and computer-assisted reporting
Fluent in Spanish
Scripps Howard Scholarship for College Journalism

Activities: [List only important activities and memberships, especially those that show leadership or skills related to the job you are seeking. This category may be omitted.]

References: [List only two or three people who have given you permission to list them. References may be listed on a separate page if you run out of room. List people's titles, addresses and phone numbers. Do not write "Available on request."]

Sample of scannable résumé

Interviews

The interview is your chance to explain how much you want to work for the employer and why you would be a good choice. It is also your chance to find out more about the employer and to assess whether you would really like to work there.

Here are some tips:

Dress Conservatively: Wear the type of clothing that employees at that organization would wear to work. Women might wear casual attire such as a skirt and blouse or more businesslike outfits such as a suit or dress, depending on the company. Men should wear a suit or sport jacket with a shirt and tie. No jeans and no sneakers!

Be Prompt: Be on time for your interview. You may arrive 15 minutes early, but don't get there too early. Never be late. That's equivalent to missing a deadline. And that's equivalent to saying you are not fit for the job.

Be Prepared: Be informed about the publication, organization or station. Read copies of the publication, particularly the most recently published ones, or view video on the station's Web site if possible. Public relations applicants should try to gather research about the company and the types of promotions the firm does. Memorize the names of key editors in advance.

The Gannetteer, Gannett Co., Inc.

Newspaper newsroom

Understand the Costs: Some organizations will pay for your transportation and hotel. If not, be prepared to pay for them yourself. Small newspapers and other organizations may not have the budget for your travel costs. You have to decide if the cost is worthwhile to you. If the organization is out of state, it's fair to ask if your transportation and lodging costs will be reimbursed.

Concentrate: When you are introduced to people, try to remember their names, especially those of key editors—such as the city editor or, if you are applying for a sports job, the sports editor. Homework helps.

Be Enthusiastic: Your enthusiasm is your best asset, especially if you don't have experience. Show that you're interested in the job. Smile and enjoy the interview just as if you were doing an interview for a story. If you don't really want to work for the firm, don't waste everyone's time.

Be Polite: Thank the editor or key person for granting you an interview, and thank the person at the end of it as well.

Be Pleasant: Even if you are frightened, smile and be responsive.

Be Yourself: Do not try so hard to make a good impression that you are insincere. Be honest about what you can and cannot do and what you want to learn. Never try to give a false impression of yourself.

Ask Questions: The questions you ask are as important as the ones you answer. They show your curiosity and your concern about the job—qualities of a good reporter, editor or publicist.

Editors have their favorite questions, so it is hard to prepare for the interview. However, almost all of them will ask why you want to work for their organization and why you want to be a journalist. Try to be creative but sincere. "I've always wanted to write" is such a boring answer.

Here are some other questions that are popular with newspaper editors (similar questions are often asked in other fields):

Why Do You Want to Work for This Organization? The answers are up to you: because you grew up in the area, want to remain in the area, are familiar with the community and so on. It's best to specify something you like about the organization if you are familiar with it. Or you could say you are seeking a variety of experiences, particularly if it's a small newspaper or television station, where reporters tend to do all types of stories. If it's a large organization, you could say you're attracted by the prestige of the publication or station or the chance to learn from very experienced journalists. If you are so eager that you will work anywhere, it's OK to say so. Just be honest.

Why Did You Want to Become a Journalist or Public Relations Practitioner? Because it's more interesting than selling used cars, because you seek adventure, because you love the language, whatever. Here is your chance to give your real reason. It could be that someone influenced you or that you just like the type of work.

What are Your Goals as a Journalist? You could say, "To get your job some day" or "To work here until *The New York Times* begs me to come there." A preferred answer might be because you like the work of this paper or station and you are familiar with the community (if that's true). If your goal is to be a foreign correspondent, at this point you might consider joining the Navy. Small papers don't have much use for foreign bureaus. Again, be sincere.

What Books, Magazines and Newspapers Do You Read? Editors love this question. It tells them something about you.

What Other Interests Do You Have? This is another favorite question.

What Can You Do for This Organization, or Why Should I Hire You? Don't say you can turn the organization around or make it wonderful. But do say something about the types of stories you would like to do, or say that you would be willing to do all types of stories. Don't be arrogant.

What Do You Think of This Newspaper, TV Station or Public Relations Firm? Be cautious with this one. Don't say it's terrible and you can save it. Point out something good first. Then you might point out some weakness or area that you think could be improved. Perhaps you think it could use more human approaches to stories or more hard news. If you've read it, you have a right to your opinion. Just be diplomatic.

What Was Your Favorite Story (or Public Relations Project) That You Wrote or Produced, and Why Did You Like It? This is another question that gives insight into you—as well as your professional interests.

How Would You Cover This Issue? The editor might give you an example of a topic that is of concern in that community. You'll have to think and do the best you can to come up with some interesting approaches.

What Questions Do You Have? This question is very important. Here's where you get your chance to ask about the company, the workload, perhaps what the editors want or expect from reporters and copy editors. You could ask about a probationary period. You could also ask about salary, benefits and other compensation; generally, however, that shouldn't be your first question.

At the end of the interview, don't forget to thank the interviewer for his or her time and interest.

Interview Follow-Up After you have had an interview, wait a few weeks and then call to let the editor know you are aggressive and interested in the job. But don't be a pest.

Even if you are not interested in the job, send a note thanking the editor for the interview. That's just basic courtesy. And if you are interested in the job, the thank-you note lets the editor know something else about you: You're thoughtful.

? What Do You Think

Do you think it's better to start your resume with an objective or a summary?

☐ Objective
☐ Summary
☐ Not sure

Exercises

1 **Interview people in your field:** Depending on your field of interest, interview three newspaper editors, television news directors, magazine editors or public relations employers about the qualities they seek in job candidates and the kinds of applications they want.

2 **Describe yourself:** Write a few descriptive paragraphs about yourself in the third person (*she* or *he*). This exercise will give you a clue to what makes you special, and it may help you find a lead for your cover letter.

3 **Cover letter and résumé:** Write a cover letter and a résumé for a job or internship you would be interested in getting.

4 **Online résumé.** Write an online résumé.

☞ **Featured Online Activity** Log on to the book Web site for Chapter 24 and choose at least three resources that will link you to jobs or internships in your field of interest at

academic.cengage.com/masscomm/rich/writingandreportingnews6e

Appendix 1

Grammar and Usage

The difference between the right word and the nearly right word is the same as that between lightning and the lightning bug.
Mark Twain

COACHING TIPS

When in doubt, check it out.

Don't depend on computer spellers and grammar checkers.

Don't turn in copy without checking it for grammar, spelling and style.

Keep a dictionary and stylebook on your desk as you write. Use them.

Test Your Knowledge:

Whom or *who* should you contact for jobs and internships?

Will grammar have an *effect* or *affect* on your career?

Do you expect to go *further* or *farther* in your career if you get a good journalism background?

Do you know how the media *is* or *are* changing the way news is covered?

Does this sentence look *alright* to you? If it does, you need to study this chapter well.

The correct usage is in this paragraph: *Whom* should you contact for an internship? Check directories in your field. A good grasp of grammar will have a beneficial *effect* on your career, but poor grammar will *affect* your chances of getting a good job. You will go *further* in your career if you understand how the media *are* changing the way news is covered. It is never *all right* for you to write *alright*.

Many news organizations require you to take a grammar and style test if you are applying for a job as a reporter or copy editor. Public relations practitioners also need good writing skills. If you don't have a good grasp of grammar and usage, you won't be considered a good writer. And you can't rely on an editor or your computer to catch all your errors.

Some of these items are also in the style guide, but the repetition will reinforce the need for you to learn this information. Now that you understand how to write a news story, this chapter will help you avoid these common errors in grammar, spelling and usage:

Advise/advice: *Advise* is what you do; *advice* is what you receive.
   I advise you to study this chapter. If your professor has *advised* you to buy an Associated Press Stylebook, she gave you good *advice*.

Affect, effect: *Affect* is an active verb, and *effect* is a noun. Think of *affect* with an *a* for action and *effect* with an *e* for the end result. *Effect* can be used as a verb with *to*, as in "to effect change," but that is not a common use.
   Failing your style tests will *affect* your grade. But the *effect* on your writing will be more serious.

Aggravate/annoy: *Aggravate* means to make a condition worse; *annoy* means to irritate. People don't get aggravated; conditions do.

If you continue to smoke, you will *aggravate* your lung disease.

If you don't turn off your cell phone in class, you will *annoy* me.

A lot, alot: Two words, please. Always. If you can't remember, use *many* instead of *a lot.*

Alright: *Alright* is listed in the dictionary as all right in informal dialogue, but it is not all right, according to the Associated Press Stylebook, which says *never* use that spelling. Use two words, *all right,* to mean OK.

It is not *all right* to use *alright.*

Altogether/all together: *Altogether* means completely or thoroughly. *All together* means people or items are all gathered in one place.

Among, between: *Among* is used with more than two items; *between* is used with two items.

The conflict was *between* two students. The pay increases were divided *among* 10 employees.

Ampersand: Do not use the ampersand (&) as a substitute for *and.* This symbol should be used only when it is part of a company's name, such as Dun & Bradstreet.

Anxious, eager: *Anxious* means you are worried; *eager* means you are excited or looking forward to something.

In your cover letter, don't say you are *anxious* to work for a company.

Even if you are worried about the job, you are probably *eager* to get it.

As, like, as if, as though: Use *as, as if* or *as though* to introduce a sentence or clause with a verb. *Like* means "similar to" and should be used only to compare nouns or pronouns. Whenever you are confused, just see if *similar to* would fit in the sentence. If the sentence or clause contains some action, use *as.* Think *a* for *as* for action.

As I said (not *like I said*), she plays basketball *like* a professional. It looks *as if* she will become a professional basketball player.

Bad, badly: *Bad* is an adjective that modifies a noun, as in "You wrote a *bad* paper." *Badly* is an adverb that modifies a verb, as in "You played *badly* in the game." These words are used *badly* most of the time when used with the linking verb *feel.* "You *feel bad*" means that your health, emotional or mental state is bad. "You *feel badly*" means that your sense of touch is poor. (See *Linking verbs* for more explanation.)

Don't *feel bad* if you have made this common mistake, but don't write *badly* anymore in this context.

Before, prior to: *Before* is appropriate and less formal for most uses. *Prior to* is appropriate when the connection between the two events makes it clear that one event must precede the other.

Every passenger must show identification *before* a ticket will be issued. Every passenger must show identification *prior to* boarding the plane. (*Before* would also be acceptable here.)

Between, among: See *among.*

Between you and I or you and me: Never use *I* in this case. *Between* is a preposition that must be followed by a pronoun in the objective case: *me, her, him, them, us.*

Every time you are tempted to use *I*, mentally substitute *he* or *we*. You're not as likely to say "between you and he" or "between they and we."

Biannual/semiannual/biennial: *Biannual* means twice a year. So does *semiannual*. *Biennial* means every two years. Note that these words are not hyphenated.

Bimonthly/semimonthly/biweekly/semiweekly: *Bimonthly* means every other month; *semimonthly* means twice a month. Same with biweekly—every other week—and semiweekly—twice a week.

Board with singular verb: A reference to a board of directors or a board of education or any other board followed by a phrase describing it takes a singular verb, such as *is, was* or *votes*. The board is considered a singular entity; it's still one board even if it has 30 members. Ignore the modifying phrase.

> The *Board of Education is* meeting tonight. The *Board of Regents votes* on the issue tomorrow. (If that sounds awkward, you might say "*Members of the Board of Education are meeting* tonight.")

Can, may: *Can* means you are capable of doing something; *may* means permission or the chance to do something.

> You *may* get a promotion if you *can* create Web pages.

Clause, phrase: A clause is a group of words containing a subject and a verb. An independent clause forms a complete sentence; a dependent one depends on the rest of the sentence to make sense. Use a comma after an introductory clause. A phrase is a group of words without a subject or a verb. If you want to write well (that's a dependent clause), don't interrupt your subject and verb with a long clause.

> *Poor:* The student, who was fond of writing long, complicated sentences with clauses between his subject and verb, was an English major.

> *Better:* The student, who was an English major, was fond of writing long, complicated sentences.

> *Phrase: After the game,* the fans celebrated at a local pub.

Convergence Coach

Online sites with poor grammar and spelling errors lack credibility. Online news stories use Associated Press style. TV "crawls," the print that scrolls across the bottom of a screen, must also adhere to good grammar and usage even though these headlines are brief.

■ Proofread your copy carefully before you post anything online.

■ Most people's e-mail messages are notoriously sloppy. Check spelling and grammar before you send your e-mail messages, particularly if you are sending an e-mail for an interview, an online résumé or other career-related activities.

■ Although broadcast journalists also use Associated Press style, the medium features the spoken word. Therefore, you may want to use a phonetic spelling of a name that is difficult to pronounce. But anything that is shown on the screen, such as a name or a title, should be checked for accurate spelling and grammar.

Comma: Use a comma between two independent clauses joined by a conjunction—*and, but, for, or, no, so, yet*—unless the clauses are short. Use a comma after an introductory clause unless it is short. Always put commas inside the quotation marks in a direct quote. Check the *Associated Press Stylebook* for a more complete discussion.

> "When a sentence includes a direct quote (that's an introductory clause), the comma always goes inside the quotation marks," the professor said. "So does the period."

Comma splice: Never join two sentences with a comma. That's called a comma splice. Learn to love the period, especially in newswriting. If the sentences are closely related, you might use a semicolon.

> People who use commas to join sentences are making a dreadful mistake; comma splices indicate bad writing.

Compared to/compared with: Use *compared to* when you liken one thing to another. Use *compared with* when you examine the similarities and differences of two or more items.

> She is very smart *compared to* her sister. *Compared with* all the other students in her class, she is the best writer.

Complement, compliment: *Complement,* with *e,* means "to complete," also with *e. Compliment,* with *i,* means to flatter or praise.

> "If you can't get a *compliment* any other way, pay one to yourself," Mark Twain said.

> If you want a scarf to *complement* your outfit, buy one.

Consensus: This word means an agreement of opinion, so do not say "*consensus of opinion.*" That's redundant.

> After six hours of debate, the board of commissioners reached a *consensus* about building a new parking garage.

Council/counsel: A *council* is an appointed or elected group of people who give advice or make decision. *Counsel* is the advice or consultation you receive.

Credible/creditable: *Credible* is believable. *Creditable* is deserving of credit, honor or esteem.

> He gave a *credible* explanation for his absences.

> He is doing a *creditable* job in the department, but it would be better if he were just doing a good job. The use of *creditable* in this case is awkward.

Criteria, criterion: *Criteria,* referring to the factors that will be used to judge something, is plural. If only one factor is involved, it is a *criterion.*

> The *criteria* to get an A in this class are good writing, spelling, grammar and punctuation. The *criterion* for expulsion from the journalism school is plagiarism.

Currently, presently, now: *Currently* means now; *presently* means soon, although it can mean now. If you are confused, just use *now.*

Dangling modifier: A phrase or a participle (an adjective made from a verb ending in *ing*) is said to dangle if it is not placed directly before the noun or pronoun it modifies.

> *Dangling participle:* After *studying* for three hours, the *test* was canceled. (The test did not study for three hours. The student did.)

> *Correct:* After *studying* for three hours, the *student* learned that the test was canceled.

Desert, dessert: A desert is a barren place; a dessert is something to eat.

You probably won't find a delicious *dessert* in a *desert*.

Directions/regions: Capitalize regions of the country—*Midwest, North, South, West, Northeast, Southwest, East Coast* and *West Coast.* Use lowercase for directions: Go *west* and turn *east.*

She is hoping to get a job on the East Coast, but right now she lives in the Midwest.

He said the party is about five blocks east of the university.

Either, neither: Each of these words requires a singular verb and a singular pronoun. Think of *either one* or *neither one.* But if *either* joins a singular word and a plural word, the verb agrees with the closer subject.

Either student *is* qualified for the position.

Neither the president nor the vice president *is* available for comment.

Neither of the students *plans* to present *her* project tomorrow.

Either the president or several members *are going* to attend *their* fraternity's philanthropic event.

Embarrassment, harassment: These words are often spelled incorrectly. *Embarrassment* has two *r*'s and two *s*'s; *harassment* has just one *r*. You are probably embarrassed more than you are harassed, so give it the extra *r* for being a regular occurrence.

Etc.: This is an abbreviation for the Latin word *et cetera,* meaning "and other things." You can substitute *and so on* or *and so forth,* but it is best to avoid this term. It leaves the reader wondering what else should follow. As the late John B. Bremner, a renowned authority on usage, wrote, "Above all, don't use *etc.* as a cover for ignorance when you have run out of ideas."

Everyone, everybody, every one, each: Each of these words takes a singular verb and a singular pronoun. If the previous sentence sounds strange to you, mentally eliminate the prepositional phrase (*of these words*). The phrases that intervene between *everyone, each* and *everybody* and the verb or pronoun are what cause the confusion. If you really get confused, substitute *all* or another plural word for *everyone, each* or *everybody.*

Every one of the students *is* seeking a good job in *his* or *her* field. (Stress the *one* in this sentence. You wouldn't say *everyone are* or *everybody are seeking.*)

Farther, further: *Farther* is distance; *further* involves length of time, quantity or intensity.

How much *farther* do we have to drive?

I'll give this *further* thought.

Feel: This word indicates a state of being or a sense of touch. Don't use it to mean "think" or "believe."

You will *feel* bad if you don't get an A on the quizzes at the end of the chapter.

You *think* or *believe* you are doing well (not you *feel* you are doing well) in the course.

Fewer, less: Use *fewer* to refer to a specific number of items that you can count; use *less* to refer to a collection of items, a period of time or a quantity. *Less* is often used with a sum of money.

Fewer than 10 graduates took jobs in which they made *less* than $15,000.

Fragment: An incomplete sentence, sometimes just a word or phrase. (That is a fragment.) Fragments can be effective as a writing technique for emphasis but should be used cautiously and rarely.

Full-time/full time: Use the hyphenated version when you are using the word to describe something such as a *full-time* job. But use two words without a hyphen when it is not followed by a noun. *He works full time.*

Goes without saying: If it does *go without saying,* then why say it? This is a stupid expression often used in corporate memos.

Half-mast, half-staff: On naval ships and at naval stations, flags are flown at *half-mast.* Other flags are flown at *half-staff,* usually to commemorate a person or tragic event.

Hyphenate compound modifiers: When two or more adjectives are used together to modify a noun that follows them, use a hyphen. Don't use a hyphen for *very* or adverbs ending in *ly.* Do not use a hyphen if a compound adjective follows an action verb.

> The *3-year-old* child had a chronic ear infection. But: The child is 3 years old.

She was an *honor-roll student* in high school (compound adjective modifying *student).* But: The student was on the honor roll in high school (no modifier).

The *part-time job* pays well (compound adjective modifying *job).* But: I work *part time* in the office (compound adjective after an action verb).

The student had a *poorly furnished apartment* (no hyphen after *ly* adverb).

A *very strong wind* blew off the roof (no hyphen after *very).* Limit the use of *very* in your writing; it's a weak modifier.

I, me: *I* does the action; *me* receives it. The same rule applies to the pronouns *he, she* and *we.* Don't use these words after the prepositions *to* or *with. I, he, she* and *we* are in the nominative case, meaning they should be used as subjects. *Me, her, him, us* and *them* are in the objective case and should be used as objects in sentences.

> Whenever the newspaper needs someone to work overtime, Julie and *I* always get picked.

> The chancellor gave the report to several journalism students and *me* to review before he made a decision.

If I were: Do not use *if I was. If* is a word used in the subjunctive mood, meaning it expresses a condition; it should always be used with *were.*

> *If I were you,* I'd learn to use *were* with *if* when I mean it in a conditional sense. *If I were he,* I'd probably reword the sentence, because it is correct but it sounds weird. *If she were* in my reporting class, she wouldn't use *was* in a sentence starting with *if.*

Irregardless: There is no such word, *regardless* of what you may believe and *regardless of the fact that it is listed in the dictionary as nonstandard usage.* Don't use it.

It's, its: Wordsmith John B. Bremner calls the misuse of *it's* and *its* "possibly the most sickening example of literary ignorance." *It's* is a contraction for *it is; its* is a possessive word meaning "belonging to it."

> *It's* going to cost more to attend college next year because the university raised *its* tuition.

Join, not join together: *Join* means to connect. Can you *join* something apart? *Together* is superfluous.

Judgment: No *e*. There is no judge in *judgment.*

Lay, lie, laid, lain: *Lay* means to place or put something somewhere; it always takes an object when used in this sense. If you can substitute the verb *place*, use *lay. Laid* is the past tense. *Lie* means to recline. Its past tense is *lay,* and therein lies the confusion. It might help you to mentally use *down* with *lie* or to substitute *recline. Lain* is the perfect tense of *lie.*

> Please *lay* the book on the desk. She *laid* the book on the desk yesterday.

> *Lie* down and take a nap for a few hours. She *lay* on the beach for three hours yesterday and was badly sunburned. (This still sounds awkward, and it might be preferable to say, "She *was lying* on the beach" or "She *had lain* on the beach for three hours. . . .")

> He *had lain* on the sofa for three hours.

Layoffs/lay off: *Layoffs* without a hyphen is one word when used as a noun. When you lay off people as a verb, you must do it in two words.

> Newspapers had many *layoffs* this year. The station was forced to *lay off* several reporters.

Less than/under: When you are using a collection of items rather than a specific number of items, *less than* or *under* is acceptable. For a comparison of a specific number, use *fewer than* (see *fewer*).

> She makes *less than* $20,000 per year.

> She makes *under* $20,000 per year.

> He weighs *less than* 200 pounds.

> He weighs *under* 200 pounds.

Like, as: See *as, like.*

Linking verbs: The *to be* verbs are linking verbs: *am, is, are, was, were, have been.* Verbs expressing the senses are also considered linking verbs: *appear, feel, smell, sound, taste, look.* Linking verbs join the subject with a predicate nominative, meaning a noun or pronoun in the same case as the subject. The pronoun that follows a linking verb could be used as a subject. The adjective after a linking verb modifies the subject and is called a predicate adjective.

> It *is* she. She *is* it. (You wouldn't say "Her *is* it.") The food *tastes good* and the music *sounds good,* but I still *feel bad.* (*Good,* a predicate adjective, modifies *food* and *music,* not the verb. You wouldn't say "The food *tastes well* and the music *sounds well,* but I still *feel badly.*")

Lose, loose: If you *lose* your assignment, you're in trouble. If your pants fall down because they are too *loose,* you'll be embarrassed. You might also be in trouble. You'll certainly be in trouble if you mix up the spelling of these two words.

Media: This word is plural and takes a plural verb for agreement. Television is one *medium,* but newspapers, magazines and television are the *media.*

> The *media are planning* major coverage of the election. The *media are changing* the way *they* cover news.

Memento/not momento: If you want to give students something to remember at their graduation, you will give them a *memento.* There is no such word as a momento although your graduation might be a *momentous* occasion, meaning it was of great moment or something to remember.

ETHICS

Ethical Dilemma: Should you clean up quotes? If a speaker uses poor grammar, should you fix the grammar?

Ethical values: Accuracy, fairness, sensitivity.

Ethical Guidelines: The Associated Press Stylebook says, "Never alter quotations even to correct minor grammatical errors or word usage. . . . Do not routinely use abnormal spellings such as *gonna* in attempts to convey regional dialects or mispronunciations."

The guidelines reinforce the concept that a quote must be someone's exact words. However, what is stylistically correct may not be ethically sensitive. If you are trying to convey that a politician uses poor grammar and that concept is relevant to a profile or to the person's way of speaking, you may want to use the ungrammatical language. However, if you are interviewing someone who may be an immigrant and does not speak English well, it could be insensitive to quote exactly. Instead of using the exact quote, consider paraphrasing or using a partial quote. Avoid using too many partial quotes because they disrupt the flow of a sentence and cause the reader to wonder what was left out.

Morale/moral: *Morale* means a mental or emotional attitude; *moral* is the distinction between right and wrong.

In his ethics course, he studied *moral* reasoning methods, but when he failed the course, his *morale* plummeted.

More than, over: *More than* is better when referring to numbers; *over* is better when referring to spatial relationships, as the opposite of *under.* In some cases, *over* can be used with numbers, such as ages or amounts of money.

More than 300 people attended the hearing.

The car went *over* the bridge. He is *over* 20. She earns *over* $400 per week. (This last sentence is acceptable, but so is *more than* $400 per week.)

Needless to say: If it's *needless to say,* don't say it. This is another stupid expression.

None: When you use *none* as in *not one,* use a singular verb. Use a plural verb when you mean *no two or more* or *not any* in a collective sense.

None (*not one*) of these students *is* going to graduate school.

None (*not any*) of the student fees *are* being used for health care.

Nonprofit/not-for-profit: A *nonprofit* organization is not supposed to make any profits, nor is it supposed to have a hyphen. The term *not-for-profit* can mean the same thing. If you are using it as an adjective to describe an organization, join the words with hyphens.

Off of: *Off* is enough. *Off of* is unnecessary and ugly usage.

The manager took 10 percent *off* the regular price.

Part-time/part time: When this term is used as an adjective to describe another word, treat it as one word by hyphenating it, such as your *part-time* job. When you say you work only part time, meaning part of the time, use two words.

Passive voice, active voice: Avoid passive voice whenever possible. You are using passive voice when you indicate that something has happened to you or the subject. You are using the active voice when you indicate that you or the subject is doing the action. The action verbs that characterize the active voice have more impact than passive verbs. But sometimes you need the passive voice. Place the most important information first in the sentence, and that will determine if you need active or passive voice. Active voice is preferable for print media and essential for broadcast media.

Active voice: Three students *received* scholarships.

Passive voice: Scholarships *were received* by three students.

Appropriate use of passive: The serial killer *was sentenced* to death by the judge. (That's probably better than saying "The judge *sentenced* a serial killer to death today" because the emphasis should be on the killer, not the judge.)

Pleaded, pled: *Pled* as the past tense of *plead* is considered acceptable in English usage, but the Associated Press Stylebook considers it colloquial and prefers *pleaded*.

The defendant *pleaded* guilty, but if he *pled* guilty, he would still go to jail regardless of whether the Associated Press style gurus approved of the term he used.

Precede/proceed: *Precede* means what goes before; *proceed* means to go ahead or continue.

Proved/proven: *Proved* is the past tense of an action. *Proven* is an adjective and should be used to describe someone.

You have *proved* that you are ready to graduate.

He is a *proven* leader.

Prerequisite/perquisites: If you have to take a beginning reporting course before you can take magazine writing, the first course is a *prerequisite,* meaning it is required to precede something. You know that because you have many prerequisites (without hyphens). If you get a good job, you might get some *perks,* which is really an abbreviation for *perquisites.*

Publicly, not publically: If you want to run for president of the student government, you should announce your intentions *publicly.* Be careful not to commit the common mistake of omitting the *l* from the word.

Restaurateur: No *n* as in restaurant. Think of a *restaurateur* as the person who manages the place where you ate, not a place for an ant.

Seasons: Use lowercase for seasons—spring, summer, autumn and fall. That goes for springtime and summertime, too. However, if the season is part of a formal title such as *Spring Break* or *Winter Olympics,* capitalize it.

Should have, not should of: *Of* should never be used as a verb. Also wrong: *could of* and *would of* in place of *could have* and *would have.*

By the time you are in college, you *should have* learned never to write *should of.*

Stationary, stationery: *Stationary* means something stays the same (note the *a*'s); *stationery* is the paper you use for letters (note the *e*).

Subject–verb agreement: The verb must agree with the subject. If the subject is singular, the verb must be singular as well. Plural subjects take plural verbs. Here's why that is not as easy as it seems:

The number of students who drop classes *is* increasing. The subject is *number,* not *students.* When you have a noun, *number,* followed by a prepositional phrase with a plural word such as *students,* identify the subject. Don't be misled by the phrase. When *number* is the subject, it always takes a singular verb.

The rate of dropouts *is* increasing. The subject is *rate,* not *dropouts.*

There *are* fewer students enrolled in the print journalism program. The subject is *students,* not the expletive *there.* Avoid starting sentences with *There* because you are forced to use a weak verb. Better: Fewer students are enrolled in the print journalism program.

A singular subject, followed by the phrase *as well as,* takes a singular verb. The city budget, as well as the tax proposal, *was* approved. Better to say: The city budget *and* the tax proposal *were* approved.

Everyone, each, either, neither, every take singular verbs. Imagine the word *one* as the subject when you use those words. *Each* (one) of the students *is* creating a Web page. If that sounds awkward, use *All* of the students *are* creating a Web page.

When a compound subject (two or more subjects) is joined by *and,* it takes a plural verb. The *professor and the students were* sick.

Singular or plural: When a compound subject is joined by *or, nor, but, either, neither,* the verb agrees with the subject closest to it. *Neither* the mayor *nor* the council members *have* proposed a solution. The desk *or* the computers *have* to be sold to raise the money.

Collective nouns such as *audience, jury, board* take singular verbs. The *Board of Commissioners is* scheduled to meet after the holidays. If that sounds awkward, just say The *commissioners are* scheduled to meet after the holidays.

The audience *was* enthusiastic about the performance.

See other entries for *none, board, everyone.*

Than, then: *Than* is used for comparison; *then* is used for time. Think of *then* and *when.*

That, which: When a clause is essential (or restrictive), meaning the sentence won't make sense without it, use *that.* If the sentence can stand alone without the clause (if the clause is nonessential or nonrestrictive), use *which.* Use a comma before a clause with *which;* don't use a comma to precede a clause with *that.* And don't use either word to refer to people. Use *who.*

The committee *that* banned reporters from the hearing was fined. (What committee was fined? The clause is essential to the meaning of the sentence.)

The Lawrence School Board, *which* meets regularly on Tuesdays, will discuss changing school boundaries this week. (The sentence is clear without the clause telling when the board meets.)

The school board members, *who* will vote next week, were elected to two-year terms. (Use *who* when referring to people.)

Their, there, they're: *Their* means "belonging to them"; *there* means "where" or is sometimes used to begin a sentence; *they're* is a contraction for *they are.*

Students who did not qualify for *their* loans this year said *they're* going to file new applications while *there* is still time.

There is or there are: Avoid starting sentences with these words. They always force you to use the weak *to be* verbs. Turn the sentence around and insert an active verb.

Poor: There are no internships being offered at that newspaper.

Better: That newspaper is not offering any internships.

Toward, towards: Use *toward* without the *s.*

Unique: *Unique* means "one of a kind, incomparable." You cannot have something that is more unique or most unique or very unique. If it's unique, it is beyond comparison or qualification.

Who, whom: *Who* is the subject; *who* does the action. *Whom* is the object and receives the action. These words are confusing in clauses. Try to reverse the sentence or clause and see if *who* can be the subject. Deciding on the right word is even trickier when *who* or *whom* is the subject of a clause.

Are you the person *who* called me about the job? (*Who* is the subject of this clause; *who* does the action; *who* called.)

Are you the student *who* is seeking the job? (*Who* is the subject of the clause *is seeking*.) Are you the student *whom* I hired last week? (*Whom* is the object of *I hired*; *whom* received the action.)

Whom do you wish to see about the job opening? (*You*—the subject—wish to see *whom*—the object, the person who receives the action of your wish.)

The personnel director will choose *whoever* she thinks is the most qualified. (She thinks *whoever* is qualified; *whoever* is the subject of the clause *whoever is most qualified*.)

Who's, whose: *Who's* is a contraction for *who is*; *whose* is a possessive meaning "belonging to whom."

Whose team project was late, and *who's* responsible?

Your, you're: *Your* is possessive, meaning "belonging to you," and *you're* is a contraction for *you are*.

Now *you're* ready to test *your* skill by doing the following exercises.

ZIP code: ZIP should be all in capital letters and code should be in lowercase. It is a trademark of the U.S. Postal Service, and it stands for Zone Improvement Program.

For more tips on usage, see Appendix 2, "Style Guide."

What Do You Think ?

Which of the following errors do you think are the most common in media publications?

- ☐ It's/its
- ☐ Their/there/there's
- ☐ Alright/all right
- ☐ Effect/affect

Exercises

1 Grammar A–K: Study the grammar and usage tips from A to K, and correct the errors in the following sentences. Not all sentences contain errors; some may contain more than one error. Type the errors and the corrections, or type the entire sentence in correct form if your instructor prefers.

a She felt bad about missing the school board meeting, but her editor fired her irregardless of her excuse.

b We will all join together in prayer for the students who died in the shooting, and we will fly the flags at half-mast.

c It's alright if you miss class for a job interview, you can make up the test tomorrow.

d We'll divide the workload between three students.

e The St. Joseph Board of Commissioners are planning to submit a proposal for a bond issue to pay for road improvements, and they are hoping the election committee will reach a consensus of opinion to put the issue on the ballot.

f I know you are anxious to get this job, but each of the applicants will have a chance to discuss their strengths and weaknesses with the personnel director.

g Based on your writing skills, it looks like you could be a good journalist.

h Each of the students is going to receive a plaque with their diplomas at graduation.

i She was embarrassed that she had less than five answers correct on the quiz.

j After the boss read the report, he gave it to Jim and I to rewrite and said its due back by Monday.

2 **Grammar L–Y:** Study the grammar and usage tips from L to Y, and correct the errors in the following sentences. Not all sentences contain errors; some may contain more than one error, and some of the errors may include information from A to K. Type the errors and the corrections, or type the entire sentence in correct form if your instructor prefers.

a The people that attended the gay rights rally said it was one of the most unique events the school had sponsored.

b However, the participants in the rally said the media was annoying when they converged on the speakers with cameras and microphones.

c Some of the speakers felt badly that the crowd became unruly and the organizer said he was embarassed when some of the participants complained.

d Needless to say, next year the rally will be planned better.

e None of the five students involved in the fracas is going to be punished.

f The first-place award, that was an engraved silver bowl, was received by the class valedictorian.

g The three top restauranteurs in the city provided food for the banquet, but over 200 people got sick after the event.

h The City Board of Health, that investigates such cases, said the food smelled and tasted well, but they are withholding judgement on the cause of the illness until the food can be tested.

i Irregardless, alot of people were laying on the ground, holding their stomachs in pain.

j The city health inspector wanted to know who he should blame, and he said he was moving towards a solution to the mystery of revealing whose responsible for the food poisoning outbreak.

3 **Edit a story:** The following poorly written story would never be accepted for publication. Ignore the wordiness, and edit it only for grammar and usage errors. When you retype the story, underline, circle or use boldface to identify the errors, and type in the corrections.

In 1918 William Strunk Jr. produced a little book for his English course at Cornell University, it had a great affect on his students. E.B. White, one of the students who the professor taught, published the book in 1957. Today, the book, that was originally known as "The Little Book," is still having a great effect on writers. Its called *The Elements of Style.* Like I said, it's still popular, and every writer should have their own copy. It's presently available on the World Wide Web.

Strunk never thought it was alright to use alot of unnecessary words. One of his famous sayings are "Omit needless words". Between you and I, that advice is still good today, and I feel badly that this story is filled with errors that would of made Strunk cringe. It goes without saying that Strunk would have been embarrased if I was in his class. None of these sentences are perfect, and if this was the way a student wrote, Strunk would have issued stern judgement. Poor grades were received by students who wrote this badly.

Their is no excuse for writing badly, Strunk might have said. "Vigorous writing is concise", Strunk wrote. The media does not always follow Strunk's advice. He was the most unique teacher of his time. If your anxious to be a good writer, you'll check out his book online.

☞ **Featured Online Activity** Log on to the book Web site for the grammar appendix and take the interactive quizzes on grammar and spelling at

academic.cengage.com/masscomm/rich/ writingandreportingnews6e

Appendix 2

Style Guide

The *Associated Press Stylebook* is an essential tool for all media writers. It is filled with valuable guidelines for punctuation, spelling, word use and clear writing. Although many newspapers have their own guidelines, the *Associated Press Stylebook* is widely accepted. It is also used for public relations writing and Web style. However, many of the guidelines for magazines and broadcast writing differ from those for newspaper and public relations releases. This abbreviated style guide is in no way a substitute for the printed version of the Associated Press Stylebook. However, for a quick reference on common problems and uses, the following material, which is based on the *Associated Press Stylebook* and is used with permission, may be helpful. The *AP Stylebook* is also online at *www.apstylebook.com* for a registration fee. Check the Web site for this book for interactive, online quizzes: *academic.cengage. com/masscomm/rich/writingandreportingnews6e.*

A

acronyms: Acronyms are words formed with the initials from of a name for an organization or company. Avoid acronyms that the reader would not easily recognize. Do not follow an organization's full name with the acronym in parentheses. If the acronym would not be clear on second reference, don't use it.

academic degrees: Avoid abbreviations when possible. Preferred: *John Jones, who has a doctorate in psychology.* Use an apostrophe in *bachelor's degree* and *master's degree.* Use *Ph.D.* for a doctorate, and use other abbreviations, such as *M.S.* and *B.A.,* only when needed after a name. Don't use both *Ph.D* and *Dr.* to identify someone. Wrong: *Dr. Sam Jones, Ph.D.* Right: *Dr. Sam Jones, a chemist.*

academic departments: Use lowercase except for proper names such as *English* and *Spanish* but not *history department.*

academic titles: Capitalize and spell out formal titles such as *chancellor* and *chairman* when they precede a name—*Chancellor Robert Smart.* Use a lowercase letter after a name—*Robert Smart, chancellor, spoke yesterday*—and when an academic title is used elsewhere without a name. Use lowercase for *professor* and for modifiers before a name: *history professor William Oldtime.* Don't use the title *professor* before the name on second reference; just use the last name.

addresses: Use the abbreviations *Ave., Blvd.* and *St.* only with a numbered address: *1600 Pennsylvania Ave.* Spell out these words when they are part of a street name without a number: *Pennsylvania Avenue.* Do not use abbreviations for *Road, Drive, Terrace* or other such words. Use figures for street numbers: *6 University Drive.* Spell out and capitalize *First* through *Ninth* when they are used as street names; use figures with two letters for 10th and above: *7 Fifth Ave., 100 21st St.*

affect, effect: *Affect* is a verb, meaning to influence. *Effect* is most commonly used as a noun, meaning the result. Consider *affect* as action and *effect* as the end result. *The style quizzes will affect your grade. A college degree will have a positive effect on your career. Effect* as a verb is less commonly used and means to cause or create, as in *He will effect changes in the department.*

ages: Always use figures: *He is 9 years old* or *The boy, 9, is missing.* When age is used as an adjective, as in *a 9-year-old boy,* use hyphens.

AIDS: The acronym is acceptable in all references to acquired immune deficiency syndrome, a virus that weakens the immune system. The scientific name for the virus that causes AIDS is the human immunodeficiency virus, or HIV. People who test positive for the virus, who are said to be HIV-positive, do not have AIDS; they have the AIDS virus. People do not have AIDS until they develop several serious symptoms of the disease. When writing about the deaths of people who have AIDS, say they died from AIDS-related illnesses, not from AIDS. The actual cause of death is not AIDS; it is the illnesses that result from the weakened immune system.

allege: Use this word with great care, and avoid it when possible. It does not spare you from a libel suit. Use it when you need to make it clear that the unproved action is not being treated as a fact: *the alleged rape.* Specify the exact charge and the source—police or court records—somewhere in the story. Avoid redundancy. Wrong: *Police accused her of allegedly stealing the bicycle.* Right: *Police accused her of stealing the bicycle.*

all right: two words, not *alright.* Even though *alright* is listed as in the dictionary as being used in some manuscripts, it is not acceptable in journalism or modern usage.

alumnus, alumni, alumna, alumnae: *Alumnus* is one man, *alumni* is the plural for graduates, *alumna* is one woman graduate and *alumnae* is plural for women graduates. *Alumni* is the most common plural because it includes men and women.

a.m., p.m.: Use lowercase letters with periods. Avoid redundancy: *10 a.m. this morning.*

among, between: Use *between* for two items and *among* for more than two: *The money was divided between two students; the money was divided among six students.* Equally important, when using *between,* always follow it with objective pronouns such as *me, him,* or her, as in *between you and me,* not *between you and I.*

anybody, anyone, any one, any body: one word for indefinite reference: *Anyone can master this;* two words for singling out a person: *Any one of you can master this.*

average, mean, median, norm: The *average* is the number obtained when the totals are added and divided by the number of quantities—2, 4 and 6 equals 12, divided by 3 equals an *average* of 4. The *mean* is the figure between two extremes obtained by adding all the figures and dividing by the total number of items: The *mean* of 2, 4, 6, 8 and 10 is 6. The *median* is the middle number in a series arranged in order: The *median* grade of 60, 70 and 80 is 70. *Norm* is a standard of average performance for a group.

B

backward: not *backwards.*

bad, badly: *Bad* is an adjective but can be used with *feel* for a condition of health, meaning *I feel bad. Badly* is an adverb: *He played badly.*

because, since: *Because* denotes a cause–effect relationship; *since* is used more to denote a sense of time or when the result was related but not the direct cause. *Because you studied, you will pass the test. Since you have been in the department, the rules have changed.*

beside, besides: *Beside* means at the side of; *besides* means in addition to.

Bible: Capitalize when referring to the Old Testament or New Testament. Capitalize related terms: *Gospels, Scriptures, Holy Scriptures.* Lowercase *biblical* in all uses. Lowercase *bible* as a nonreligious term: *Her textbook was her bible.*

biweekly: every other week.

black: preferred term for people of African descent. Check with sources to see if they prefer *African-American.* Although not specified in the *AP Stylebook,* in some cases members of minority groups prefer the term *people of color.* You should always check with your sources for usage of appropriate terms.

blond, blonde: *blond* for males and all adjectives; *blonde* as nouns for females. *She had blond hair.*

brand names: Capitalize them: *She drank a Coke.*

brunet, brunette: Use *brunet* as a noun for males and as an adjective for both sexes. Use *brunette* as a noun for females.

burglary, larceny, robbery, theft: *Burglary* is unlawful entry of a building involving a crime, *larceny* is the legal term for taking property, *robbery* involves violence or threat in committing larceny and *theft* is taking property without threats or violence. *Robbery* can be committed without a person present in a property, such as *his house was robbed,* but it is usually used with the threat of violence.

bus, buses: These are transportation vehicles. *Busses* means kisses.

C

cancel, canceled, canceling, cancellation

cannot: one word.

capital, capitol: *Capital* is the city where a seat of government is located. Do not capitalize. *Capitol* is the building for the seat of government in Washington or in the states: The legislators met in the *capitol;* the *capital* of Connecticut is Hartford; the capitol in Hartford looks like a white fairy-tale castle with a gold dome.

Catholic: Use *Roman Catholic Church* in the first reference. Second or more references may be the *Catholic Church* or *Catholicism*—capitalized when referring to the religion.

Centers for Disease Control and Prevention: Plural for *Centers.*

cents: Spell out the word *cents* and use lowercase. Use numerals for amounts less than a dollar: *5 cents.* Use the dollar sign and a decimal system for larger amounts: *$1.05.*

city council, city commission: Capitalize either term when it is part of a proper name: *the Hartford City Council* or the *Lawrence City Commission.* Retain the capitalization if the reference is to a specific council but the context does not require the city name: *The City Council passed an ordinance.* Use lowercase when the term is used in a generic sense, not referring to a specific body: *Every city in our state has a city council.*

city hall: Capitalize if it refers to a specific city hall, with or without the name: *Hartford City Hall.* Lowercase when used in a generic sense: *You can find records in any city hall.*

civil cases, criminal cases: Civil cases are brought by individuals or organizations seeking damages; criminal cases are filed by a government agency against people involved in a crime.

collective nouns: Nouns denoting a single unit take singular verbs and singular pronouns for agreement: The Board of Supervisors made *its* ruling; the committee *is* going to meet; the family *is* going on a picnic; the jury reached *its* verdict.

complement, compliment: *Complement* means to complete; *compliment* means to praise.

compose, comprise: *Compose* is to create or put together: She *composed* the music for the school play; The country *is composed* of 50 states. *Comprise* is to contain or include all, best used in active voice: The jury *comprises* 12 members.

composition titles: Put quotation marks around titles of books, movies, plays, poems and songs, but not the Bible or reference works, newspaper or magazine names or software titles. Even though books and other publications are italicized in manuscripts, the convention of quotes is still used in journalism because typewriters did not have italicized capabilities. Do not underline these titles as you might in a term paper bibliography.

Congress, congressional: Capitalize *U.S. Congress* and *Congress* when referring to the U.S. Senate and House of Representatives. Lowercase *congressional* unless it is part of a proper name, such as the *Congressional Record.*

Constitution, constitutional: Capitalize references to the U.S. Constitution, with or without the modifier *U.S.* Capitalize when referring to constitutions of other nations or states and using the name of the nation or state: *the Massachusetts Constitution.* Lowercase when not using the name of a state, for general references: *the state constitution, the organization's constitution.* Lowercase *constitutional* in all uses.

county, counties: Capitalize the word when it is part of a proper name: *Broward County.* Lowercase it in general references—*the county agency*—and when it is not used as a title—*the county of Broward*—and when it is part of a plural—*Broward and Westchester counties.* Capitalize *county* if it is part of a board's or agency's name: *the County Commission.*

couple: When used for two people, use a plural verb: *The couple were married.* When used as one unit, use a singular verb: *Each couple was awarded a prize for participating in the dance contest.*

courtesy titles: On first reference, do not use the courtesy titles *Miss, Mr., Mrs.* or *Ms.* For second references, eliminate courtesy titles in most cases unless your newspaper prefers to use them for all or for specific stories, such as obituaries. For example, use

Elma Smith for the first reference, *Mrs. Smith* for second reference in these selected cases. When courtesy titles are used for women, ask if they prefer *Miss, Ms.* or *Mrs.* When writing about a couple with the same name, on second reference use their full names: *John and Betty Smith.*

court names: Capitalize the full proper names of courts at all levels. Retain capitalization if *U.S.* is dropped: *U.S. Supreme Court* or *Supreme Court, 2nd District Court, 8th U.S. Circuit Court of Appeals.*

D

dangling modifiers: Make sure that the modifier is followed by a noun that did the action. Wrong: *Driving at high speeds, the car crashed into a tree.* The car wasn't driving. Right: *Driving at high speeds, she crashed the car into a tree.*

data: A plural word that takes a plural verb: *The data are missing.*

database: one word.

datelines: Datelines should contain a city name all in capital letters, followed in most cases by the abbreviated name of the state in uppercase and lowercase letters: *KANSAS CITY, Mo.* Major cities that are clearly identified with their states do not need to be followed by the state name; some examples are *ATLANTA, PHILADELPHIA, NEW YORK, SAN FRANCISCO, SEATTLE, DALLAS.* See the *state names* item for a full list. The *AP Style Guide* does not recommend ZIP code abbreviations in text or datelines.

days of the week: Capitalize *Monday, Tuesday* and so on. Do not abbreviate days except in tabular form.

dean's list: lowercase in all cases.

different: Use *different from,* not *different than.*

dimensions: Use figures and spell out *inches, feet, yards* and so on. Hyphenate when used as adjectives before nouns: *She is 5 feet 6 inches tall; the 5-foot-6-inch woman; the 5-foot woman; the basketball team signed a 7-footer; the car is 17 feet long, 6 feet wide and 5 feet high.*

directions and regions: Lowercase *north, south, east* and *west* when they indicate directions: Go *south* for three miles; then turn *east.* Capitalize when they indicate regions: She lived in the *South* for three years before she moved to the *Midwest.*

dollars: Use the dollar sign, *$,* with a figure in all cases except casual references, usually only for a dollar: He paid *$3* for the book; please give me *a dollar.* For amounts of $1 million or more, use the word *million* or *billion.* For amounts less than $1 million, use numerals only: *$2,000,* not *$2 thousand.*

E

effect, affect: See *affect, effect.*

either, neither: The verb agrees with the nearest subject: *Either Jane or John is going to the play; either John or the other students are going to the play.*

embarrass, embarrassment: two r's and two s's.

employee: not *employe*.

espresso

essential and nonessential clauses and phrases: An essential clause cannot be eliminated without changing the meaning of the sentence. It should not be set off by commas: *Students who do not study their stylebook should not blame professors for taking points off their papers.* The clause *who do not study their stylebook* is essential; only students who do not study their stylebook are affected. If the clause is used in a nonessential way, it should be set off by commas: *Students, who do not study their stylebook, should not blame professors for taking points off their papers.* This sentence means that all students should not blame their professors, whether they use the stylebook or not. To determine whether a phrases or clause is essential or nonessential, cross out the phrase or clause and see if the sentence makes sense without it. If it doesn't, then you know the phrase or clause is essential. Use *who* or *whom* to introduce a clause or phrase referring to a human being. Use *that* for all other essential clauses and phrases; use *which* for nonessential ones. These constructions are also called *restrictive* and *nonrestrictive* phrases and clauses.

everyone, every one: *Everyone* is a pronoun that takes a singular verb: *Everyone has his or her book. Every one* means each item: *Every one of these papers is good.*

F

farther, further: *Farther* is physical distance; *further* means more time or degree. *He will walk farther to get home. She will study the matter further.*

federal: Use a capital letter when the word is part of a title: the *Federal Trade Commission.* Use lowercase when it is an adjective: *the federal court.*

felony, misdemeanor: *Felony* is a serious crime; *misdemeanor* is a minor offense. The punishments vary, but at the federal level, a misdemeanor is punishable by less than a year in jail, and a sentence for a felony is usually more than a year in prison.

fewer, less: Use *fewer* for individual items and *less* for quantity: *She had fewer than three mistakes on the test. She has less money in her bank account this month.*

fiscal year: The 12-month period used for budgets, not always starting with the calendar year. Many government organizations start their fiscal year in July.

flier, flyer: *Flier* is a handbill or notice; *flyer* is a proper name for trains and buses. If you distribute posters about an event, you are giving out *fliers.*

fractions: Spell out amounts less than one, using hyphens between the words: *two-thirds.* When you use fractions with a whole number, write the whole number, a space and then the fraction: *2 1/2.*

french fries: lowercase.

G

geographic names: Do not use postal abbreviations for state names. See *state names.*

governmental bodies: Capitalize the full proper name of governmental agencies, and retain capitalization if referring to a specific body; lowercase terms used in a general sense: *the Boston City Council, the City Council* (when referring to the Boston City Council); *the city councils decide how to spend the money.*

governor: Capitalize and abbreviate in a formal title—*Gov. John Jones.*

grand jury: lowercase.

grisly, grizzly: *Grisly* is gruesome or horrible; *grizzly* is a type of bear.

H

half-mast, half-staff: On ships, flags are flown at *half-mast;* on shore, they are flown at *half-staff.*

handicapped, disabled, impaired: Do not describe people as disabled or handicapped unless the description is crucial to a story. If it is, ask the people how they prefer to be described. Avoid euphemisms such as *mentally challenged* and *afflicted with;* instead, say the woman *has multiple sclerosis,* not she *suffers from* or is *afflicted with multiple sclerosis.*

hang, hanged, hung: If someone commits suicide by hanging, he *hanged* himself. Past tense for *hanging* as in hanging a picture is *hung.*

Hanukkah: The preferred spelling for the Jewish holiday.

harass, harassment

his, her: Use the pronoun *his* when it is not clear whether the antecedent is male or female. Although the author of this textbook objects to this rule, she has followed it throughout the book with a few exceptions.

holidays: Capitalize them: *New Year's Eve, Easter, Hanukkah, Memorial Day* and so on.

homicide, murder, manslaughter: *Homicide* is the legal term for slaying; *murder* is premeditated homicide. Do not call anyone a murderer until the person is convicted of the charge.

hopefully: Avoid it. It means in a hopeful manner and should not be used as *Hopefully, I will pass. I hope I will pass* is better.

HTML: Use this acronym for hypertext markup language. Capitalize HTML when used alone; lowercase when used as part of an Internet address as in www.cengage.com.

HTTP: Use this acronym for hypertext transfer protocol. Note that *AP Stylebook* still capitalizes *Web, Web site* and *Internet.* (See those terms.)

I

imply, infer: A speaker *implies* something; a listener *infers* something from what is said.

incorporated: Abbreviate as part of a company name, but do not set off in commas: *Dow Jones & Co. Inc.*

initials: Use periods and no space when a person uses initials instead of a first name: *I.F. Stone.*

Internet addresses: AP recommends that URLs (Uniform Resource Locators), which are Web site addresses, and other Internet addresses be placed as the last line in a story or in a self-contained paragraph at the end of a story. However, many documents on the Web and chapters in this book now include links and URLs in or at the end of a sentence where they are discussed. Capitalize *Internet, World Wide Web* and *Web.*

it's, its: Learn the difference. *It's* is a contraction meaning it is. *Its* is a possessive pronoun: *The dog lost its collar.*

J

Jell-O

judge: Capitalize before a name when it is part of the person's title: *U.S. District Judge Joanne Jones.* Do not use *Judge* to precede the name on second reference; use only the last name: *Jones.* Do not capitalize when used without the name: *The judge issued a ruling.*

judgment: Spell this word correctly, without an *e*—not *judgement.*

junior, senior: Abbreviate in names, but don't precede with commas: the late *John F. Kennedy Jr.*

K

kidnap, kidnapped, kidnapping, kidnapper: Double the *p.*

kindergarten

Kleenex: A trade name; capitalize.

Ku Klux Klan: Capitalize and also capitalize *Klan,* but *KKK* may be used on second reference when referring to this organization.

L

lay, laid, lie, lain: *Lay* means to place something, and it takes an object: *Lay the book on the table.* The past tense is *laid. Lie* means to recline or lay down. The past tense is *lay* or *had lain. She is lying down because she has a headache; she lay down for an hour because she had a headache. She has lain on the sofa for an hour.*

legislative titles: For congressmen and congresswomen, *U.S. Rep.* and *Rep.* are the preferred first-reference forms: *U.S. Rep. Barbara Bates.* Capitalize the titles when used before a name. On second reference, the word *congressman* or *congresswoman,* in lowercase, may be used when the name of the person is not used.

legislature: Capitalize the names of specific bodies: *the Kansas Legislature,* or *the Legislature* when referring to the specific Kansas body. Lowercase the term when used in a general sense: The *legislature* of each state must approve the amendment. Lowercase when using it as a plural: The Kansas and Missouri *legislatures* approved the amendment.

likable: not *likeable.*

like, as: *Like* should be used to compare nouns and pronouns and must be followed by an object: *He plays basketball like a professional. As* introduces clauses with verbs: *As I said, you should study your stylebook.*

ly words: No hyphens after adverbs ending in *ly.*

M

magazine names: Capitalize but don't use quotation marks. Lowercase *magazine* unless it is part of the magazine's title.

majority, plurality: *Majority* is more than half; *plurality* is more than the highest number.

Mass: Mass is celebrated, not said.

master's degree: lowercase. A *master's* is acceptable on second reference.

media: The plural for news organizations such as broadcast, print and magazines is *media;* use it with a plural verb. The news *media are* upset about the ruling.

miles per hour: *mph,* no periods, is acceptable in all references.

military titles: Capitalize formal titles on first reference; use the last name only, without the title, on second reference. You may abbreviate titles: *Sgt. Maj. John Jones, Lt. Col. James Comolli.* See the *Associated Press Stylebook* for a complete list of such abbreviations.

million, billion: Use either word with figures: *$1 million, $13 billion, $1.3 billion, 2 million people.* In casual reference, you may use the word without figures: *I'd like to make a million dollars.*

months: Capitalize the names of months. When they are used with a specific date, abbreviate only *Jan., Feb., Aug., Sept., Oct., Nov., Dec.* For example, *Jan. 12, 2007, was the coldest day on record.* Spell out the name of a month when used without a specific date: *July 2004 was the warmest month on record.* Spell out other uses of months: *July 4 is a holiday.*

N

nationalities and races: Capitalize names of nationalities and races: *Arab, Asian, African-American, Caucasian.* Lowercase *black, white.*

newspaper names: Do not use quotation marks. Include *The* if it is part of the name.

No. 1: Use *No.* as an abbreviation before a number: *Their team is No. 1 in its league.*

none: It means no single one and takes a singular verb: *None of the council members was willing to approve the measure,* meaning not one of the members.

Use a plural verb only if the sense is no two or no amount: *None of the taxes have been paid.*

numerals: Spell out numbers that start a sentence: *Twenty-one people attended the event.* Spell out the numbers one through nine; use figures for 10 and above.

O

off of: Eliminate the *of.*

OK: Use *OK,* not *okay.*

on: Do not use before days of the week unless it would be confusing otherwise: *The meeting will be held Monday.*

P

people, persons: Use *person* when speaking of an individual, *people* when referring to persons in all plural uses: *Hundreds of people attended the lecture.*

percentages: Use figures and spell out the word *percent: Taxes will increase 1 percent.* Use decimals, not fractions, for partial percentages—*3.5 percent*—and repeat *percent* after each item.

Ph.D., Ph.D.s: It's easier to say the person has a doctorate, but *Ph.D.* may be used after a name as part of a person's title. Do not use *Dr.* as a prefix for an academic title.

plead, pleaded: *Pleaded,* not pled, for past tense: *He pleaded guilty.*

police department: Capitalize the term when used with the formal title or when referring to a specific department: *The Los Angeles Police Department has a new chief. He will reorganize the Police Department.* Lowercase the term when it stands alone and when it's used in a general sense: *You can get the form at a police department.*

political parties: Capitalize the name of the party and the word *party* if it is part of the title: the *Republican Party, the Democratic Party.* Capitalize *Republican, Democratic, Liberal* and *Socialist* when they refer to individuals who are members of a specific political party. Lowercase these words when used to signify a way of thinking: *She is democratic in her views.*

politicians: When identifying a representative or a senator, use the party affiliation and the abbreviation for the state: *Sen. Sam Brownback,R-Kan.*

possessives: For plural nouns indicating possession, add only an apostrophe: *the boys' club.* For singular possessive nouns, add an apostrophe and an *s: The boy's book was lost.*

presently: Means in a while; do not use for *now.*

principal, principle: *Principal* is a noun and adjective meaning someone or something in authority or first in rank: *She is the school principal and the principal player on the team. Principle* is a noun that means a fundamental truth or motivating force: *They fought for the principle of democratic rule.*

prostate gland: not *prostrate gland.*

Q

questionnaire

quotations in news: Don't alter quotations to correct grammar or change any words; paraphrase if the quotation is not clear.

R

race: Specify only when pertinent in a story. Capitalize specific races, but lowercase *black, white,* and so on. See also *nationalities and races.*

ratios: Use figures and hyphens: *a 2-1 ratio.*

re-elect, re-election: Use a hyphen after the *re* prefix.

reference works: Do not use quotation marks around reference works, including catalogs, almanacs, dictionaries, encyclopedias and the like.

religious titles: The first reference to a clergyman or clergywoman should include a capitalized title before the person's name. In many cases, *the Rev.* is the designation that is appropriate. For example, use *the Rev.* before a priest's name, not *Father: The Rev. Vince Krishe is the priest at St. Lawrence Roman Catholic Church.* On second reference, just use the last name: *Krishe.* If a person is known only by a religious name, repeat the title on second reference: *Pope Benedict XVI.* For rabbis, use the word *Rabbi* before the name for first reference; use only the last name for second reference. For nuns, use *Sister* or *Mother* before the name in all references if the nun uses only a religious name: *Sister Agnes.*

restaurateur: not *restauranteur.*

room numbers: Capitalize *Room* with a figure: *Room 231.*

S

seasons: Don't capitalize *spring, summer, winter, fall.*

sheriff: Capitalize the word when used as a formal title before a name; use only the last name on second reference: *Sheriff Bob Jones resigned Tuesday.* Lowercase when used after the name: *Bob Jones, sheriff of Ourcounty, resigned Tuesday.*

software titles: Don't use quotation marks: *Microsoft Word.*

speeds: Use figures: *7 mph.*

state names: Spell out state names when they stand alone; abbreviate when they are used in conjunction with the name of a city, town, or village or with a dateline. Do not abbreviate the following state names: *Alaska, Hawaii, Idaho, Iowa, Maine, Ohio, Texas* and *Utah.* Use a comma after the state name if it follows the city in a sentence, as in *She is from Philadelphia, Pa., but now lives in Alaska.* The abbreviations for the other states are as follows (note that many differ from ZIP code abbreviations): *Ala., Ariz., Ark., Calif., Colo., Conn., Del., Fla., Ga., Ill., Ind., Kan., Ky., La., Md., Mass., Mich., Minn., Miss., Mo., Mont., Neb., Nev., N.H., N.J., N.M., N.Y., N.C., N.D., Okla., Ore., Pa., R.I., S.C., S.D., Tenn., Vt., Va., Wash., W.Va., Wis., Wyo.*

subjunctive mood: Use the subjunctive mood of a verb to convey wishes. Use the verb *were,* not *was,* to follow the singular pronoun used in a subjunctive sense: *If I were a rich woman, I would still teach. I wish it were possible to meet all the students who use this book.*

T

teenage, teenager: Do not hyphenate; this is a recent change in AP style, which used to require the hyphen.

temperatures: Use figures for the degrees and words for *minus* or *plus: It was minus 30 in Barrow, Alaska, today* or *It was 30 below zero.*

that, which, who, whom: Use *who* and *whom* when referring to people and to animals with a name. Use *that* and *which* when referring to inanimate objects and to animals without a name: *He is the man who has the book; she is the woman to whom I spoke yesterday; Fluffy is the dog who was lost; get the record that the police filed.*

their, there, they're: *Their* is possessive, *there* is a place and *they're* means they are.

time: Use *a.m.* and *p.m.* with the specific time: *9:30 a.m., 10 p.m.*—not *10:00 P.M. Noon* and *midnight* stand alone. Use the day of the week in stories referring to any of the seven days before or after the current date, not *yesterday* or *tomorrow.*

titles: Capitalize titles when they are used before the person's name as part of the official title: *Sheriff John Jones made the arrest.* Lowercase titles when they are used to identify the person after her or his name or when used without the person's name: *John Jones, the sheriff, made the arrest. The sheriff made the arrest.*

trademarks: Capitalize brand names: *Coke, Kleenex.* Use lowercase for generic terms: *a cola drink, a tissue.*

T-shirt

U

United States: The abbreviation *U.S.* is acceptable as a noun or adjective for *United States.* The *AP Stylebook* allowed this change in 2005; it previously required spelling out the words except when used as a modifier: *She came to the U.S. last year, and she is now a U.S. citizen.*

URL: Use this acronym for Uniform Resource Locator, the computer address for a Web page.

U.S. Postal Service: Capitalize when referring to the formal title; lowercase in generic references: *The U.S. Postal Service* or the *Postal Service* operates the mail; *I went to the post office.*

U.S. Supreme Court: Capitalize and also capitalize *Supreme Court.*

Usenet: Use this term to refer to a particular worldwide system of discussion groups.

V

verbs: Don't split infinitives (*to be* verbs): *She was ordered to leave immediately,* not *she was ordered to immediately leave.*

vice: Use two words with no hyphen: *vice chairman, vice principal, vice president.*

vote tabulations: Use figures separated by a hyphen: *The House voted 230–205.* Spell out votes below 10 in other phrases: *The City Council needed a two-thirds majority.*

W

weather: Spell out the word *degree: The temperature was 75 degrees.*

who, whom: Use *who* to refer to people and animals with names; use *that* or *which* for inanimate objects. *Who* is a subject of a sentence or clause; *whom* is an object: *Whom do you wish to see?* Turn the sentence around to find the subject when you are confused. *You* is then the subject: *You wish to see whom?*

who's, whose: *Who's* means who is; *whose* is possessive, belonging to whom.

World Wide Web: Use the full term on first reference or *Web* on second reference. Capitalize these words.

Y

years: Don't use an apostrophe for plurals: *the 1990s,* not *the 1990's.*

yesterday: Use the day of the week instead of *yesterday.*

youth: The term is applicable to boys and girls from ages 13 to 17. Use *man* or *woman* for people 18 and older.

Z

ZIP code: Use all capital letters for *ZIP* but lowercase *code.*

Credits

This page constitutes an extension of the copyright page. We have made every effort to trace the ownership of all copyrighted material and to secure permission from copyright holders. In the event of any question arising as to the use of any material, we will be pleased to make the necessary corrections in future printings. Thanks are due to the following authors, publishers, and agents for permission to use the material indicated.

Chapter 1. 4: Courtesy of the Lawrence Journal-World **5:** ©Bill Snead **6:** ©Bill Snead **12:** "26 hurt as school bus crashes head-on," The Louisville (Ky.) Courier-Journal. Reprinted with permission. **13:** "71-year-old gets 8 years in drug case," The (Portland) Oregonian. Reprinted with permission. **13:** "Couple spends $6,000 looking for lost cat," Rocky Mountain (Denver) News. Reprinted with permission. **13:** "Man ticketed for walking his lizard," St. Petersburg (Fla.) Times. Reprinted with permission. **14:** "Family sues in corpse mix-up," St. Petersburg Times. Reprinted with permission. **14:** "Palmer facility would benefit from warning system upgrades," Zaz Hollander, Anchorage (Alaska) Daily News. **14:** "The proof is in the medical studies," Knight-Ridder/Tribune News Service. Reprinted with permission. **15:** "80-year-old gets draft notice," The Associated Press. Reprinted with permission. **16:** "Minority teens, police goals collide," St. Cloud (Minn.) Tribune. Reprinted with permission **16:** "Today's libraries have more to check out than books," The Milwaukee Journal Sentinel. Reprinted by permission. **17:** "Damage catches residents by surprise," Topeka (Kan.) Capital-Journal. Reprinted with permission. **17:** "Shawnee Heights ducks as funnels twist through," Topeka (Kan.) Capital-Journal. Reprinted with permission. **19:** ©Paul Horn and Dave Hardman. Reno (Nev.) Gazette-Journal. Reprinted with permission.

Chapter 2. 25: Gary Bivings, "The Use of the Internet by America's Newspapers," The Bivings Group. Reprinted by permission. **26:** Courtesy of OhmyNews International.

Chapter 3. 37: "Beware the freshman 15," Lawrence (Kan.) Journal-World. Reprinted with permission. **38:** "Salmon spawn a new crisis," Los Angeles Times. Reprinted with permission. **39:** Ball State University **40:** "11-year-old begins grad school," The Associated Press. Reprinted with permission. **40:** "Amnesia victim recalls abduction," The Associated Press. Reprinted with permission. **40:** Santa Cruz (Calif) Sentinel **41:** "Teen stabbed in school fight," St. Petersburg (Fla.) Times. Reprinted with permission. **41:** The Vancouver Sun **42:** "Man prowls dorms," Iowa City (Iowa) Press-Citizen. Reprinted with permission. **44:** "Papers a lesson in criminology," St. Petersburg (Fla.) Times. Reprinted with permission. **47:** Infographic by Andrew Rohrback, University Daily Kansan. Reprinted with permission. **48:** "Thousands gather on Capitol steps for animal rights," The Associated Press. Reprinted with permission. **49:** "Throw the book at them," The Associated Press. Reprinted with permission. **53:** "Apartment blaze blamed on toddler." Reprinted by permission of The Wichita Eagle.

Chapter 4. 61: South Florida Sun-Sentinel **61:** KXAN-TV (Austin, Texas) **62:** Courtesy of KTUU-News Channel 2, Anchorage, Alaska. **64:** ©Fred Pearce **65:** "Police search for another hit-and-run driver." Courtesy of KTUU-News Channel 2, Anchorage, Alaska. **65:** "Pedestrian in critical after hit-and-run," Anchorage (Alaska) Daily News. Reprinted with permission. **66:** "Child alerts family to duplex fire," Anchorage (Alaska) Daily News. Reprinted with permission. **66:** "Family left homeless after fire," KTUU, Anchorage, Alaska. Reprinted with permission. **67:** Courtesy of Gannett Co,. Inc. **67:** Screen shots of "Step-by-Step: A Murder Story Unfolds" from "Anatomy of a News Story", Reprinted by permission of Gannett Co., Inc.

Chapter 5. 71: Courtesy of Martha Miller **71:** "Reno woman arrested in killing of boyfriend," Reno (Nev.) Gazette-Journal. Reprinted with permission. **73:** "Iowans get ready, The state fair will begin today," The Des Moines (Iowa) Register. Reprinted with permission. **74:** Wichita (Kan.) Eagle **74:** "Robotic squirrel part of trend to improve undergrad research," Associated Press. Reprinted with permission. **74-75:** Excerpts from "Greensburg is gone, its future, unknown," from May 6, 2007, and two excerpts from Deb Gruver in The Wichita Eagle. Reprinted by permission. **75:** "Planes collide at LAX," Los Angeles Times. Reprinted with permission.

Chapter 6. 88: Courtesy of Mark Potter **90:** ©Gannett Co., Inc. **104:** Reprinted by permission of the Society of Professional Journalists.

Chapter 7. 108: "For women on Death Row, an agonizing wait," South Florida Sun-Sentinel. Reprinted with permission. **108:** Courtesy of Barbara Walsh **109:** "Seeking answers amid the rubble," Portland Press Herald/Maine Sunday Telegram. **109:** Edna Buchanan excerpts from The Corpse Had a Familiar Face, Random House, New York, 1987, p. 265. **110:** Clark, Gerald, Capote: A Biography, Simon and Schuster, New York, 1988, p. 322. **110:** Ruas, Charles, Conversations with American Writers, McGraw-Hill Book Co., New York, 1984, p. 52. **125:** "Mianus Legacy: Pain and Anger," The Hartford (Conn.) Courant. Reprinted with permission.

Chapter 8. 131: Courtesy of Don Fry **132:** Kentucky University **133:** "It's the water . . . ," Knight-Ridder Tribune News. Reprinted with permission. **134:** East Valley Tribune, Mesa, Ariz. **134:** The Associated Press. **135:** "2 killed, 1 injured when boat flips in rough weather," The Orlando (Fla.) Sentinel. Reprinted with permission. **135:** "Sunscreen ingredient may promote cancer," The Associated Press, Reprinted with permission. **136:** "Book thief gets 7 years of probation," The Philadelphia Inquirer. Reprinted with permission. **137:** "2 charged with theft of parking coins," Minneapolis (Minn.) Star-Tribune. Reprinted with permission. **137:** "Man who confronts gunman is shot to death," St. Petersburg (Fla.) Times. Reprinted with permission. **137:** The Associated Press **138:** Reprinted by permission of the Tucson Citizen. **139:** "Open up crime reports, judge says," The Kansas (Mo.) City Star. Reprinted with permission. **141:** "College student arrested after making 'megabomb,'" The Associated Press. Reprinted with permission. **141:** "North County man, 88, killed in blaze started by smoking," St. Louis (Mo.) Post-Dispatch. Reprinted with permission. **141:** "Toddler's death tied to beating," St. Petersburg (Fla.) Times.

Reprinted with permission. **142:** "Paroled killer held in kidnap, rape of 2 girls," St. Paul (Minn.) Pioneer Press. Reprinted with permission. **142:** "Penn imposes penalties on scientist," The Philadelphia Inquirer. Reprinted with permission. **142:** "S.J. gunman left 'little signs' before killings," San Jose (Calif.) Mercury News. Reprinted with permission. **143:** "U.S. reports sharp drop in casual drug use," The Philadelphia Inquirer. Reprinted with permission. **144:** "Study focuses on link between red meat and cancer," The Associated Press. **146:** "Ex-lover must pay in video case," The Philadelphia Inquirer. Reprinted with permission. **146:** "Neighbors squealing over pigs," The Philadelphia Inquirer. Reprinted with permission. **147:** "4.7 quake leaves Southcentral shaken, not stirred," Anchorage(Alaska) Daily News. Reprinted with permission. **147:** "In Santa Barbara drought, it's not easy being green," Los Angeles Times. Reprinted with permission. **148:** "Home reaches out to teen moms," Orange County (Calif.) Register. Reprinted with permission. **148:** Story about toy gun, South Florida Sun-Sentinel. Reprinted with permission **149:** "Monster loans," The Seattle Times. **149:** "Seminole man not real doctor, detectives say," The Orlando (Fla.) Sentinel. Reprinted with permission. **150:** "1964 case gets fresh interest," St. Petersburg (Fla.) Times. Reprinted with permission. The book thief item is on p. 136. **150:** "Colo. poison-gas site now a wildlife haven," The Philadelphia Inquirer. Reprinted with permission. **150:** Public library story, The Philadelphia Inquirer. Reprinted with permission. **151:** "Lottery triangle," Los Angeles Times. Reprinted with permission. **151:** "They know all about you," St. Petersburg (Fla.) Times. Reprinted with permission. **152:** "Survivors tell of riding out the storm," The Philadelphia Inquirer. Reprinted with permission. **152:** "U.S. colleges try to confront problem of campus drinking," The Associated Press. Reprinted with permission. **153:** "L. Merion wants to ban cigarettes," The Philadelphia Inquirer. Reprinted with permission. **153:** "Postcards from sculptor carry messages via a piece of the rock," Los Angeles Times. Reprinted with permission. **153:** "True love story," St. Paul (Minn.) Pioneer Press. Reprinted with permission. **154:** "10-year-old saves choking classmate," The Orlando (Fla.) Sentinel. Reprinted with permission. **154:** "The good and bad from city hall," N.Y. Newsday. **155:** "Crack: Drug tightens grip on Niagara County," Niagara (N.Y.) Gazette. **155:** "It may be back to class for professors," St. Petersburg (Fla.) Times. Reprinted with permission. **156:** The Baltimore Sun.

Chapter 9. 161: Courtesy of Ken Fuson **166:** "Temple racism course wins support," The Philadelphia Inquirer. Reprinted with permission **167:** "Anatomy of a road, Part 1," The Tampa Tribune. **167:** Dave Barry, "Childhood is a breeze compared to stress of moving," Reprinted with permission of Dave Barry. **168:** Lansing Community College story, Lansing (Mich.) State Journal. Reprinted with permission. **170:** "Bigamist's family stunned," San Jose Mercury News. Reprinted with permission. **170:** "Doctor's AIDS death brings fear, ire," The Philadelphia Inquirer. Reprinted with permission. **170:** "Infected with AIDS, she longed to become a mother once again," The Philadelphia Inquirer. Reprinted with permission. **171:** "Double secret, double boyfriend," from series "Life at the edge of everything," St Petersburg Times. **171:** "Judiciary panel works as the night wears on," The Hartford (Conn.) Courant. Reprinted with permission. **172:**"Universities gender makeup changing," Lawrence (Kan.) Journal-World. Reprinted with permission. **174:** "Hotmail addresses shared with site," The Associated Press. Reprinted with permission. **174:** "Alzheimers steals fine minds" Des Moines (Iowa) Register. Reprinted with permission. **175:** "Judgment day for a drug dealer," The Milwaukee (Wis.) Journal Sentinel. Reprinted with permission. **175:** "Rescuers work hard, but catch is small," Anchorage (Alaska) Daily News. Reprinted with permission. **176:** "In Fort Myers: Money, mercy and murder," Fort Myers (Fla.) News-Press. Reprinted with permission. **177:** "Desperate days at the Merlin," The Spokesman-Review (Spokane, Wash.). Reprinted with permission. **178:** "Mystery call has police barking up wrong tree," Des Moines Register and Tribune Co. Reprinted with permission. **178:** "Shrimper imprisoned for not using turtle protection device," The Associated Press. Reprinted with permission. **179:** USA Today writing guidelines, courtesy of J. Taylor Buckley Jr., USA Today.

Chapter 10. 183: Courtesy of Jack Hart **184:** "Teen sentenced to read about Holocaust," The Associated Press. Reprinted with permission. **184:** "Fairview fire started outside house," KTUU-TV, Anchorage, Alaska. Used with permission. **186:** "Casinos sinking college dreams," The Associated Press. Reprinted with permission. **187:** "Hookahs gain in popularity," KUJH-TV, University of Kansas. Reprinted with permission. **189:** "Boy, 3, shoots 16-month-old," St. Petersburg (Fla.) Times. Reprinted with permission. **190:** "For drivers, grief can be just a phone call away," The Orlando (Fla.) Sentinel. Reprinted with permission. **192:** "Getting to know Mario Gonzales," The Northern Light, University of Alaska Anchorage. **193:** "They got out alive, but no one was spared," The Des Moines (Iowa) Register. Reprinted with permission. **193:** Reprinted by permission of the Anchorage Daily News. **195:** Inverted pyramid exercise based on a story from The Associated Press. Used with permission. **195:** Wall Street Journal formula exercise based on: "College students are most susceptible to online obsession, experts say," Lawrence (Kan.) Journal-World. Reprinted with permission. **196:** Hourglass exercise based on "Couriers help foil robbery," St. Louis (Mo.) Post-Dispatch. Reprinted with permission. **196:** List exercise based on release from the National Science Foundation.

Chapter 11. 199: "A cry in the night," St. Petersburg (Fla.) Times. Reprinted with permission. **200:** Courtesy of Tom French **201:** "Angels and Demons," St. Petersburg (Fla.) Times **202:** "Now's the time for State Fair," Des Moines (Iowa) Register. Reprinted with permission. **202:** Courtesy of Mary Ann Lickteig **204:** "'Fat Albert' carves out an 891-pound niche," St. Petersburg (Fla.) Times. Reprinted with permission. **204:** Comments by Bruce DeSilva, Coaches' Corner. Reprinted with permission. **205:** The Hartford (Conn.) "Crafts deines he killed wife," Courant **205:** "Penn Relays: A carnival of sociability," The Philadelphia Inquirer. Reprinted with permission. **206:** "Adventures in babysitting," St Petersburg (Fla.) Times **206:** "Fielder puts final touch on season of triumph," Detroit Free Press. Reprinted with permission. **207:** "New life begins with help of coyotes," Daily Forty Niner (Calif. State University, Long Beach), 1991. Reprinted with permission. **207:** "Read-in attracts 400 to KC library," Kansas City (Mo.) Star. Reprinted with permission. **208:** "It couldn't happen to me: One woman's story," Des Moines (Iowa) Register. Reprinted with permission. **209:** "Ghosts don't spook Down East couple," Bangor (Maine) Daily News. Reprinted with permission. **209:** "Clive woman's spell of success," Des Moines (Iowa) Register. Reprinted with permission. **210:** "Nov. 22,

1963: A day when time stopped," The Associated Press. Reprinted with permission. **212:** "Cooper Landing man revels in clover collection," The Peninsula Clarion, Kenai, Alaska. Reprinted with permission. **213:** Four-leaf clover story. Courtesy of KTUU-News Channel 2, Anchorage Alaska. **217:** "A soldier's story," Iowa City (Iowa) Press-Citizen. Reprinted with permission.

Chapter 12. 223: top, Courtesy of KTUU-News Channel 2, Anchorage, Alaska **226:** Rundown, Courtesy of KTUU-News Channel 2, Anchorage, Alaska. **228:** bottom, Courtesy of KTUU-News Channel 2, Anchorage, Alaska **231:** Courtesy of KTUU-News Channel 2, Anchorage. **233:** Web image, courtesy of KTUU-TV. **234:** "Slimed eagles get baths, TLC in Anchorage," Anchorage (Alaska) Daily News. Reprinted with permission. **242:** Nude camp excerpt, NBC News Channel wire. Reprinted with permission. **244:** Animal rights protest excerpt, Associated Press broadcast wire. Reprinted with permission. **244:** Toxic chemical spill excerpt, Associated Press broadcast wire. Reprinted with permission. **244:** Baldwin City water problems, KSNT-TV, Topeka, Kansas. Reprinted with permission. **247:** MySpace story, KTUU-News Channel 2, Anchorage. Alaska. Reprinted with permission. **247:**The (Louisville, Ky.) Courier Journal **247:** Courtesy of KTUU-News Channel 2, Anchorage, Alaska. **248:** "16-year-old boy with no license takes police on Highlands chase," The (Louisville, Ky.) Courier-Journal. Used with permission.

Chapter 13. 252: top, Courtesy of Gannett Co. **252:** bottom, Courtesy of The News Press, Fort Myers, Florida **253:** Reprinted by permission of the Department of Journalism, University of Arizona. **254:** Copyright 2009, The Roanoke Times. Reprinted by permission of The Roanoke Times. **255:** Reprinted by permission of The Poynter Institute/Stanford University Eye Trac Study. **258:** Courtesy of Jakob Nielsen **262:** Missing pig turns up as meal. The Associated Press. Reprinted with permission. **263:** "School officials cuffed, led away by couple." The Associated Press **264:** Selling yourself again: The job interview revisited, CNN.com. Reprinted with permission.

Chapter 14. 269: Courtesy of Evie Lazzarino **270:** Courtesy of Evie Lazzarino **275:** Crayola Products, Binney & Smith Inc. Crayola and the serpentine design are registered trademarks of Binney & Smith, used with permission. **276:** "Crayola Introduces Crayons That Are Literally Off The Wall," press release, Binney & Smith Inc. Reprinted with permission. **278:** www.census.gov.

Chapter 15. 290: Courtesy of The Student Press Law Center.

Chapter 16. 312: Brian Vandervliet. Used with permission.

Chapter 17. 321: Courtesy of Tim Gallimore **325:** "Dress-up Dolly," The Philadelphia Inquirer. Reprinted with permission. **326:** "How to avoid sexism, stereotypes in writing," The Gannetteer, Gannett Co., Inc. **331:** Excerpts from "AIDS in the Heartland," St. Paul (Minn.) Pioneer Press. Reprinted with permission.

Chapter 18. 335: Courtesy of Alan Richman **340:** "A time to die," Sunshine magazine,

401: Rockford sales tax story, Rockford (Ill.) Register-Star. **402:** "Alabama's Rivers: Endangered Resource," The (Montgomery) Alabama Journal. **403:** "City touts lowest rate of dropouts," St. Joseph (Mo.) News-Press. Reprinted with permission. **403:** "Single-father homes on the rise," The Associated Press. Reprinted with permission. **403:** "Universities gender makeup changing," Lawrence (Kan.) Journal-World., Reprinted with permission. **405:** ©Philip Meiring/The University Daily Kansan. Used with permission. **407:** "Storm brews over reappraisal," Atlanta Constitution. Reprinted with permission. **408:** "Homeowners getting 1st break in 20 years," The (Hackensack, N.J.) Record. **409:** Philadelphia city budget advance, The Philadelphia Inquirer. Reprinted with permission. **409:** Reprinted by permission of the St. Petersburg Times. **409:** "Governor releases capital and operating budget," Reprinted by permission of KTVA-TV, Channel 11, Anchorage, Alaska.

Chapter 22. 420: "Boy dies in car crash," Orange County (Calif.) Register. Reprinted with permission. **421:** "Rare comic books stolen from Council Bluffs store," The Associated Press. Reprinted with permission. **421:** Courtesy of KTUU-News Channel 2, Anchorage, Alaska. **422:** "Robbers sought," The Orange County (Calif.) Register. Reprinted with permission. **422:** "Robber does flipflop," Topeka (Kan.) Capital-Journal. Reprinted by permission. **422:** "Burger burglar makes off with a Whopper of a haul," The (Salem, Ore.) Statesman-Journal. Reprinted with permission. **424:** "Man charged in woman's death," The Milwaukee Journal. Reprinted with permission. **424:** "Shattered dreams; 'Perfect' kids shot, mom jailed," The Orlando (Fla.) Sentinel. Reprinted with permission. **426:** "Mom, infant escape Kodiak fire," The Associated Press. Reprinted with permission. **428:** "Simpson acquitted of murders," The Associated Press. Reprinted with permission. **430:** ©Bill Skeet **437:** "N.H. Prosecutors get Smart," The Associated Press. Reprinted with permission. **438:** "A snake in a mattress twists its way into court," The Philadelphia Inquirer. Reprinted with permission. **438:** Joy Griffiths" killing: Act of love or murder?" St. Petersburg (Fla.) Times. Reprinted with permission. **439:** "Man gambles on plea, loses," The Kansas City (Mo.) Star. Reprinted with permission.

Chapter 23. 443: Courtesy of David Handschuh **444:** Courtesy of Yuri "Hectop" Faktorovich; copyright 2001 Hecktop; http://www.maxho.com **445:** James T. Tourtellotte. Courtesy of U.S. Customs Service. **446:** "Remains of 1,161 WTC victims will go unnamed," New York Newsday. **448:** Lizz Dabrowski, The Oklahoma Daily. Used with permission. **448:** Anita Amarfio, The Oklahoma Daily. Used with permission. **449:** Excerpts from stories in The Oklahoma Daily. Reprinted with permission. **452:** "Explosion prompts blood drives, donations," The Oklahoma Daily. Reprinted with permission. **453:** The Detroit News, graphic and excerpts from "The crash of flight 255." Reprinted with permission. **456:** "Bomb cripples Oklahoma City," The Oklahoma Daily. Reprinted with permission. **458:** "Grief cuts wide swath," The Detroit News, special report. Reprinted with permission. **458:** Reprinted by permission of the Detroit News. **460:** "20 die in La Guardia crash," The Associated Press. Reprinted with permission. **462:** Los Angeles Times **462:** "Napa, Sonoma hit by floods again," San Jose (Calif.) Mercury News. Reprinted with permission. **464:** "A wicked wind takes aim," Chicago Tribune. **465:** "Weather forecast blazes on," St. Joseph (Mo.) News-Press. Reprinted with permission. **467:** "Band of brothers," The Associated Press. Reprinted with permission.

Chapter 24. 478: "Cutesy cover letters are like bricks," Quill. Reprinted with permission. **481:** Reprinted by permission of Shelly Falevits. ©Gannett Co., Inc. Used with permission.

Appendix 2. 502: Excerpts from The Associated Press Style and Libel Manual. Reprinted with permission.

9/11, 63, 443–46, 447

A roll, 231
ABC-TV, 299, 307
absolute privilege, 296
Abu Ghraib, 63, 315
access, 414–16
according to, 54
accuracy, 10, 27–8, 31, 43, 91, 115,
    146, 216, 255, 272, 288, 294–95,
    304, 308, 412, 414, 475, 497
accusations, 141, 417
active voice, 62, 136, 144, 172, 222,
    230, 259, 272
actual malice, 291, 294, 300, 305
actuality, 238
Adams, Eric, 228
advance stories, 386–87, 409
Ager, Susan, 50
aggregator, 7–8, 24
aging, 329–30
AIDS, 251, 327, 330–32, 367
airplane crashes, 460–61
Al Día, 323
Alabama Journal (Montgomery,
    Ala.), 402
Alabama State University, 291
Albany Times Union, 328
Albom, Mitch, 206, 374
Albrycht, Elizabeth, 271, 285
Alfred P. Murrah building, 447–48
alien, 321
alleged/allegedly, 141, 296, 417, 503
Amarfio, Anita, 448
ambient sound, 238
American Civil Liberties Union, 301
American Journalism Review, 310,
    314, 337, 345
American Library Association, 303
American Opinion magazine, 294
American Press Institute, 58,
    266, 445
American Red Cross of Alaska, 276
American Society of Newspaper Edi-
    tors, 99, 323, 345, 374, 445, 474

analogies, 204, 206, 219, 370, 392, 402
anatomy of a news story, 64–66
Anchorage (Alaska) *Daily News,*
    14, 65–66, 147, 175, 231, 234
Anders, Gigi, 345
Anderson, Janine, 148
Andrews, Chris, 169
anecdotal lead, 39–40, 145–46,
    185, 258
anecdotes, 336, 340–41, 368, 400, 442
anonymous sources, 28, 86, 90–94,
    127, 309, 311
AOL (America Online), 301–02
Apple Inc., 7, 31
Arab, Ranjit, 348
The (Tucson) *Arizona Daily Star,*
    138, 329
Arizona State University, 98
Armas, Genaro C., 403
Armstrong, Valoree, 42
Asian American Journalists
    Association (AAJA), 324
Associated Press Managing
    Editors, 91
Associated Press Stylebook, 82, 95,
    224, 256, 273, 327, 371, 418,
    434, 465, 490–91, 493, 497–98,
    502–14
Associated Press, 15, 24, 40, 44,
    48, 74, 91, 134–35, 137, 141,
    144–45, 152, 174, 178, 184, 186,
    204, 210–11, 213, 215, 224, 244,
    262–63, 385, 398, 403, 421, 426–
    28, 437, 445, 460, 466–67
Atlanta Journal-Constitution,
    313, 407
attribution, 41–42, 50, 52–54, 62,
    81–82, 86, 97, 140–44, 189, 207,
    217, 222, 230, 296–97, 418
Aubespin, Mervin, 322–23
Auburn University, 271
augmenting quote, 40

B roll, 231
Baber, Anne, 283

background, 42, 94, 115, 117, 119,
    124, 282, 336, 338–40, 351, 384,
    388, 412, 427, 454
backpack journalist, 254
backtiming, 246
bail, 418, 431, 433
Baker, Jim, 37
Ball State University, 39
Baltimore Sun, 8, 156
Banaszynski, Jacqui, 121, 128, 163,
    330–32
Bangor (Maine) *Daily News,* 209
Barnes, Nora Ganim, 29–30
Barnicle, Mike, 93
Barry, Dave, 167
Bartimus, Tad, 466–67
Bauer, Traci, 415
Beach, Patrick, 178
beat reporting, 356–75
Belk, Henry, 37
Bell, Dawson, 14
Bennett, Ed, 222, 225–27
Better Homes & Gardens, 70
Bhatia, Peter, 86, 91
bigotry, 324
Binney & Smith, 273, 275
Bivings Group, 25
Blair, Jayson, 10, 92–93, 216, 309
Bleiberg, Laura, 354
Block, Mervin, 131
blocking technique, 168, 215,
    259, 402
bloggers, 5, 294, 301–02, 316, 318
bloggers code of ethics, 255
blogosphere, 23, 29, 316
blogs, 3, 5, 7, 9, 11, 16, 22–32, 74–75,
    79–82, 90, 251–52, 255, 271,
    289, 328, 356, 358, 366, 381,
    428, 442, 454, 472–73, 476
Blundell, Bill, 198, 215–16
blurbs, 259–62
Boca Raton (Fla.) *News,* 18
body building, 178
bond, 433
BonziBuddy, 302

booking, 429–30
Bor, Jonathan, 366–67
Border Beat, 252–53
Borsi, Dianna, 404
Boston Globe, 93, 336
Boston University, 397
Bozeman (Mont.) *Chronicle,* 309
Breaux, Kia Shanté, 186
Bremner, John B., 494–95
Brennan, William, 291
brevity, 346
briefs, 259, 262, 433
broadcast profiles, 341
broadcast script format, 231–33
broadcast story structure, 239
broadcast style, 238–39
broadcast terms, 246–47
broadcast writing tips, 229
B-roll, 278
Bryant, Kobe, 417
Buchanan, Edna, 109, 125, 130,
    412–13, 457
Buckhead, 294
Buckley Amendment, 415
Buckley, Taylor Jr., 95
budget line, 82–83
budget stories, 404–10
budget terms, 406
Bumpus-Hooper, Lynne, 425
Burke, Jill, 65
Burnett, Carol, 296
Bush, George W., 27, 294
business writing, 368–70

Callahan, Christopher, 98–99
campaign contributions, 101
Campus Security Act, 415
Canuto, Phillip E., 14
capital budget, 406
Capote, Truman, 110–11, 201
Cappon, Jack, 398
Carlin, George, 93
Carpenter, Tim, 172, 403
Carr, David, 315
Cavalier Daily, 309
CBS, 27–28, 212, 237, 255, 294,
    313, 315
celebrities, 15, 335–36
Chan, Sharon Pian, 149
character generator, 231, 246
Charlotte (N.C.) *Observer,* 10, 113

Chicago Sun Times, 308
Chicago Tribune, 8, 36, 463
Children's Internet Protection Act, 303
Children's Online Privacy Protection
    Act, 302
Children's Online Protection Act, 303
Cho, Seung-Hui, 454
chronological order, 216, 339,
    342, 382
chronology, 119, 122, 126, 163,
    188–89, 198, 218, 412, 419,
    442, 451–52
Chyron, 246
circle kickers, 174, 244
citizen journalism, 10–11, 26, 28–29,
    316, 442, 454
civic journalism, 10
civil cases, 428
civil court process, 432
Clabes, Judith, 478
Claremont McKenna College,
    268–69
Clark, Gerald, 110
Clark, Roy Peter, 34, 219
Clery Act, 415
Clery, Jeanne Ann, 415
clichés, 398
cliffhanger, 176, 178, 193, 218–19,
    264–65
climaxes, 175
Clinton, Bill, 311
closed-ended questions, 117
CNN, 9, 11, 16, 45, 262, 264,
    369, 454
Coaches' Corner, 366
coaching method, 11
coaching tips, 2, 22, 34, 58, 70, 86,
    106, 130, 145, 160, 182, 198, 222,
    250, 268, 288, 306, 320, 334, 356,
    376, 392, 412, 472, 490
Coats, Janet, 7
Cohen, Dan, 93
College Heights Herald, 132
Collins, Huntly, 166, 387
Commercial Appeal (Memphis,
    Tenn.), 337
commitment statement, 229, 239
Committee for Open Debate on the
    Holocaust, 317
Communications Decency Act, 289,
    301–03

computer-assisted reporting, 100,
    393–95
confidential source, 91, 93
conflict, 13–15, 72
conflict of interest, 359–60
consent agenda, 387
context, 42, 230
convergence, 2–6, 60, 111
Convergence Coach, 16, 30, 44, 66,
    82, 97, 123, 144, 169, 188, 212,
    228, 260, 277, 303, 316, 328, 341,
    366, 383, 395, 428, 454, 484, 492
convergent media writing, 58–69
conversational, 22, 31, 34, 36, 61,
    118, 144, 222, 259, 264, 401, 439
Cooke, Janet, 92
Cooper, Matt, 91
copyright, 27–28, 82, 289–90,
    303–04, 310, 397
corporate publications, 283–85
corporate Web sites, 284
CorporatePR blog, 271, 285
corrections, 295
Corwin, Miles, 148, 151
Courier-Journal (Louisville, Ky.),
    12, 357–58
court reporting terms, 432–36
court stories, 427–39
courtesy titles, 55, 253
cover letters, 477–83
Cox Broadcasting Co. v. Cohn, 299
Crayola, 273, 275
credibility, 10, 28–29, 82, 86, 91–92,
    96–97, 99, 110, 115, 146, 216,
    272, 294, 310, 359, 492
crime reporting, 412–41
criminal court process, 429
critical listening, 112
cross-directories, 96, 105, 424
cross-media platforms, 60
cross-promotion, 4–5
crowdsourcing, 60, 260, 359
curiosity, 70–85
Curley, Rob, 2, 4–5
cyberjournalist.net, 16, 28, 82,
    255, 316,

Dabrowski, Liz, 448
Daily Forty Niner, 207
Daily Kos, 359
Daily Nightly blog, 27

Dallas Morning News, 252, 323, 393–94
Danish newspaper cartoons, 324
Dart Center for Journalism & Trauma, 444, 446
databases, 41, 77, 99–100, 105, 393
Dateline, 308
Datko, Karen, 150
Davis, Foster, 113, 128
Davis, Kevin, 148
Davis, Mark, 167
Dawson, Walter, 337
De Niro, Robert, 335–36
death tolls, 450, 457
deception, 10, 92, 111, 307–08
deck head, 38
deep background, 94
defamation, 290, 296–97, 300, 302
Defense Information School, 83
delayed identification, 137
Dent, Mark, 374
Denver Post, 23
Des Moines (Iowa) *Register,* 73, 79, 160–61, 174, 178, 194, 202, 208–09, 314
descriptive writing, 73, 203–15, 339, 366, 452–53
DeSilva, Bruce, 204, 215
Detroit Free Press, 14, 50, 124, 206, 350, 374
Detroit News, 453, 459–60
deView, Lucille, 220
dialogue, 170, 200–02, 207–08, 216–17
Diaz, Iris M., 409
Didion, Joan, 201
Dietemann v. Time Inc., 299
Digital Millennium Copyright Act, 304
Dionise, Jeff, 453
disabilities, 327, 329
disaster basics, 453–57
discussion groups, 364
diversity, 94–95,
Doogan, Sean, 214
Dorgan, Michael, 463
Dotson, Bob, 239
Dow Jones & Co., 29
Downey, Maria, 66
Downie, Leonard, 315
Drew, Richard, 445

Dube, Jonathan, 28, 82, 255, 316
Dubow, Craig, 60
Duke University, 313
Dunlap, Karen Brown, 371
Dwyer, R. Bud, 315

East Valley Tribune, (Mesa, Ariz.), 134
Ebert, Roger, 309
Editor & Publisher, 145, 325
education beat, 364–66
Education Writers Association, 366
Ehmke, Layton, 213
Eisenberg, Carol, 446
Electronic Frontier Foundation, 302
Elliott, Deni, 306
ellipsis, 52
e-mail interviews, 122–23, 254
e-mail news releases, 277
e-mail résumés, 475
embedded links, 256
empowerment box, 397, 442, 451
endings, 43, 161, 173–78, 180, 186, 229, 240, 245, 342
entertainment stories, 15
environmental writing, 366–68
Erin Rooney, 482
ethics, 10, 27–28, 49, 63, 76, 91, 124, 146, 165, 191, 216, 236, 255, 272, 298, 306–19, 324, 345, 359, 379, 381, 397, 426, 447, 482, 497
ethnicity, 419
eUniverse, 23
euphemisms, 328–29
exercises, 20, 32, 55, 68, 105, 128, 156, 180, 195, 219, 247, 266, 285, 304, 318, 332, 354, 375, 410, 439, 471, 489, 500
expunged, 415
external links, 256
Eye Track, 18, 255–56

fabrication, 10, 27, 92–93, 309
Facebook, 7, 24, 99, 303, 341, 359, 454, 473, 476
fact boxes, 45–46, 122, 256, 340–41, 397
fact sheet, 268, 273, 281–82
fact vs. opinion, 75
Fagan, Mark, 377–79, 381, 387
fair comment, 298
fair use, 304

Fairbanks (Alaska) *Daily News Miner,* 140, 365
Fairness and Accuracy in the Media, 325
fairness, 28, 31, 43, 89, 91, 95, 115, 216, 272, 304, 497
Falevits, Shelly, 481
Fallujah, 315
false light, 299–300, 302
FAQ (frequently asked questions), 257
Farber, Lindsay, 446
feature leads, 38–39, 133, 273
feature stories, 17, 73
feature techniques, 198–221
featured online activity, 20, 32, 57, 69, 84, 105, 128, 159, 180, 197, 220, 248, 267, 287, 305, 319, 333, 355, 375, 390, 411, 441, 471, 501
federal courts, 428–29
federal shield law, 91
Federal Trade Commission, 302
Federal Wiretap Statute, 111
fedworld.gov, 366
feed reader, 8
felonies, 429, 431, 434
Fielden, Michele, 448
Fields, Monique, 171
Finkel, David, 204, 428
fire stories, 425–26
First Amendment, 93, 288, 291, 297, 299, 301, 306, 317, 429
first appearance, 431
firstgov.gov, 366
fiscal year, 406
Fish, Larry, 152
Fletcher, Harrison, 390
Flickr, 24, 454
Florida Today, 251
focus, 11, 12, 34, 36–37, 39, 44, 115, 132, 162–63, 185, 202, 215, 229, 239–40, 258, 338, 341, 372
focus sentence, 131–32, 163, 166, 268, 284
FOI Resource Center, 103
follow-up questions, 118–19, 380
follow-up stories, 81, 254, 260, 358–59, 420, 450, 454, 459–60
Fong, Tillie, 13
Food and Drug Administration, 238
Food Lion, 299, 307
foreshadowing, 178, 209

Fort Myers (Fla.) *News-Press,* 176, 250–52
Fortune magazine, 368–69
forward spin, 61, 138, 179
Franklin, Jon, 215
fray.com, 265–66
free-choice questions, 121, 123
Freedman, Wayne, 169
Freedom of Information Act, 101, 103–04, 395
free-writing, 164, 220
French, Robert, 271
French, Tom, 171, 199–201, 205–06, 216, 218
Frontiersman (Wasilla, Alaska), 400
Fry, Don, 131
Fry, Steve, 17
Fuson, Ken, 160–61, 174, 194
Future Exploration Network, 25
Future of News study, 58, 60

Gallaga, Omar, 448–49, 452
Gallimore,Tim, 320–22
Gannett Co., 8, 19, 60, 67–68, 90, 161, 251–52, 326, 370, 486
Gannetteer, 90, 326, 370, 486
Garcia, Mario, 18
Geisel, Theodor Seuss, 353
gender, 325–27, 333
Gentlemen's Quarterly (GQ), 334–36
Gertz v. Welch, 293–94
Gilleland, LaRue W., 123
Gillmor, Donald, 290
Girard, Fred, 460
Glass, Stephen, 92–93, 216
GOAL method, 123–24, 339
Goertzen, Jeff, 453
Golden Fleece awards, 293, 296
Goldsboro News-Argus, 37
Google, 7, 23–24, 82, 95–96, 99
Gordon, Anne, 316
Gowen, Matt, 195
grammar and usage, 490–501
grand jury, 431, 434
graphics, 404, 419, 452, 454
Gross, Terry, 336–37
Gruver, Deb, 75
Gusty, Andrea, 410

Hallmark, 269, 282
Halpin, James, 235

handicapped, 327
Handschuh, David, 443–45
Hansen, Chris, 308
hard news vs. soft news, 74
hard news, 17–18, 35, 73
Hardman, Dave. 19
Hart, Gary, 310, 311
Hart, Jack, 182–83, 206
Hartford (Conn.) *Courant,* 89, 125, 171, 205, 418
headlines, 38, 259
health writing, 366–68
Hectop, 444
helpfulness, 14
Helyar, John, 368–69
Hernandez, Richard, 380
Hersh, Seymour M., 315
hidden cameras, 307–08
highlights, 45, 77, 122, 190, 257, 262, 340–41, 376, 383–84, 397, 419, 442
Hight, Joe, 446
Hill & Knowlton, 29
Hill, James, 300
Hill, Kathy, 348
Hodges, Louis, 308, 316
Hofstra University, 60, 323
Hogan, Dave, 13
Hogan, Thomas F., 91
Holenport, Tracy, 224
Holland, Megan, 147
Hollander, Zaz, 14, 147
homicides, 423
Honolulu Advertiser, 215, 252
Hopkins, Kyle, 65
Horn, Paul, 19
hourglass technique, 189, 196, 244, 422
Hower, Wendy, 365
Hoy, 323
human interest, 13–15, 17, 79, 211, 396, 451–52, 465
Hurricane Katrina, 25
Hutchinson v. Proxmire, 293
Hutchinson, Ronald, 293, 296
hyperlocal news, 251
hypothetical source, 146

icebreakers, 118, 123, 126, 128
idea budgets, 82
iFOCUS, 266

illegal alien, 321
immediacy, 12, 17, 61, 138, 227, 241, 252
impact, 14, 41, 62, 72, 118, 392
In Cold Blood, 110, 201
infographic, 46
information centers, 60, 251
injunction, 434
innocent, 434
integrated media, 4
interactive, 9, 25, 30, 41, 64, 219, 228, 251–52, 257–58, 264
International Association of Business Communicators, 283
internships, 99, 472–99
interview planning, 115
interviewing problems, 127
interviews for grief, 457
interviews (for jobs), 486–88
intrusion, 299
invasion of privacy, 298–301, 308, 314
inverted pyramid, 47, 183–84, 188–89, 195, 244, 254, 284, 420
Investigative Reporters and Editors, 91, 98, 295
Iowa City Press-Citizen, 217
iPod, 7, 31
Irby, Kenny, 63
Isaza, Rudolph, 449, 456–57
iTunes, 31
Izard, Ralph, 307

Jackman, Tom, 439
jargon, 120, 164, 173, 356, 364, 366, 370, 392, 398, 400, 412, 427
journalese, 398
Jewell, Richard, 297, 313, 314
Jha, Ashok Kumar, 26
job applications, 472–89
Johnson, Gail, 382
Jones, Patty Curtin, 409
Jones, Paula, 311
journalismnet.com, 364
Journalist's Guide to the Internet, 98
juvenile offenders, 416

Kammer, Jack, 325
Kansas City (Mo.) *Star,* 46, 139, 207, 340, 439
Keller, Julia, 463

Keller, Larry, 264
Kelley, Jack, 93, 309–10
Kelly, Kristan, 365
Kennedy, Erin, 146
Kentucky Post, 478
key words, 166, 242
kicker, 131, 173, 346
Kidder, Tracy, 201
King, Martin Luther, 291
King, Peter, 237
Kirkwood, Heather, 328
Kissinger, Henry, 296
Klinkenberg, Jeff, 200
Knight, Kenneth, 6
Knight-Ridder Inc., 8
Knight-Ridder/Tribune News
    Service, 14
Koff, Stephen, 151
Koger, Chris, 383
Koppel, Ted, 15
Krzos, Mark, 252
KSNT-TV (Topeka, Kan.), 245
KTNV-TV (Las Vegas, Nev.), 324
KTUU-TV (Anchorage, Alaska), 62,
    66,184, 214, 222–49, 421
KTVA, Channel 11 (Anchorage,
    Alaska), 410
KUJH-TV (University of Kansas), 188
Kunkel, Thomas, 337
Kuralt, Charles, 211-12
KXAN-TV (Austin, Tex.), 61

ladder of details, 203
LaFleur, Jennifer, 393–95, 402
Lang, Annie, 188
Lansing (Mich.) *State-Journal,*
    169, 400
Lawrence (Kan.) *Journal-World,* 3–7,
    11, 16, 37, 172, 195, 377–78,
    387, 403
Lawrence (Mass.) *Eagle-Tribune,* 107
Lawrence, Merlissa, 371
Lazzarino, Evie, 268–70
lead-ins, 236–37
leads, 37–38, 130–59, 165, 240,
Leaf, Brian, 401
lede, 132
Lee, Nelle Harper, 110
Lehigh University, 415
Leiby, Richard, 340
Lewinsky, Monica, 311

LEXIS/NEXIS, 100
libel, 165, 289–99, 302
libel and FOIA hotline, 103
Lickteig, Mary Ann, 73, 202–03, 209
Life magazine, 299
linear, 9, 256–57
listening tips, 111
lists, 171–72, 190–91, 196, 256–57,
    259, 264, 284, 402
literary journalists, 201
localize news, 79
location map, 46, 72
logging tape, 224
Lopresti, Mike, 370
Los Angeles Times, 8, 38, 75, 148, 151,
    153, 269, 462
Louisiana State University, 307
Louisville (Ky.) *Courier-Journal,* 248
Lovely, Dan, 475

Macon (Ga.) *Telegraph,* 309
Mailer, Norman, 204
mainbar, 18, 360, 451, 459
Malcolm, Janet, 110, 165
Malernee, Jamie, 263
manslaughter, 423
mapping, 77–78, 284
Maraniss, David, 203
Marimow, Bill, 445
market value, 406
Márquez, Gabriel García, 201
Martin, John P., 439
Martindale, Mike, 460
Martino, Stephen, 312
Marymont, Kate, 67, 250
Masson v. New Yorker, 165
Masson, Jeffery, 165
matchmaking technique, 86, 89,
    95,121, 357
Mathis, Joel, 3–4
Mathis, Joy, 447–48
McBreen, Sharon, 149
McClatchy Co., 8
McCormick, Mark, 357–59, 362
McGuire, Tim, 445
McMurray, Jose D., 322–23
McPhee, John, 201
McVeigh, Timothy, 447
mean, 406
Media Bloggers Association, 316
Media General Inc., 6

media jobs, 99, 472–99
media kit, 273, 275, 281–305
media law, 288–305
media manipulation, 379–80
median, 406
meetings, 377–81, 385–89
Meinhardt, Jane, 141
Meiring, Philip, 372, 405
metaphors, 368
metasearch engines, 98
Miami Herald, 109, 125, 130, 310,
    311, 412–13
Miami Hurricane, 317
microcontent, 259
microsites, 252
Miller, Judith, 90–91
Miller, Martha, 70, 76, 217
Miller, Stephen C., 96
Milwaukee Journal Sentinel, 16, 175,
    424, 472–73, 477
miniprofiles, 257
Minnesota Supreme Court, 93
Mirage bar, 308
Miranda warnings, 429
misdemeanors, 429, 431, 434
mobile journalists, 251
mojos, 251–52, 254
Moonves, Leslie, 295
morality, 310
morgues, 366
Morse, Dan, 402
motions, 431
motor vehicle accidents, 420
Mower, Joan, 48
MSNBC, 9, 11, 16, 25, 266
Muhammad, 324
multicultural sensitivity, 320–33
multicultural sources,
    94–95, 272
multimedia, 3–6, 9, 16, 30, 60, 68,
    251–52, 257–58, 395, 361, 452,
    454, 477
Murdoch, Rupert, 23
Murphy, Heddy, 190
Musarium, 9, 219
Myers, Dan, 409
MySpace, 7, 23–24, 26–27, 99, 223,
    226, 247–48, 303, 341, 359, 476

Nachison, Andrew, 266
names of suspects, 416

Napster, 304
narrative writing, 183, 188–89, 193, 200, 203, 207–11, 216, 219, 264, 342, 409, 438, 451–52
NASA, 80
National Association of Black Journalists (NABJ), 322
National Association of Colleges and Employers, 473
National Association of Hispanic Journalists (NAHJ), 321–22
National Enquirer, 296
National Press Photographers Association, 447
National Public Radio, 237, 336
natural disasters, 461
natural sound, 238
NBC, 27, 87–88, 228, 237, 239, 242, 288, 308
Nederbrock, Mike, 223–24
neutral reportage, 297–98
Nevins, Buddy, 83
New Republic, 92
New York Daily News, 315, 443
New York Times, 10, 37, 90, 92, 96, 216, 269, 291, 309, 315, 336, 397
New York University, 443
New Yorker magazine, 300, 315
News & Observer (Raleigh, N.C.), 345
news conferences, 384–85
News Corporation, 303
news releases, 191, 271–80
Newsday, 18, 138, 154, 323, 446
Newslab, 188
newslink.org, 364
Newspaper Association of America, 324
News-Press (Fort Myers, Fla.), 67
Nguyen, Dong-Phuong, 171
Niagara (N.Y.) *Gazette,* 155
Nichols, Terry, 447
Nicholson, Jim, 349
Nielsen, Jakob, 258
Nifong, Michael B., 313
No Electronic Theft Act, 304
nolo contendere (no contest), 431–32, 435
nonlinear, 9, 219, 256
Northern Light (University of Alaska Anchorage), 192
not for attribution, 94

note-taking, 113–15, 128
numbers, 369, 402
nut graph, 37–40, 83, 130–159, 166, 185, 190, 202–03, 216, 240, 258, 273, 338–39

O'Brien, Mark, 273, 275
O'Hanlon, Kevin, 400
obituaries, 348–54
obscenity, 303
observation, 73–84, 112, 203, 346, 453
off the record, 93–94, 127
O'Harra, Doug, 147
OhmyNews, 26, 28, 316
Oklahoma Daily, 447–49, 452, 456–57
Olympic Park bombing, 297
Omer, Sevil, 356, 359–62
on the record, 94, 127
online documents, 361
online journalism, 8, 250–67
online legal issues, 301–03
Online News Association, 253, 359
online readers, 255
open-ended questions, 117, 123
Orange County (Calif.) *Register,* 148, 220, 354, 390, 420, 422
Oregonian, 13, 86, 91, 182–83, 345
organization, 160–80, 341
Orlando (Fla.) *Sentinel,* 135, 149, 154, 190, 425
Orwell, George, 173
Outing, Steve, 22
Overholser, Geneva

pacing, 161, 170, 178, 180, 400
Pape, Tiffany, 447–48
Papper, Robert, 60, 323
parallelism, 170, 178, 190
parroting, 50, 152, 164, 341
participatory journalism, 11, 26
Parton, Dolly, 325–26
passive voice, 62, 136, 230
Paul, Corey, 132
Pazniokas, Mark, 171
People magazine, 336
Pepper, Jon, 458
Permalink, 24
person of interest, 297, 416, 436
personal tragedy, 466–70

personalized journalism, 9, 265
perspective, 451, 454–55, 460, 465
Perverted Justice, 308
Pesznecker, Katie, 66
Peters, Mike, 376
Pett, Saul, 210–11
Pew Internet and American Life Project, 23
Philadelphia Daily News, 349
Philadelphia Inquirer, 8–9, 37, 124, 136, 143, 146–47, 150, 152–53, 166, 170, 205, 315, 326, 328, 343, 387, 409, 439
Pittsburgh Press, 371
plagiarism, 10, 27, 52, 77, 81–82, 92, 212, 309–10
Plame, Valerie, 91
plea bargain, 432, 435
Plessinger, Alison, 83
podcasts, 3, 7, 29, 31, 252, 268, 271
point of emphasis, 134–35
points of entry, 18
political correctness, 32
Pool, Bob, 153
pornography, 204, 303, 319
Portland Press Herald/Maine Sunday Telegram, 108–09
Post-Standard (Syracuse, N.Y.), 367
Potter, Deborah, 188
Potter, Mark, 87–89
Powazek, Derek, 265–66
Power Line, 25
Poynter Institute, 18, 28, 63, 91, 219, 237, 255, 314, 316–18, 324, 333, 371, 374
Pozner, Jennifer L., 325
PR Quest, 271
preliminary hearing, 431
present tense, 222, 230, 272
Presstime, 324
primary sources, 90, 105
privacy, 298, 305, 310–11
private figures, 293–94
privilege, 296
PRNewswire, 98
probate courts, 429
profiles, 79, 334–55
Profnet, 98
proximity, 12, 15
Proxmire, William, 293, 296
PRWeb, 29, 271

PSA (public service announcement), 246
pseudonyms, 92
public figures, 292–93, 297, 300, 316
public journalism, 10–11
public officials, 109, 292, 296, 310, 316
public records, 100–103, 300, 364, 414–15
Public Relations Society of America (PRSA), 29, 270–72, 285, 318, 475
Public Relations Student Society of America (PRSSA), 99, 475
public relations writing, 268–87, 475
public service announcements, 280–81
Pulitzer Prize, 92–93, 107, 109, 121, 163, 200, 203, 208, 215, 308–09, 314, 330, 345, 370, 413, 463
pull quote, 45, 401
Purdy, Matthew, 170, 343

qualified privilege, 296
qualities of news, 12
question/answer format, 192, 256–57, 264, 341–42
Quill magazine, 295, 478
quotes, 40, 50–52, 142, 165, 179, 381, 388, 392, 401, 497

race, 419
racism, 205
radio, 237–38
Radio/Television News Directors Association (RTNDA), 59, 99, 165, 191, 236, 278, 318, 323, 397, 474
Rae-Dupree, Janet, 463
Raffensperger, Terry, 399
Ramsay, Yvonne, 184
rape, 92, 299, 313, 416–18
Rather, Dan, 27, 294
Reader's Guide to Periodical Literature, 96
records, 100–03, 105, 360
Reno (Nev.) *Gazette-Journal,* 19, 71, 356, 359, 361, 397
Reno v. ACLU, 301
repetition of key words, 166–67
Reporters Committee for Freedom of the Press, 111

reporting techniques, 396, 418, 449
Research and Training Center for Independent Living, 329
résumés, 483–86, 492
Reuters, 8
reverse directories, 96, 105
revision, 164, 245, 265
Reynolds, Rachel, 458
rhythm, 161
Ric Bohy, Ric, 460
Rice, Donna, 311
Richman, Alan, 334–36, 355
Rinearson, Peter, 370
Roanoke (Va.) *Times,* 254
Roberts, Eugene, 37
Robertson, Lori, 310
Rockford (Ill.) *Register Star,* 401
Rocky Mountain (Denver) *News,* 13
Rohrback, Andrew, 47
Rojas, Patricia, 79
role play, 72, 77, 120, 288, 419, 442, 450
Rood, Lee, 16
Roosevelt, Theodore, 442
Rosenblatt v. Baer, 292
RSS (Really Simple Syndication), 7–8, 24–25, 29, 80–82, 271, 302, 359
Ruas, Charles, 110
Rudolph, Eric, 313
Ruehlmann, William, 203

Saavedra, Tony, 400
Sabo, William, 176
said or says, 54, 62
Salsini, Paul, 472–73, 477–78
Samsung, 301
San Jose (Calif.) *Mercury News,* 8, 142, 170, 463
Santa Cruz Sentinel, 40
Sarasota Herald-Tribune, 7
Savalli, Carla, 26
scene, 206, 208, 216, 219
Schoonover, Dylan, 188
Schorer, Jane, 208, 209, 314
Scott, Patrick, 147
Scripps Howard Foundation, 478
Seattle Times, 149, 370
secondary sources, 90
second-day leads, 138, 389
sections technique, 193, 215, 218, 342

Security on Campus, 411
Sedalia (Mo.) *Democrat,* 309
sej.org, 368
self-sponsorship, 89
Sellers, Lauren, 425
sequence of events, 216, 243, 451
sequencing, 183
serial narratives, 218
sex offender registries, 98, 415
sexism, 205, 326
Sharp, Adrian, 39
Shattered Glass. 92
Shefchik, Rick, 153
Sher, Julian, 99, 364
Sherman, Mark, 407
shield laws, 91
Shields, Tom, 209
show-in-action technique, 73–74, 198, 205–07, 216, 341, 347, 366
sidebar, 18, 27, 72, 185, 257, 347, 360, 420, 451–52, 462
Sidis v. F-R Publishing Corp., 300
Sidoti, Liz, 385
silent treatment, 120
Simons, Dolph C. Jr., 5–6
Simpson, O.J., 427–28
slander, 290, 302
slug, 82–83, 231
Smith, Bradley R., 317
Smith, Joel, 460
Smith, Patricia, 93
Smith, Stephen A., 379, 380
Smolkin, Rachel, 314
snapshot profiles, 345–55
Snead, Bill, 5–6, 384
SNN6 (Six News Now, Lawrence, Kan.), 3, 7, 377
SOC (standard out cue), 246
social networking sites, 7, 23, 28–29, 31, 99, 251, 289, 301, 303, 316, 328, 341, 358, 428, 454, 472–73, 476
Society of Environmental Journalists, 366, 368
Society of Professional Journalists, 10, 28, 76, 91, 124, 146, 165, 255, 307, 316, 345, 359, 381, 426
soft leads, 38, 132–33, 145–53
soft news, 17
SOT (sound on tape), 64, 151, 231–32, 246

sound bites, 40, 224, 227–29, 231, 238, 243
source book, 87, 98–99, 364
sources, 86–105, 359–60
South Florida Sun-Sentinel, 61, 83, 108, 148, 340, 449
Southwest Missouri State University, 415
specialty beats, 9, 364–74
speeches, 379–83
Spokesman-Review (Spokane, Wash.), 26–27, 177, 345, 347
sponsorship technique, 89, 116
Sporich, Brett C., 207
sportswriting, 370–74
St. Cloud (Minn.) *Times,* 16
St. Joseph (Mo.) *News-Press,* 304, 399, 466
St. Louis (Mo.) *Post-Dispatch,* 141
St. Paul (Minn.) *Pioneer Press,* 93, 142, 152, 331
St. Petersburg (Fla.) *Times,* 13–14, 41, 44, 137, 141, 150–51, 155, 171, 199, 200–01, 204, 206, 263–64, 409, 426, 438
Stalking the Feature Story, 203
stand-up, 247
Stanford University, 18, 255
Star Tribune (Minneapolis), 8, 93, 137, 401, 445
Starr, Kenneth, 311
state courts, 428–29
Statesman-Journal (Salem, Ore.), 422
statistical stories, 402–04
statistics, 122, 392–411, 451, 465
Stecklow, Steve, 150
Steele, James, 392
Steele, Robert M., 317
Stephens, Mark, 176
Steve Brandt, Steve, 401
Stevens, Jane, 254
Stevens, John Paul, 301
stitching, 166
stoplight technique, 163
story ideas, 70–85, 282, 358
story organization, 160–81, 263
storyboard, 256
storytelling, 198–221, 215–16, 264, 403–04
Strunk, William Jr., 265
Student Press Law Center, 289

style guide, 502–14
Sullivan, Julie, 177, 345–47
Sullivan, L. B., 291
summary blurb, 38, 44, 157
summary judgment, 432, 435
summary lead, 47, 132–33, 138, 145, 190, 263, 273
Sunflower Channel, 6
Sun Herald (Port Charlotte, Fla.), 9, 350
Sunline, 350
suspects, 297, 312, 419
Sussman, Lawrence, 16
Swarns, Rachel, 14
Sweeney, Frank, 463

tag, 228, 247
Tampa (Fla.) *Tribune,* 6–7, 167, 261, 426, 446
tape recorders, 110–11
Taschler, Joe, 17
tax terms, 406
teasers, 225, 236, 247
Technorati, 24–25, 82
telephone interviewing, 125–27
teleprompter, 247
tell-a-friend technique, 36, 412
The American Editor, 445
The Corpse Had a Familiar Face, 109
The Elements of Style, 266
The Fabulist, 92
The New Republic, 216
The Oklahoman, 446
The Record (Hackensack, N.J.), 408
The Story of a Shipwrecked Sailor, 201
The Sun (Baltimore, Md.), 366, 445
The Sun (San Bernadino, Calif.), 55, 400
theme, 202–03, 216, 334, 338–39, 345, 372, 466
Thomson Company, 8
tickler file, 70, 80, 356, 358, 363
tightening stories, 179
time frames, 215, 342
Time Inc. v. Hill, 300
time lines, 9, 72–73, 254, 256–57
Time magazine, 91
timeliness, 12, 255, 273
Times v. Sullivan, 291–92
Tipton, Lori, 248
titles, 55, 239, 353

To Catch a Predator, 308
Tofani, Loretta, 170
Tompkins, Al, 237
tone, 209
Topeka (Kan.) *Capital-Journal,* 17, 423
topic sentence, 284
Topousis, Tom, 408
Tourtellotte, James, 445
Trackbacks, 24, 29
Tracy, John, 223, 227, 228–30
Tracy, Nancy, 89,125
transitions, 50, 164, 166–70, 179, 242
transparency, 26–27, 316
trends, 16, 81
Tribune Company, 8
Tribune Media Services, 376
tsunami, 446
Tucson (Ariz.) *Citizen,* 138
Tulsa (Okla.) *World,* 330
Tuohy, Lynne, 205
turning points, 337, 339, 372
TV job qualities, 229–30
tvjobs.com, 474
TV rundown, 224–26
tvspy.com, 474
Twain, Mark, 216, 350, 490, 493

U.S. Census, 94, 97, 278–79, 321, 329, 411
U.S. Constitution, 298, 428
U.S. Court of Appeals, 429
U.S. Department of Agriculture, 278
U.S. District Court, 429
U.S. Supreme Court, 91, 93, 110, 291, 292–94, 300–03, 429
U.S. Web portal (*usa.gov*), 80
undercover techniques, 299
undocumented immigrant, 321
University Daily Kansan, 46, 309, 312, 319, 348, 372, 374
University of Alaska Anchorage, 64, 192, 223
University of Arizona, 252–53
University of California Berkeley, 254
University of Iowa, 42
University of Kansas, 5, 11, 46, 188, 240, 269, 309, 311–12, 328, 347
University of Maryland, 98
University of Massachusetts–Dartmouth, 30

University of Miami, 317
University of Missouri, 128, 314, 322, 330
University of Montana, 345
University of Oklahoma, 447
University of South Florida, 273, 306
University of Virginia, 309
University of Washington, 444
university records, 415
unusual nature, 13, 25
updated leads, 138, 230, 389
updating, 12, 254
USA Today, 90, 93, 95, 138, 179, 275, 309
Usenet, 99
user-generated content, 11, 26
Utsler, Max, 240

Vancouver Sun, 41
Vandervliet, Brian, 311
verbs, 179, 198, 206, 260, 284, 399
vidcast, 31
video news releases (VNRs), 81, 278
vignettes, 347
Virginia Polytechnic Institute, 24–25, 254, 454
visuals, 16, 18, 43, 63, 76, 121, 268, 272, 340, 397
VO (voice over), 247
vodcast, 31
voice, 240
voicer, 238

Vorsino, Mary, 252
vortex, 292
Vosburgh, Mark, 190

The Wall Street Journal formula, 37, 148, 185–86, 188, 195, 241, 400
Walsh, Barbara, 106–08, 118
Washington and Lee University, 308
Washington Post, 92, 203, 311, 315, 384
WashingtonPost.Newsweek Interactive, 2, 5
weather stories, 461, 463–66
Web profiles, 341
webcasts, 26
weblog, 7, 23, 81
Weinberg. Steve, 91, 295
Welch, Robert, 294
Western Kentucky University, 132
WFLA-AM, (Tampa, Fla.), 426
WFLA-TV (Tampa, Fla.), 6–7
Whah Anielam, 225–26
What do you think?, 19, 31, 55, 68, 83,103, 127, 156, 179, 193, 219, 247, 266, 285, 304, 318, 332, 353, 374, 389, 409, 436, 466, 488, 500
White, E. B., 266
White, Vanna, 301
Whois database, 97, 362
Wichita (Kan.) *Eagle*, 53, 74–75, 359, 379–80

Williams, Brian, 27
Wired.com, 359
wiretapping, 111
Wittenauer, Cheryl, 465–66
Woestendiek, John, 150
Wohlforth, Charles, 175
Wolfe, Tom, 201
Wonkette, 25
Woods, Keith, 324
World Trade Center, 63, 443–45, 457
wrap, 238, 245
Writing Broadcast News, 131
Writing for Story, 215
writing process, 161–65
writing techniques, 398, 407–08
Wykes, S. L., 170

Yahoo!, 7, 24, 98
Yeon-ho, Oh, 26
YouTube, 3, 23, 26, 99, 289–90, 473, 476
you voice, 264

Zell, Sam, 8
Zeran v. America Online, 301
Zeran, Kenneth, 301–02
Ziegenmeyer, Nancy, 314
Zilko, 121, 223–28, 231
Zollman, Peter M., 4
Zuckman, Jill, 175